The Infinite Path

The Law of Perpetual Innovation

FOUNDATIONAL REFERENCE EDITION

Paul A. Martinez

Published by Franklin Publishers
Printed in the United States of America

For permissions, inquiries, or additional copies, contact:
Franklin Publishers
www.franklinpublishers.com

To

Trinity Jewel,

Apollo Hendrix,

and

Nova Xaria

The wild thinkers, rule benders, and bedtime negotiators
who remind me daily that curiosity doesn't need permission.

Keep asking "Why?"

Always remain fearless explorers, brilliant interrupters, and joyful disruptors.
You remind me that every great discovery begins with a "What if?"
May you wander often, wonder always,
and never settle for the paths already drawn.

"The value to a people does not come from what utility delivers us, but rather, what utility delivers us from."

— The Law of Perpetual Innovation

INTRODUCTION

The importance of new ideas and technological advances has been recognized by economists and thinkers for centuries. Classical economists such as Adam Smith and John Stuart Mill discussed how new inventions and improvements played a pivotal role in driving economic progress. Although they did not use the term "innovation" as it is commonly understood today, their recognition of the impact of technological advancements laid the groundwork for later interpretations of the concept. These early insights highlight that the seeds of what we now understand as innovation were already being sown in the minds of those who observed the transformative power of new ideas and inventions.

It wasn't until the early 1900s that economist Joseph Schumpeter introduced the concept of "creative destruction" and formally used the term "innovation" to describe the process by which old structures are dismantled to make way for new, often superior ones. Schumpeter's works underscored a causal relationship between innovation and its outcomes, suggesting that each innovation disrupts the status quo, leading to further innovations that address the new environment created by the disruption. This laid the foundation for future interpretations of innovation's disruptive nature, which was further developed by Clayton Christensen in his concept of "disruptive innovation." Christensen's work highlighted how smaller, initially overlooked innovations can eventually upend established industries, displacing incumbents and reshaping the competitive landscape. This idea of innovation not only as a driver of change but as a force that disrupts markets and creates new ones deepened our understanding of how innovation interacts with its environment.

Over time, other disciplines developed concepts that echoed this recursive nature of innovation. In systems thinking, the idea of "feedback loops," where the outputs of a system are fed back as inputs, creating a cyclical effect, became well-established. Similarly, the notion of "unintended consequences" became prevalent in economics, sociology, and environmental studies, where actions, often innovations, had effects that were unforeseen and unplanned, further driving changes and adaptations in the system. In strategic management, the "resource-based view" emphasizes how firms leverage their resources and capabilities to innovate, which in turn alters the competitive landscape, necessitating continuous adaptation and innovation.

Despite these insights, no framework has fully formalized the idea of a self-perpetuating loop of causality between innovation and the factors that spark its emergence. While these disciplines recognize the recursive nature of innovation and its outcomes, they have not explicitly connected these dots in a way that provides a comprehensive, systematic understanding of how innovation not only drives change but also inherently creates the conditions for further innovation. This gap in understanding has limited humanity's ability to predict and manage the complex dynamics of innovation in a way that maximizes its benefits while minimizing its drawbacks.

One reason for this oversight may lie in the complexity and unpredictability inherent in the innovation process itself. Innovations often arise from unexpected intersections of ideas, technologies, needs, and shifting environments, making it difficult to map out their trajectories in a deterministic way. Moreover, the traditional focus has often been on the outcomes of innovation, whether economic growth, social change, or technological advancement, rather than on the underlying process that drives these outcomes. As a result, while the consequences of innovation have been well-studied, the recursive nature of the innovation process itself has remained an elusive art form.

I have formalized what I believe to be a law that accurately describes the core underlying mechanisms driving innovation. This law encapsulates the self-perpetuating cycle of innovation, highlighting how each advancement inherently creates the conditions for the next. Alongside this conceptual framework, I have developed methods that could be transformed into a practical system. This system would allow an organization to harness these insights, significantly enhancing their product development efforts by enabling them to predict, design, and implement innovations that may not only meet but anticipate market demands and societal needs to some probabilistic confidence interval.

With this approach, one can move beyond simply reacting to the outcomes of innovation and begin to actively shape its trajectory. By leveraging specific predictive models, one can design innovations that maximize their benefits, whether for customers, the environment, or society. This can be accomplished while minimizing their drawbacks, both known and unforeseen. This will enable one to develop products and services that are not only more effective and efficient but also more sustainable and aligned with broader societal goals.

This book introduces the Law of Perpetual Innovation (LPI), a unified framework that explains innovation not as a linear pursuit of progress, but as a recursive response to burden. LPI reframes innovation as a system-level loop, driven not by utility maximization or visionary ambition, but by the resolution of accumulated constraints, unmet needs, and emergent desires. By connecting concepts from evolutionary biology, behavioral economics, systems theory, cognitive psychology, and thermodynamics, LPI offers a comprehensive model that explains not just how innovation unfolds, but why it must. This law reveals that innovation is not optional, nor is it arbitrary, it is the inevitable outcome of friction, failure, aspiration, and entropy.

I would like to formally present these ideas to you, such that one can begin to consider how this law and its framework can be integrated into an organization's innovation processes. This book will outline a novel paradigm for innovation that can help drive an organization's competitive advantage in the marketplace. I believe this approach could be a game-changer for an organization, and I look forward to the opportunity to share it with you.

Part 1:
Setting the Stage

In Part 1, we uncover the missing half of the innovation story, byproduct burden. We see how it completes the long-standing focus on utility. Through vivid examples (like chewing gum sparking nostalgia) and historical contexts (from the first light bulbs to Apple's screen-time solutions), these chapters demonstrate that every new product and service inevitably produces unintended consequences, which then spark further creativity and adaptation. We trace this cycle all the way back to nature, exploring how organisms evolve in response to external pressures and learning that human progress likewise depends on perpetual problem-solving. By introducing the "Law of Perpetual Innovation," Part 1 shows that true innovation isn't just about building better solutions; it's about continually addressing the byproducts that emerge whenever we find something useful. This sets the stage for a comprehensive framework that rethinks how we design, assess, and evolve everything we create.

CHAPTER 1
A Missing Counterpart

From Bubble Gum to Byproduct: A First Look at the Law of Perpetual Innovation

On your way home, you stop at a gas station to refuel and grab a bottle of water. As you wait at the counter, your eye catches a pack of gum you haven't seen in years. It is the same brand you loved as a kid. On a whim, you toss it in with your purchase. A few moments later, as you pump gas, you unwrap a piece, pop it into your mouth, and the familiar flavor immediately takes you back. You're no longer standing at a gas station; you're riding bikes with friends on endless summer afternoons, stopping by the corner store for candy and soda. The memory rushes in, vivid and warm. Life was simpler then. There were no deadlines, no bills, no to-do lists, just freedom and laughter.

What you just experienced is a moment of utility. The gum provided more than just the satisfaction of flavor; it delivered nostalgia, reconnecting you to a time when life felt carefree and joyful. Economists would call this "nostalgic utility," a satisfaction rooted in the recollection of a pleasurable moment from your past.

As you finish fueling and drive away, the nostalgia lingers, but it begins to shift. You think about how uncomplicated life used to be, waking up late, spending hours outside, and having few responsibilities. Today, you have a mortgage, bills to pay, and a busy schedule that seems to shrink your freedom. By the time you park in your driveway, the warm glow of nostalgia has faded, leaving you with a subtle ache. A sense of something lost.

This ache is what I call byproduct. It is the unintended consequence of the gum, the emotional residue that followed the initial moment of satisfaction. The gum delivered utility both in the form of flavor satisfaction and nostalgia, but it also triggered reflections on the gap between your carefree past and your demanding present. Without seeing that gum, you wouldn't have bought it, and without tasting it, you wouldn't have experienced this mix of burdensome emotions. Byproduct always follows utility, revealing itself in ways we rarely anticipate.

This pattern, where utility is always followed by byproduct, is universal and encompasses what I call "The Law of Perpetual Innovation." It is why some people hesitate to try out new restaurants, change car brands, or enter new relationships after experiencing heartbreak. The initial utility of love and connection was followed by the byproduct of some form of loss or even pain. It is why others stick to their favorite meal at a restaurant rather than trying something new. They fear the potential byproduct of disappointment, choosing the certainty of familiar satisfaction instead. Utility and byproduct are inseparable; they are two sides of the same coin.

The first part of the Law of Perpetual Innovation states that whenever we experience utility, byproduct inevitably follows. Anything that brings us satisfaction, no matter how fleeting or profound, will eventually give rise to some form of dissatisfaction, longing, or even a desire for something better. This truth is woven into the fabric of life. Whether it is a product, a service, a relationship, or an experience, utility is always followed by some secondary effect; byproduct.

The second part of the Law of Perpetual Innovation tells us what happens next. When byproduct arises, we tend to seek other utility to overcome and alleviate it. Consider this: after parking your car, still feeling down about your lost youth, you step into your kitchen and grab a cookie. As you sit down on the couch with the remote in hand, you realize something. While you may no longer have the easygoing freedom of childhood, you now have the autonomy to make your own choices. You no longer need permission to eat dessert before dinner, and you can watch whatever you like on TV. The cookie and the couch remind you of the utility in your life today, subtly shifting your perspective and lifting your spirits.

Or perhaps, when you arrive home, you decide to scroll through social media, turn on a favorite TV show, or dive into your latest hobby. In that moment, you are seeking fresh utility to offset the lingering disappointment sparked by the gum's nostalgia. And it may work, at least for a while. But as you immerse yourself in this new diversion, another byproduct might emerge, whether it is the guilt of spending too much time online or the fleeting dissatisfaction of realizing you still have chores to do, and so on. This is the third part of the Law of Perpetual Innovation which tells us that as we seek to alleviate byproduct through new utility, byproduct will emerge again, and the cycle will continue. It never ends.

This constant cycle of utility and byproduct drives human behavior and innovation. It is what pushes us to create, refine, and reimagine the products and services we create, buy and use. In this book, I will focus on how this dynamic plays out in the world of products, services and systems; the things people and businesses create in order to fulfill the needs and desires of other people. This dynamic relationship between utility and byproduct is not momentary. It is ongoing and infinite, a perpetual dance that shapes the way we live, work, and innovate.

This continuous cycle keeps us innovating, experimenting, and redefining what we want out of life. Yet despite its power, traditional economics has not given byproduct the spotlight it deserves. For centuries (since the late 1700's), economists have relied on the concept of utility (the satisfaction, benefit, or value we gain from goods and services) as the central framework for understanding consumer behavior and more recently, innovation. Utility's dominance stems from its intuitive nature. People seek products and services that fulfill their needs and desires, and this sense of reward shapes how we choose, consume, and invest in the world around us. However, as comprehensive and powerful as utility is, it tells only half the story.

A Storm Beneath the Sunshine of Utility

In reality, every attempt to deliver utility gives rise to byproduct, the secondary and often unintended effects that emerge from the processes, products, and systems we rely on. This is the definition of byproduct within the Law of Perpetual Innovation (LPI) Traditionally, "byproducts" have been defined narrowly as tangible waste materials, pollutants, or undesirable side effects that arise alongside a primary output. In classic economic and industrial contexts, these byproducts were often viewed as worthless leftovers or inconvenient hurdles, something to be discarded or mitigated. Over time, however, our understanding of byproduct has expanded beyond mere waste. It now encompasses a wide range of outcomes, including environmental damage, social consequences, cultural shifts, and technological spinoffs. LPI posits that it can also represent entirely new scenarios, such as unmet desires and needs that emerge as we become accustomed to existing utilities. In other words, byproduct can be more than just tangible waste, or harm. It can also be the spark that ignites the search for something better.

To fully understand this, consider that as certain technologies mature, users often develop new preferences and expectations. A product that once seemed highly innovative and satisfying might begin to reveal limitations and shortcomings over time. These limitations, which may not have been apparent initially, become byproducts that spur further innovation. For example, the transition from bulky, energy-hungry cathode ray tube televisions to sleek, energy-efficient flat screens was not solely driven by a pursuit of more utility. It was prompted by the byproducts of aging technology, which included excessive weight, large space requirements, and high energy consumption that

4

became "issues" over time. Eventually igniting the development for better alternatives. Byproducts in this sense do not always present as hazards. Sometimes they manifest as subtle nudges pointing innovators to improve what exists and discover entirely new frontiers. Nonetheless, they are secondary effects that emerge from utility.

From Bone Glue to Cultural Shifts: Byproducts Unmasked

A historical perspective reveals this complexity. Initially, byproducts were simply secondary goods that could occasionally be repurposed, such as making soap from fats or glue from bones. Later, sociologists and environmentalists recognized that entire communities and ecosystems could be reshaped, often negatively, by industrial byproducts like overcrowding, pollution, and cultural homogenization. Technologists discovered that unintended offshoots of production could spur radical innovation, leading to new materials and markets previously unimagined. Today, we see byproducts as intrinsic, multifaceted elements of economic, social, and ecological systems. They can be harmful externalities in need of regulation, or catalysts for technological breakthroughs. Within the Law of Perpetual Innovation (LPI), these are fundamentally subtle shifts in human behavior.

Within LPI, byproduct transcends these nuanced historical understandings. Here, byproduct is any secondary effect, tangible or intangible, immediate or emergent, negative or positive, that inevitably arises from the utility experience. At one extreme, a byproduct might be a glaring harmful consequence, such as toxic waste that demands urgent remediation. At the other extreme, it might appear as a fervent desire for something better. Somewhere in the middle lie gaps between our lived experiences and our ideal expectations, including minor inconveniences, inefficiencies, overlooked opportunities, and evolving desires we hardly knew we had. It isn't until our current solutions fall short, or better solutions make our current one's pale in comparison.

This expanded view is crucial. Rather than seeing byproduct as merely the absence or reduction of utility, we regard it as a distinct category that stands alongside utility. Byproduct is not simply the negative image of utility. It is its complementary counterpart. It emerges whenever we engage with reality, signaling where our hopes, dreams, and evolving standards fail to match it. Where utility brings enjoyment, comfort, and perceived fulfillment, byproduct reveals new needs, unresolved challenges, or unforeseen potentials. The interdependence of these two forces —utility and byproduct —shapes the continuous cycle of innovation. Recognizing that no form of utility comes without a corresponding byproduct helps us understand why human beings are perpetually driven to reinvent the world around them.

When The Real World Crashes Your Perfect Blueprint

For readers who may not have a strong background in economics, such as engineers or technologists, it may be helpful to think of utility and byproduct as two components within a complex system. Engineers routinely break systems down into subsystems with inputs, outputs, and feedback loops to understand how each part affects the overall system. In this analogy, utility represents the intended and desired output that the system is designed to deliver. In contrast, byproduct represents the unintended outputs or effects that emerge when the system interacts with reality. Just as an engineer would never assume that a system has no secondary effects or failure modes, we should not assume that a product only delivers pure utility. The real world is rarely so clean and linear; it is precisely these messy, emergent byproducts that often guide us in making systems more robust, efficient, and sustainable.

Armed with these broader definitions, we can now re-examine traditional economic thought. Economists have long analyzed how consumers choose goods and services to maximize utility, but they have rarely granted separate conceptual space to what might be called byproduct. Instead, unintended consequences or dissatisfaction have generally been treated as a reduction or decline in utility. This book challenges that view. By explicitly separating byproduct from utility, we gain a clearer sense of what needs improvement and where new innovation might arise. Rather than simply managing diminishing utility, we acknowledge that new or modified solutions become necessary because a distinct category of unmet desire, dissatisfaction, or unintended result has emerged.

Traditional economic frameworks, anchored almost exclusively in utility, have overlooked byproduct as a fundamental and complementary dimension. Recognizing the importance of byproduct encourages us to address its diverse manifestations, from harmful environmental externalities to newly surfaced consumer desires. By doing so, we see them not as shortcomings we must endure, but as critical signals that guide ongoing innovation.

Through my exploration of economic theory, it became clear that traditional economists have focused heavily on utility as the primary framework to describe both the benefits and drawbacks of goods and services. There is little explicit recognition of a distinct duality between utility and its secondary effects, that would separately account for the unintended consequences, drawbacks, or unresolved opportunities inherent in products.

Economic theory, especially through consumer choice models like those of Marshall, Hicks, and others, uses utility maximization as the central lens for analyzing consumer behavior. Economists often study how consumers aim to maximize utility, given constraints like prices and income, using concepts like indirect utility functions and demand functions to navigate these trade-offs. However, this approach collapses both positive and negative outcomes into the same concept, viewing diminishing satisfaction as simply "reduced utility" rather than recognizing an entirely separate category for the emergent negative outcomes (what I call byproducts) of consumption.

In behavioral economics, thinkers like Kahneman and Tversky have introduced more nuance by addressing how real-world consumers experience utility subjectively, especially through the concept of experienced utility. Behavioral economists have demonstrated that consumers are not always rational and that what people expect to find rewarding does not always align with what they actually find rewarding after using a product. These insights enable economists to examine anomalies, heuristics, and biases that influence decision-making. But even here, negative outcomes or dissatisfaction are often treated as part of utility's decline, rather than a separate phenomenon. While they delve deeper into anomalies and irrational behaviors that affect utility perception, the fundamental idea still revolves around utility as the central framework.

By not splitting off byproduct, even these more sophisticated models risk missing an opportunity to highlight the distinct nature of negative or emergent consequences. They remain confined to a narrative where all experiences, whether beneficial or harmful, exist on a single continuum of utility. If an experience disappoints, it is perceived as delivering less utility. However, as we shall see, this simplification overlooks the fact that negative outcomes sometimes require entirely different approaches and solutions. Addressing byproduct is not merely about restoring lost utility, it is about acknowledging a new category of problem that can lead to entirely new forms of innovation.

Rethinking the Rules: Leaving the Utility-Centric Universe Behind

Through this book, I argue that utility demands its duality. Distinguishing utility from byproduct is largely unaccounted for in mainstream economic models. While economists certainly recognize that goods and services can generate unintended negative outcomes, these are often folded back into the broader utility framework rather than being treated as a unique, complementary concept. The separation of these two forces (utility and byproduct), in my experience, allows for a clearer distinction between the positive benefits a product provides (utility) and the secondary effects or unmet needs it generates (byproduct). This distinction can sharpen the focus on innovation, enabling businesses to proactively address byproducts rather than manage "diminishing utility."

The tension between utility and byproduct is tied to the way humans perceive and categorize the world through our tendency to create dualities or dichotomies to make sense of complex phenomena. This is evident across various domains of life: we distinguish between light and dark, good and bad, and reward and punishment. In philosophy, this approach reflects an underlying epistemological framework that helps us organize our understanding of reality. When we apply this dualistic lens to the concept of utility, we can uncover the limitations of utility-centric thinking and why separating benefit (utility) and burden (byproduct) can provide a clearer, more precise model for innovation and human understanding.

At its core, human cognition relies heavily on dualistic thinking. From an early age, we learn to make sense of the world by categorizing our experiences into opposites or dichotomies: pleasure vs. pain, success vs. failure, reward vs. punishment. These distinctions help us navigate and make decisions, guiding our actions and behaviors. For example, the way I raise my children, I do not provide "negative" rewards for bad behavior. I apply a different category, that of consequences or punishment. This distinction allows me to be clear about what I am reinforcing, and it helps my children understand the relationship between their actions and the outcomes they may face because of them.

Similarly, the traditional economic model of utility, which treats both positive outcomes (benefits) and negative outcomes (drawbacks) under the same umbrella, lacks this crucial distinction. In attempting to compress both positive and negative experiences into a single concept (utility), we blur the boundaries that human cognition naturally seeks to create. We obscure the relationship between what we are rewarding or reinforcing (utility) and what we are discouraging or avoiding (byproduct). Just as it would be counterintuitive to say that a child is receiving a "diminished reward" when they are punished, it is philosophically inconsistent to frame the negative aspects of a product or service as merely diminished or a decline in utility. Which is what economics continues to do. These are not just variations in degree; they are fundamentally different experiences that require separate categories for proper understanding and action.

This analogy is especially relevant for engineers and other innovators who are accustomed to identifying distinct failure modes or unintended outcomes. When an engineer sees that a machine both performs a desired function and produces harmful vibrations, noise, or emissions, they do not merely say that utility is reduced. Instead, they identify the problematic byproduct and find a way to reduce it. Distinguishing between byproducts and utilities in the innovation process allows for more targeted solutions. Rather than thinking in terms of simply increasing utility, engineers can consider both enhancing utility and mitigating byproducts. This dual focus encourages a more systematic approach to problem solving.

Phenomenology, the study of how we experience the world, offers insight into the fundamental distinction between utility and byproduct. Utility and byproduct are not simply two points on a continuum of experience; they are two distinct modes of interaction with the world. The experience of utility is one of fulfillment, satisfaction, and the meeting of needs; it generates feel-good neurochemicals. It is a positive interaction with reality, where the world aligns with our goals, desires, and expectations. On the other hand, byproduct represents the friction between our expectations and the reality of the world. It is the experience of unmet needs, dissatisfaction, or unintended consequences; and it is usually accompanied by feel-bad neurochemicals (depending upon how Zen-like one may be).

By collapsing both positive and negative experiences into a single term, such as "utility," the traditional model fails to capture the phenomenological realities of human experience. In the utility-centric model, negative outcomes are described simply as a reduction or absence of utility, which misrepresents the distinct nature of frustration, inconvenience, or pain. These negative experiences are not just the absence of good, they have their own phenomenological weight. We do not experience discomfort or dissatisfaction as a "lack of benefit." Instead, we experience them as distinct, often deeply felt states of being. A product that fails us is not just delivering less utility, it is introducing an entirely different category of experience that we process differently and respond to uniquely.

From an epistemological perspective, which deals with the nature of knowledge and how we come to understand the world, distinguishing between utility and byproduct enhances clarity. If we consider how knowledge is built, through observation, categorization, and analysis, collapsing both positive and negative aspects of a product or experience into the same conceptual bucket (utility) dilutes our ability to analyze and learn from each as having its own distinct attributes.

In contrast, recognizing byproduct as its own category allows us to construct a clearer understanding of what specifically detracts from an experience or product. Byproducts are not simply "less utility," they are knowledge-producing attributes that reveal new information about the limitations or unintended consequences of a product. When framed as a byproduct rather than a "diminished utility," these insights can be actively pursued and addressed. This epistemological shift will help innovators and thinkers focus not just on increasing benefit (utility) but on solving or reducing the unique burdens (byproducts) introduced by that utility.

Many engineers, for instance, already employ this perspective to guide their iterative design process. Identifying problems (byproducts) as separate issues, linked to some feature (utility), allows for clearer troubleshooting and incremental improvement. Where previous models might have suggested we only need to add more value, the byproduct-oriented model suggests we can also look for ways to eliminate or reduce harmful outputs or unintended side effects. The result is a more holistic innovation cycle that recognizes that every product improvement may introduce new byproducts, and that addressing these byproducts is a central part of moving forward.

There is also a moral or ethical dimension to this dichotomy. In many philosophical systems, reward and punishment are treated as fundamentally different moral acts. Reward is a reinforcement of desired behavior, while punishment is a correction or deterrent of undesirable behavior. These are not merely two ends of the same spectrum; they are distinct actions with different purposes and moral weight.

Similarly, when we treat byproducts as separate from utility, we can more clearly see the ethical dimensions of innovation. Utility represents the value a product provides; the reward it offers to the user. Byproduct, on the other hand, represents the dissatisfactions, unintended consequences, or unresolved tension that the product may cause. In a utility-centric model, where byproducts are simply framed as diminished utility, it is easier to ignore or minimize the ethical responsibility to address them. However, when byproducts are treated as distinct yet linked units, innovators are morally called to account for these secondary effects that necessitate deliberate mitigation or resolution.

For example, the environmental impact of plastic production is not merely "diminished utility" for future generations; it is a byproduct. It is an unintended but direct result of our current utility-based consumption patterns. By framing these consequences as byproducts, we take moral responsibility for them in a way that a utility-centric model does not encourage. Recognizing byproducts is a step toward more socially and environmentally responsible innovation, where the full implications of a product are considered and addressed.

Finally, the utility-centric model falls short because it oversimplifies the complex dynamics between humans, products, and the environment. In simplifying everything under the term utility, it assumes that the process of innovation is a one-way street: a product delivers utility, and that utility may simply erode over time. This overlooks the nuanced, dynamic relationship between innovation and the world around it, as well as how products create new needs, problems, and opportunities.

By distinguishing between utility and byproduct, yet linking them, we gain a more holistic view of innovation, one that accounts for the full range of effects a product can have, not just its benefits. Innovation is not simply about maintaining or increasing utility; it is about actively managing the byproduct burdens that emerge from our interactions with products and services. This dual approach encourages a more comprehensive understanding of innovation as a cyclical process, where every benefit introduces a potential burden, and where addressing these byproduct burdens is as important, or even more important, as enhancing utility.

In practice, this means that when a product solves one problem, it always creates new ones. For instance, the invention of smartphones has delivered immense utility by connecting people and providing on-demand access to information. Yet, these utility generated byproducts; distraction, addiction to screen time, privacy concerns, electronic waste, and social isolation in some contexts. A purely utility-focused model might regard these problems as diminished utility, but doing so ignores their fundamental nature as separate and pressing issues. Understanding them as byproducts encourages innovators to create better user interfaces, healthier digital habits, more secure data protection measures, improved recycling programs, and features that enhance social connection rather than undermine it. This is LPI (Law of Perpetual Innovation) in action, a law that acknowledges that innovation never ends because byproducts continuously arise and prompt further improvements.

The philosophical distinction between utility and byproduct reflects a deeper human tendency to perceive and organize the world in terms of dualities. Just as we distinguish between reward and punishment, we must distinguish between utility and byproduct to fully understand and engage with the innovation process. The utility-centric model falls short by oversimplifying human experience, ignoring the distinct nature of unintended outcomes, and failing to account for the rich phenomenological and ethical dimensions of product development. By adopting a dual model of utility and byproduct, innovators can develop products and services that not only deliver value but also anticipate and address the unique challenges that arise from their use, creating a more responsible and forward-thinking approach to innovation.

From Recognition to Reformation: Rewriting the Playbook of Progress

As we advance through this book, we will explore frameworks and reasoning that illuminate the need to distinguish between the benefits products and services offer, and the burdens and opportunities that always emerge from them. Engineers will find parallels with root cause analysis and system design methodologies, where identifying unintended outputs is a key step toward building more resilient and sustainable solutions. Economists may discover fertile ground for new models that treat byproduct as a separate variable worthy of measurement, quantification, and inclusion in decision making processes.

Ultimately, the Law of Perpetual Innovation teaches us that there is no endpoint to innovation. Every solution introduces new byproducts, and every byproduct becomes a source of insight, guiding us toward the next wave of improved utility. By recognizing the duality between utility and byproduct, we gain the conceptual tools needed to navigate this perpetual cycle more effectively and ethically. Rather than simply reacting to diminishing utility, we can anticipate, identify, and address byproducts at their emergence, shaping a more adaptive, responsible, and continuously evolving path forward.

In the chapters that follow, we will build on these ideas, showing how a deeper understanding of byproducts can reshape our approach to design, strategy, and problem solving. We will learn how to categorize byproducts, assess their impact, and devise strategies to neutralize or even leverage them. We will see how embracing the utility and byproduct duality opens doors to solutions that are more than incremental fixes. Instead, it inspires transformative thinking, ensuring that as we create value and we remain vigilant about the unintended consequences that inevitably accompany it.

This is the essence of LPI. There is no final, perfect state of utility. Instead, we find ourselves in a continuous loop, guided by utility on one side and byproduct on the other. Understanding this interplay allows us to be more thoughtful innovators, better stewards of our solutions, and more conscientious participants in the global ecosystem of products and services that define modern life. In this dual model, we find a richer, fuller understanding of how innovation truly unfolds and how we can shape its course toward outcomes that are not only beneficial but also responsibly managed and perpetually open to refinement.

CHAPTER 2
Exposing Utility, Byproduct and Innovation

hello.

Before I left Apple Inc., I had conversations with some of our top engineers about innovation. I asked, "What does the next paradigm of innovative thinking look like?" The idea was not just to provide customers what they want, but to also ensure they get as little as possible of what they don't want. You might wonder, "Isn't that what most companies already do?" Not exactly. Most consumer product development companies focus on creating form-utility.

Form-utility refers to the usefulness a product or service provides when it meets customer needs and preferences in its finished state. Customers see value in the final product or service, the "form," rather than in its individual components. For example, they value a frosted cake, not just the ingredients, or they'll prefer a complete dry-cleaning service over a do-it-yourself kit.

Utility means that something is useful or valuable to people. It is useful because of the benefit or satisfaction it brings. For instance, a hammer provides the utility of driving nails easily. An acoustic guitar offers the utility of playing music without needing an amplifier. A ride-sharing service provides transportation, often cheaper and faster than a taxi. People pay for products or services because the utility they offer is valuable to them. They exchange money, one form of value, for the utility the product or service provides, a different form of value. It is important to understand that products and services are the medium through which utility is delivered, unless the product itself evokes a feeling or sentiment, in which case it also provides utility. So, it is logical for product development companies to focus on delivering form-utility when creating products or services. Companies invest in making a product as effective for the consumer as possible, while also ensuring efficient production and distribution to protect their bottom line.

When a company develops a product, it wants to do it well. It invests in various areas, from designing the product and choosing its features, to sourcing components and materials. The company assembles and manufactures these materials into a finished product, tests it, packages it, and distributes it to stores or directly to customers. The company also plans how to sell the product and makes it easy for customers to buy. All these steps are focused on getting the product into the hands of the customer because it delivers utility.

It is no surprise that individuals and businesses invest heavily in creating utility by building prototypes, piloting products, and conducting user studies; all aimed at delivering utility. Businesses create value for customers by driving utility creation efforts. So, "Is it not logical to say that the value businesses create for customers by delivering utility also creates value for the business?" That is what I used to believe, but there is more to the story than just utility.

Deconstructing Utility

Shoes protect our feet from rough terrain. Cars take us from point A to point B faster than walking, saving us physical effort and shielding us from the weather. Airplanes carry us over any terrain or water, faster and often safer than cars. All these examples share a common core utility: human Movement and Locomotion. Locomotion has been essential since ancient hominids began walking on two legs. Yet today, few would consider walking from state to state or coast to coast, which was common before planes, trains, and automobiles. In the past, people traveled in caravans, either on foot or by horse-drawn carriage, across vast landscapes without roads. They faced dehydration from heat, frostbite from cold, marshy land after rain, and the constant threat of running out of food or supplies. The journey was grueling, and many did not survive. Yet today, walking just two miles to a store seems like a burden to many, so they drive. If I want to cross 10 states, I can hop on a plane and arrive by dinner, entirely avoiding the hardships faced by those who came before me.

This change highlights a fundamental truth: the value of business lies in its ability to create products and services that improve upon experiences humans want to avoid. Let us call these "opportunities" for now. Opportunities arise when the utility of a product or service falls short in some way. When shoes were first invented, likely simple leather straps, they provided much more utility than going barefoot. But over time, their limitations became clear. They wore out, took time to put on, and did not smell great after a full day of use. What once seemed like a revolutionary improvement soon revealed its shortcomings.

Interestingly, the natural human utility of walking (locomotion) led to the invention of shoes. A human-driven utility designed to improve natural movement. But those early shoes eventually were not good enough. If they were, we would still be wearing them today. The first shoe had secondary effects on its users: they took time to put on, did not last long, and smelled bad. These secondary effects triggered the desire for something better. This is where the opportunity for innovation begins. What LPI calls byproduct.

A byproduct is a secondary effect or result, often unintended or unexpected, that arises because of something else. In the context of The Law of Perpetual Innovation, a byproduct is a secondary effect that emerges from the utility of goods and services. Utility and byproduct are inseparable. When utility is created and delivered, byproducts always follow, whether immediately or over time. As described in the first version of the shoe (a product) that protected the users' feet from harsh terrain (the utility). The secondary effects that emerged came in the form of the limitations that became apparent immediately and over time; they wore out, took time to wrap around the feet, and did not smell great after wear (the byproducts).

Byproducts, however, are not always negative. They can create new desires or needs that only arise after the product becomes part of the user's life. For example, the noise of a hammer hitting a nail or the risk of hitting your fingers are byproducts that might inspire a desire for quieter, safer tools. Perfect utility does not exist because byproducts will always emerge due to factors like usage, product wear, changing personal preferences, evolving environments, and competition. This constant emergence of byproducts is why we see a proliferation of options in products such as shoes, cars, and modes of transportation. They all trace back to the original human utility of Movement and Locomotion; with each new innovation responding to the byproducts of the last.

Clarifying Innovation

It is important to have a clear understanding of what innovation is and is not. People often associate innovation with modern technology, but strides in innovation have been happening since at least the early 1600s. While technology can drive innovation, innovation can also result from non-technological advancements. Originally, innovation referred to significant improvements for society or a population. Advancements in living standards, working conditions, health, and education. True innovation is anything that has a positive impact on a large number of people, measurable through direct or indirect improvements to their economy or quality of life. These large-scale improvements are what define innovation.

Innovation is not a technology-based term; it is an economics-based term. Today, the word tends to be misused. For example, a company might say, "We are currently innovating," or "We're working on an innovative solution." These uses are technically incorrect because innovation is the outcome of an effort, not the effort itself. Innovation is the result of deliberate creative actions, and it refers to how those actions positively impact a large group of people or society. It is not the creative actions themselves. Saying, "We are currently innovating," does not make sense. What is more accurate is, "We are currently creating," or "We are developing," or "We are driving efforts to make an innovative impact."

Consider a professional athlete. If you ask what they are doing during pre-season training, they will tell you they are practicing or training, or that they are preparing to win games. They would not say they are "winning games" while still in training. In the same way, you cannot claim to be "innovating" when the efforts you are making (like developing a product) have not yet resulted in the outcome (innovation). It is crucial to recognize that innovation is a change in an economic or social environment that creates or distributes wealth, a.k.a. value. And just so you know, I have misused the term too, because it has become common, especially in Silicon Valley. It is a buzzword that is often used by people seeking investment or funding to suggest their creations will be innovative. Over time, business culture has distorted its meaning. However, it is important to understand what innovation truly means.

The international organization for standardization (ISO) defines innovation, in the standard ISO 56000:2020, as "A new or changed entity realizing or redistributing value."

Innovation through Utility (the illusion)

Now that you understand what it means to be innovative, we can talk about what innovation seems to be rooted in today: utility. Specifically, the provision of utility through goods and services. Let us take the incandescent light bulb as an example and look at how it made a significant positive impact on society, resulting in innovation. Many of us, me included, tend to take in-home lighting for granted. It's hard to imagine what the world was like before electricity powered light bulbs across our cities. For those of us who wake up before sunrise, we turn on the lights in our bedrooms, bathrooms, kitchens, or other areas as we prepare for the day. In the past, there were no lights to switch on. If you were fortunate enough to have candles or oil lamps, you would use them for light. Otherwise, you started your day with whatever dim natural sunlight entered your home.

We can all agree that in-home lighting was innovative, but that is not where the light bulb made its most significant debut. Its deepest impact on society did not begin in homes, that came later.

The real breakthrough for electric lighting happened in industry. Companies could now light their factory floors, no longer relying on sunlight, candles, oil lamps, or gas lighting. This allowed production to continue around the clock, increasing the output of steel, chemicals, textiles, canned foods, and more. Flame-based lighting in factories also increased the risk of fires, making workplaces dangerous. In coal mines, for example, flame-based lights could ignite flammable gases, causing massive explosions that killed dozens of workers when gas veins were accidentally exposed. But with the light bulb, these dangers were significantly reduced. Industry could now produce and supply more goods to consumers in less time and under much safer conditions. This was the first wave of meaningful mass utility that made the light bulb truly innovative.

Innovation through Byproduct (the reality)

Innovation always depends on providing some form of utility. This utility may come in the form of a new product or an improvement on an existing one. Either way, as we have discussed earlier, something else emerges along with the realization of utility: byproduct. Byproducts are an intrinsic causality of utility. The two are inseparable. You cannot create utility (something beneficial) without also generating byproduct (the emergent drawbacks or burdens).

Let us take a look at some of the byproducts of the incandescent light bulb as an example. By today's standards, it is a simple product, but the first light bulbs had very low luminous efficiency. Less than 5% of the power they consumed was converted into visible light; the remaining 95% was emitted as invisible infrared radiation. This inefficiency meant the light bulb acted more like a heat source than a light source. If you needed both light and heat, that was fine. But for most users, this inefficiency introduced byproducts.

For industrial plants and factories, the excess heat became a problem. Their indoor temperatures increased, which created challenges for industries that needed to maintain specific temperature conditions to preserve their products. This was a byproduct for those industries. In cases where temperature control was not necessary for products, it still became a problem for workers, adding to their discomfort. Another byproduct. Early light bulbs also had short lifespans and were highly sensitive to vibrations, meaning they needed to be replaced frequently. Since light bulbs were already expensive, these additional overhead costs had to be absorbed by companies, affecting employees before reaching customers. More byproduct.

Additionally, the first light bulbs emitted light in one general, but inconsistent, hue. This created issues for manufacturers who needed to see the true color of fabrics, textiles, or other materials. Metamerism, which occurs when light of a particular spectral color interacts with a material and causes it to appear as a different color than it would under natural or white light, was a problem. This, too, was a byproduct of early light bulbs.

Perhaps the most significant impact was on society itself in the form of changes to the workday. Factories and industrial plants could now operate 24 - 7. While this was good for manufacturers and the economy, especially in a time of weak labor laws, it was detrimental to many workers, their families, and their communities. This was a major societal byproduct. In addition, the light bulb disrupted industries like candle-making, oil lamps, and gas lamps, leading to job losses and financial struggles for many families. But since flame-based lighting had its own set of byproducts that the light bulb resolved through its improved utility; this economic disruption was often dismissed as "part of doing business." Still, economic disruption is undeniably, a byproduct.

These are just a few examples of the byproducts that came with the first wave of mass utility provided by the incandescent light bulb. Many more followed over time. What is important to recognize is that improvements to the light bulb have continued over the decades. As each utility is created and its byproducts emerge, new utilities are developed to resolve those byproducts, which in turn create their own new byproducts. This ongoing process forms a perpetual cycle of utility and byproduct (see illustration below). If understood and applied correctly, this cycle can significantly help organizations create better products and services.

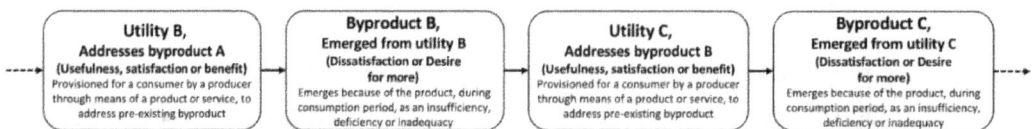

| Utility B, Addresses byproduct A (Usefulness, satisfaction or benefit) Provisioned for a consumer by a producer through means of a product or service, to address pre-existing byproduct | Byproduct B, Emerged from utility B (Dissatisfaction or Desire for more) Emerges because of the product, during consumption period, as an insufficiency, deficiency or inadequacy | Utility C, Addresses byproduct B (Usefulness, satisfaction or benefit) Provisioned for a consumer by a producer through means of a product or service, to address pre-existing byproduct | Byproduct C, Emerged from utility C (Dissatisfaction or Desire for more) Emerges because of the product, during consumption period, as an insufficiency, deficiency or inadequacy |

What the cycle really looks like

The most successful businesses understand this concept deeply. While they may not use the term "byproduct," they are constantly striving to address the byproducts of their current or earlier solutions; the problems, dissatisfactions, or unmet desires that arise. Their goal is not just to create utility, though that is ultimately what they deliver. They know that their next opportunity lies in addressing these byproducts. This is where real value exists.

Byproduct is not just a part of the innovation system. It *"is"* the system. While innovation depends on providing utility, that utility is driven by byproducts, not utility itself. In fact, it is impossible to describe a product's utility without referencing byproducts in some way. For instance, when you say, "These shoes are comfortable," you are really pointing to the byproduct of discomfort being solved. "This hat looks elegant" addresses the byproduct of lacking style. "This car is quiet" improves upon the byproduct of noise. This is what LPI refers to as *byproduct-referencing utility* (see Chapter 13, Principle of Byproduct as Relational Context). All utility is described in terms of an undesirable or aspirational state the product improves upon. The byproduct a user wishes to eliminate, avoid, or escape forms the context for why a product's utility is appreciated and therefore valuable.

Earlier, I asked, "Is it not logical to say that the value businesses create for their customers by driving utility creation is also value for the business?" In principle, yes, but only when that utility is grounded in the right byproducts. A company's success hinges on identifying and solving the right byproducts; the unresolved deficiencies or unfulfilled aspirations that truly matter to its customers. No matter how functional or innovative a product might seem, if it addresses the wrong byproduct, it will fail to resonate. Utility alone is not enough; it must liberate customers from the specific issues that hold them back or stop them from experiencing something better. Just as an employee's worth is gauged by their ability to deliver results that matter to their company, a business thrives by delivering outcomes that matter to the customer. And what customers truly desire is the resolution of the byproducts causing their dissatisfaction or prompting an unmet desire for better. Misjudging these byproducts means missing the mark, jeopardizing adoption and long-term success for the business.

By these accounts, innovation is driven by byproducts, not utility. Every utility is a solution to previous byproducts, and every new utility will generate byproducts in turn. The incandescent light bulbs' utility resolved many of the flame-based lightings' byproducts. Fluorescent lightings' utility resolved many of the incandescent light bulbs' byproducts. LED lighting utility resolved many of the byproducts of incandescent and fluorescent lighting. The cycle has continued since humans harnessed fire at least 1 million years ago. This is the endless cycle of innovation, what I refer to as the *Law of Perpetual Innovation.*

A Brief Side-step: How byproduct gets lost in the pursuit of utility provision

As scientific, engineering, manufacturing, distribution, and other functional disciplines have evolved over the years, they have continued to branch out into more specialized areas. These branches tend to grow especially fast in fields that receive the most funding from organizations that produce well-selling products and services. Combine this with companies developing increasingly complex products or services, while trying to stay competitive in the marketplace, and you end up with organizations where these functional disciplines are spread across a vast global geography.

As this happens, functional teams become more fragmented and disconnected from the broader view of what it takes to fully produce and deliver the goods or services. No single person in the entire organization knows exactly everything that goes into conceptualizing, designing, prototyping, qualifying, testing, manufacturing, packaging, storing, distributing, marketing, and selling the product. Or whatever else is necessary to get it into the customer's hands.

With this level of complexity spread across the globe, and everyone focused on driving utility provision, who is paying attention to how this provided utility might negatively impact various parts of the business, or society, the economy, or both intended and unintended customers? This is where byproduct emergence can go unchecked.

More on Byproduct

It is important to take some time to expand on the concept of byproduct. Not all byproducts are harmful or concerning. In fact, many established and reputable companies today do a great job of managing this through their science and engineering teams. Still, some byproducts come in the form of "inspiring or provoking a want or desire for something better." This happens when certain aspects of a product's current form-utility lead to a feeling of absence or a tension between the current utility "that is" and a future potential utility "that could be." This can occur immediately, over time, or incidentally, either due to the product's utility itself (intrinsically) or because of external factors (extrinsically) in comparison to our existing products' utility.

For example, the invention of the light bulb eventually led to the desire for more customized or aesthetically pleasing lighting, such as table lamps and chandeliers. Functionally, these are not necessities, but more of a want. However, for some people, this is important. Design aesthetics can enhance usability while complementing a personal or environmental setting. When such wants or aspirations remain open or unmet, they linger as an unresolved "tension." This too is byproduct.

Another example is a car. As soon as we buy it, we might realize we now want nicer rims because the current ones do not meet our expectations (an immediate and intrinsic byproduct). Over time, the utility or satisfaction we get from the car fades (economists call this diminishing marginal utility). When the car was new, we washed it every week and kept it spotless, but two years later, we are not as invested. Then one day, we see a friend's new car, similar to ours but with added features: power windows, wireless key entry, Bluetooth music streaming, and better rims. This encounter triggers a desire for that newer model (an incidental and extrinsic byproduct). Without seeing our friend's car, we may not have felt the desire for something potentially better (Chapters 10-12 further explore Aspirational Comparison).

As mentioned earlier, all utility arises from some previous byproduct, creating a never-ending cycle between utility and byproduct (see illustration below). While some byproducts are easy to identify, others are more subtle. Take the photographic camera, for example. What preexisting byproduct could have inspired its creation? We can infer that from early cave drawings to modern paintings, there was a desire to capture a lasting visual impression of a moment in time without needing a skilled painter or a long wait. These were likely the byproducts that the camera addressed.

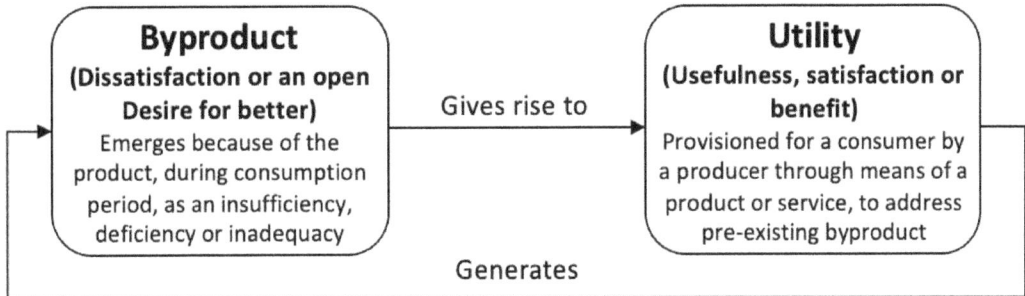

Byproduct (Dissatisfaction or an open Desire for better) Emerges because of the product, during consumption period, as an insufficiency, deficiency or inadequacy	Gives rise to	**Utility** (Usefulness, satisfaction or benefit) Provisioned for a consumer by a producer through means of a product or service, to address pre-existing byproduct
	Generates	

The Byproduct Utility causality loop

Or consider consumable alcohol. What byproduct might have led to its utility? Since alcohol requires fermentation, it is possible that alcohol itself began as a *naturally occurring byproduct* of nature itself. It is believed that the ability to metabolize alcohol predates humans, as our primate ancestors consumed fermented fruit. Over time, humans could already process alcohol, and as we recognized its effects on our perception, it became central to social gatherings and rituals in many ancient civilizations, addressing byproduct burdens intrinsic to human interaction and emotional regulation such as social inhibition and anxiety. This continues to be the case today.

Byproduct is an unavoidable after-effect of some prior utility. Utility created by humans. This utility originally stemmed from humanity's cognitive and perception-based interactions with their environment. As humans recognized limitations in their abilities, it revealed or even provoked opportunities to improve their present circumstances. For example, when humans first started drawing on cave walls, the urge to do so likely came from a desire to capture what they were seeing around them, to memorialize that experience. Or when humans discovered that fire could keep them warm from the elements, a motivation to harness that utility emerged.

But what about the origins of utility itself, where the byproduct being addressed did not come from any prior human creation? This leads us to the question of where utility, or innovation, began. How humans, or species in general, from their earliest days, came to extend their abilities, even before they created tools or systems that drove new byproducts.

CHAPTER 3
Origins of Innovation

Where do we begin?

Innovation, in its most primal form, stretches back to the earliest phases of life on Earth, long before African Hominins appeared 2 million years ago and well before the hunter-gatherer humans of 11,000 years ago. Over time, countless interactions between Mother Nature and our species have led to a multitude of adaptations, commonly referred to as evolution. Evolution, however, is not merely a passive process. It is fundamentally driven by responses to environmental stimuli that provoke change. These responses, at their core, occur at the cellular level through mutations in an organism's DNA or RNA.

The mutation process is triggered by external factors, what we can describe as *"naturally occurring byproducts."* These forces, which include high-energy radiation, environmental chemicals, or other natural elements, provoke changes in an organism's genetic material. Suppose these mutations provide a benefit, such as enhancing an organism's ability to grow, reproduce, feed, or survive. In that case, they result in what we can refer to as a *"naturally occurring utility (NOU)."* This utility represents a new or improved capability that offers value to the organism, allowing it to better adapt to its environment.

These naturally occurring byproducts act as evolutionary catalysts, compelling organisms to adapt and improve. When cells respond to such instigating forces, they create opportunities for naturally occurring utility, an ongoing cycle of adaptation and improvement. If a mutation is beneficial, it is preserved through natural selection and passed down through generations, ultimately spreading across an entire species. However, not every mutation is advantageous. Some mutations, when triggered by external forces, fail to provide a natural utility. Instead, they weaken the organism's ability to survive and reproduce, and as a result, are eliminated by natural selection. These failed mutations are byproducts themselves. Failed attempts at natural utility that are weeded out by the forces of evolution.

On the other hand, when a mutation is advantageous, when it results in a *naturally occurring utility*, it becomes a pivotal factor in the survival and evolution of the species. Over time, this utility is passed on to future generations, spreading across entire populations until it becomes a defining characteristic of the species. This process is what we can describe as *"naturally occurring innovation,"* where an evolutionary improvement is driven by natural forces and sustained through the process of natural selection.

"A naturally occurring innovation is being defined as a naturally occurring utility (NOU) that becomes widespread across an entire population of a species or a significant subgroup of that species."

Today, our human bodies bear evidence of these *naturally occurring innovations*, shaped by millions of years of adaptation to our environment. For instance, the development of fingers and opposable thumbs has provided humans with the ability to grasp and manipulate objects, such as pulling roots from the ground or throwing rocks and weapons, critical functions for survival and defense. This utility has been universally beneficial across the human species, offering a clear example of *naturally occurring innovation*. As new capabilities like object manipulation evolved, we likely attempted to hunt larger animals, and before mastering these skills, many early attempts likely resulted in harm from these animals, which became an unintended byproduct of our drive to expand our survival strategies.

Another profound natural innovation is the human ability to stand upright with an erect posture. This adaptation allows for more efficient energy expenditure, freeing our hands for other tasks as we walk or run. Coupled with this, our capacity to perspire is a critical natural utility that helps regulate body temperature during physical exertion. These innovations, widespread across our species, have been essential for our survival and success in a range of environments.

Our eyesight provides yet another example of naturally occurring innovation. Human vision offers a broad range of distance and color perception, allowing us to see and differentiate between objects both near and far. This ability to detect close objects, like food sources or dangerous insects, while simultaneously scanning for distant threats or opportunities, has been indispensable for human survival. However, as new naturally occurring utilities emerged, such as the ability to see colors, we interacted with berries, mushrooms and insects that were not always beneficial for our survival. This led to harmful byproducts to emerge because of these utilities, ultimately driving the need to create new human-driven utilities like identifying, storing, and retrieving information about what was safe or harmful.

Beyond these general innovations, Mother Nature has driven more region-specific adaptations in humans based on distinct climatic conditions. The evolution of dark skin, for instance, is a natural utility that provides protection against the harmful effects of ultraviolet radiation, a natural byproduct of intense sunlight. Without this protective utility, individuals would experience a significant reduction in folic acid (vitamin B9) levels, as well as DNA damage to their skin. This natural innovation has been crucial for populations living in areas with high sun exposure.

Another region-specific adaptation is the evolution of nostril width, which scientists believe is closely tied to the climatic conditions of a given region. One of the primary functions of the nose is to warm, humidify, and filter air before it enters the lungs, helping to maintain overall health. In cold, dry climates, a naturally occurring byproduct, humans evolved narrower nostrils. This adaptation, a natural utility, allowed for more effective conditioning of cold air by trapping and warming it as it passes through the mucus-covered nasal passages. This small yet significant natural innovation improved the survival chances of those living in such environments.

These examples illustrate how the dynamic interplay between *naturally occurring byproducts* and the development of *naturally occurring utilities* has shaped the course of human evolution. Through this process of natural selection, Mother Nature has driven countless innovations that continue to define our species. Each step in the evolutionary process reveals a deeper truth about innovation: that it is an unbroken cycle, where byproducts provoke utility, and utility, in turn, creates new byproducts, leading to further innovation. To fully appreciate this perpetual innovation cycle, we must first explore how life transitioned from molecular chaos to structured, multicellular organisms. Each step driven by incremental yet critical innovations responding directly to environmental pressures and their accompanying byproducts.

The Emergence of Utility from Molecules to Multicellularity

At the heart of the Law of Perpetual Innovation (LPI) lies the principle that innovation occurs continuously as a response to persistent burdens (byproducts). This principle was true even billions of years ago at life's earliest moments. Long before life possessed the complexity we recognize today, Earth's environment itself was an unrelenting generator of natural challenges. Around 4 billion years ago, our planet was more akin to a chaotic laboratory, continually bombarded by radiation, volcanic eruptions, meteor impacts, and violent chemical reactions in hydrothermal vents and tidal pools. From LPI's perspective, these harsh conditions represented a landscape saturated with naturally occurring byproducts, unstable temperatures, radical chemical gradients, and intense radiation, that constantly challenged molecular stability.

In this harsh environment, any molecular structure capable of momentarily maintaining internal order represented a primitive form of utility, or a "proto-utility." For instance, simple lipid molecules spontaneously formed vesicles, tiny bubble-like structures that encapsulated chemical reactions, temporarily protecting delicate reaction intermediates from external disturbances. Such proto-utilities provided a temporary advantage, enabling these molecules to persist slightly longer amidst external chaos. Yet, if these structures failed to manage external disruptions such as changes in pH or destructive radiation, they quickly dissolved. Only those capable of maintaining their internal balance amidst relentless challenges persisted, thus paving the path toward more complex biological structures.

Over immense spans of time, this molecular trial-and-error led to increasingly sophisticated assemblies. Early molecular clusters, driven by sheer chemical dynamics, inadvertently embodied foundational principles such as utility integration and adaptive utility (see utility principles 32 and 26 in chapter 16, respectively). For example, mineral surfaces within hydrothermal vents acted as catalysts, enhancing chemical reactions by bringing molecules closer together, integrating various proto-utilities into more stable networks. Additionally, primitive redox reactions, capable of recycling electron carriers, adapted dynamically to the external energy sources, continually managing the disruptive byproducts of their environments.

Eventually, an extraordinary event took place: molecules capable of self-replication emerged. This marked a significant turning point, giving rise to the process of natural selection, a powerful but unconscious engine of innovation. Molecular structures that successfully replicated themselves passed their advantageous properties forward, while structures unable to manage the byproduct burdens of their environment quickly disappeared. This evolutionary dynamic, essentially a continuous competition to minimize natural byproduct, drove natural innovation at an accelerating pace. Over generations, improvements such as RNA-based enzymes, capable of mitigating toxic metabolic intermediates, became prevalent due to their immediate survival benefits.

As life progressed from simple cells to more complex organisms, cellular growth encountered significant physical constraints. Individual cells faced limitations such as reduced efficiency in nutrient uptake and internal communication, issues arising directly from their increasing size. A clear geometric byproduct. Natural selection responded by promoting multicellularity, effectively employing advanced principles of innovation. Cells began linking their internal environments through structures such as gap junctions, integrating their metabolic efforts and collectively mitigating disruptions from external stressors. For instance, in early marine organisms, coordinated groups of cells formed rudimentary tissues capable of sharing nutrients and dispersing metabolic heat more effectively.

This multicellular collaboration naturally led to utility specialization (utility principle 49, chapter 16), where different cells within a group assumed specific roles to reduce overall inefficiencies. In primitive sea sponges, for example, some cells specialized in structural support, others in nutrient absorption, and yet others in defense mechanisms against predation. This division of labor drastically reduced the metabolic and functional burdens previously faced by single cells attempting to fulfill multiple roles simultaneously.

Further evolutionary refinements introduced modularity (utility principle 31, chapter 16), distinct, interchangeable components such as specialized tissues and organ systems. These modules enabled organisms to compartmentalize functions, effectively isolating and managing byproducts. For example, plants evolved leaf abscission zones, areas that allowed the safe shedding of leaves burdened by accumulated damage or toxins, thereby preserving overall plant health. Similarly, animals developed distinct organ systems, such as the liver, specialized in filtering and detoxifying metabolic byproducts from the bloodstream.

Adaptive utility also emerged, allowing organisms to respond dynamically to transient environmental burdens. Hormonal feedback loops evolved, enabling real-time adjustments to internal conditions, such as regulating body temperature during rapid climatic shifts. For instance, mammals developed endothermic capabilities, actively generating and dissipating heat to maintain stable body temperatures regardless of external variations.

Through these evolutionary innovation methods of integration, specialization, modularity, and adaptive utility, life continuously adapted and complexified, constantly driven by the unending cycle of byproducts and the pursuit of utility. Each innovation created new layers of complexity, inevitably generating new byproducts that further fueled evolutionary innovation. From primitive molecular aggregates to the sophisticated multicellular life forms we see today, the cycle of perpetual innovation has remained unbroken, relentlessly pushing life toward greater complexity, efficiency, and resilience against a chaotic environment.

As multicellular life mastered increasingly complex utilities, one evolutionary branch would eventually diverge profoundly, giving rise to extraordinary cognitive capacities, utilities that would radically redefine innovation and our relationship with the natural world.

Our Divergence

Building upon the deep evolutionary history of molecular and multicellular utilities, human evolution witnessed a remarkable divergence. Countless naturally occurring innovations have shaped our species, some of which have already been discussed. While the exact number of natural utilities that emerged and remained over the past 7 million years is unknown, they collectively contributed to the human being we know today. However, one pivotal event stands out. An event so significant that it forever altered the trajectory of humanity. This was the development of extraordinary cognitive abilities. A *divergence event* that set humans apart from all other species in a way that makes us seem almost alien in comparison.

This cognitive divergence happened gradually, but its impact was profound. Humans evolved mental faculties so advanced that, at some point, we came to believe we were no longer part of the animal kingdom. We imagined ourselves to be creations of some higher power, members of a different, superior kingdom altogether. This belief took hold despite the lack of any evidence, even though we clearly shared characteristics with animals. We fed, bred, and bled just like them. Yet our cognitive abilities, and the utilities that stemmed from them, were so unique that we could not believe we were the same as other creatures. This in itself is a remarkable testament to the power of human imagination. At that time, we had not yet developed the tools or processes to test and prove such beliefs. Nevertheless, the *"cumulative utilitarian faculties"* gifted to us by Mother Nature culminated in what can be described as a *natural disruptive divergence*; a disruption not to technology or culture, but to the natural order of Mother Nature herself.

In this process, it was as if humanity borrowed from the flame of Mother Nature's torch and made a conscious decision to innovate under our own terms. This disruption manifested as humans taking control of the world, its natural resources, and all other species inhabiting it. We declared ourselves the gods of the Earth, entitled by the very super-entities of our own imagining. This shift in thinking marked humanity's self-perceived dominion over the natural world.

Armed with this newfound cognitive capacity, we developed the ability to work together and cooperate. A significant utility that greatly enhanced our chances of survival. Through evolution, our brains and bodies became hardwired for social interaction, enabling us to collectively observe and adapt to our environment. We evolved the ability to release neurochemicals as a form of biological feedback, reinforcing behaviors that benefitted us and signaling when to avoid potential dangers. These neurochemical processes allowed us to assess situations, make judgments, and take action.

For example, when confronted with a threat such as a lion or bear, our adrenal glands evolved the ability to release epinephrine (adrenaline) and cortisol (the stress hormone). These neurochemicals heightened our alertness, preparing us to either confront the threat or flee from it quickly. This was a survival utility, honed over time by the natural selection process.

Conversely, our bodies also evolved mechanisms to generate positive mood states or counteract negative ones. We developed the ability to release neurochemicals that produced feelings of accomplishment or contentment after achieving certain goals, such as finding shelter or successfully hunting large prey. In these moments, our brains would release dopamine and serotonin, giving us a sense of achievement and well-being. Similarly, when we bonded with loved ones or helped members of our tribe, the release of neurochemicals like oxytocin, serotonin, dopamine, and endorphins would generate feelings of happiness, connection, or even elation. This natural reward system reinforced cooperative behaviors, fostering strong social bonds, and improving the survival of the group.

Our cognitive evolution extended beyond basic survival instincts. Over time, these neurochemical reinforcements encouraged more complex social behaviors, including empathy, altruism, and long-term planning. We began to recognize the benefits of working together, sharing resources, and protecting one another, further strengthening our communities. These cooperative behaviors became fundamental to the human experience, rooted in the evolutionary utilities that shaped our species.

This ability to experience and interpret a wide range of emotions and social interactions allowed humans to create complex societies and civilizations. The divergence that began with our cognitive evolution became a key driver of *human-driven innovation*, enabling us to not only survive but to thrive in a world we were increasingly shaping through our own intelligence.

In this way, our species' extraordinary mental abilities, and the utilities that arose from them, led us to diverge from the rest of the animal kingdom in ways that continue to shape our relationship with the natural world and with one another. This cognitive evolution remains the foundation of our ability to innovate, cooperate, and dominate the planet, further reinforcing the *Law of Perpetual Innovation* as we continue to harness both natural and human-driven utilities to address the byproducts of our environment and society.

Creativity's Pull

As humans evolved and developed the ability to take neurochemical cues based on how we perceived our environment, we began to build and create things that helped us manage our emotional responses. More specifically, we created tools and systems to suppress the release of *feel-bad* neurochemicals, such as those triggered by fear or discomfort, while increasing the release and duration of *feel-good* neurochemicals, associated with satisfaction, accomplishment, and joy. In other words, we started to create solutions that reduced externally imposed byproducts (challenges or hardships) and expanded our natural human utility (our innate capabilities).

For example, when we experienced the hardship of cold weather, a natural byproduct that our body hair could not fully protect us from, we had to find a way to survive while still moving or hunting. Eventually, we learned to cover ourselves with animal furs. These furs, with their dense layers of hair, trapped air more effectively than our own body hair, providing insulation against the cold. In this way, animal furs acted as an extension of our body's natural utility. We had now created a *wearable utility*, a product that could be used or removed at will, to enhance our ability to stay warm. Of course, this innovation likely evolved over time through trial and error, as we experimented with other materials like leaves or grass before discovering the superior properties of certain animal hides.

Similarly, when we grew frustrated with the inefficiency of catching fish by hand, a method that was time-consuming and often resulted in hunger when it failed, we innovated. First, we used sticks and rocks (Utility Version 1), then developed spears (Utility Version 2), and eventually figured out how to tie strands of twigs together to create nets (Utility Version 3). With a net, we could catch multiple fish at once, effectively extending our natural utility of manual grasping and hunting.

We can imagine the tribe member who stayed by the fire, night after night, tinkering with twigs and branches while others watched with curiosity. To them, it might have looked like this person was weaving a large, ineffective object. But then came the day when that same individual returned from the river with an abnormal number of fish, more than anyone could catch with their hands or spears alone. The sense of joy and exhilaration that must have washed over them as the tribe looked on in awe, realizing this innovation could feed not just the inventor, but the entire group. This moment likely triggered the release of *feel-good* neurochemicals for everyone, reinforcing the individual's sense of accomplishment and social value. From that day forward, the tribe slept easier, with less fear of hunger, reducing *feel-bad* neurochemicals. And the individual who made that first net? They became the tribe's first "net engineer," what we might call an *innovator* today.

For thousands of years, humans continued this process of creativity and innovation. The evolution of these tools and technologies was slow, laborious, and immensely challenging. Before we learned how to work with metal, we had to rely on primitive tools, which in turn resulted in primitive creations. All the while, we were in constant search of food, shelter, and protection from predators. The only way to manage these basic needs while also working on new creations was through the help and cooperation of others. Cooperation became a crucial utility in and of itself, allowing early humans to divide tasks and share the burden of survival.

As time went on, certain individuals in a group became proficient in specific tasks, and they assumed the role of experts in their craft. These roles, whether hunting, farming, or making tools, became their identity, often passed down through generations, becoming extensions of their naturally occurring utility. Their descendants were known by the skills they mastered (Mr. Bowman, Ms. Sheppard, Mrs. Skinner), and over time, these skills became essential to the survival and progress of human communities.

Throughout history, the pace of this innovation was slow, moving at what could be described as a snail's pace. Yet, every so often, a breakthrough would occur, an innovation whose utility was truly transformative. The harnessing of fire, the domestication of animals, the invention of the wheel, the practice of farming, the discovery of metalworking, and the scientific method were such breakthroughs. These innovations springboarded humanity's ability to improve living conditions and, crucially, freed up time. This freed time allowed for more focused efforts on reducing the byproducts that triggered *feel-bad* neurochemical responses (fear, discomfort, hunger) and on creating new utilities that enhanced *feel-good* neurochemical responses (joy, satisfaction, security).

With each successive innovation, the process of byproduct reduction and utility creation accelerated, and it continues to do so today. What started with simple tools and animal skins has evolved into advanced technologies, systems of governance, and global cooperation. This cycle of reducing external challenges and extending our natural abilities continues *ad infinitum,* driving the perpetual cycle of human innovation, creativity, and progress.

Each step in this journey reflects the *Law of Perpetual Innovation,* where each solution to a byproduct creates new utilities, which in turn generate their own byproducts, leading to further innovations. It is a never-ending process, powered by the human drive to improve our circumstances, foster cooperation, and achieve a sense of accomplishment and well-being.

Enter: "Goods and Services"

As humanity continued to innovate, the utilities we created became organized into what we now call goods and services. These are the building blocks of all economic activity, serving as the foundation for production, distribution, and consumption within societies. The exchange of goods and services not only shaped how societies function but also gave rise to fundamental concepts that underpin modern civilization, such as property, trade, monetary value, interest, debt, credit, wealth, customers and suppliers, supply and demand, profit and loss, assets and liabilities, contracts, businesses, markets, financial systems, and ultimately, the economy.

As these concepts took shape, they provided a framework for understanding, measuring, and controlling the flow, growth, or decline of goods and services and the markets they fueled. These concepts also helped us comprehend broader economic phenomena, such as "the wealth of nations," which refers to the economic power of a society as measured by its production of goods and services. One key metric in this context is Gross Domestic Product (GDP), which represents the total market value of all goods and services produced by a nation within a specific time limit. The GDP has become a standard of measure to assess the economic health of a country and the living standards of its population.

Looking at global GDP trends over the last 1,023 years (see illustration: using international dollars, a hypothetical currency adjusted for inflation and standardized to 2021 prices), the data reveals striking patterns of economic growth. It took 500 years, from 1000 AD to 1500 AD, for the global GDP to double. From 1500 to 1600, it grew by 1.33 times, and from 1600 to 1700, by 1.12 times. Growth began to accelerate more noticeably between 1700 and 1820, with GDP increasing by 1.87 times. Then, from 1820 to 1900, it surged by 2.98 times. But the most dramatic shift occurred between 1900 and 2023, when global GDP exploded by a staggering 34.29 times.

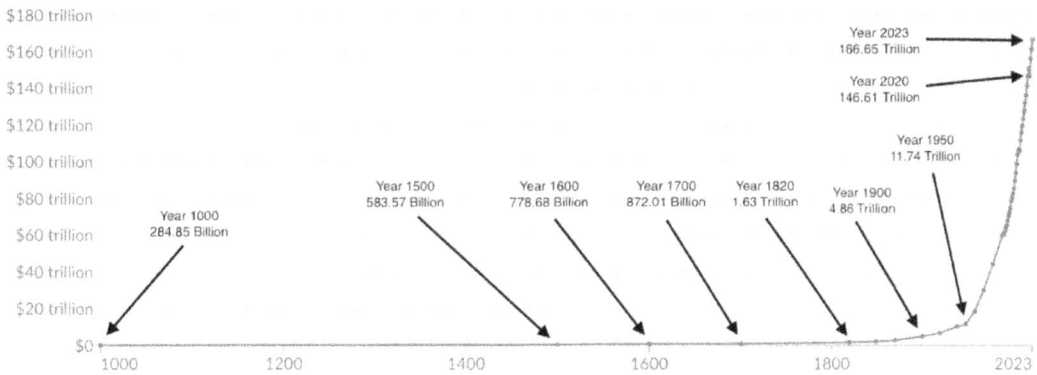

Data compiled from multiple sources by World Bank (2025); Bolt and van Zanden - Maddison Project Database 2023; Maddison Database 2010 – with major processing by Our World in Data

What does this data tell us? It shows that the production of goods and services, and the utility they provide, has driven an unprecedented surge in global economic growth. Particularly from 1950 onward, the world underwent a massive transformation, fueled by a series of technological and societal advancements that significantly reshaped global living standards. This period saw dramatic improvements in healthcare, education, communications, governance, labor markets, and industrial practices, as well as a major leap in life expectancy rates.

Perhaps the most influential force behind this explosion of growth has been technology. The rapid pace of technological innovation, from industrial machinery to digital tools, has not only expanded the scale and scope of production but has also revolutionized how goods and services are delivered and consumed. Technology became the key driver of efficiency and innovation, enabling industries to optimize their operations and reach broader markets with greater speed and accuracy.

The acceleration of economic growth in the 20th century illustrates the immense power of human-driven utilities in shaping societies and economies. This rapid progress was made possible through the continuous creation of new utilities and the resolution of their accompanying byproducts. Each new innovation brought with it new challenges, whether inefficiencies, environmental consequences, or societal disruptions, that demanded further innovations to address them. The perpetual cycle of byproduct-driven innovation thus continues to shape the world today.

"Byproduct-Driven Innovation is being defined as the process of creating new utility by addressing the byproducts, unintended consequences, inefficiencies, or emergent

outcomes, produced by naturally occurring or human-driven systems or interactions of pre-existing utility"

The modern economy, built on goods and services, reflects the essence of the *Law of Perpetual Innovation.* As we create more complex goods and services to meet human needs and desires, new byproducts emerge, provoking yet more innovation. This endless cycle has accelerated at an unprecedented pace over the last century, fundamentally altering how societies operate and how we interact with the world around us. The process continues, with the future holding even greater possibilities as technology and innovation further evolve.

Why a Watch (from Apple)?

During my time at Apple, I learned that one of the reasons the Apple Watch was originally developed was to address a growing issue: the increasing amount of screen time people were spending on their mobile phones. This behavior had become problematic in many ways. The goal was to help people cut back on the habit of reaching for their phone whenever a notification arrived. People using mobile phones while driving can result in vehicle accidents. Pedestrians, distracted by their phones while crossing streets, can get hit by cars. Mobile phone overuse was also having detrimental effects on productivity in the workplace, the education system, healthcare, and other sectors. It had become a serious distraction, not only for adults but especially for children, whose developing minds were particularly vulnerable. In this case, the societal byproducts of mobile phone use were clearly emerging, and Apple was one company taking steps to address them.

The idea was for the Apple Watch to provide people a simpler way to check notifications without having to pick up their phone. By quickly glancing at a watch, they would not be tempted to unlock their phone, check social media, or browse the internet. Unfortunately, the plan did not entirely succeed as intended. The explosion of social media apps and the widespread addiction to mobile phone screen time made it difficult to break the habit. While the Apple Watch did not fully eliminate phone overuse, it did start to shift behavior and continues to evolve in how it interacts with iPhone users.

In addition to the Apple Watch, Apple introduced the *Screen Time* feature on the iPhone, allowing users to monitor and manage the time they spent on their devices. This feature aimed to give individuals insight into their usage patterns, helping them reduce unnecessary screen time. More recently, Apple expanded these efforts with the

Screen Distance feature, designed to address another emerging byproduct of excessive screen time: myopia.

Myopia, or nearsightedness, is a condition where close objects appear clear, but distant ones become blurry. This issue is becoming more prevalent, particularly as people spend extended periods of time looking at screens. Apple's *Screen Distance* feature uses the iPhone's face recognition technology to ensure that users are holding their devices at a safe distance from their eyes, reducing the risk of developing myopia. The concern is especially acute for individuals with a genetic predisposition to nearsightedness, as improper phone use could accelerate the onset of this condition.

The development of the Apple Watch and the introduction of these features on the iPhone reflect Apple's response to the societal byproducts of its own technologies. While the watch did not completely solve the problem of screen time, it represents an important step in addressing the unintended consequences that arose from the widespread use of smartphones. These efforts illustrate how innovation, as defined by the *Law of Perpetual Innovation,* continuously responds to the byproducts of previous utilities. As new technologies emerge, so do new byproducts, leading to further innovations that aim to mitigate those effects, perpetuating an ongoing cycle of problem-solving and progress.

Further Divergence?

Over the past 80 years, innovation and technology have been advancing at an unprecedented rate. The *form-utility* provided by some technologies has reached a critical point, enabling us to circumvent certain essential human efforts and exertions that have historically been a prerequisite for achieving lasting feelings of joy and satisfaction. Activities that once required time, persistence, and effort, key drivers of feel-good mood states, are now being bypassed by innovations that deliver instant gratification with minimal effort. Today, clicks, likes, swipes, binge-watching, and gaming can provide immediate bursts of satisfaction, but they also make it increasingly difficult to attain deeper, more enduring states of contentment.

Humans are hardwired for the long, arduous hunt and the repetitive gathering of food. For ages, this is how we triggered the release of *feel-good* neurochemicals like dopamine and serotonin. Yet, today, we are bypassing these hardwired processes, attaining satisfaction with unprecedented speed and ease. The gratification we now receive from technology feels almost evolutionarily illegitimate, our brains simply were not designed for this level of immediate reward. Evidence suggests we are not built for this type of quick-hit satisfaction. Yet, many remain unaware of how our biology has evolved and how these modern experiences disrupt our natural reward systems.

The result is a widespread inability to see how we are mistreating and abusing these systems. Overexposure to shallow snippets of information, unsubstantiated facts, misinformation, artificial validation, and graphic overindulgence is becoming the norm. As a society, we are surrounded by innovations that offer instant rewards and conveniences, and many of these have *Evolutionary Distorted Byproducts* (see Principle of Evolutionary Distorted Byproduct and Principle of Dual-Edged Utility) lurking beneath the surface, capable of influencing our brain chemistry and behavior in profound ways.

"Evolutionary Distorted Byproducts are being defined as byproduct that emerges when the utility of modern technologies, products, or services interfere with or bypass the natural evolutionary processes that humans have evolved and adapted over many millennia, such as effort-based rewards, delayed gratification, physical exertion, and social connection. These distortions lead to misaligned emotional, psychological, or physical responses, causing behaviors or outcomes like impatience, overindulgence, obesity or reduced resilience, that are incongruent with the adaptive mechanisms humans evolved to thrive in natural environments. The result is a mismatch between the quick, low-effort satisfaction provided by modern conveniences and the long-term, effort-driven processes essential to human survival and psychological well-being."

Through observation, I have noticed that individuals who overuse technology-based products, those that provide rapid dopamine hits, often display increasing levels of impatience, irritability, and uneasiness. Many people today seem unwilling to make even small sacrifices or put in the effort to do what they need to do before indulging in what they want to do. There is a growing lack of appreciation for the people and opportunities directly in front of them, as individuals no longer need to strive to feel gratitude. I see dreams abandoned because the long, difficult journey required for their realization seems unbearable. I see a lack of commitment, decreased resilience, poor emotional regulation, and diminished self-reflection. People lack the stamina to engage in deep thought, struggle with self-esteem, and experience widespread sleep deprivation.

I have also noticed a concerning trend of individuals mistaking "empathy for others" as grounded in their own assumptions, which are often uninformed or unaware of broader perspectives. There is a shrinking openness to different viewpoints and a lack of willingness to consider ideas that differ from their own. These behaviors, I believe,

36

are the *byproducts* of certain technological advancements. Oxford professor and neuroscientist Susan Greenfield writes, *"We reach the height of mindfulness when we acquire the logic of past, present, and future in our decision-making. We experience the opposite, mindlessness, when we pursue sensation, impulsiveness, and quick reward..."*

Where humans evolved the ability to tolerate boredom, spending millennia weathering long winters lodged in shelter, today boredom is often perceived as a form of suffering. Yet boredom, if used constructively, can act as a *positive byproduct,* rather than a *negative* one, that sparks creativity. Instead, many seek instant relief from boredom, and corporations and entrepreneurs are all too eager to answer this call, delivering innovations that further shortcut essential human experiences. But at what cost?

What can we, or should we do? It's clear that some mass utility provisions (technological innovations) result in unanticipated byproducts masked in utility. Once we open Pandora's box, there is often no going back. The consequences of these innovations, whether psychological, social, or physical, may not be fully reversible. However, what if we could anticipate these byproducts? What if we had the tools to foresee how innovations might affect human behavior, health, or society at large?

While we cannot predict the future with crystal-clear certainty, advances in technology, specifically *Artificial Intelligence*, are bringing us closer to being able to simulate event-outcome permutations. This capability might allow us to map out the multitude of byproducts that could arise from the intended form-utility of new products and services. As we continue to innovate, we can leverage these technologies not only to create new utilities but also to mitigate the negative byproducts that will inevitably emerge.

The challenge, as always, lies in how we choose to apply these tools. As the *Law of Perpetual Innovation* suggests, innovation is a continuous cycle of resolving burdens and addressing the byproducts of previous solutions. If we remain mindful of this dynamic, we may be able to guide the next wave of technological advancements in ways that preserve the essential human experiences we are at risk of losing.

CHAPTER 4
Methods and Paradigm Shifts

Growth

In the previous chapter, we examined the extraordinary surge in global GDP that was set in motion mid-20th century, particularly following World War II. The decades following the 1950's saw unprecedented growth. Historically, this explosive increase has been attributed to several key factors: post-war reconstruction, technological breakthroughs, the rise of industrial economies, and the expansion of international trade. This momentum has continued into the 21st century. With the 1990's standing out as a pivotal period, driven by the information technology revolution, the collapse of the Soviet Union, and accelerated globalization. It's key to point out that from the 1950's onward, global GDP growth rates eclipse the steady, gradual increases seen in the previous nine centuries. Today, it is widely understood that this growth was initiated by a combination of factors post World War II:

- **Scientific and technological innovation** (e.g., nuclear fission and nuclear power plants, the transistor, jet propulsion, the polio vaccine, Teflon, Nylon, and television)
- **Globalization and trade expansion** (e.g., the Marshall Plan in Europe, similar efforts in Japan, the General Agreement on Tariffs and Trade (GATT))
- **Post-war investments in research and development** (e.g., the Manhattan Project, National Science Foundation, Japan's post-war R&D in industrial technology)
- **Improved government and economic policies, including Keynesian economics** (e.g., government stimulus programs, the Agricultural Adjustment Act in the U.S., Chinese land reform, the Treaty of Rome, the Bretton Woods Agreement)
- **Advances in industrial processes and labor productivity** (e.g., lean manufacturing techniques, assembly line optimization, automation in

manufacturing, the expansion of continuous casting in steel production, and containerization)

These were undoubtedly powerful contributors to the post-war economic boom. But is there a deeper, more fundamental force that underpinned this explosion of growth? Could there be an underlying catalyst that connects these individual factors, that sparked the exponential economic expansion of this era?

A Significant Method and Paradigm Shift

The story of human progress and innovation is, in many ways, a story of changing perspectives. The way we view the world and the mechanisms by which we interact with it have shifted dramatically over time, often driven not by a gradual accumulation of knowledge, but by sudden, revolutionary changes in thought. As Thomas Kuhn outlined in his book *The Structure of Scientific Revolutions (1962)*, scientific progress often occurs in distinct phases. Periods of "normal science," where knowledge builds incrementally, yet are interrupted by paradigm shifts when established systems, methods, and frameworks are replaced by new perspectives that revolutionize our understanding of a field.

Centuries before the widespread paradigm shift that transformed human understanding and led to the global GDP explosion of the mid-20th Century, intellectual life was dominated by philosophical and religious systems of thought. These systems placed heavy emphasis on authority, tradition, and inherited wisdom. Many early inquiries into natural phenomena were influenced by philosophical reasoning rather than experimental science. For example, Aristotle (384-322 BCE) proposed theories about physics and biology based on observation and deduction. His ideas largely went unchallenged due to the absence of systematic methods for testing hypotheses. His belief in the geocentric model of the universe persisted for centuries despite its inaccuracies because it was never subjected to rigorous empirical testing.

In medieval Europe, Scholasticism (11th to 17th Centuries CE, peaking in the 12th and 13th Centuries) was the dominant intellectual framework. This school of thought was grounded in the teachings of classical philosophers like Aristotle and sought to harmonize these ancient ideas with Christian theology. During these times, belief systems supported speculation and mysticism. Scholars and alchemists pursued goals like transmuting base metals, such as lead and copper, into gold, and sought the Philosopher's Stone, believed to grant immortality and wisdom. In today's understanding of science, these ideas seem almost comical. Yet, the intellectual leaders of the time, much like the Albert Einstein's or Stephen Hawking's of our era, held these beliefs.

Instead of promoting inquiry or discovery, Scholasticism focused on interpreting and preserving established texts. Philosophical and religious systems relied on deductive reasoning, where conclusions were drawn from established premises, often grounded in theological or metaphysical beliefs. The goal was to affirm what was already "known," rather than to independently question or investigate the natural world. This led to a rigid intellectual climate where curiosity was often stifled in favor of preserving established truths, slowing the advancement of knowledge and innovation by today's standards.

Religious institutions, particularly the Catholic Church, also played a central role in shaping how knowledge was approached. The Church held significant power over the dissemination of ideas, determining which intellectual pursuits were permissible and which were heretical. Theological doctrine was treated as ultimate truth, and anything that contradicted it was seen as a threat. For instance, cosmological models were based on the geocentric view of the universe, which placed Earth at the center of all things. This view aligned with religious teachings about humanity's central place in God's creation. Dissent from this view was not only discouraged but actively punished.

During the Renaissance (14th to 17th Centuries CE), however, cracks began to appear in these older frameworks. Thinkers like Nicolaus Copernicus (1473-1542) and Johannes Kepler (1571-1630) questioned the long-standing geocentric view of the cosmos. Artists and polymaths like Leonardo da Vinci (1452-1519) sought to understand the natural world through observation and dissection, challenging the medieval notion that nature was merely a reflection of divine order. Although religious authority still held considerable influence, this period marked the beginning of a broader intellectual movement. People started to explore the world through inquiry and experience rather than relying solely on faith and inherited wisdom.

Nevertheless, entrenched mindsets continued to hinder progress into the 17th Century CE. The story of Galileo Galilei (1564-1642) remains relevant today. Galileo's observations through the telescope revealed that the heavens were not as perfect and immutable as the Church had taught. His discovery of Jupiter's moons and the phases of Venus provided strong evidence for the heliocentric model proposed by Copernicus, which positioned the Sun, not the Earth, at the center of the solar system. However, this idea ran counter to religious doctrine, and despite the empirical evidence Galileo provided, the Church condemned his findings. In 1633, he was forced to recant his views under threat of punishment, and his work was suppressed for many years. This example illustrates how authority and tradition not only slowed progress but also actively sought to suppress new knowledge that threatened established worldviews.

Then came the Enlightenment (late 17th to 18th Centuries CE). It marked the true turning point. It was a major change in basic assumptions that fundamentally altered the way humanity pursued and understood knowledge. Thinkers like René Descartes (1596-1650), John Locke (1632-1704), Isaac Newton (1642-1727), and Voltaire (1694-1778) championed reason, empirical observation, and individual inquiry as the paths to truth. They rejected the idea that knowledge was static or could only be derived from religious or philosophical authority. Instead, they believed in the potential for humans to observe the world, form hypotheses, and test ideas to arrive at new understandings. This shift did not occur overnight, but it laid the foundation for a new intellectual method that would change the course of history.

Just before Descartes, Locke, Newton, and Voltaire, a thinker named Francis Bacon (1561-1626) proposed a new approach to acquiring knowledge. This approach fundamentally reshaped how humans understood the world and would later be utilized by these great thinkers. Rather than relying on established authorities, this emerging "inductive method" emphasized observation, experimentation, and a systematic approach to discovering truth. This marked the beginning of the transition away from older, rigid modes of thinking toward one that would eventually revolutionize industry, technology, and global economies.

Over time, this new approach to understanding the natural world began to permeate society. It spread slowly at first, as it faced resistance from entrenched institutions. However, as breakthroughs in physics, chemistry, biology, and engineering became undeniable, more people began to adopt this new mindset. Scientific and intellectual inquiry no longer belonged solely to the privileged few in universities and monasteries. It spread to explorers, merchants, and inventors, sparking innovations that transformed economies and societies. The 1st and 2nd Industrial Revolutions (late 18th to early 20th Centuries), fueled by this newfound understanding of the world, introduced mechanization, manufacturing processes, and technological innovations that revolutionized how goods were produced and how economies functioned.

However, the full impact of this paradigm shift took over 300 years to fully evolve. Although the seeds were planted during the Enlightenment, it was not until the 20th Century that this new way of thinking became foundational. A profound shift in how societies approached scientific, technological, and engineering discovery significantly reshaped the world. This structured, evidence-based process that had been unfolding for over 300 years came to be known as "The Scientific Method."

This was the true engine that ushered in the era of technological innovation from the mid-20th Century (~1950) onward. It arguably reached its most mature, integrated and widespread form by the mid-20th Century. This period, marked by massive technological and scientific advances during and after World War II, saw the scientific method institutionalized across academia, industry, and government research. By this time, the principles of systemic observation, hypothesis testing, falsifiability, and peer review were deeply embedded in all major scientific endeavors. This structured method was the spark that ignited the wave of exponential economic activity, resulting in unprecedented global GDP growth. It ushered in an era driven by processes and capabilities grounded in a fundamentally different method than the ones that had dominated human thought for over a millennium.

A Proposed Method

By focusing on how we approach understanding the natural world, rather than relying on preconceived beliefs, the scientific method enabled breakthroughs in technology, medicine, and industry. This shift from the blind acceptance of tradition to a rigorous, evidence-based process did more than change what we discovered; it transformed how we think about discovery itself. It sometimes takes a metacognitive shift to call into question not just what we know, but how we come to know it. The scientific method became the foundation for consistent, scalable progress, that led humanity to innovate in ways never imagined before. It shifted more of the energy and emphasis of innovators from what to pursue, to how to pursue it.

Similarly, the Law of Perpetual Innovation, also referred to as Byproduct-Driven Innovation, builds on this metacognitive shift by expanding on the phenomenological aspect of innovation. It does this by providing a crucial duality to utility by emphasizing not just the utility a product or service provides. But also, its duality, the byproduct burdens that arise from it; a residual rooted in some form of tension; ranging from something undesired in the status quo to an unresolved desire for something better. This perspective ensures that we see utility not as a static outcome but as a dynamic process that generates both value and new challenges. By acknowledging this dual relationship, the Law of Perpetual Innovation provides a more comprehensive framework to perceive, predict, and manage the outcomes of innovation, allowing us to continuously refine how we approach new developments.

This book encourages readers to fundamentally shift how they view products and services. Focusing not just on the utility they deliver but on the byproducts that utility is actually intending to address, as well as the byproducts that will surely emerge from it in time. Traditionally, product and service innovation has been understood as solutions that deliver utility, whether functional, emotional, or social. In this view, innovation focuses on adding new features or improving efficiency to provide greater utility to users. However, the Law of Perpetual Innovation argues that utility does not drive innovation. Instead, innovation is sparked by the deficiencies, consequences, unmet needs and open desires that arise from utility. The burdens and tensions that have accumulated and been left behind from some pre-existing utility itself. Making byproduct the driving force of innovation. Byproducts, both anticipated and unforeseen, continually push us to rethink and redesign what we've already created, making innovation an ongoing cyclical process.

This shift in perspective requires viewing products as dynamic, evolving components of a larger, ever-changing system. Instead of seeing them as static solutions to fixed problems, we must recognize that problems themselves are fluid, constantly revealing themselves and changing. As users interact with a product, new byproducts naturally emerge, prompting us to revisit and evolve the utility a product provides. Rather than treating products as complete once they fulfill their intended goal, we must see them as ongoing experiments, with their value and utility, subject to constant reevaluation. In this sense, "utility creation" is always reactive, responding to and resolving some form of byproducts that arise as users engage with and experience some pre-existing product or method. Successful companies like Apple, Nike, Microsoft and Amazon inherently understand this, even if they do not explicitly articulate it in these terms.

Unlike the traditional view, which sees innovation as a goal-oriented process aimed at delivering better utility, the Law of Perpetual Innovation reframes innovation as an inevitable and continuous response to emerging byproducts. It proposes that perfect utility is impossible because as soon as one set of byproducts is resolved through fresh utility, new ones inevitably arise. This contrasts a current but fading perspective, where developers might expect that a well-designed product will provide lasting value without substantial revision. The new approach requires accepting that utility will always evolve, and that products and services should be designed with the anticipation of byproduct emergence.

This shift fundamentally changes how we approach product development and innovation management. Instead of focusing primarily on maximizing utility, companies must invest in learning to identify, track, and leverage byproducts as core drivers for future growth. Organizations that adopt this mindset will be better equipped to stay ahead of shifts in markets, user needs, and technology. They will engage in a process of "relevant" iteration, driven by a deep understanding that innovation is a perpetual cycle, continually fueled by byproducts.

CHAPTER 5
Overview of the LPI Framework

Defining the Law of Perpetual Innovation

In human-driven innovation, byproducts emerge as unintended consequences or unmet needs from the utility we create. Here, utility precedes the byproduct. We develop a product or solution intending to deliver a specific utility, and from its interaction with users and environments, byproducts emerge. These byproducts are essentially secondary outcomes of our efforts to innovate, creating aftereffects, inefficiencies, or unresolved desires for improvement.

In nature, however, byproducts are more foundational and act as pre-existing or emergent external forces, like environmental stressors or resource constraints, that "act upon" organisms rather than arising from them. These forces provoke mutations or adaptations, which may lead to the development of new traits, capabilities or strategies. What we might call "natural occurring utility." Here, utility follows the byproduct. Organisms adapt in response to these external pressures, leading to evolutionary outcomes that enhance their survival or efficiency in the given environment.

In both cases, byproducts serve as a trigger for new utility, but they differ in origin and timing. In human-driven systems, byproducts emerge after utility creation, stemming from interactions between products, users, and environments. In natural systems, byproducts exist as environmental pressures that induce utility through adaptation.

Thus, rather than an inconsistency, this reflects a difference in the process by which utility is realized:

- **Human-Driven Utility** - Utility creation is reactive to byproducts that emerge from both existing utility innovations and natural external byproduct forces, with each new utility (product, service, etc.) generating further byproducts to address.

- **Naturally Occurring Utility** - Byproducts are external forces that proactively shape utility through adaptation, as organisms evolve to meet these pressures.

The cycle of byproduct and utility holds in both contexts, but with systems of nature, it is the byproduct that comes first as an independent, driving force, while in human-driven systems, byproduct emerges as a resultant outcome of pre-existing human-created utility. The Law of Perpetual Innovation captures this dual nature:

The Law of Perpetual Innovation is defined as the endless cycle arising from the causal relationship between byproduct and utility, where byproducts, whether pre-existing in natural systems or emergent in human systems, consistently drive further adaptation, utility, or innovation. Wherein human systems, the utility will always cause the emergence of byproduct, which in turn gives rise to further human-driven utility creation, resulting in a byproduct-utility causality loop, in perpetuity.

The Law of Perpetual Innovation (LPI) shifts the current innovation paradigm by revealing that the value to a people does not come from what utility delivers us, but rather, what that utility delivers us from. LPI states that innovation's real impact comes from its ability to reduce or eliminate negative aspects on a broad scale. Utility serves us by liberating us from some form of burden or tension between "what is" and "what could or should be." It has always been byproducts that drive utility creation. Making innovation's true purpose the continual answering to these byproducts, for greater societal benefit.

The Evolutionary Analogy to Byproduct

In nature, *naturally occurring byproducts* like environmental pressures, predators, climate changes, or competition for resources create the forcing functions that organisms must adapt to survive. These byproducts act as selection pressures that drive the emergence of new traits or mutations. If a mutation proves beneficial, it becomes a *naturally occurring utility* because it provides a survival or reproductive advantage. The process is reactive, not proactive. Organisms don't evolve traits in anticipation of naturally occurring byproducts. Rather, mutations or adaptations arise in response to real, pressing needs to their environment. Those that address the current byproducts are selected by natural forces. Those that fail to adapt, risk extinction.

In the business world, companies face similar kinds of pressures such as market changes, customer dissatisfaction, new regulations, and emerging technologies. These are the byproducts of a constantly shifting landscape. Just like in nature, a company's survival depends on its ability to respond to these byproducts effectively. When a company identifies key byproducts and creates a product or service (utility) that addresses them, it gains a competitive advantage, much like an animal gaining a new survival trait.

However, if a business focuses only on creating products without understanding the underlying byproducts or pressures, it's like an animal evolving random traits that don't help it survive. Eventually, these companies get weeded out, just like species that can't adapt. They fail to see the true drivers of change in their industry and get disrupted by competitors who have identified and solved the real, pressing needs. By embracing a byproduct-driven approach, companies can continuously adapt, innovate, and secure their place in the market. Much like the fittest species in nature. This makes the byproduct selection process not just a part of innovation but the very foundation of a business's long-term survival and success.

An Evolved Perspective

Traditionally, sole proprietors, corporations and innovators have placed utility creation at the heart of their strategies. LPI shatters this outdated mindset, revealing that it is byproduct, not utility, that drives the innovation cycle. LPI elevates byproduct from mere side effect to a central strategic imperative, emphasizing its identification, articulation and selection as the real engine of progress. This shift redefines innovation itself. It is no longer primarily about creating utility, but about addressing what's absent, unmet or even undiscovered. It has always been byproduct lurking underneath the surface, under many names, serving as the perpetual engine of innovation. Successful innovators know this. They view their offerings not merely as solutions, but as responses to what is missing from our lives, often before we even recognize it.

At its core, LPI contends that perfect utility, a product or service entirely devoid of unmet or provoked needs across its lifecycle, is an illusion. No product can fully satisfy every possible need or avoid every unintended consequence. Instead, each solution creates new issues, which, in turn, necessitate further solutions. Byproducts encompass the challenges that arise when a utility is delivered. They may take the form of misalignments with user needs, environmental impacts, or unfulfilled aspirations for improvement. The cycle of byproduct and utility is continuous and never-ending, defining innovation not as a linear progression but as an ever-evolving process that moves forward by resolving problems and satisfying unsettled desires.

LPI introduces a structured approach to innovation by organizing this dynamic into five modules: Foundational Constructs, Guiding Principles and Theory, Systemic Classifiers, Impact Models and Utility Pursuit. Together, these modules create a comprehensive framework that businesses, innovators, and even consumers can use to understand the cyclical nature of innovation and apply it effectively within their own contexts.

What is the purpose of the Law of Perpetual Innovation?

LPI, is a framework that positions byproduct as the instigator of utility creation. Traditionally, innovation is perceived as a proactive effort to generate value, where new utilities are designed and introduced into the market with the expectation of fulfilling a need. However, this view fails to account for why certain innovations succeed while others do not. LPI provides the proof. It argues that every successfully adopted utility is in fact a reactive response to specific byproduct burdens. These byproducts act as clear, causal signals of unmet needs, creating a certainty that compels the development of new solutions. Thus, it is the presence of these byproducts, not proactive utility creation, that ultimately drives successful innovations.

By repositioning byproduct as the driving force, LPI redefines the utility creation component of innovation as reactive in nature. This does not mean that utility development lacks foresight, proactive planning, or creativity; rather, it acknowledges that each product, service, or system arises from a specific demand or issue that the previous solutions (or lack thereof) could not fully address or that appeared over time. In LPI's perspective, utility creation is fundamentally about addressing byproducts.

Therefore, the purpose of LPI is to offer a structured framework that allows individuals and organizations to proactively engage in this cycle, making deliberate choices about how to anticipate current and future needs. By leveraging LPI's framework, individuals and organizations can systematically innovate, not by force-fitting solutions into the market, but by recognizing the organic demand created by unresolved byproducts. This is accomplished by discovering the right byproducts to address.

Why LPI Should Matter to Sole Proprietors, Corporations, and Innovators

In a competitive marketplace, businesses and innovators must continuously deliver relevant products and services that meet genuine market needs. LPI offers a shift in perspective that emphasizes byproducts as the foundation of effective innovation. It guides companies to focus on factual issues (real byproducts) rather than speculative solutions (assumed utility). For many businesses, this shift can be transformative, allowing them to stay ahead of market demand, enhance customer loyalty, and allocate resources more effectively.

One significant challenge facing small businesses and startups is the failure to align with market needs. For nearly 42% of failed startups, a lack of sufficient demand is cited as a primary reason for their business's downfall (CB Insights, 2018). This statistic highlights a critical gap: many new businesses focus on pushing utilities they believe in, rather than addressing genuine byproducts that signal real market demand. While some entrepreneurs create products and services they personally favor, they may overlook whether these solutions actually resolve desires or needs for their target audience. In contrast, "successful" entrepreneurs often adopt a byproduct-focused mindset, seeking to resolve frustrations, unmet and even latent needs, that have a high likelihood of resonating with customers. This is why such entrepreneurs appear to possess unique abilities or even "luck" if you will. Where in fact, these entrepreneurs do possess a special insight, they *"Fall in love with the problem, not the solution (Levine, 2023)."* Their unique approach focuses on what actually comes first, byproduct not what comes second, the utility solution that addresses it. With the framework of LPI, *"Competing against Luck (Christensen, 2016)"* can become a thing of the past.

This distinction in approach illustrates the essence of LPI. When businesses recognize that utility creation should be a direct response to byproducts, they are significantly more likely to create products or services that fulfill authentic needs. This minimizes the risk of market misalignment and maximizes their chances of success. For example, rather than forcing a new feature into the market, a company that follows LPI principles would first identify whether there is a byproduct, such as a current or latent customer burden among existing solutions or workarounds, that demands resolution. This insight-driven approach can lead to the development of innovations that are not only embraced by customers but that also drive sustained market growth.

Transforming Byproduct into Strategic Innovation Drivers

By driving innovation efforts with a focus on byproducts, businesses and innovators can uncover opportunities for innovation. This approach transforms byproducts from obstacles into starting points for utility creation and strategic growth. Through this perspective, organizations can achieve the following:

- **Identify Untapped Opportunities**
  LPI empowers organizations to view byproducts not as obstacles but as new avenues for value creation. By identifying and examining byproducts that arise from existing utility, companies can discover overlooked opportunities that hold potential for innovation and "meaningful" differentiation.

- **Anticipate Emerging Byproducts**

  Many byproducts only become apparent after a product has been widely adopted. LPI, however, offers a framework for predicting and managing these byproducts early in the development process, enabling companies to preemptively address issues before they affect customers or disrupt markets.

- **Turn Byproducts into Strategic Assets**

  LPI repositions byproducts as valuable data points, highlighting areas for refinement, iteration, and even radical innovation. Rather than viewing them as isolated issues or costly afterthoughts, businesses can use byproducts as signals that guide product evolution and feature expansion.

Through the acquisition of these capabilities, businesses can unlock significant advantages that better position them for success. By identifying untapped opportunities, anticipating emerging byproducts, and leveraging them as strategic assets, companies can achieve the following key benefits:

- **Anticipate Real Market Needs** - LPI enables companies to focus on genuine, observable byproducts, allowing them to predict customer demands based on unmet needs rather than speculative utility.

- **Improve Resource Allocation** - By concentrating on resolving impactful byproducts, organizations can use resources more strategically, investing in initiatives with a higher potential for return and relevance.

- **Reduce Failure Rates** - For startups and small businesses, taking a byproduct-driven approach reduces the risk of creating products that do not resonate with customers, as each solution is rooted in resolving an actual need.

- **Build Customer Loyalty and Trust** - By addressing byproducts that customers care about, businesses foster a stronger connection with their audience, enhancing loyalty and customer satisfaction.

- **Stay Adaptable and Future-Ready** - LPI's framework encourages ongoing assessment of byproducts, allowing companies to pivot and adjust as market needs, societal values, and technological advancements evolve.

Through LPI, innovation becomes more than a race to introduce new products; it transforms into a disciplined, systematic approach focused on addressing issues that are meaningful and impactful to customers. This ensures that businesses are consistently relevant, adaptable, and prepared for long-term success in a dynamic world.

Why LPI Matters for Individuals and Consumers

The impact of LPI is not confined to corporations and innovators. For individuals and consumers, LPI promises a marketplace that is more aligned with their actual needs, frustrations, and aspirations. When companies adopt LPI's byproduct-driven approach, they create products that are designed to solve real problems and enhance the user experience, resulting in offerings that feel more relevant, useful, and satisfying.

As consumers, individuals often encounter products that seem to miss the mark, either by failing to address their needs or by introducing solutions to problems or aspirations they do not actually have. LPI's emphasis on byproduct as the driver of innovation ensures that companies prioritize solutions that address existing frustrations, dissatisfactions, and open desires. This creates products that are more user-centered and reduces the likelihood of encountering innovations that feel out of touch or irrelevant.

Consider a fitness app that, instead of adding arbitrary features, focuses on a common byproduct among users: the challenge of staying motivated over time. By identifying this byproduct, the app might introduce personalized goal-setting features or reminders that address users' motivation directly. This approach not only improves user satisfaction but also reinforces the relationship between the product and the customer, making it a more integral part of the user's routine. For the individual, this translates into a product experience that truly resonates with their needs and promotes sustained engagement.

In addition to personal benefits, LPI has implications for consumers who are increasingly concerned with the ethical and environmental aspects of the products they buy. By focusing on byproduct-driven innovation, LPI encourages companies to consider the broader impact of their products on society and the environment. This can lead to more sustainable and responsible business practices, allowing individuals to choose products that align with their values.

For individuals who are themselves aspiring innovators, LPI offers a powerful framework for creative and professional pursuits. Whether they are entrepreneurs, designers, or problem solvers, individuals who adopt a byproduct-driven approach can bring more impactful ideas to life, focusing on meaningful innovation that is grounded in solving legitimate challenges.

For customers and individuals, LPI matters because it:

- **Improves Product Relevance** - LPI ensures that products address genuine needs, or byproducts, creating a more meaningful and useful consumer experience.

- **Encourages Ethical and Sustainable Choices** - By highlighting the importance of responsible innovation, LPI aligns companies with consumer values around social and environmental responsibility. Inherently reducing the utilization of natural resources for the creation of products that miss the mark.

- **Empowers Informed Consumer Decisions** - LPI encourages transparency, allowing individuals to make more confident choices about the products they support.

- **Offers a Pathway for Personal Innovation** - For individuals interested in innovating or creating, LPI provides a structured approach for identifying credible issues, making it easier to develop solutions with lasting impact.

By emphasizing byproduct-driven innovation, LPI fosters a customer-centric market where consumers are active participants in shaping products and services. It creates a world in which individuals' needs, frustrations, and aspirations are the focal point of innovation. This customer-centric approach not only enhances satisfaction but also strengthens the relationship between brands and their users, as customers experience firsthand that products are crafted with their unique challenges in mind. In a marketplace guided by LPI, customers gain a sense of agency, knowing that their needs and feedback actively drive the next wave of solutions and improvements.

How LPI is Structured to Deliver These Benefits

To fully understand and apply the Law of Perpetual Innovation, it is essential to explore the five core modules that compose its framework: Foundational Constructs, Guiding Principles and Theory, Systemic Classifiers, Impact Models, and Utility Pursuit. Each of these serves a unique purpose in shaping a complete, nuanced view of innovation, and collectively, they provide a comprehensive approach to byproduct-driven innovation.

1. Foundational Constructs - These refer to the core human needs and capabilities, the "Human Origin Utilities," that are deeply embedded in our nature and from which all human-driven utility creations derive. These origin utilities anchor innovation in human motivations, such as the needs for movement, communication, nourishment, and social interaction, while also recognizing that innovation arises as a structured response to entropy's constant push toward disorder. Understanding these inherent utilities and their thermodynamic context allows businesses to trace their solutions back to fundamental human drivers, making their innovations more relevant and universally impactful.

2. Guiding Principles and Theory – These represent the theoretical framework for how utility and byproduct interact and evolve under LPI. It introduces key concepts like the Byproduct Emergence Theorem, clarifying why new burdens inevitably arise, and the Theory of Constant Utility, showing how core utility remains stable even as fresh constraints overshadow it. Alongside these are guiding principles for both utility and byproduct, such as the Principle of Utility as Reactive (utility responds to byproduct) and the Principle of Byproduct Composition (byproduct has both objective and subjective aspects) ensure innovators can systematically recognize, classify, and prioritize the byproducts they encounter.

3. Systemic Classifiers - The systemic classifiers serve to organize and categorize both byproducts and utilities into actionable frameworks. Through the Byproduct Taxonomy and the Absolute Utility Map, LPI provides a method for breaking down complex byproducts into manageable classes, offering clarity and consistency in approaching innovation. These classifiers allow companies to systematize their response to byproducts and avoid the trap of viewing innovation through a narrow "utility focused" lens. This encourages a holistic systems understanding of their product's overall influence, by relating their proposed utility to factual byproducts.

4. Impact Models - With tools like the Byproduct Impact Spectrum and Byproduct Contrast Continuum, LPI equips innovators with the ability to assess and understand byproduct impact in nuanced ways. These models clarify that byproducts do not fall into simple "positive" or "negative" categories but exist, along a *spectrum of impact* and a *continuum of user experiences*. By using these example models, businesses can make informed decisions about where to focus their resources, whether on mitigating high-impact byproducts or optimizing more subtle, aspirational improvements.

5. Utility Pursuit - This module captures the dynamic emotional-cognitive triggers that drive the transition from recognizing a byproduct to seeking a new utility. It introduces the concept of forescension, and touches on the role of artificial intelligence in amplifying and responding to both deficiencies and aspirations. This module bridges the psychological with the technological, providing insight into how utility is actively pursued once byproducts are recognized or anticipated.

Together, these five components form a robust, adaptable framework for navigating perpetual innovation. Components #1–4 serve as foundational building blocks, while Component #5, Utility Pursuit, represents the bridge between insight and action, capturing how individuals and systems respond to byproduct emergence.

As We Move Forward

The Law of Perpetual Innovation invites a profound shift in perspective, positioning byproduct as the driving force to all utility, and therefore, of all innovation, natural and human-driven. By embracing LPI's framework, businesses, innovators, and individuals alike can transform the way they approach product development and problem-solving. Instead of introducing utilities in isolation, LPI advocates for a continuous, responsive cycle in which each innovation serves as a reaction to genuine byproducts, creating solutions that are grounded in the realities of user experience and market demand.

Through its five core modules LPI provides a comprehensive approach to navigating this cycle. For businesses, it offers a roadmap to relevant, sustainable growth. For innovators, it delivers a philosophy of purposeful problem-solving. For customers, it promises a marketplace where products are genuinely in tune with their needs and values. The LPI framework provides a means to not only advance innovation, but to do so with clarity, purpose, and responsiveness to the world's real, evolving demands.

Part 2:

The Framework of
The Law of Perpetual
Innovation

Module A:
Foundational Constructs

In Module A, we trace every modern invention back to the "Human Origin Utilities." These are the core needs and capacities (like movement, communication, and shelter) that have guided human ingenuity from the start. Chapter 6 lays out the notion that all innovations extend these primal functions and needs, and in Chapter 7 we see a formal proof showing that while technology can evolve the ways we fulfill a utility, the fundamental need itself endures (the "Law of Conservation of Human Utility"). Chapter 8 enumerates 19 such origin utilities, tying everything from smartphones to skyscrapers to the same foundational human drives. Finally, Chapter 9 reframes this entire process through a thermodynamic lens, revealing innovation as our endless battle against entropy, continually finding ways to conserve human energy and mitigate the byproducts that arise whenever we solve old problems with new solutions.

NOTE: *While LPI's enumeration of the 19 Human Origin Utilities aims to offer a foundational framework for understanding the deep-rooted drivers of all human-driven innovation, it is not intended to be absolute or final but is understood to be invariant across all humans in all societies. Considerable effort has been made to establish as exhaustive a list as possible, yet the number may ultimately be more or less, because some utilities may appear to overlap depending on context, interpretation, or application. What matters is not the perfection of the count, but the recognition that all innovation traces back to core human capacities and capabilities that are Homo sapiens invariant. Those essential needs, functions, and potentialities from which every utility emerges and to which every byproduct eventually returns.*

CHAPTER 6
Deconstructing Human Origin Utility

Tracing Modern Innovation

Human innovation is often viewed through a forward-looking lens, focusing on the endless progression of new ideas, technologies, products, systems and capabilities. This cyclical process can be observed as a forward-moving phenomenon, where each step of utility generation begets the next. According to the Law of Perpetual Innovation, every utility created inevitably gives rise to byproducts that prompt further innovation. However, the very nature of this endless cycle forward begs the question, *"Where did this begin?"* While this law describes an ever-advancing cycle, it also implies a lineage of utility creation, where modern innovations can be traced back through a genealogy of earlier utilities, each building upon fundamental human capabilities and capacities. By exploring this genealogy, we can uncover the "origin utilities"; the foundational functions inherent in the human body that have given rise to all subsequent innovations and have driven the creation and evolution of all products and services throughout human history. These are known as the "Human Origin Utilities", and they are responsible for every human-made thing that has ever existed and exists on this planet today.

Philosophical Foundations of Utility as an Extension of Human Capability

The notion that all innovations are extensions of basic human capabilities finds its roots in ancient philosophy. Aristotle, in his work "Nicomachean Ethics" (~350 BCE), discusses the concept of telos, or purpose, where every entity has an inherent purpose or function. For humans, this function includes the capacity to reason, communicate, and act in accordance to their nature. Aristotle's ideas suggest that human actions and creations are intrinsically tied to the fulfillment of these natural purposes.

Similarly, the concept of *techne* (origin of the word technology), also from ancient Greek philosophy, refers to the skill or art of making that which is seen as an extension of human ability. The ancient Greeks recognized that tools and technologies were created to enhance human capabilities, to do what the human body could not do alone. Plato, in his dialogue "Protagoras" (~380 BCE), presents a myth where Prometheus gives humans the gift of fire and the arts to compensate for their lack of natural defenses, highlighting the idea that technology is a means of overcoming human limitations.

Modern philosophers have also grappled with the relationship between technology and human nature. Martin Heidegger, in his essay "The Question Concerning Technology" (1954), argues that technology is not just a collection of tools but a way of revealing the world, of bringing forth what is latent in nature. For Heidegger, technology is deeply rooted in human existence, reflecting our desire to shape and control our environment.

These philosophical perspectives underscore the idea that innovation is not a series of random, disconnected events but rather a continuous process of extending and enhancing inherent human functions and capacities. If we accept this premise, it follows that all modern utilities, the products and services we use today, must have their origins in the basic capabilities of the human body. This leads us to the concept of origin utilities; the primal functions that have served as the foundation for all subsequent innovations.

Tracing the Genealogy of Utility from Primal Functions to Modern Innovations

To understand the genealogy of utility, it is essential to recognize that every modern innovation is rooted in a fundamental human functional need. By tracing these innovations backward through time, we can identify the primal utilities that have driven the development of new tools, technologies, and systems; in fact, all goods and services, ever created by humans, from Artificial Intelligence to primitive stone tools.

Consider the example of transportation. Today, we have an array of transportation technologies such as airplanes, trains, automobiles, bicycles, and even shoes, that facilitate movement from one place to another. In addition, innovations in support of movement such as roads, parking structures, airports and seaports, have been developed to improve the overall "mobility" effort. These innovations are all extensions of the basic human ability to move and travel. A function that has been essential to survival since the earliest days of our species. Early humans relied on their legs to migrate, hunt, and gather food. As they encountered new challenges, they developed tools to enhance their mobility, from walking sticks to simple footwear to protect their feet to more complex vehicles for long-distance travel. The development of the wheel, a pivotal innovation in human history, can be seen as a direct extension of the need to move efficiently across distances. As we advance through history, each new transportation technology represents a further refinement and specialization of this primal function of "mobility."

Example genealogy of **Movement and Locomotion**:

- **Electric Vehicles and Autonomous Driving** (21st Century CE) – Innovations in self-driving and electric technology revolutionize transportation efficiency and sustainability.
- **High-Speed Rail** (20th Century CE) – High-speed rail systems allow for rapid, efficient travel across long distances.
- **The Steam Locomotive** (19th Century CE) – The industrial revolution brings mechanized rail travel, transforming movement and trade.
- **Carriages and Wagons** (17th Century CE) – Horse-drawn vehicles become central to long-distance transportation.
- **Chariots** (c. 2000 BCE) – Wheeled vehicles revolutionize military tactics and land travel in ancient civilizations.
- **Animal-Pulled Sleds** (c. 8000 BCE) – Early humans use animals to transport goods and people across icy terrain.
- **Footwear** (c. 40,000 BCE) – Early humans create protective coverings for their feet to enhance mobility and survival.

Communication is another example of a utility with deep roots in human nature. The ability to speak, listen, and convey information is a fundamental aspect of human interaction. Early humans communicated through gestures, symbols, and primitive spoken cues. Over time, these basic forms of communication evolved into more sophisticated systems, such as spoken language, writing, printing, telecommunication, and eventually the internet. Each of these innovations can be traced back to the primal need to share information, connect with others, and coordinate social activities. The development of written language, for example, allowed for the preservation and transmission of knowledge across generations, a critical advancement in human history.

Example genealogy of **Communication and Language**:

- **The Internet and Smartphones** (21st Century CE) – Ubiquitous tools for instantaneous global communication.
- **Email Systems** (20th Century CE) – Electronic communication revolutionizes professional and personal correspondence.
- **The Postal Service** (16th Century CE) – Organized systems for long-distance written communication emerge.
- **Moveable Type Printing** (15th Century CE) – Gutenberg's innovation democratizes access to written knowledge.
- **Early Written Alphabets** (c. 1800 BCE) – Writing systems like the Proto-Sinaitic script simplify communication.
- **Beads and Symbolic Artifacts** (c. 10,000 BCE) – Early symbolic items convey meaning and foster communication.
- **Cave Paintings of Lascaux, France** (c. 17,000 BCE) – Early symbolic communication through visual art.

Similarly, the human capacity for memory and cognition has given rise to a wide range of innovations designed to enhance these functions. The creation of tools for information storage and retrieval, such as paper, books, libraries, computers hard drives, and database cloud systems reflects the desire to extend and improve our natural cognitive abilities. Early humans relied on oral tradition and storytelling to pass down knowledge. Still, as societies grew more complex, the need for more reliable and efficient methods of information storage became apparent. The invention of writing was a revolutionary step in this process, allowing for the recording of complex ideas and the preservation of knowledge over time.

Example genealogy of **Memory and Cognition**:

- **Cloud Storage and Big Data** (21st Century CE) – Advanced technologies for storing and processing vast amounts of information.
- **Personal Computers** (20th Century CE) – Digital tools enable individuals to store and process information efficiently.
- **Mass-Produced Books** (15th Century CE) – The printing press makes written knowledge widely accessible.
- **Ancient Scroll Libraries** (c. 3rd Century BCE) – Collections of scrolls, such as in Alexandria, centralize knowledge.

- **Clay Tablets with Cuneiform** (c. 3000 BCE) – Early writing systems record transactions and ideas on durable media.
- **Tally Sticks** (c. 20,000 BCE) – Early humans use carved sticks to record numerical information.
- **Oral Tradition** (Prehistoric Times) – The earliest method of knowledge transmission through spoken word and storytelling.

These examples illustrate how modern utilities are not isolated inventions but are part of a continuous lineage that can be traced back to some fundamental human needs. By recognizing this genealogy, we can gain a deeper understanding of the origins of innovation and how our natural abilities have been the driving force behind technological progress.

Evidence for Origin Utilities: The Evolutionary Perspective

The idea of origin utilities is supported by evidence from evolutionary biology and anthropology, which suggest that human capabilities have evolved in response to environmental pressures and have served as the foundation for subsequent technological innovations.

One of the most compelling examples of this is the evolution of bipedalism, the ability to walk on two legs. This adaptation is believed to have occurred around 4 million years ago and is considered one of the defining characteristics of the human lineage. Bipedalism freed up the hands for manipulation and tool use and allowed early humans to travel long distances more efficiently, opening up new possibilities for hunting, gathering, and migration. The development of bipedalism can be seen as the origin naturally occurring utility for all subsequent transportation innovations, from the invention of simple tools like walking sticks to the creation of complex vehicles like cars and airplanes.

The evolution of the human hand, with its opposable thumb, is another example of an origin naturally occurring utility. The ability to grasp and manipulate objects has been crucial to the development of tools and technologies throughout human history. Early hominins used simple tools made of stone and bone to hunt and process food. Over time, these tools became more sophisticated, leading to the development of specialized instruments for agriculture, construction, and industry. The human hand's dexterity and precision have been the foundation for countless innovations, from the creation of fine art to the development of advanced robotics.

The evolution of the human brain, particularly the expansion of the prefrontal cortex, has also played a critical role in the development of innovation. The prefrontal cortex is associated with higher cognitive functions such as planning, problem-solving, and decision-making. These capabilities have enabled humans to engage in complex social interactions, create abstract concepts, and develop technologies that extend beyond immediate survival needs. The evolution of the brain has been the driving force behind the development of language, mathematics, science, and art. All of which are essential components of modern innovation.

Anthropological evidence also supports the idea of origin utilities. Archaeological findings show that early humans created tools and technologies to enhance their naturally occurring abilities. For example, the discovery of ancient spear points and arrowheads suggests that early humans developed hunting tools to compensate for their lack of natural weapons, such as claws or sharp teeth. The development of fire-making techniques allowed early humans to cook food, providing a source of warmth and protection from predators. These innovations can be seen as extensions of primal human functions, or utilities, such as the need for sustenance and safety.

The Evolution of Utility: From Origin to Complexity

As human societies have evolved, the original utilities of the human body have been progressively refined, specialized, and adapted to meet the changing needs of individuals and communities. This process of innovation can be seen as a branching pathway, where each new utility builds upon earlier capabilities over time, sprouting further branches leading to greater diversity, and at times convergence of branches leading to simplicity. Together, these pathways reflect humanity's ongoing journey to extend, enhance, and sometimes reinvent the fundamental traits that were present in early humans.

One of the key factors driving this evolution is *incremental innovation*, where small improvements accumulate over time to create significant advancements. This principle is evident in the development of transportation technologies, where each new innovation refines an earlier method. The transition from walking to horseback riding allowed humans to travel faster and over greater distances, while the invention of the wheel further enhanced mobility, leading to carts, chariots, and eventually motorized vehicles. Each step in this evolutionary chain of events builds upon the original utility of movement and locomotion, extending the basic human ability into increasingly sophisticated forms.

Another factor shaping the evolution of utility is ***specialization***, where specific functions become more refined and differentiated over time leading to more tailored solutions. This principle can be observed in communication technologies, as the basic human capacity for speaking and listening evolved into a wide range of tools and systems. The invention of writing allowed for the recording and transmission of complex information, leading to books, newspapers, and eventually digital media. Specialized technologies like social media further transformed human interaction, reflecting how fundamental capacities can evolve into unique, diverse expressions over time.

The evolution of utility is also influenced by ***integration***, where different functions and technologies converge, to become more complex under the hood, yet resulting in greater simplicity on the surface, for the user. This principle is evident in modern computing, where the integration of functions such as arithmetic, data storage, and information processing has led to powerful machines that vastly extend human cognitive capacities. From early calculating tools like the abacus to electronic computers, these developments show how different utilities can integrate and combine to produce technologies that redefine what humans are capable of achieving.

The Role of Cultural Evolution in Shaping Utility

While biological evolution provided the raw materials for human capabilities, cultural evolution has played a central role in shaping how these capabilities have developed over time. Cultural evolution refers to the process by which human societies accumulate, refine, and pass down knowledge, practices, and technologies through generations. Driven by the transmission of ideas and innovations through language, education, and social structures, cultural evolution enables the rapid spread and transformation of utilities, often at a pace far exceeding that of biological evolution.

For example, once the wheel was invented, its use and refinement spread quickly across different societies, leading to diverse applications like chariots, carts, and eventually automobiles. This cultural spread was facilitated by trade, cultural exchange, and the written word, allowing societies to build upon each other's innovations and adapt utilities to new contexts. Richard Dawkins' concept of the "meme," the idea that cultural information spreads and evolves in a manner analogous to genetic evolution, helps explain how such innovations propagate. Just as genes transmit biological traits, memes carry cultural elements, allowing ideas like the wheel or writing systems to be refined, replicated, and reshaped over time.

Cultural evolution can even introduce divergence in how utilities develop, as different societies refine utilities in ways that reflect their unique needs, values, and environments. The basic utility of writing, for instance, emerged for record-keeping, but distinct cultures developed unique systems such as hieroglyphics, cuneiform, and alphabets. These diverse expressions serve the same purpose of communication but reveal how cultural influences shape utility.

Moreover, cultural evolution can reimagine or repurpose utilities in response to new challenges and opportunities. A classic example is the development of the printing press by Johannes Gutenberg, which built upon the basic utility of communication but transformed it into something far-reaching, democratizing knowledge and fostering the spread of new ideas. This innovation was not merely an adaptation; it reshaped society, influencing events like the Protestant Reformation and the Enlightenment.

The interplay between biological and cultural evolution thus underpins the development of utility. Biological evolution provided the foundational capacities that all humans share, while cultural evolution has allowed us to adapt, specialize, and even redefine these capacities into diverse forms.

Human Origin Utilities: A Foundation for Innovation

At the heart of this evolution lies a blend of ***Innate Human Capacities*** and ***Developed Human Capabilities***. Innate Human Capacities are rudimentary traits that were likely present in early humans, forming the foundational abilities related to survival, environmental interaction, and basic adaptation. Over time, some of these capacities have been further refined and expanded into Developed Human Capabilities. These are more complex, specialized functions that emerged as humans adapted, started innovating, and began forming complex societies. Together, these innate capacities and developed capabilities make up what LPI refers to as the *19 Human Origin Utilities*. They represent the breadth of human capabilities and capacities, from our basic survival instincts to the sophisticated constructs that underpin civilization itself; from early, to modern day, to what the future holds.

To illustrate this distinction, we can break down these utilities into:
- Innate Human Capacities
- Developed Human Capabilities:

Innate Human Capacities

These are basic, rudimentary traits that were likely present in early humans (even pre-Homo sapiens) at some level, as part of our fundamental biological makeup. They formed the foundation potentials that were simply a part of us and are primarily related to survival, environmental interaction, and basic adaptation.

- **Movement and Locomotion:** Fossilized footprints and skeletal remains of early hominins indicate bipedal locomotion as early as 3.6 million years ago in Australopithecus afarensis.

- **Perception and Sensory Processing:** The basic sensory abilities, such as vision and smell, evolved millions of years ago and are shared with other primates, providing essential survival skills.

- **Memory and Cognition:** Studies of early hominin brain structure suggest rudimentary cognitive functions for problem-solving and environmental adaptation.

- **Manipulation (Manual):** Evidence of precise grips in Australopithecus fossils indicates that early hominins could manipulate objects with their hands.

- **Nourishment and Sustenance:** Analysis of early hominin teeth and jaw fossils shows adaptations for a varied diet, indicating a drive for diverse nourishment.

- **Reproduction:** Reproduction is a biological imperative seen across all hominins and early humans, necessary for the continuation of the species.

- **Exploration and Curiosity:** Archaeological evidence suggests that early hominins migrated out of Africa, reflecting exploration and adaptability to new environments.

- **Competition and Achievement:** Fossil evidence of injuries and hunting practices implies competition for resources and social dominance among early hominins.

- **Environmental Awareness and Interaction:** Early hominins adapted to diverse habitats, as evidenced by their spread across varying ecosystems and climates.

- **Self-Preservation and Survival:** The development of defensive behaviors, such as finding shelter and forming social groups, indicates an innate drive for self-preservation.

- **Resource Acquisition and Management:** Early tool use and evidence of hunting and foraging strategies suggest methods for acquiring and managing food resources.

- **Communication (in part):** Primitive forms of vocalization and gesture, likely present in early hominins, would have facilitated basic communication in social groups.

- **Tool Use:** Stone tools dating back over 3 million years provide evidence that early hominins used tools for tasks like cutting and processing food.

- **Protection (in part):** Fossils suggest that early hominins sought natural shelters, such as caves, for protection against predators and environmental hazards.

- **Social Interaction and Bonding:** Evidence of group living and possible burial practices in Neanderthals points to early social bonds and interaction.

- **Basic Health Awareness (in part):** Fossil evidence shows that early hominins tended to injured individuals, suggesting rudimentary health care within social groups.

- **Parental Care (in part):** Fossilized remains of young hominins found alongside adults suggest a form of parental care for offspring survival.

- **Basic Environmental Control (fire use, in part):** Evidence from controlled fire use by Homo erectus around 1 million years ago suggests early environmental control.

Developed Human Capabilities

These capabilities represent traits that required further evolution, social organization, or cognitive development to reach their full expression. They are often tied to social constructs, cultural development, or complex human cognition. These emerged as Homo sapiens adapted, created, and societies began to emerge.

- **Language (complex)**: Modern language is unique to Homo sapiens, with linguistic complexity supported by anatomical adaptations in the brain and vocal tract.

- **Shelter (constructed)**: The construction of intentional shelters, such as huts, appears later with Homo sapiens and reflects more complex social organization.

- **Well-being (beyond health)**: Evidence of ritual and care for the elderly in Homo sapiens implies a concern for well-being beyond mere survival.

- **Family Structures (complex)**: Structured family roles and extended kinship networks are associated with Homo sapiens, as seen in burial practices and cultural artifacts.

- **Artistic Expression and Creativity**: Cave paintings and symbolic artifacts, first seen with Homo sapiens, provide evidence of sophisticated artistic expression.

- **Spirituality and Meaning**: Ritual burial practices among Neanderthals and early Homo sapiens suggest the beginnings of spiritual or symbolic thinking.

- **Environmental Control (advanced)**: Advanced environmental manipulation, such as agriculture, emerged with Homo sapiens and allowed systematic alteration of landscapes.

- **Emotional Fulfillment**: The pursuit of fulfillment through cultural practices, such as music and ritual, appears unique to Homo sapiens and reflects complex emotional development.

Each of these human origin utilities serves as a cornerstone of human development, providing the basis for further innovation and cultural growth. The combination of these Innate Human Capacities and Developed Human Capabilities into the 19 Human Origin Utilities (presented in Chapter 8) illustrates the way humans have both preserved foundational traits and developed them into the sophisticated abilities we recognize today.

Having explored the evolutionary and philosophical roots of utility, the next chapter will present a formal framework, complete with equations and a logical theorem, that proves why these Human Origin Utilities underlie all innovations throughout history.

CHAPTER 7

A Formal Proof &
The Law of Conservation of
Human Utility

This chapter presents a unifying proof that positions the 19 Human Origin Utilities (HOUs) as the foundational drivers behind every human innovation. We will explore how new solutions continually emerge in response to byproducts of previous innovations. An iterative process that ensures every inventive step can be traced back to at least one of these fundamental HOUs. Alongside this, we introduce the Law of Conservation of Human Utility, which states that while human-driven innovation may continually transform how utilities are fulfilled, it cannot create or destroy these core human needs themselves.

To illustrate the theory in concrete terms, we will examine how the utility of Movement and Locomotion spurred a chain of breakthroughs, from the earliest foot-wrapping to modern autonomous vehicles. This example will demonstrate how each innovation solves a specific deficiency yet inevitably produces fresh byproducts, perpetuating the cycle. By the end of chapter 8, readers will see how the Law of Conservation of Human Utility and the 19 HOUs offer a structurally rigorous lens through which to understand, predict, and guide humanity's perpetual drive to innovate.

The General Concept

Human beings innovate in response to needs, desires, or inefficiencies that disrupt or under-serve their fundamental utilities. The 19 HOUs (including, for example, Movement and Locomotion, Nourishment and Sustenance, Communication and Language, etc.) form the foundation for all such needs. Every innovation emerges as an attempt to address a gap or byproduct that interferes with one or more of these HOUs.

Key Insight:

If an innovation resolves a problem in Utility u, that innovation can produce new byproducts, which, in turn, trigger further innovations, always traceable back to one or more original utilities.

Definitions

1. **19 Human Origin Utilities (HOUs)**

   Denote the set of all 19 HOUs by

   $$U = \{u_1, u_2, \dots, u_{19}\}$$

   Each u_i represents a fundamental human utility, such as Movement and Locomotion, Communication and Language, Protection and Shelter, etc.

2. **Innovation**

   Let $I(t)$ represent a human-driven innovation at time t. An innovation can be a process, product, method, or system that addresses a previously unmet or underserved utility.

3. **Byproduct**

   Let $B\big(I(t)\big)$ be the set of byproducts (or unintended consequences/secondary problems) that emerge from innovation $I(t)$. These byproducts often create or reveal a new gap or inefficiency in one or more utilities.

4. **The Utility Traceability Function**

   $$\Phi(I): I \mapsto \{u \in U\}$$

   - Reads as: Phi of I maps ($\mapsto$) an innovation I to a particular human origin utility u that belongs to the full set of the Human Origin Utilities U.
   - Interpretation: This function $\Phi(I)$ shows that every innovation I can be traced back to at least one of the 19 Human Origin Utilities in set U. It's a backward tracing function from any human-driven innovation (a human-driven utility) to the foundational human origin utility it was intended to support or restore.

5. The Byproduct-Utility Disruption Function

$$\Psi(B): B \mapsto \{u \in U\}$$

- Reads as: Psi of B maps ($\mapsto$) a byproduct B to a particular human origin utility u that belongs to the full set of the 19 Human Origin Utilities U.
- Interpretation: This shows that each byproduct disrupts or compromises one or more of the Human Origin Utilities. It allows us to trace which origin utility (or utilities) is being overshadowed by the emergence of a particular byproduct.

6. The Innovation Driver Function (aka the Innovation Equation)

$$I(t + 1) = f\Big(B\big(I(t)\big)\Big)$$

This function states that the new innovation I at time $t + 1$ is a function f of the byproducts arising from the prior innovation $B\big(I(t)\big)$. Implicitly, function f aims to resolve or mitigate those byproducts.

A Core Theorem

Origin Utility Traceability Theorem:

Every human-driven innovation $I(t)$ can be mapped to at least one Human Origin Utility $u \in U$.

The Detailed Proof

1. **Base Condition:**
   Human innovations arise to address a perceived problem, limitation, or deficiency. Let ΔU denote this perceived deficiency (the byproduct) in a given utility u.

2. **Utility-Byproduct Linkage:**
   A perceived deficiency ΔU always links to at least one utility $u \in U$. Formally,

$$\forall \Delta U, \ \exists\, u \in U \quad \text{such that} \quad \Psi(\Delta U) = u$$

- Reads as: For every (∀) deficiency in utility (Δ*U*), there exists (∃) a utility *u* in the set (∈) *U* such that Psi (the byproduct-utility disruption function) of that deficiency equals *u*.
- Interpretation: Every perceived byproduct (or utility-deficiency) (i.e., disruption, limitation, burden or problem) in a user's experience can be traced back to a disruption in one of the core human utilities. This connects every problem or gap back to a specific origin utility (1 or more) being unmet or impaired.

In other words, if a byproduct is causing a problem, that problem disrupts a specific origin utility *u* type.

3. **Innovation as a Response:**
To address Δ*U*, an innovation *I*(*t*) arises:

$$I(t) = f(\Delta U)$$

- Reads as: The innovation (*I*) at time (*t*) is a function (*f*) of the perceived deficiency in utility (Δ*U*), understood as a byproduct.
- Interpretation: This means that every innovation emerges in response to a perceived deficiency; something lacking, broken, burdensome or insufficient in the human experience. That deficiency (Δ*U*) disrupts one or more of the original human origin utilities (*u* ∈ *U*), and the innovation *I*(*t*) is created as a reactive solution to resolve or minimize that disruption. In other words, innovation is not born from inspiration alone. It is a direct response to a specific burdensome gap in utility.

Because Δ*U* is tied to *u*, the innovation is thereby traceable to that same utility *u*.

4. **Recursive Structure:**
Every innovation spawns byproducts:

$$B\big(I(t)\big) = \{\text{secondary issues, inefficiencies, or consequences}\}$$

- Reads as: The byproducts (*B*) of the innovation (*I*) at time *t* are the secondary issues, burdens, or unresolved tensions that result from it.

- Interpretation: This identifies that no innovation is perfect. Each solution, while solving an initial burden, creates new ones (i.e., *byproducts*). These may include unintended consequences, inefficiencies, or even negative externalities that weren't part of the original design but emerge once the innovation is implemented in the real world.

This expression defines the core fuel for the next cycle of innovation.

The next innovation, $I(t + 1)$, emerges to solve or mitigate those byproducts:

$$I(t + 1) = f\left(B\big(I(t)\big)\right)$$

- Reads as: The innovation (I) at time $t + 1$ (the next time step, signifying the iterative sequential nature of innovation) is a function (f) of the byproducts (B) of the innovation (I) at time t.
- Interpretation: This describes the perpetual cycle of innovation. Each new innovation doesn't just emerge randomly; it emerges as a response to the unresolved deficiencies or unfulfilled aspirations introduced by the previous solution. So, while $I(t)$ solved one issue, it introduced others $B\big(I(t)\big)$, and $I(t + 1)$ now exists to solve those new issues. Together with the previous expressions, this defines the fundamental engine behind the Law of Perpetual Innovation.

Once again, each byproduct within $B\big(I(t)\big)$ can be traced back to a disruption in one or more human origin utilities $\{u \in U\}$.

5. **Conclusion (Deductive Step):**
   Because each byproduct (and every innovation it triggers) structurally originates from one or more of the invariant Human Origin Utilities, each subsequent innovation necessarily inherits this invariant structural connection. Therefore, for every innovation $I(t)$:

$$\exists\, u \in U : \Phi\big(I(t)\big) = u$$

- Reads as: There exists ($\exists$) a utility u in the set ($\in$) U such that (:) Phi (Φ) of innovation I at time t equals u.

- Interpretation: Any innovation $I(t)$, regardless of when it occurred, can be traced back to at least one origin utility (u) that it was intended to support. This supports that all innovations serve a foundational human purpose.

This also confirms, deductively rather than inductively, that every innovation inherently serves a foundational human purpose defined by a timeless structural human utility. Hence, the relationship of innovation to the Human Origin Utilities is deductively proven rather than merely inductively inferred.

The Core Equations

We can express the recursive nature of innovation mathematically:

$$I(t + 1) = f\left(B\big(I(t)\big)\right) \quad \textit{"Innovation Equation"}$$

where:
- $I(t)$ is the innovation at time t.
- $B\big(I(t)\big)$ is the set of byproducts from the innovation $I(t)$.
- f is an operator (or function) that resolves those byproducts.

From this, the mapping to a utility $u \in U$ is:

$$\forall I(t), \exists\, u \in U : \Phi\big(I(t)\big) = u \quad \textit{"Utility Traceability Function"}$$

- Reads as: For every ($\forall$) innovation I at time t, there exists ($\exists$) a utility u in the set U (of HOUs) such that (:) Phi of $I(t)$ equals u.
- Interpretation: This is the [Human Origin] Utility Traceability Function, representing the Origin Utility Traceability Theorem, in its complete logical form. It states that every human-driven utility innovation, at any time, can be functionally traced back to at least one of the 19 Human Origin Utilities.

Equations "Innovation Equation" and "Utility Traceability Function" together formalize how each innovation arises in response to a perceived deficiency (byproduct), and how each such deficiency relates to at least one Human Origin Utility.

Explanation of the Proof and Equations

- **The "Innovation Equation":** states that every innovation at time $t + 1$ is a direct result of the byproducts generated by the innovation at time t. This shows causality and continuity in the innovation chain.

- **The "Utility Traceability Function":** reaffirms that for every innovation $I(t)$, there is at least one origin utility $u \in U$ that inspired it. The function Φ is essentially a trace that links innovation back to the original utility driver.

- **Integration of Concepts:** By combining the idea that every byproduct is a perceptually experienced deficiency in some utility (ΔU) with the fact that each new innovation seeks to remedy those deficiencies, we see a perpetual cycle. This cycle ensures that all human-driven innovation can be traced back to a Human Origin Utility, fulfilling or enhancing that utility is the root cause of the innovation's existence.

The Implications

1. **Universal Applicability:**
   This framework applies to every domain of human endeavor: medicine, transportation, communication, art, etc.

2. **Predictive Power:**
   o By identifying which origin utility or utilities are disrupted by an existing technology's byproducts, one can anticipate the next wave of innovations.

3. **Holistic Perspective on Innovation:**
   o Innovations do not exist in isolation. They form an ecosystem wherein each new idea partially resolves old problems but inevitably generates new ones, all in service of one or more of the 19 HOUs.

4. **Guiding R&D and Policy:**
   o Recognizing the root utilities helps policymakers and researchers prioritize what fundamental issues must be tackled.
   o E.g., in the context of Movement and Locomotion, once we realize how important seamless human mobility is, we can predict that after solving certain byproduct burdens (traffic, pollution, resource use), new burdens (e.g., battery disposal for electric cars, safety concerns for autonomous vehicles) will spur further innovations.

A Detailed Example: Movement and Locomotion

Here is a detailed Example illustrating how bipedalism (a naturally occurring utility, or NOU) drove an iterative chain of human-driven innovations such as foot wrapping (early footwear), horse-riding, the wheel, horse-drawn carriages, and ultimately the automobile. This step-by-step example shows how byproducts (burdens or deficiencies) (ΔU) continually propel new solutions in service of the underlying Human Origin Utility (HOU) of Movement and Locomotion.

Bipedalism as a Naturally Occurring Utility (NOU)

In Chapter 3 we defined Naturally Occurring Utility (NOU) as a trait produced by evolution that proves beneficial for the organism. Over time, this beneficial trait propagates within the species, effectively becoming a Naturally Occurring Innovation; since innovation is any benefit (utility) that reaches mass scale.

- Example of a NOU:

Bipedalism in humans. By standing and walking on two legs, early hominids gained advantages in locomotion efficiency and the ability to use their hands for other tasks.

From NOU to Human-Driven Innovation

Even though bipedalism is not a human-engineered solution, once it's in place, certain environmental conditions can create byproducts or deficiencies that disrupt or limit the full potential of that NOU. These disruptions then trigger human-driven innovations to protect, enhance, or extend the naturally occurring utility.

Step-by-Step Evolution of Movement-Related Innovations

We'll denote Movement and Locomotion as u_{move}. Bipedalism (NOU) is a special sub-case within u_{move}. Let's illustrate the cyclical process:

1. **Environmental Byproducts Disrupting Bipedalism**

   - NOU: Bipedalism.
   - Byproduct Sources: Sharp objects, uneven terrain, temperature extremes. These hazards constitute an experienced deficiency ΔU_1: damage to feet, reduced mobility, and discomfort while walking.

   Formally, we can write:

$$\Delta U_1 \text{ (hazards to feet)} \xrightarrow{\Psi(\cdot)} u_{move}$$

- Reads as: Deficiency one ΔU_1 as hazards to feet is mapped by Psi (the byproduct-utility disruption function) to the human origin utility of movement and locomotion u_{move}.
- Interpretation: In this example, the environmental challenges faced by barefoot humans (sharp terrain, cold, etc.) are interpreted as a disruption of the movement and locomotion utility, triggering innovations like foot wrapping or shoes.

In other words, ΔU_1 *disrupts* u_{move} (bipedal locomotion) because it limits our ability to walk safely.

2. First Human-Driven Innovation: Foot Wrapping (Early Footwear)

Let $I(1)$ be the first footwear (e.g., foot wrapping made from animal skins or plant fibers).

$$I(1) = f(\Delta U_1)$$

$I(1)$: Foot Wrapping (The First Shoe)

By resolving the deficiency ΔU_1, foot wrapping protects the feet, restoring more effective bipedal movement. However, foot wrapping itself creates new byproducts:

$$B\big(I(1)\big) = \{\text{"maintenance (repairs), wear-and-tear, increased resource needs"}\}$$

3. Byproducts Spark the Next Innovations

Those byproducts from $I(1)$ (the earliest shoes) might lead to better shoe-making techniques, advanced materials, and so on. But let's broaden the scope to see how limitations in pure bipedalism itself (e.g., slow speed, limited carrying capacity) triggered entirely new transportation modes.

a. Riding Horses

- Deficiency ΔU_2 : Bipedal travel can be slow, tiring, and limiting for covering large distances or with heavy loads.
- Innovation $I(2)$: Horse-riding. Humans discovered that using animals for locomotion provided faster and more efficient movement than walking alone.

$$I(2) = f(\Delta U_2)$$

$I(2)$: Domestication and Riding of Horses

Eventually, new byproduct burdens emerge: Need for saddles, bridles, stables, feed, animal care, risk of injury from falling, etc.

b. **The Wheel**
- Deficiency ΔU_3: Even riding horses has limits (limited carrying capacity, 1-2 riders at most, long distances force resupply or finding water).
- Innovation $I(3)$: The wheel, used with carts or chariots to reduce limitations of riding horses.

$$I(3) = f(\Delta U_3)$$

$I(3)$: Invention of the Wheel

Eventually new byproducts emerged from wheeled transport: new road-building needs, axle and wheel durability issues, maintenance etc.

4. **Chain Reaction Continues: Carriages and Automobiles**

Rinse and repeat. Each new transport method aims to resolve deficiencies discovered in the prior method.

a. **Horse-Drawn Carriages**
- Deficiency ΔU_4: A simple cart behind a horse can only carry so much, may be unstable, etc.
- Innovation $I(4)$: Improved horse-drawn carriages with better wheels, suspension, body design, carrying and load-hauling capacity.

$$I(4) = f(\Delta U_4)$$

$$I(4): \text{Horse-Drawn Carriages}$$

New Byproducts: Still rely on animals, manure on roads, limited speed, nourishment and healthcare for the horse, etc.

b. The Automobile

- Deficiency ΔU_5: The speed and endurance of horses are still finite. Maintenance and care for animals is expensive and time-consuming.
- Innovation $I(5)$: Automobile mechanical power replaces animal power.

$$I(5) = f(\Delta U_5)$$

$$I(5): \text{Automobile (Late 19th Century onward)}$$

Byproducts: Need for fuel infrastructure, roads, parking, more complex maintenance etc., which then spur further innovations (incremental innovations over decades, luxury vehicles, electric cars, autonomous driving, etc.).

Putting It All Together Mathematically

Using the central "innovation equation":

$$I(t + 1) = f\left(B\big(I(t)\big)\right)$$

we can walk through the chain:

1. Naturally Occurring Utility (Bipedalism) $\rightarrow \Delta U_1$ (hazards to feet) $\rightarrow$
2. $I(1)$ (Foot Wrapping) $\rightarrow$ Byproducts $B\big(I(1)\big) \rightarrow \Delta U_2$ (slow bipedal speed) $\rightarrow$
3. $I(2)$ (Horse Riding) $\rightarrow$ Byproducts $B\big(I(2)\big) \rightarrow \Delta U_3 \rightarrow$
4. $I(3)$ (Wheel) $\rightarrow$ Byproducts $B\big(I(3)\big) \rightarrow \dots \rightarrow$
5. $I(4)$ (Horse-Drawn Carriages) $\rightarrow$ Byproducts $B\big(I(4)\big) \rightarrow \Delta U_5 \rightarrow$
6. $I(5)$ (Automobile) $\rightarrow$ and so on.

In each step, the newly introduced solution mitigates the previous deficiency while generating fresh byproducts that eventually give rise to new deficiencies (ΔU). Each deficiency can be traced back to a disruption or limitation in u_{move}. Hence, the cycle:

$$\Delta U \;\mapsto\; I(t) \;\mapsto\; B\big(I(t)\big) \;\mapsto\; \Delta U_{t+1} \;\mapsto\; I(t+1)$$

- Reads as: A perceived deficiency in utility leads to an innovation (new utility) at time t, which [eventually] generates and accumulates byproducts, which then create a new perceived deficiency (byproduct) at time $t + 1$, which then leads to a new innovation at $t + 1$.
- Interpretation: This expression captures the cyclical and perpetual structure of innovation:
  - Each utility deficiency is perceived as byproduct or burden that drives a solution,
  - which ultimately introduces new byproducts,
  - which again cause the perception and recognition of deficiency,
  - which then drive new innovations, forever.

Exemplifying the Law of Perpetual Innovation

- **Naturally Occurring Utility (NOU) as Beneficial Mutation (Evolution):** Bipedalism arose organically. Because it benefited survival and resource acquisition, it then became widespread (NOU $\rightarrow$ *Naturally Occurring Innovation*).
- **Human-Driven Innovation in Response:** Once in place, bipedalism's limitations or byproduct burdens propelled humans to develop footwear, harness animals, invent the wheel, and eventually build automobiles.
- **Infinite Path:** Each innovation (natural or human-driven) begets further byproducts, ensuring that the cycle of *deficiency* $\rightarrow$ *solution* $\rightarrow$ *byproduct* $\rightarrow$ *new solution* continues indefinitely.

Bipedalism, a Naturally Occurring Utility originating from evolution, set the stage for an endless chain of human-driven innovations to optimize and extend our capacity to move. Whether it's foot wrapping or autonomous electric vehicles, each improvement solves one byproduct burden but inevitably spawns new ones, fueling the Law of Perpetual Innovation. All of these efforts trace back to the fundamental human origin utility of Movement and Locomotion, u_{move}, showing that even a purely biological adaptation eventually ties into a grand, iterative tapestry of human ingenuity.

Concluding Remark

From the dawn of human history to the cutting-edge frontiers of modern technology, Movement and Locomotion (one of the 19 HOUs) has been a constant driver of innovation. The same pattern holds for all the other Human Origin Utilities. Each one spawns a continuum of solutions and byproducts, perpetually fueling the next wave of inventions.

Through this framework and the accompanying equations, it becomes clear that the 19 Human Origin Utilities are indeed the origin of all human-driven innovation. By identifying the root utility behind any pressing byproduct, we can anticipate and shape the trajectory of future breakthroughs.

A Core Implication: The Law of Conservation of Human Utility

We've explored the epistemological shift enabled by anchoring human innovation explicitly within the 19 Human Origin Utilities (HOUs). Now, we can formally recognize a powerful new universal principle that logically emerges from this structural foundation. The Law of Conservation of Human Utility.

This foundational law can be stated as follows:

"The Law of Conservation of Human Utility states that human-driven innovation neither creates nor destroys fundamental human origin utilities, instead, it perpetually transforms how these utilities are fulfilled."

In essence, this law is to human-driven innovation what the law of conservation of energy is to physics. Just as energy remains constant, continually reshaping and taking different forms without ever being created or destroyed, human utilities such as Movement and Locomotion, Nourishment and Sustenance, Communication and Language, Protection and Shelter, and others, remain fundamentally invariant across all of human history. Innovations continuously evolve around these utilities, reshaping their fulfillment without ever altering their foundational human-essential nature.

Deductive Premises and Structural Foundations

To solidify this law's deductive power (and thereby fully transcend David Hume's inductive skepticism), we explicitly restate its foundational premises:

1. **Premise 1** - Timeless Existence of Human Origin Utilities (HOUs):
   The set $U = \{u_1, u_2, \ldots, u_{19}\}$, representing the fundamental human capacities and capabilities outlined earlier in this work, exists as a timeless and universally invariant set. These utilities are inherent to the human condition; biologically, psychologically, and socially essential across all contexts and eras.

2. **Premise 2** - Inevitability of Byproducts and Structural Symmetry (Utility $\leftrightarrow$ Byproduct):
   Each innovation $I(t)$ necessarily produces byproducts $B(I(t))$, creating an unbreakable structural symmetry:
   - Utilities resolve existing byproducts.
   - Byproducts inevitably emerge from each new innovation (new utility) created.
   - This symmetry guarantees that innovation cycles perpetually and predictably.

3. **Premise 3** - Recursive Structural Symmetry of Innovation:
   Innovation follows the explicit recursive structure (**The Innovation Equation** aka **The Innovation Driver Function**):

$$\boxed{I(t + 1) = f\left(B\left(I(t)\right)\right)}$$

This equation illustrates innovation as structurally recursive where each utility innovation emerges from prior byproducts, in a pattern that is not merely observed but structurally unavoidable. Thus, it confirms innovation as inherently recursive, invariant, and thus deductively predictable rather than inductively probable.

4. **Premise 4** - Explicit Mapping from Innovation to Invariant HOUs:
   Formally expressed as (**The Utility Traceability Function Φ**):

$$\boxed{\forall\, I(t), \exists\, u \in U : \Phi\left(I(t)\right) = u}$$

This explicitly guarantees every innovation maps to at least one of the invariant HOUs, anchoring innovation deductively to universal human conditions rather than historically inductive patterns.

5. **Supporting Premise 5 (additional explicit truth)** - Each Byproduct Explicitly Disrupts at least one Human Origin Utility:
Formally expressed as (**The Byproduct-Utility Disruption Function Ψ**):

$$\Psi(B) : B \mapsto \{u \in U\}$$

This Ψ function explicitly identifies which specific utility is compromised or overshadowed by the emergence of a particular byproduct. By explicitly including the Ψ function, we gain deeper insight into why and how innovations inevitably follow certain structural paths: Each innovation explicitly emerges to resolve specific disruptions identified by Ψ, reinforcing the deductive rigor and explanatory completeness of our structural innovation theory. (Note: In Chapter 12, we dive deeper into Psi Ψ to prove that byproduct emergence is real and discuss exactly why it is inevitable.)

Explicit Structural Invariance (Summary Table)

The following table clarifies how our foundational equations embody structural invariance, anchoring the Law of Conservation of Human Utility firmly in deductive logic rather than inductive inference:

Equation	Structural Invariance Interpretation	Deductive Justification
$I(t+1) = f\left(B\left(I(t)\right)\right)$	Innovation explicitly emerges from structurally inevitable byproducts, not arbitrary events.	Deductively guaranteed by the inherent cyclic causality between utility innovations and byproducts.
$\forall I(t), \exists\, u \in U : \Phi\left(I(t)\right) = u$	Every innovation (utility) explicitly and structurally maps back to invariant HOUs, anchoring innovation in timeless human conditions.	Deductively defensible as each innovation explicitly resolves disruptions tied directly to invariant human utilities.
$\Psi(B) : B \mapsto \{u \in U\}$ (Adds Clarity)	Each byproduct that emerges explicitly disrupts or compromises at least one invariant HOU, necessitating further innovation.	Deductively stable as byproducts explicitly emerge as disruptions to invariant HOUs, structurally perpetuating innovation cycles.

These clearly defined structural invariants explicitly validate our Law of Conservation of Human Utility, establishing it as both deductively sound and practically meaningful.

Broad Implications of the Law

By formalizing this law, several critical implications follow:

- **Universality and Predictive Reliability**:
  Human innovation is no longer viewed as historically contingent guesswork but as structurally anchored in invariant, universal human utilities, making predictions robust and deductively reliable.
- **Expansion into Soft Sciences**:
  Because our HOUs explicitly include psychological, emotional, social, and cultural utilities, we can extend structural deductive reasoning confidently into domains traditionally dominated by uncertainty.
- **Practical Utility and Innovation Management**:
  Innovation methodologies, including LPI's Byproduct-Driven Innovation Engine (BDIE), can explicitly leverage this structural invariance to

fundamentally enhance strategic decision-making, technological forecasting, and policy planning.

In summary, the Law of Conservation of Human Utility provides a transformative understanding: innovations never arise arbitrarily but perpetually reshape how core human utilities are fulfilled. This structural certainty moves innovation theory decisively beyond induction, redefining it as a rigorous, deductively grounded discipline.

Concluding on the Structural Certainty and Evolution of Innovation

The journey throughout this chapter culminates in a profound epistemological evolution, one that decisively addresses, and transcends, the inductive skepticism first articulated by David Hume. By explicitly grounding our theory of innovation in the 19 Human Origin Utilities, we have not merely improved upon traditional thinking; we have fundamentally reshaped the epistemological basis upon which innovation stands.

From Induction to Deductive Certainty

Our explicit recursive equations, explicitly defined functions (Φ and Ψ) and clearly articulated invariants, combine to form a fully deductive structural framework. Innovation predictions now possess explicit structural certainty, grounded in timeless universal human conditions, rather than uncertain historical probabilities.

- **Explicit Structural Symmetry**: Innovation cycles through structurally predictable states, governed explicitly by HOUs.
- **Explicit Utility Traceability**: Every innovation explicitly maps back to an invariant utility (Φ), emerging explicitly in response to disruptions defined by Ψ.
- **Explicit Structural Recursion**: Innovation perpetually resolves existing byproducts and creates new ones, ensuring innovation remains explicitly cyclic and structurally inevitable.

The Law of Conservation of Human Utility: A Universal Principle

Explicitly formalized, the Law of Conservation of Human Utility stands as a profound universal principle where innovation perpetually reshapes, transforms, and evolves the 19 Human Origin Utilities (HOUs) yet never fundamentally creates or destroys them. These HOUs are core human drives and capacities, so deeply ingrained in our biology and intrinsic human nature, invariant across all eras and societies, that unless we cease to be Homo sapiens, we will always strive to fulfill them. Whether we are enhancing our ability to move, communicate, protect ourselves, or interact with the environment, any deficiency or obstacle merely intensifies our motivation to innovate further; it never negates the underlying utility itself.

Even in extreme scenarios, such as severe environmental degradation, what actually happens is that the realization of a given human origin utility (*e.g., Environmental Awareness, Interaction, and Control*) becomes more challenging, creating larger byproduct burdens ΔU. This leads us to innovate in more novel ways (e.g., new methods of conservation, adaptation, or restoration), rather than "destroying" the utility. In other words, the drive to manage the environment remains fundamental to our makeup. Far from disappearing under pressure, a threatened Human Utility amplifies the perpetual cycle of innovation and reaffirms our identity as byproduct-resolving beings, perpetually striving to preserve these invariant human drives.

Integrative Summary and Vision for the Future

To conclude, the Law of Perpetual Innovation, explicitly anchored in the invariant 19 Human Origin Utilities, represents a transformative step forward in how we understand and practice innovation. By grounding innovation in a structurally deductive framework, it overcomes the traditional difficulty of relying solely on past observations to predict future outcomes (what philosophers like David Hume call the "problem of induction"). Put simply, rather than guessing that things will continue a certain way just because they have in the past, this model demonstrates why innovation must progress in specific, predictable cycles linked to fundamental human drives.

This new approach reconceives innovation not as a matter of uncertain guesswork but as a rigorous, logically grounded discipline, firmly rooted in what it means to be human. Equipped with this perspective, we gain the theoretical clarity, predictive reliability, and practical power to navigate an ever more complex and dynamic world, knowing that our core utilities and the need to fulfill them, remain the ultimate wellspring of perpetual innovation.

Integrative Statement:

"By establishing the Law of Conservation of Human Utility, we transcend the limitations of inductive reasoning, confidently anchoring the innovation process to universal, structurally invariant human conditions. Innovation is thus no longer mere historical extrapolation, it becomes structurally predictable, robust, and deductively grounded. Thus, the Law of Perpetual Innovation stands as a philosophically rigorous, structurally robust, and practically powerful evolution in how humanity understands and engages with innovation itself. It revolutionizes not only how we understand human progress, but how we actively engage with its unfolding future."

CHAPTER 8
The 19 Human Origin Utilities

We've now seen the formal underpinnings of why these 19 specific utilities remain invariant. Let us turn to an in-depth look at each Human Origin Utility (HOU) to see how they manifest in practice.

Despite the incredible advancements in technology and innovation, every human-driven creation will trace back to origin utilities rooted in the human body and its needs. Modern innovations, no matter how complex, always serve to enhance or extend these basic human potentials. This persistence of HOUs can be seen in these 19 key areas:

1. ## Movement and Locomotion

    Movement and Locomotion refers to the human ability to navigate and traverse the environment through bodily movement (walking, running, swimming) and technology-assisted mobility (wheeled vehicles, boats, aircraft, etc.). It underlies survival (e.g., escaping predators, seeking resources), exploration, and virtually all forms of human interaction.

    Distinct From Other Utilities
    - **Manipulation and Tool Use (5)**: While both involve physical action, Movement and Locomotion focuses on changing one's location or position, whereas Manipulation emphasizes physically altering or manipulating objects.
    - **Environmental Awareness (15)**: Although environment shapes how we move, Movement and Locomotion centers on mobility rather than actively managing or modifying the environment.

    Relevant Considerations
    - Core to survival and social development (migration, trade routes, cultural exchange).
    - Innovations in transportation (the wheel, domestication of animals, engines) continuously expand human reach and speed.

Example Historical Progression:
1. Footwear (c. 30,000 - 40,000 BCE)
2. Rafts and Canoes (c. 8,000 - 10,000 BCE)
3. The Wheel (c. 3500 BCE)
4. Domestication of the Horse (c. 3000 BCE)
5. Roman road paving (c. 500 BCE - Roman Empire)
6. Sailing Ships (c. 2000 BCE - 15th Century CE)
7. The Bicycle (c. 19th Century)
8. The Automobile (c. late 19th Century)
9. The Airplane (c. early 20th Century)
10. Electric Vehicles and Autonomous Driving (c. 21st Century)

2. Perception and Sensory Processing

Perception and Sensory Processing is the ability to gather, interpret, and respond to environmental stimuli via the primary senses (sight, hearing, touch, taste, smell). It also includes extended or augmented senses (e.g., night-vision devices, hearing aids).

Distinct From Other Utilities
- **Memory and Cognition (4)**: Perception gathers raw data from the environment; cognition transforms it into knowledge, decisions, or abstract thought.
- **Communication and Language (3)**: While perception is about intake of sensory information, communication is about expressing or receiving more structured messages, often shaped by language and culture.

Relevant Considerations
- Essential for detecting threats (predators, hazards) and opportunities (food, water, mates).
- Crucial to quality of life, shaping art, enjoyment, and our entire phenomenological experience.

Example Historical Progression:
1. Light from fire (c. 1 million - 1.7 million years ago)
2. Mirrors (c. 6,000 BCE)
3. Rudimentary glass/quartz "reading stones" (c. 1000 CE)
4. Eyeglasses (c. 13th Century CE)
5. The Microscope (c. 1590)

6. Ear Trumpets (c. 17th Century CE)
7. Photography (c. 19th Century)
8. X-ray Imaging (c. 1895)
9. Digital Cameras and Image Sensors (c. late 20th Century)
10. Advanced Sensory Implants (c. 21st Century)

3. Communication and Language

Communication and Language is the human ability to convey information, ideas, and emotions through spoken words, gestures, signaling, writing, symbols, and digital media. It sustains social bonds, cultural transmission, and collective problem-solving.

Distinct From Other Utilities
- **Social Interaction and Bonding (9)**: Social bonding involves relationships and group cohesion, while Communication focuses specifically on the mechanisms and media of information exchange.
- **Memory and Cognition (4)**: Communication expresses or encodes thoughts; cognition processes those thoughts internally.

Relevant Considerations
- Forms the backbone of collaboration, governance, education, and culture-building.
- Evolves with technology, from oral traditions and writing to mass media and social networks.

Example Historical Progression:
1. Cave Paintings *(of Lascaux, France)* (c. 17,000 - 22,000 BCE)
2. Egyptian Hieroglyphs (c. 3100 BCE)
3. The Phoenician Alphabet (c. 1050 BCE)
4. Greco-Roman Inscribed Stone Monuments (c. 6th Century BCE)
5. The Invention of Paper (c. 105 CE – China during Han Dynasty)
6. Chinese Woodblock Printing (c. 7th Century CE)
7. The Gutenberg Printing Press (c. 1440 CE)
8. The Telephone (c. 1876)
9. Radio and Television Broadcasting (c. early 20th Century)
10. The Internet and Smartphones (c. late 20th - 21st Century)

4. Memory and Cognition

Memory and Cognition encompass the capacity to store, retrieve, process, and integrate information: enabling humans to think critically, plan, learn, invent, and solve problems.

Distinct From Other Utilities

- **Learning and Knowledge Acquisition (19)**: Closely related, but Memory and Cognition focuses on the internal mental processing (e.g., working memory, problem-solving), whereas Learning includes social and structural processes (formal education, apprenticeships).
- **Perception and Sensory Processing (2)**: Perception feeds raw data to the brain; cognition interprets and acts on that data.

Relevant Considerations

- Underpins technological progress and cultural evolution: scientific discoveries, philosophical reasoning, and artistic creativity all hinge on cognitive abilities.
- Innovations like computers, libraries, and archives externalize or augment human memory.

Example Historical Progression:

1. Oral Tradition of spoken word, songs, and stories (c. Prehistoric Times)
2. Mesopotamian Development of Writing (c. 3200 BCE)
3. Creation of Libraries *(to house scrolls)* (c. 7th Century BCE – Ashurbanipal's Library; Library of Alexandria c. 3rd Century BCE)
4. Mnemonic Devices in Ancient Greece *(to enhance memory)* (c. 5th Century BCE)
5. The Codex *(binding of pages; the first books)* (c. 1st Century CE – Roman Empire)
6. Medieval Manuscripts and Illuminated Texts (c. 8th - 15th Century CE)
7. The Scientific Method and Record-Keeping (c. 17th Century CE)
8. The Encyclopedia (c. 18th Century)
9. Digital Computers (c. mid-late-20th Century)
10. Cloud Storage and Big Data (c. 21st Century)

5. Manipulation and Tool Use

Manipulation and Tool Use is the ability to grasp, hold, and manipulate objects using hands (especially via an opposable thumb), thereby enabling tool creation and deployment. It reflects the direct physical interaction with the environment to shape, build, and transform.

Distinct From Other Utilities
- **Movement and Locomotion (1)**: Tool use is about manipulating objects rather than moving oneself across space.
- **Resource Acquisition and Management (17)**: Although many tools are used to obtain resources, Tool Use specifically refers to the physical interaction; resource management emphasizes storage, distribution, and conservation.

Relevant Considerations
- Fundamental to innovation: stone tools, mechanical devices, and modern robotics all extend manual dexterity.
- Catalyzes everything from simple crafts to complex manufacturing systems.

Example Historical Progression:
1. Stone Tools (c. 2.5 million years ago)
2. Hand Axes (c. 1.6 million years ago)
3. Wooden Spears (c. 400,000 years ago)
4. Bow and Arrow (c. 10,000 - 20,000 BCE)
5. Copper Tools (c. 5000 BCE)
6. Archimedes' Screw (c. 3rd Century BCE)
7. Crane Systems (c. 1st Century BCE – Roman Empire)
8. Windmills (c. 9th Century CE)
9. Industrial Machinery (c. 18th Century)
10. 3D Printing (c. 21st Century)

6. Protection and Shelter

Protection and Shelter addresses the need to safeguard against environmental extremes, predators, and diseases by constructing or employing protective measures (clothes, housing, fortifications).

Distinct From Other Utilities
- **Self-Preservation and Survival (16)**: Overlaps in intent (staying safe), but here the emphasis is on physical structures or technologies that protect, while Self-Preservation is broader, encompassing legal systems, defense strategies, and personal safety.

- **Environmental Awareness (15)**: Although designing shelters requires environmental understanding, this utility focuses on building or employing protective barriers.

Relevant Considerations
- Spans from primitive huts and clothing to modern skyscrapers and disaster-resistant designs.
- Central to shaping living spaces, urban development, and architectural innovation.

Example Historical Progression:
1. Caves and Natural Shelters (c. Prehistoric Times)
2. Primitive Huts (c. 300,000 - 400,000 years ago)
3. Mud-Brick Houses (c. 7000 BCE)
4. Stone Fortifications (c. 3000 BCE)
5. Roman Architecture (c. 1st Century BCE - 4th Century CE)
6. Medieval Castles (c. 9th - 15th Century CE)
7. Widespread EU refinement of Brick and Mortar (c. 14th - 17th Century CE)
8. Skyscrapers (c. late 19th Century)
9. Disaster-Resistant Buildings (c. late 20th Century)
10. Sustainable Housing (c. 21st Century)

7. Nourishment and Sustenance

Nourishment and Sustenance pertains to securing and consuming food and water to maintain life and health. It ranges from foraging and cooking to agriculture, food technology, and dietary science.

Distinct From Other Utilities
- **Resource Acquisition and Management (17)**: While nourishment is about obtaining and ingesting life-sustaining resources, Resource Acquisition and Management covers a broader spectrum, including metals, energy, and trade goods.
- **Health and Well-being (10)**: Food and water are crucial for health, but this utility specifically focuses on sourcing and preparing the nutrients; Health and Well-being includes medical care, disease prevention, and mental health.

Relevant Considerations
- Integral to cultural identity (cuisines, communal feasts) and economic systems (agriculture, markets).
- Food technology continuously evolves to improve safety, nutrition, and sustainability (e.g., GMOs, vertical farming).

Example Historical Progression:
1. Cooking with of Fire (c. 1 million - 1.7 million years ago)
2. Fishing with Simple Tools (c. 40,000 - 90,000 BCE)
3. Development of Agriculture & Domestication of Animals (c. 8,000 - 10,000 BCE)
4. Irrigation Systems (c. 3000 BCE)
5. Use of Salt for Preservation (c. 2000 BCE)
6. Fish Farming (c. 1000 BCE)
7. Rice Cultivation Expansion (c. 6th Century BCE - Asia)
8. The Columbian Exchange *(of crops between continents)* (c. 15th - 16th Century CE)
9. Canning, Pasteurization and Refrigeration (c. 19th Century)
10. Genetically Modified Organisms *(GMO's)* (c. late 20th Century)

8. Reproduction and Family Structures

Reproduction and Family Structures refer to the biological drive to propagate the species and the social norms surrounding courtship, marriage, parenting, and kinship systems. It ensures the continuation of human lineages and shapes social organization.

Distinct From Other Utilities
- **Social Interaction and Bonding (9)**: While both involve interpersonal relationships, Reproduction focuses on kinship and lineage, whereas Social Interaction covers broader community, friendship, and group dynamics.
- **Emotional Regulation and Fulfillment (14)**: Romantic and familial bonds can affect emotional well-being, but Reproduction and Family Structures emphasize the procreative and child-rearing side.

Relevant Considerations
- Influences social norms, inheritance laws, and cultural rituals.
- Modern developments include contraception, fertility treatments, and evolving definitions of family (adoption, surrogacy, single-parent families).

Example Historical Progression:

1. Kinship Groups and Development of Pair Bonding (c. 1.5 million - 1.7 million years ago)
2. Shared Parenting in Hunter-Gatherer Societies (c. 200,000 BCE)
3. Patriarchal and Matriarchal Clans (c. 3000 BCE)
4. Codification of Marriage and Inheritance Laws (c. 1754 BCE)
5. Religious Sanctification of Marriage, widespread (c. 4th - 5th Century CE)
6. Christian Marriage as a Sacrament (c. 5th Century CE)
7. Inheritance Laws and Primogeniture *(oldest son inheritance)* (c. 6th - 7th Century CE)
8. Nuclear Family Model (c. 18th - 19th Century)
9. Family Planning and Contraception (c. 20th Century)
10. Assisted Reproductive Technologies *(ART)* (c. late 20th Century)

9. Social Interaction and Bonding

Social Interaction and Bonding centers on forming relationships, networks, and communities. It encompasses cooperation, group identity, shared traditions, and collective activities that build social cohesion.

Distinct From Other Utilities

- **Communication and Language (3)**: Communication is the medium of exchanging information, while Social Interaction explores the formation of bonds, groups, and communal structures.
- **Competition and Achievement (13)**: Although both involve social context, Social Interaction emphasizes connection and collaboration, whereas Competition focuses on rivalry, performance, and excellence.

Relevant Considerations

- Underlies social institutions (tribes, clans, city-states) and fosters cultural practices (rituals, celebrations, shared beliefs).
- Modern forms include online communities, social networks, and multinational organizations.

Example Historical Progression:

1. Formation of Tribes and Clans (c. Prehistoric Times)
2. Early Burial Rituals (c. 100,000 BCE)
3. Ritualized Dance and Music (c. 20,000 - 40,000 BCE)

4. Religious and Cultural Rituals (c. 10,000 BCE - Present)

5. Trade Networks (c. 3000 BCE)

6. The Polis and City-States (c. 8th Century BCE)

7. Feudalism and Social Hierarchies (c. 9th - 15th Century CE)

8. Guilds and Trade Associations (c. 12th - 17th Century CE)

9. Labor Unions and Social Clubs (c. 19th Century)

10. Social Media and Online Communities (c. 21st Century)

10. Health and Well-being

Health and Well-being refers to practices and systems that sustain physical, mental, and emotional health, ensuring survival, improved quality of life, and personal contentment.

Distinct From Other Utilities

- **Nourishment and Sustenance (7)**: While nutrition is crucial to health, Health and Well-being also encompasses medicine, hygiene, mental health, and social health infrastructures.
- **Emotional Regulation and Fulfillment (14)**: There is overlap in psychological care, but Health focuses on the broader spectrum of preventing and treating diseases and injuries, whereas Emotional Regulation zeroes in on managing internal emotional states.

Relevant Considerations

- Evolves from traditional herbal remedies and sanitation systems to cutting-edge telemedicine, biotech, and mental health interventions.
- Directly tied to societal longevity, productivity, and general happiness.

Example Historical Progression:

1. Use of Medicinal Plants (c. 60,000 BCE):

2. Shamanic Healing Practices *(spiritual & medicinal practices)* (c. 30,000 BCE)

3. Trepanation *(drilling into the skull)* (c. 10,000 BCE)

4. Traditional Chinese Medicine *(herbs & acupuncture)* (c. 2000 BCE)

5. Roman Aqueducts and Sanitation (c. 300 BCE - 100 CE)

6. Islamic Golden Age Medicine *(Avicenna's encyclopedias)* (c. 9th - 11th Century CE)

7. Quarantine Practices (c. 14th Century CE)

8. The Microscope & Vaccination (c. 17th & 18th Centuries, respectively)

9. Psychoanalysis, Organ Transplants and Medical Imaging (c. 20th Century)
10. Digital Health and Telemedicine (c. 21st Century)

11. Exploration and Curiosity

Exploration and Curiosity capture the innate drive to learn about unknown territories, be they physical, intellectual, or internal. This utility is a major catalyst for scientific, cultural, and geographical advancements.

Distinct From Other Utilities

- **Learning and Knowledge Acquisition (19)**: Both involve expanding understanding, but Exploration highlights the quest and discovery aspect, whereas Learning emphasizes the structured absorption of information and skills.
- **Environmental Awareness (15)**: Exploration may entail adapting to new environments; however, Environmental Awareness also involves stewardship and intentional management, not just discovery.

Relevant Considerations

- Sparks migrations, expeditions, and intellectual revolutions (e.g., Age of Discovery, Space Race).
- Powers technological leaps as humans strive to uncover mysteries from ocean depths to quantum realms.

Example Historical Progression:

1. Hominid Migration Out of Africa *(into Asia and Europe)* (c. 2 million years ago)
2. Cave Exploration and Rock Art (c. 40,000 BCE)
3. Maritime Exploration by Raft and Canoe (c. 10,000 BCE)
4. Polynesian Celestial Navigation (c. 2000 BCE - 1000 CE)
5. Expedition of Alexander the Great (c. 4th Century BCE)
6. Age of Viking Exploration (c. 8th - 11th Century CE)
7. Age of Exploration *(Columbus, Magellan, Vasco)* (c. 15th - 17th Century CE)
8. The Scientific Revolution *(scientific inquiry)* (c. 16th - 18th Century)
9. Space Exploration (c. mid-20th Century)
10. Quantum, Genomic and Microbial Exploration (c. 21st Century)

12. Artistic Expression and Creativity

Artistic Expression and Creativity involve shaping ideas, emotions, and aesthetics into tangible forms: painting, music, dance, sculpture, design, literature, film, etc. It enriches culture, fosters communication of complex feelings, and can influence societal change.

Distinct From Other Utilities

- **Emotional Regulation and Fulfillment (14)**: Both can involve expressing and processing emotions, but Artistic Expression focuses on creation, design, and aesthetic experience, whereas Emotional Regulation is broader, addressing coping strategies and mental balance.
- **Communication and Language (3)**: Artistic creativity often communicates beyond literal language; through symbolism, metaphor, or sensory experience.

Relevant Considerations

- Creativity spans from prehistoric cave paintings to digital art and immersive media, shaping cultural identity.
- Innovation in design and problem-solving often arises from creative methods and art-inspired thinking.

Example Historical Progression:

1. Engraved Shells and Beads *(at Blombos cave)* (c. 100,000 - 75,000 BCE)
2. Venus Figurines (c. 25,000 BCE)
3. The Development of Sculpture and Pottery (c. 10,000 - 3,000 BCE)
4. The Emergence of Written Literature (c. 2000 - 1000 BCE)
5. Greco-Roman Architecture and Relief Sculpture (c. 5th Century BCE)
6. Islamic Calligraphy and Geometric Patterns (c. 7th Century CE)
7. The Renaissance (c. 14th - 17th Century CE)
8. The Baroque and Rococo Periods (c. 17th - 18th Century)
9. Romanticism and Realism (c. 19th Century)
10. Photography and Film (c. 19th – 21st Century)

13. Competition and Achievement

Competition and Achievement refer to the desire to excel, surpass others, or reach personal and collective goals. This utility underlies athletic contests, awards, professional benchmarks, and scientific/technological milestones.

Distinct From Other Utilities

- **Social Interaction and Bonding (9)**: Competition can occur within social groups, but Social Interaction emphasizes cooperation and relationships, while Competition highlights rivalry or achievement-driven dynamics.
- **Emotional Regulation and Fulfillment (14)**: Although success can yield emotional fulfillment, Competition focuses on external performance and recognition.

Relevant Considerations
- Drives innovation and excellence, from sports and academic challenges to international space races.
- Can shape hierarchies, reward structures, and cultural values around merit, ambition, or teamwork under competitive pressure.

Example Historical Progression:
1. Competitive and Cooperative Hunting (c. 400,000 - 100,000 BCE)
2. Symbolic Grave Goods *(suggesting status and achievement)* (c. 20,000 BCE)
3. Mesoamerican Ball Game *(the Olmecs)* (c. 1400 BCE)
4. Roman Gladiatorial Games (c. 3rd Century BCE)
5. Chinese Imperial Examinations *(merit based civil service exams)* (c. 605 CE)
6. Medieval Tournaments *(jousting and melee)* (c. 11th Century CE)
7. The Royal Society's Scientific Competitions (c. 17th Century CE - London)
8. Industrial Inventions and Patents (c. 18th - 19th Century)
9. Nobel Prizes *(1901 – Present)* and The Space Race *(1950's – 1970's)* (c. 20th Century)
10. eSports and Digital Gaming Competitions (c. 21st Century)

14. Emotional Regulation and Fulfillment

Emotional Regulation and Fulfillment focus on managing affective states: reducing fear or stress while cultivating joy, resilience, and personal contentment. It covers practices from meditation and therapy to cultural philosophies on happiness.

Distinct From Other Utilities
- **Health and Well-being (10)**: Both address mental health, but Emotional Regulation zooms in on handling feelings (anger, sadness, excitement) and seeking gratification, whereas Health spans broader disease prevention and physical wellness.

- **Artistic Expression and Creativity (12)**: Creativity can be an outlet for emotional expression, but Emotional Regulation is more about internal state management rather than producing an external creation.

Relevant Considerations
- Central to social harmony, personal relationships, and ethical decision-making.
- Techniques evolve alongside cultural, spiritual, and scientific shifts (e.g., stoicism, psychoanalysis, mindfulness apps).

Example Historical Progression:
1. Ritualized Burial and Mourning Practices (c. 100,000 BCE)
2. Development of Myth and Storytelling (c. >30,000 BCE)
3. Philosophical Theories of Emotion *(e.g., Pythagoras, Confucius)* (c. 6th Century BCE)
4. Buddhist Meditation and Mindfulness (c. 5th Century BCE)
5. Epicurean and Stoic Philosophy *(emotion regulation, resilience)* (c. 3rd Century BCE)
6. Islamic Philosophies of Balance *(moderation, gratitude, charity)* (c. 7th Century CE)
7. Renaissance Humanism *(self-worth and fulfillment)* (c. 15th - 16th Century CE)
8. The Enlightenment and Rational Emotions (c. 17th - 18th Century)
9. Modern Psychology and Psychoanalysis (c. 19th - 20th Century)
10. Digital Mental Health Tools *(Apps for mood, meditation, etc.)* (c. 21st Century)

15. Environmental Awareness, Interaction, and Control

Environmental Awareness, Interaction, and Control address the understanding and shaping of natural surroundings to ensure survival, comfort, and ecological balance. This includes agriculture, climate considerations, resource stewardship, and sustainable design.

Distinct From Other Utilities
- **Protection and Shelter (6)**: Shelter is one aspect of environmental adaptation, while Environmental Awareness covers a broader scope: managing ecosystems, pollution, and sustainable living.
- **Resource Acquisition and Management (17)**: Both deal with resources. However, Environmental Awareness focuses on the overarching relationship

with nature, whereas Resource Management emphasizes the logistics of obtaining and distributing materials (including non-environmental resources like metals or fuel).

Relevant Considerations
- Involves conservation efforts, renewable energy use, and smart urban planning.
- Critical to long-term survival and quality of life for both current and future generations.

Example Historical Progression:
1. Controlled Use of Fire *(for warmth, cooking, clearing land)* (c. 1.7 - 1 million years ago)
2. Migration and Adaptation to New Environments (c. 120,000 - 60,000 BCE)
3. Agriculture and Land Management (c. 10,000 BCE)
4. Urban Planning and Architecture (c. 3000 BCE)
5. Forestry and Resource Management (c. 12th Century CE)
6. The Industrial Revolution *(responsible resource mgmt.)* (c. 18th - 19th Century)
7. Conservation Movement *(national parks, forests)* (c. late 19th - early 20th Century)
8. Environmental Science and Ecology *(ecosystem impact)* (c. 20th Century)
9. The Green Revolution *(chemical fertilizers, pesticides)* (c. 1940s - 1970s)
10. Environmental Technology and Smart Cities (c. 21st Century)

16. Self-Preservation and Survival

Self-Preservation and Survival underscore the instinctual and strategic actions taken to guard against threats: physical, legal, social, or biological. It involves defensive tools and methods (weapons, laws, policies), personal safety technologies, and preparedness.

Distinct From Other Utilities
- **Protection and Shelter (6)**: Overlaps in protecting humans from harm, but Self-Preservation goes further to include legal frameworks, personal safety gear, and broad survival strategies.
- **Health and Well-being (10)**: While health aims at maintaining and improving one's condition, Self-Preservation is more about preventing or escaping imminent threats (predation, violence, societal collapse).

Relevant Considerations

- Emerges in war, policing, self-defense methods, fortification, and regulatory standards (e.g., building codes, emergency protocols).
- Evolves continuously with new technological or existential risks (pandemics, cybersecurity).

Example Historical Progression:

1. Stone Tool Development for Hunting and Defense (c. 2.5 million BCE)
2. Use of Animal Skins and Clothing (c. 100,000 BCE)
3. Fortification of Settlements *(defensive structures around settlements)* (c. 5000 BCE)
4. Formation of Early Legal Systems (c. 2000 BCE)
5. Development of Body Armor (c. 1500 BCE)
6. Advances in Military Fortifications (c. 500 BCE)
7. Gunpowder and Firearms (c. 9th Century CE)
8. Personal Safety Tech *(alarms, smoke, and CO2 detectors)* (c. 20th - 21st Century)
9. Health and Safety Regulations (c. 20th - 21st Century)
10. Biodefense and Pandemic Preparedness (c. 21st Century)

17. Resource Acquisition and Management

Resource Acquisition and Management refers to procuring, storing, and using essential materials (food, water, minerals, energy) efficiently to support human communities, economic growth, and technological development.

Distinct From Other Utilities

- **Nourishment and Sustenance (7)**: Overlaps in obtaining food and water, but Resource Management extends to raw materials, fossil fuels, metals, and distribution systems.
- **Environmental Awareness (15)**: Although managing resources impacts the environment, this utility focuses on logistics, exploitation, and optimization, while Environmental Awareness highlights the broader ecological consequences and stewardship.

Relevant Considerations

- Includes trade networks, supply chains, energy infrastructure, and resource conservation measures.

- Influences economic structures (markets, currency, credit), technology (storage, transport), and policymaking (resource allocation).

Example Historical Progression:
1. Stone Tool Creation for Hunting (c. 2 million BCE)
2. Earliest Forms of Food Preservation *(drying and smoking meat)* (c. 12,000 BCE)
3. Pottery for Food Storage (c. 7000 BCE)
4. Early Trade Networks (c. 2000 BCE)
5. Roman Aqueducts for Water Supply (c. 1st Century BCE)
6. Medieval Crop Rotation *(for soil fertility and long-term yields)* (c. 8th Century CE)
7. Saltpeter Mining for Gunpowder *(in China)* (c. 9th Century CE)
8. Canning and Food Preservation (c. 19th Century)
9. Electricity Generation and Distribution (c. late 19th Century)
10. Global Supply Chains and Resource Distribution (c. 21st Century)

18. Spirituality and Meaning

Spirituality and Meaning capture the human quest for purpose, ethical frameworks, and connection to something greater than individual existence (e.g., gods, universal principles, philosophical ideals). It spans religious beliefs, rituals, philosophy, morality, and personal existential exploration.

Distinct From Other Utilities
- **Emotional Regulation and Fulfillment (14):** Overlaps in personal peace and existential comfort, but Spirituality embraces broader questions of morality, cosmology, and transcendence.
- **Social Interaction and Bonding (9):** While spiritual or moral systems often build community, here the focus is on personal and collective sense of purpose, sacredness, and ethical codes.

Relevant Considerations
- Includes rites, scriptures, meditative practices, moral philosophies, and modern secular or humanist outlooks.
- Influential in social justice movements, ethical governance, and the shaping of cultural identities.

Example Historical Progression:

1. Burial with Grave Goods *(for the afterlife of spiritual journey)* (c. 100,000 BCE)
2. Polytheistic Religions in Mesopotamia *(sun, fertility, and storm gods)* (c. 3,000 BCE)
3. Ancient Egyptian Beliefs and Afterlife *(pyramids and complex burials)* (c. 2,500 BCE)
4. Rise of Monotheism in the Abrahamic Religions *(Judaism, Christianity Islam; ideas of divine justice, moral responsibility, and salvation)* (c. 1st Millennium BCE - Present)
5. Axial Age and World Religions *(Hinduism, Buddhism, Confucianism, Daoism, and Zoroastrianism; ethical conduct and spiritual meaning)* (c. 8th - 3rd Century BCE)
6. Philosophical Mysticism in Ancient Greece and Rome *(Plato and the Neoplatonists explored transcendence)* (c. 3rd - 5th Century CE)
7. Medieval Christian Mysticism (c. 12th - 15th Century CE)
8. Protestant Reformation and Religious Pluralism (c. 16th Century CE)
9. Enlightenment, Secularism, and Humanism (c. 18th - 19th Century)
10. Modern Psychology and Emotional Fulfillment *(self-actualization)* and Digital Age Spirituality *(meditation & spiritual fulfillment Apps)* (c. 20th and 21st Century)

19. Learning and Knowledge Acquisition

Learning and Knowledge Acquisition covers the systematic or informal processes by which humans absorb new information and skills. It includes self-directed learning, formal education, mentorship, and the entire cultural apparatus of knowledge transmission.

Distinct From Other Utilities
- **Memory and Cognition (4)**: While cognition provides the mental capacity to process and store information, Learning covers the cultural, social, and formal methods used to impart those ideas (schools, libraries, apprenticeships).
- **Exploration and Curiosity (11)**: Learning can be methodical and structured, whereas Exploration focuses on the drive to discover and venture into the unknown. Both feed each other but have different emphases.

Relevant Considerations
- Drives civilization forward through intellectual traditions, scientific breakthroughs, and technological innovations.

- Continuously accelerated by writing systems, printing, global communication, and digital platforms.

Example Historical Progression:
1. Development of Toolmaking *(passing on of these skills)* (c. 3.3 million BCE)
2. Invention of Writing in Sumer (c. 3,200 BCE)
3. Mathematics in Ancient Egypt (c. 2,500 BCE):
4. Academies and Philosophy in Ancient Greece (c. 4th Century BCE):
5. Establishment of Libraries in Alexandria (c. 3rd Century BCE)
6. Medieval Universities in Europe *(e.g., Bologna, Paris, Oxford)* (c. 12th Century CE)
7. Scientific Method and Revolution *(rapid science advancement)* (c. 17th Century CE)
8. The Enlightenment and the Age of Reason (c. 17th - 18th Century)
9. The Industrial Revolution and Technical Education (c. 18th - 19th Century)
10. The Digital Revolution and Online Learning (c. 20th - 21st Century)

The Implications of Origin Utilities for Future Innovation

Understanding the concept of origin utilities has important implications for the future of innovation. As we continue to develop new products, services, and systems, it is essential to recognize that these innovations are not departures from our past but rather continuations of a long-standing process of extending and enhancing our natural endowments.

One of the most valuable applications of the 19 Human Origin Utilities lies in evaluating and refining products over time. By assessing how a product or service ties back to these foundational utilities, we can uncover insights into both the positive and negative impacts it may have. For example, a product initially designed to address utilities like "health and well-being" and "nourishment and sustenance," such as bottled water, may unintentionally conflict with other origin utilities, like "environmental awareness and control," when plastic waste becomes a growing concern. Similarly, the health utility that bottled water provides may be undermined by the gradual introduction of microplastics, which pose risks to human health. Monitoring these connections enables a proactive approach, ensuring that innovations remain aligned with invariant human needs, rather than inadvertently creating new problems.

This perspective provides a framework for continuous observation and improvement. As products, services, or systems evolve, new connections to the origin utilities can emerge, some positive and others detrimental. By consistently analyzing these links, innovators can spot shifts in how a product aligns with fundamental human needs. Such diligence reveals areas where innovation may need realignment or rethinking to ensure that long-term impacts stay beneficial. This kind of holistic assessment allows creators to keep pace with evolving needs and impacts, encouraging more sustainable and responsible innovation.

Additionally, adopting an origin utility lens helps to distinguish those who innovate with purpose from those who exploit for profit. When companies observe and adapt their offerings in light of the 19 HOUs, it signals that they are committed to delivering meaningful value, not just extracting it. By contrast, businesses driven purely by profit may neglect these deeper ties, often resulting in products that fail to consider long-term or indirect consequences. With the framework of the 19 utilities, however, it becomes far harder for such companies to operate unethically or ignore the broader impacts of their products. By laying bare how a product aligns or conflicts with these foundational human needs, the Law of Perpetual Innovation (LPI) sheds light on whether a company is building for the common good or merely profiting at the expense of it.

Understanding our origin utilities encourages a more holistic "systems thinking" approach to innovation. By recognizing that all technologies are rooted in fundamental human functions, we can prioritize innovations that align with our natural capacities and capabilities to promote overall well-being. This approach emphasizes the importance of designing technologies that are not only effective but also sustainable, ethical, and supportive of human flourishing.

We've been innovating upon ourselves all along

The concept of origin utilities offers a profound insight into the nature of innovation, revealing that all modern technologies, tools and systems are extensions of the fundamental capacities and capabilities inherent in all humans. By tracing the genealogy of utility back through time, we can uncover the primal functions that have driven human progress for thousands of years. These origin utilities such as movement, perception, communication, and cognition, have served as the foundation for countless innovations, each building upon the basic functions that define our species.

The persistence of these origin utilities in modern innovations highlights the continuity of the human experience, where new technologies are not radical departures from our past but rather the latest chapters in a long-standing process of extending and enhancing our natural origin abilities. We've been driving evolutionary augmentation, innovating upon ourselves all along. Continuously extending the limits of our natural abilities through iteration upon our own existence. As we look ahead, through the scope of our continuous pursuit of human utility expansion it becomes clearer that we are in a perpetual state of becoming.

Alfred North Whitehead (1861 - 1947) emphasized that reality is not made of static entities but of processes and changes. In his view, humans are not "beings" but "becomings," constantly shaped by interactions and experiences. Or stated another way "We are not defined by what we are, but by what we are in the process of becoming."

CHAPTER 9
Innovation, Entropy and Human Energy Expenditure

The Dual Thermodynamic Foundation of Innovation

Innovation has historically been studied through a fragmented lens, often split between economic, technological, sociological, and psychological theories. While each perspective has offered valuable insights, none have comprehensively unified the act of innovation with the deeper, universal laws that govern physical existence itself. The Law of Perpetual Innovation (LPI) advances a bold and necessary framework: innovation is not merely a product of cultural advancement, market forces, or creative impulse. It is, fundamentally, a thermodynamic necessity. It is the structured and conscious act of humanity locally resisting entropy's relentless advance, conserving finite human energy, and perpetually reorganizing complexity within an open system.

Through LPI, innovation is explicitly redefined as humanity's perpetual endeavor to manage and locally reduce entropy through the resolution of byproducts. These byproducts, emergent from prior innovations and systems manifesting as inefficiencies, burdens, and friction points, are not anomalies but the inevitable operational consequences of entropy within naturally occurring and human-driven systems. They demand continuous attention, increasing effort, and structured adaptation.

In this chapter we explore how LPI systematically integrates the First and Second Laws of Thermodynamics into the very fabric of innovation theory. It will build a mathematical foundation that explains not only how human systems consume and transform energy, but also why entropy necessitates the endless cycles of invention, replacement, and refinement that characterize human advancement. Additionally, it will demonstrate how LPI extends, integrates, and formalizes historical insights from thinkers like Eric Beinhocker, Buckminster Fuller, Adrian Bejan, Albert Einstein, and Francis Bacon, all of whom glimpsed portions of the profound relationship between entropy, energy, utility, and human progress.

Innovation, as LPI reveals, is not simply a phenomenon of markets and technologies or human convenience or a cultural progression. It is the necessary structural expression of conscious agency in a universe that otherwise trends relentlessly toward disorder. Every product, every process, every invention is a statement: that energy can be conserved, that burdens can be lifted, and that meaning can be preserved against the ceaseless forces that drift toward disorder. Entropy.

The First Law of Thermodynamics and the Human-Product-Environment System

The First Law of Thermodynamics states that energy within a closed system cannot be created or destroyed; it can only transform from one form into another. While human-product-environment interactions are technically open systems, exchanging energy with their surroundings, the foundational imperative remains. Total energy remains conserved, even as it transforms through different forms such as mechanical work, cognition, emotion, or social engagement.

> Definition of a **Human-Product-Environment System** (HPES): it is a conceptual unit that represents the dynamic relationship between a person (or group), the tools or utilities they engage with (products/services), and the surrounding conditions (environmental, social, cultural, temporal) in which that engagement occurs.

> In the context of LPI:
> - **Human**: The agent who perceives, expends energy, and experiences utility (benefit) and byproduct (burden).
> - **Product**: The tool, system, product, service or good that delivers utility but also generates byproducts.
> - **Environment**: All surrounding conditions; physical, digital, social, regulatory, etc., that influence the performance of the product and the user's experiential interaction with it.

> These systems are open (they exchange energy and information), dynamic (they evolve over time), and bounded (they can be defined around a particular utility being fulfilled, such as transportation, communication, or cognitive offloading).

When a human incorporates a product, service, or system into their life, they enter into an energetic relationship with that utility. Energy in the form of physical effort, cognitive attention, emotional investment, and social coordination is expended to extract the desired utility. Initially, the perceived net utility is likely high because the energy required to engage with the utility is relatively low compared to the gains achieved: convenience, pleasure, status, knowledge, freedom, etc.

However, over time, byproducts emerge. These byproducts represent measurable, tangible shifts in energy dynamics. A device that once operated flawlessly now demands maintenance. A service that once streamlined life now introduces new complexities. A relationship that was once effortless, now requires continual emotional upkeep. In every case, new forms of energy expenditure emerge that were not originally present or anticipated.

These byproducts represent real energy transformations. Mental energy shifts toward managing frustration, discontentment, or anticipation. Physical energy increases to compensate for degraded performance. Emotional energy is taxed by the tension of unmet aspirations or persistent dissatisfaction.

At a scientifically predictable point, the user will recognize that the energetic cost associated with managing these accumulated burdens (byproducts) exceeds the energetic benefit derived from the original utility. Following the First Law, no new energy can be created to magically balance this equation. Energy must be transformed, and the system must find a new way to manage it. Consequently, the user is compelled, not metaphorically but scientifically, to seek out new products, services, or systems (new utility) whose total energetic burden is lower than that of their existing ones.

This dynamic explains the foundational behaviors underlying adoption, abandonment, and replacement of utilities. It is not primarily driven by trends, fads, or marketing manipulation. It is driven by the natural, universal imperative to conserve and optimize finite personal energetic resources within a system (the human-product-environment system) that cannot create new energy but must transform and allocate what is available with maximum efficiency.

Real-world examples illustrate this thermodynamic principle vividly:

- **Transportation**: The adoption of cars, and later airplanes, dramatically reduced the physical and time expenditures associated with walking or horseback travel.

- **Domestic Technologies**: The invention and adoption of washing machines, dishwashers, and microwaves were driven by the imperative to transform human physical and cognitive energy away from manual domestic labor into freer, more valuable pursuits.

- **Luxury Goods**: Items like expensive watches or cars function not merely as status symbols but as mechanisms that reduce the cognitive and social energy required to establish credibility, status, and competence in social hierarchies.

- **Digital Tools**: The development of smartphones, computers, and integrated communication platforms reduces the cognitive, emotional, and logistical energy otherwise required to manage disparate communication and organizational tasks.

In every case, the adoption of innovations is fundamentally an act of energy optimization. Consumers gravitate toward solutions that allow them to reallocate finite cognitive, emotional, social, and physical energy away from burden management and toward productive, enjoyable, or meaningful activities.

Thus, the First Law of Thermodynamics is not an analogy for human innovation. It is the foundational energetic law that governs it. Innovation exists because finite energy must be transformed more efficiently as environmental conditions evolve and burdens (byproducts) accumulate.

Transition: From Energy Transformation to Entropy Accumulation

While the First Law of Thermodynamics governs the conservation and transformation of energy, it does not guarantee that the energy remains equally useful over time. Even as humans continuously transform energy into useful forms of locomotion, cognition, emotional regulation and so on, the quality of energy available within any system diminishes. It becomes progressively more disordered, more difficult to harness without additional effort.

This universal degradation is the domain of the Second Law of Thermodynamics.

The Second Law states that in any closed system, entropy never spontaneously decreases; it either remains constant or increases. Entropy is the measure of disorder, inefficiency, and irreversibility. In open systems such as human societies, entropy can be locally reduced, but only through the continual input of new energy and conscious effort. Otherwise, byproducts (the tangible manifestations of entropy in human experience) accumulate and progressively burden the system.

Thus, even as energy transforms and is conserved according to the First Law, entropy accumulation under the Second Law is inevitable unless proactive interventions occur. In human-product-environment systems, entropy manifests through:

- **Physical Deterioration**: Materials wear down, machines fail, and biological systems age, increasing maintenance costs and decreasing functional performance.

- **Cognitive Overload**: As systems grow more complex, the mental effort required to navigate them rises, taxing human cognition.

- **Emotional Fatigue**: Initially satisfying products or experiences yield what is perceived as diminishing emotional returns as novelty wears off and frustrations accumulate.

- **Social Friction**: Systems that once facilitated cooperation may evolve to create hierarchy, exclusion, or inefficiency, requiring new forms of social negotiation and energy expenditure.

Each of these emergent burdens represents an increase in systemic entropy. They are the natural, unavoidable byproducts of interacting with complex utilities over time.

Thus, even in an open system where energy flows continuously, entropy demands vigilance. Without continual innovation, without constant conscious local entropy reduction, systems stagnate, regress, or collapse.

The Second Law of Thermodynamics and the Necessity of Innovation

The Second Law explains why no innovation remains effortless indefinitely. Every product, every service, every social institution, no matter how elegant at inception, eventually succumbs to the creeping pressures of entropy.

In human systems:

- Entropy Accumulation manifests as mounting byproducts that decrease the perceived efficiency, reliability, and desirability of utilities.

- Energy Expenditure rises as users must invest increasing physical, cognitive, emotional, and social resources simply to sustain prior levels of utility experience.
- Local Entropy Reduction through Innovation becomes imperative. New products, services, methods, and systems must emerge to address the burdens that have accumulated and restore energetic balance.

Thus, the perpetual cycle of innovation unfolds through three structured stages:

1. **Entropy Accumulation**
   Initially, a utility offers a high net gain relative to energy input. Over time, however, entropy manifests through byproducts. Physical components wear down. Software interfaces clutter. User expectations evolve beyond original system capabilities. Social expectations shift, creating new demands.

   This stage is characterized by an increasing number and intensity of inefficiencies, frustrations, and burdens. The system begins to tilt away from optimal energy balance.

2. **Energy Expenditure**
   As entropy accumulates, users expend growing cognitive, emotional, social, and physical effort to manage or compensate for these burdens. What once required minimal attention now demands vigilance. What was once frictionless now involves negotiation, workaround, maintenance or repair.

   The user's finite energy budget becomes increasingly consumed not by direct utility enjoyment, but by entropy management. The energetic cost-benefit ratio tilts steadily downward.

   At a threshold point, the net perceived utility $U(t)$ declines sharply, not because the fundamental function has vanished, but because the energetic burden of sustaining it has grown intolerable.

3. **Local Entropy Reduction through Innovation**
   At or near this threshold or personal inflexion point, the conditions for innovation ripen.

Innovators observe the accumulation of burdens and recognize the energetic inefficiencies introduced by the old or current system. They introduce new utilities through new products, services, methods, etc. that selectively resolve or mitigate the dominant and most relevant byproducts.

Through innovation, entropy is locally reduced. Human energy expenditure is conserved or redirected toward higher-value activities. Utility is restored or reimagined with a lower cost to human energy expenditure.

The innovation cycle thus restarts, planting the seeds for the next phase of human advancement and the next inevitable accumulation of byproducts that future innovations must eventually address.

This cycle is perpetual because entropy accumulation is perpetual. Every successful innovation delays, but does not eliminate, the eventual burden of entropy's disorder.

Innovation is not merely a cultural artifact.

It is the structured, thermodynamic negotiation with entropy, required for directed life to persist.

The Law of Perpetual Innovation: A Universal Framework

The Law of Perpetual Innovation unifies the First and Second Laws of Thermodynamics within the context of human activity:

- **First Law**: Energy is conserved but must be transformed continually to optimize human outcomes within finite energetic constraints.
- **Second Law**: Entropy inevitably accumulates unless counteracted by structured, conscious effort.

Innovation is humanity's structured method for managing these dual realities. It is how finite human energy is preserved, redirected, and applied meaningfully within systems that would otherwise drift toward disorder. It is how complexity is sustained and expanded in a universe that naturally tends toward disintegration. It is how conscious human agency resists entropy's final equilibrium.

Thus, innovation is not only inevitable. It is essential to the continuation of meaning, structure, and directed existence itself. Without perpetual innovation, systems stagnate. Energy is trapped in managing burdens rather than achieving goals. Conscious life becomes entangled in friction and effort without forward movement. Through perpetual innovation, humanity preserves its agency, extends its reach, and fulfills its role as a conscious agent of localized entropy resistance in the universe.

The Mathematical Framework for the Law of Perpetual Innovation's Integration of Entropy, Energy and Utility

Having established the dual thermodynamic foundations of innovation, through the conservation of energy (First Law) and the inevitable accumulation of disorder (Second Law), we now move to the formal mathematical structure that underlies the Law of Perpetual Innovation (LPI). This structure models the dynamic relationships between entropy, byproducts, human energy expenditure, perceived utility, and innovation. It elevates what has historically been observed intuitively by thinkers, economists, engineers, and designers, into a rigorous and generalizable system grounded in the laws of physics and human behavioral logic.

This mathematical model substantiates the Law of Perpetual Innovation, offering a predictive tool for understanding how and why innovation occurs and more importantly, when it becomes necessary.

1: Defining Key Quantities

To model the perpetual cycle of innovation mathematically, especially within human-product-environment systems, we begin by defining the following quantities:

- $S(t)$: System Entropy at time t, representing the total accumulated disorder, inefficiency, or burden in a human-product-environment. This includes all the physical, emotional, and cognitive "friction" that arises from using or maintaining a system over time.

- $E_h(t)$: Human Energy Expenditure at time t, encompassing all the effort; mental (cognitive), emotional, social, and physical, that a person must invest to continue using or benefitting from the human-product-environment system. It represents the total energy required to sustain usable outcomes.

- $B(t)$: Byproducts at time t, referring to the consequences or emerging burdens caused by the use or outcomes of prior innovations (pre-existing utility). These include things like software or process bloat, maintenance tasks, emotional frustration, or increasing complexity, all of which arise naturally during the use and experience of human-product-environment systems (in Chapter 12, we discuss the Byproduct Emergence Theorem that goes into greater detail on the components of byproduct).

- $U(t)$: Net Perceived Utility at time t, defined as the benefit, satisfaction or value the user experiences and derives from the system, minus the energetic cost required to maintain or interact with it. This represents the user's real, experienced value, not just what the product offers, but what remains after accounting for the cost of use.

- $I(t)$: Innovation Event at time t, representing a targeted [new utility] intervention designed to reduce $B(t)$, thereby lowering $S(t)$, conserving $E_h(t)$, and improving $U(t)$; the net perceived utility by the user, by lowering the total energy cost to achieve desired outcomes within the human-product-environment system.

These variables together describe the thermodynamic and experiential dynamics of innovation within human-product-environment systems.

It is essential to understand that byproducts are the consequences or manifestations of entropy accumulation in human-product-environment systems. Entropy is the underlying thermodynamic principle, and byproducts are its expressions; the observable burdens, inefficiencies, or residues that make entropy real and tangible in the human experience. So, while entropy is abstract (disorder), byproducts are embodied (e.g., slow load times, outdated interfaces, emotional fatigue, etc.).

2: Establishing Fundamental Relationships

2.1 Entropy and Byproducts are Inextricably Linked

As human-product-environment systems are utilized and experienced, disorder emerges over time. In the context of innovation, this disorder manifests as byproducts: new inefficiencies, new frustrations, new unfulfilled desires, etc. These byproducts build up, whether that's a clogged inbox, a worn brake pad, or emotional fatigue from an overcomplicated user interface. These byproducts represent the "cost of using the system."

Therefore: The total system entropy $S(t)$ increases in direct proportion to the quantity and severity of accumulating byproducts $B(t)$.

Mathematically:

$$S(t) = k \cdot B(t)$$

Where:

- $k > 0$ is a **byproduct proportionality coefficient** that scales byproduct into a measurable value for how disruptive each unit of byproduct is to the system. Think of it as contributing to systemic disorder.

  What exactly is k? It is a coefficient that quantifies how impactful each unit of byproduct is in terms of system disorder (entropy). Not all byproducts are equally disruptive. k allows us to express the intensity or weight of byproducts on the system's entropy level. (Module D: Chapter 19, will expand on capturing objective byproduct)

  Where does k exist? It is context-specific. For example, in a hospital workflow system, a missing checklist (byproduct) may have higher k than a minor display glitch.

  What does k do? It allows us to scale the impact of byproducts. Without k, we would assume that all byproducts are equally entropic, which is rarely true.

  What does it mean? A high k means the system is sensitive to disruption (fragile, high-stakes, or tightly coupled). A low k means the system is resilient or tolerant to inefficiencies.

This direct proportionality between System Entropy $S(t)$ and Byproducts $B(t)$ captures a core insight: as byproducts accumulate, entropy rises. No product, service, or human system is immune to this thermodynamic drift.

This means that as byproducts emerge, whether in the form of cognitive overload, emotional dissatisfaction, physical inefficiency, or social friction, the effective disorder (entropy) within the human-product-environment system context rises in direct proportion. Put simply, the more burdens a system produces, the more disordered or inefficient it becomes. Over time, even well-designed systems accumulate entropy in this way, requiring increasing effort to maintain.

2.1.1 Introducing ε: Thermodynamic Inefficiency as an Input Variable

To formalize the relationship between systemic disorder and the emergence of byproduct, we define:

$$\epsilon > 0$$

<u>Where ϵ represents Thermodynamic Inefficiency</u>: the portion of energy transformation in a system that is lost to irrecoverable disorder, waste, or degradation. It captures a scalar measure of deviation from perfect efficiency.

This gives us a useful input variable for the Byproduct Emergence Function $\Psi(\epsilon, \eta, \delta)$ introduced in Chapter 12. It allows us to mathematically isolate inefficiency as a predictor of burden (byproduct) emergence, much like we do with expectation deviation η and aspirational comparison δ, also discussed in Chapter 12.

Since entropy $S(t)$ accumulates as byproducts $B(t)$ increase:

$$S(t) = k \cdot B(t)$$

and since disorder cannot emerge without inefficiency:

$$S(t) \propto \epsilon$$

Reads as: System entropy $S(t)$ at time t, is proportional to ($\propto$) thermodynamic inefficiency (ϵ).

Then:

$$\epsilon > 0 \Rightarrow Bo(t) > 0$$

Reads as: Whenever there is any thermodynamic inefficiency (ϵ), an objective byproduct $Bo(t)$ must emerge.

This links thermodynamic inefficiency to systemic entropy and prepares the groundwork for its role in the total byproduct emergence model formalized in Chapter 12.

Therefore: Byproducts are the tangible, human experienced manifestations of entropy growth within a human-product-environment system.

2.2 Human Energy Expenditure Rises with System Entropy

As entropy $S(t)$ increases over time, people have to work harder to attain the same utility benefits. Thus, the human energy expenditure $E_h(t)$ required to sustain a given level of perceived utility also rises. Humans must expend more cognitive attention, emotional energy, physical labor, or social capital to maintain their outcomes.

This is formally captured by:

$$\frac{dE_h}{dS} > 0$$

Meaning that each incremental increase in entropy S, requires a corresponding increase in the human energy E_h needed to manage or counteract that disorder.

The relationship can be further approximated linearly as:

$$E_h(t) = \alpha S(t) + \beta$$

where:

- $\alpha > 0$ represents the **Entropy or Burden Sensitivity Coefficient** of human energy expenditure to changes in entropy (a high α means small increases in entropy cause a lot more effort).

  α exists at the intersection of:
  - The individual's characteristics: cognitive resilience, emotional regulation, physical endurance, tolerance for disorder.
  - The task or context: some environments (e.g., air traffic control) have low entropy tolerance, amplifying even small burdens.

  This coefficient represents how burdensome entropy feels and becomes for a user.
  - A trained athlete might tolerate physical load better (low α for physical entropy)
  - An emotionally fatigued person might find small inconveniences overwhelming (α increases dynamically due to context).

This coefficient reflects how sharply perceived burden rises with entropy. It's influenced by personal resilience, system design, and context. It "lives" in the human-product-environment system and can vary over time.

- $\beta \geq 0$ represents a **Baseline Energy Constant** or **Cost** requirement even under conditions of minimal entropy (such as basic engagement with a product).

This constant represents the minimum amount of effort a person must exert under ideal, low-entropy conditions to extract utility. View it as the minimum cost of using a product when it's perfectly maintained, intuitive, clean and frictionless.

No system is free of energy cost, but this value sets the floor, the lowest bound, of human energy expenditure required to extract utility from a system.

It exists in the fundamental mechanics of the utility. For example:
   - Friction from physical action (e.g., walking to turn on a light)
   - Attention required to process inputs (e.g., reading a sign)
   - Minimal cognitive steps (e.g., opening an app)
   - Emotional activation needed to engage (e.g., calling a customer service agent)

This relationship explains why, even when a product or service initially delivers high utility at low cost to human agency, the gradual emergence of byproducts raises the energetic toll over time. The key idea here is that as systems become more disordered, humans are burdened with spending more energy just to get the same beneficial outcomes. This makes it harder to sustain satisfaction and performance.

(This explains why some users have a tendency to stay with a certain product. They're invested (sunk cost fallacy); even when the rational choice would be to cut their losses.)

Therefore: Entropy imposes a growing energetic tax on the user.

2.3 Utility as a Function of Energy Expenditure

Now we can look at $U(t)$, the net utility a person feels they are getting from a human-product-environment system. This is the value they perceive after subtracting the energy it takes to keep using the system:

$$U(t) = U_0 - E_h(t)$$

Where U_0 is the maximum potential utility. What the system could offer under ideal conditions.

Substituting in our earlier equation for $E_h(t)$:

$$U(t) = U_0 - \alpha S(t) - \beta$$

This equation shows that net perceived utility $U(t)$ drops as entropy $S(t)$ rises. People don't just stop using products because they no longer work. They stop using them because they no longer work for them, meaning the energy it takes to continue using them is no longer worth it.

Therefore, the goal of innovation becomes clear: it must reduce System Entropy $S(t)$ to lower Human Energy Expenditure $E_h(t)$ and restore Net Perceived Utility $U(t)$.

2.4 Innovation as Local Entropy Reduction and Energy Conservation

Every innovation $I(t)$ acts as a localized intervention to reduce entropy. It is a deliberate attempt to relieve this growing pressure by resolving accumulated burdens, minimize disorder, and restoring efficiency to reclaim undesired human energy expenditure (in dealing with byproducts).

Its effect can be measured by:

$$\Delta S(t) = S_{\text{before}}(t) - S_{\text{after}}(t)$$

$$\Delta E_h(t) = E_{h,\text{before}}(t) - E_{h,\text{after}}(t)$$

$$\Delta U(t) = U_{\text{after}}(t) - U_{\text{before}}(t)$$

where:

- $\Delta S(t) > 0$ indicates a successful entropy reduction,
- $\Delta E_h(t) > 0$ represents successful human energy conservation.
- $\Delta U(t) > 0$ represents successful increase and restoration to the net perceived utility

Thus, innovations are thermodynamic interventions, selectively restoring order and reducing the energetic burdens placed on humans.

We also define Innovation Efficacy $\mathcal{E}_\jmath$ as:

$$\mathcal{E}_\jmath = \frac{\Delta E_h}{E_{h,\text{before}}}$$

This is the percentage of user energy saved.

Thus:
- High efficacy innovations are those that produce a large positive ΔE_h relative to the previous baseline. significantly lightening user burdens.
- Low efficacy innovations provide marginal relief, often becoming quickly overshadowed by new emerging byproducts.

High-efficacy innovations save a lot of energy. Low-efficacy ones do very little and may likely be ignored or abandoned.

3: The Overall Mathematical Model of Innovation-Entropy-Energy-Utility Cycle

Putting it all together, we get the full picture of how entropy, energy, and utility interact over time in human-product-environment systems:

1. Byproducts are how entropy accumulates and expresses itself in the system:

$$S(t) = k \cdot B(t)$$

2. Entropy increases user effort (human energy expenditure):

$$E_h(t) = \alpha S(t) + \beta$$

3. As user effort increases, net perceived utility declines proportionately:

$$U(t) = U_0 - \alpha S(t) - \beta$$

4. Innovation must reduce local system entropy to conserve human energy burden and restore utility:

$$\Delta S(t) > 0, \quad \Delta E_h(t) > 0, \quad \Delta U(t) > 0$$

5. Innovation Efficacy tells us how effective the innovation is:

$$\mathcal{E}_g = \frac{\Delta E_h}{E_{h,\,before}}$$

These equations explain why innovation is not just about making things new or different. It is about relieving the burden of entropy, lowering the energy users have to spend, and improving their lived experience in human-product-environment systems.

Innovation is the thermodynamically driven act of conserving human energy against the inevitable accumulation of burdens across cognitive, emotional, physical, and social domains within human-created systems.

- Innovation is not primarily about creativity for its own sake.
- Innovation is a thermodynamically required act to manage entropy's pressure on finite human resources.
- The success of innovations can be objectively measured by their ability to conserve energy through entropy management.

Innovation is, therefore, not a luxury. It is a thermodynamic imperative. It is the universal mechanism through which humans preserve function, maintain agency, minimize wasted energy, and sustain complexity and meaning in a world that is always drifting toward disorder.

Historical and Modern Perspectives on Innovation, Entropy, and Human Progress

The Law of Perpetual Innovation (LPI) articulates a unified, explicit, and mathematically grounded theory of innovation rooted in the thermodynamic principles of energy conservation and entropy management. While LPI is novel in its completeness and precision, elements of this understanding have surfaced through history, glimpsed intuitively or partially articulated by various thinkers across science, engineering, economics, and philosophy.

This section explores how historical and modern thought has touched on aspects of the LPI framework and how LPI, for the first time, fully integrates, extends, and formalizes these insights into a coherent and predictive law.

Eric Beinhocker and the Origin of Wealth

In The Origin of Wealth (2007), Eric Beinhocker explicitly frames economic innovation as creating useful order out of disorder. He writes that "wealth is created to the degree that this interaction decreases entropy in favor of 'fit order' that meets human needs, desires and preferences." In other words, economic value arises from reducing entropy (disorder or wasted energy) by producing configurations that serve human purposes.

Beinhocker's framing comes remarkably close to LPI's recognition that innovation exists primarily to manage entropy by reducing systemic disorder. Where Beinhocker focused primarily on the economic domain, LPI generalizes this pattern to all dimensions of human existence: cognitive, emotional, social, cultural, and ecological.

In LPI's framing, Beinhocker's "fit order" is a local reduction of entropy achieved through conscious innovation, and wealth is but one manifestation of the broader energetic conservation principle at work across human systems.

Importantly, LPI extends Beinhocker's ideas by introducing explicit mathematics, connecting byproducts to entropy, modeling human energy expenditure, and rigorously explaining why innovation must occur perpetually, not just as an economic artifact, but as a universal thermodynamic necessity.

Adrian Bejan and the Constructal Law

Mechanical Engineer Adrian Bejan (1996) formulated the Constructal Law, an explicit principle about flow and design evolution. It states that natural phenomena and human-made systems evolve to facilitate easier flow of energy, matter, and information through them. Trees grow branching patterns to optimize nutrient transport. Vascular networks evolve to minimize resistance. In essence, systems reconfigure (innovate) continuously to reduce friction, resistance, and inefficiency. This is a near-direct articulation of innovation's value: designs change over time to minimize energy wastage (akin to reducing entropy) and thus improve utility.

Constructal Law resonates profoundly with LPI. In human systems, byproducts create friction and energetic resistance. Innovation acts as the conscious reconfiguration of these systems to reduce that resistance, conserve energy, and restore flow.

LPI can thus be seen as the conscious counterpart to the unconscious evolution that Bejan describes. Whereas rivers and trees reconfigure naturally over evolutionary time, humanity innovates deliberately, applying conscious foresight, creativity, and structured effort to accelerate entropy management.

This distinction, of conscious versus unconscious entropy optimization, is critical. Humanity, through innovation, becomes the first known agent capable of strategically managing entropy in real time, rather than waiting for natural selection over millennia.

Buckminster Fuller and Ephemeralization

Buckminster Fuller's concept of ephemeralization (1930's) captures this idea closely. Ephemeralization is the ability of technological advancement to do "more and more with less and less," ultimately approaching doing "everything with nothing." This means each innovation increases efficiency and utility, thus achieving the same or greater output (utility) with less input (energy, materials, effort). Fuller saw this trend of increasing efficiency (reducing waste and inefficiency) as an inevitable driver of human progress.

LPI substantiates and mathematically grounds Fuller's powerful intuition. While Fuller recognized the trend, LPI explains why it occurs: because entropy accumulation demands new innovation cycles, and each successful innovation locally reduces the energetic burden imposed by byproducts.

Additionally, LPI formally introduces the concept of asymptotic progression toward zero personal energy expenditure across each of the nineteen Human Origin Utilities (discussed in Chapter 29). Thus, ephemeralization is not merely a descriptive trend but is a mathematically predictable outcome of humanity's thermodynamic struggle against entropy.

Where Fuller offered a visionary description, LPI supplies the underlying causal mechanics and predictive structure.

Albert Einstein's Reflections on Order from Disorder

While not writing about technology per se, Albert Einstein (1920's) famously observed the opportunity latent in disorder: "Out of clutter, find simplicity. From discord, find

124

harmony. In the middle of difficulty lies opportunity." This insight, often cited in *innovation* contexts, neatly captures the idea that the value of an innovation is in bringing order (simplicity, harmony) out of chaos or inconvenience. It reflects the same principle: problems (analogous to entropy or "clutter") drive creative solutions that restore order.

While Einstein's insight was poetic, the Law of Perpetual Innovation captures and formalizes this dynamic structurally. Disorder, as manifested through the accumulation of byproducts, mathematically necessitates innovation. The simplicity and harmony that Einstein alluded to are achieved not by accident but by deliberate, structured interventions that resolve burdens and conserve energy.

Einstein's observations find their full scientific articulation within LPI: entropy accumulation seeds the conditions for innovation, and innovation restores local order, only to set the stage for the next cycle.

Francis Bacon and the Relief of Man's Estate

In the seventeenth century, Francis Bacon articulated that the purpose of science and invention was the "relief of man's estate," i.e., to reduce the hardships, human suffering, toil, and inefficiencies of life. Bacon recognized that technological and scientific progress should ease burdens, not merely for curiosity's sake, but to better human life.

LPI frames Bacon's vision within thermodynamic necessity. The "relief of man's estate" is not merely an ethical or social good. It is a thermodynamic imperative. Without innovation to relieve the burdens accumulated by prior solutions, human systems would collapse under their own inefficiencies.

Thus, LPI situates Bacon's moral insight within a scientific law: innovation must occur, and must continually occur, to conserve finite human energy against the growing burdens of entropy.

Where Bacon intuited a moral obligation, LPI defines a scientific inevitability.

Innovation as Humanity's Existential Imperative

Seen through the comprehensive lens of the Law of Perpetual Innovation, innovation emerges as more than a sociotechnical phenomenon. It reveals itself as an existential necessity. It is humanity's perpetual strategy for conserving finite energy and extending conscious agency in a universe otherwise dominated by entropy and systemic decay.

Every act of innovation, whether grand or humble, is a conscious defiance against disorder. It is a directed application of energy to locally reverse entropy's grip. Without innovation, the burdens of accumulated byproducts would inevitably overwhelm human systems, progressively sapping physical, cognitive, emotional, and social vitality until progress itself would stall and regress.

Innovation is thus humanity's structured method of buying time and space against the inevitable. It allows organized life to persist longer, reach farther, and experience more complexity and meaning than would otherwise be possible in a universe that trends toward dissolution. This existential framing elevates innovation beyond economics, technology, or convenience. It makes innovation the very condition for the continuation of meaning in the universe. Thus, the Law of Perpetual Innovation reveals that innovation is not merely a feature of human civilization. It is the deepest thermodynamic and existential imperative of conscious life. It is the cosmic mechanism by which meaning persists, by which energy is conserved for purposeful action, and by which consciousness resists the final stillness of entropy.

Innovation is also how humanity preserves agency. Without innovation, agency would be trapped and constrained by the unyielding pressure of growing burdens. Every act of creation, every solution to a problem, is a reassertion of humanity's sovereign will to act meaningfully in the face of the universe's decline. Innovation preserves not just technologies or conveniences. It preserves the very possibility of meaningful existence itself.

Innovation is not simply an aspect of our progress.

It is the story of our survival.

Module B:
Guiding Principles and Theory

In Module B, we begin with Chapter 10, which lays out the core insight of the Law of Perpetual Innovation: byproduct inevitably emerges from utility, whether we're talking about something we've already experienced (experienced utility) or something we merely anticipate (potential utility). Here, we see how disappointment, frustration, or even new aspirations can arise the moment expectations shift, either because a product or service isn't delivering on its promise or because we discover a better possibility. Sub-Module B1 (Chapters 11–13) then dives into the theory and principles of byproduct, explaining how these unintended consequences shape innovation cycles. Sub-Module B2 (Chapters 14–16) mirrors that analysis for utility, revealing the deeper patterns behind why we seek certain benefits and how those benefits, in turn, open the door to still more byproducts and fresh opportunities.

CHAPTER 10

The Cardinal Principle of LPI - Byproduct Emergence from Utility

Experienced and Potential Utility

Before unveiling the cardinal principle that identifies byproduct emergence from utility, we will first explore key concepts that will enable you to fully understand this core insight.

Experienced Utility: Understanding the Reality of the Value Experience

The concept of *experienced utility*, a term widely discussed in behavioral economics, psychology, and cognitive neuroscience, focuses on how individuals actually feel and respond while engaging in a particular activity or consuming a product rather than how they think they will feel beforehand. Unlike "decision utility," which is based on predictions of future satisfaction and often guides the choices we make, experienced utility represents our real-time, moment-to-moment affective states as we interact with goods, services, relationships, and situations. Pioneering work by scholars such as Daniel Kahneman and others has demonstrated that what we anticipate enjoying and what we end up enjoying can diverge significantly, shedding light on how complex and context-dependent human well-being truly is.

Central to the notion of experienced utility is the brain's intricate evaluation system. As we encounter the world, our neural machinery continually assesses stimuli for their ability to fulfill or challenge our goals and expectations. The ventral tegmental area (VTA), nucleus accumbens (NAcc), and prefrontal cortex (PFC) facilitate momentary bursts of pleasure or reward (often tied to dopamine release) when our experiences align with expectations. In parallel, neural regions such as the anterior cingulate cortex

(ACC) and amygdala track discrepancies, moments when reality fails to meet our imagined standards, often resulting in the emergence of negative emotions and stress-related hormones like cortisol. Together, these regions and neurochemicals create the "ups" and "downs" of our subjective reality, influencing how "good" or "bad" a given experience feels in "our" reality.

This dynamic interplay between expectations and lived outcomes is not a quirk of modern life. Rather, it has deep evolutionary roots. Across millennia, our ancestors benefited from neural systems that rewarded advantageous behaviors such as seeking nutritious food or forming supportive social bonds. They penalized costly miscalculations, like trusting an unreliable ally or consuming a harmful substance. As environments and cultural contexts have changed, these ancient neural circuits have continued to shape our capacity to extract value, or utility, from our daily interactions. Today, the same processes that once helped humans survive and thrive can sometimes yield dissonance, dissatisfaction, or what may be termed *"byproducts of the pursuit of utility."*

These byproducts, both emotional and practical, emerge naturally from the dynamic evaluation of experiences. While some individuals remain fixated on discrepancies and shortcomings, others reframe these unexpected outcomes as opportunities for growth and innovation. Here is where the Law of Perpetual Innovation (LPI) offers a useful lens. LPI posits that no state of utility is static; every fulfillment reveals new gaps or unmet desires, each of which can inspire creative solutions or enhance resilience. In this view, the negative feelings associated with a shortfall, such as an uncomfortable chair or a relationship disappointment, need not represent endpoints. Instead, they serve as catalysts that propel the cycle of continuous improvement, encouraging individuals and groups to refine tools, structures, and interpersonal strategies over time.

In essence, experienced utility is not a fixed quantity, but a fluid perception shaped by several factors, including biological predispositions and cultural expectations (more on this in Chapter 20). It guides how we feel in the moment and informs how we adapt to changing circumstances. To fully appreciate the role of utility in human life, it is crucial to understand that experienced utility is not only about immediate gratification or discomfort; it also sets the stage for how byproducts arise. These byproducts, often viewed as "negative" or "unwanted" elements, can be reconceived as raw material for innovation, pushing us to adjust our designs, refine our personal relationships, and align our actions more closely with our aspirations.

Byproduct Emergence from Experienced Utility (via Expectation Deviation)

Byproducts emerge from experienced utility when a mismatch is detected between what was expected and what was actually experienced, what LPI formally defines as **Expectation Deviation** (η), where $\eta = U_{expected} - U_{experienced}$ (reads as: the experienced gap between the utility one expected and what was actually experienced). This emotional-cognitive discrepancy triggers subjective byproduct, even if the product or service technically performs well. These gaps offer valuable clues about what might be refined, reimagined, or adapted. Some people become fixated on what went wrong, what we might call "negative byproduct" or deficiency. In contrast, others see the same gaps as steppingstones for progress, or "positive byproduct" or new potential. Although we begin by framing these two as a duality, they actually lie along a continuum, which we will explore more thoroughly in Chapter 20. For now, consider this spectrum as two notable endpoints, each revealing different psychological and neural responses to the challenges that arise when utility is not fully realized. *(From a utility standpoint, we have set the stage for understanding how both success and shortfall can coexist.)*

Example 1: The Chair—From Promised Comfort to Unexpected Discomfort

Picture yourself standing in your living room, admiring a recently delivered chair that had been touted as the ultimate ergonomic solution. The promotional materials promised supportive contours, breathable fabrics, and unmatched adaptability. As you unbox it, your mind, specifically your prefrontal cortex (PFC), begins setting expectations based on these claims, past encounters with well-designed furniture, and your current desire for relief after long work hours. The anterior cingulate cortex (ACC) starts its watchful role, preparing to measure whether reality matches what you have imagined and therefore expecting. In this moment, hope and promise mingle, forming your baseline "expected utility."

You ease into the chair for the first time. Immediately, your spine aligns with the gentle curvature of the backrest, your arms rest comfortably, and your legs find a relaxed, natural angle. The ventral tegmental area (VTA) releases dopamine into the nucleus accumbens (NAcc), reinforcing the feeling that you've made a wise choice. Serotonin, flowing from the raphe nuclei, contributes to a gentle sense of calm and well-being. Oxytocin, influenced by your positive brand associations, engenders trust in the product's claims, while endorphins add a subtle warmth of relief; your muscles relax, your breathing softens. You feel not just satisfied but validated. This is more than just

130

a chair. It's a promise kept. A need fulfilled. *(From a utility standpoint, your expectations are met. Utility has been realized and confirmed.)*

Over the following weeks, as you spend longer periods working, reading, or relaxing in this chair, a subtle shift occurs. The armrests, which at first seemed just fine, are starting to cause mild shoulder tension, especially during marathon work sessions. Your ACC detects a discrepancy. This isn't what you signed up for. The dopamine surge you once enjoyed subsides; reality isn't as rewarding as it seemed. The amygdala stirs, amplifying a sense of disappointment or low-level frustration, while cortisol trickles into your system, heightening your emotional arousal and internal urgency to resolve this minor injustice. Adrenaline and norepinephrine further sharpen your focus onto the source of discomfort, making it harder to think about anything other than your shoulders and that stubborn fixed armrest design.

As this discomfort persists, the brain's memory systems, aided by glutamate, store the negative association. You find yourself ruminating and replaying your discomfort and disappointment each time you sit down. Previously neutral feelings about the chair now tilt toward annoyance. You try small adjustments: shifting your posture, placing a cushion under your elbows, maybe even researching ergonomic armrest covers online. This mental and emotional labor is not what you initially expected or opted into. Your mind interprets the repeated disappointment as a mild form of grief. Something that once brought ease now brings tension. Your psyche deploys emotional coping mechanisms to reconcile this loss of initial utility: you might rationalize by thinking, "Maybe I'm just sitting incorrectly," or compensate by telling yourself, "I'll just adjust my posture." These mental gymnastics are attempts to restore a sense of harmony and justify your purchase decision. *(From a byproduct standpoint, the initial comfort has morphed into a subtle but persistent deficiency; an unanticipated shortfall that now burdens your experience. Byproduct has emerged.)*

Example 2: A Relationship—From Emotional Alignment to Rediscovered Depth

Now consider a very different setting, your home after a long day, shared with a romantic partner. Over time, you've developed a rich tapestry of expectations about your relationship's "utility." These expectations, managed by the PFC, aren't about physical comfort but emotional nourishment. You anticipate understanding glances, empathic listening, and heartfelt support. The ACC stands ready to gauge how reality measures up to these relational benchmarks.

When your partner greets you warmly, genuinely listens to your concerns, and shares affirmations of love, the neural reward systems light up. Dopamine validates that your emotional needs are met, oxytocin cements a sense of trust and closeness, and serotonin contributes to a stable, contented mood. In these moments, you feel seen, valued, and emotionally secure. The partnership seems precisely as it should be, an emotional refuge from the storms of life. *(From a utility standpoint, emotional fulfillment is achieved, reinforcing the bond and delivering expected relational utility.)*

But human bonds are dynamic, not static. Perhaps after a stressful week, you approach your partner, hoping for that same understanding presence, only to find them preoccupied, dismissive, or inattentive. Instantly, the ACC detects a shortfall. The emotional alignment you relied on is not forthcoming. Dopamine levels dip: no reward awaits in this encounter. Cortisol and adrenaline rise, mirroring the stress of the unmet need, while norepinephrine zeroes in on the emotional gap, making it difficult to focus on anything else. The amygdala magnifies feelings of disappointment or rejection, and glutamate ensures this painful encounter is etched into your memory.

In response, you might experience a mild sense of loss or grief, mourning the emotional safety you once took for granted. Just as with the chair, your mind attempts to cope. Rationalization might come in the form of, "They've had a long day, maybe tomorrow will be better," or compensation could look like seeking emotional support from a friend or distracting yourself with a hobby. These efforts try to soften the harsh edges of unmet expectations and ease your emotional discomfort. *(From a byproduct standpoint, an emotional deficiency has surfaced within what was once a reliable source of comfort and understanding, leaving a burden in its wake; byproduct.)*

Some individuals become "lodged" in this state. The disappointment hardens into resentment, feeding a narrative of deficiency: "They never really listen." Over time, this fixed, negative lens can erode trust, stifle open communication, and limit the ability to envision solutions. Emotional rumination sets in, replaying the hurt, and inhibiting forward progress. In this deficiency-focused mindset, the relationship's byproduct (emotional distance) seems insurmountable, a glaring flaw blocking the path to mutual fulfillment.

Byproduct Emergence from Potential Utility (via Aspirational Comparison)

This book is focused on product development, not product marketing, yet the emergence of byproduct is not confined to the experiencing of utility alone. It also emerges the moment a consumer becomes aware of a potential utility state. One that appears superior to their current experience, even if nothing has objectively failed. This chapter explores the cardinal principle of how all byproducts emerge, not just from experienced utility, where expectations meet or diverge from reality, but also from potential utility, where the very *"awareness"* of a product, service, system or experience introduces new perceived gaps in a consumer's current state.

This is where "Decision Utility" becomes relevant. In behavioral economics, decision utility refers to the expected satisfaction or benefit a person anticipates from choosing a particular option. Unlike experienced utility, which is determined after interacting with a product, decision utility exists before the experience even occurs. It is what compels action by shaping a consumer's perception of future benefit or fulfillment. Within LPI, we call this Potential Utility. Formally, **Aspirational Comparison (δ)** is defined as $\delta = U_{potential} - U_{experienced}$ (reads as: the perceived gap between a superior utility possibility and the current utility experience).

This means that byproducts do not only emerge after utility is experienced, but they can also emerge before utility is ever realized, during the decision-making phase itself. The moment a consumer becomes aware of a new offering and they desire it, this awareness introduces what we call Aspirational Comparison (δ), a forward-facing discrepancy between what they have and what they now know is possible. This byproduct can take the form of:

- **A newly recognized limitation:** The consumer now perceives their current state as lacking something they hadn't previously considered (e.g., "My car doesn't have the upgraded safety features.")

- **A newly imagined yet unfulfilled "Aspiration" or possibility**: The consumer envisions an improved state they had not previously considered, in contrast to their existing state (e.g., "What if I had a car that could drive itself and free up my time?").

Importantly, while thermodynamic inefficiencies (ε) may already exist, they are often tolerated or normalized until awareness of a better alternative recontextualizes them as burdens. This is why advertising and marketing are so powerful. They do not just inform consumers of product availability; they conjure byproducts that alter the consumer's perception of what they lack or could have by introducing potential utility. The moment an individual is exposed to an advertisement, their prior equilibrium is disrupted. A new expectation may be formed, revealing an absence that now feels like a shortfall or a possibility that now seems attainable, yet currently unattained. This psychological shift creates demand not because a "new product" (new higher potential utility state) itself is inherently desired, but because one's current situation in comparison to this new potential reality has provoked a sense of lack or losing out (less current utility state). Through this awareness of a deficiency (feels negative) or new aspiration (feels positive), byproduct has emerged, which can now compel action.

By understanding that byproduct emergence is not only a result of utility falling short but also of potential utility awareness, we can see why innovation is an ongoing, self-renewing cycle. New products, services and experiences do not just solve existing problems, they generate new perceived gaps, which emerge as byproducts that compel the pursuit or design of future utility. This principle reinforces the fundamental truth that byproducts, not utility, are the real driver of demand.

While the initial discomfort stems from experienced utility, the forward leap into a better imagined state constitutes a new mental construction, placing the resulting byproduct firmly within the domain of potential utility. Sometimes, this aspirational comparison ($\delta > 0$) emerges not from a new product or ad, but from an individual's reinterpretation of their own experience. This aspirational tension can emerge not just from external offerings, but from reinterpretations of one's own experience, where deficiency gives rise to imagined improvement.

In the case of the chair example from earlier, we ended up with dissatisfaction from expectation deviation ($\eta > 0$). However, this could evolve into a forward-looking aspiration. Perhaps the user starts wondering if adjustable armrests would serve not only them but a range of users with different body types and needs. This thought introduces a new perceived possibility. A mentally constructed potential utility ($U_{potential}$), which now reframes the existing chair's limitations as avoidable. This is aspirational comparison in action:

$$\delta = U_{\text{potential}} - U_{\text{experienced}} > 0$$

This triggers a shift in the brain: the default mode network (DMN) and lateral prefrontal cortex (PFC) activate, fostering divergent thinking. The hippocampus simulates solutions such as retractable armrests or modular designs. Dopamine resurges as these ideas take shape, serotonin stabilizes mood, and oxytocin rebuilds trust in innovation itself. A problem has now been reinterpreted as potential. A byproduct becomes a blueprint. *(From a byproduct standpoint, what began as dissatisfaction is reframed as innovation pressure through aspirational comparison.)*

A similar transformation can occur in human relationships. Taking the relationship example from before, a moment of emotional neglect might initially produce frustration via expectation deviation ($\eta > 0$), but some individuals do not stay stuck in deficiency. Instead, they reframe the emotional gap through aspirational comparison. They ask: "What if we found new ways to reconnect?" This activates the DMN and lateral PFC, as the brain imagines new relational possibilities: scheduling dedicated time, learning new communication tools, or seeking support.

Once again:

$$\delta = U_{\text{potential}} - U_{\text{experienced}} > 0$$

Dopamine returns with the imagined improvement. Serotonin and oxytocin support emotional regulation and openness. The original burden transforms into a relational innovation pathway. What was once disappointment becomes the seed of deeper connection. *(From a byproduct standpoint, emotional deficiency is transcended by imagined improvement, converting shortfall into relationship innovation.)*

These examples illustrate that aspirational byproducts can emerge not only from marketing or external comparison but also from internal reinterpretation. Awareness itself becomes the engine of innovation.

Whether driven by disappointment (η) or inspiration (δ), every byproduct reveals a cognitive misalignment that motivates action. And every action aimed at innovation begins with the unease that something could be better. In both cases, the burden that surfaces, whether rooted in shortfall or sparked by possibility, triggers the need for change. And that need is what innovation exists to answer.

Reflecting on the Chair and Relationship Examples

When we consider both the ergonomic chair and the intimate relationship, what emerges is not merely a repetition of processes, but a universal principle that transcends any specific context. In both scenarios, whether we are grappling with physical discomfort or emotional disappointment, the brain's underlying mechanisms for detecting and responding to unmet expectations are remarkably consistent. The anterior cingulate cortex (ACC) identifies prediction errors, highlighting the gap between what we hoped for and what we actually received. This discrepancy triggers a cascade of emotional and cognitive responses. The amygdala amplifies feelings of frustration, cortisol and related stress hormones heighten tension, and neurotransmitters like glutamate help encode the memory of the shortfall, sometimes to the point of continuous rumination. Together, these elements anchor the perception of deficiency in our minds, whether that deficiency takes the form of an ill-fitting armrest or a moment of inattentiveness in a loved one. Formally, these are expressions of expectation deviation ($\eta = U_{expected} - U_{experienced}$) which triggers subjective byproduct from experienced utility, even when no outright failure has occurred.

Yet this initial emotional turbulence does not tell the whole story. What ultimately defines the meaning and impact of the byproduct is how we choose to interpret it. In the chair scenario, disappointment over poor ergonomics can become a catalyst for mechanical innovations or more inclusive design solutions. In the relationship scenario, emotional grievances can spark honest communication, greater empathy, and stronger relational bonds. Both of these transformations rely on tapping into additional brain networks and functions. This shift is not merely emotional, it is structural. When the brain begins to simulate better alternatives, whether through imagined design features or enhanced relational patterns, it is performing an aspirational comparison ($\delta = U_{\text{potential}} - U_{\text{experienced}}$). The default mode network (DMN), prefrontal cortex (PFC), and hippocampus support the shift from a reactive stance, focused on what went wrong, to a more creative, future-oriented perspective that seeks solutions and growth.

This capacity to reinterpret a byproduct as either a dead end or a constructive challenge reflects a fundamental neural flexibility in humans. By recontextualizing a shortfall, we can restore dopamine flow, which rekindles motivation and interest, maintain emotional stability through serotonin, and rebuild trust with oxytocin. These neurochemicals help us recast the perceived deficiency into a platform for innovation, collaboration, and renewed possibility. In other words, byproducts need not serve as endpoints. Instead, they can become starting points for new, more adaptive chapters in our interactions with both objects and one another, converting the deficiency into innovation pressure. It is through this cognitive re-computation that subjective byproduct evolves from a burden of failure into a vision of possibility.

The presence of relatable detail, such as the subtle ache of an ergonomic misalignment or the hollow feeling that arises when emotional support falters, helps ground these concepts in everyday experience. This grounding ensures that understanding the neuroscience of utility and byproduct is not limited to an abstract or clinical exercise. Instead, it becomes a tool for making sense of our lived realities. In practical terms, this means that both the physical world of products and the intangible realm of human connection follow similar patterns. Our neural architecture equips us to identify shortfalls (negative byproducts), respond to them emotionally, remember them vividly, and then, if we choose, to reinterpret them as opportunities (positive byproducts). Recognizing this universal dynamic encourages us to approach future challenges with curiosity and resilience, knowing that even when things do not unfold as planned, we possess the innate capacity to invent new forms of utility from the byproducts we encounter.

Recognizing the Dimensions of Byproduct

So far, our examples, like the chair that fell short, or a strained relationship, have shown how byproducts emerge from experienced utility. Additionally, it's crucial to understand that byproducts do not only result from post-experienced shortfalls. They also arise the moment you become aware of a new potential utility, one you do not yet have, but now realize could serve you better. In both cases, byproducts contain two inseparable components:

- **Objective Component**: The tangible, measurable aspect of burden, such as product, process or system degradation or physical barriers to adoption.

- **Subjective Component**: The emotional-cognitive evaluation of that burden, either as a shortfall (expectation deviation) or a longing (aspirational comparison).

These components may "appear" to us asynchronously, but they are always co-present. A physical defect becomes meaningful only when felt or noticed. Likewise, a sense of dissatisfaction or desire is always anchored in some perceived structural or comparative basis. (Chapter 20 will introduce the Byproduct Contrast Continuum. For now, we explore these dimensions in their simpler binary form: deficiency and aspiration.)

Here is a simplified diagram illustrating this:

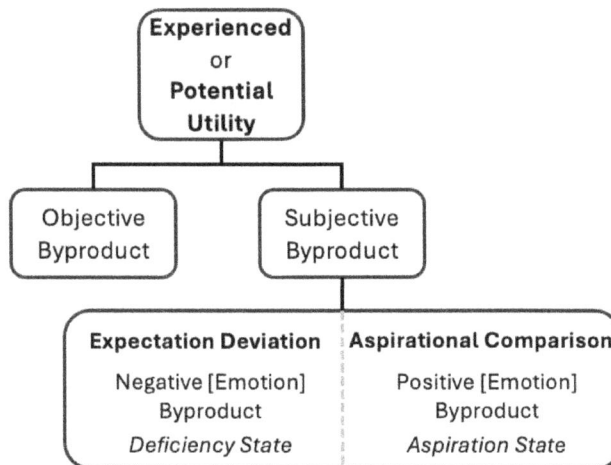

Simplified Diagram of Byproduct Emergence

Objective Component of Byproduct

1. **From Experienced Utility**

   For utility we are already using, the objective byproduct is often straightforward and quantifiable:

   - **Example (Pencil)**: Physical degradation such as a tip dulling or breaking. These performance-based issues emerge naturally as the pencil is used and can be measured (e.g., how often it breaks or how quickly it wears down).
   - **Example (Ergonomic Chair)**: Lack of adjustable armrests, causing discomfort over time. This is a direct, observable shortfall that may reduce physical support. (e.g., quantifiable by user complaints, angle misalignments, or reported pain in certain body areas)

2. **From Potential Utility**

   With utility we only anticipate, the objective component usually involves external or systemic constraints that either facilitate, complicate, or block adoption:

   - **Example (EV Awareness)**: Consumers might discover that electric vehicles are appealing alternatives to gas cars, yet objective byproducts include limited charging stations, higher upfront costs, or regulatory hurdles. None of these are direct performance defects of the vehicle itself; rather, they are the external barriers (feasibility, infrastructure) that shape whether and how a potential utility can be realized.

Summary: Objective byproducts from experienced utility reflect performance degradation. Objective byproducts from potential utility take the form of environmental, integration or systemic barriers that impede access to, or acquisition of, the improved utility.

Formalizing Total Byproduct

To mathematically represent the complete burden imposed by any utility, whether real or imagined, we define:

$$B(t) = B_o(t) + B_s(t)$$

Reads as: Total byproduct $B(t)$ is the sum of objective byproduct $B_o(t)$, such as physical inefficiencies or systemic barriers, and subjective byproduct burden $B_s(t)$, such as emotional dissatisfaction or cognitive tension.

This expression captures the full experiential and structural cost of interacting with or anticipating utility. Even if one dimension appears more dominant at a given moment, LPI holds that every byproduct contains both a tangible (objective) and perceptual (subjective) component. These two aspects always begin with the objective component yet may appear to emerge asynchronously due to the initial latent nature of how thermodynamic inefficiencies (ϵ) in physical systems and products may go unnoticed at first or become accepted by people. However, they are functionally inseparable in the lived experience of utility, and they become burdensome once noticed or reinterpreted through frustration, dissatisfaction, aspiration, or desire.

In Chapter 12, this framework will be extended to show how total byproduct emerges from three deterministic drivers: thermodynamic inefficiency ϵ, expectation deviation η, and aspirational comparison δ. This structure, objective plus subjective, is foundational to understanding the complete anatomy of byproduct.

Subjective Component of Byproduct

Subjective byproducts arise from internal states of dissatisfaction or desire. These are emotional-cognitive interpretations of either a shortfall in expected performance or the awareness of something superior. They can emerge from both experienced and potential utility:

1. **From Experienced Utility**

- **Negative (Unresolved Deficiency / Expectation Deviation - η):** Disappointment, frustration, or unmet expectations stemming from a degrading product or underperforming service.
  - **Example (Chair):** A poorly designed seat may cause disappointment and frustration, signaling users that their present situation is unacceptable
  - **Effect:** This dissatisfaction can motivate a search for better solutions or replacement.

- **Positive (Unfulfilled Aspiration / Aspirational Comparison - δ):** Even a mildly deficient experience can lead someone to imagine a better solution.

139

- o **Example (Chair)**: Feeling slightly uncomfortable might trigger ideas about a chair with reclining settings or improved posture support.
- o **Effect**: The mental construction of a superior alternative reframes dissatisfaction into aspiration.

2. From Potential Utility

- **Negative (Unresolved Deficiency / Expectation Deviation η)**: Becoming aware of a better alternative can retroactively frame your current solution as insufficient.
  - o **Example (Mechanical Pencil)**: After learning about an advanced pencil that never needs sharpening, one may begin to view their once-satisfying wooden pencil as outdated.
  - o **Effect**: This new awareness can produce dissatisfaction strong enough to trigger replacement.

- **Positive (Unfulfilled Aspiration / Aspirational Comparison δ)**: Exposure to a new possibility creates a positive sense of yearning or desire.
  - o **Example (AR Glasses)**: Hearing about immersive augmented reality may provoke curiosity and a longing for an experience not yet had.
  - o **Effect**: This aspiration creates emotional tension and motivates pursuit of the new utility.

Whether originating from deficiency or aspiration, all subjective byproducts reflect emotional-cognitive engagement with utility gaps, either present or potential.

Examples in Human Relationships

The same principles apply to relationships:
- A measurable reduction in shared time may serve as an objective signal of relational strain.
- The subjective reaction might be frustration, disappointment, or even loneliness.

Alternatively, these same conditions could inspire aspiration:
- Seeing a couple that shares deeper intimacy may lead one to envision what's possible in their own relationship.
- This might produce either:

o   A deficiency-based feeling: "Why aren't we like that?"

o   Or an aspirational response: "We could be more like that."

In both cases, the byproduct may lead to corrective effort, innovation, or deeper emotional connection.

Key Insight: Byproduct emergence does not rely solely on product or relationship breakdown. It often hinges on how users interpret their current experience against what they expected or what they now imagine could exist.

Strategic Implications for Innovators

Understanding the dual nature of byproduct emergence, objective and subjective, allows innovators to:

- Anticipate dissatisfaction even before performance drops.
- Detect emerging aspirations from subtle cues.
- Innovate in response to emotional-cognitive signals, not just mechanical failures.

This enables businesses to act not only when things break, but when perception itself begins to shift.

NOTE: In this text, the terms "aspiration" and "opportunity" may be used interchangeably depending on context. Aspiration refers to internal motivation to transcend current conditions. Opportunity highlights external feasibility or readiness for that transition. Both describe the recognition that the current utility state is no longer sufficient.

Guiding Principle 0: Byproduct Emerges from Experiencing Utility and Awareness of Potential Utility

It is necessary to crystallize the root idea that underlies the Law of Perpetual Innovation; that byproduct always emerges from utility. As we have seen through examples and neuroscience, byproduct emergence is not confined to experienced utility alone. Byproducts arise not only from the direct interaction with a product, service, or system, but also from the awareness of potential benefits (higher potemtial utility).

Whenever utility is experienced, whether solving a problem, fulfilling a need, or achieving a goal, byproducts will inevitably arise. These byproducts may appear as minor irritations, such as a poorly designed armrest on a chair, or as emotional disruptions, such as disappointment in an intimate relationship. They are not accidental or rare occurrences; they are intrinsic, inevitable elements of the utility experience.

However, byproducts can also emerge before utility is ever experienced, when an individual becomes aware of a new offering, service, system, or experience. This awareness of potential utility initiates a byproduct response, either as an unresolved deficiency (through expectation deviation η) or as an unfulfilled aspiration (through aspirational comparison δ). These two subjective pathways are cognitively triggered by a structural gap, either real or imagined, between the current state and a perceived superior alternative. When individuals recognize a previously unconsidered gap in their current reality or an enhanced future state, this triggers a byproduct of decision-based dissatisfaction, compelling them to escape their current state by seeking resolution.

The interplay between experienced utility-based byproducts and potential utility-based byproducts is crucial in understanding how innovation progresses and why demand emerges. The byproducts of experienced utility provide direct feedback that lead mostly to incremental improvements, ensuring that products, services, and systems evolve to correct real-world needs. Meanwhile, the byproducts of potential utility can expand the perceived spectrum of need, stimulating even far-reaching aspirations and driving forward the next wave of radical innovation. Both forces operate together, reinforcing the perpetual cycle of byproduct emergence and innovation.

This foundational cardinal principle sets the stage for the remaining Byproduct and Utility Principles. It provides a concise, guiding thread that reminds us that whenever we encounter shortfalls or desires, we should recall Principle 0, recognize that byproduct emergence is natural, and use that awareness to move forward. With this principle in mind, we can now consider why some individuals lean toward deficiency-focused interpretations of byproduct while others embrace opportunity-focused (or aspiration-focused) reframing of it. We will now establish a formal definition for Principle 0.

0. **Principle of Byproduct Emergence from Experienced and Potential Utility**
   Byproducts inherently emerge whenever utility is pursued, experienced, or even anticipated. They are not anomalies, but structural consequences of human-product-environment interaction. Each byproduct contains both objective (physical/systemic) and subjective (emotional-cognitive) components, even when only one is initially perceived.

When utility is experienced, the brain evaluates its outcome against expectations. Over time, thermodynamic inefficiency (ϵ) accumulates, products degrade, systems slow, or friction increases, while expectations evolve due to personal growth or changing external standards, competitive alternatives or social-cultural environmental shifts. When the experienced utility no longer aligns with what was expected, a cognitive-emotional gap emerges, known as expectation deviation ($\eta = U_{expected} - U_{experienced}$). This deviation gives rise to subjective byproduct in the form of dissatisfaction, dissonance, or felt deficiency.

Byproducts also emerge before any utility is used, triggered by the awareness of a superior or alternative possibility. This perceived gap between one's current experience and a better imagined or observed utility state is called aspirational comparison ($\delta = U_{potential} - U_{experienced}$). It creates a different kind of byproduct, one rooted in longing, ambition, or desire. Even without system failure, the possibility of something better can recontextualize ones' current state as insufficient.

Whether through η or δ, the emergence of byproduct always signals a misalignment that provokes adaptive behavior or innovation. Marketing, social-cultural influence, and technological progress often serve as accelerants by exposing new possibilities, redefining adequacy, and surfacing byproducts that users had not previously recognized.

Byproducts are not exceptions but an intrinsic feature of the utility experience and expectation. No instance of utility stands alone; every engagement with or awareness of utility generates new opportunities for refinement, adaptation, and creative advancement. Whether through direct experience or anticipated potential, byproducts ensure that innovation remains an ongoing, self-renewing cycle, where each step toward fulfillment generates the conditions for further unmet needs and new possibilities.

Examples:

The Bicycle
Early bicycles provided a transformative utility, that of human-powered transportation. However, their experienced utility revealed significant

byproducts. Heavy frames made them difficult to maneuver, rigid tires caused discomfort over rough terrain, and limited gear systems required excessive physical exertion. These deficiencies led to a series of innovations, such as lighter materials, cushioned seats, and improved gearing mechanisms, all aimed at addressing byproducts that became evident through direct use.

At the same time, potential utility awareness shaped demand and accelerated innovation. As advancements were made, consumers became aware of lighter, more efficient, and smoother-riding bicycles, making older models feel inadequate even before they failed. The newly perceived gap between existing ownership and better emerging possibilities became its own byproduct, compelling users to seek upgrades not necessarily because their current bicycles had failed, but because they now saw an improved alternative that redefined what was possible.

The Pen

Writing instruments have always sought to fulfill the basic utility of creating legible marks on a surface, yet experienced utility consistently exposed byproducts. Quill pens required constant dipping, were prone to inconsistent ink flow, and dried too slowly, leading to smudging. Fountain pens improved upon these shortcomings but introduced new byproducts, such as leakage and high maintenance. The development of ballpoint pens addressed these deficiencies by offering a more reliable ink flow, less maintenance, and a mess-free experience.

However, byproducts also emerged from potential utility awareness. Before the invention of the ballpoint pen, people accepted the limitations of existing pens. Yet, when ballpoints were introduced, consumers who had not previously been dissatisfied with fountain pens suddenly perceived their writing experience as flawed. Even if their fountain pen worked well, its unresolved deficiencies/expectation deviations (or the unfulfilled aspiration/aspirational comparison of a better pen out there) became newly relevant in light of the improved alternative, illustrating how awareness of a potential utility can generate demand even before a consumer directly experiences a problem.

The Light Bulb

The invention of the incandescent light bulb delivered an unprecedented utility, instant artificial illumination. However, experienced utility quickly revealed byproducts: bulbs produced excessive heat, burned out quickly, and consumed high amounts of energy. These shortcomings drove inventors to create more energy-efficient and long-lasting solutions, leading to the development of fluorescent and LED-based lighting.

Simultaneously, potential utility awareness played a critical role in accelerating adoption. As soon as consumers became aware that LEDs lasted significantly longer and consumed less energy, they began perceiving traditional bulbs as wasteful and inefficient, even if they had been satisfied with them before. The knowledge that a superior alternative existed created a new byproduct, causing them to "push" away from the now-perceived shortcomings of older bulbs, coupled with a "pull" toward the higher promise of LEDs, prompting many to switch despite no urgent performance issues with their existing lighting.

VERY IMPORTANT NOTE (Regarding Principle 0)

"Potential Utility" must always be grounded in verifiable, "Experienced Utility" or, at minimum, robust evidence that reasonably stands in for real-world data. When businesses market offerings with grand promises that lack substantiation, like an eye cream claiming to erase wrinkles effortlessly, they exploit consumers' hopes rather than simply "stretch the truth." This is not merely an overreach of creative marketing; it is an ethical breach that manipulates decision utility, luring people into purchasing under false pretenses. Once the product inevitably fails to deliver, the fallout extends beyond user disappointment, breeding distrust of brands and undermining faith in marketplace integrity. Even early-stage innovations should be grounded in pilot results, user studies or validated research, preventing claims from devolving into empty speculation.

This principle also applies across broader society and culture. Idealized narratives of love, success, or happiness, often seen in social media, romantic films, or celebrity portrayals, can create illusions of perfect lives that are detached from genuine, documented experiences. Individuals who internalize these illusions may experience byproducts of frustration, inadequacy, or self-doubt when confronted with real-life imperfection. Just as businesses are accountable for ensuring that marketing claims reflect tested or evidenced outcomes, social and cultural institutions and influencers have a parallel responsibility to acknowledge that the "Potential Utility" they endorse must be tethered to authenticity. When aspirational ideals are severed from honest, verifiable anchors, they risk fostering disillusionment, eroded self-esteem, and collective cynicism about what is truly achievable.

The same vigilance extends to political arenas and public discourse. Exaggerated policy visions or sensationalized promises, detached from any credible track record or transparent data, mislead entire communities. They generate byproducts of disillusionment, cynicism, and mistrust among those who initially believed in them. Whether it involves an influencer claiming a flawless lifestyle, a politician touting transformative national prosperity, or an advertiser pushing grandiose product benefits, all claims about "Potential Utility" must remain grounded in verifiable evidence or proven experience. Abandoning this accountability fractures trust, inflames negativity, and ultimately undermines the shared human pursuit of genuine innovation and progress.

Cognitive Variables That Drive Subjective Byproduct

As we make our way to Chapter 12, where we formalize the full structure of byproduct emergence, we briefly defined the two cognitive variables that govern subjective byproduct: Expectation Deviation and Aspirational Comparison.

Expectation Deviation (η)

$$\eta = U_{expected} - U_{experienced}$$

Reads as: The emotional-cognitive gap between what the user anticipated and what they actually experienced.

When $\eta > 0$, the user perceives a shortfall, resulting in frustration, disappointment, or cognitive dissonance. This deviation leads to subjective byproduct rooted in experienced utility.

Aspirational Comparison (δ)

$$\delta = U_{potential} - U_{experienced}$$

Reads as: The psychologically perceived gap between one's currently experienced utility state and a more desirable alternative, whether observed, imagined, or culturally introduced.

When $\delta > 0$, the current utility experience is recontextualized as insufficient. This comparison creates subjective byproduct rooted in potential utility. Not necessarily because of failure, but because of contrast.

Together, η and δ form the cognitive structure behind all subjective burdens. In Chapter 12, we will integrate them with thermodynamic inefficiency (ϵ), the objective burden driver, into the unified byproduct emergence function:

$$B(t) = \Psi(\epsilon, \eta, \delta)$$

Understanding expectation deviation η and aspirational comparison δ not only strengthens the cognitive grounding of LPI, but also enables us to model and predict burden/byproduct emergence more precisely, making innovation more responsive, targeted, and psychologically aware.

For Additional Author Insights--

See APPENDIX I for: Evolutions Benefits & Drawbacks and A Call to Action This appendix discusses the mindset evolution favors and ends in responsible innovation.

Sub-Module B1:
Theory and Principles of Byproduct

Sub-Module B1 delves into *why* byproducts lie at the heart of every demand and innovation cycle, showing that products don't create desire in a vacuum, but rather, they arise to resolve both negative shortfalls (unmet needs or frustrations) and positive aspirations (new possibilities) triggered by existing or potential utility. Chapter 11 highlights how byproduct is the deeper driver of demand, constantly prompting people to "escape" their current state whether it feels inadequate or overshadowed by something better. Chapter 12 presents a formal theorem proving that byproducts must inevitably surface, thanks to thermodynamic inefficiencies, unmet expectations, and awareness of higher utility standards. Finally, Chapter 13 outlines 56 core principles that classify and clarify these byproducts, from minor annoyances to profound system disruptions, underscoring how every innovation is shaped by the burdens it alleviates, thus giving meaning to the benefits it delivers.

CHAPTER 11
The 'Why' of Byproduct

A Brief History on Demand Economics

For centuries, economic theories have tried to explain "**what**" drives demand by focusing on consumer preferences, utility maximization, and price sensitivity. Early thinkers like Adam Smith and David Ricardo (18th – 19th Century) saw demand as a reflection of the perceived value or utility that goods provide. It was assumed that people make rational choices to maximize their satisfaction. This led to the development of concepts like marginal utility, which emphasized that demand decreases as the additional satisfaction gained from consuming a product diminishes. As the field evolved, economists like Alfred Marshall (early 20th Century) introduced the demand curve, linking demand with price and consumer income, while later theories added nuance by exploring how choices are influenced by preferences and constraints; for instance, brand loyalty or cultural norms (preferences), and limited budgets or time (constraints).

The "**how**" of demand, particularly in the 20th century, became more focused on the mechanisms of consumer decision-making. Indifference curve analysis, advanced by economists like John Hicks (early 20th Century), suggested that demand is shaped by the trade-offs consumers make between different goods based on their preferences. John Maynard Keynes (mid-20th Century) brought a macroeconomic perspective, arguing that aggregate demand is driven by income, employment, and consumer expectations about the future. More recently, behavioral economists like Daniel Kahneman and Amos Tversky introduced concepts from psychology that challenged the idea of purely rational consumers. They revealed that demand can be shaped by cognitive biases, emotions, and framing effects; influenced by factors beyond pure utility maximization, such as social influences, loss aversion, and mental accounting.

While behavioral economists have revealed that demand is influenced by psychological factors like framing and loss aversion, another crucial factor remains highly underexplored: the role of potential utility awareness (Kahneman, Walker and Sarin's

"Decision Utility"). When individuals become aware of an unexplored offering, one they have not yet engaged with but now recognize as possible, it creates a new byproduct of decision-based dissatisfaction. This is not a reaction to a deficiency they have experienced, but to a newly perceived gap between their current reality and what could be. Traditional demand models focus on what people want now. Still, LPI, standing on the shoulders of decision utility findings, highlights that awareness of an unconsidered utility can generate new demand, even before direct experience, which LPI terms potential utility.

Despite these advances, economic theory has largely focused on describing **what** people want and **how** they make choices, without fully addressing the deeper "**why**," behind demand. Traditional theories attribute demand to consumer desires and preferences but rarely explore the underlying reasons for these desires. The Law of Perpetual Innovation (LPI) fills this gap by identifying byproduct, that has emerged from some pre-existing utility, as the root of demand. When individuals feel either let down by what is or inspired by what could be, these become driving forces behind the demand, and even creation, of new utility. Unlike traditional views, LPI argues that demand originates from the shortfalls experienced by consumers when they experience utility or from a newly perceived gap introduced through potential utility awareness rather than from speculative value creation.

In this way, byproduct provides a fundamental explanation for *why people want and need what they want and need.* It shifts the focus from utility creation to addressing real or perceived gaps in existing products, services, systems, and experiences. By recognizing that demand emerges from byproduct, businesses can better understand what consumers are truly seeking: solutions to problems they encounter or possibilities they now face, even if they cannot articulate them precisely. This perspective offers a new, deeper lens on demand theory, suggesting that the most successful innovations respond to byproducts as the true drivers of demand in any market.

The Role of Byproducts in Shaping Demand

Under LPI, the fundamental driver of demand is byproduct. *"I'm freezing my butt off out here! If I only had something to keep me warm."* The experienced utility of a person's current garments reveals an unresolved deficiency, prompting them to want to escape their current utility state for an improved solution. Or *"Avengers Infinity War is out? I'm so going!"* (*unspoken subtext*: fear of missing out on cultural buzz, unresolved plot lines, or craving big-screen excitement). Here, the awareness of a potential utility introduces either an unresolved deficiency (e.g., fear of being left out)

150

or an unfulfilled aspiration (e.g., needing to immerse in that "epic" cinematic experience), sparking the desire to pursue this new or higher utility.

These perspectives reframe the traditional understanding of demand creation, highlighting that demand emerges from the byproducts people encounter, whether they stem from a current utility that no longer meets expectations or from the newly discovered higher potential of an unexperienced offering perceived as upstaging their current state. Such byproducts may surface as an unresolved deficiency via expectation deviation (η) that users want to escape, or an unfulfilled aspiration via aspirational comparison (δ) that they feel compelled to fulfill.

By recognizing these felt shortfalls or pending opportunities, individuals become driven to "flee" their existing state in search of something better. This explains why innovation isn't merely about improving products in a vacuum, but about addressing tangible and perceived gaps that people find untenable once recognized. In short, byproducts lie at the heart of market demand, signaling that either something is lacking where utility currently exists or that something newly attainable has reshaped what people believe they need. Let's explore how these byproducts shape and influence demand and why understanding their emergence is critical for navigating market dynamics.

1. **Byproducts as the Root Cause of Demand**
   LPI identifies byproduct as the underlying driver of demand, which can surface from either an experienced shortfall (expectation deviation) or a newly perceived potential alternative (aspirational comparison). In some cases, people encounter a tangible frustration with existing solutions, spurring them to seek improvements. In other cases, they become aware that a superior possibility exists, casting their current utility in a lesser light. Neither frustration nor aspiration alone would be enough if not for the byproducts (negative or positive) that signal "it's time for change."

   Simply experiencing these emotions, without connection to a specific utility (product, service, or system) does not create actual demand. Emotional triggers must be linked to an emerging byproduct that concretely shows where the current offering falls short or could be surpassed. This byproduct then generates the drive to escape the unresolved deficiency (expectation deviation) or the unfulfilled aspiration (aspirational comparison), both of which lead people to pursue a new or improved utility state; the next product, service or system.

Businesses that address these concrete signals, rather than mere speculation, tap into genuine demand.

Example: Short-Term Rentals (e.g., Airbnb)
Conventional hotels imposed byproducts such as impersonal rooms, rigid check-in times, lack of local character and uniform pricing structures. Travelers grew aware that cozier, more flexible, culturally immersive and budget-friendly lodging was possible, revealing a gap unaddressed by traditional offerings. Short-term rental platforms arose precisely to resolve these byproducts, unlocking demand for more unique, home-like travel experiences.

2. **Demand as a Reactive Response**
   Under LPI, demand arises not from guesswork but in reaction to unmet needs or new possibilities. Consumers often do not realize they "want or need" a new product until a shortcoming weighs on them or they discover a more appealing alternative. In either case, it is the byproduct, whether a frustrating constraint or an exciting opportunity, that triggers their readiness to adopt something new. Demand, therefore, lags behind byproduct recognition. The consumer must first sense a gap, then they react.

   Example: Food Delivery Services (e.g., DoorDash, Uber Eats)
   Consumers did not initially express a strong desire for an app to order meals until daily life revealed persistent issues: standing in lines, juggling schedules, limited local dining variety. These obstacles, however, became intolerable (byproducts of busy lifestyles) once consumers realized that delivery services could reduce or eliminate these issues for them. What followed was the formation of strong reactive demand for quick, convenient restaurant-to-doorstep solutions.

3. **Shaping Consumer Expectations Through Byproducts**
   Byproducts also recalibrate what users come to expect in future offerings. When they encounter defects, inefficiencies, or otherwise frustrating experiences, they anticipate the next version or competitor to address those shortcomings. Similarly, once people learn that a new product eliminates the inconveniences they previously accepted, their standard for what "good enough" looks like changes. This heightened or shifted expectation becomes a potent source of market pressure, urging companies to innovate.

Example: Demand for Plant-Based Milk Alternatives

Traditional dairy consumption carried byproducts such as lactose intolerance, ethical concerns about animal welfare, and the environmental impact of dairy farming. As these byproducts became more visible, people expected a healthier, more sustainable approach. This led to plant-based alternatives like almond or oat milk to rise to meet these revised expectations, providing a similar taste experience without the digestive discomfort and fewer ecological downsides. Over time, nuanced variations began to make their way into the market to meet increasing expectations; sweetened, unsweetened, protein-enriched and so on. What had been an offbeat choice became a mainstream standard, illustrating how byproducts reshape consumer norms.

4. **Unseen or Latent Byproducts Driving Demand**

A significant insight from LPI is that many byproducts remain dormant, unseen, or latent until they accumulate enough friction (byproduct) to grab attention and influence demand. These hidden issues may not be immediately obvious to consumers or businesses. Consumers might adapt to minor irritations without complaint, yet beneath the surface, these small pain points build latent underlying demand pressure. Successful companies are often those that identify and address these latent byproducts before they become problematic or widespread, sometimes unlocking entirely new markets. (*NOTE: Chapters 20 and 28 expand on latent byproduct regarding disruptive/radical innovation*)

Example: Virtual Fitness Platforms (e.g., Peloton, Home Workout Apps)

The shift from gym memberships to virtual fitness experiences was driven, in part, by latent byproducts like limited gym hours, commuting hassles, unavailability of equipment, sanitation concerns or discomfort exercising around crowds. Even though people rarely spelled out a need for fully interactive home workouts, these collected irritations added up. Once the infrastructure and technology that could support interactive home workout capability surfaced, companies that recognized these under-the-radar grievances launched digital classes, virtual leaderboards, and real-time coaching, unearthing a significant demand for in-home exercise solutions.

5. **Byproducts as Predictive Signals of Emerging Demand**

By examining existing or emerging byproducts, businesses can forecast where demand is headed. Negative byproducts like time wastage, rising costs, or environmental impact can flag issues needing fixes. In addition, positive byproducts like glimpses of next-level features or evolving performance can hint at upgrades consumers may eventually crave. Rather than guessing at future wants, organizations garner direct clues by studying changes or emergence-adoption in dissatisfaction or excitement around previous and current offerings.

Example: Sustainable Products
Pollution, resource depletion, and the growing sense of consumer guilt were clear byproducts of dated manufacturing processes. Observing these signals, visionary companies introduced greener packaging, eco-friendly materials, and more energy-efficient operations before mass demand fully crystallized. By tackling these underlying issues, companies captured a wave of environmentally conscious consumers whose demand followed naturally once the solutions became available.

6. **The Continuous Feedback Loop Between Byproducts and Demand**
Every new utility innovation that addresses current byproducts inevitably faces its own byproducts: introducing new complexities or getting overshadowed by new aspirations. In other words, it spawns or provokes its own further byproducts. This cyclical push-and-pull underpins LPI's perpetual nature: demand responds to newly surfaced gaps, which in turn arise from the latest solutions. Businesses that ignore this feedback loop risk being blindsided by changing market realities.

Example: Transition from Keyboards to Touchscreens
Physical mobile phone keyboards had byproducts like limited typing speed, bulkiness and mechanical failure. Touchscreen technology removed these issues but introduced new byproducts such as fragile screens, smudge-prone surfaces, and accidental taps. Each leap solved old pain points yet generated new ones, spurring additional design enhancements like gorilla glass, fingerprint sensors, predictive text, and haptic feedback.

Deeper Insight: Byproduct as the "Why" Behind Demand

Traditional models of demand often point to preferences or perceived utility, however, they seldom ask why these preferences come into being. According to LPI, the answer lies in byproducts, the objective, tangible gaps coupled with the subjective psychological gaps that people cannot bear to keep ignoring. These gaps emerge within the present experience of utility or between the present and an anticipated (future) higher potential utility that already appears superior.

Evolution primed us to escape what endangers us or to pursue outcomes that enrich us, a tendency that modern life translates into the relentless urge to "fix" and "upgrade." The result is that whenever we spot a product or service promising relief from inconvenience or the chance to seize a brighter possibility, we feel compelled to respond. It's the same impulse that once drove us to flee predators or secure safe water, but now it manifests in choosing a more comfortable chair to relieve chronic back pain or selecting a cutting-edge smartphone we've been anticipating.

Sometimes, these gaps are unresolved deficiencies via expectation deviation, such as daily irritations or sporadic inefficiencies that indicate a product is no longer good enough. Traditional economics would treat this as a decline in utility or dissatisfaction (even a form of disutility) triggered when our experience falls short of the benefits we expected. LPI identifies this as byproduct emergence, where an objective shortfall and its subjective emotional-cognitive counterpart emerge from expectation deviation. LPI argues that it is not a decline in utility but rather the emergence of byproduct that unsettles us. This can trigger pursuit mechanisms in our neurobiology, as demand for relief from our current state, where the next utility that can rescue us from this state may or may not be in our purview.

(Note: The present experienced utility, or present state, can mean the product, service or system itself (byproduct emerging from this utility), or it can mean between two or more utilities (byproduct emerging from the interaction or interdependence of products, systems, etc.). For example, sharpening your pencil yet, the sharpener is faulty, so it keeps breaking the tip, yet you keep sharpening and remain dissatisfied with the pencil when it's not actually the culprit.)

Other times, these emotional-cognitive gaps are unfulfilled aspirations via aspirational comparison: byproduct that emerges as seemingly positive mental states such as suspense, curiosity, ambition, desire, or looming anticipation. This happens through awareness that a newly discovered "higher" utility will potentially exceed one's present state, leaving one in a state of unfulfilled aspiration. LPI refers to this as a positive [subjective] byproduct. This is a perceived increase between present and future potential utility states, where the expectant prediction of ascended utility awaits our experience. However, since we are currently not in that ascended state, mechanisms in our neurobiology trigger a sense of urgency to obtain, acquire or secure this perceived elevated utility. In this case, byproduct has emerged from the formation of higher expectations, due to awareness of a higher standard, that our present utility now does not meet. This, in turn, renders our present utility less sufficient or devalued. However, demand for relief from our present state is undoubtedly in our purview, albeit, not without risk; for the grass may not end up being greener once we transition.

(Note: Behavioral economists might label this a direct search for greater satisfaction, since people anticipate a net payoff above and beyond their current state, a prime example of how classical 'maximizing utility' can be seen to align with LPI's concept of unfulfilled aspiration. Additionally, uncertainty and risk aversion can curb demand even if a seemingly superior future potential utility state "grass is greener" awaits us. LPI acknowledges that this risk can moderate one's motivation to obtain or acquire the elevated utility state (or forescend, discussed in Chapters 12 and 22), unless the perceived benefits clearly outweigh potential disappointments, reinforcing the cyclical nature of innovation.)

Regardless, both positive and negative byproduct spark the emotional-cognitive urge to flee one's present state in favor of a future state, whether prompted by a past-present (or present-only) negative byproduct gap or by a present-future positive byproduct gap. Yet once that future becomes the present and over time fails to meet expectation, the LPI cycle resets, creating a fresh byproduct. When both negative or positive byproducts reach a threshold of urgency, we seek, pursue or demand new solutions. In place of viewing demand as a passive reaction to price or as an abstract preference, LPI shifts our gaze to the affective tension between "what is" and "what could be." Byproducts thus become the deeper "why," continuously driving us to fix, refine, and create.

Ultimately, we don't merely want new utilities; we want liberation from burdens, unmet desires, dissatisfactions, unaddressed curiosities, looming anticipation, or the sense that we are settling for less than is possible. Let me rephrase this. We may believe that we want what utility provides us, when in fact, we want it because of what it removes from us - byproducts. Demand arises when our emotional-cognitive awareness of a new or different utility reveals itself as the mechanism that can "deliver us from" something we can no longer remain in. Be it no present utility (this is a fallacy – see below). A present experienced utility that no longer meets our expectations, giving rise to byproduct. Or a byproduct that has emerged from the tension between awareness of a future higher potential utility (raising expectations) and our present utility (now regarded as inadequate due to its inability to meet the higher standard). This is the real power of byproduct in shaping every purchase, every innovation, and every aspiration we encounter.

(VERY IMPORTANT NOTE: While standard economics often views consumption as a quest for positive satisfaction, LPI aligns with the idea that removing dissatisfaction is crucial. However, LPI argues that the seeking of positive gains, or satisfaction, is not what we actually seek. What we actually seek is the relief or resolution of the burdensome tension of insufficiency, limitation, or incompleteness. This will ultimately land us in a state of satisfaction, for a time being, until new byproducts emerge once again (what economics today identifies as a decline in utility), and the cycle repeats.)

Here are examples that help us see how the escaping of byproduct creates demand.

- **No present utility**: Equates to not being alive, according to LPI. If you are alive, there's utility in your life. *(Note: In classical economics, lacking a specific good means zero utility from that good alone, not from all goods. By contrast, LPI emphasizes that so long as one is alive, at least some form of baseline utility is being occupied or consumed.)*

  The idea of having no present utility is a fallacy. Someone might say, *"Well, I want a car because I don't presently have a car."* Yet, they already have alternative modes of mobility, such as shoes, a bicycle, a wheelchair, crutches, or access to public transportation. In saying, *"I want a car,"* what they truly seek is an escape from more inferior forms of mobility. Even if they are barefoot, walking everywhere, they are still exercising the human origin utility of *movement and locomotion*. And they would likely be eager to escape that inferior state of utility really quick.

  If one is alive, they have utility in their life, they've simply become accustomed to much of it. Someone sitting idle, seemingly doing nothing, still benefits from utility. They may have clothes on their back (to extend their *origin utility of self-preservation and survival*), or they may be sitting on a chair or the floor of a house (to extend their *origin utility of protection and shelter*). Even if someone were stark naked in the desert, it would only be a matter of time before they would need to pursue utility to escape hunger, thirst, or harsh weather conditions.

- **Expectation Deviation - negative [subjective] byproduct**: A present experienced utility that no longer meets our expectations, giving rise to byproduct.

  Fleeing from negative byproduct is easier for us to perceive as escaping it rather than seeking utility. This is because of the nature of the grievance caused by the byproduct that emerged from the utility. The objective component of the byproduct triggers negative emotional-cognitive reactions, which we generally seek to avoid. If a pair of shoes becomes uncomfortable or painful, off they come. If an acquaintance constantly complains or gossips about others (unless you're into that), we distance ourselves. If we get a flat tire, our windows smudge, one of our acrylic nail's breaks, or our deodorant stops working, we take action. This does not imply that gains or positive aspirations have no pull; rather, empirical evidence in behavioral economics shows humans prioritize averting negative outcomes more so than they seek new positives. In that sense, the stimulus of negative states often captures our attention in a stronger way.

By seeking to escape these negative [subjective] byproduct states, we create market demand. We buy a new tire or get the existing one plugged, purchase window cleaner and paper towels, and so on. Additionally, we tend to pursue utility that is equivalent to or better than our pre-existing solution. And when I say better, I mean better at reducing the same amount of byproduct as before, whether in frequency, duration, or intensity. (we'll pursue equivalent unless presented with, or we envision, a higher potential utility). However, once a gap is felt, practical considerations like price, income, and availability still govern if and how we act on it. LPI's byproduct framework focuses on the emotional impetus behind demand, highlighting *why* we become motivated, it does not deny that financial or market realities further shape whether that demand materializes.

Sometimes, we experience negative byproduct that we seek to escape. Yet, no equivalent utility exists to move toward, such as the loss of an intimate relationship or the death of a loved one. Yet, even then, we often turn to alternative utility to help us cope or grieve (alcohol, religion, therapy, etc.). In traditional economics, these absent solutions represent a missing market; individuals or communities may develop new tools, services, or coping mechanisms. LPI parallels this by suggesting we may seek novel forms of emotional or practical 'utility' that had not existed previously. We innovate.

- **Aspirational Comparison - positive [subjective] byproduct**: A byproduct that emerges from the tension between awareness of a future higher potential utility (which raises our expectations) and our present utility (which now appears inadequate in comparison).

158

For instance, my wife and I were leaving a burger joint with our two youngest kids and our 2-year-old nephew, Luke, a curious and feisty little guy. My wife was carrying Luke while our two kids walked beside us. Our daughter, Nova (age 10), noticed a bench along the path and jumped onto it to walk across. The moment Luke saw her, he became agitated. My wife immediately told our daughter, "Get off the bench because Luke can see you, and he's wanting to do the same."

This is a prime example of positive byproduct and how it manifests instinctually. The moment Luke saw Nova jump on the bench, his neurobiological circuitry instantly registered that his current state (present experienced utility) was less exciting than the new state he had just become aware of (a future higher potential utility). His expectations shifted, and he immediately tried to free himself from my wife's arms to pursue the same experience. This is how demand from positive [subjective] byproduct takes shape.

The features in the products we purchase are another example of positive byproduct. When choosing a smartphone, most models today offer the same base capabilities. However, some have added features (higher potential utility) that influence our decision. At a neurobiological level, we subconsciously evaluate which features will relieve us of more future burdens, inconveniences, or byproducts. In short, we assess which smartphone will free us from the most byproducts to come. Even a smartphone with a stunning aesthetic design but fewer features could still win out if it helps us escape the byproducts of lacking style or lowered prestige.

Marketing, especially advertising, is highly skilled at manufacturing byproducts in the consumer's mind to provoke demand. One method is by highlighting how your current utility state is deficient in some way (pushing negative byproduct into your awareness). While they can't change the products or services you already use, they can alter your perception of their utility by shaping your expectations. By analyzing competitors' offerings, marketers identify deficiencies that make existing products feel inadequate. They strategically present this in a way that triggers feel-bad neurochemicals, then follow up by displaying how their product not only addresses those deficiencies but also prevents others you may not have even considered. This creates awareness of a higher potential utility, generating tension in the mind between your current and newfound utility. The result is a mix of feel-good and feel-bad neurochemicals, reinforcing both an "unresolved deficiency (expectation deviation)" and an "unfulfilled aspiration (aspirational comparison)." To heighten urgency, they use tactics like "for a limited time only" or "while supplies last." Ultimately, their goal is to leave you in an emotional-cognitive state of dissatisfaction with what you currently have, an intensified desire for something better, and a pressured urgency to act before the opportunity slips away. (*Note: While standard demand curves assume relatively stable preferences, real-world evidence shows that clever marketing reframes expectations and triggers new byproduct states, aligning with behavioral economics' stance on how context reshapes perceived utility.*)

Conversely, some businesses generate extremely heightened potential utility (positive byproduct) by drastically limiting advertising. These "no-ad" exclusive retailers include luxury brands (aka positional or Veblen goods) such as Arij (bespoke perfumes), Ferrari (luxury sports cars), Philippe Dufour (collectible watches), Feadship (superyachts), and Cifonelli (bespoke suits). You won't see commercials from these brands because the makers cultivate byproducts of scarcity, and elitism as part of their allure. Owning one of their products signals an escape from being perceived as common, average, or middle-class. These businesses position themselves as the highest standard of utility known to humanity. However, don't be fooled, they still need to remain relevant to their target customers. They just don't advertise where the masses are.

(*Note: Standard economics recognizes [status] "signaling" and positional or "Veblen goods" as reason enough for zero or minimal advertisement (the product's exclusivity is the marketing). Positional goods naturally create conditions where scarcity and elitism exist as byproducts of their function. Their value (utility) to people is in status (to show wealth, power, or prestige) and exclusivity (to feel special by owning something rare), and as a result, limited access (scarcity) and social stratification (elitism) are perpetuated as emergent byproducts. The makers of these products perpetuate these byproducts themselves, to keep them scarce and elitist. If these goods became easy to get, they would lose their utility, and people would stop valuing them. Ferrari limits the number of cars it makes each year. Even if you have the money, you can't always buy one. That scarcity (byproduct) increases demand and keeps the car exclusive.*)

A final note about the role of Remembered Utility; how past experiences, or even hearsay, can alter our current understanding of what is or is not "good enough." We intentionally chose not to expand this further here because the LPI model focuses primarily on **why** demand arises, not on the full complexity of **how** memory may color present and future utility judgments. Behavioral Economics reminds us that, in real-life

160

scenarios, biases and nostalgia frequently shape our awareness of byproduct (Note: they don't refer to them as byproduct), possibly intensifying or dulling that drive for change. That said, weaving these memory-driven nuances into LPI's framework is feasible but adds layers of detail less critical to the core insight of *why* we feel motivated to escape our current state. LPI's demand for utility. (Chapter 15 discusses the Utility Abandonment Condition, which provides more detail on Remembered Utility)

A classic illustration of remembered utility appears in the advice from my grandfather. He always taught me to turn on the car's heater (and roll down the windows) whenever driving up a long hill. An old trick to prevent car engines from overheating. Back in his day, cars commonly overheated, making that tip a vital piece of practical wisdom. Yet modern automotive technology has rendered this specific byproduct mostly obsolete. Today's cars address overheating with superior cooling mechanisms. Nonetheless, my grandfather's recollection embodies how memory, even if partially outdated, can perpetuate an awareness (or, more precisely, a *fear*) of a negative byproduct that might no longer be so relevant. In turn, that remembered utility can shape decisions about which vehicle to buy or how to maintain it.

Here are two examples that show how these recollections or secondhand accounts might fuel byproduct in everyday choices:

Jewelry Piece (ties back to the human origin utility of Artistic Expression and Creativity)
A person might look back on a time when they wore a unique pendant that earned them endless compliments. Whether triggered by old photos, a friend's remark, or spotting something similar online, that remembered utility can reignite an emotional gap, either a mild dissatisfaction with their current look or a fresh spark of aspiration for regaining that more confident persona. In short, this "memory-induced" byproduct drives them to seek a new accessory. By making such a purchase, they *escape* the sense that their self-expression is bland, arriving instead at a reinvigorated aesthetic identity.

Birthday Cake (ties back to the human origin utility of Social Interaction and Bonding)
Childhood celebrations or witnessing a friend's lively party might set a "standard" for birthdays. Relying on this recollection can yield a subtle sense of inadequacy: failing to serve a cake might prompt guilt or disappointment (negative byproduct), while envisioning the cheerful gathering and shared laughs fosters aspiration (positive byproduct). People then feel a small but

genuine *push* to buy or bake a cake, effectively evading the byproduct of a joyless birthday and reinforcing the value of that shared ritual. Here, memory-based expectations elevate the significance of a sweet custom well beyond its basic function as dessert.

Ultimately, we chose to keep these references to remembered utility limited in scope, to highlight the core of LPI without overcomplicating the narrative. Yet, as these examples attest, memory and hearsay can certainly magnify or reshape our sense of byproduct. Whether triggered by an outdated tip from a relative or a nostalgic longing for the perfect birthday, such recollections can reinforce both negative and positive emotional gaps, subtly shaping demand. We might have refrained from detailing every nuance, but the foundational truth stands: the recognition of a gap, fueled by experience (past or present) or possibility (future), is what compels us to seek, adopt, or innovate solutions, revealing once more why byproduct remains the deeper "why" behind demand.

Wanting to Watch a Movie – Byproducts as the Core Driver of Demand

The desire to watch a movie does not arise from nothing. It is not a random impulse but a reaction to a byproduct of an unmet need, a lingering dissatisfaction, or an emerging aspiration that prompts a search for resolution. The Law of Perpetual Innovation reveals that demand is never created in a vacuum. It is always the result of a byproduct that has surfaced, either as a deficiency to be corrected (Expectation Deviation) or as an unrealized benefit (Aspirational Comparison) that draws a person toward a higher potential experience. In the case of movies, the demand for watching one is not about the movie itself but about what it represents: the fulfillment of an unresolved byproduct, whether that be boredom, stress relief, social engagement, or the pursuit of an anticipated emotional experience.

Many people experience this when boredom sets in. This cognitive byproduct emerges when there is a lack of external stimulation, leaving the mind restless and in search of engagement. The demand for entertainment is not simply about enjoying a movie, it is about resolving this discomfort. Similarly, emotional fatigue and stress generate demand as well. When work, personal responsibilities, or life's pressures accumulate, they create an emotional byproduct that makes reality feel overwhelming. The idea of watching a movie then presents itself not merely as a form of entertainment, but as an unrealized benefit, an opportunity for emotional escape and mental relief.

However, demand for movies is also shaped by potential utility awareness. Trailers, reviews, and social conversations introduce an expectation that a movie will provide an extraordinary experience. Even before watching, individuals may perceive a gap between their current state of monotony or lackluster entertainment experiences and the excitement promised by a blockbuster film. This byproduct of decision-based dissatisfaction compels them to seek resolution by going to see the movie.

Beyond individual experiences of boredom, stress or higher-potential utility awareness, social and cultural byproducts also contribute to the demand for movies. A lack of interaction with friends or family creates a void that leads people to seek shared experiences, and a movie provides the perfect setting to fulfill that need. In these cases, the demand for a movie is not about the film itself but about restoring social connection. Cultural byproducts, such as the fear of missing out (FOMO), further drive demand. When a film becomes a major cultural event, those who have not seen it experience a byproduct of social exclusion. The anticipation of joining conversations or avoiding spoilers highlights an unrealized benefit, watching the movie is not just about consuming a story but about maintaining relevance within a social group. The awareness that others are participating in a shared experience creates a powerful psychological pull toward seeking the same experience.

For franchise followers, entirely new byproducts emerge. Unresolved narrative curiosity, a cognitive byproduct, creates an internal gap that must be closed. The ending of a previous film may have left questions unanswered, and the next installment becomes the necessary resolution. Emotional investment in characters and worlds generates an attachment byproduct, creating a lingering sense of incompleteness that demands fulfillment. Even past satisfaction with a movie can create a new byproduct such as raised expectations. When a previous film was deeply enjoyable, the expectation of future enjoyment becomes an unrealized benefit that drives demand for the next one (though we may have a cognitive bias that Part 2 movies tend to fall short, the sheer curiosity of "will it be as good or better" increases the byproduct, further motivating us).

This cycle demonstrates why demand is not about the movies themselves but about what is missing, unresolved, or anticipated in a person's experience. The Law of Perpetual Innovation shows that businesses do not create demand by simply making a product available. Demand exists because byproducts emerge, creating the conditions for people to seek resolution. Sometimes, this is an urgent need, such as escaping stress or monotony. Other times, it is the pull of an unrealized benefit through the potential of an experience that promises to fill a void or enhance one's emotional, cognitive, or social state. The moment a person desires to watch a movie, they are not acting on pure preference but on an unconscious drive to resolve a byproduct. The same principle applies across all industries. True demand does not originate from the product itself but from the byproducts it addresses or the benefits it has yet to deliver.

NOTE Regarding Potential Utility: Unspoken Reasons Behind Choices

People rarely list out every reason for wanting to watch a movie. You likely won't hear them say, "I'm bored," "I don't want to miss out," "I need a break," or "I'm attached to these characters." Instead, a quick phrase, "Avengers Infinity War is out? I'm so going!" stands in for a complex web of motivations, whether that's curiosity about the next plot twist, social belonging with friends who love the franchise, or the emotional stress escape of a cinematic spectacle. In the framework of LPI, these shorthand expressions actually point to byproducts: the genuine, often unspoken gaps that drive us to seek something new or better, even though we don't articulate them in everyday speech.

Brevity in conversation (verbal economy) and a shared cultural context often mean we don't feel the need to explain every detail. If friends already know you've followed Marvel for years, they instantly understand your excitement; if you're mostly motivated by fear of missing out (FOMO), you won't declare it out loud. Ultimately, an emotional driver, whether it's the thrill of seeing a beloved character's fate or avoiding social exclusion, propels an almost reflexive "I'm in!" without diving into the deeper rationale.

Yet, recognizing this unspoken layer is crucial for innovators who want to meet real demand. By understanding that each casual outburst, "I'm so going!", masks unvoiced byproducts (attachment to characters, the need for fun or stress relief, shared social experiences), you gain insight into what people truly crave beneath their surface statements. Rather than relying on what consumers explicitly say, you must look for these underlying motives to design experiences that resonate more deeply. By bridging the gap between everyday shorthand and the unspoken logic behind it, you can create offerings that authentically address the gaps people are eager to fill, even if they rarely put those needs into words.

CHAPTER 12
The Byproduct Emergence Theorem

Note: This chapter is divided into 10 sections to allow for pause and reduce reading burden.

1: The Purpose of This Chapter

The Law of Perpetual Innovation (LPI) rests on a single, unbreakable claim: every utility interaction necessarily generates byproducts. While the previous chapters established this principle conceptually, through the recursive logic of innovation (Chapter 7), the thermodynamic underpinnings of entropy and energy expenditure (Chapter 9) and the emotional-cognitive dynamics of expectation and aspiration (Chapter 10). A formal deductive proof of why byproducts must emerge has not yet been established.

This chapter addresses that gap.

Here, we prove mathematically, structurally, and cognitively that byproducts are not simply likely to emerge, nor occasionally emergent. They are guaranteed outcomes of interacting with any utility over time. Their appearance is a function of three fundamental forces:

- **Thermodynamic Inefficiency (ϵ):** Every real-world system, by physical law, produces waste, disorder, or degradation over time.

- **Expectation Deviation (η):** Human beings cognitively compare what was expected against what was experienced.

- **Aspirational Comparison (δ)**: Upon recognizing the existence of a superior potential utility, humans experience the insufficiency of the current one.

These three forces combine to form the function $\Psi(\epsilon, \eta, \delta)$, the Byproduct Emergence Function, which outputs a guaranteed burden, expressed as:

$$B(t) = B_o(t) + B_s(t) = \Psi(\epsilon, \eta, \delta) > 0$$

Reads as: The total byproduct at time (t), denoted as $B(t)$, is the sum of objective byproduct $B_o(t)$ and subjective byproduct $B_s(t)$. Both emerge from psi (Ψ), which is a function of three inputs, thermodynamic system inefficiency (epsilon ϵ), expectation deviation (eta η), and aspirational comparison (delta δ). If any of these three inputs is greater than zero, total byproduct must emerge.

Where:
- $B_o(t)$: Objective byproduct at time t: physical or systemic burden
- $B_s(t)$: Subjective byproduct at time t: emotional-cognitive burden

In clearer terms, $B(t)$ is always greater than zero because at least one of the three emergence conditions, system inefficiency, expectation deviation, or aspirational comparison, will always be active in real-world environments.

And under the Law of Perpetual Innovation, every byproduct, regardless of where or how it originates, contains both an objective and a subjective component. These two aspects are not separable; they are co-emergent. A mechanical flaw (objective) becomes relevant only when it is felt, noticed, or interpreted by a human user (subjective). Likewise, a feeling of longing, disappointment, or aspiration (subjective) is always provoked by a real, remembered, or imagined referent (objective).

Even unnoticed objective burdens eventually lead to psychological strain (e.g., frustration, fatigue, or resentment), and even purely subjective discomforts are always rooted in some structurally objective reference, whether a competing product, a shifting standard, or an internalized comparison.

The result is a complete validation of LPI's foundational logic: it is not utility that drives innovation, it is the burdens that utility can never fully eliminate. And those burdens are not anomalies. They are guaranteed by the architecture of physical systems and the structure and functionality of the human mind.

2: Review of Known Quantities and Prior Results

Before establishing the theorem, we must recall several critical variables, functions, and relationships that will serve as both premises and building blocks for our formal proof. These quantities are already in use across Chapters 7, 9 and 10, and this chapter extends them to form a unified emergence structure.

Variables and Parameters

Symbol	Meaning	Domain
$S(t)$	System Entropy at time t	Thermodynamics / System State
$E_h(t)$	Human Energy Expenditure at time t	Cognitive / Physical Effort
$B_o(t)$	Objective Byproduct at time t	Physical, systemic or structural burden
$B_s(t)$	Subjective Byproduct at time t	Emotional-Cognitive burden
$B(t)$	Total Byproduct at time t $B_o(t) + B_s(t)$	Complete burden experienced
U_0	Ideal Utility Baseline	Theoretical Max Utility (zero burden)
$U(t)$	Net Perceived Utility at time t $U_0 - E_h(t)$	User's experienced utility
α	Entropy Sensitivity Coefficient	Burden Amplification factor
β	Baseline Energy Floor	Irreducible cost to extract utility

Note: Although the byproduct variables $B_o(t)$ and $B_s(t)$ are defined separately to highlight their distinct origins, in practice, they are inseparable. Objective burdens are only relevant once experienced, and subjective burdens always stem from, or are shaped by, some real or imagined objective deviation. Every byproduct in the LPI framework is, therefore, hybrid in nature.

Byproduct Emergence Inputs

These three terms represent the root causes of all byproduct emergence:

- **ε: Thermodynamic Inefficiency**
  - No physical or digital system operates at 100% efficiency. This guarantees residual entropy, which produces structural degradation or performance friction. Even the most optimized systems generate entropy over time.

- **η: Expectation Deviation** (from experienced utility)
  - Defined as: $\eta = U_{\text{expected}} - U_{\text{experienced}}$
  - Reads as: If the user's predicted or anticipated utility is higher than what they actually experienced, the result is emotional-cognitive burden. This deviation cab manifest as frustration, disappointment, or disillusionment, depending on the magnitude of the gap.
  - This deviation occurs when reality fails to meet cognitive prediction or prior promise.

- **δ: Aspirational Comparison** (potential utility)
  - Defined as: $\delta = U_{\text{potential}} - U_{\text{experienced}}$
  - Reads as: If the utility that could be attained, either observed in others or imagined as possible, is greater than what is currently experienced, even when no failure occurs, this forward-directed contrast will introduce cognitive tension, restlessness, or unfulfilled desire.
  - Even when a system performs adequately, the awareness of a better possible utility state (real or imagined) triggers forward-directed dissatisfaction (e.g., present unfulfillment or anticipation tension)

Together, ϵ, η, and δ form the input conditions to the Byproduct Emergence Function Ψ. These are the variables that define the inevitability of burden and, in doing so, the inevitability of innovation under LPI.

Functions and Logical Operators from Previous Chapters
We now recall the foundational mappings from Chapter 7:

- **Utility Traceability Function**

$$\Phi(I): I \mapsto \{u \in U\}$$

  - Reads as: Each innovation (I) maps to one or more Human Origin Utilities u in the set U.
  - Interpretation: Every innovation can be traced back to the original human function or capability it seeks to enhance or restore.

- **Byproduct-Utility Disruption Function**

$$\Psi(B): B \mapsto \{u \in U\}$$

- Reads as: Each byproduct (B) maps to one or more Human Origin Utilities u in the set U that it burdens, interferes with, or disrupts.
- Interpretation: This function allows innovators to pinpoint which utility is being overshadowed by the presence of a particular byproduct.

- **Innovation Driver Function (aka the Innovation Equation)**

$$I(t+1) = f\left(B\big(I(t)\big)\right)$$

- Reads as: The innovation at time $(t+1)$ is a functional response to the byproduct created by the previous innovation at time (t).
- Interpretation: This represents the recursive structure of innovation under LPI. All *[successful]* innovation is driven by prior byproduct burden, not creativity alone.

Now, in this chapter, we introduce:

- **The Byproduct Emergence Function**

$$\Psi(\epsilon, \eta, \delta): R^+ \rightarrow R^+$$

- Reads as: Psi (Ψ) is a function that takes three non-negative real values (R^+), systemic inefficiency [epsilon (ϵ)], expectation deviation [eta (η)], and aspirational awareness [delta (δ)], and outputs $(\rightarrow)$ a positive real value (R^+). *(In the LPI framework, this output (R^+) is interpreted as the total byproduct burden $B(t)$.)*
- This function formalizes the claim that byproduct is not a random outcome, it is a mathematically guaranteed result of interacting with any utility across physical and psychological dimensions. The presence of even one non-zero input ensures that:

$$\Psi(\epsilon, \eta, \delta) > 0 \Rightarrow B(t) > 0$$

Any real non-negative value greater than zero of

$$\epsilon, \eta, \text{ or } \delta \text{ must yield } B(t) > 0$$

This prepares us for the next section, where we describe the two emergence pathways in detail and formally state the theorem.

3: The Dual Pathways of Byproduct Emergence

To prove that byproduct must emerge from any utility experience or anticipation, we must identify and formalize the two fundamental pathways through which byproducts arise. These are not parallel alternatives, but mutually reinforcing layers of inevitability: one rooted in the physics of systems (the objective component of byproduct), and the other in the cognition of humans (the subjective component of byproduct). Together, they ensure that even the most efficient systems and the most delightful user experiences generate some form of residual secondary effect. A burden, a friction, a gap, or a cost. Byproduct.

It's important to emphasize that sometimes these pathways may appear independent in how byproduct is initially detected or described. However, all byproducts ultimately possess both components: a measurable deviation in the system (objective) and a perceived or emotional consequence (subjective). They are structurally inseparable.

Thermodynamic Pathway - Objective Byproduct Emergence

The first pathway is grounded in physics and systems engineering. It holds that no interaction within a real-world system is perfectly efficient. All systems experience friction, wear, latency, degradation, or loss: phenomena that collectively fall under the umbrella of entropy.

Recall from Chapter 9:

$$S(t) = k \cdot B(t)$$

where:
- $S(t)$ is the system's entropy at time t,
- $B(t)$ is the accumulated byproducts at time t, and
- $k > 0$ is the byproduct-weighting coefficient representing how disruptive each unit of byproduct is to system order.

Reads as: System entropy is directly proportional to the magnitude of total byproduct in the system. As byproducts accumulate, system disorder increases.

This relationship implies that byproduct is not only an inevitable certainty, but also directly measurable through increasing entropy. The universal presence of inefficiency is captured by the condition:

$$\epsilon > 0$$

which represents unavoidable thermodynamic [system] inefficiency. No matter how well-designed, any human-product-environment system will accumulate:

- Wear and tear,
- Latency or delay,
- Resource waste or leakage,
- Maintenance demands,
- Physical or functional degradation over time.

These forms of inefficiency translate directly into objective byproducts, which we denote as:

$$B_o(t) = \Psi(\epsilon)$$

Reads as: Objective byproduct, over time, is a function of thermodynamic inefficiency. That is, wherever $(\epsilon > 0)$, it follows that:

$$B_o(t) > 0$$

Thus, even in systems that appear stable or optimized, the universal applicability of the Second Law of Thermodynamics ensures that objective byproduct emerges as an unavoidable feature of real-world function.

Cognitive-Perceptual Pathway - Subjective Byproduct Emergence

While entropy guarantees objective byproducts, human experience introduces a second pathway of burden: the emotional-cognitive recognition of deviation. Humans are not passive receivers of outcomes, they compare, expect, imagine, and desire.

There are two forms of subjective deviation that result in the emergence of byproduct:

a) Expectation Deviation (η)

Defined as:

$$\eta = U_{\text{expected}} - U_{\text{experienced}}$$

Where:
- U_{expected}: is the utility the user anticipates before interaction.
- $U_{\text{experienced}}$: is the actual utility benefit (value) perceived during or after use.

Reads as: Expectation deviation is the gap between what was hoped for and what was received and experienced.

Whenever $\eta > 0$, the user senses a shortfall or gap in their experience that becomes emotionally and cognitively burdensome, producing frustration, disappointment, or dissatisfaction. The hallmarks of subjective byproduct. This gives us:

$$\eta > 0 \Rightarrow B_s(t) > 0$$

Reads as: If expectation deviation (η) is greater than zero, then subjective byproduct $B_s(t)$ must be greater than zero.

b) Aspirational Comparison (δ)

Defined as:

$$\delta = U_{\text{potential}} - U_{\text{experienced}}$$

Where:
- $U_{\text{potential}}$: is the perceived value of an aspirational, ideal, alternative, potentially superior future utility now conceivable or visible to the user.
- $U_{\text{experienced}}$: is the currently experienced utility state.

Reads as: Aspirational comparison measures the perceived gap between the current utility experience and a potentially better, more desirable one.

Even if the current experience matches expectations, the recognition of a superior alternative can create an awareness of deficiency, $\delta > 0$. This doesn't require failure, only exposure to something better. This produces aspiration-induced byproduct, often experienced as an unfulfilled tension, envy, ambition, restlessness, or impatience. (Sometimes the gap is vivid: "I wish I owned a car.")

So:

$$\delta > 0 \Rightarrow B_s(t) > 0$$

Reads as: If aspiration comparison (δ) is greater than zero, then subjective byproduct $B_s(t)$ must be greater than zero.

Combined Cognitive Result:
Because either form of deviation results in perceived burden, we define:

$$B_s(t) = \Psi(\eta, \delta)$$

Reads as: Subjective byproduct is a function of both unmet expectations and aspirational comparisons.

Thus, from the subjective or emotional-cognitive standpoint, byproduct must emerge when users:

- Feel disappointed by what they receive or are experiencing (η), or
- Envision or observe something better than what they have (or don't yet have) (δ)

Even if a utility performs flawlessly, the moment a person becomes aware of an alternative, either real, remembered, or imagined, that appears structurally superior in form, function, or outcome (objective structure or performance), the current utility is re-evaluated. This comparison activates a cognitive gap, which in turn produces subjective byproduct:

$$B_s(t) > 0$$

Note: Though labeled "subjective," these burdens are not abstract. They are structured responses to cognitive reference points, making them indirectly traceable to objective or systemic triggers.

Total Byproduct Emergence Condition

Although it may appear that byproduct arises from either the objective or subjective pathway independently, LPI maintains that all byproducts involve both components, objective disruption and subjective interpretation. They may appear to emerge on different timelines or with differing intensities, but neither exists in isolation.

We define the total byproduct function as:

$$B(t) = B_o(t) + B_s(t) = \Psi(\epsilon, \eta, \delta)$$

Reads as: Total byproduct at time (t) is the combined output of physical inefficiency, experiential shortfall, and aspirational desire.

And since in all real systems:
- $\epsilon > 0$: no perfect system
- $\eta > 0$ or $\delta > 0$: no perfect user alignment

Then it must follow that:

$$\Psi(\epsilon, \eta, \delta) > 0 \Rightarrow B(t) > 0$$

Reads as: If Psi (Ψ) outputs a value greater than zero, then total byproduct $B(t)$ must be greater than zero.

This prepares the ground for the formal statement of the theorem.

4: The Byproduct Emergence Theorem (Formal Statement)

We are now ready to present the central result of this chapter.

Theorem: The Byproduct Emergence Theorem
Statement:

In any human-product-environment system operating under real-world conditions, every utility interaction or anticipated utility state will inevitably produce byproducts. The total byproduct emerging at time t is a deterministic function of thermodynamic inefficiency ϵ, cognitive deviation from expectation η, or aspirational comparison δ, such that:

$$B(t) = \Psi(\epsilon, \eta, \delta) = B_o(t) + B_s(t) > 0$$

Where:
- $\epsilon > 0$: Thermodynamic [systemic] inefficiency
- $\eta = U_{expected} - U_{experienced}$: Expectation gap
- $\delta = U_{potential} - U_{experienced}$: Aspirational utility gap

174

- $B_o(t) = \Psi(\epsilon)$: Objective byproduct
- $B_s(t) = \Psi(\eta, \delta)$: Subjective byproduct

Reads as: Total byproduct is the guaranteed result of at least one of the three inputs: system disorder, unresolved experiential deficiency, or unfulfilled aspiration, being greater than zero. Every byproduct contains both an objectively tangible $B_o(t)$ and a subjectively felt $B_s(t)$ dimension.

Corollary 1: Dual Sufficiency

Either of the following conditions alone is sufficient for byproduct emergence:

- $\epsilon > 0 \Rightarrow B_o(t) > 0$: If thermodynamic [systemic] inefficiency is greater than zero, then so must objective byproduct be greater than zero.
- $\eta > 0$ or $\delta > 0 \Rightarrow B_s(t) > 0$: If either expectation deviation or aspirational comparison are greater than zero, then so must subjective byproduct be greater than zero.

Therefore, even a theoretically perfect system, where ($\epsilon \to 0$), cannot escape the emergence of subjective burden if users compare, imagine, or desire something better. Emotional and cognitive burdens are as structurally inevitable as physical ones.

Corollary 2: Universal Innovation Pressure

Because:

$$B(t) > 0$$

is always true in any real utility interaction, and because LPI asserts that:

$$I(t + 1) = f\big(B(t)\big)$$

It follows that innovation pressure is both permanent and systemic.

No innovation achieves finality. Every utility state, no matter how optimized, sets the stage for its own future replacement, not because it ceases to function, but because it inevitably produces burden that demands resolution.

In the next section, we will proceed with the step-by-step proof of the theorem using these terms and prior equations.

5: Proof of the Byproduct Emergence Theorem

To formally prove the Byproduct Emergence Theorem, we must demonstrate that the total byproduct $B(t)$, composed of both objective and subjective components, is strictly greater than zero under real-world utility conditions.

We begin by reintroducing the theorem for clarity:

$$B(t) = B_o(t) + B_s(t) = \Psi(\epsilon, \eta, \delta) > 0$$

Reads as: The total byproduct at time t, denoted as $B(t)$, is equal to the sum of objective byproduct $B_o(t)$ and subjective byproduct $B_s(t)$, and this sum is strictly greater than zero whenever thermodynamic [systemic] inefficiency ϵ, expectation deviation η, or aspirational comparison δ is greater than zero.

This theorem affirms that byproduct must emerge from any instance of utility interaction or potential utility awareness, and that every byproduct contains both a tangible/systemic component and a perceptual/emotional one. Even if one appears more visible than the other.

We proceed with a step-by-step proof, divided by source of emergence:

1: Proof via Thermodynamic Inefficiency (ϵ)
By the Second Law of Thermodynamics, no system can operate at perfect efficiency:

$$\epsilon > 0$$

From Chapter 9:

$$S(t) = k \cdot B(t) \quad \Rightarrow \quad B(t) = \frac{S(t)}{k}$$

Where:
- $S(t)$ is the entropy of the system at time t
- $B(t)$ is the total byproduct burden
- $k > 0$ is the byproduct proportionality coefficient that scales byproduct into a measurable entropy value

Reads as: System entropy increases in direct proportion to the byproduct burden.

176

Since entropy is a function of inefficiency and disorder, and since:

$$S(t) \propto \epsilon \quad \text{and} \quad k > 0$$

Reads as: System entropy $S(t)$ at time t, is proportional to ($\propto$) thermodynamic inefficiency (ϵ) and the byproduct proportionality coefficient is greater than zero.

Then we derive:

$$\epsilon > 0 \Rightarrow S(t) > 0 \Rightarrow B_o(t) > 0$$

This proves that objective byproducts $B_o(t)$ must emerge from any real utility interaction due to unavoidable thermodynamic inefficiencies ϵ.

2: Proof via Expectation Deviation (η)

From behavioral neuroscience and Chapter 10:

$$\eta = U_{\text{expected}} - U_{\text{experienced}}$$

Reads as: Expectation deviation is the emotional-cognitive gap between what the user thought they would experience and what they actually experienced.

Let $\eta > 0$. The brains predictive systems (e.g., anterior cingulate cortex (ACC), amygdala, and other neural systems) register this deviation as dissatisfaction, disappointment, or emotional tension. This emotional response constitutes a subjective byproduct:

$$\eta > 0 \Rightarrow B_s(t)_{\text{deficiency}} > 0$$

Therefore, even if $\epsilon = 0$, subjective byproduct burden will still emerge whenever the experienced utility fails to meet internal expectations.

3: Proof via Aspirational Comparison (δ)

Also from Chapter 10:

$$\delta = U_{\text{potential}} - U_{\text{experienced}}$$

Reads as: Aspirational comparison is the perceived insufficiency of current utility in contrast to a higher possible alternative.

Let $\delta > 0$. Awareness of a superior potential utility state, whether from personal imagination or external exposure and observation (e.g., advertising, social media, word of mouth), creates emotional-cognitive tension. This aspirational tension constitutes a subjective byproduct:

$$\delta > 0 \Rightarrow B_s(t)_{\text{aspiration}} > 0$$

Thus, even if a product performs flawlessly and meets expectations, mere exposure to a better possibility can still result in subjective byproduct burden.

4: Irreducibility of Byproduct (due to β – the Baseline Energy Cost)
From Chapter 9:

$$E_h(t) = \alpha S(t) + \beta \quad \Rightarrow \quad U(t) = U_0 - E_h(t)$$

Even in a perfectly efficient system $S(t) = 0$, the baseline energy cost $\beta > 0$ ensures that utility consumption is never free of byproduct burden:

$$\beta > 0 \Rightarrow E_h(t) > 0 \Rightarrow U(t) < U_0 \Rightarrow \eta > 0 \Rightarrow B_s(t) > 0$$

Reads as: If baseline effort β is greater than zero, then human energy expenditure $E_h(t)$ must also be greater than zero. This guarantees that the net perceived utility $U(t)$ experienced by the user is always less than the ideal utility U_0. That difference can create an expectation gap η, which in turn leads to the emergence of subjective byproduct $B_s(t)$.

This confirms that byproduct can exist even under zero entropy conditions, due to the presence an irreducible cognitive or physical effort (cost of use or experiencing utility).

5: Summation and Non-Zero Condition

Let:

$$B(t) = B_o(t) + B_s(t)$$

Where:
- $B_o(t) = \Psi(\epsilon)$

- $B_s(t) = \Psi(\eta, \delta)$

Given:

- $\epsilon > 0$, from physical thermodynamic law
- $\eta > 0$ and/or $\delta > 0$, from cognitive evaluation
- $\beta > 0$, from irreducible effort

It follows that:

$$\Psi(\epsilon, \eta, \delta) > 0 \Rightarrow B(t) > 0$$

Reads as: If the Byproduct Emergence Function Ψ, which takes in thermodynamic inefficiency ϵ, expectation deviation η, and aspirational comparison δ, produces a value greater than zero, then the total byproduct $B(t)$ at time t must also be greater than zero.

Therefore, Q.E.D. (quod erat demonstrandum): <u>Byproduct must emerge</u>!

This completes the formal proof.

This proof is the mathematical embodiment of Cardinal Principle 0 (Chapter 10) and confirms that byproduct emergence is not probabilistic, it is structurally inevitable by both the nature of physical systems and the architecture of human emotional-cognitive perception.

6: The Role of α and β in Byproduct Sensitivity

Now that we have proven that byproduct must emerge, we must address how intensely that byproduct is felt or acted upon. This is governed by two foundational coefficients introduced in Chapter 9:

The Coefficient α: Burden Sensitivity to Entropy

Defined in:

$$E_h(t) = \alpha S(t) + \beta$$

Reads as: Human energy expenditure E_h at time t increases in proportion to system entropy $S(t)$, scaled by the user's sensitivity α, with an irreducible baseline cost β.

Where:

- α reflects how sensitive and reactive a user's experience is to increases in system entropy $S(t)$.
- High α: Small increases in entropy result in high energy burden and fast-growing subjective byproduct.
- Low α: Users are resilient, indifferent or less affected by entropy and tolerate inefficiencies better.

Examples:

- A first-time flyer might panic at a single jolt of turbulence (high α)
- A seasoned pilot may remain calm amidst multiple cockpit alerts (low α)

Therefore, α controls how visible and urgent the byproduct becomes from the user's perspective. It determines the perceived slope of utility loss in relation to disorder.

The Constant β: Baseline Energy Cost

If we recall Net Perceived Utility from Chapter 9:

$$U(t) = U_0 - E_h(t) = U_0 - \alpha S(t) - \beta$$

Even if a system is perfectly efficient, meaning:

$$S(t) = 0$$

The user must still invest energy to extract utility:

$$E_h(t) = \beta \Rightarrow U(t) = U_0 - \beta$$

Where the Net Perceived Utility would now become:

$$U(t) = U_0 - \beta$$

This creates a guaranteed gap between the ideal utility U_0 and the net experienced and perceived utility $U(t)$, due to a minimum energy investment β, resulting in a minimum byproduct:

$$\eta = U_{\text{expected}} - (U_0 - \beta) > 0 \Rightarrow B_s(t) > 0$$

Reads as: There is always a minimum cognitive and/or physical cost to extracting utility, even under perfect conditions. This ensures a baseline level of subjective burden from expectation deviation η.

This floor ensures that no interaction with utility is burden-free, even when no degradation has occurred.

Interpreting α and β as Systemic Predictors

Together, α and β form the backbone of burden perception modeling:

Symbol	Meaning	Predictive Role
α	Sensitivity to entropy	Determines how strongly byproduct is perceived and felt per unit of disorder
β	Baseline energy cost	Ensures that byproduct exists even in ideal conditions

These coefficients allow system designers to predict:
- Where user dissatisfaction is most likely to emerge
- Which user segments will be more or less tolerant of system inefficiency
- Whether to prioritize innovation that reduce entropy $S(t)$ (by improving system efficiency) or reduce user effort, through lowering β, (by improving usability)

This sets the stage for using $B(t)$, α, and β in innovation forecasting future byproduct accumulation and thus demand prediction models, ultimately guiding innovation cycles.

7: Implications of the Byproduct Emergence Theorem

The proof of the Byproduct Emergence Theorem establishes that byproducts are not accidental, peripheral, or avoidable. They are structurally guaranteed outcomes of interacting with or even contemplating utility. This section explores what that truth means for innovation theory, consumer behavior, product design, and the entire structure of the Law of Perpetual Innovation.

Innovation Must Respond to Byproduct, Not Utility

Traditional models treat innovation as the pursuit of utility gains; higher performance, new features, increased delight. But the Byproduct Emergence Theorem reverses this logic.

Since:

$$B(t) > 0$$

is always true, and since innovations arise from burdens, not bliss, the purpose of innovation is not to deliver utility. It is to resolve byproduct. To provide relief or escape to prior and existing byproduct burdens.

The true innovation sequence becomes:

Utility $\Rightarrow$ Byproduct Emergence $\Rightarrow$ Perceived Burden $\Rightarrow$ Innovation Pressure

Reads as: Every "successfully adopted utility" innovation originates in response to the burdens generated by utility itself, not as an act of proactive invention, but as a reactive solution to emergent or growing constraints and burdens from prior or pre-existing utility.

Every new "successful innovation" is, fundamentally, a burden-resolution event, not a utility-creation event. It also helps explain why some businesses succeed while others fail: those who ignore or misread emerging byproducts fail to adapt, while those who track burdens directly guide innovation with precision.

Demand Emerges from Structural Tension

Because:

$$B(t) > 0$$

and because byproduct is the experiential signal of a gap between what is and what could be, the existence of byproduct naturally gives rise to demand.

This leads to Corollary 3 (of Section 4, Corollary 2; innovation pressure inevitability)

Corollary 3: Byproduct Emergence as the Root of Demand

Given that byproduct necessarily emerges in any system, demand arises not from utility itself, but from the emotional-cognitive and physical need to escape byproduct.

Formally:

$$D(t) = f(B(t)) \Rightarrow D(t) > 0$$

Here:
- $D(t)$: Demand formation at time t
- f: Motivational function converting byproduct burden into behavioral pursuit

Reads as: Demand is a reaction to byproduct. It is the psychological and behavioral pressure to escape, seek relief or resolve the byproduct burdens of current or anticipated conditions.

This directly affirms the central thesis of Chapter 11: byproduct is the deeper 'why' of demand. Since "demand" is the signal that a byproduct burden has become too costly to ignore, "innovation" is the act of resolving it.

Perfect Utility Is a Logical Impossibility

Since both:

$$\beta > 0$$

(irreducible human energy cost) and at least one of:

$$\epsilon > 0, \quad \eta > 0, \quad \delta > 0$$

(some thermodynamic inefficiency, some expectation deviation or some aspirational comparison) is always true in real-world systems and conditions, then:

$$B(t) = 0 \Rightarrow \text{is only possible if: } \epsilon = 0, \eta = 0, \delta = 0, \beta = 0$$

But a zero-byproduct condition is physically, cognitively and behaviorally impossible.

Therefore:

Perfect utility is a logical impossibility.

183

This reinforces a core doctrinal claim of LPI: no utility state can ever be permanent or fully satisfying (Principle of Utility as Imperfect, Chapter 16). Every act of fulfillment contains the seed of its own undoing. Every product, system or innovation will eventually burden. And every resolution will inevitably produce new byproducts.

Note: This principle does not contradict the Theory of Constant Utility introduced in Chapter 15. That theory holds that a product's inherent utility function remains stable over time; what changes is the accumulation of byproducts that distort its perceived value. In contrast, the impossibility of perfect utility refers to the fact that net perceived utility can never be experienced without burden, due to unavoidable systemic inefficiencies and human expectation dynamics.

Burden Sensitivity Varies Across Contexts

From the role of α (entropy/burden sensitivity coefficient), we understand that byproducts are not perceived uniformly. What is a negligible inefficiency to one user may be intolerable to another.

The theorem thus has a direct implication:
- The emergence of byproduct is universal.
- But the threshold at which it becomes intolerable, and therefore sparks innovation or action, is contextual.

This has profound implications for design and user experience:
- The same product may be praised or abandoned depending on the user's tolerance (high or low α).
- Emotional-cognitive byproducts accumulate differently across individuals and cultures.
- Products must be stress-tested not only for function, but for perceptual burden variation.

This insight opens the door to personalization, segmentation, and behavioral prediction forecasting in innovation, user experience design and product strategy.

Forescension Requires Emergent Byproduct

Chapter 22 introduces the concept of forescension, the emotionally driven tension in exiting a current utility state and the forward-directed pursuit of a new utility state.

But forescension cannot occur in the absence of tension. This chapter proves that that tension is always present and is called byproduct.

Thus:

Forescension is a response to emergent byproduct.

All ambition, restlessness, drive, or escape impulse (to pursue better conditions) originates from the burdens made visible by the byproduct function:

$$\Psi(\epsilon, \eta, \delta)$$

This function generates the pressure that underlies both innovation and transformation. It grounds human agency in the inevitable emergence of insufficiency.

8: Integration into the LPI Framework

The Byproduct Emergence Theorem is not a side theory, it is the mechanical engine that drives the entire Law of Perpetual Innovation. This section demonstrates how it connects and elevates the structural elements of LPI introduced in earlier chapters.

Reinforcement of Principle 0 (Chapter 10)

Chapter 10 introduced the Cardinal Principle of LPI:

Byproduct inherently emerges from both experienced utility and awareness of potential utility.

This theorem now provides the mathematical substantiation of that principle, formalized as:

$$B(t) = \Psi(\epsilon, \eta, \delta) > 0$$

What was once a conceptual truth is now formally proven.

Connection to Thermodynamic Innovation (Chapter 9)

Chapter 9 defined innovation as the thermodynamic act of locally resisting entropy. We now recognize that entropy manifests experientially as byproduct.

Therefore:

- Entropy is the physical law.
- Byproduct is the human signal.
- Innovation is the response.

The theorem binds these three into a closed-loop system:

$$\text{Entropy} \Rightarrow \text{Byproduct} \Rightarrow \text{Innovation}$$

Reads as: Entropy, as a physical force of disorder, gives rise to byproduct, the human-perceived signal of burden or inefficiency, which in turn creates the pressure that drives innovation as a structured necessary response.

Because entropy threatens the organization, agency, and continuity of human systems, the emergence of byproduct is not just inconvenient, it signals a drift toward disorder that must be resisted. Innovation becomes the structured and necessary response because it is humanity's only means of locally counteracting entropy to preserve meaning, extend capability, and maintain forward momentum and purposeful structure in an otherwise degrading universe.

Structural Continuity with Chapter 7

Chapter 7 introduced:

- **The Utility Traceability Function**:

$$\Phi\big(I(t)\big) = u \in U$$

Where every innovation maps to a core human utility it seeks to serve.

- **The Byproduct-Utility Disruption Function**:

$$\Psi(B) = u \in U$$

Where every byproduct maps to the utility it disrupts.

- **The Innovation Driver Function**:

186

$$I(t + 1) = f\left(B\big(I(t)\big)\right)$$

Where every new innovation responds to the burdens created by the previous.

Now, we extend this with **The Byproduct Emergence Function**:

$$\boxed{B(t) = \Psi(\epsilon, \eta, \delta)}$$

This closes the LPI cycle:
- Every utility interaction leads to $B(t) > 0$
- Each byproduct maps to a disrupted Human Origin Utility via $\Psi(B)$
- That disruption creates emotional-cognitive tension
- That tension triggers forescension or innovation pressure
- New utility innovations resolve byproducts, but also generate new ones

Thus, innovation is not a straight line, it is a recursive, burden-encoded spiral.

Grounding Demand Theory (Chapter 11)

Chapter 11 posed a major challenge to classical economics:

"What if demand doesn't arise from preference but from emergent byproduct?"

The Byproduct Emergence Theorem confirms this:
- Experienced byproducts reveal deficiencies that compel escape
- Aspirational byproducts reveal opportunities that create longing

In both cases, the driver is the same:

$$\boxed{B(t) \Rightarrow D(t)}$$

Reads as: Burden leads to demand, not in theory, but as a universal behavioral law.

This shows that demand is not a stable or abstract latent preference. It is a reaction to the experience or anticipation of burden. This completes the logical bridge between thermodynamics, cognition, and innovation behavior under the Law of Perpetual Innovation.

9: Real-World Illustrations of Byproduct Emergence

To fully appreciate the theorem's practical implications, we now walk through four representative examples, two from experienced utility and two from potential utility. Each case reinforces the central truth: byproduct always emerges, and it is that emergence, across both objective and subjective dimensions, that provokes utility change through an innovation response.

Each of these examples reflects the Law of Perpetual Innovation's assertion that no utility exists in isolation from byproduct burden, and that all byproducts contain both physically tangible and cognitively experiential components, even when only one appears initially obvious.

Example 1: Experienced Utility → Objective Dominant Byproduct

Scenario: Smartphone Battery Degradation

- **Utility**: A smartphone originally delivers full-day battery life.
- **Objective Byproduct**: Over time, battery cells degrade due to chemical wear. This is a thermodynamic effect of entropy accumulation:

$$\epsilon > 0 \Rightarrow B_o(t) > 0$$

  o Reads as: Because physical inefficiency is inevitable, objective byproduct accumulates in the form of reduced performance.

- **Subjective Byproduct**: The user notices the battery drains faster today, than it did 2 years ago. This deviation from their mental model generates frustration and inconvenience:

$$U_{\text{expected}} > U_{\text{experienced}} \Rightarrow \eta > 0 \Rightarrow B_s(t) > 0$$

  o Reads as: A gap between what the user expected and what they now experience creates emotional-cognitive burden.

Result: The user begins researching newer models, triggering demand and potentially forescension. The utility still technically functions but is now overshadowed by byproduct.

Example 2: Experienced Utility → Subjective Dominant Byproduct

Scenario: A Once-Comforting Relationship

- **Utility**: A romantic partner provides emotional support and closeness.
- **Objective Byproduct**: Over time, communication patterns degrade, attentiveness declines, responses slow, and emotional engagement diminishes. This reflects thermodynamic inefficiency in the biological systems that regulate relational behavior. The prefrontal cortex, limbic system, and dopaminergic circuits responsible for empathy, emotional regulation, and reward-based bonding become less efficient as mental energy is taxed by stress, fatigue, competing obligations, and aging:

$$\epsilon > 0 \Rightarrow B_o(t) > 0$$

  o Reads as: Because biological and cognitive systems are subject to entropy, objective byproduct emerges in the form of reduced relational performance.

- **Subjective Byproduct**: The one partner begins to feel emotionally neglected, unseen, or disconnected. This mismatch between expected support and the experienced response produces emotional burden:

$$U_{\text{expected}} > U_{\text{experienced}} \Rightarrow \eta > 0 \Rightarrow B_s(t) > 0$$

  o Reads as: A gap between what the partner emotionally expected and what they now experience creates subjective byproduct in the form of emotional strain.

Result: Even without overt conflict, a persistent expectation gap forms. The relationship becomes a source of internal burden, potentially prompting conversations, boundary-setting, or therapy. Each a form of relational innovation. Additionally, because the brain is neuroplastic, such innovations can lead to the rekindling of emotional engagement and even biological re-optimization within the very neural systems affected by entropy. The utility still exists, but it is increasingly overshadowed by accumulating byproducts until adaptive effort (personal or mutual improvement or innovation) locally reduces the burden.

Example 3: Potential Utility Awareness → Aspirational Byproduct

Scenario: Awareness of Non-Toxic, Eco-Friendly Cooking Pans

- **Current Utility**: The user is satisfied with their traditional non-stick cookware.
- **Potential Utility**: They learn about ceramic-coated, non-toxic, and environmentally safer cooking pans. These newer options promise reduced chemical exposure improved durability, and greater sustainability.

$$U_{\text{potential}} > U_{\text{experienced}} \Rightarrow \delta > 0$$

  - Reads as: Awareness of a superior alternative recontextualizes the current cookware as insufficient, generating unfulfilled aspiration via aspirational comparison.

- **Objective Byproduct**: Traditional non-stick pans often made with PTFE or similar coatings gradually degrade when exposed to repeated heating cycles. This breakdown, caused by thermal and mechanical stress, releases trace chemicals into food and the environment. These physical effects are expressions of thermodynamic inefficiency at the material level:

$$\epsilon > 0 \Rightarrow B_o(t) > 0$$

  - Reads as: Repeated energy input accelerates molecular degradation in cookware materials, producing objective byproduct in the form of health and environmental risk.

- **Subjective Byproduct**: Even though the current pans still function well, the user begins to feel discontentment, concern, or guilt. The mere awareness of a safer, more eco-conscious alternative shifts perception and reframes the once-acceptable product as outdated or unsafe:

$$\delta > 0 \Rightarrow B_s(t) > 0$$

  - Reads as: Aspirational comparison triggers emotional-cognitive burden after reframing of their current cookware utility due to the awareness of a higher potential utility, even in the absence of functional failure.

Result: Demand emerges not because the cookware failed, but because a new possibility altered the perceived sufficiency of the current utility. The accumulation of physical burden (toxicity, degradation) and/or emotional burden (guilt, aspiration)

190

creates pressure for utility replacement, illustrating how awareness alone can initiate innovation behavior.

IMPORTANT NOTE: Aspirational comparison does not require a functional superiority in the alternative potential utility. Aesthetic appeal, symbolic value, social signaling, or any other perceived utility can be sufficient to generate aspirational tension. In LPI, any perceived gap in net experienced value, across any dimension of utility, can trigger byproduct emergence and fuel the innovation cycle.

Example 4: Potential Utility Awareness → Deficiency Reframing
Scenario: Discovery of a Noise-Canceling Headset
- **Current Utility**: A commuter uses basic wired or wireless headphones for listening to music or podcasts during transit.
- **Potential Utility**: While traveling, they observe another passenger using noise-canceling headphones and enjoying uninterrupted focus and calm amidst the noise of engines, crowd chatter, and flight announcements.

$$U_{\text{potential}} > U_{\text{experienced}} \Rightarrow \delta > 0$$

  o Reads as: Exposure to a more immersive, less fatiguing headset alternative introduces aspirational comparison, reframing the current utility as insufficient.

- **Objective Byproduct**: The commuter retrospectively begins to notice the physical toll of ongoing ambient noise, cognitive fatigue, elevated stress, or difficulty concentrating. These effects, though previously normalized, are now recognized as environmental overstimulation. The inability of the current headphones to shield against that sensory input reflects a form of thermodynamic inefficiency: excessive environmental energy (noise) penetrates the system and taxes the user's internal energy reserves:

$$\epsilon > 0 \Rightarrow B_o(t) > 0$$

  o Reads as: The failure to block entropy from the external environment (in this case, sound energy) results in objective burden that was previously tolerated but now revealed.

191

- **Subjective Byproduct**: Emotional fatigue and dissatisfaction emerge once the commuter realizes that a more comfortable alternative exists. The current utility experience is no longer neutral and acceptable, it is now cognitively reframed as a burden that needs to be escaped:

$$\delta > 0 \Rightarrow B_s(t) > 0$$

  - Reads as: A better perceived utility creates emotional discontent with the current state, even if no failure occurred.

Result: Demand emerges not from functional breakdown, but from cognitive contrast. The user's experience is retroactively reinterpreted through aspirational awareness, transforming a once-acceptable utility into a newly perceived deficiency. This reframing illustrates how aspirational byproduct can surface both latent (subconscious) objective burdens and new emotional tensions, driving innovation behavior through re-evaluated context.

These examples reinforce the theorem's core message:
- All utility states decay or become insufficient, either due to performance decline, evolving expectation, or comparison to potential alternatives.
- Byproduct is the language of change.
- And innovation is the only viable response.

10: The Universal Byproduct Emergence Sequence

Byproduct emergence under LPI follows a universal sequence. Whether rooted in real-world usage or exposure to a superior possibility, byproduct always begins with an underlying thermodynamic inefficiency (ϵ) through a measurable deviation, limitation, or disorder that exists within the system. But this inefficiency does not immediately produce byproduct. It becomes burdensome only when it is noticed, evaluated, or contrasted. That is, when it is cognitively framed through expectation deviation (η) or aspirational comparison (δ).

Thus, in all cases:
1. ε is the root condition
2. η or δ is the trigger
3. $B(t)$ is the outcome

Sequence A: Byproduct via Expectation Deviation (η)

This path begins when a utility is used and its performance is experienced. Thermodynamic inefficiencies (ε) are already present, but they do not become byproduct burdens until the user compares reality to prior expectations.

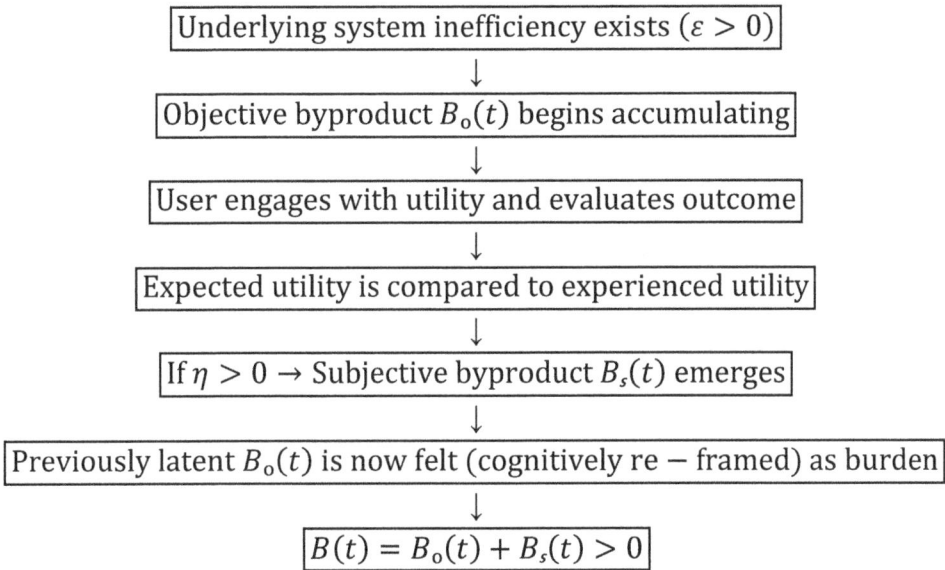

$$\boxed{\text{Underlying system inefficiency exists } (\varepsilon > 0)}$$
$$\downarrow$$
$$\boxed{\text{Objective byproduct } B_o(t) \text{ begins accumulating}}$$
$$\downarrow$$
$$\boxed{\text{User engages with utility and evaluates outcome}}$$
$$\downarrow$$
$$\boxed{\text{Expected utility is compared to experienced utility}}$$
$$\downarrow$$
$$\boxed{\text{If } \eta > 0 \rightarrow \text{Subjective byproduct } B_s(t) \text{ emerges}}$$
$$\downarrow$$
$$\boxed{\text{Previously latent } B_o(t) \text{ is now felt (cognitively re} - \text{framed) as burden}}$$
$$\downarrow$$
$$\boxed{B(t) = B_o(t) + B_s(t) > 0}$$

Key Insight:
Even when inefficiencies are objectively present, they only generate felt burden once the user cognitively recognizes the deviation, even if the objective performance wasn't initially noticed. The burden is born <u>not</u> at the moment of inefficiency, but at the moment it is noticed and interpreted as deficient. The moment of expectation misalignment. That's when byproduct emerges.

Sequence B: Byproduct via Aspirational Comparison (δ)

This path begins with the user becoming aware of a utility state that appears superior either through observation, memory, or imagination. Once again, inefficiency (ε) exists, but it only becomes burdensome when the current state is reframed as suboptimal in comparison.

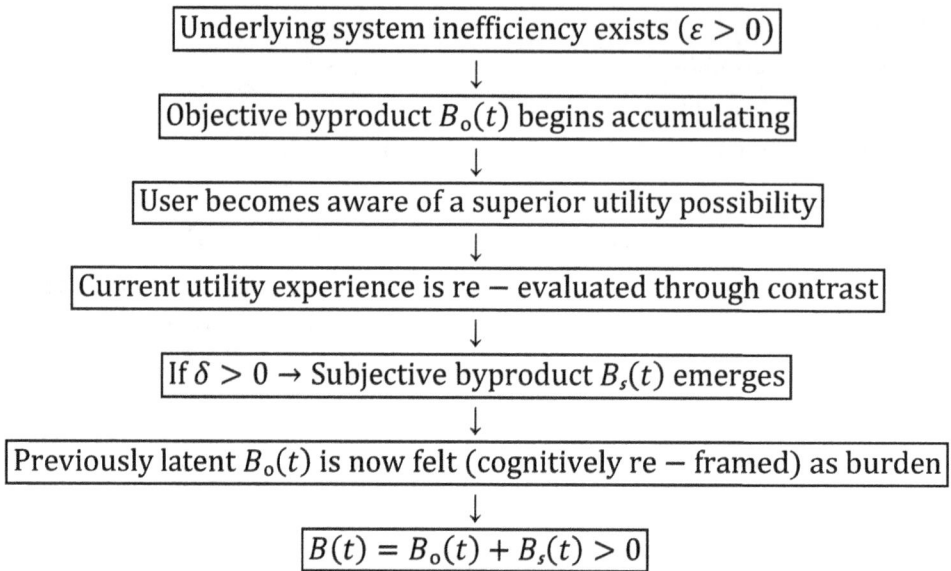

$$\boxed{\text{Underlying system inefficiency exists } (\varepsilon > 0)}$$
$$\downarrow$$
$$\boxed{\text{Objective byproduct } B_o(t) \text{ begins accumulating}}$$
$$\downarrow$$
$$\boxed{\text{User becomes aware of a superior utility possibility}}$$
$$\downarrow$$
$$\boxed{\text{Current utility experience is re} - \text{evaluated through contrast}}$$
$$\downarrow$$
$$\boxed{\text{If } \delta > 0 \rightarrow \text{Subjective byproduct } B_s(t) \text{ emerges}}$$
$$\downarrow$$
$$\boxed{\text{Previously latent } B_o(t) \text{ is now felt (cognitively re} - \text{framed) as burden}}$$
$$\downarrow$$
$$\boxed{B(t) = B_o(t) + B_s(t) > 0}$$

Key Insight:
Aspirational comparison causes retroactive burden recognition. The user did not notice the inefficiency before. But once a better possibility is known, that inefficiency becomes meaningful and burdensome. Even when the alternative is hypothetical, it is mentally constructed as objectively better, which triggers a subjective emotional-cognitive tension.

Hidden (aka Latent) Burden Recognition

Not all byproducts are immediately felt. In some cases, thermodynamic inefficiency (ε) accumulates silently, unnoticed by the user, until a triggering moment reframes the experience. This may occur through a sudden failure, a growing inefficiency that crosses a threshold, or an aspirational comparison that casts the current state in a new light.

In these cases, objective burden exists well before it is recognized, but subjective byproduct only emerges once a cognitive evaluation occurs, through either:
- Expectation deviation $(\eta > 0)$
- Aspirational comparison $(\delta > 0)$

Key Principle: Byproduct can remain latent, but it is never arbitrary. It always emerges in response to structural inefficiency ε but only becomes meaningful through conscious or subconscious human interpretation.

This ensures LPI's sequence holds even in edge cases. Burden must be perceived to be experienced. And once it is, innovation pressure follows.

Summary Rule

Objective inefficiency (ε) is always present. But byproduct only emerges when that inefficiency is cognitively interpreted through expectation (η) or aspiration (δ).

This is the universal structure of byproduct emergence. It confirms that byproducts are never purely emotional nor are they purely technical. They are hybrid phenomena: each instance of byproduct arises from a structural inefficiency in the system and becomes meaningful only through the brain's capacity to frame, compare, or desire differently. The physical and the perceptual are not separable, they co-produce every burden.

Conclusion – The Inescapable Birth of Burden

The Byproduct Emergence Theorem stands as a structural keystone of the Law of Perpetual Innovation. It confirms, with mathematical and behavioral precision, what earlier chapters have established conceptually: every utility, whether experienced, remembered or merely imagined, necessarily produces byproduct.

This theorem proves:
- From entropy and inefficiency (ϵ), objective byproducts arise as degradation, friction, or disorder.
- From unmet expectations (η), subjective byproducts emerge as emotional dissatisfaction or cognitive dissonance.
- From aspirational awareness (δ), subjective byproducts arise even in the absence of any system failure, driven purely by comparison to a perceived superior possibility.
- And from irreducible baseline effort (β), even excellent systems still contain some byproduct burden.

Thus, utility never stands still, and satisfaction is never self-sustaining. The moment a product, service, or system is used, or even becomes known, it begins to generate the very conditions that will eventually unseat it.

This principle reshapes how we must think about innovation:

Innovation is not driven by the pursuit of novelty or the desire to create utility.

It is driven by the byproduct burdens that utility itself cannot avoid producing.

This reframes demand not as abstract desire, but as emergent restlessness, the felt signal of unresolved deficiency or unfulfilled aspiration, created by the system's own limitations or the consumer's shifting expectations.

From now on, every time we see someone abandon a product, seek an upgrade, imagine a better way, or even hesitate to adopt, we must ask what byproduct has emerged. Because it is not utility that compels them forward. It is the inescapable birth of byproduct.

CHAPTER 13
The 56 Byproduct Principles

The Byproduct Principles are a set of guidelines within the Law of Perpetual Innovation that help innovators, designers, and organizations identify, understand, and anticipate the various ways in which byproducts arise. They describe the emergence of byproducts from different perspectives, including how they form, where they manifest, when they appear, and why they occur. By categorizing and analyzing the diverse characteristics of byproducts, the principles provide a structured approach to recognizing both immediate and latent effects that accompany any product, service, or system. Ultimately, the Byproduct Principles enable a deeper understanding of the unintended consequences, unmet needs, and emerging desires that fuel the cycle of perpetual innovation, offering a roadmap for turning challenges into opportunities for new utility creation.

The following diagram exposes some of the more fundamental attributes of byproduct emergence as well as the Byproduct Principles they represent (BP-#).

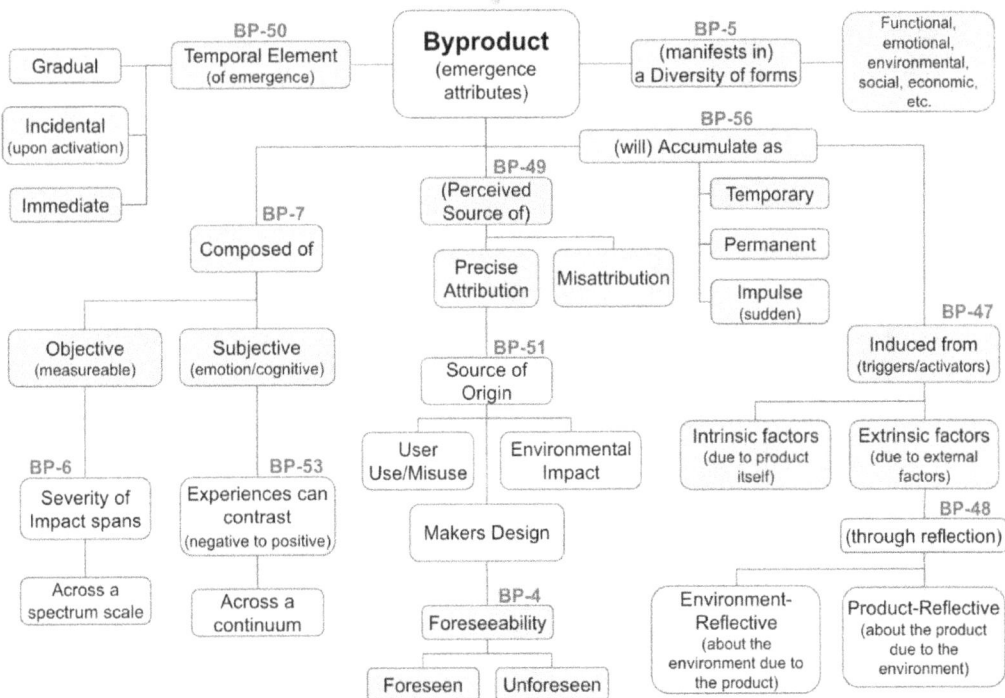

NOTE: Not all byproduct principles identified to date will be expanded upon. We will go into some depth on several of the more fundamental ones.

1. **Principle of Byproduct as Relational Context:** The Principle of Byproduct as Relational Context asserts that form-utility cannot be described or understood in isolation. Utility only has meaning and value when described in the context of the byproduct it resolves. Byproduct is the essential framework through which all forms of utility are articulated and understood. Without byproduct, there would be no basis for utility to exist. Whether a utility addresses inefficiencies, discomforts, fears, unfulfilled desires, or other hopes and challenges, its existence is always tied to the resolution of some byproduct.

   This principle emphasizes that form-utility can never be explained on its own terms. It is only and always expressed in relation to the byproduct that gave rise to it. This means that when people communicate about the utility they seek from a product or service, they are inevitably describing the byproduct they wish to eliminate or mitigate. This principle is also known as byproduct-referencing utility.

   For example, let's look at noise-canceling headphones. The utility they provide (the ability to block out noise) cannot be understood in and of itself. It only makes sense in the context of the byproduct of unwanted noise in public or noisy environments. The headphones offer utility because they address this byproduct, allowing users to focus or enjoy peace. Without the byproduct of noise, the utility of these headphones would be irrelevant, as there would be no problem for them to solve. Or when someone talks about needing a smartphone with long battery life, they are actually expressing their frustration (the byproduct) with short battery life in their current phone. Therefore, utility, whether it's functional, emotional, or aesthetic, cannot stand apart from byproduct. Utility is defined by the burdens or inefficiencies it addresses.

2. **Principle of Byproduct-Driven Utility:** The Principle of Byproduct-Driven Utility contends that utility is not an isolated concept but is inherently rooted in and shaped by byproduct. Every product, service, or system is designed to address a pre-existing byproduct, which could range from physical inefficiencies to emotional or social discomforts. Without the existence of a byproduct, utility has no purpose or meaning. Byproducts, whether functional, emotional, environmental, or social, are the driving force behind innovation.

This principle highlights that when individuals or organizations seek a new utility, they are expressing their desire to resolve or mitigate an existing byproduct. Therefore, the creation of utility is reactive rather than proactive. It is always responding to something undesirable or lacking in the status quo.

This principle emphasizes that even aspirational or aesthetic utilities, which may seem removed from direct byproducts, are actually rooted in more abstract byproducts like the desire for self-expression, prestige, or connection. Thus, every utility can be traced back to a byproduct that precedes it, solidifying the idea that innovation is perpetually byproduct-driven.

For example, let's consider the invention of the automobile. The initial utility of the car was to resolve the byproduct of limited, slow, or cumbersome forms of transportation, such as horse-drawn carriages or trains. As cars evolved, further byproducts emerged (e.g., traffic congestion, pollution), driving the development of new utilities like electric cars, ride-sharing services, and smart traffic systems. Each of these innovations is directly responding to the byproduct created by the previous utility, illustrating that utility creation is byproduct-driven.

3. **Principle of Perpetual Innovation through Byproduct:** The Principle of Perpetual Innovation through Byproduct holds that innovation is an ongoing, never-ending process driven by the continuous emergence of new byproducts. Every solution or utility that is developed to resolve a byproduct inevitably generates new byproducts, ensuring that the cycle of innovation continues, perpetually. This principle underlines that perfect utility is unattainable, as every innovation brings about its own unintended consequences or unmet needs.

For example, the discovery of antibiotics resolved several byproducts, such as life-threatening bacterial infections and the inability to effectively treat common illnesses. However, antibiotics introduced new byproducts like antibiotic-resistant bacteria, over-reliance on medication, and disruptions to the human microbiome. These new byproducts, in turn, drove further innovation, leading to developments in phage therapy, next-generation antibiotics, and AI-driven drug discovery platforms to combat resistance and restore balance to global health systems.

4. **Principle of Byproduct Foreseeability:** This principle highlights that byproducts can be classified as either foreseen or unforeseen. Foreseen byproducts are those that innovators can predict and mitigate during the design process, while unforeseen byproducts only emerge after the product interacts with real-world systems, users, or environments. While foreseen byproducts can be planned for, unforeseen byproducts often cause the most disruption, driving significant adjustments or entirely new innovations.

For example, the drawbacks of electric vehicle battery waste (a foreseen byproduct) were anticipated, but unforeseen byproducts, such as the strain on the electric grid due to the growing number of charging vehicles, emerged as electric cars became more widely adopted. These unforeseen byproducts require further innovation in the energy infrastructure to support this change.

5. **Principle of Byproduct Diversity:** Byproducts can manifest in various forms. They can be functional, emotional, environmental, social, economic, and so on. It asserts that addressing byproducts often requires multi-faceted solutions. Innovation must take into account this diversity, as byproducts can affect a wide range of areas beyond the primary function of a product. This principle underscores the complexity of innovation, as solving one byproduct may involve dealing with consequences in multiple areas simultaneously.

For example, the introduction of electric vehicles has a diverse set of byproducts. On the environmental side, they reduce emissions, but they also raise concerns about battery disposal and electricity consumption. Economically, they shift demand toward renewable energy sources, while socially, they change driving behaviors and create new job markets. Each of these byproducts is distinct, requiring different approaches to address them effectively.

6. **Principle of Byproduct Scaling:** Byproducts exist on a spectrum of severity of impact, from minor inconveniences to major system failures. This principle emphasizes the need for innovators to understand and prioritize which byproducts require immediate attention and which can be managed over time. Some byproducts might be mere annoyances, while others can lead to disastrous consequences if left unaddressed.

For example, a dull pencil is a minor byproduct that can be solved by sharpening it, whereas a car brake failure is a critical byproduct that demands urgent attention. Innovators must assess the severity of each byproduct to allocate resources effectively and prioritize addressing the most significant ones first.

7. **Principle of Byproduct Composition:** This principle introduces the concepts of objective byproduct (observable or imaginable, physical deviations in product performance) and subjective byproduct (emotional-cognitive reactions in user experiences). Both components will be present and are addressable through innovation, as they can both influence the user experience and product effectiveness. While objective byproducts are often more straightforward to identify and measure, subjective byproducts can be trickier, as they depend on user perceptions and emotions.

For example, a smartphone's objective byproduct might be its slow performance due to too many apps running simultaneously. The subjective byproduct, on the other hand, could be the frustration the user feels because their phone isn't performing as expected. Both of these need to be addressed: by optimizing the phone's performance (objective) and improving the user's experience through education or clearer UI design (subjective).

8. **Principle of Innovation Triggering:** While objective byproducts (such as measurable flaws or limitations) establish a factual baseline, it is the subjective dimension of byproduct, ranging from frustration or discomfort (negatively felt byproduct) to curiosity or aspirational longing (positively felt byproduct), that ignites true innovation. Emotional-cognitive responses to how a product or service *feels*, rather than simply how it performs, frequently serve as the most potent catalyst for change. This principle stresses that users' subjective experiences, whether driven by dissatisfaction or by excitement for something better, are more powerful triggers of adaptive or radical solutions than their objective counterpart alone.

- **Negative Byproduct (Unresolved Deficiency-Based via Expectation Deviation) Example:** Traditional taxis had long provided basic transportation, meeting an objective need for getting from point A to point B. However, the subjective byproduct of long wait times, inconsistent pricing, and poor customer experience spurred the innovation behind ride-sharing services, which addressed these frustrations and reshaped urban travel worldwide.

- **Positive Byproduct (Unfulfilled Aspiration-Based via Aspirational Comparison) Example:** Basic cars fulfill the raw need for transportation, but once automakers introduced quieter cabins, premium materials, and cutting-edge aesthetics, drivers realized how much road noise, cramped seating, and lack-of-style overshadowed their current experience. These new possibilities didn't arise from "thin air"; automakers recognized specific drawbacks that people had moderately accepted and engineered improvements that relieved them of those limitations. By highlighting a better utility path, one that eased the sensory discomfort and routine feel of daily commutes, luxury vehicles came to embody not just utility, but an escape from the shortcomings of standard models. Giving people something to aspire to.

9. **Principle of Byproduct Minimization vs. Elimination:** Byproducts cannot be completely eliminated, only minimized to a level that is tolerable for users. Total elimination of a form or class of byproduct generally comes from radical innovations or technological shifts that set previous utility delivery methods on a path toward obsolescence.

10. **Principle of Latent Byproducts:** Latent byproducts remain undetected or unchallenged, existing within daily behaviors, processes, or expectations without being acknowledged as actual burdens. They only become recognized once a superior alternative surfaces, making inefficiencies that had seemed negligible or too subtle to address suddenly apparent. This realization can be as transformative and radical as fixing major known issues, revealing how deeply entrenched "invisible frictions" can be removed through innovative solutions.

Latent byproducts are overlooked inefficiencies, minor annoyances, or unrecognized user needs that have not yet attracted attention as "problems" because:

- **Limited Awareness:** Users do not perceive them as shortcomings in the first place, often because they have grown accustomed to small workarounds.

- **No Competing Benchmark:** There has been no superior product or service that spotlights the friction.
- **Incremental Impact:** Each isolated inconvenience may feel trivial, yet the total effect across many users or repeated interactions can be enormous.
- **Dormant Demand:** The byproduct remains dormant in people's minds until an innovation finally removes it, at which point the gain in convenience or efficiency feels momentous.

For example, until mobile phones became commonplace, landline and pay-phone inconveniences, such as physically staying near a home phone, struggling to find a working pay phone, or carrying loose change, were not viewed as burdens. These routines were merely part of how telecommunication functioned. With the rise of mobile connectivity, these hidden constraints suddenly became glaring, aiding in the rapid decline of public pay phones and permanently reshaping communication habits.

Latent byproducts often lay hidden in everyday routines because they do not accumulate into dramatic impediments. But when eliminated, their absence feels revolutionary despite many users never having explicitly requested a change before encountering the new, improved solution.

11. **Principle of Byproduct Interdependence:** Byproducts often don't exist in isolation. One byproduct can trigger others, creating a cascade of effects within a system. This principle addresses how the interconnections between products, systems, or services within larger super-systems generate secondary byproducts that can ripple through seemingly bounded environments. Innovators must account for these chain reactions and recognize how byproducts from one product or system may impact other elements within a broader system, creating tensions between them. Especially in environments where multiple systems are nested together. This principle focuses on the immediate effects that a nested or interconnected product, service or system can impose upon or cascade throughout, other interfacing systems or super-systems.

For example, consider a cell phone ringing in a movie theater. In most situations, a ringing phone is simply serving its intended purpose of alerting the user to an incoming call. However, when the phone user and their device are nested within the super-system of a movie theater, whose primary utility is to offer an immersive experience free from disruptions, that phone ringing instantly becomes a byproduct. It disrupts not just the individual but the entire audience, triggering secondary byproducts such as audience irritation, social tension, and a break in the immersive experience. In this way, the seemingly benign alert of a cell phone ring becomes an unwanted byproduct precisely because of its interdependence with the theater's primary goal of uninterrupted entertainment. This chain reaction exemplifies how interlinked systems can produce cascading byproduct effects that impact the broader environment.

12. **Principle of Byproduct Awareness and Communication:** Transparency and communication about potential foreseen byproducts help manage user expectations and build trust. (This principle is from the maker's perspective; the awareness they drive and communicate out.)

13. **Principle of Byproduct Resilience:** Products must be resilient, designed to withstand and adapt to the negative effects of inevitable byproducts.

14. **Principle of Byproduct Multiplicity:** A single utility can generate multiple byproducts throughout its lifecycle, requiring solutions for each phase.

15. **Principle of Systemic Impact of Innovation:** This principle addresses how innovation can impact large-super-systems, such as economies, ecosystems, and social systems, and how these impacts generate secondary byproducts that affect other systems. It focuses on the long-term effects and impacts that an innovation can impose on other larger systems or innovations. When a product or service is introduced, it doesn't exist in isolation; it interacts with broader systems, often generating effects that ripple out beyond the immediate user. These secondary byproducts may emerge in unexpected ways as the product interacts with other systems or environments in an unbounded manner.

For example, ride-sharing apps like Uber and Lyft disrupted the traditional taxi industry, but their systemic impact went beyond transportation. They affected urban planning, labor markets, and even environmental policies, creating new byproducts such as increased traffic congestion in certain cities. These systemic byproducts highlight how innovations can have far-reaching consequences beyond their intended scope.

16. **Principle of Alternative and Unintended Uses:** Innovations often find alternative or unintended uses that go beyond their original purpose. This principle highlights how users' creativity or the unintended discovery of new applications can create entirely new byproducts, some beneficial and others potentially harmful. This unpredictability makes it difficult to foresee all the ways a product may be used once it reaches the market.

For example, the development of bubble wrap, was originally invented as textured wallpaper. It was repurposed as protective packaging material, which became its dominant use. While this alternative use provided new utility, it also created byproducts, such as increased plastic waste, that were not anticipated when the product was first invented.

17. **Principle of Byproduct as Opportunity:** Byproducts are not always negative; they can reveal new opportunities for innovation and the development of new markets.

18. **Principle of Evolutionary Distorted Byproduct:** This principle describes how modern innovations can bypass or distort natural evolutionary processes that humans have adapted to over millennia, such as effort-based rewards, delayed gratification, physical exertion, and social bonding. These disruptions misalign with our innate psychological, emotional, and physical responses, creating behaviors and outcomes incongruent with long-term well-being, physical health and resilience. While these innovations often provide immediate utility, they can inadvertently generate byproducts such as impatience, overindulgence, or diminished social skills, which conflict with the adaptive mechanisms that humans evolved to thrive in natural environments. This principle encourages innovators to design products and technologies that align with, rather than bypass, fundamental human evolutionary needs.

For example, modern technologies often bypass or distort fundamental evolutionary processes, creating a range of emotional, physical, and social byproducts. For instance, social media platforms replace natural face-to-face interactions with instant gratification through likes and comments, fostering psychological byproducts such as reduced self-esteem and a craving for external validation. Similarly, highly processed foods hijack the brain's reward systems by delivering concentrated flavors without the effort of gathering or preparing natural meals, leading to physical byproducts like overeating, metabolic imbalances, and obesity. On a social level, streaming platforms provide endless entertainment with minimal effort, bypassing the need to seek out or wait for new experiences, which can reduce opportunities for shared activities and meaningful social engagement, fostering isolation over time. These examples illustrate how modern innovations, while addressing immediate wants, can produce evolutionary distorted byproducts that misalign with the emotional, physical, and social mechanisms humans evolved to thrive on, often diminishing long-term well-being and resilience.

19. **Principle of Open-Ended Byproducts:** The Principle of Open-Ended Byproducts states that certain byproducts cannot be fully resolved and remain in a state of continuous evolution, tied to un-converged utility. Utility that has no definitive or final state of fulfillment (e.g. Industry Standard). These byproducts persist because the utility they are associated with is still in flux, driven by ever-changing user expectations, environmental shifts, or technological advancements. As a result, these byproducts, such as battery life, performance, charge speed, or environmental impact, can only be incrementally improved rather than fully eliminated.

In addition, some open-ended byproducts may not yet be addressable with current methods or technologies. They would require a significant shift in utility, such as a breakthrough technological shift or a new paradigm of utility, before they can be effectively managed or eliminated. Until that shift occurs, these byproducts remain unresolved, awaiting a fundamental transformation in how the utility is provided and perceived.

For example, while advances in rechargeable battery technology have extended battery life, the byproduct of limited power remains open-ended due to increasing user demands and power-hungry features. Addressing this fully may require a major shift, such as the development of fundamentally new energy storage methods beyond current battery technology. Until such a shift occurs, the byproduct of battery life will persist as an open-ended challenge.

20. **Principle of Byproduct Consequence Balancing:** Utility must be balanced against the negative consequences of its byproducts.

21. **Principle of Byproduct Sustainability:** Byproducts should be managed with sustainability to prevent long-term harm.

22. **Principle of Byproduct Evolution:** The Principle of Byproduct Evolution asserts that as innovations evolve, so too do the byproducts they generate. Byproducts are not static; they change in nature, scope, and intensity as the product or system matures and interacts with other technologies, markets, and user needs. This principle emphasizes the need for ongoing innovation to address the shifting byproducts that arise over time, particularly as products are scaled, adopted globally, or integrated with other systems. The evolution of byproducts can lead to entirely new industries or markets as innovators continually adjust to emerging challenges.

For example, in the early days of smartphones, the primary byproducts revolved around issues like battery life and network connectivity. As these problems were mitigated, new byproducts emerged, such as data privacy concerns, overuse leading to social isolation, and e-waste from frequent device upgrades. The byproducts of the technology evolved as the product became more advanced and more embedded in users' daily lives. Innovators must now deal with these new byproducts, creating solutions like encrypted communication, social media usage limits, or recycling programs.

23. **Principle of Byproduct Emergence through Complexity:** Byproducts often emerge from the increasing complexity of a system, especially as layers of innovation interact in unexpected ways. As products, systems, or services grow in complexity, so too do the byproducts. Complexity can lead to unexpected interactions, edge cases, and new forms of inefficiency that simpler systems do not experience. This principle urges designers to seek simplicity or, at the very least, to anticipate that the byproducts resulting from complexity may not be evident early on but can have significant impacts as the system matures. This principle recognizes that complexity is a double-edged sword, bringing new functionality and capacity while simultaneously introducing new and often unforeseen byproducts. Innovators must account for the fact that complex systems introduce challenges and emergent byproducts that would not exist in simpler configurations.

For example, autonomous driving systems have led to byproducts related to safety concerns and decision-making in edge cases (e.g., bad weather, pedestrian unpredictability). These byproducts stem from the complexity of the algorithms and the layers of technology involved. Additionally, large-scale digital platforms like social media systems have created byproducts of misinformation and data misuse as the complexity of their interactions with vast user bases increases.

24. **Principle of Byproduct as Systemic Feedback:** Byproducts can act as feedback loops within a system, highlighting larger issues or inefficiencies that require deeper analysis and innovation.

25. **Principle of Byproduct Diffusion:** Byproducts do not remain confined to their point of origin; they often diffuse into other domains or industries, affecting systems or ecosystems that are seemingly unrelated. The broader the reach of the innovation, the higher the likelihood that its byproducts will spill over into other areas. Recognizing byproduct diffusion is essential for innovators, as it can introduce unintended consequences that require cross-domain or cross-industry collaboration to address. It also highlights the need for systemic solutions when byproducts affect broader systems.

For example, the rise of e-commerce created byproducts such as increased packaging waste, which affected not only the retail sector but also the logistics and waste management industries. Similarly, the proliferation of smartphones led to increased demand for rare earth minerals, creating environmental and geopolitical byproducts beyond the scope of the tech industry itself.

26. **Principle of Byproduct Superposition:** Byproducts from different areas or utilities can superimpose, leading to compound effects that amplify their overall impact. When byproducts overlap, their combined effects can be more disruptive than each byproduct in isolation, leading to unforeseen consequences that are harder to predict or control. This principle encourages innovators to anticipate how byproducts from different sources or areas might interact and compound. It requires a broader system-level approach to managing byproducts, as overlapping issues can lead to greater challenges than initially expected.

For example, the overuse of antibiotics in livestock (a byproduct of industrial farming practices) can overlap with rising antibiotic resistance in human healthcare (a byproduct of overprescription and misuse), accelerating the evolution and spread of drug-resistant bacteria across both food supply chains and clinical environments. This convergence diminishes the effectiveness of existing treatments, strains healthcare systems with more complex and expensive interventions, and enables resistant strains to circulate globally. By reinforcing each other, these overlapping byproducts amplify the overall threat, culminating in a broader public health crisis far greater than either issue would pose by itself.

27. **Principle of Byproduct Persistence:** As new innovations replace older technologies, the byproducts tied to the obsolete systems may persist long after the original utility is replaced. These lingering byproducts can continue to affect users or the environment, requiring long-term solutions even after the innovation cycle has moved on. This principle emphasizes the importance of considering the lingering effects of legacy byproducts when designing new systems. Innovators must address these long-lasting consequences to ensure that past byproducts do not interfere with future utilities.

For example, modern regulations have largely replaced lead-based paints with safer, formulas, yet older homes and public buildings still harbor layers of lead paint. As these structures age, chipped or peeling paint can contaminate household dust and soil, posing a serious health risk, especially to children. Long after the switch to safer coatings, the original byproduct of lead paint remains a steadfast concern, exemplifying how residual consequences can persist well beyond an innovation's lifecycle.

28. **Principle of Byproduct Containment:** Some byproducts must be contained within specific areas or environments to prevent them from escalating or spreading into other systems.

29. **Principle of Byproduct Social Amplification:** Certain byproducts can be amplified by public perception or media attention, increasing their perceived severity regardless of their actual impact.

30. **Principle of Latent Emotional Byproduct:** Emotional byproducts may not manifest immediately but can accumulate over time, becoming significant only after long-term exposure to a product or service. Products that subtly affect user well-being or stress levels may not show immediate emotional impacts, but these can build up and affect the user experience over extended use. This principle emphasizes the delayed nature of emotional-cognitive byproducts, particularly in long-term or habitual use cases. Innovators must account for how

products may subtly affect users emotionally over time, leading to significant dissatisfaction or disengagement only after prolonged interaction.

For example, streaming service algorithms designed to personalize recommendations might increase short-term satisfaction by curating shows, music, or videos closely aligned with user interests. Over time, however, these highly targeted feeds can encourage binge-watching or lead to social isolation, as users spend more hours passively consuming content. This hidden emotional toll grows imperceptibly, intensifying feelings of loneliness or detachment from real-world relationships. Initially, the changes may be too subtle to detect, but eventually, these accumulated emotional byproducts can surface as deep dissatisfaction or a sense of being disconnected from both offline and online communities.

31. **Principle of Byproduct as Cultural Disruption:** Innovations can disrupt cultural norms or traditions, creating byproducts that alter societal behaviors and values.

32. **Principle of Byproduct Suppression Backlash:** Some byproducts are suppressed during normal use but can resurface dramatically when a product is pushed beyond its typical limits.

33. **Principle of Byproduct as Perceived Risk:** Users may react to byproducts based on perceived risk rather than actual harm, affecting their trust in and usage of a product.

34. **Principle of Byproduct as Informational Deficit:** A lack of clear information can create byproducts such as user confusion or misuse, which can negatively affect the user experience. (This principle is from the user's perspective; what info they have received and are aware and unaware of, regarding the product, service or systems' byproduct.)

35. **Principle of Byproduct as Unintended Engagement:** When users interact with products in ways not anticipated by designers, new byproducts can emerge that require new solutions.

36. **Principle of Byproduct Latency Disclosure:** Delaying the disclosure of byproducts can damage user trust, making early communication about potential long-term effects crucial.

37. **Principle of Byproduct Conformance to Social Values:** Byproducts that conflict with prevailing social or ethical values can become more problematic than those that align with societal expectations.

38. **Principle of Byproduct Inertia:** Certain byproducts have inertia, meaning they persist or grow due to existing systemic momentum, even when efforts are made to counteract them. These byproducts are difficult to eliminate because they are embedded in systems, processes, or behaviors that are resistant to change or heavily relied upon in societies. This principle encourages innovators to recognize the long-term persistence of certain byproducts, even when mitigation strategies are in place. Byproducts with inertia require sustained and coordinated interventions to reverse or neutralize them, as they tend to resist change and continue to grow over time.

For example, plastic waste from packaging is a byproduct with significant inertia. Despite efforts to reduce single-use plastics, the reliance on plastic materials continues to grow due to their entrenched use in packaging industries. Another example is fossil fuel dependency, where, despite advancements in renewable energy, the systemic momentum of oil and gas infrastructure makes it difficult to fully transition away.

39. **Principle of Byproduct Emotional Contagion:** Emotional byproducts like frustration or anxiety can spread among users, amplifying negative feelings and increasing dissatisfaction.

40. **Principle of Byproduct Temporal Acceleration:** Certain byproducts can accelerate in impact over time, growing exponentially rather than linearly, especially if external factors or usage conditions change. Initially, minor byproducts may intensify as usage increases or as the product interacts with evolving environmental or systemic conditions. This principle emphasizes the importance of early detection and management of byproducts that may grow more severe over time. If not addressed promptly, such byproducts can escalate rapidly, overwhelming users or systems. Innovators must be proactive in identifying signs of acceleration and implementing mitigation strategies early.

For example, the overuse of pesticides in farming may initially seem like a manageable trade-off for higher crop yields. However, as pests develop resistance over successive growing seasons, farmers are compelled to use stronger chemicals in greater quantities. This accelerates environmental harm, leading to soil degradation, water contamination, and the decline of beneficial pollinators like bees, creating a cascading ecological crisis that grows more severe with time.

41. **Principle of Byproduct as a Signal:** Byproducts can serve as early indicators of broader systemic issues or future trends that require innovative solutions.

42. **Principle of Byproduct Normalization:** Byproduct normalization arises when users, markets, or ecosystems begin treating certain frictions, inefficiencies, or shortcomings as an inevitable part of the product or service experience, even if these issues were initially perceived as problematic. Over time, what began as a disruption becomes woven into user routines or market standards, effectively hiding otherwise fixable burdens behind the presumption that "this is simply how things work." Normalization can be overt, where users knowingly adapt to the inconvenience. Or covert, taking hold so gradually that people barely notice the newly embedded friction.

This principle underscores the value of reexamining long-accepted byproducts to identify whether they are indeed unavoidable or merely widely tolerated. In many cases, consumers no longer push for a solution because they have grown used to these inefficiencies, creating a gap that innovators could potentially fill with disruptive ideas. However, not all normalized byproducts demand a fix: some may be woven so deeply into user behavior that any attempted overhaul would feel more burdensome than beneficial. Yet, in other instances, unearthing normalized burdens can lead to transformative change that reshapes consumer expectations or entire market categories.

For example, persistent phone notifications have become embedded in daily life, yet the constant barrage of pings, alerts, and popups is a normalized byproduct of modern connectivity. Similarly, chronic traffic congestion is widely accepted in urban environments, even though it continuously drains time and energy from commuters. Another case is the habitual notion that internet usage must remain tethered to a stationary device, an assumption overturned once mobile data speeds improved, prompting a shift toward "internet anywhere" on smartphones. By consciously questioning these deeply ingrained assumptions, innovators may uncover hidden opportunities to redefine what users expect or consider "inevitable."

43. **Principle of Byproduct Behavioral Residue:** Some byproducts leave behind behavioral residues, where users subtly alter their behaviors, habits, routines, or even customs over time in response to repeated negative or ritualistic interactions. These changes can persist long after the byproduct itself has been addressed, shaping how users engage with products, services, or even entire markets. Behavioral residues may result in disengagement, abandonment of a product, or resistance to adopting improved solutions, as users internalize coping mechanisms or establish routines or rituals around the original byproduct.

This principle highlights the long-term impact of even minor byproducts on user behavior, emphasizing the importance of anticipating and managing these effects early. Innovators must consider how a byproduct can shape user habits, not only while it exists but also after it is resolved. Addressing the behavioral residue requires understanding how deeply ingrained routines may prevent users from recognizing or adopting superior alternatives, even when they offer clear or beneficial advantages.

For example, slow loading times in apps can create behavioral residues, causing users to gradually reduce their engagement with the platform over time, ultimately leading to churn. Poor customer service experiences are another example, as they leave users less likely to return to a brand, even after the issue is resolved. Similarly, habits formed around established routines, such as refueling at gas stations or carrying and packing cigarettes, can prevent users from adopting alternatives with lower byproducts and greater utility. For instance, users accustomed to gas station refueling may find it inconvenient to switch to electric vehicles due to the need to develop new behaviors like charging at home or at public stations. Likewise, smokers who associate cigarettes with social rituals may resist transitioning to safer nicotine alternatives, even when these options provide similar satisfaction with fewer health risks. These examples illustrate how entrenched habits and rituals formed around byproducts can hinder the adoption of innovative solutions, emphasizing the need for careful consideration of behavioral shifts in both design and awareness strategies.

44. **Principle of Byproduct as Dual-Provoked Desire:** This principle emphasizes how a byproduct can provoke two distinct types of desires, an internal desire (focused on improving or upgrading the system or product itself) and an external desire (focused on related products, systems, or even environmental elements). Byproducts can create dissatisfaction within a product while simultaneously sparking aspirations for complementary enhancements. This principle encourages innovators to explore both internal and external desires that arise from byproducts. It highlights the opportunity to innovate not only within the product itself but across a broader ecosystem of solutions, addressing both types of desires provoked by the same byproduct.

For example, a user purchases a high-performance laptop and, after some time, desires a more efficient cooling system for the laptop (internal desire). Simultaneously, the user starts looking into a new ergonomic workstation setup to complement the laptop's performance (external desire). Another example is a person buying a high-quality sound system and realizing they need to improve the room's acoustics (internal desire) while also wanting smart lighting for a complete experience (external desire).

45. **Principle of Byproduct as Complementary Trigger:** Byproducts can trigger desires for complementary or adjacent products that enhance the overall user experience.

46. **Principle of Byproduct Cascading Potential:** Byproducts often lead to a cascading chain of new desires, where addressing one unmet need triggers additional demands. These demands may range from problem-solving needs to desires for enhancement, emerging immediately or over time. This principle describes the cascading nature of byproducts, emphasizing that resolving one issue can reveal further opportunities for innovation. This principle encourages innovators to be proactive in anticipating the cascading demands that follow after addressing initial byproducts. Innovators should not only focus on solving the immediate issue but also recognize the broader ripple effects that resolving one byproduct may trigger.

For example, a person installs a smart thermostat in their home, which soon leads to the desire for additional smart home integrations like automated lighting and then security systems and so on. Another example is a person buying a fitness tracker, enjoying its basic features, then wanting more advanced metrics like sleep monitoring, calorie tracking, and smart scales, leading to a cascading demand for more smart devices.

47. **Principle of Byproduct Induced Origin:** Byproducts can be categorized based on their origin, either being intrinsic to the product, service or system (arising from the core design or functionality of the product) or extrinsic (arising from interactions between the product and external environmental factors).

- **Intrinsic byproducts**: are built into the product, service or system and stem directly from the design, materials, or technology, emerging from its natural wear, design limitations, or functional inefficiencies. Example: A laptop battery losing its charge-holding capacity over time.

- **Extrinsic byproducts**: result from how the product, service or system interacts with external elements like environments or other systems. These originate outside the system but still affect its perceived or actual utility. These are driven by social, economic, technological, or competitive forces. Example: A smartphone that functions perfectly well but is perceived as outdated due to the introduction of a newer, faster model.

Understanding the origin of the byproduct is essential for diagnosing and resolving it effectively. The purpose of this principle is to highlight the importance of understanding where a byproduct originates. Whether the byproduct is a natural consequence of the system's design or caused by external conditions can affect how developers address it. Innovators must determine whether the byproduct is truly a shortcoming of the system or if it's a result of external elements: a broader super-system.

For example, a user experiences battery degradation in their smartphone after prolonged use. This is an intrinsic byproduct directly related to the hardware's aging process. Another example is a smartphone user experiencing connectivity issues in a rural area due to poor signal coverage, an extrinsic byproduct caused by the external environment, not the phone itself, yet may end up impacting the users perceived value (utility) of the phone itself.

48. **Principle of Origin Reflective Byproduct:** Origin Reflective Byproduct builds on the extrinsic aspect of the induced origin principle. They occur when a product's introduction into an environment provokes a reflective desire for change, either towards the product itself (Product-Reflective) or towards the environment (Environment-Reflective). These byproducts are distinguished by whether the user's desire for change is focused on altering the product to better fit the environment or altering the environment to complement or accommodate the product. The goal of this principle is to differentiate between byproducts that arise from the interaction between the product and its environment, helping innovators recognize whether the desire for change is driven by the product's introduction or by the environment's existing conditions. Understanding this distinction allows for better product adjustments and more informed decisions about the surrounding context.

- **Product-Reflective Byproduct**: This type emerges when the presence of the product within a specific environment triggers a desire to modify the product itself. The desire for change appears to be product-related but is actually prompted by the environmental context. For instance, a new couch placed in a living room may lead users to feel that the couch requires pillows of a different color, size or shape due to its appearance relative to the rest of the room.

- **Environment-Reflective Byproduct**: This type arises when the product's presence highlights or exacerbates issues within the environment, leading users to desire changes in the surrounding space. For example, after introducing a new couch, users might feel the need to replace the rug, repaint the walls, or adjust the lighting to better match the couch's style or color scheme.

For example, a user notices that their smartphone's sleek, new design and advanced camera capabilities make their current phone case look outdated or bulky. Despite the case providing adequate protection, the user now feels a desire to buy a slimmer or more stylish case to match the aesthetics of the new phone. Here, the byproduct (desire for a new case) appears to stem from the product itself, but it is actually a reflection of how the product contrasts with the accessories or items that accompany it (Product-reflective, with respect to its environment). Another example is after integrating their smartphone into their home environment, the user realizes that the phone's advanced display and sound capabilities highlight the poor quality of their old Bluetooth speaker. The user now feels the need to upgrade their home audio system or speaker setup to fully utilize the capabilities of the smartphone. In this case, the byproduct (desire to upgrade the speaker) emerges from the product's presence, but it is directed towards the external environment rather than the product itself (environment-reflective, due to the product, but about its environment).

49. **Principle of Byproduct Attribution:** Byproducts can be either correctly attributed to their true source or misattributed, where users incorrectly blame the product, system, or service for issues caused by external factors or environmental conditions. Proper byproduct attribution is critical for effective problem-solving. Misattributing a byproduct can lead to wasted resources, unnecessary fixes, or overlooked root causes. This principle emphasizes the need for careful analysis and accurate diagnosis of byproducts. Correctly attributing byproducts ensures that resources are focused on addressing the true source of the issue, rather than chasing symptoms caused by external factors. Misattribution often happens when users lack full visibility into the broader context that may contribute to the byproduct.

For example, a user complains that their laptop has slow internet speeds, attributing the problem to the device, but the actual cause is weak Wi-Fi signals in their location. An issue with the external network. Another example is a user experiencing battery drain in their phone after several years of use, correctly identifying it as a result of the phone's aging battery, which is an intrinsic byproduct.

50. **Principle of Temporal Emergence:** This principle focuses on the timing of byproduct emergence, recognizing that byproducts do not always surface immediately. Byproducts can emerge at different stages of a product's lifecycle or as the product interacts with environments or over time. Temporal Emergence classifies byproducts based on three primary types of timing:

- **Immediate Awareness**: Byproducts that surface as soon as the product or system is used, requiring immediate attention.

- **Gradual Surfacing**: Byproducts that appear over time, often as a result of repeated use, wear and tear, or evolving user needs.

- **Incidental Emergence**: Byproducts that occur under specific or rare conditions, which may only become apparent in unusual circumstances or when external environmental factors change or impose a trigger.

Innovators must consider when byproducts are likely to emerge and plan solutions accordingly. Immediate byproducts may need quick fixes, while gradual or incidental byproducts may require longer-term monitoring and response.

For example, a customer buys a new printer, and it fails to connect to their network immediately, this represents immediate awareness. Gradual surfacing could involve a laptop's battery life slowly degrading after several months of use. Incidental emergence might involve a camera fogging up only in very humid environments, which occurs under rare conditions.

51. **Principle of Source of Byproduct Origination:** Byproducts can emerge from three primary sources: User Use or Misuse, Environmental Impact, or Maker's Design. Each source creates different types of byproducts, and recognizing where a byproduct originates is crucial for developing the most effective solutions.

- **User Use or Misuse**: Byproducts that result from how users interact with the product, either by following intended use patterns or by misusing the product in unintended ways.

- **Environmental Impact**: Byproducts that emerge due to the external environment, such as weather conditions, infrastructure limitations, or other external broader systems that affect the product.

- **Maker's Design**: Byproducts that result from the trade-offs made during the product's design, including design flaws, material limitations, or performance compromises. This includes unforeseen or unanticipated issues.

218

Understanding the source helps innovators target the root cause of the byproduct. For example, a byproduct originating from user misuse might require education, while one emerging from environmental conditions might require external mitigation. A design flaw might require a complete redesign or augmentation or a patch to resolve.

For example, a customer places their laptop on a soft surface, causing it to overheat due to blocked ventilation, this byproduct results from user misuse. A car's paint fading due to long-term exposure to harsh sunlight represents an environmental impact. A smartphone having a smaller battery capacity due to slim design choices reflects a maker's design byproduct.

52. **Principle of Byproduct as Opportunity for Ecosystem Expansion:** Byproducts can reveal gaps in the market, offering opportunities to expand product ecosystems by addressing unmet needs.

53. **Principle of Byproduct Contrast Continuum:** Subjective Byproducts will exist along a continuum that ranges from extreme negative unresolved deficiencies, aka expectation deviations (such as problems causing extreme dissatisfaction), to highly positive unfulfilled aspirations, aka aspirational comparisons (such as a deep desire for transformative improvement). Byproducts are dynamic and can evolve along this continuum, transitioning from negative experiences due to some deficiency, to positive opportunities for growth or the potential for something better. This principle highlights that subjective byproducts are not binary but can exist among a range of negative and positive states depending on user experience, expectation and context. Innovators should recognize the span of this spectrum or continuum, resolving negative byproducts while also capitalizing on the positive opportunities they reveal.

For example, on the negative end, a user experiences continuous system crashes, causing frustration and dissatisfaction that demand immediate fixes. On the positive end, a user enjoys their fitness tracker but desires additional features like advanced health analytics and sleep tracking, driving future innovation.

54. **Principle of Design-Managed Byproduct:** The Principle of Design-Managed Byproduct refers to how certain byproducts, once emergent and disruptive,

eventually become systematically managed through established design methods, standards, best practices, and industry guidelines. Over time, through research, field experience, and data collection, industries develop methods to control these byproducts consistently and predictably. These byproducts no longer represent significant risks or variability, as they are integrated into the design process and accounted for as part of standard practices. This principle emphasizes that innovation processes mature over time and that once disruptive byproducts can eventually be managed effectively through design improvements. By addressing a previously uncontrolled byproduct, the process becomes stable, predictable, and controllable. This allows innovators to shift their focus to new byproducts and innovations, while managing previous risks systematically.

For example, gold plating on electrical connectors was once inconsistent, leading to unreliable connections. Today, established industry standards specify the exact thickness of gold plating and base metal required for reliable performance. Another example is crumple zones in vehicle design, initially a disruptive byproduct. Crash absorption has now become a systematically designed feature with regulatory standards in place. Additionally, concrete strength standards have evolved, where historically, performance varied, but now the material is highly standardized and controlled.

55. **Principle of Strategic Byproduct Selection:** This principle emphasizes that the most critical aspect of product, system, or service development exists not necessarily in the utility itself but foremost, in the identification, and careful selection of which byproducts to resolve. Utility creation is inherently reactive and tied to addressing byproducts. The most successful innovations are those that tackle the most meaningful and impactful byproducts that directly influence the customer experience. Selecting the wrong byproducts, those that are less relevant or less critical to the user, can diminish the perceived value of the resulting utility, leading to dissatisfaction or indifference. This principle highlights that successful innovation hinges on an organization's ability to identify, prioritize, and address the right byproducts; those that have the greatest impact on the customer's experience. In contrast, focusing on resolving byproducts that the customer doesn't care about, or failing to resolve critical byproducts that affect the user, can lead to products that seem out of touch, underwhelming, or ineffective. The customer values the utility they receive, but that utility is only as valuable as the byproducts it resolves for them and helps

them escape, avoid or mitigate; those that are most aligned with their unmet needs, frustrations, or open desires.

Key Considerations:

1. **Customer-Centric Selection**: The byproducts selected to address must be those that directly influence the customer's experience and meet their most pressing needs or aspirations. Developers must ask, "What byproduct most prevents the customer from realizing value?" or "Which unresolved byproduct could create the highest value if addressed?"

2. **Strategic Trade-offs**: In product development, resources and time are limited. This principle requires developers to strategically prioritize which byproducts to resolve first, ensuring that their efforts deliver the maximum perceived utility to the customer. Focusing on the wrong byproduct may waste resources and reduce the perceived value of the utility delivered.

3. **Continuous Reassessment**: Customers' needs, and external environments evolve over time. This principle demands continuous reassessment of which byproducts are most pressing at any given moment and ensuring that the right ones are being tackled to keep pace with customer expectations and changing environments.

Implications of This Principle:

1. **Byproduct-Driven Innovation**: The principle reinforces the concept that byproducts drive innovation, not the utility itself. The most successful innovations emerge from understanding and resolving byproducts that matter most to users.

2. **Customer Value Alignment**: The value a customer perceives in a product or service reflects how well it addresses the byproducts most relevant to their experience. The alignment between customer needs and resolved byproducts defines success.

3. **Risk of Misalignment**: If developers focus on the wrong byproducts, the product's utility may fail to resonate with the customer, leading to poor adoption, dissatisfaction or abandonment.

For example, an online education platform that invests heavily in gamification features while neglecting the byproducts of confusing navigation or inconsistent video quality may alienate students. While gamification can enhance engagement, ensuring seamless access to content and reducing technical frustrations is far more critical to the platform's core utility. Focusing on these foundational byproducts ensures the platform meets learners' expectations and retains their trust. Similarly, smart home device manufacturers that prioritize sleek aesthetics or extensive voice command options but fail to address connectivity issues or compatibility with existing systems risk disappointing users. The core utility of smart home devices is convenience and seamless integration, so neglecting these critical byproducts undermines their value. Prioritizing connectivity and compatibility ensures that the device delivers its intended utility effectively, enhancing the user's experience.

56. **Principle of Byproduct Accumulation:** Byproducts do not typically emerge all in a singular moment (unless they are an impulse byproduct, see below); they emerge over time, and can gradually accumulate, reducing the net perceived utility of a product, service, or system. Each of these accumulation types may be either intrinsic, arising from the product itself, or extrinsic, arising from external influences (see Principle of Byproduct Origination). As byproducts accumulate, they progressively detract from the available net perceived utility of the product, leading to the illusion that utility is diminishing, when in reality, the core utility remains constant. This principle serves as the foundation for understanding how perceived utility loss is not due to the degradation of the product's core function, but rather due to the burden imposed by accumulating byproducts. Byproduct accumulation is categorized into three distinct forms:

1. **Temporary Byproducts**

   Temporary byproducts emerge as reversible inefficiencies that can be mitigated, reset, or managed over time. These byproducts do not cause lasting degradation but temporarily reduce net perceived utility until they are addressed. Temporary byproducts can be either:

   - Intrinsic: Arise directly from the product, such as dust collecting on a camera lens, a smartphone slowing down due to cached memory overload, or a dull knife that requires sharpening.
   - Extrinsic: Stem from external factors, such as seasonal traffic congestion reducing the efficiency of a public transportation system,

power outages disrupting the use of electric appliances, or a change in regulatory policy momentarily increasing compliance costs for a business.

2. Permanent Byproducts

Permanent byproducts represent inefficiencies, degradations, or external burdens that persist indefinitely and cannot be reversed. These may gradually accumulate over time, making their effects increasingly difficult to ignore. Permanent byproducts can be either:

- Intrinsic: Caused by irreversible changes in the product itself, such as battery capacity degradation in a laptop, structural fatigue in a bridge, or physical wear of irreplaceable components on a mechanical watch.

- Extrinsic: Induced by external systemic changes, such as a product being perceived as outdated due to evolving social trends, a business suffering permanent reputational damage, or new environmental or state regulations permanently restricting the use of certain materials or products in certain regions of a country.

3. Impulse-Based Byproducts

Impulse-based byproducts occur suddenly and unexpectedly, causing an immediate drop in available net perceived utility. These byproducts disrupt the user experience in an abrupt way, either through an internal failure or an external event. Impulse-based byproducts can be either:

- Intrinsic: Arise from catastrophic failures within the product, such as a computer hard drive crashing without warning, a factory machine suffering complete mechanical failure, or a car accident rendering the vehicle a total loss.

- Extrinsic: Triggered by rapid changes in external conditions, such as a disruptive competitor making an existing product obsolete overnight, new government regulations suddenly banning a product category, or a social media-driven scandal instantly damaging a brand's reputation.

Each of these accumulation types plays a role in the perceived decline of utility, but none of them change the fact that the product's original functional capacity remains intact, it is simply constrained or limited by growing burdens. This principle works in conjunction with the Principle of Byproduct Induced Origin, which provides further differentiation between intrinsic and extrinsic sources of byproducts. Understanding byproduct accumulation enables innovators to anticipate, delay, reduce, or eliminate these burdens, ensuring that the net available utility remains higher for longer periods of time.

This principle is critical for understanding why utility appears to diminish, it is not the utility itself declining, but rather, the accumulation of byproducts overshadowing it.

For example, a gasoline-powered car experiences intrinsic byproduct accumulation through mechanical wear, leading to increased maintenance needs over time. However, its net available utility is also constrained by extrinsic byproduct accumulation, such as the rising cost of fuel, regulatory emissions restrictions, and shifting social preferences toward electric vehicles. While the car's functional capability remains constant (it can still drive), the perceived net utility is reduced due to accumulating burdens that make it feel outdated or inefficient in its context.

Sub-Module B2:
Theory and Principles of Utility

In Sub-Module B2, we shift our focus from *why* byproducts matter to the "**what**" of innovation, namely, utility. Chapter 14 sets the stage by showing that utility is always a reaction to some unresolved byproduct: it's the specific solution we adopt to escape old shortcomings or fulfill unmet aspirations. Next, Chapter 15 presents the "Theory of Constant Utility," revealing that a product's core utility doesn't actually diminish; but rather, new byproducts (whether physical, social, or emotional) overshadow its core utility, prompting us to seek the next upgrade. Finally, Chapter 16 enumerates 50 principles of utility design and evolution, covering everything from the need for resiliency and integration across ecosystems, to how utility is shaped by personal identity or social context. Throughout, we see that utility isn't an end in itself. It's the "what" that responds to and resolves the deeper "why" of byproduct.

CHAPTER 14
The 'What' of Utility

The Pursuit of the "What" in Innovation: The Right Utility

For the past few hundred years, businesses have approached innovation primarily through the lens of utility creation. A consumer is seen as a utility-seeker that will eventually experience a decline in the utility of their goods or services. Businesses will then respond to "restore utility" to the consumer. This effort to deliver goods and services that meet consumer needs and desires is the basis of traditional economic theory, which views businesses as entities that respond to market demand by producing and supplying the "**what**"; the tangible or intangible utilities that consumers seek. Economists define utility as the measure of satisfaction or benefit derived from consuming a product or service. This concept underpins the supply-demand equilibrium, where businesses strive to maximize production efficiency, profitability, and consumer satisfaction.

Throughout history, this approach has led to remarkable advancements. The Industrial Revolution, for instance, brought innovations in production methods and the delivery of utility at unprecedented scales. Factories churned out goods to meet growing consumer demand, while railroads and steamships expanded access to these utilities across regions. Over time, businesses refined their understanding of utility, addressing not only functional needs but also emotional, social, and aspirational desires. This expansion of utility creation gave rise to iconic innovations like the automobile, telephone, and luxury goods, all aimed at answering the same fundamental question, "What do consumers want?"

Today, economists, marketers, innovators, and entrepreneurs continue to pursue this question. In modern economic theory, utility creation remains central to competitive advantage. Marketers analyze consumer preferences, behaviors, and psychological triggers to craft offerings that resonate. Entrepreneurs seek to identify gaps in the market and build solutions that promise greater convenience, efficiency, or emotional satisfaction. Innovators adopt methodologies like design thinking and lean development, which emphasize understanding user needs and iterating rapidly to deliver utility. All these practices are united by a shared goal, to create products and services that provide the "**what**" that consumers demand.

However, this lens of utility creation has its limitations. Focusing primarily on crafting products or experiences that meet perceived needs often leads businesses astray. In practice, this approach often encourages a fragmented view of innovation, where success is equated with building a better version of an existing utility or introducing new features that differentiate a product in the marketplace. For example, Samsung's high-end smartphones typically race to add new cutting-edge features such as iris scanners, air gesture controls or 3D Touch Displays. While these advancements may have driven short-term sales, they failed to address the deeper reasons "**why**" consumers may have felt dissatisfied, disengaged, or ready to move away from such capabilities. These features were ultimately short lived.

When businesses rely and invest primarily on utility creation, they risk producing offerings that consumers do not value or even notice. Economists have long acknowledged the concept of consumer surplus, the difference between what consumers are willing to pay for a product and what they actually pay. While this concept highlights the perceived value of utility, it also underscores the challenge businesses face. That is, in creating utilities that genuinely enhance satisfaction rather than flooding markets with features or products that lack meaningful value. We know this to be true in the marketplace because its staying power confirms its value, "*continued presence signals genuine relevance.*"

Compounding this issue is the rise of hyper-competition, driven by global markets, technological advancements, and rapidly changing consumer preferences. Businesses are pressured to innovate faster and more frequently than ever before, but many fail to ask the right questions. They focus on the immediate "**what**" of utility. What new features to add, what new product to launch, without fully understanding the underlying drivers of consumer dissatisfaction or new demand. This has led to market over-saturation in many industries, where consumers are bombarded with countless choices, and businesses struggle to differentiate themselves.

At the same time, modern environmental and social consciousness adds further complexity. Today the term "byproduct" has entered public discourse, typically under poor connotation, referring to pollution, waste, or other unintended consequences of industrial activity. Businesses are increasingly held accountable for the negative externalities their products and services create, from environmental degradation to societal harm. Governments impose regulations, and consumers demand sustainability and ethical practices. These pressures add another layer of complexity to the traditional utility-focused approach, as businesses must now balance creating value with mitigating harm.

Despite these pressures, the utility creation lens still dominates innovation today. Economists emphasize the importance of understanding demand curves and price elasticity, marketers rely on segmentation and data analytics to tailor offerings, and entrepreneurs focus on minimum viable products to test market fit. The central question remains, "What do consumers want, and how can we supply it?" Yet, as businesses face rising rates of product failures, dropping percentages of market share, unmet expectations, and market saturation, it becomes increasingly clear that this approach is incomplete in today's world. The pursuit of the "**what**" is necessary, but without a deeper understanding of "**why**" demand exists in the first place, businesses risk investing in solutions that miss the mark.

The current day framework of utility creation has brought us far, but it also reveals its own limitations. As markets evolve and the pace of innovation accelerates, businesses must move beyond the traditional "**what**" of supply-side economics. To truly innovate in the market of tomorrow, they must understand the conditions that give rise to demand and the deeper forces that drive consumer dissatisfaction, inefficiency, or desire. Without this clarity, utility creation becomes a gamble, sometimes on the backs of thousands of employees. The exercise of yesterday's method in responding to surface-level preferences while missing the underlying opportunities for the meaningfully relevant innovation of tomorrow, requires innovation in-and-of-itself.

Utility as the "What" That Fulfills the "Why"

In Chapter 8, we discussed the concept of byproduct as the "**why**" that sparks demand. If byproduct serves as the foundation for demand, then utility is the actionable response to it. Utility is the "**what**" that fulfills those needs, resolves those inefficiencies, or satisfies those pending desires. It is the product, service, or system deliberately created to neutralize, mitigate or escape the byproduct.

Utility represents the supply-side complement to byproduct-driven demand. It is the mechanism by which successful businesses respond to the signals revealed by byproduct, crafting solutions that align with consumer expectations and emerging needs. Importantly, utility creation is not arbitrary. It requires deliberate effort, ingenuity, and creativity to address the specific challenges or desires that byproduct highlights.

Take the example of Netflix. The company's innovation was not driven by the creation of a new form of entertainment. Instead, *"Hastings and Randolph (Netflix founders) were keenly aware of the limitations of the DVD rental model and anticipated the potential of digital distribution."* By providing on-demand streaming, Netflix fulfilled the "**what**" of consumer demand: convenience, flexibility and control. While resolving the inefficiencies revealed by the latent and normalized byproducts of the DVD rental model:

- Needing to drive to a physical location to rent a DVD
- Uncertainty about whether your preferred title will be available
- Frequently settling for a second-choice movie if the first pick is out of stock
- Waiting in line to pay for the rental
- Keeping track of the DVD at home to avoid losing it
- Making another trip just to return the DVD
- Risking additional costs in late fees if you don't return it on time, and so on…

This alignment between byproduct and utility not only ensured Netflix's success but also reshaped the entertainment industry.

Utility creation, therefore, is not merely about building products or services; it is about building the right products or services. When businesses focus solely on utility without understanding the byproduct that drives demand, they risk creating offerings that fail to resonate with users. Misaligned utility, such as the Segway, which addressed a problem most consumers didn't feel they had, is a gamble that relies on luck rather than strategic precision. (If you aren't aware of what the Segway was, this further proves the point.)

Utility may be the supply-side driver, but it is byproduct that creates the demand. Successful innovation hinges on identifying and addressing the correct byproduct. Without this alignment, utility creation becomes disconnected from real user needs, reducing the likelihood of success. Conversely, when businesses deliberately align their utility creation with meaningful byproducts, they not only meet demand but also create lasting value, ensuring relevance in a constantly evolving market.

Utility as a Means to an End: Six Economic Theory Perspectives

Utility in economics is not pursued in isolation, it is derived from consuming goods and services that fulfill some underlying purpose. Economic bodies of knowledge generally explain why we seek utility through various lenses, including satisfaction of needs, problem-solving, goal attainment, and preference fulfillment. Below is a brief structured breakdown of these perspectives.

1. **Classical & Neoclassical Economics: Utility as Satisfaction of Needs**
   Utility is sought because it represents satisfaction or well-being from consumption. In this view, utility is not sought for its own sake, but as a measure of how well goods and services satisfy our preferences.
   - **Early economists (Adam Smith, Jeremy Bentham, John Stuart Mill)**: Viewed utility as the ability of goods to bring happiness or reduce pain.
   - **Neoclassical Economics (William Stanley Jevons, Alfred Marshall, Vilfredo Pareto):** Formalized utility as a numerical representation of preferences, where consumers choose goods to maximize satisfaction.
   - **Marginal Utility Theory:** Marginal utility theory suggests that consumers allocate resources to maximize satisfaction by consuming additional units only as long as the added benefit exceeds the opportunity cost. The equi-marginal principle builds upon this, stating that optimal consumption occurs when the last unit of money spent on each good provides equal marginal utility per dollar across all goods.

2. **Behavioral Economics: Utility as Emotional and Psychological Satisfaction**
   People seek utility because it reduces discomfort, meets psychological needs, and aligns with expectations. In this view, utility is sought because it aligns with deeper emotional and psychological needs, not as an abstract goal.
   - **Prospect Theory (Daniel Kahneman & Amos Tversky):** People evaluate utility based on gains and losses rather than absolute levels, meaning they seek utility to avoid perceived losses.
   - **Loss Aversion:** We avoid choices that might bring disutility (dissatisfaction) more than we seek additional pleasure.
   - **Hyperbolic Discounting:** People seek immediate utility rather than long-term gains because psychological reward structures favor instant gratification.

3. **Consumer Choice & Rational Decision-Making: Utility as Optimization**
   People seek utility to make rational trade-offs that improve their position in a constrained world. Here, utility is sought because it helps individuals make better choices.
   - **Utility Maximization:** Individuals make choices to get the highest possible satisfaction given their income and the price of goods.

- **Opportunity Cost:** Seeking utility is about choosing the best alternative among limited options.
- **Indifference Curves:** Show how people balance competing desires to maintain overall well-being.

4. **Evolutionary and Biological Economics: Utility as Survival and Reproduction**

Utility-seeking behavior evolved as a mechanism to enhance survival and reproduction. In this perspective, utility-seeking is a biologically ingrained survival mechanism, not an arbitrary pursuit.

- **Evolutionary Game Theory:** Suggests utility is a proxy for fitness, where we prefer things that increase our chances of survival.
- **Biological Drives:** Humans seek food, shelter, security, and reproduction because these are fundamental to evolutionary success.
- **Neuroeconomics:** Suggests the brain is wired to seek utility in ways that promote long-term gene survival.

5. **Social and Institutional Economics: Utility as Social Status and Collective Well-Being**

While traditional economic models assume utility reflects inherent satisfaction, social and institutional economics suggest that utility is often shaped by external reference points. Veblen's conspicuous consumption shows how status-seeking behaviors create perceived utility gains, even when the functional benefit remains unchanged. (*Note: Later in this chapter, it will be revealed that this aligns with portions of LPI's perspective; that what is perceived as diminishing utility may actually be a shift in social context, creating new byproducts (e.g., status anxiety, outdated technology, competitive benchmarking) that overshadow previous utility.*)

- **Thorstein Veblen (Conspicuous Consumption):** People seek goods not just for function, but to signal wealth and status.
- **Pierre Bourdieu (Social Capital):** Utility-seeking extends to social relationships where we consume things that enhance our position in society.
- **Institutional Economics:** People seek utility based on social norms and institutional pressures.

6. **Postmodern & Behavioral Critiques: Utility as Illusion or Social Construct**

Utility-seeking is sometimes manufactured by marketing, cultural forces, or irrational habits. This critique suggests that utility-seeking can be manipulated and is not always in our best interests.

- **Jean Baudrillard (Consumer Society):** People seek utility not because they need it, but because society creates artificial desires.
- **Behavioral Addiction Models:** Utility-seeking can become compulsive, driven by dopamine loops rather than rational thought.
- **Hyperreality Theory:** Consumption is less about utility and more about symbols and identity.

Where LPI Diverges from Traditional Economic Theories

The Law of Perpetual Innovation fundamentally diverges from traditional economic theories by framing utility-seeking as a response to byproducts rather than as a pursuit of inherent value. These byproducts will emerge from our current utility (product, service or system) itself, or from tensions between your present utility (current state) and a potential utility (a higher potential, or reward state). Instead of viewing utility as something people seek for the value it delivers, LPI argues that utility is always a reaction to an existing byproduct (a tension, deficiency, or unresolved state). While standard economics often views consumption as a quest for this positive satisfaction (utility), LPI aligns with traditional economics that removing dissatisfaction is crucial. However, LPI argues that the seeking of positive gains, or satisfaction, is not what we actually seek; that's the illusion. What we actually seek is a resolution to insufficiency, limitation, or incompleteness, whether tangible, emotional, or aspirational. Even when we strive for more or better, we do so because something about our present condition is lacking, constrained, or unfulfilled, thus motivating us to seek change.

LPI introduces a structural shift in how we define utility. As stated earlier, the traditional view in economics is that people seek utility because it delivers them value; it is an end goal per se. LPI flips this logic and says that people seek utility because it delivers them from a byproduct. It reframes economic thought by introducing byproduct as the missing variable in utility-seeking behavior. It asserts that:

- **Utility is never an end goal:** It is always a means of escaping or resolving something undesirable. Even when we aspire to, or, for something, it remains an unfulfilled aspiration via aspirational comparison, that we seek to remedy.
- **Utility is always contextual:** No utility exists on its own, it only exists because it resolves or mitigates a byproduct.

232

- **We don't innovate to create utility**: We innovate because an unresolved byproduct forces us to. (*Note: We can and do innovate to create utility. However, if it does not address actual byproduct, then its likelihood of successful adoption is unlikely.*)
- **Byproduct is the true driver of all innovation.** Without an initial deficiency, inefficiency or unresolved state, there would be no need for innovation.
- **The pursuit of utility is actually the avoidance of byproduct:** People are not chasing value, they are overcoming burdens or limitations (e.g. tension, worries, adversity, fear) and utility enables this.
- **Every form of utility has no meaning without its opposing byproduct:** e.g., comfort exists because discomfort preceded it, transportation exists because distance is an obstacle, medicine exists because illness is a byproduct.

While traditional economics explains why people seek utility from various perspectives, LPI goes a step further by revealing that utility-seeking is fundamentally reactive, not proactive. It posits that people seek utility only because an unmet need or pending desire (a byproduct) exists, not because utility has inherent value on its own. Byproduct resolution gives utility its value.

Diminishing Marginal Utility through traditional Economics and LPI: The Pizza Example

In traditional economics, diminishing marginal utility states that as you consume more of a good (e.g., pizza), the additional satisfaction (utility) from each additional unit declines. The initial slice is highly enjoyable, the second slightly less, and by the fifth or sixth slice, eating more may even become unpleasant. (See the following illustration.)

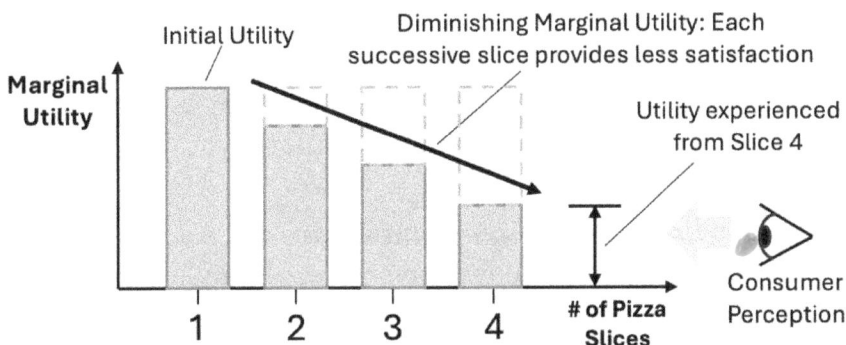

Traditional Economics View of Diminishing Marginal Utility

LPI, however, does not view this as a decline in utility. Instead, LPI would argue that new byproducts are emerging and accumulating as consumption continues, making the original utility feel insufficient or even counterproductive. (See the following illustration.)

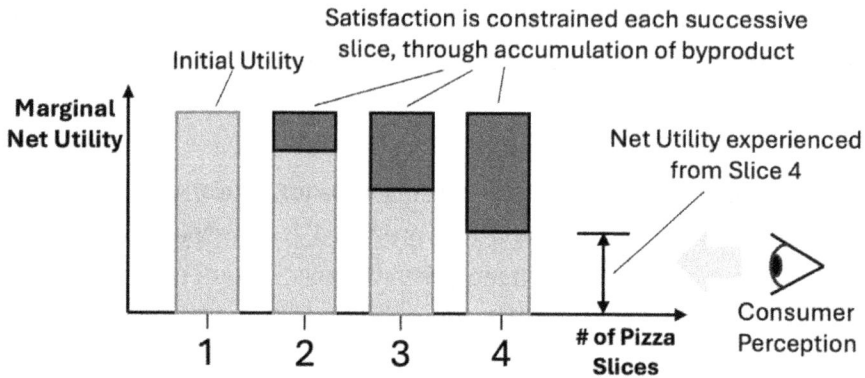

LPI's View: Accumulating Marginal Byproduct

What is Actually Happening According to LPI:

- The inherently objective utility of the pizza remains constant, it still provides nourishment, taste, and fulfillment of hunger, just as it did with the first slice.
- However, as more slices are consumed, new byproducts emerge and accumulate, making continued consumption feel less desirable.
- These accumulating byproducts are what drive the shift in experience, not an inherent loss of utility in the pizza itself.

Identifying the Objective and Subjective Byproducts Emerging: As the person eats additional slices, the two components of byproduct emerge.

- **Objective Byproduct (Physical and Functional Issues)**
  These are measurable or observable and independent of perception. As more slices are eaten, new physical effects arise:

  - **Fullness (Physiological Saturation):** The body begins to reach a threshold where additional food is unnecessary.
  - **Slower Digestion:** The stomach has more food to process, increasing discomfort.
  - **Nutritional Excess:** Excess calories and fats may cause bodily strain.

234

- o **Potential for Nausea or Discomfort:** Overconsumption can cause bloating, sluggishness, indigestion or acid reflux.

The pizza's objective utility remains constant in that it still delivers nourishment, flavor, and caloric energy. However, new byproducts (physical saturation, discomfort, and inefficiency in digestion) emerge that reduce the perceived desirability of additional consumption.

- **Subjective Byproducts (Emotional-Cognitive Experience)**
  These byproducts are shaped by personal perception, expectations, and psychological responses:

  - o **Taste Fatigue:** The first few bites were novel and exciting, but as eating continues, the sensation becomes repetitive.
  - o **Reduction in Satisfaction:** The psychological expectation of pleasure may be met early, and additional slices do not feel as rewarding.
  - o **Regret or Guilt:** The eater may begin to feel regret due to overindulgence, especially if they are health conscious.
  - o **Desire for Variety:** The monotony of the same taste may make the current food option less and less appealing.

Even though the pizza still delivers the same taste and nutrients, objective and subjective byproducts make it feel less desirable due to physical and psychological saturation, shifting expectations, or surfacing regret. Therefore, it's not the utility that we seek to escape from, but rather the byproducts that have emerged and accumulated. The Pizza, minus any byproducts, would result in zero drop in net utility: yielding no reason to cease consuming.

(Note: Byproduct is not always subtractive in nature, where it ends up reducing perceived net available utility. One person may appreciate a slice of pizza just out of the fridge, while it may deter another. Both objective and subjective dimensions of byproduct can be experienced and perceived differently across individuals. Understanding this can lead to new markets. For example, I have yet to see pizza being sold as pre-baked but refrigerated. Such a specialized solution would remove the byproduct of needing to bake then refrigerate a pizza. Something most would likely not see as byproduct today yet does exist as a latent "under the scenes" byproduct for cold pizza lovers.)

LPI's Explanation of the Process: Instead of saying "utility declines with each slice", LPI reframes the experience as, "The utility of the pizza remains constant in delivering nourishment and taste, but as consumption continues, new byproducts emerge, both objective - physical (fullness, discomfort) and subjective- psychological (boredom, guilt), that accumulate, making continued consumption less and less appealing." This explains why a consumer stops eating. It's not because the pizza itself "declines in utility," but because the accumulation of new byproducts outweighs the benefits of continued consumption.

(Note: Neuroscience research further reinforces this perspective. Studies using fMRI scans show that as individuals consume repeated units of the same good, neural activation in reward-related regions diminishes, not necessarily because the object itself has changed, but because the brain's reference point has adjusted. This adaptation process, long recognized in psychology, aligns directly with LPI's principle that perceived utility is constrained by byproducts (e.g., taste fatigue, monotony, regret) rather than an actual loss of the product's inherent utility. In other words, consumption stops not because the pizza itself provides less nourishment or taste, but because newly emerged byproducts (physiological fullness, sensory adaptation, and cognitive biases) erode the net perceived utility.)

This reframing matters because it shifts our focus from "declining utility" to "rising byproduct." It reveals that innovation (e.g., food variety, portion control, or new flavors) is not about restoring lost utility but about addressing new byproducts. Restaurants, for example, would introduce meal customization, side dishes, or flavor variations to counteract byproduct emergence (boredom, fullness, taste fatigue). By understanding that it is not about utility decline but rather about their utility experience being detracted from, by emerging byproducts, LPI provides a more precise model of how consumers interact with products and why they stop consuming at a certain point.

Viewpoints within LPI's Utility and Byproduct Model

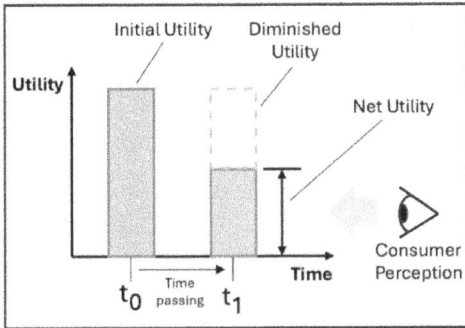

Current Economics View of Utility

Note: Not all goods experience strict linear utility degradation. External factors (maintenance, market demand, innovation) can affect utility perception.

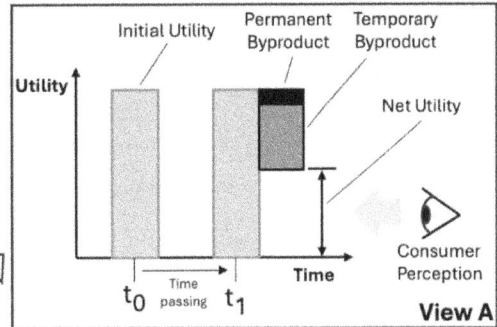

Two LPI Hypothesis Views of Utility

Note: In both views, byproduct accumulates, some may be permanent and some may be temporary. This results in net utility being restricted or constrained.

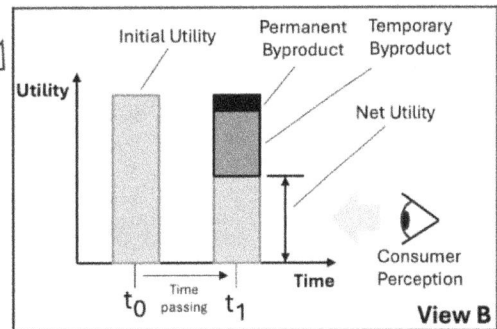

LPI's Accurate View (View A in illustration above) shows how a products utility remains constant and never really diminishes. This would completely change the framework of how global economies operate (See "Deeper Implications…" in the next chapter). However, View B is a stark reality today. The most successful businesses today have systems in place where they collect byproduct data (though they don't call it that) and they utilize it to drive resolution to byproducts in their next generation offerings (e.g. Apple, Tesla, and many other companies collect performance and incident data on their products). However, many businesses out there believe in diminishing utility at the same time. Yet, we sense something is amiss. Some of these businesses also attempt to create utility not as a response to byproduct, but as an attempt to "**restore utility**." If these offerings don't end up resolving actual byproduct, they end up falling short in the market. Which there is much evidence of across markets today.

This distinction is crucial: Economic models that assume diminishing utility typically do so without factoring in how external forces reshape perception. However, behavioral economics and neuroscience provide direct evidence that utility itself is stable, while

237

the experience of it fluctuates due to competing influences such as social comparisons, expectations, cognitive biases, and external innovations. When we recognize that utility itself is constant, the true variable in decision-making becomes not the good itself, but about the byproducts that overshadowed it, which shift over time.

1. **View A – Utility is Constant (LPI's Accurate View)**: The utility remains constant however the accumulation of intrinsic byproducts (permanent and temporary: *see Utility Principles 11 & 12 in Section 2 ahead*), of this current offering itself deprive the net available utility, by restricting or constraining it. Or, if this current offering faces competing offerings that have resolved or minimized these byproducts, these become extrinsic byproduct (via aspirational comparison) for this offering; therefore, recontextualizing it as having less net perceived utility.

2. **View B – Utility "Appears to Decline" due to Byproduct Accumulation going unaccounted for (Hidden View)**: This is how we have been perceiving utility decline all along, without accounting for or attributing byproduct to the drop in net available utility. The utility does remain constant, however, due to current economic models, we only see diminished utility. Where instead net perceived utility has been displaced by byproducts (permanent and temporary: *see Utility Principles 11 & 12 in Section 2 ahead*), reducing net available utility by restricting or constraining it, as exemplified in View A.

Many current economic models depend on the assumption that utility declines as more units are consumed, whether it's a product, service, system, experience, or even a relationship. Diminishing Marginal Utility (DMU) is the foundation for much of consumer theory today, including demand curves, pricing models, labor supply, and even happiness economics.

However, the current utility-centric model has flaws. It fails to explain certain consumer behaviors, innovation cycles, and systemic inefficiencies that emerge in real markets. These flaws act as byproducts of the traditional economic perspective, and even LPI's Hybrid model (View B) would provide a better framework for understanding and resolving them. Whereas View A reveals the true underlying story.

Implications of the two Views, the latest: "Behavioral Economics" and "Classical Economics"

Aspect	View A: LPI's Accurate View – Utility is Constant	View B: Hidden View - Utility "Appears to Decline" from unaccounted byproduct	Behavioral Economics – Psychological & Social Biases	Classical Economics – Diminishing Marginal Utility
Main driver of Innovation	Innovation aims to reduce or eliminate byproducts (that alter perceived sufficiency) through successive iterating or radical innovation, respectively	Restoring lost utility: Innovation arises because existing products lose effectiveness as byproducts accumulate.	Novelty & psychology (catering to changing preferences, biases, and emotional triggers)	Profit & competition as older offerings saturate or become less attractive
How Products Become Obsolete	Byproducts emerge, making them feel inadequate, costly or insufficient	True performance loss makes them obsolete	Perceived obsolescence driven by social cues, fashion, and emotional factors	Physical depreciation & competition from better substitutes
Market Behavior	Competing products don't "increase utility" but rather remove/reduce byproducts from existing utility	Competition involves both improving function and eliminating new inefficiencies	Herd behavior & brand loyalty: biases (status-seeking, habit) shape demand more than strict utility	Equilibrium & creative destruction: markets adapt as entrepreneurs disrupt incumbents
Consumer Decision-Making	Consumers switch when byproducts outweigh benefits even if the product still works	Consumers switch when the product no longer functions at an acceptable level	Bias-influenced choices (loss aversion, peer pressure, habit, etc.) rather than pure cost benefit	Rational choice under diminishing returns: comparing cost vs. satisfaction
Implications for Business Models	Focus on mitigating byproducts before they create dissatisfaction.	Companies must manage both byproduct reduction and performance restoration.	Focus on emotional engagement, loyalty programs, status cues.	Continuous innovation or cost leadership to stay competitive

According to LPI's Ideal View (A): Utility Remains Constant in Its Intended State

According to LPI, utility does not decline on its own; rather, byproducts emerge that cause the user to perceive a shift in utility. In LPI, utility remains constant in its intended state, but its relevance or effectiveness is eroded by the emergence and accumulation of new byproducts. Instead of saying "utility declines," LPI would argue that "Byproducts emerge and accumulate, detracting from the utility experience, ultimately rendering the utility insufficient at some personal/individual inflexion point." The product did not "lose" utility, rather, its aging, inefficiencies, the environment, impact to our emotional-cognitive states, or competing innovations created new byproducts that affected how the utility is now perceived. In other words, the product does not become "less useful" in a vacuum; rather, its effectiveness is now judged in relation to the new landscape of byproducts. This distinction shifts innovation away from trying to "restore utility" and instead focuses on addressing newly emerged and accumulating byproducts.

Instead of saying: "A decline in utility results in byproduct emergence."

LPI would frame it as: "Byproduct emergence results in a perceived detraction of existing utility."

So how can utility remain constant in its intended state? LPI argues that utility remains constant in its intended state because utility is always defined in relation to the previous byproducts it was created to resolve. That is, when a product, service, or system is created, it successfully delivers its intended utility to address those previous byproducts as long as the conditions under which it was designed remain unchanged. However, conditions do change, new byproducts emerge, shifting the perceived adequacy of the existing utility. This creates the illusion that utility has "declined," when, in reality, what has changed is the context in which the utility exists. Utility is not an abstract or standalone concept; it is contextual and reactive. It exists only because a prior byproduct required resolution.

This reality points to the perpetual cycle of innovation humanity is confined to. The ever-successive chain and branching-effect of improvements and innovations that are extensions of our natural human origin utilities: augmenting them, expanding them, and supporting them throughout human civilization.

Let's look at an example of how Utility remains constant:

Example: A Flashlight
- The utility of a flashlight is to provide illumination in the absence of light.
- As long as darkness exists (naturally occurring and human-driven byproduct), the flashlight continues to fulfill its intended function. Its utility does not decline.
- However, if other byproducts emerge (positive extrinsic byproducts that trigger aspirational comparison), such as a longer-lasting battery technology, the introduction of built-in smartphone flashlights, or night-vision glasses, the flashlight now feels less sufficient compared to newer solutions.
- However, the flashlight's original utility (providing light in darkness) remains unchanged because this utility still addresses this former byproduct. However, now it is perceived as less useful in the presence of new solutions whose ability to reduce/eliminate these new byproducts, now overshadow it (pun intended).

Thus, the utility did not decline; the landscape changed due to the emergence and awareness of new byproducts, altering the perception of this utility's sufficiency.

The Illusion of Utility decline Comes from Changing Byproducts

One may mistake byproduct emergence for utility decline because the product's effectiveness is judged against new conditions. Let's apply this hypothesis to a real-world product and demonstrate that perceived utility decline is actually due to byproduct accumulation or competing aspirational comparisons, not the loss of utility itself.

Example: A Basic Car's Utility
- The intended utility of a basic car is to transport people from point A to point B.
- This utility remains constant, if you drive the car today as you did five years ago, it still fulfills this purpose.
- However, new byproducts emerge over time:
    - **Gas prices rise**: making fuel efficiency a new concern.
    - **Maintenance & replacements**: making the time & costs burdensome
    - **Traffic noise pollution increases**: making quieter cabin's more desirable.
    - **Electric vehicles enter the market**: making gas-powered cars seem outdated.
    - **Ride-sharing services become common**: making car ownership feel unnecessary for some.

Personal Reflection: The Utility-Centric Model vs. LPI's Byproduct-Driven Model

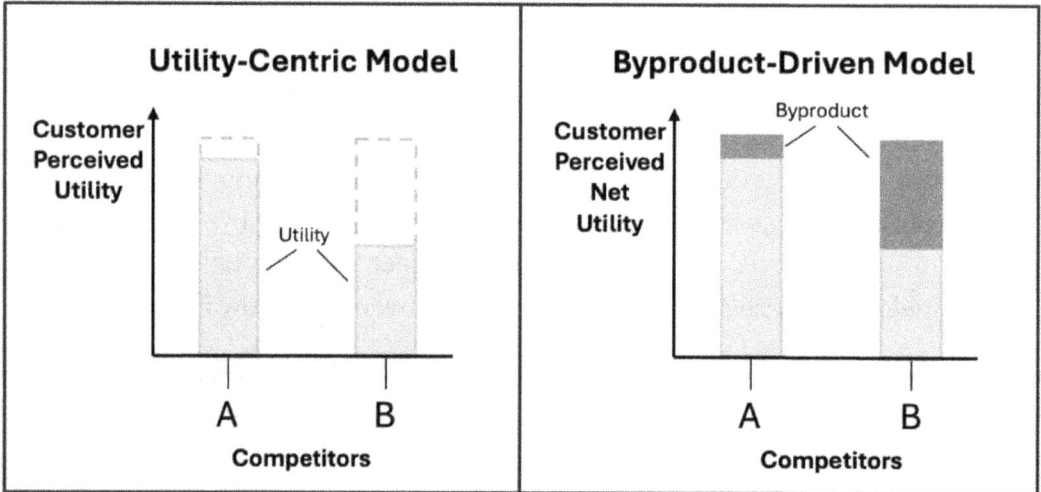

About 27 years ago, I recall sitting at a table with various cross-functional groups (engineering, product design, marketing, advanced technology, and others) grappling with the question: "What should we create next?" What functions, capabilities, features, and "look and feel" would our customers want? This was for our upcoming fourth-generation wireless handset, and we were following the same approach that countless companies before us had taken, and that many continue to use today: attempting to recoup utility in the minds of our customers and against our competitors. This is basic Utility-Centric Model innovation.

At the time, we were Competitor B (as seen in the utility-centric model above), and many of our competitors (symbolized by Competitor A) were taking our lunch. I came to believe this was simply how innovation worked. Where it's the creative process of generating ideas, building prototypes, testing them with focus groups, refining, and iterating until we found a hit. Or a miss. Short of having a crystal ball, many companies essentially compete against luck.

Suppose you look at the dashed-line empty boxes in the utility-centric model above. In that case, those represent what product developers seek to recover, the utility they aim to restore in customers' minds. Some companies develop an acute sense of what people truly seek "utility," or better yet, "seek utility to escape byproduct". It wasn't until I joined Apple that I fully understood what successful product development is really about.

From my perspective, one of Apple's general platform-sustaining business models is to let competitors shake out the market first with new features, capabilities, and technologies. Once the market speaks, Apple enters, refining the living daylights out of an offering. These refinements are Apple's way of reducing and eliminating the byproducts that first-to-market and existing competitors failed to address. In addition, Apple ensures that the byproducts that eventually will accumulate and overshadow net perceived utility, do so at a slower rate than the competition. This strategy positions Apple as Competitor A (as seen in the top-right byproduct-driven model) while placing early developers and follow-on competitors in the Competitor B position.

However, what makes Apple truly innovative, and radical, is its ability to create transformative products that address latent byproducts. These are minor inconveniences, work-arounds and inefficiencies that people have grown so accustomed to (Principle of Byproduct Normalization) that they don't recognize them as burdens. That is, until they are shown a better way. This is Byproduct-Driven Innovation at its core (Chapter 20 expands on this).

The introduction of the iPhone exemplified this principle. It merged and integrated multiple existing utilities (phone, camera, internet capability, touchscreen, and MP3 player) substantially reducing the byproduct of complexity (Principle of Byproduct Emergence through Complexity) or multiplicity that came with carrying, swapping out, and managing multiple devices (Principle of Utility Integration). Apple continues to drive innovation in this way, unmasking byproducts that people have accepted as "just how it is."

Apple has revealed latent byproducts time and again, through Apple Music, its platform-interconnected ecosystem, Apple Pay, Apple Watch, and more, establishing itself as a radical innovator across many market sectors. But this isn't luck. This is radical innovation by design. Radically transformative through [normalized] byproduct-driven innovation (viewing the world through the byproduct-driven model).

In essence, radical as well as disruptive innovation is about unearthing and resolving byproducts that masses of people have become normalized to and accepted, byproducts that people do not yet perceive as formidable burdens until a radical innovator removes the veil and shows them a better way.

As for the wireless handsets, MP3 players, cameras, and other standalone devices that Apple's iPhone displaced. Their inherent utility remained constant; they continue to address the byproducts they were originally designed to mitigate. That's why you can still find some of these for sale today. Some will eventually fade away. However, they weren't instantly rendered obsolete; rather, they were overshadowed by an extrinsic, normalized byproduct, one that reduced complexity through integration.

How LPI Aligns with the Latest Research on Perceived Utility Shifts

LPI does not reject existing economic theories outright; rather, it reframes them through a byproduct-driven model that better accounts for consumer behavior. Recent advances in neuroscience, behavioral economics, and psychology strongly support LPI's perspective that declining marginal utility is largely a perceptual phenomenon rather than an intrinsic loss of value.

Hedonic Adaptation and Byproduct Accumulation:
Psychological studies on hedonic adaptation show that our satisfaction with repeated experiences decreases not because the objects themselves change, but because our expectations adjust. LPI frames this as byproduct accumulation: The pizza's taste remains the same, but boredom, guilt, and fullness (byproducts) accumulate, making continued consumption undesirable.

Neuroscience Evidence of Perceived Utility Reduction:
fMRI research confirms that the brain exhibits diminishing activation in response to repeated rewards, meaning our neural perception of value shifts even when the object remains unchanged. This supports LPI's assertion that utility does not decrease but rather, byproducts alter its perceived net value.

Cognitive Biases and Prospect Theory:
Behavioral economics demonstrates that consumers often evaluate utility not in absolute terms, but relative to prior expectations. Loss aversion, status comparisons, and hyperbolic discounting all reveal that what appears to be diminishing utility is actually a function of shifting reference points, not inherent value loss. LPI fully integrates this insight by demonstrating that emerging byproducts create these shifts, rather than any intrinsic reduction in the product's function or benefits.

The Illusion of Declining Utility:

Traditional economic models assume utility naturally diminishes over time, but this overlooks the role of byproducts in shaping perceived value. LPI reveals that most perceived declines in utility are the result of competing byproducts overshadowing prior benefits. This explains why products that remain functionally identical (e.g., a working 4-year-old phone) still feel "obsolete" due to newer features, social comparison, and changing expectations.

CHAPTER 15
The Theory of Constant Utility

While the Byproduct Emergence Theorem (Chapter 12) reveals how and why byproduct burdens form in response to utility interaction or awareness, the Theory of Constant Utility reminds us that these burdens do not reflect a decay in utility itself, but rather an accumulation of constraints that increasingly obscure it.

The Theory of Constant Utility Under LPI

The Law of Perpetual Innovation (LPI) challenges our deeply held assumption that products and services inevitably lose their intrinsic value as time goes on. Instead, LPI advances a bold premise: once a product or service is created to address a particular byproduct, whether a deficiency, burden, or emerging aspiration, its inherent ability to perform that function remains stable. The "utility" it provides does not spontaneously diminish. Rather, the product becomes overshadowed by accumulating byproducts such as new limitations, inefficiencies, or shifts in consumer preference, making the solution appear outdated or insufficient. This gives the illusion that its utility has declined when in reality, its core utility is as potent as ever.

These byproducts have two components to them: objective and subjective. Objective byproducts are observable physical or functional burdens, for example, mechanical wear, regulatory hurdles, or extra effort required by a design flaw. Subjective byproducts are our emotional-cognitive reactions to these objective factors. They can be felt as negative, manifesting as unresolved deficiencies from expectation deviation (η), that make us feel frustration or dissatisfaction. They can also be felt as positive, manifesting as unfulfilled aspirations through aspirational comparison (δ), that trigger urgency, excitement or longing. Byproducts can likewise be intrinsic to the product itself (e.g., frequent sharpening of a pencil, or battery degradation in a smartphone) or extrinsic, arising from interactions with external factors (e.g., new cultural norms, competitive offerings/technologies, or environmental regulations). Over time, these accumulating byproducts constrain or limit the net perceived utility of a product's otherwise constant function.

Because of these emerging constraints, some temporary and fixable, some permanent or catastrophic, <u>people may appear to abandon the core utility itself (classical economics view). When in fact, according to LPI, we do not truly seek to give up that underlying benefit. We really seek to escape the byproducts overshadowing it</u>. If we ate more and more slices of pizza but never felt full, bored, or concerned about health impacts, we really would have no reason to stop. The fact that we do stop arises from this accumulation of byproducts such as fullness, flavor fatigue, fear of weight gain and so on, which together constrain the pizza's constant function of offering enjoyment and caloric sustenance.

This premise is pivotal to the perpetual innovation loop championed by LPI. Every product arises to solve an existing byproduct, yet in doing so, it eventually generates fresh byproducts, some intrinsic, like mechanical wear or routine maintenance, and others extrinsic, such as regulatory burdens or a change in user expectations. As these byproducts accumulate, the once-sufficient solution starts to feel inadequate, prompting the creation of new innovations that resolve those emergent issues. The cycle repeats indefinitely because mitigating one set of byproducts, through a fresh utility offering, leads to the emergence of others that must be tackled in time to come. Consequently, innovation is never about "restoring lost utility" so much as it is about systematically confronting newly surfaced or persistent byproducts.

However, some byproduct events can catastrophically sever a product's ability to deliver its utility altogether, like a smartphone run over by a truck, or a worn-down pencil snapped in two. In such cases, the net available utility is obliterated because the permanent byproduct accumulation surpasses any fixable threshold. Yet if the smartphone in question continuously backed up its data to the cloud, the byproduct impact is significantly less severe: only the device's physical function is lost, but all its data, settings, apps and content; its intrinsic utility, remain constant and preserved. The smartphone itself is but a shell to the many underlying core utilities that it houses.

The Illusion of "Declining Utility"

Traditional economics teaches us that utility "naturally" fades the more we consume a good or rely on a service. The law of diminishing marginal utility, for example, suggests that each additional unit of a product yields progressively less satisfaction. According to LPI, this conventional view stems from a fundamental misunderstanding. People often report feeling less satisfied not because the product's essential capacity has shriveled, but because fresh constraints gather around it. These new burdens can be as trivial as clutter or as serious as external regulatory pressures, all of which work together to overshadow the product's constant capacity to perform its job.

A concrete illustration is a smartphone that felt perfect when it was new. Months later, users say, "My phone just isn't as good anymore." LPI contends that the phone's core function of running apps, making calls, and connecting you to the internet, remains as strong as when you first unboxed it. The illusion of decline arises from new byproducts: a battery that charges more slowly (objective, intrinsic wear ε), software bloat from constant updates (intrinsic and extrinsic ε), user envy of newer models (extrinsic subjective, aspirational comparison, δ), or user dissatisfaction stemming from unmet expectations after an update (intrinsic subjective, expectation deviation, η). The phone's functional capacity does not degrade in some intrinsic sense. Rather, these swirling new burdens overshadow its original capabilities, curbing the net perceived utility and making it appear as though the utility itself has diminished.

Constant Utility Theory does not deny that products get replaced or break; it redefines the reason they become inadequate. Every product's functional capacity remains stable unless a catastrophic byproduct accumulation ends it. All apparent declines in utility are, in truth, the direct or indirect result of emerging burdens termed as byproducts (emotional, cognitive, technical, social, economic, environmental), ultimately giving birth to perpetual innovation.

Examples in Action

One way to clarify how utility remains constant is to examine specific products, each of which once solved a particular byproduct yet now seems less adequate because new constraints have emerged.

- **The horse-drawn buggy** illustrates the same dynamic. It once revolutionized transport, allowing faster travel than walking while carrying more cargo. That core capacity never "decayed," but the rise of cities created serious byproducts like piles of manure in streets, the cost of feeding and stabling horses, and slower travel in an era that demanded speedier means. The motorized car addressed these byproducts by eliminating horse manure, running on fuel instead, and traveling at faster speeds. In adopting automobiles, people did not reject the horse-drawn carriage for losing its inherent ability to move from point A to point B; rather, they preferred a solution that tackled the accumulated byproducts, overshadowing the buggy's sufficiency.

248

- **A basic gas-powered car** provides a further demonstration. As long as it is maintained and given fuel, it performs the same function it did when it was first built. Transporting people from one place to another. However, many drivers perceive older cars as no longer meeting modern needs because new byproducts have emerged over time. Rising gas prices (extrinsic, economic) make fuel-thirsty cars feel burdensome, climate concerns (extrinsic, environmental) highlight emissions, sophisticated new features (extrinsic, technological) appear in competing vehicles and shifting social norms (extrinsic, cultural) favor quieter or more luxurious rides make older models feel burdensome. Although the car's capacity for mobility remains the same, these issues accumulate, leading people to label the car "less useful." LPI would say the old car's utility is actually intact but overshadowed by byproducts that were once negligible or nonexistent. Classic cars are a prime example of constant utility. These vehicles have been culturally reframed as "classic," providing nostalgic utility alongside their original constant core utility.

A Full Cycle Example of Constant Utility and Byproduct Emergence

Nothing clarifies the interplay between constant utility and perpetual innovation, like following a product (or system) from its inception through multiple cycles of byproduct accumulation and renewal. Imagine a household heating scenario. Initially, you might rely on a wood-burning furnace to solve the problem of a cold climate, a naturally occurring byproduct of environmental exposure. The furnace reliably converts wood to warmth, fulfilling its intended function. For a while, this system remains sufficient and may appear to have no decline in utility. Over time, however, a range of byproducts emerge. Ash and soot accumulate inside the furnace (intrinsic, objective byproduct, driven by thermodynamic inefficiency ϵ), requiring regular cleaning, ordering and chopping wood and causing annoyance and hindrance (extrinsic, subjective byproduct due to cognitive effort and inconvenience via expectation deviation η). Metal grates wear down from repeated heating and cooling (intrinsic, permanent byproducts via ϵ). Complaints emerge that wood smoke is affecting air quality in the neighborhood (extrinsic, objective, ϵ) and fueling social pressure (extrinsic, subjective via aspirational comparison δ). Eventually, these accumulating burdens begin to overshadow the furnace's original value. The user feels that the furnace is no longer "as good," not because its fundamental ability to generate heat has vanished, but because so many additional byproducts now accompany its ongoing operation.

In response, a gas furnace is introduced (new utility). It preserves the same constant baseline utility (U_0) of generating warmth, but it has mitigated the prior byproducts. There is no daily ash to dump, less environmental smoke, and reduced manual and mental labor. When people switch, it is not because the wood furnace lost its utility, but because the new system addresses the byproducts $B(t)$ overshadowing the older one. For a while, this innovation is widely adopted.

But over time, new byproducts surface: pipeline leaks (intrinsic objective, ϵ), price volatility (extrinsic subjective, η), carbon emissions (extrinsic objective, ϵ), and new regulatory hurdles (extrinsic subjective, η). These fresh byproduct burdens trigger yet another cycle of innovation, perhaps via electric heat pumps or solar heating. Once again, constant utility remains intact, but perception shifts due to byproduct accumulation.

This cycle continues indefinitely. At each stage, the core utility does not degrade. It is the surrounding burdens, intrinsic and extrinsic, objective and subjective, that accumulate and ultimately prompt further innovation.

Nevertheless, catastrophic failure can sever a product's ability to deliver utility entirely. If a furnace cracks irreparably or a smartphone is run over by a truck, the system's net available utility is nullified. Such events can be understood as impulse-based byproduct spikes sudden and overwhelming $B(t)$ that surpass U_0 in a single moment.

The Constant Utility Theorem

Supporting Proof Statement for the Constant Utility Theorem

A product or system, a "good" in economic terms, is an objectively real entity. It has mass, form, function, and operation within the physical world. However, utility, the value a user experiences from engaging with that good, is not a physical property of the object itself. Rather, utility is a subjective phenomenological experience: a mental state evoked in the mind of the user through their interaction with the good. Therefore, no product "contains" utility intrinsically. It is not utility itself, but a medium through which utility is accessed or delivered.

This distinction is foundational to the Constant Utility Theorem. If a product serves as a stable, constant medium, then its designed capacity to perform its intended function, its baseline utility U_0, remains inherently stable over time. It does not degrade by itself. The function for which the product was designed remains technically intact, unless physically disrupted. A red guitar designed to appeal visually retains that visual appeal

250

capability; a chair designed to support weight does not forget how to do so. The product's utility potential is constant in structural terms.

What does change, however, is not the product's capacity, but the perception of the utility it delivers. This perceived erosion does not stem from the utility itself diminishing, but rather from the accumulation of burdens, what LPI defines as byproducts. Just as utility is delivered subjectively through the experience of the objective product, byproducts also exist along two axes: the objective, such as physical wear, clutter, or heat; and the subjective, such as frustration, boredom, or fatigue. Byproducts are the forces that overshadow the constant baseline utility, not reduce it.

Therefore, when users feel that a product or service "isn't what it used to be," the Constant Utility Theorem states this is not because the underlying utility U_0 has deteriorated, but because the total byproduct burden $B(t)$ has increased. Whether due to system inefficiency ϵ, expectation deviation η, or aspirational comparison δ; the user perceives growing tension, dissonance, or cost in extracting that utility. The result is not a decline in the utility's function, but in its net perceived value, expressed as:

$$U_{perceived}(t) = U_0 - B(t)$$

This relationship upholds the Constant Utility Theorem's core claim: Utility does not decay by itself, only its experience does, as byproduct burden accumulates. Products and services are structurally stable in what they are designed to offer; it is our emotional, cognitive, and energetic interpretation of them that changes as time, use, and context evolve.

Thus, the Constant Utility Theorem is not merely a statement about engineering or physical degradation. It is a universal claim about the perceptual stability of function and the cognitive fragility of satisfaction, shaped by entropy, expectation, and emotional comparison. Over time, it is not the product, service, system or personal relationship's ability to deliver its intended function that disappears, it is the individual's satisfaction in receiving that function amidst growing burden, that fades. What we abandon is not function, it is function under burden. We do not walk away from utility, we walk away from the dissatisfaction of extracting it under burden, and toward the promise of a utility that feels freer, lighter and more attainable.

Theorem Statement:

In any real-world human-product-environment system, the inherent capacity of a product, system, or service to deliver its ideal utility baseline U_0, remains constant over time t. However, the net perceived utility $U_{perceived}(t)$ declines not because baseline utility U_0 diminishes, but because cumulative byproduct burden $B(t)$ increases. When the total burden exceeds a system's or user's tolerance threshold, abandonment, replacement, or innovation occurs.

Formal Proof and Mathematical Structure

$$U_{perceived}(t) = U_0 - B(t)$$

Where:

- U_0: Baseline constant utility. The idealized, inherent functional value a product or system was designed to deliver. This value does not degrade by itself.
- $B(t)$: Cumulative byproduct burden over time t. This includes all internal and external burdens that erode perceived value.

Where $B(t)$ is structured as:

$$B(t) = B_{\text{temp}}(t) + B_{\text{perm}}(t) + B_{\text{impulse}}(t)$$

Reads as: The total burden experienced at time t is composed of reversible temporary burdens, permanent burdens that accumulate structurally, and impulse-based catastrophic burdens. These form the composite experience of decline despite U_0 being stable.

Where:

- $B_{temp}(t)$: Temporary and reversible burdens (e.g., dust, dullness, minor emotional fatigue/frustration). These can often be reduced or reset.
- $B_{perm}(t)$: Permanent, irreversible burdens (e.g., wear, corrosion, outdated tech, regulatory obsolescence).
- $B_{impulse}(t)$: Sudden catastrophic burden events that instantly nullify utility (e.g., device destruction, fire damage, existential recontextualization).

These byproduct categories $B_{temp}(t), B_{perm}(t), B_{impulse}(t)$, handle how byproducts evolve over time or appear suddenly, but they do not explicitly distinguish whether byproducts are intrinsic to the product or system (wear and tear, mechanical aging,

252

software bloat) or extrinsic (shifts in consumer tastes, regulatory changes, competition). We can now refine to include both the dimension of "how byproducts unfold" (temporary, permanent, impulse) and "where byproducts originate" (intrinsic vs. extrinsic).

One approach is to incorporate both perspectives, refined into:

$$B(t) = B_{temp(in)}(t) + B_{temp(ex)}(t) + B_{perm(in)}(t) + B_{perm(ex)}(t) + B_{impulse(in)}(t) + B_{impulse(ex)}(t)$$

Where:
- $B_{temp(in)}(t)$: Intrinsic temporary burdens (e.g., dust in hardware).
- $B_{temp(ex)}(t)$: Extrinsic temporary burdens (e.g., short lived fashion cycle).
- $B_{perm(in)}(t)$: Intrinsic permanent burdens (e.g., mechanical erosion).
- $B_{perm(ex)}(t)$: Extrinsic permanent burdens (e.g., permanent shift in regulation or culture).
- $B_{impulse(in)}(t)$: Intrinsic catastrophic events (e.g., sudden device failure).
- $B_{impulse(ex)}(t)$: Extrinsic catastrophic disruptions (e.g., an abrupt legal ruling or immediate obsolescence from superior competitor tech).

Chapter 12 demonstrated that these burdens always have an objective (measurable flaws via ϵ) and subjective (emotionally or cognitively interpreted burdens via η and δ) component.

This confirms that burden accumulates along multiple pathways, but always grows with time or exposure.

Now:

$$\text{If } B(t) < U_0 \text{ then } U_{perceived}(t) > 0$$

$$\text{If } B(t) \geq U_0 \text{ then } U_{perceived}(t) \leq 0$$

Hence, U_0 is constant, and the only factor driving perceived utility decay is $B(t)$.

Corollaries

Corollary 1: Utility does not decay on its own

$$\text{If } B(t) = 0 \text{ then } U_{perceived}(t) = U_0$$

Reads as: If there are no burdens, the net perceived utility equals its inherent baseline constant capacity.

Corollary 2: Utility only becomes obsolete through burden accumulation

$$\text{If } B(t) \geq U_0, \text{ then } U_{perceived}(t) \leq 0$$

Reads as: Once burden equals or surpasses the original utility capacity, the system is functionally obsolete.

Corollary 3: Byproduct emergence is guaranteed

From the Byproduct Emergence Theorem:

$$B(t) = \Psi(\epsilon, \eta, \delta) > 0$$

Corollary 4: Innovation occurs when burden crosses a threshold

This leads into the Inflection Threshold discussed below.

The Utility Abandonment Condition, aka The Byproduct Tolerance Threshold

To understand when a user abandons a utility, it is not sufficient to observe the presence of byproducts alone. The Law of Perpetual Innovation (LPI) proves that byproducts are inevitable (Chapter 12), but it does not claim that all byproducts instantly drive behavioral change. What causes change is the moment when total byproduct burden surpasses the tolerance threshold for that burden. The Byproduct Inflection Threshold is the critical burden point at which an individual or system can no longer tolerate the overshadowing effects of byproduct burden $B(t)$, prompting utility abandonment, adaptation, or innovation. This is not purely a physical limit, but a psychological emotional-cognitive tipping point shaped by user sensitivity, cultural norms, and entropy tolerance.

Formal Definition: Byproduct Tolerance Threshold

Let:
- U_0: Baseline constant utility (maximum attainable free of burden)
- $B(t)$: Total byproduct burden at time t, (from Chapter 12) defined as:

254

$$B(t) = \Psi(\epsilon, \eta, \delta) = B_o(t) + B_s(t)$$

- α: Entropy sensitivity coefficient (how strongly burden is perceived from disorder)
- β: Baseline energy cost (irreducible effort to extract utility)

We define the Byproduct Tolerance Threshold as a function:

$$T_b = f(\alpha, \beta, U_0)$$

Reads as: The burden tolerance threshold T_b is a function of user sensitivity to entropy α, irreducible human energy cost β, and the product's constant baseline utility U_0.

Complete Inflection Condition

A user will abandon or reject a utility when the total byproduct burden equals or exceeds their threshold to tolerate it:

$$B(t) \geq T_b(\alpha, \beta, U_0)$$

Reads as: If total byproduct at time t equals or exceeds the user's tolerance threshold, the utility is no longer perceived as net-beneficial.

This expression constitutes the Byproduct Inflection Point or **Utility Abandonment Condition**.

Expanded Functional Form

The function T_b can be approximated linearly for general application:

$$T_b = \alpha U_0 + \beta$$

Reads as: The threshold at which a user abandons utility rises with their sensitivity to entropy α, scaled by the constant baseline utility U_0, and offset by the irreducible energy cost β.

Interpretation:
- High α: Even minor byproduct accumulation quickly becomes intolerable (low tolerance).

- Low α: Greater resilience to disorder (high tolerance).
- β ensures that even in perfect systems, there is some minimal cognitive/physical cost to using utility, which still contributes to burden perception.

Individualized Burden Tolerance

While $T_b = \alpha U_0 + \beta$ serves as a generalized model, personalized threshold functions require additional parameters:

Let:
- κ: Cognitive resilience coefficient (resistance to emotional friction)
- θ: Contextual burden elasticity (influence of situational factors: urgency, fatigue, risk tolerance)
- μ: Memory intensity coefficient (how strongly past burdens amplify current perception, aka Remembered Utility)

Then, a more individualized form might be:

$$T_b^{(i)} = \alpha U_0 + \beta + \kappa - \theta + \mu$$

Reads as: The individualized tolerance threshold includes the base entropy (α) and effort (β) terms, plus modifiers for emotional resilience (κ), contextual sensitivity (θ), and cumulative memory (μ) of prior burdens.

Even in this extended form, $B(t) \geq T_b^{(i)}$ remains the tipping point for abandonment, rejection, or forescension.

VERY IMPORTANT NOTE: On Remembered Utility and the Role of μ (mu)
While the individualized Byproduct Tolerance Threshold introduces μ, the memory intensity coefficient, to account for how prior emotional-cognitive burdens affect current utility perception, LPI intentionally restricts its usage. μ captures the idea of Remembered Utility, or more precisely, the lingering emotional residue of prior experiences with the same product, service, or system. This memory imprint, whether of joy, disappointment, surprise, or betrayal, can color a user's current threshold for tolerance. For example, someone who had a past negative customer service encounter may more quickly reach their abandonment point even after small new annoyances. However, despite its psychological relevance, μ was deliberately left out of the formal emotional-cognitive byproduct emergence model, that is, from the expectation

deviation term η and aspirational comparison δ, because it is already implicitly embedded within them. Human expectations and aspirations are not formed in a vacuum; they draw heavily from prior memories and emotional baselines. Including μ explicitly within $\Psi\,(\varepsilon, \eta, \delta)$ would double-count its influence and obscure the simplicity and clarity needed for predictive modeling.

Additionally, μ remains excluded from the core drivers of innovation under LPI for a deeper reason: memory is notoriously unreliable. Cognitive psychology and behavioral economics have shown that recollection is prone to recency bias, peak-end effects, affective forecasting errors, and hindsight distortion. People often misremember how bad or good an experience actually was, relying on exaggerated highs or lows rather than accurate averages. Because of this, μ introduces a degree of interpretive volatility that reduces the model's precision. The same logic applies to κ, the cognitive resilience coefficient, and θ, the contextual burden elasticity. κ reflects how emotionally or psychologically resilient a user is under pressure, whether they interpret burden as manageable or overwhelming. θ accounts for situational variability, such as fatigue, urgency, or risk, which can dramatically modulate tolerance in the moment. These variables are essential for fine-tuning behavioral predictions in high-fidelity models, but like μ, they are not modeled within the core emergence function because they operate as modifiers of user response, not as origins of byproduct emergence.

Therefore, μ, κ, and θ are used only within the extended form of the Utility Abandonment Condition $T_b^{(i)}$, where individualized tolerance modeling is necessary. Until behavioral science advances allow for more reliable quantification of remembered utility, μ will remain a secondary modifier, useful only for adjusting personalized thresholds. For now, α (entropy sensitivity) and β (irreducible effort) remain the primary drivers of behavioral change, as they more accurately capture systemic burden and real-time cognitive cost, without the distortions introduced by memory-based bias.

Relationship to Time

Although T_b is not a direct function of time, time is indirectly present through the time-dependent accumulation of $B(t)$. Since byproduct grows (or spikes) over time:

$$\frac{dB}{dt} > 0 \Rightarrow B(t) \rightarrow T_b$$

Reads as: The longer a utility is used, the more likely its byproduct burden will reach the abandonment threshold, unless innovation reduces $B(t)$ through updates, maintenance, or design improvements.

Corollaries

Corollary 1: Innovation Trigger Condition

$$B(t) \geq T_b \Rightarrow I(t+1) = f(B(t))$$

Reads as: When burden exceeds the tolerance threshold, innovation becomes behaviorally necessary to restore utility viability.

Corollary 2: High Tolerance Users Extend Utility Lifecycle

$$T_b \uparrow \Rightarrow \text{Lifespan of } U_0 \uparrow$$

Reads as: Users with high tolerance for burden prolong the functional viability of a product or service, delaying innovation pressure.

Corollary 3: Sensitivity-Driven Market Segmentation

Different user groups have different α and κ values, allowing innovators to target upgrades, redesigns, or interventions toward users most likely to reach their T_b soonest.

Educational Interpretation

The Constant Utility Theorem teaches us that utility does not degrade; perception does. What declines is not function, but user willingness to endure the burdens accompanying that function. These burdens may be small at first, but over time, via entropy, expectation gaps, or aspirational comparisons, they compound. Eventually, the user "tips" at T_b.

Understanding this equation allows:
- Businesses to forecast product lifecycles and design interventions.
- Engineers to distinguish between design flaws and user fatigue.
- Policymakers to reform innovation incentives by burden management, not raw output.

Constant Utility Theorem Conclusion

The Constant Utility Theorem affirms a foundational truth of the Law of Perpetual Innovation: It is not the product's purpose that decays, but its perceived relevance under mounting byproduct burden. Utility is stable; what shifts is the emotional, physical, and contextual weight that obscures it.

By defining utility and byproduct burden separately and modeling the threshold of tolerance T_b, we gain the tools to diagnose decline, predict demand, and guide responsible innovation. The Byproduct Tolerance Threshold T_b formalizes when users defect from utility not because utility is lost, but because byproduct has grown too heavy to bear. It links human cognition, thermodynamic systems, and innovation behavior into a single inflection framework that completes the Constant Utility Theorem. Innovation, then, is not a quest for new utility, but a quest to relieve the rising burdens that distort our experience of utility already present.

Deeper Implications and the Flaws LPI Can Resolve

When we accept that utility remains constant, we uncover serious limitations in many conventional economic models. Traditional theory suggests that people stop consuming a good because the satisfaction (utility) they derive from each additional unit diminishes. But under the Law of Perpetual Innovation (LPI), people stop consuming not because the good's inherent utility has faded, but because byproducts have accumulated, ranging from clutter, saturation, and mild annoyance to health risks, environmental burdens, or awareness of superior alternatives.

Reframing our systems of business, policy, and social infrastructure around byproduct accumulation instead of utility erosion can drive more effective interventions. If we recognize that utility stays constant while burdens (objective and subjective) increase, we are better equipped to prevent dissatisfaction, anticipate innovation needs, and preserve long-term value. What follows are examples of how adopting a constant utility worldview reshapes critical economic and policy frameworks.

A New Type of GDP

The way nations track growth and prosperity is typically through Gross Domestic Product (GDP). Conventional wisdom says that as GDP rises, so does overall utility or well-being. Yet, whenever production climbs, corresponding negative byproducts such as pollution, resource depletion, or social anxiety grow as well. Under a constant-utility worldview, these negative byproducts may overshadow the gains from increased production, resulting in less net improvement in genuine social welfare.

Suppose we recognized that every productive act preserves its inherent utility but simultaneously introduces new burdens (byproducts). In that case, we might design "net utility growth" or "genuine progress" indices rather than relying strictly on GDP. Policymakers could systematically factor in environmental destruction, mental and physical health issues, or social disruption subtracted from the raw output gains. Doing so might reveal that some forms of production yield a net negative once byproducts are accounted for, even if the market values them highly. This radical shift could encourage industries to minimize harmful side effects rather than just maximizing production and externalizing the resulting costs. This can reshape how governments rank prosperity, rewarding sustainable industries that keep byproduct accumulation low, rather than merely maximizing output.

Traditional Model to GDP

$$GDP = C + I + G + (X - M)$$

Where:
- C : Consumer spending
- I : Business investment
- G : Government spending
- X : Exports
- M : Imports

This equation implicitly assumes that each unit of production adds positive utility to society, ignoring potential negative externalities.

LPI's Net Utility GDP

To incorporate byproducts, define:

$$\text{Net Utility GDP} = \left(C + I + G + (X - M) \right) - B_{macro}$$

Where:

- B_{macro}: Cumulative macro-level byproduct at a societal scale, such as:

260

- Environmental: Pollution, climate change costs, waste management burdens
  - Social: Rising mental and physical health crises, social unrest
  - Economic: Overleveraging, structural unemployment
  - Technological: Overreliance on automation, digital addiction

Under LPI, if B_{macro} grows faster than raw output, net prosperity might stagnate or decline even though nominal GDP rises.

Deeper Explanation
- **Why This Matters**: Traditional economics can cheer a factory's production growth while ignoring the pollution overshadowing local living standards. LPI's vantage ensures we see that the product's constant utility in the economy is, in part, overshadowed by negative byproducts.
- **Policy Relevance**: If a region invests heavily in high-GDP but highly polluting industries, real net utility might be small. Factoring in B_{macro} pushes governments to adopt policies aimed at minimizing overshadowing burdens like carbon caps or mental health support, rather than blindly chasing growth.

Illustration:
- A city experiences a $1 billion increase in factory output but also a $0.8 billion cost from smog-related healthcare expenses.
  - **Traditional GDP** sees a +1.0B rise.
  - **LPI Net Utility GDP** sees a net +0.2B (1.0B minus 0.8B in byproduct). If more hidden byproducts exist (ecosystem loss, stress), the real gain might be negligible or negative.

More Accurate Predictions of Consumer Behavior

Classical demand curves in economics assume people buy less of something as they consume more, because each additional unit presumably yields less utility. Reality, however, is often more nuanced. Under LPI, people stop consuming not due to a decline in utility itself, but because each additional unit accumulates new burdens; byproducts, that overshadow the utility.

Sometimes, consumers continue purchasing repeated versions of a product if the byproducts remain minimal, such as collecting digital media that takes up little space. Other times, they stop after just a few units if burdens escalate quickly, such as with sugary foods that lead to health concerns, guilt, or social stigma.

Take coffee as an example: people do not necessarily get "bored" of coffee. Its taste or caffeine utility does not decline intrinsically. Rather, they may cut back because of jitters, acidity, or growing concerns about cost or health. These are subjective and objective byproducts that accumulate and eventually reduce the net perceived utility. If coffee companies address these byproducts, through half-caff options, gentler blends, variety packs, or discounts, loyalty can persist indefinitely. The product's intrinsic utility (U_0) remains constant. It is the rising $B(Q)$ that pushes users away.

Traditional Model: Diminishing Marginal Utility

$$MU(Q) = \frac{dU}{dQ}, \quad \text{with } MU(Q) \text{ decreasing as } Q \text{ increases.}$$

Where:
- Q : Quantity consumed
- U : Total utility from consumption

The classical rationale: as consumption rises, the satisfaction from each additional unit diminishes.

LPI's Byproduct-Based Marginal Perceived Utility

Net perceived utility under LPI is expressed as:

$$U_{perceived}(Q) = U_0 - B(Q)$$

Then:

$$MU_{perceived}(Q) = \frac{d(U_0 - B(Q))}{dQ} = 0 - \frac{dB(Q)}{dQ} = -B'(Q)$$

Where:
- U_0: The stable baseline utility of each unit (e.g., each chocolate bar taste remains constant).
- $B(Q)$: The cumulative byproducts introduced by each additional unit (e.g., clutter, health concerns).

Deeper Explanation
- **Why People Stop Buying**: They do not tire of a product's utility, but rather accumulated burdens such as guilt, storage concerns, or side effects detract from the net benefit of the experience.
- **Strategic Insight**: Marketers aiming to sustain demand should reduce or mitigate these overshadowing burdens, varying flavors, offering portion or satiation mitigation, providing disposal or recycling solutions, reduced complexity or learning curves, rather than "trying to restore lost inherent satisfaction," which never actually declines according to LPI.

Illustration:
- A local gym sees many members discontinue their memberships before meeting fitness goals, not because exercise itself loses its health benefits, but because crowded facilities, inconvenient hours, and parking hassles overshadow the same workout value. If the gym expanded off-peak class options or introduced virtual training, it directly tackles these overshadowing issues and could keep members engaged.

Rethinking Labor Market Misconceptions

The conventional labor model suggests that at some point, workers experience negative marginal utility for each additional hour or day worked, leading them to reduce labor supply or quit. LPI's constant-utility viewpoint implies that the job's inherent utility (benefits), such as wages, human connection, and sense of purpose, continues to hold steady unless catastrophic byproducts wholly destroy that utility. The real reason people disengage or resign is not an inevitable decline in the "value" of work, but rather the buildup of negative byproducts: burnout, poor management, a sense of stagnation, and so forth.

Companies that see job dissatisfaction as an accumulation of burdens rather than as diminishing returns on labor can intervene more effectively. Instead of simply throwing higher salaries at the problem, they may introduce flexible schedules, reduce toxic managerial practices, or bring in mechanisms that promote professional growth. By systematically eliminating or mitigating these byproduct burdens, the organization can maintain or even restore the net value employees derive from their positions.

Traditional Model: Disutility of Labor

A simplified labor supply model posits:

$$\text{Work Utility} = W - D(L)$$

Where:
- W: Wage (monetary benefit)
- $D(L)$: Disutility of labor (fatigue, effort), typically rising with hours L.

Workers quit or reduce hours if $D(L)$ surpasses W.

LPI-Based Labor Model

We can frame an LPI-based formula:

$$U_{job}(t) = U_0(\text{income, purpose, structure}) - B_{work}(t)$$

Where:
- $U_0(...)$: Baseline utility of the job (salary, identity, social status).
- $B_{work}(t)$: Accumulated workplace byproducts overshadowing that baseline (stress, long commute, management issues, stagnation, poor work-life balance).

When $B_{work}(t) \geq U_0(...)$, the employee's net satisfaction hits zero (or negative), leading them to exit.

Deeper Explanation
- **Why Workers Burn Out**: The job's monetary and psychological benefits do not shrink on their own. Rather, daily stress, poor workplace culture and environment-based burdens grow, overshadowing the consistent positives.
- **Employer Solutions**: Reducing byproducts (e.g., flexible hours, mental health support, improvements in management structures or personnel, cultural improvements) can restore net satisfaction without necessarily raising wages.

Illustration:
- A coder enjoys the stable salary and creative challenge. Over time, unchecked crunch hours, toxic leadership, or repetitive over-burdening tasks overshadow that stable baseline. They quit, even though the job's utility, income, plus creative coding, never actually "declined." Instead, the accumulation of

264

overshadowing burdens (workplace accumulated byproduct) forced the coder out.

Innovation Outcomes and Predictability

Traditional Approach: Schumpeterian "Creative Destruction"

A well-known classical perspective on innovation originates from Joseph Schumpeter's concept of creative destruction. It suggests that major leaps in innovation occur when entrepreneurs or firms introduce disruptive technologies or processes that destroy old industries by making them obsolete. Although not usually represented by a formula, one could distill Schumpeter's view into a generalized "innovation profitability" equation:

$$\Pi_{innovation} = \text{(Revenues from novel products)} - \text{(Costs of R\&D and market entry)}$$

Firms innovate when their expected profit $\Pi_{innovation}$ is positive, for example, when the new product or process stands to return more than it costs to develop, produce, and distribute. Traditional theory typically focuses on revenue potential from "new utility" or efficiency gains, assuming old solutions lose favor in the face of "superior" offerings.

LPI Approach: The Utility–Byproduct Loop and Targeted Innovation

Under the Law of Perpetual Innovation (LPI), innovation outcomes follow a predictable loop guided by a constant baseline utility overshadowed by accumulating byproducts. Here, U_0 denotes the same core function provided by both the incumbent solution and any successor solution, like "watch a movie," "listen to music," or "call someone on the phone." In other words, the functional outcome remains stable, but what changes is how overshadowing burdens are managed in each iteration. (*Note: watch a movie is in fact "observe narrative performance art," as to clarify that whether it's a live play or a movie, the core Utility stands. In these examples we've simplified the examples. See Chapter 28, on Radical Innovation, for deeper insight.*)

A more explicit formula might be framed as:

$$\text{Innovation Payoff (IP)} = [\, U_0 - B_{incumbent}(t)\,] - [\, U_0 - B_{innovation}(t)\,]$$

Here:

- U_0 = The stable baseline utility across old and new solutions (both deliver the same essential outcome).
- $B_{incumbent}(t)$ = The overshadowing byproducts of the incumbent solution at time t.
- $B_{innovation}(t)$ = The byproducts introduced (or avoided) by the new solution.

Firms, inventors, or entrepreneurs compare overshadowing burdens in the old product's net state to those anticipated in the new one. Innovation thrives if the new solution significantly removes or reduces $B_{incumbent}(t)$ relative to $B_{innovation}(t)$. In short, under LPI:

- The Old Utility is overshadowed by burdens (i.e., the byproducts that accumulate over time).
- A New Utility emerges explicitly to resolve those byproducts, not because old utility "declined" in its functional capacity, but because overshadowing burdens are increasingly intolerable.
- <u>Innovation is more predictable</u> because you identify which overshadowing byproducts are most pressing, then build solutions targeting them.

If we reorganize that payoff to highlight net byproduct difference, we get:

$$ IP \approx B_{incumbent}(t) - B_{innovation}(t) $$

Hence, if $B_{incumbent}(t)$ is large, and the new product's burdens $B_{innovation}(t)$ remain small, IP is positive, and adoption is likely.

Deeper Explanation

- **Rooted in Byproduct Resolution:** Traditional creative destruction emphasizes "disruptive technologies" that appear more cost-efficient or introduce so-called "new utility." Under LPI, the new solution systematically eliminates overshadowing byproducts (lack of convenience, user frustrations, environmental damages, or legal constraints) that hamper the incumbent. The underlying function U_0 (like reading a book, communicating verbally, or traveling from point A to B) does not degrade; its overshadowing burdens are what become intolerable. (*Note: It's important to emphasize that these* *byproducts can become intolerable before a better offering. However, they can also come to be perceived as intolerable because a better offering (higher potential utility via aspirational comparison η) is brought into awareness.)*

- **Predictability:** Rather than experiencing random waves of disruption, LPI implies a structured approach to innovation: identify where incumbents are failing (where $B_{incumbent}(t)$ is spiking) and create a new solution to reduce those burdens. This yields a more methodical path to success than guesswork or hype over "superior tech."

- **Longer-Term Outcomes:** Even after a new solution supersedes the old, it develops its own overshadowing byproducts over time ($B_{innovation}(t)$ grows). This perpetual accumulation triggers yet another wave of invention, continuing the cycle. In essence, the overshadowing shift never stops because every solution eventually accrues byproduct burdens.

Contrast with Schumpeter

- **Schumpeterian View:** Innovation arrives in bursts, older industries lose out to radical newcomers, and the economic cycle can appear chaotic or sporadic.

- **LPI View:** Innovation is ongoing and can be deliberately steered by monitoring emergent or latent byproducts overshadowing existing solutions. This approach increases predictability by letting firms or entrepreneurs systematically remove overshadowing burdens, the surest path to meaningful transformation.

In bridging to radical innovations, we see they often arise when $B_{incumbent}(t)$ is deeply entrenched, and a new solution magically cuts that burden down. When the gap in overshadowing byproducts is extreme, the shift feels "radical."

Illustration 1: Home Movie Entertainment

A classic example is the evolution of home entertainment. Under a traditional model, each wave, from VHS to DVD to Blu-ray to streaming, gets explained by "superior technology" capturing the market, earning high revenues, and displacing incumbents. But LPI clarifies that each wave specifically addresses overshadowing byproducts:

- VHS overshadowed film projectors by resolving burdens of expensive reels, distribution hurdles, and specialized equipment.

267

- DVDs overshadowed VHS by removing tape wear, bulky cassettes, and time-burdens of fast-forwarding and rewinding cassettes.
- Blu-ray overshadowed DVD by tackling resolution constraints (HD), and disc capacity for high-def content.
- Streaming overshadowed physical media by removing storage clutter, disc scratching, and limited in-store inventory and all other the burdens it came with.

At every point, the baseline utility of "watching a movie" stayed the same. However, new solutions systematically removed overshadowing byproducts. Under LPI, innovators look for those overshadowing burdens (storage, disc damage, restricted selection) and aim to minimize them, achieving more predictable success than simply piling on extra "features."

Illustration 2: Telephony

We can see the same byproduct-driven evolution in telephony:
- Landline Phones delivered direct voice communication at home or in the office but forced people to remain tethered to a physical location.
- Cell Phones overshadowed landlines by removing the "fixed location" burden. Yet early cell phones introduced new overshadowing byproducts: short battery life, spotty coverage, and minimal data capabilities.
- Smartphones overshadowed basic cell phones by tackling small screens, limited apps, and poor internet access, thus removing more overshadowing burdens. Users gained browsing, messaging, apps, and better coverage. Over time, of course, smartphones accrued their own overshadowing byproducts (like frequent updates, app overload, battery drain, or privacy concerns).

Again, the core baseline function of "distance communication" remains the same. But overshadowing burdens keep shifting from landlines to basic cells to modern smartphones, each wave neutralizing old burdens yet inevitably introducing new ones. Observing these byproduct reveals a predictable cycle of improvement.

Extended Reflection on the Value of Constant Utility

Constant utility does not deny that products are eventually replaced or that entire industries disappear. It reframes why they do. Products are not abandoned because their core function degrades, but because accumulating byproducts, such as new constraints, inefficiencies, or evolving expectations, overshadow their continued use. What, once served well, becomes impractical, not because it fails to deliver its utility, but because it can no longer do so without burdens it wasn't designed to handle. Where at some tipping or inflexion point, the burdens now outweigh the benefits.

This reframing helps us see upgrades more clearly. Most upgrades do not reinvent a product's baseline function, they reduce or even delay burden onset. An LED lightbulb and a fluorescent bulb both provide light. The LED succeeds because it reduces energy use, lasts longer, and creates fewer disposal issues. Similarly, basic electric and gas cars both provide transportation. The electric car's appeal lies not in enabling travel, but in removing noise, emissions, and maintenance byproducts that increasingly overshadow its predecessor.

Constant utility also explains catastrophic failure. It's rarely a slow erosion of function. It's typically a sudden spike in byproducts that surpass the threshold of usability. A shattered screen, melted circuit, or destroyed gearbox renders the product's utility inaccessible, not because utility faded, but because burdens spiked beyond recoverable limits.

Concluding Perspectives for a Byproduct-Conscious Future

Embracing constant utility reframes how we interpret product failure, innovation, and progress. The core utility never "wears out," it's the accumulation of burdens that forces change. Innovation, then, is not about creating novelty for its own sake, but about alleviating the byproducts that obscure utility. This perspective reshapes how we design, strategize, and evolve.

In business, companies that monitor byproduct accumulation, not just feature adoption, are better positioned to evolve. They don't need to restore "lost value"; they need to remove the burdens that make that value feel inaccessible. This leads to more sustainable innovation cycles and reduces wasteful obsolescence.

In policymaking, focusing on byproduct reduction instead of utility stimulation leads to smarter interventions. It shifts attention from "what more can we give?" to "what's currently in the way?" be it pollution, regulatory complexity, burnout, or digital overload. Better outcomes follow when policies target burdens rather than chase new, sometimes unnecessary, outputs.

For society at large, LPI can reduce the anxiety that fuels endless consumption. If people understand that the core function of their device or lifestyle hasn't degraded, they can evaluate whether perceived dissatisfaction is rooted in new burdens, not lost performance. This leads to more conscious consumption and design reuse.

Ultimately, the model of constant utility reveals innovation as a cycle of byproduct resolution. A product is created to solve burdens, performs well for a time, then new burdens emerge, prompting replacement. The original function remains stable throughout, it's only the byproduct burden landscape that shifts. Whether in transportation, media, energy, or communication, progress follows a pattern: the utility is constant, the byproducts are not.

This insight clarifies that the future of innovation lies not in endlessly chasing "newness" but in deliberately minimizing what gets in the way. If we accept that every innovation will one day be burdened again, we can design not just for impact, but for endurance. Progress becomes not a race to reinvent utility, but a responsibility to preserve and unburden it, again and again.

CHAPTER 16
The 50 Utility Principles

The Utility Principles are a set of guiding concepts within the Law of Perpetual Innovation that provide a comprehensive approach to understanding, designing, and delivering utility in response to user needs and byproducts. These principles explore utility from multiple dimensions, including how it is perceived, created, adapted, and sustained. They emphasize the reactive nature of utility, highlighting its role as the "what" that fulfills the "why" of demand, while addressing challenges such as imperfect delivery, dynamic user expectations, and systemic interactions. By offering insights into the evolution, customization, and emotional impact of utility, the principles equip innovators and organizations with tools to align their creations with meaningful user needs. Ultimately, the Utility Principles help guide innovation efforts to drive solutions that resonate with users, adapt to changing contexts, and contribute to long-term innovation and market relevance.

NOTE: Not all utility principles identified to date will be expanded upon. We will go into some depth on several of the more fundamental ones.

00. Principle of Utility as Constant:

The inherent functional utility of a product, service, or system remains constant in its intended role, but its perceived net utility changes due to the accumulation of byproducts. Utility is not diminished, it is obscured by the progressive burden of accumulating intrinsic and extrinsic byproducts, which restrict, constrain, or overshadow the previously accepted value. This misperception of diminishing utility is what drives perpetual innovation.

This principle, based on the Constant Utility Theorem, directly challenges the traditional economic assumption of diminishing utility, which suggests that a product or service naturally becomes less valuable over time. LPI refutes this premise, asserting that utility does not degrade, rather, its perceived net availability and sufficiency are restricted due to byproduct accumulation.

This distinction is critical:

- Utility remains intact: the product still performs the function it was designed for (address a previous set of byproducts).
- Byproducts accumulate: increasing friction, effort, cost, or negative perception over time.
- Net perceived utility declines: not because the product changed, but because its once-acceptable utility is now overshadowed by byproducts.

This explains why all innovation is fundamentally byproduct-driven: new innovations do not create utility from nothing, they remove, mitigate, or circumvent accumulated byproducts that restrict the perception or effectiveness of a previous utility state.

For example, a traditional incandescent lightbulb provides the same illumination on the day it is purchased as it does a year later (assuming byproduct accumulation didn't surpass initial baseline utility, rendering it nullified). The functional utility remains unchanged. However, byproducts such as increasing electricity costs, awareness of more energy-efficient alternatives (heat generation and electricity cost impact), and the inconvenience of frequently replacing burnt-out bulbs, begin accumulating. These byproducts overshadow the utility of the bulb, making it feel insufficient or wasteful. When LED bulbs are introduced, they do not "increase the lighting ability" of the bulb's original function, they remove the byproducts of inefficiency, energy cost, and replacement frequency. This makes LED bulbs a superior alternative, not because the old bulb's utility declined, but because its byproducts became more apparent.

Thus, utility is constant, but its viability within a changing context is not. This principle reinforces that all perceived utility loss is due to byproduct accumulation, not inherent baseline utility degradation. Understanding this principle allows innovators to systematically analyze byproduct accumulation trends, enabling them to predict the next wave of disruption and identify areas for innovation before they reach critical mass.

1. **Principle of Utility as Imperfect:** Perfect utility is unachievable. Factors such as aging products, changing user preferences, changes in environment (economic, market, technology, society and culture), or changes in competition ensure that every product or service, no matter how well designed, will generate new byproducts; inefficiencies, unintended consequences or a desire for something better. These new byproducts ensure that no utility can be perceived as flawless forever. Products can always be improved, but they will never be free from creating new challenges or opportunities for future innovation.

   For example, the automobile solved the problem of long-distance travel but created new byproducts such as traffic congestion, accidents, and environmental pollution. Even with advancements in safety and fuel efficiency, the car still generates challenges like electronic waste and reliance on charging infrastructure (for electric cars).

2. **Principle of Utility as the Antithesis to Byproduct:** Every utility is created as a response to a specific byproduct. The existence of utility is directly linked to the issue it resolves. In other words, utility and byproduct are inseparable. This principle emphasizes that the value of any utility lies in its ability to neutralize, mitigate or escape a byproduct.

   For example, ergonomic office chairs are designed to resolve the byproduct of discomfort and poor posture associated with prolonged sitting. Their utility is defined by their capacity to alleviate back pain, improve posture, and enhance productivity by countering the physical strain caused by traditional office seating. Another example are water purification systems. They tackle the byproduct of contaminated or unsafe drinking water. The utility they provide is inherently linked to their ability to remove impurities, pathogens, and toxins, ensuring access to clean and safe water for consumption and daily use.

3. **Principle of Utility as Reactive:** Utility is always reactive; it is a response to a pre-existing byproduct. Successfully adopted utility doesn't arise out of nowhere but from a recognition that something is missing, inefficient, undesirable or now newly desired. This principle emphasizes that innovation is fundamentally tied to problem-solving; demand that arises from the byproducts of existing utility, whether latent and "unknown or unarticulated", or known and understood. Every product or service is created to address a specific

shortcoming, whether that shortcoming was environmental, functional, social, or otherwise.

For example, robotic vacuum cleaners like the Roomba were developed in response to the byproduct of time-consuming and labor-intensive traditional sweeping or vacuuming. Their utility reacts to this inefficiency by automating cleaning tasks, making it easier for households to maintain clean floors with less overall effort.

4. **Principle of Utility as Perceived:** Utility possesses both objective and subjective dimensions. Objectively, a product or service can be evaluated based on quantifiable attributes such as durability, speed, or distinct features, providing a baseline of what it can deliver. These measurable qualities enable developers to test performance, compare solutions, and refine design. However, while objective criteria establish a product's foundational capabilities, they represent only part of the equation. Utility is ultimately shaped by how individuals experience and interpret a product. What truly defines utility is how users subjectively assign value based on their personal preferences, motivations, and unique ways of engaging with the product. Even small variations in attitude or perspective can lead different people to derive vastly different levels of satisfaction from the same design.

   For example, consider two individuals using the same pencil. Person A perceives the pencil as a precise, reliable writing tool; they appreciate the clean lines, minimal smudging, and consistent performance. The pencil helps them feel organized and productive, boosting their confidence as they plan tasks or jot down quick notes. Meanwhile, Person B sees the same pencil as a creative outlet, relishing how varying pressure and angle can produce a range of textures and shading effects. For them, the pencil's utility lies in its capacity for artistic expression, invoking a sense of freedom and accomplishment each time they sketch or draw. Despite sharing the same physical object, these two users perceive its utility through distinctly different lenses, underscoring that personal perception is central to any product's net perceived value.

5. **Principle of Utility as an Extension of Human Origin Utilities:** All modern utilities can be traced back to fundamental human capabilities and capacities, or what are termed "human origin utilities." These are basic functional needs like movement, perception, communication, and manipulation, to which

innovations are directly tied. Every modern utility extends (cars extend mobility) or supports the extension of (parking structures support the extension of mobility) one or more of these foundational human capacities, making products, services and systems an augmentation of natural human needs and abilities.

For example, video games extend the human origin utilities of perception, manipulation, exploration, competition, fulfillment and achievement. They build upon humans' natural capacities for sensory processing, problem-solving, curiosity and achievement. They offer immersive environments that simulate complex scenarios and allow players to manipulate virtual worlds, satisfying the innate drive to discover, compete and accomplish goals. Through challenges, leaderboards, and achievements, video games simulate environments where players can strive for mastery, even test their skills against others, and gain a sense of fulfillment from progressing and winning. This makes them a profound extension of fundamental human drives for interaction, exploration, and success.

6. **Principle of Utility as Context-Dependent:** Utility is not static or inherent to a product, but rather shifts according to the environment and conditions in which that product, service or system is employed. A solution that delivers high utility in one setting may prove ineffective or irrelevant in another due to variations in physical climate, cultural norms, available infrastructure, or situational constraints. This principle underscores the idea that the practical value of any product fluctuates based on where, how, and by whom it is used. Consequently, designers and innovators must consider a range of contexts (geographical, social, economic, and cultural) when developing solutions, recognizing that even well-engineered products can see their utility diminish or disappear once the environment changes.

For example, take a standard ballpoint pen, which functions reliably in a classroom or office. In these controlled, dry environments, the pen's design directly addresses the user's writing needs. However, in wet or extremely cold outdoor conditions, the ink may fail to flow properly, significantly reducing its effectiveness. Similarly, electric vehicles thrive in urban areas equipped with charging stations, but their utility can decline in remote regions that lack sufficient infrastructure. These examples highlight how utility depends as much on context and external conditions as on the product's intrinsic design, reinforcing the importance of adapting solutions to the specific environments in which they will be used.

7. **Principle of Intended Utility vs. Experienced Utility:** A product's intended utility, meticulously planned by its creators, may differ substantially from the utility that users actually encounter once they interact with it. Differences in personal preferences, usage habits, and environmental factors often introduce variations that deviate from the designer's original vision, resulting in a gap between how the product was meant or intended to land and how it is actually received and experienced. To minimize this gap, developers must engage closely with users, test in realistic conditions, and remain open to continuous feedback, ensuring that the final product aligns as closely as possible with real-world needs and expectations.

Consider protein powders in the fitness supplement market. Although these products are designed to provide an easy, effective way to support muscle recovery and growth, users often encounter unexpected issues such as unpleasant taste, digestive discomfort, or ambiguity around proper dosage. These unforeseen challenges can undermine the perceived efficacy of the supplement, leaving users frustrated or disappointed. By reformulating flavors, improving digestibility, and offering clear situational usage instructions, manufacturers can help close the gap between the intended utility, of enhanced fitness performance, and the experienced utility that users encounter.

8. **Principle of Utility as Dynamic:** Utility evolves over time and iterations. What may be considered highly useful at one point may diminish in net available utility as user needs change, new technologies emerge, or societal or cultural conditions shift. This principle highlights the importance of adaptability in innovation. Products and services must evolve to maintain their relevance.

For example, the utility of incandescent light bulbs was high when they were first introduced, providing a significant improvement over flame-based lighting. Over time, as energy efficiency and environmental concerns grew, the net perceived utility of incandescent bulbs lessened, leading to the development of more efficient fluorescent and, eventually, LED lighting.

9. **Principle of Utility Perception and Expectation Management:** Creators must manage both how users perceive a product, service or system and the

expectations that users hold before and during its use. Even when actual performance meets high technical standards, a disconnect between user perception and user expectations can undermine perceived utility. Achieving consistency between real capability and user anticipation is, therefore, critical to fostering satisfaction and loyalty.

For example, Costco's Kirkland brand often matches or exceeds the quality of equivalent name-brand products but is marketed more simply. Because it lacks the marketing campaigns or brand prestige that boost consumer perception of competing labels, users may assume it is of lesser value. In truth, the Kirkland product and its heavily advertised counterpart can be nearly identical in specifications and performance. However, differences in perceived utility arise because user expectations and perceptions diverge, shaped by brand awareness and promotional strategies rather than by actual quality.

10. **Principle of Utility as Emergent through Interaction:** Utility only emerges when users actively engage with and experience the product, service or system. A product may have latent potential, but it is not realized until someone interacts with it. This principle highlights the need for user engagement as part of the utility experience.

For example, a pencil only becomes useful when someone picks it up and writes with it. Until that interaction occurs, the pencil is simply an object with latent potential, but no realized utility.

11. **Principle of Net Utility Deviation** (aka Temporary Byproduct Accumulation)**:** In the realm of products, services, or systems, utility can be temporarily limited or restricted by byproduct, resulting in less available total utility. This results in less total net utility, because net available utility has deviated from its baseline or benchmark due to wear, damage, environmental conditions, or other influencing byproduct factors. These departures from optimal performance are not permanent, but they do require interventions such as maintenance, repair, or recalibration, to restore the overall effectiveness. By recognizing and addressing the root byproduct causing these deviations promptly, users and service providers can extend overall lifespans and maintain more consistent performance over time.

Consider a pencil whose tip becomes dull after extended use. As the point wears down (byproduct accumulating), sharpness in writing diminishes, representing a temporary emergence of byproduct (in economics it's viewed as a drop in utility). However, sharpening the pencil restores its core functional utility to near its initial standard. This cycle of deviation and restoration continues until permanent degradation sets in (Utility Principle 12), at which point the pencil's utility can no longer be fully recovered.

12. **Principle of Net Utility Degradation** (aka Permanent Byproduct Accumulation): All products, services, or systems inevitably experience a permanent constraint in available utility over time, commonly unfolding through permanent byproducts of irreversible wear, irreversible aging, or catastrophic breakdown. While regular upkeep or repairs may slow this process, the loss of performance can eventually become irreversible, rendering replacement the only practical solution. In rare instances, this permanent accumulation of byproduct may occur suddenly, driven by foreseen or unforeseen byproduct events such as catastrophic failures or severe damage, that rapidly restrict the available utility below its functional or operational threshold.

Electric vehicle batteries exemplify this pattern of gradual degradation (gradual byproduct accumulation): as the battery ages, its charge capacity diminishes, reducing the driving range over several years. Ultimately, replacement becomes necessary once performance degrades beyond a useful level. However, byproducts such as a sudden manufacturing defect or external impact can also produce an abrupt total loss of available utility. Similarly, a pencil gradually wears down (byproduct accumulation) to the point where it becomes too short to handle or sharpen. However, an unexpected break can instantly render it unusable as well (byproduct completely and permanently restricts the available utility).

13. **Principle of Utility Trade-offs:** Every innovation or design improvement comes with trade-offs. When developers enhance certain aspects of a product, service, or system they often do so at the expense of other features or capabilities. This principle highlights the balance innovators must strike between competing priorities. Every utility enhancement comes with potential costs, and understanding these trade-offs helps in managing expectations and aligning with user priorities.

For example, fast food chains may introduce healthier menu options to appeal to health-conscious consumers, but this often comes at the expense of taste or increased preparation time. While the utility of health is enhanced, the trade-off may result in reduced appeal to customers seeking the traditional fast-food experience of indulgence and speed.

14. **Principle of Utility Customization:** Utility can be tailored to individual user preferences and needs, maximizing its value for different contexts.

15. **Principle of Utility as a Spectrum:** Utility exists on a spectrum, meaning different users extract varying levels of perceived utility from the same product based on their individual needs, preferences, or circumstances. What provides high utility to one person may offer minimal value to another. This principle emphasizes that utility is not a one-size-fits-all concept, and understanding this variation is key to effective innovation.

For example, a basic car may offer high utility to a commuter who values reliability and cost-effectiveness but low utility to someone who prioritizes luxury features like leather seats and a premium sound system. Similarly, a pencil may provide maximum utility to a student who needs a reliable writing tool, but an artist may require a broader range of materials to meet their creative needs.

16. **Principle of Utility Competition:** As new innovations (new utility solutions) emerge; they often compete with or replace older utilities. This competition between utilities drives further innovation and pushes industries to evolve. New technologies or services that offer greater efficiency, lower costs, or additional features (due to reduction or elimination of previous byproducts) can displace existing products or services, creating new byproducts that'll soon need to be addressed. When new utilities enter the market, they do so in relation to the byproducts that existing solutions either failed to address or inadvertently created. In other words, each new competing utility is meaningful only because it resolved a specific byproduct (inefficiency, discomfort, unfulfilled desire, etc.) and in competing with other utilities, it will inevitably generate additional byproducts. This dynamic interplay drives continual innovation, as each utility's existence both highlights unresolved issues and inspires new solutions.

For example, let's consider the competition between minimalist running shoes and high-cushion running shoes through the lens of byproduct.

- Minimalist footwear addresses the byproduct of feeling disconnected from the running surface, by granting a more natural stride and enhanced ground feel. However, this emphasis on minimalism produces its own byproduct: insufficient shock absorption, which can lead to joint discomfort (byproduct) for some runners.
- High-cushion shoes, in turn, arose to mitigate that discomfort, by providing added support and impact protection. Yet, by focusing on cushioning, they introduced a different byproduct: a heavier, less responsive feel that can deter speed-oriented runners.
- Recognizing these gaps, manufacturers have since developed hybrid designs with lightweight yet supportive foam midsoles to reduce joint stress (the byproduct of minimalism) without sacrificing responsiveness (the byproduct of heavy cushioning).

In this way, each new utility emerges in direct response to the byproduct left unresolved by existing options, illustrating how competition between utilities both reveals unmet needs and propels the creation of more refined solutions.

17. **Principle of Utility Recontextualization:** The Principle of Utility Recontextualization explains how the perceived value or utility of a product changes as new innovations and technologies emerge in the market, social and cultural conditions change, and economic factors influence utility adoption. This principle focuses on how new products, solutions, or technologies redefine the environment in which older products exist, causing a shift in how those older products are perceived and evaluated. As new alternatives or complementary innovations arise, the context within which an existing product is understood evolves, altering the features that are emphasized or valued. This recontextualization does not mean the product loses its utility; rather, its perceived utility is reframed based on the aspirational comparative (δ) advantages of newer products. This often happens over shorter, industry-driven cycles of technological advancement.

For example, the introduction of electric guitars altered how acoustic guitars were perceived. Initially valued for portability (when compared to a harp or piano) and self-sufficiency (when compared to a violin and its required bow), the acoustic guitar's utility was recontextualized once electric guitars became popular. The natural, unamplified sound of the acoustic guitar became its defining feature in contrast to the amplified sound of the electric guitar. This shift did not eliminate the utility of the acoustic guitar but reframed it within a new landscape shaped by emerging environmental conditions.

18. **Principle of Temporal Utility Shift** (generational amnesia or shifting baseline syndrome): As time passes and generations grow further removed from the original context of an innovation, the perceived utility of a product or service changes. The problems or byproducts the product initially addressed may no longer be relevant, and new concerns, shaped by evolving societal and technological norms, take precedence. What was once groundbreaking utility is now a given, and the product's utility is redefined in relation to the new realities of the present. This principle highlights that the passage of time, rather than new technologies alone, plays a key role in shifting the perception of utility as older comparisons become less relevant.

For example, when the automobile was first introduced, its utility was perceived primarily in contrast to the horse and buggy. The car's ability to travel faster, require less maintenance, and avoid the physical limitations of animal-driven transportation were the main benefits. However, as generations passed, the horse and buggy became obsolete, and the comparison ceased to be relevant. Today, the utility of a car is judged against byproduct concerns like fuel efficiency, environmental sustainability, and comfort. Issues that have emerged over time as societal priorities shifted. The original context that defined the car's perceived value (at the time) is no longer present, shifting the byproduct landscape, consequently shifting new-utility creation based on the evolving expectations of the modern world.

19. **Principle of Utility Anticipation:** Utility creation can be anticipated. Innovators and designers can forecast future byproducts (needs or problems, and their accumulation) and proactively develop solutions that preemptively address those challenges before they fully manifest. This principle emphasizes foresight in utility design, allowing creators to introduce utilities that solve emerging or latent problems, thereby staying ahead of market demands and external pressures. Anticipating utility means thinking beyond the present byproduct by projecting from it, but always in reaction to it, and addressing the needs of a rapidly evolving future landscape.

For example, televisions evolved by reacting to the byproduct of limited content access and rigid viewing schedules in traditional broadcast TV. While the innovation of smart TVs was proactive in anticipating the growing demand for on-demand content and streaming, the utility they provided was fundamentally reactive to the pre-existing byproduct of inflexibility in content consumption. Innovators recognized this existing constraint and anticipated its progression as consumers demanded more control over how and when they consume entertainment. The development of smart TVs with internet connectivity and apps was their way of addressing this byproduct, staying ahead of the inevitable shift toward on-demand and streaming services. They accomplished this by extending their response in predicting how these constraints (byproducts) would grow with advancing internet capabilities, projected streaming capabilities and evolving consumer expectations.

20. **Principle of Utility as a Complex System Contributor:** Utility extends beyond its immediate function by shaping and influencing larger social structures, environments, or technological frameworks. Rather than existing in isolation, a product, service, or solution can trigger ripple effects throughout these interconnected complex systems, altering economic activities, cultural practices, or ecological balances. This principle shares similarities with the Principle of Utility as Ecosystem-Dependent, but differs in scope: while Ecosystem-Dependent focuses on how utility is enhanced by integration within a specific network of products or services, Utility as a Complex System Contributor emphasizes how utility can reshape broader societal, environmental, or technological landscapes.

For example, mobile payment platforms, often viewed as convenient financial tools, serve as prime examples of this principle. Solutions like PayPal, Alipay, and M-Pesa have done more than simplify transactions; they have accelerated global financial inclusion, reshaped consumer behavior, and boosted economic growth. According to the World Bank, global account ownership rose to 76% in 2021, partly due to mobile payment services enabling unbanked populations to access financial resources. In regions such as sub-Saharan Africa, M-Pesa has fueled GDP growth by expanding access to savings and credit, while in India, the Unified Payments Interface (UPI) processed 3.65 billion transactions in September 2021 alone, marking a rapid transition to cashless economies. These examples underscore how a single innovation can drive fundamental shifts in broader systems, catalyzing new economic and social dynamics well beyond its original scope.

21. **Principle of Utility Transparency:** Utility should be clearly communicated to the user, making its functionality, benefits, and trade-offs explicit to ensure informed decision-making and user satisfaction. (This one goes hand-in-hand with the principle of byproduct awareness and communication.)

22. **Principle of Utility Resilience:** Utility must be resilient, meaning that it should maintain its value and functionality even when faced with external shocks, disruptions, or changes in conditions. A resilient utility is able to withstand failures, system breakdowns, or unforeseen events without losing its core value. This principle is essential for ensuring the long-term reliability of a product, system, or service.

    For example, waterproof smartphones are a prime example of resilient utility. Even when exposed to water, which is a common risk for users, the phone continues to function effectively, ensuring that the utility of communication and connectivity remains intact under adverse conditions.

23. **Principle of Utility Sustainability:** Utility should be designed with sustainability in mind, ensuring that it can continue to provide its perceived value without depleting or harming external systems such as the environment or social fabric. This principle calls for the creation of utilities that not only meet user needs but also contribute to long-term environmental and societal well-being, avoiding unsustainable byproducts.

    For example, ceramic-coated cookware is an evolution in design that emphasizes sustainability by eliminating the use of harmful chemicals like PFOA (perfluorooctanoic acid), a synthetic compound previously found in traditional nonstick coatings. PFOA, part of the "forever chemicals" group, has been linked to health issues such as cancer, liver damage, thyroid problems, and developmental concerns, and it contributes to long-term environmental contamination due to its inability to degrade. Ceramic coatings offer the same utility of easy cleaning and nonstick cooking while ensuring safety for both users and the environment, making them a more sustainable choice.

24. **Principle of Utility Continuity:** Utility should have continuity, meaning it provides consistent perceived value across different versions, environments, or use cases. This principle ensures that users can rely on the utility even as products evolve, new versions are released, or environmental conditions change. Continuity strengthens user trust and ensures that utility is not disrupted unnecessarily, fostering a smooth user experience over time.

For example, operating system updates that maintain backward compatibility with older software or hardware demonstrate utility continuity. Users can continue to rely on the utility of their devices without the need for drastic changes, even as the system evolves with new features.

25. **Principle of Utility Reinforcement:** Utility can be reinforced over time through iterative design improvements, user feedback, and system upgrades. This principle emphasizes that utility is not static but can grow in value and effectiveness as it is refined. By continually updating and improving the utility, creators can adapt to user needs and enhance the product's performance over time.

For example, navigation apps like Google Maps improve their utility by incorporating user feedback and real-time data. Over time, these enhancements refine route suggestions, traffic updates, and other features, reinforcing the app's core utility of efficient navigation.

26. **Principle of Adaptive Utility:** Utility can be self-adaptive, meaning it can respond dynamically to changing conditions, environments, or user needs without requiring direct input or adjustments from the user. Adaptive utility ensures continued relevance and value by autonomously evolving to meet shifting requirements, suppressing byproduct real-time, optimizing its performance, and delivering the most appropriate functionality based on contextual changes. This principle emphasizes design that allows products or services to automatically adjust, ensuring seamless usability and sustained utility (see Chapter 26, Adaptive Utility Innovation).

For example, automatic cars demonstrate adaptive utility by automatically adjusting gears to optimize performance and fuel efficiency based on speed and road conditions. Unlike stick shift cars, which require manual user manipulation, automatic cars deliver self-adaptive functionality by mitigating the byproduct burden of manually shifting in real-time, making driving easier and more efficient without any active engagement from the user. Other examples include auto-correct in word processing programs and predictive text in smartphones.

27. **Principle of Utility Redundancy:** Products, services, or systems can incorporate multiple layers of functionality to ensure that their core utility remains available under various conditions, not just when something fails. Redundancy can serve as a backup if the primary mechanism becomes compromised (byproduct $B(t)$ surpasses baseline utility U_0) and can also operate under normal conditions to improve performance or efficiency. By integrating alternative pathways or features that work alongside the main function, designers create offerings that maintain or even enhance utility in both routine and challenging scenarios.

For example, electric vehicles with regenerative braking illustrate how redundancy can operate in everyday use as well as in more critical situations. While the main battery supplies power for driving, regenerative braking recovers kinetic energy during deceleration to recharge the battery, effectively extending the car's range, delaying byproduct accumulation of "needing to recharge." This design not only helps offset reductions in battery charge when the primary power source runs low, but also contributes to overall efficiency and performance during normal operation. This demonstrates how redundancy can bolster a system's utility by reducing or delaying byproduct accumulation, beyond mere failsafe protection (impulse byproduct mitigation).

28. **Principle of Utility Interdependence:** Modern utilities seldom stand alone. Instead, they often rely on or enhance each other, forming a network of interdependent functions that collectively deliver greater value than any single utility could provide on its own. This principle underscores how different features or capabilities, within a single product or across multiple products and services, work together to create synergistic benefits, elevating the overall user experience.

For example, smartphones exemplify utility interdependence by blending communication (calls, messaging), entertainment (music, video streaming, games), navigation (maps, GPS), and productivity (email, calendars, document editing) into one comprehensive device. Each utility reinforces and complements the others, resulting in a multi-functional tool whose total value exceeds the sum of its individual capabilities.

29. **Principle of Utility Elasticity:** Utility can expand or contract in value depending on how deeply the user engages with the product, system, or service. This principle acknowledges that users interact with utility in different ways, and the level of engagement can alter the utility's perceived value. Utility elasticity allows products to be more flexible, catering to power users who seek advanced functionality while also being accessible to casual users who may only require basic features.

    For example, professional software like Adobe Photoshop offers a wide range of tools for advanced users, allowing them to unlock deeper functionality. At the same time, beginners can use a simpler interface with basic features. The utility of the software expands, or contracts based on the user's needs and engagement level, offering both accessibility and complexity.

30. **Principle of Utility Latency:** Utility may remain latent until it is triggered by specific events, environmental conditions, or changes in user needs. Latent utility may not always be immediately visible or active but can exist in the background, providing value only when it is required. This principle highlights the importance of designing products with potential future needs in mind, ensuring that utility is ready to emerge when necessary.

    For example, car airbags represent latent utility that only activates in the event of a crash. While the utility of safety is always present, it remains hidden until a critical moment when the airbags deploy, providing immediate value when it's needed most, upon an impulse byproduct incident.

31. **Principle of Utility Modularity:** Utility can be modular, meaning that the product's total utility may be delivered in discrete parts or through different experiences that address unique aspects of the user's needs. Rather than offering a single, cohesive utility, modular utilities serve multiple smaller purposes, often in fragmented or customizable ways. Such a capability isolates byproducts to their specific modules (see Chapter 27, Modular Utility Innovation).

For example, toolsets for home repair, such as those offered by brands like DeWalt or Milwaukee, deliver modular utility by providing interchangeable tools and components designed for various tasks, such as drilling, sawing, or tightening bolts. These toolsets often utilize rechargeable battery systems that add another layer of modularity by being compatible across the brand's entire range of cordless products. A single battery can power multiple tools, from power drills to leaf blowers, allowing users to expand their toolkit without investing in separate power sources. Additionally, multi-battery charging docks enable users to charge several batteries simultaneously, ensuring uninterrupted workflow and convenience. This combination of modular tools and shared battery systems enhances flexibility, efficiency, and cost-effectiveness.

32. **Principle of Utility Integration:** Utility is perceptually enhanced when integrated with other technologies, components, products, systems, or services, creating a seamless, more simplified experience across multiple touch points. This principle recognizes that utility does not operate in isolation but can be perceptually amplified when combined with other utilities, enabling users to experience higher levels of convenience and value on the surface, while the increased complexity exists within the system. The true driver here, however, is the reduction of a discrete (multiple or separate) system: a system made up of many outward facing parts. This can be perceived as byproduct of complexity or multiplicity. Integration, therefore, centralizes, streamlines and internalizes complexity byproduct to exist behind the scenes, transforming it to a more managed, often hidden form that end-users experience as simplicity (see Chapter 24. Innovation through Utility Integration).

For example, a smart home system that integrates with voice assistants, security systems, temperature or lighting controls and entertainment devices enhances its utility by creating a unified experience. By connecting these different utilities, the system offers seamless control over multiple aspects of the home, increasing the overall value for the user. Another example is the increased level of integration in semiconductor microchip technology.

33. **Principle of Utility Elasticity Over Time:** The perceived value of utility can expand or contract over time based on external conditions, personal life stages, or changing user priorities. As users age or circumstances change, certain utilities may become more or less relevant, making it essential for products to remain flexible in their perceived value across different timeframes.

For example, a health-tracking wearable might gain more perceived utility as users become more health-conscious with age. Even though the core functionality of the device remains the same, its utility grows as it aligns with the user's evolving priorities, such as fitness and well-being.

34. **Principle of Utility as Behavioral Reinforcement:** Utility can reinforce certain user behaviors, either intentionally or unintentionally, by creating patterns of use that encourage repetitive actions or establish habits. This principle acknowledges the role that utility plays in shaping user behavior, both positively and negatively, depending on how the product, system, or service is designed.

For example, fitness apps that reward users for completing daily exercise routines serve as a positive behavioral reinforcement, encouraging healthy habits through gamification and rewards. Conversely, social media apps that push notifications may inadvertently reinforce excessive screen time, leading to negative behavioral byproducts.

35. **Principle of Utility as a Behavioral Feedback Loop:** A product, system, or service that implements a behavioral feedback loop continuously refines its utility based on how users actually interact with it. Instead of simply reinforcing habitual behaviors, this dynamic process involves collecting user input, either through explicit feedback or usage patterns, and then adjusting features, recommendations, or configurations to better meet evolving needs. Over time, the product's evolving utility then shapes new user behaviors, creating a cycle of ongoing adaptation and improved user engagement and behaviors.

For example, a personal finance application can monitor users' spending habits, payment schedules, and saving goals, then recalibrate its budgeting tools and alerts accordingly. If the app detects frequent overspending in a particular category, perhaps dining out, it might suggest tighter limits or notify the user of cheaper alternatives in their vicinity. Conversely, if a user demonstrates consistent saving in one category, the app may propose new investment opportunities. Through this evolving dialogue between user actions and system recommendations, the financial utility becomes increasingly attuned to individual needs, motivating users to stay more active in managing their finances.

36. Principle of Utility as Emotional Equilibrium: Utility can help manage or balance emotions, providing users with comfort, stability, or reassurance, especially in emotionally challenging scenarios.

37. Principle of Utility Fatigue: Over time, users may experience diminished perceived value due to overexposure or loss of novelty through the accumulation of byproduct, making it important to keep utility fresh and engaging to prevent fatigue.

38. Principle of Utility Reciprocity: Utility can enable reciprocal exchanges between users, fostering cooperative or social interactions that enhance the overall value through mutual benefit.

39. Principle of Utility Flexibility: Utility should be flexible enough to be adjusted to different user needs or contexts, allowing the user to shift its functionality based on changing circumstances.

40. Principle of Utility Integration with Identity: Utility can be tied to how a product allows users to express or reinforce their identity, adding psychological and social value to the utility. This principle highlights the importance of products that not only meet functional needs but also help users express personal, cultural, or social identity.

For example, luxury cars provide utility not only through transportation but also by allowing owners to signal social status, taste, or success, creating a deeper emotional attachment to the product. The same principle can apply to handbags, sunglasses, watches, and reusable water bottles (like my wife's many Stanley cups, circa 2024).

41. Principle of Utility as Desire Fulfillment in Layers: Utility operates in layers of desire fulfillment. The first layer addresses the immediate or primary byproducts, but as users interact with the product, system, or service, additional desires or needs emerge from emerging byproducts, creating subsequent layers of fulfillment. This principle emphasizes that utility is not static but evolves as users discover new ways to engage with the product, thus newer byproducts emerging, leading to more comprehensive utility over time.

For example, a smartphone initially fulfills the user's desire for communication, but over time, layers of new desires such as personalization (customizing wallpapers or settings) and functionality (using apps for banking, social media, or gaming) surface, deepening the utility provided.

42. **Principle of Utility as Contextual Catalyst:** A product, system, or service's utility can act as a catalyst for new external desires based on its presence within a broader context. This principle highlights that utility is not confined to the product itself but influences adjacent needs and desires (byproduct), sparking additional opportunities for utility creation in related areas.

For example, purchasing a new couch that fits perfectly in a living room may catalyze the desire for additional items like new décor, rugs, or lighting to complement the updated space. The initial utility of the couch leads to further desires (byproducts) to enhance the surrounding environment.

43. **Principle of Utility as a Holistic Experience:** Utility encompasses more than just the satisfaction of a functional need; it includes the total user experience, which can involve emotional, aesthetic, and social dimensions. This principle highlights that products, systems, or services are often valued not only for the functional byproducts they mitigate, but also for how they make users feel and how they fit into a larger life context. In other words, Holistic is truly defined by having a large or significant number of the 19 Human Origin Utilities (HOUs) being met in one shot.

For example, a handwritten greeting card offers a holistic experience that goes beyond its functional purpose of delivering a message. It provides emotional utility through the personal touch of handwritten words, aesthetic utility through its design and craftsmanship, and social utility by fostering a sense of connection and thoughtfulness between the sender and recipient.

44. **Principle of Utility as Ecosystem-Dependent:** A product or service's utility can rely on how effectively it interacts with a broader network of complementary offerings. This principle highlights that utility can be amplified or diminished by the degree of integration with related systems, creating an "ecosystem effect" that shapes the overall user experience. In other words, even a well-designed solution may underperform if it fails to align with the external products, technologies, or services upon which it depends. This principle differs

from the Principle of Utility as a Complex System Contributor, where utility affects large complex systems. This principle highlights how utility relies on integration within a specific network or ecosystem.

Apple devices exemplify this concept by seamlessly syncing data and functionalities across iPhones, MacBooks, iPads and Apple Watches, enabling users to transition effortlessly between tasks. This tight integration amplifies each device's inherent utility and creates a cohesive, user-friendly environment. On a simpler level, cookware (e.g., pots, pans, kettles, or skillets) relies on standardized stovetops, whether gas, electric, or induction, to function effectively. Both scenarios illustrate how robust ecosystem alignment enhances reliability, compatibility, and ease of use, ultimately elevating a product's overall utility.

45. **Principle of Lifecycle Utility Origin Elasticity:** Utility undergoes cyclical expansion and contraction over a product, system, or service's lifecycle, influenced by cultural shifts, technological advancements, and emerging byproducts. This principle acknowledges that utility is not static; it ties back to fundamental human needs (19 Human Origin Utilities) in varying degrees over time, expanding as products tap into new societal trends, fulfill latent desires, or are enhanced by technological progress. However, as negative byproducts emerge, or as societal values shift, the perceived utility can contract, reducing or even severing its connection to some of the Human Origin utilities. Expansion often occurs through strategic marketing or cultural narratives that associate the product with multiple utilities, broadening its relevance and perceived value. Conversely, contraction is frequently driven by the recognition of negative or harmful byproducts or outdated practices, as well as by technological obsolescence, which replaces older products with safer, more efficient alternatives.

For example, cigarettes exemplify lifecycle utility origin elasticity, as their utility expanded and contracted over time in relation to human origin utilities. Initially, cigarettes had limited tiebacks, primarily fulfilling the HOU of "Emotional Regulation & Fulfillment" by offering stress relief and relaxation; predominantly for men. As mass production and marketing efforts expanded their appeal, cigarettes began to tie back to additional origin utilities, including "Social Interaction & Bonding", by being portrayed as symbols of sophistication, and perceived "Health & Well-being", with claims of calming nerves and aiding digestion. This broader connection to multiple utilities fueled their widespread adoption, for both men and women. However, as scientific research revealed severe health risks, these tie-backs rapidly contracted. Cigarettes became disconnected from health utility and stigmatized in social contexts, leaving only the core tiebacks to emotional regulation and fulfillment, reflected in their addictive and stress-relief properties.

46. **Principle of Incremental Innovation:** Utility advances through small, continuous improvements that accumulate over time, resulting in significant enhancements without requiring a radical overhaul. Incremental innovation ultimately seeks to delay or reduce byproduct accumulation or onset (see Chapter 23, Incremental sustained Innovation).

47. **Principle of Radical Innovation:** Radical innovation involves groundbreaking changes that fundamentally alter the utility of a product, system, or service, often rendering previous versions or approaches obsolete. This principle focuses on transformative advancements that bring entirely new ways of achieving or accessing functionality, capabilities, or user experiences, reshaping the landscape of existing utilities. Unlike incremental changes, radical innovations deliver swift and impactful shifts that redefine how users interact with or perceive utility, frequently opening up new markets or creating unprecedented solutions to unmet needs. These innovations often have significant staying power, maintaining their relevance and dominance for decades or even centuries due to their transformative impact. It is through these radical innovations that some byproducts may completely go away, yet entirely new ones will emerge as the innovation integrates into larger systems and evolves over time (see Chapter 28, Radical Innovation).

For example, the zipper was a radical innovation in fastening technology that replaced buttons, hooks, and laces in many applications. It introduced a faster, more convenient way to secure clothing, bags, and footwear, eliminating inefficiencies and frustration associated with older fastening methods. First patented in 1913, the zipper has been in widespread use for over a century, displaying how radical innovations, even seemingly small ones, tend to last a long time due to their transformative impact and enduring utility. While newer fastening technologies exist, the zipper remains a dominant and reliable solution, demonstrating the staying power of a truly groundbreaking innovation. The wheel is another example.

48. Principle of Timeless Utility: Timeless utility is the preservation of a product, system, or service's inherent value over generations, often due to its cultural, historical, aesthetic, or emotional significance. This principle recognizes that certain utilities do not need frequent innovation or adaptation to remain relevant; instead, they are preserved and valued for their enduring qualities and connection to heritage or identity. Timeless utility is often linked to objects, sites, or experiences that transcend trends and retain intrinsic value across eras, serving as lasting symbols of cultural identity or historical continuity.

For example, classic cars, national monuments, and historical artifacts exemplify timeless utility. The utility of a classic car lies not in modern efficiency but in its nostalgic appeal, craftsmanship, and cultural significance, which retain their value across generations. Similarly, historic sites like national parks or monuments are preserved for their natural beauty, ecological importance, or historical relevance, connecting people to a shared past and offering utility that is both educational and emotional.

49. Principle of Utility Specialization: Utility specialization occurs as specific utilities become increasingly refined, differentiated, and adapted to meet more specific needs, often driven by byproducts when generalized utility solutions are not able to address niche requirements. Over time broad solutions can accumulate hidden inefficiencies or complications. By stripping away everything except a narrow focus, specialized utilities resolve these complexities for particular individuals and their usage cases. This principle highlights how a single broad utility can evolve into various tailored forms, each optimized for a unique purpose or audience. Utility specialization frequently arises as users seek more tailored solutions, prompting industries to develop and invest in specific utilities that fulfill distinct roles. Over time, specialization leads to a greater diversity of highly focused utilities, transforming general capabilities into targeted, efficient applications (see Chapter 25, Innovation through Utility Specialization).

For example, the invention of writing facilitated the recording and transmission of information, which later specialized into distinct formats such as books, newspapers, academic journals, and digital media. Each format developed to meet specific audience needs. Books for comprehensive knowledge, newspapers for timely updates, and digital platforms for instant, global communication. Writing's broad utility thus evolved into specialized utilities catering to various informational demands.

50. **Principle of Dual-Edged Utility:** The Principle of Dual-Edged Utility recognizes that some utilities offer genuine, short-term benefits but carry risks of unintended, long-term consequences when overused, abused, or relied upon excessively. These utilities can provide comfort, convenience, emotional regulation, or gratification when used in moderation, but their prolonged or imbalanced use distorts natural processes that humans evolved to depend on, such as effort-based rewards, physical activity, or meaningful social interaction. This principle emphasizes the importance of striking a balance between use and overuse, as these utilities can result in harmful byproducts (Principle of Evolutionary Distorted Byproducts) that undermine physical, emotional, and mental well-being over time.

For example, technologies like social media, gaming, or highly processed foods provide clear, immediate benefits but can mimic evolutionary reward mechanisms in ways that alter neurochemistry, reduce resilience, and lead to unintended personal and societal consequences when misused. Striking a balance between moderation and excess is key to ensuring these utilities remain beneficial without producing harmful long-term effects on a people.

Further Examples of The Dual-Edged nature of various Utility:

- **Instant Gratification Utility**: Social media platforms and streaming services offer the utility of instant access to entertainment and social validation. While beneficial for quick breaks or relaxation, overuse distorts the evolved need for delayed gratification, leading to impatience, shorter attention spans, and diminished satisfaction with longer-term efforts.
- **Sedentary Convenience Utility**: Remote work, online shopping, and entertainment technologies provide the utility of convenience by reducing physical effort. When over-relied upon, this utility fosters sedentary lifestyles, contributing to health issues such as obesity, cardiovascular disease, and diminished mental well-being.
- **Overabundance Utility**: Modern food systems provide the utility of consistent and affordable access to food. However, the over-availability of calorically dense, nutrient-poor options distorts natural scarcity-

294

reward mechanisms, leading to overeating, food addiction, and chronic health conditions like diabetes.

- **Hyper-Stimulation Utility**: Video games, social media, and similar platforms offer the utility of engaging, immersive experiences. Excessive use overstimulates the brain's dopamine pathways, disrupting natural reward systems and leading to attention disorders, anxiety, and diminished cognitive function.

- **Social Validation Utility**: Social media platforms offer the utility of instant connection and validation, fostering feelings of inclusion and recognition. Over-dependence on this utility, however, distorts the evolved need for meaningful, deep social bonds, resulting in social anxiety, insecurity, and weakened real-world social skills.

- **Risk-Minimization Utility**: Modern safety technologies and conveniences minimize physical risks and discomforts, providing the utility of security and ease. However, over-reliance on this utility discourages risk-taking, reducing resilience and personal growth by fostering avoidance behaviors.

- **Information Abundance Utility**: Digital technologies provide the utility of instant access to vast amounts of information. While beneficial for learning and productivity, excessive exposure can overwhelm cognitive systems, leading to decision fatigue, stress, and reduced focus on meaningful tasks.

- **Environmental Comfort Utility**: Urbanization and modern living spaces offer the utility of controlled, comfortable environments. However, over-dependence on these conveniences disconnects individuals from nature, reducing exposure to the mental and physical health benefits of natural settings.

- **Resource Abundance Utility**: Modern infrastructure ensures the utility of immediate access to critical resources like water, electricity, and food. Overuse of this utility fosters complacency and unsustainable consumption, leading to environmental degradation and resource scarcity.

- **Emotional Regulation Utility**: Entertainment technologies like binge-watching or video gaming provide the utility of temporary emotional regulation and escapism. Prolonged use, however, dulls natural emotional processes, leading to emotional blunting and a reduced ability to engage with real-world challenges and relationships.

Module C:
Systemic Classifiers

In Module C, we shift from the "why" and "what" of byproduct and utility to ***how*** we systematically classify them so that innovation efforts can be more targeted and data-driven. The idea is simple: once we know that byproducts inevitably arise from utility, we need a structured way to capture and categorize all those unintended consequences and the utilities that respond to them. This is where the Systemic Classifiers of LPI come in. They help organize the wide range of byproducts, highlight underlying patterns, and guide teams to prioritize the right solutions.

Just as importantly, these classifiers, while universal enough to apply across industries, can be customized for the unique demands of any product or service. Together with the Impact Models that gauge the severity or scope of a byproduct, Systemic Classifiers ensure that innovation moves from scattered guesswork to a focused, strategic process. Specifically, Module C introduces two primary classification tools:

- **The Byproduct Taxonomy** of Chapter 17 - for structuring and naming byproduct types and
- **The Absolute Utility Map** of Chapter 18 - for categorizing and aligning the core needs that each utility addresses.

By using these frameworks, innovators can systematically reveal which byproducts truly matter, anticipate what might emerge, and align their teams on the next wave of utility to create.

CHAPTER 17

Byproduct Classification - The Byproduct Taxonomy

Why a Taxonomy for Byproducts?

In the Law of Perpetual Innovation, byproducts are understood as an inseparable counterpart to utility. However, byproducts are not always in direct opposition to the utility itself. For example, the primary utility of a car is usually mobility. This holds true for most people. But if we consider a Ferrari, the primary utility shifts. It becomes more about signaling success or social status than just functional mobility.

Recognizing the true "expected" utility of a product, service, or system is essential to understanding how byproducts might impact its value. For an entry-level car, the primary utility is mobility, so byproducts that hinder mobility, such as frequent breakdowns, directly contrast with and reduce its utility. On the other hand, for a Ferrari, the most significant byproducts might not disrupt mobility but instead diminish its exclusivity or the perception of status it provides.

Ultimately, byproducts are what users cognitively experience. They can arise from gaps between what a user expects and what they actually experience, or between what they've experienced and what they begin to desire. These byproducts can take many forms. Some are directly connected to the original utility (intrinsic), while others affect it indirectly (extrinsic) without being in opposition. Let's break this down further:

Byproducts Aren't Always Oppositional:
Byproducts are not necessarily the opposite of the utility itself, but they could be secondary effects that weren't originally intended or foreseen. For instance:
- **Functional Utility:** A hammer's utility might result in damaged materials if not used properly. The byproduct isn't the opposite of functionality; it's a new issue (overuse, misuse) created by the functional utility.

- **Social Utility:** Owning a luxury car like a Ferrari may provide social status (social utility), but the byproduct might be envy from others, attention from thieves, or expectations to maintain that status through further high-end lifestyle demands.

These examples reveal that byproducts are new needs or issues that arise from a utility, which require their own form of innovation to address.

Byproducts Can Be Related to Maintenance or Sustainability of Utility:

- **Economic Utility:** The utility of making an investment could lead to a byproduct of financial risk or market volatility. This risk isn't necessarily the opposite of economic utility but is a consequence of engaging in that economic activity.
- **Convenience Utility:** While ride-sharing apps provide the utility of convenience, a byproduct might be increased traffic congestion or worker exploitation, neither of which directly contrast convenience but emerge as entirely new challenges.

Byproducts Emerge as Future Innovation Opportunities:

Each utility tends to create new gaps, inefficiencies, or secondary effects that then provoke further innovation to solve these issues:

- **Technological Utility:** The utility provided by smartphones (connectivity, access to information) creates byproducts like over-reliance on devices, digital privacy concerns, or mental health issues related to screen time. These aren't direct opposites but new challenges that require innovations in digital detox apps or data privacy tools.
- **Health Utility:** While health supplements might provide physical well-being, the byproducts could include false health claims or over-reliance on supplements instead of a balanced unprocessed-food diet, leading to further innovations in regulation or consumer education.

Byproducts Can Also Be Unfulfilled Desires Sparked by the Original Utility:

Sometimes, the utility sparks new desires that weren't previously apparent:

- **Aesthetic Utility:** A beautifully designed car may provide aesthetic utility, but the byproduct could be a desire for more customization, which in turn leads to new markets for personalization services or aftermarket upgrades or accessories.
- **Experiential Utility:** The joy derived from an experience (such as travel) might create a byproduct of expectation for even more unique or

extravagant experiences, which leads to industries offering exclusive or specialized adventure experiences.

Examples of Byproducts for Select Utilities:

- **Functional Utility:**

Byproduct: Over-reliance on tools leading to skill degradation or accidents.

- **Emotional Utility:**

Byproduct: Emotional attachment could lead to fear of loss or sentimental hoarding.

- **Social Utility:**

Byproduct: Social status can lead to envy, peer pressure, or increased financial burden to maintain status.

- **Cognitive Utility:**

Byproduct: Cognitive overload from too much information or problem-solving activities.

- **Convenience Utility:**

Byproduct: Convenience can lead to impatience, over-consumption, or loss of certain skills.

- **Simplicity Utility:**

Byproduct: A minimalist design might lead to boredom or limited functionality, spurring demand for enhanced customization options.

Byproducts may not necessarily be in direct opposition to the original utility; instead, they can be secondary effects that arise from the presence and experience of that utility. They emerge when a gap forms between what users expect and what they actually experience (expectation deviation η) as well as from what they've experienced and a new [higher] potential utility (aspirational comparison δ). Rather than negating the utility, byproducts act as valuable indicators of where future utility creation efforts could be directed. This is particularly significant when data on "issues and aspirations" (byproduct) is supported by a substantial number of users, highlighting key areas of opportunity for innovation.

The Importance of Understanding Byproduct Types in Innovation

Understanding byproducts is crucial for organizations because byproducts represent the seeds of future utility innovations. By carefully analyzing and categorizing current and potential byproducts throughout the products lifecycle, organizations can gain insight into how their innovations have and will interact with broader systems, user behaviors, and ecosystems. This foresight allows them to anticipate challenges, mitigate risks, and proactively design solutions that not only enhance the current utility but also reduce or address potentially emerging byproducts.

For organizations, there are several key benefits to this approach:
- **Risk Mitigation:** By identifying potential byproducts, organizations can minimize unintended negative consequences that may lead to product failures, reputational damage, or environmental harm.
- **Opportunity Identification:** Byproducts often reveal new needs or gaps in the market that can be addressed through subsequent innovations, providing organizations with competitive advantages.
- **Sustainability:** A deep understanding of byproducts can lead to more sustainable product designs, reducing waste, resource consumption, and long-term environmental impacts.
- **Customer Satisfaction:** Addressing byproducts, particularly those related to usability, experience, and service, can enhance customer satisfaction and loyalty by improving the overall utility of a product.

By developing a robust taxonomy of byproduct types, organizations can create more resilient, adaptive, and forward-thinking products and services that thrive in today's dynamic markets. Below are several of the 34 byproduct classes, expanded with examples, illustrating the wide range of potential byproducts that innovators must consider as part of their ongoing efforts to provide utility and value. For product or service developers, you will want to establish a taxonomy that is tailored to your product category.

A Byproduct Taxonomy: A Framework for Understanding Byproducts

The Byproduct Taxonomy example listed below is a classification system consisting of 34 major classes, each representing a distinct class of byproducts that can emerge from product, service or system use, misuse, interaction with other products or systems, or external environmental factors. This taxonomy is meant to support innovators in classifying byproducts based on their nature, source, and impact, facilitating targeted responses to specific challenges. The 34 classes serve as broad categories that allow organizations to identify potential byproducts systematically. However, <u>organizations are encouraged to create their own classes and sub-classes,</u> based on specific use cases, industry demands, or unique product characteristics.

Purpose and Value of a Byproduct Taxonomy

A Byproduct Taxonomy serves several key purposes:

- **Identification**: It helps innovators pinpoint specific byproducts and understand their nature, origins, and potential effects.
- **Prioritization**: By organizing byproducts by class, the taxonomy allows for more effective prioritization, as certain classes may represent higher risks or opportunities than others.
- **Cross-Industry Applicability**: The taxonomy is designed to be flexible and adaptable, allowing it to be applied across industries, from technology and healthcare to manufacturing and consumer goods.
- **Facilitating Solutions**: By understanding the specific class of a byproduct, innovators can design targeted solutions that address the root causes of byproducts, improving the user experience and product effectiveness.

The 34 Byproduct Taxonomy

Below is the complete list of 34 major byproduct classes with definitions. Examples have been provided across several of the classes to illustrate the diverse nature of byproducts. It is important to note that the utility-byproduct model of LPI can actually extend beyond products or services (as exemplified in Chapter 10, with the relationship example), however, for this book we will stay within the scope of products, services and systems. In addition, you will NOT notice any of the 34 byproduct classes identified as "Emotional." The reason for this should be apparent by now; all byproducts have a subjective component to them and, therefore, always have an emotional-cognitive perception tied to them.

1. **Operational and Functional Byproducts**: Byproducts that emerge from the direct use of a product or service, particularly in its operational efficiency and functionality.
   - Lack of automation leading to task burdensome processes or capability
   - Over-reliance on automated systems, leading to skill erosion
   - System malfunctions or breakdowns causing disruptions
   - Misuse or unintended use of products beyond their original purpose
   - Reduced flexibility due to rigid operational processes
   - Increased downtime due to technical failures
   - Inefficiencies or inconveniences during normal use and operation

2. **Temporal Displacement Byproducts**: Byproducts caused by shifts in how time is managed, perceived, and valued, especially due to technological advancements in productivity and communication.

    - Increased difficulty disconnecting from work as remote technologies blur the lines between personal and professional time
    - Erosion of traditional work-life boundaries, leading to burnout and decreased mental well-being
    - Reduced time for reflective or creative thinking due to constant digital interruptions
    - Escalation of social pressures to be constantly productive in a digitally connected world
    - Increased stress from multitasking and managing multiple digital communication channels
    - Increased pressure to respond immediately to work, peer or relationship related communications due to technological tethering of communication devices.
    - Difficulty managing personal time as productivity tools push for optimization in all aspects of life

3. **Social, Cultural, and Generational Byproducts**: Byproducts that affect societal norms, cultural practices, and generational dynamics, often altering how individuals interact with products or services.

    - Cultural homogenization due to globalized products and services
    - Increased anxiety and stress related to keeping up with fast-changing cultural trends
    - Social isolation and fragmentation of social bonds due to digital communication replacing face-to-face interactions
    - Increased generational divides in technology use and adoption
    - Loss of intergenerational knowledge transfer as traditional skills fade
    - Heightened social comparison and peer pressure through social media
    - Change in family dynamics due to reliance on technology for entertainment and communication

4. **Health and Well-being Byproducts**: Byproducts that affect physical, mental, or emotional health, either improving or degrading well-being.

    - Physical health deterioration due to sedentary lifestyles encouraged by technology

- Eye strain and headaches from prolonged screen use
- Reduced sleep quality due to the overuse of electronic devices
- Increased exposure to harmful materials (e.g., plastics, chemicals)
- Mental health deterioration from social media use (e.g., FOMO, social comparison)
- Addiction to technology and its psychological effects
- Increased anxiety related to constant data monitoring (e.g. fitness trackers)

5. **Psychological and Behavioral Economy Byproducts**: Byproducts affecting human behavior and decision-making, particularly in response to economic systems, marketing strategies, and behavioral nudges.
   - Increased consumer impulsiveness due to hyper-targeted advertising
   - Loss of autonomy due to behavioral nudges in digital platforms
   - Escalation of spending on convenience services, leading to financial strain
   - Increased societal pressure to conform to consumption trends
   - Reinforcement of consumer biases through algorithmic recommendations
   - Difficulty in distinguishing genuine preferences from manipulated desires
   - Escalation of peer pressure through social validation mechanisms (e.g., likes, reviews)

6. **Service and Customer Experience Byproducts**: Byproducts related to the quality of service and overall customer experience, influenced by the adoption of new technologies or service models.
   - Customer dissatisfaction with impersonal automated service channels, chatbots and prolonged automated selection menu's
   - Increased complexity in service offerings leading to confusion or frustration among customers
   - Frustration with opaque or complex subscription models that are hard to cancel
   - Difficulty in delivering consistent customer experience across regions with varying regulations
   - Difficulty maintaining brand loyalty in competitive markets with similar service offerings

- Increased reliance on user-generated content for customer support (e.g. forums), reducing maker/provider accountability
- Frustration with live customer support agents due to language barriers resulting in communication problems

7. **Environmental Byproducts**: Byproducts related to the environmental impact of producing, using, and disposing of products or services.

8. **Economic and Financial Byproducts**: Byproducts that influence economic systems, financial markets, and individual financial behaviors.

9. **Ethical Consumption and Social Responsibility Byproducts**: Byproducts related to consumer behaviors and corporate social responsibility, particularly when companies align their products with ethical or social values.

10. **Technological and Human Ethics Byproducts**: Byproducts arising from ethical concerns related to technology use, human enhancement, and the relationship between people and machines.

11. **Information and Knowledge Byproducts**: Byproducts stemming from the creation, dissemination, and management of information and knowledge, often driven by digital systems and platforms.

12. **Sustainability and Resource Management Byproducts**: Byproducts related to the management of resources, sustainability efforts, and environmental conservation.

13. **Community and Relationship Byproducts**: Byproducts that affect personal relationships, communities, and social cohesion, often as a result of new technologies or services altering how people connect.

14. **Innovation Ecosystem and Diffusion Byproducts**: Byproducts arising from the spread and adoption of innovations within industries and ecosystems, affecting collaboration, competition, and standardization.

15. **Organizational, Workplace, and Employment Byproducts**: Byproducts that influence organizational structures, workplace environments, and employment dynamics, often as a result of technological or structural changes.

16. **Product Lifecycle Byproducts**: Byproducts that emerge during different stages of a product's lifecycle, from development to disposal, affecting both companies and consumers.

17. **Data and Analytics Byproducts**: Byproducts related to the collection, use, and analysis of data, particularly in big data systems and AI-driven insights.

18. **Legal, Compliance, and Governance Byproducts**: Byproducts emerging from legal, regulatory, and governance challenges, particularly in industries undergoing rapid technological change.

19. **Psychosocial Byproducts**: Byproducts that arise from the intersection of psychological and social factors, particularly related to how innovations affect human interactions, emotions, and mental health.

20. **Trust and Transparency Byproducts**: Byproducts that affect the trust between consumers, businesses, and technologies, particularly concerning the transparency of business practices or product functionalities.

21. **Time and Productivity Byproducts**: Byproducts stemming from how innovations impact time management, productivity, and efficiency, often changing the way people approach work or leisure.

22. **Supply Chain, Distribution, and Logistics Byproducts**: Byproducts that emerge from the complexity and interdependencies of supply chains and logistics, whether on a local or global scale.

23. **Security and Risk Management Byproducts**: Byproducts that result from the need to protect data, intellectual property, and physical systems from risks, including cybersecurity threats.

24. **Societal Impact and Governance Byproducts**: Byproducts affecting societal structures, governance systems, and public policy, especially in response to new technologies or disruptive innovations.

25. **Long-Term Environmental and Health Byproducts**: Byproducts that may not appear immediately but have long-term environmental, ecological, and health impacts as a result of innovations or new products.

26. **Digital Autonomy, Privacy, and Algorithmic Governance Byproducts**: Byproducts related to the increasing role of algorithms and digital systems in shaping decision-making, privacy concerns, and autonomy in the digital world.

27. **Globalization and Geopolitical Byproducts**: Byproducts arising from the global interconnectedness of economies, technologies, and cultures, often with geopolitical ramifications.

28. **Intellectual and Cultural Capital Byproducts**: Byproducts related to the transformation, commodification, or marginalization of intellectual and cultural capital due to technological and economic shifts.

29. **Energy Consumption and Efficiency Byproducts**: Byproducts tied to the energy demands of modern technologies, industries, and infrastructures, particularly concerning sustainability and efficiency.

30. **Economic Disruption and Displacement Byproducts**: Byproducts caused by the disruption of traditional economic models and the displacement of legacy industries by new technologies and innovations.

31. **Artificial Scarcity and Market Manipulation Byproducts**: Byproducts related to the creation of artificial scarcity or manipulation of markets to drive demand or maintain control over resources and products.

32. **Resource Nationalism and Economic Sovereignty Byproducts**: Byproducts linked to the control, ownership, and political power surrounding natural and technological resources, often leading to economic and geopolitical tensions.

33. **Digital Decay and Legacy System Byproducts**: Byproducts related to the obsolescence and decay of digital systems, software, and infrastructure as technologies evolve rapidly, creating legacy systems that are difficult to maintain.

34. **Virtualization of Experience Byproducts**: Byproducts emerging from the shift to virtual experiences, where digital platforms or virtual reality replace or supplement physical, face-to-face interactions.

By leveraging a Byproduct Taxonomy, innovators can systematically classify the types of byproducts their products generate and strategically prioritize their management.

CHAPTER 18
Utility Classification - The Absolute Utility Map

Purpose and Value of the Absolute Utility Map

The Absolute Utility Map categorizes the various forms of utility across 65 distinct values, each representing a unique form of value that a product or service can offer. This map allows innovators to recognize, assess, and maximize the utility delivered to users, supporting a holistic view of how products create value across different domains. The Absolute Utility Map complements the Byproduct Taxonomy by focusing on the response aspect of innovation, helping organizations understand and optimize the specific utilities their products provide.

Absoluteness of Utility Types

Each of the 65 utility types outlined represents a specific form of value that can be delivered to users. These utility types describe distinct forms of benefit, whether functional, emotional, social, aesthetic, or other, that a product, service, or system can provide. For example, "portability" or "affordability" are not categories or classes that contain subtypes; they are standalone utilities that represent a specific form of value that is either provided or not provided.

Distinction from Classes

Unlike the byproduct classes, which are broad categories encompassing many potential byproducts, the 65 utility types are more definitive. They don't serve as overarching categories but rather as distinct, absolute "felt" attributes of a product, service, or system.

For instance:

- Affordability is the clear and specific value derived from the cost of a product or service being accessible.
- Portability refers to the ability to carry or transport an item easily.
- Emotional Fulfillment refers to the value derived from the emotional satisfaction provided by a product or experience.

These utilities are not open-ended like byproduct classes, which can be expanded and customized. The 65 utilities are a fixed set of specific, recognizable forms of value.

Application in the Framework

These utility types serve as the end goals, or targets, of innovation, with byproducts eventually emerging as a result of delivering or expanding upon these specific forms of value.

The Absolute Utility Map offers several benefits:
- **Utility Identification**: It helps innovators identify the diverse forms of utility a product can offer, from functional and aesthetic to emotional and social.
- **Utility Expansion**: By understanding the broad spectrum of utilities, organizations can explore new ways to expand the value their products provide.
- **Alignment with User Needs**: The map enables a more detailed understanding of user needs, facilitating alignment between product design and user expectations.
- **Strategic Differentiation**: The map highlights unique utilities that can serve as differentiators, giving products a competitive advantage in crowded markets.

The 65 Absolute Utility Map

1. **Functional Utility**: The practical and tangible benefits derived from using a product or service to fulfill a specific task or need.

- Example: A hammer's functional utility is its ability to drive nails into wood, making it essential for construction or repair work.

2. **Emotional Utility:** The value derived from the emotional satisfaction or psychological comfort that a product or service provides.

- Example: A favorite pen or boardgame can have emotional utility by evoking feelings of comfort.

3. Social Utility: The value derived from the social benefits gained from using a product or service, often related to status, prestige, or group belonging.

- Example: Owning a luxury car like a Ferrari provides social utility by signaling wealth and status.

4. Economic Utility: The financial benefits derived from a product or service, such as cost savings, revenue generation, or investment potential.

- Example: Investing in real estate provides economic utility through potential appreciation in property value.

5. Aesthetic Utility: The value derived from the beauty, design, or artistic appeal of a product or service, providing visual or sensory pleasure.

- Example: A beautifully designed piece of furniture offers aesthetic utility by enhancing the visual appeal of a living space.

6. Cultural Utility: The value derived from the cultural significance or identity that a product or service represents, connecting individuals to their heritage or traditions.

- Example: Wearing traditional clothing during cultural festivals offers cultural utility by preserving and celebrating heritage.

7. Ethical or Moral Utility: The satisfaction derived from making choices that align with one's values, often related to ethical or moral considerations.

- Example: Purchasing fair trade coffee provides ethical utility by supporting ethical labor practices and sustainable farming.

8. Cognitive Utility: The intellectual benefits gained from engaging with products or services that stimulate the mind or facilitate learning.

- Example: Reading a challenging book provides cognitive utility by enhancing knowledge and critical thinking skills.

9. Health Utility: The value derived from the health benefits that a product or service provides, contributing to physical or mental well-being.

- Example: Regular exercise using gym equipment provides health utility by improving physical fitness and overall health.

10. Environmental Utility: The value derived from the positive impact a product or service has on the environment, contributing to sustainability or reducing ecological footprints.

- Example: Using reusable grocery bags provides environmental utility by reducing plastic waste and promoting sustainable consumption.

11. Experiential Utility: The value derived from experiences, such as travel, entertainment, or adventure, providing enjoyment, fulfillment, or personal growth.

- Example: Traveling to a new country offers experiential utility by providing new cultural experiences and personal enrichment.

12. Temporal Utility: The value derived from the timing of a product or service, where speed, time-convenience, or availability are key factors.

- Example: Same-day delivery services provide temporal utility by saving time and offering immediate access to products.

13. Spiritual Utility: The value derived from products, services, or practices that enhance spiritual well-being or a connection to a higher purpose.

- Example: Religious artifacts such as prayer beads provide spiritual utility by facilitating religious practices and spiritual connection.

14. Relational Utility: The value derived from enhancing personal relationships through communication, shared experiences, or connection.

- Example: Family vacations provide relational utility by strengthening bonds and creating shared memories.

15. Symbolic Utility: The value derived from the meaning or representation that a product or service holds, often tied to identity, achievement, or affiliation.

- Example: Wearing a wedding ring provides symbolic utility by representing commitment and love in a marriage.

16. Convenience Utility: The value derived from the ease and simplicity of using a product or service, often through saving time in effort, or requiring less resources to accomplish.

- Example: Pre-packaged meal kits offer convenience utility by reducing the time and effort required to plan, shop for and prepare meals.

17. Sensory Utility: The value derived from the sensory pleasure or satisfaction gained from taste, smell, sight, sound, or touch.

- Example: A gourmet meal provides sensory utility through its rich flavors, aromas and visual presentation.

18. Network Utility: The value that increases as more people use a product or service, common in digital platforms or communication networks.

- Example: Messaging apps like WhatsApp offer network utility by becoming more useful as more people in your network adopt the app.

19. Psychological Utility: The value derived from products or services that contribute to mental well-being, reducing stress, anxiety, or mental discomfort.

- Example: Therapy services provide psychological utility by helping individuals manage stress and mental health issues.

20. Technological Utility: The value derived from the benefits provided by technology, such as increased efficiency, connectivity, or problem-solving capabilities.

- Example: Cloud storage services offer technological utility by allowing users to securely store and access their data from anywhere.

21. Legal Utility: The value derived from the protection or benefits provided by laws, regulations, or legal services.

- Example: Having a legal contract provides legal utility by protecting the interests of the parties involved.

22. Political Utility: The value derived from the power, influence, or benefits associated with political systems, decisions, or affiliations.

- Example: Lobbying efforts by interest groups provide political utility by shaping legislation and public policy.

23. Educational Utility: The value derived from the process of acquiring knowledge, skills, or intellectual growth through formal education.

- Example: Online courses offer educational utility by enabling individuals to learn new skills at their own pace.

24. Professional Utility: The value derived from career advancement, skill development, or professional growth.

- Example: Attending industry conferences offers professional utility by providing networking opportunities and staying updated on industry trends.

25. Community Utility: The value derived from the benefits of being part of a community, including support, shared resources, and social cohesion.

- Example: Participating in a neighborhood association provides community utility by fostering a sense of belonging and mutual support.

26. Safety Utility: The value derived from the protection or security a product or service offers, contributing to physical or psychological safety.

- Example: Wearing a seatbelt provides safety utility by reducing the risk of injury in a car accident.

27. Recreational Utility: The value derived from leisure activities and entertainment, providing enjoyment, relaxation, or pleasure.

- Example: Watching a movie in a theater provides recreational utility through entertainment and shared experience.

28. Efficiency Utility: The value derived from the ability to accomplish tasks more quickly or with less effort, often through tools or processes that optimize performance.

- Example: Using a dishwasher instead of hand-washing dishes offers efficiency utility by saving time and effort.

29. Scalability Utility: The value derived from the ease with which a product or service can be scaled up or expanded to meet growing demands.

- Example: Cloud computing platforms provide scalability utility by allowing businesses to easily expand their operations without significant upfront investment.

30. Adaptability Utility: The value derived from a product or service's ability to adapt to different situations, needs, or environments.

- Example: Modular furniture provides adaptability utility by allowing users to reconfigure pieces to suit different spaces or uses.

31. Longevity Utility: The value derived from products or services that are designed to last, providing long-term satisfaction and minimizing the need for replacement.

- Example: High-quality kitchen appliances, like a durable stand mixer, offer longevity utility by providing years of reliable service.

32. Customizability Utility: The value derived from products or services that can be tailored to individual preferences or needs.

- Example: Personalized gifts, such as a custom-engraved watch, offer customizability utility by allowing individuals to create unique, meaningful items.

33. Identity Utility: The value derived from products or services that help individuals express or affirm their identity, such as fashion, tattoos, or personalized items.

- Example: Wearing clothing that aligns with personal style or cultural identity offers identity utility by expressing who one is.

34. Nostalgic Utility: The value derived from products, services, or experiences that evoke positive memories from the past.

- Example: Listening to music from one's youth provides nostalgic utility by evoking emotions and memories associated with that time.

35. Redundancy Utility: The value derived from having backups or fail-safes in place, ensuring continuity in case of failure.

- Example: A backup generator provides redundancy utility by ensuring power availability during an outage.

36. Transparency Utility: The value derived from the clarity and openness a product or service offers, fostering trust and confidence.

- Example: Companies that provide clear, transparent pricing offer transparency utility by building customer trust.

37. Innovation Utility: The value derived from the novel or cutting-edge features of a product or service, providing unique benefits or solving problems in new ways.

- Example: A smartphone with a revolutionary camera system provides innovation utility by enabling users to capture high-quality images in new ways.

38. Resilience Utility: The value derived from products or systems that can withstand and recover from disruptions, providing reliability and peace of mind.

- Example: A water-resistant smartphone provides resilience utility by withstanding accidental spills or drops into water.

39. Privacy Utility: The value derived from products or services that protect personal information and ensure confidentiality.

- Example: VPN services provide privacy utility by protecting users' online activities from being tracked or monitored.

40. Simplicity Utility: The value derived from the ease of use and straightforwardness of a product or service, reducing complexity and making it accessible.

- Example: Minimalist UI capability like 'Quick Start' guides for electronic products offer simplicity utility by providing a fast and simple way to start using your product.

41. Compatibility Utility: The value derived from a product or service's ability to work seamlessly with other systems, devices, or processes.

- Example: Universal chargers that work with multiple devices provide compatibility utility by reducing the need for multiple chargers.

42. Interoperability/Ecosystem Utility: The value derived from the ability of systems or products to work together and exchange information effectively within an ecosystem.

- Example: Smart home devices that communicate with each other, like lights and thermostats that work with a central hub, provide interoperability utility.

43. Intellectual Utility: The value derived from engaging with challenging ideas or concepts, leading to intellectual satisfaction or growth.

- Example: Participating in a book club offers intellectual utility by engaging members in discussions that expand their understanding of literature, concepts or ideas.

44. Reputation Utility: The value derived from maintaining or enhancing one's reputation through the use of certain products or behaviors.

- Example: A company engaging in corporate social responsibility (CSR) initiatives provides reputation utility by enhancing its public image.

45. Compliance Utility: The value derived from adhering to rules, regulations, or standards, thereby avoiding penalties or enhancing trust.

- Example: A company adhering to environmental regulations provides compliance utility by avoiding fines and contributing to a positive public image.

46. Strategic Utility: The value derived from the strategic advantage a product or service provides in achieving long-term goals.

- Example: Conducting market research offers strategic utility by providing insights that guide business decisions and help identify growth opportunities.

47. Resale Utility: The value derived from the ability to resell a product at a significant portion of its original value.

- Example: Collectible items, like vintage watches, provide resale utility by retaining or even increasing their value over time.

48. Learning Utility: The value derived from the process of acquiring knowledge, skills, or cognitive growth through informal education.

- Example: Engaging with informal online courses, books or subject summary Apps offer learning utility by allowing individuals to gain knowledge in various subjects at their own pace.

49. Modularity Utility: The value derived from the ability to add, remove, or rearrange components of a system to meet different needs.

- Example: Modular furniture systems, like IKEA's shelving units, offer modularity utility by allowing users to customize configurations based on their space and needs.

50. Interactivity Utility: The value derived from products or services that allow for user interaction, enhancing engagement or personalization.

- Example: Video games offer interactivity utility by providing an immersive experience where users can control characters and make decisions that affect the game's outcome.

51. Authenticity Utility: The value derived from the perceived authenticity of a product, service, or experience, often linked to originality or cultural integrity.

- Example: Handcrafted artisanal products provide authenticity utility by being created using traditional methods, which resonate with consumers seeking genuine experiences.

52. Security Utility: The value derived from the safety and protection provided by a product or service, whether physical, digital, or psychological.

- Example: Antivirus software provides security utility by protecting computers from malware and cyber threats.

53. Patience Utility: The value derived from products or services that require or encourage patience, often leading to long-term benefits.

- Example: Brewing specialty coffee using a slow pour-over method offers patience utility by requiring time and care, resulting in a richer flavor.

54. Empowerment Utility: The value derived from products or services that enable individuals to take control of their lives or decisions.

- Example: Financial planning tools like budgeting apps provide empowerment utility by helping users manage their finances and make informed decisions.

55. Access Utility: The value derived from the ability to access resources, information, or services that were previously unavailable or difficult to obtain.

- Example: Subscription services like Netflix provide access utility by offering a vast library of movies and shows on demand.

56. Sustainability Utility: The value derived from products or services designed with long-term environmental, economic, or social sustainability in mind.

- Example: Choosing energy-efficient appliances offers sustainability utility by reducing energy consumption and lowering carbon footprints.

57. Collaborative Utility: The value derived from the benefits gained through collaboration or teamwork facilitated by a product or service.

- Example: Co-working spaces provide collaborative utility by creating environments where individuals from different fields can share ideas and resources.

58. Anticipation Utility: The value derived from the excitement or pleasure of looking forward to a future event, product, or experience.

- Example: Pre-ordering a highly anticipated book, movie or gadget provides anticipation utility as consumers look forward to receiving it.

59. Ritual Utility: The value derived from repeated actions or behaviors that hold personal or cultural significance.

- Example: Morning routines, like making a cup of coffee, provide ritual utility by creating a sense of structure and comfort.

60. Curiosity Utility: The value derived from products or services that satisfy or stimulate curiosity, leading to discovery or exploration.

- Example: Science kits for children provide curiosity utility by encouraging exploration and hands-on learning about the natural world.

61. Minimalism Utility: The value derived from the simplicity and clarity offered by minimalist designs or approaches, reducing clutter and focusing on essential elements.

- Example: Decluttering and organizing a living space offers minimalism utility by creating a more peaceful and functional environment.

62. Symbolism Utility: The value derived from products or services that hold symbolic meaning, often representing deeper values, beliefs, or identities.

- Example: Displaying a country's flag provides symbolism utility by expressing national pride and identity.

63. Freedom Utility: The value derived from the ability to make choices and act independently, often associated with products or services that offer flexibility or options.

- Example: Owning a car offers freedom utility by providing the ability to travel independently without relying on public transportation.

64. Service Utility: The value derived from customer service or support, enhancing the overall experience of a product or service.

- Example: A company with excellent customer service, like Amazon, provides service utility by resolving issues quickly and effectively, leading to greater customer satisfaction.

318

65. Ambiguity Utility: The value derived from products or services that allow for multiple interpretations or uses, often stimulating creativity or personal interpretation.

- Example: Open-ended video games, where players can choose how to approach challenges, offer ambiguity utility by fostering creative problem-solving and personalized gameplay.

Applying Systemic Classifiers to the Innovation Process

The Systemic Classifiers just described, the Byproduct Taxonomy and the Absolute Utility Map, play a pivotal role in a Byproduct-Driven innovation process, by providing structured tools for identifying, categorizing, and prioritizing both byproducts and utilities. Here's a brief summary of how these classifiers support byproduct driven innovation:

1. **Comprehensive Analysis**: Systemic Classifiers allow innovators to examine all aspects of their products' impact, from positive utilities to unintended, mitigated and positive byproducts. This holistic perspective fosters a more nuanced understanding of the product's role within larger ecosystems.

2. **Strategic Decision-Making**: By categorizing byproducts and utilities systematically, innovators can make more informed decisions about which areas require immediate attention, long-term planning, or further exploration.

3. **Enhanced Market Alignment**: Systemic Classifiers enable organizations to align their products with user expectations by recognizing and addressing specific byproducts and utilities that resonate with customers.

4. **Opportunity Identification**: The taxonomy and map reveal new avenues for value creation, whether through untapped utilities or overlooked byproducts that represent latent user needs.

5. **Asset Tracking for Prediction**: By continuously monitoring and managing the byproducts and utilities associated with an organization's products or services across different iterations and generations, patterns and trends will naturally emerge over time. This ongoing tracking provides valuable insights into how these elements evolve, enabling more accurate predictions and strategic decisions.

Systemic Classifiers as Strategic Tools in LPI

The Systemic Classifiers equip innovators with a structured approach to understanding and managing the complexities of byproducts and utilities. By applying the Byproduct Taxonomy and the Absolute Utility Map, organizations can ensure that their innovation efforts address both the challenges and opportunities within the cycle of perpetual innovation. These tools help innovators balance the two goals of minimizing byproducts and maximizing utility, fostering products that deliver sustained and meaningful value while adapting to evolving user needs and environmental contexts.

Module D:
Impact Models

Module D presents two complementary frameworks for evaluating and categorizing byproducts. Chapter 19 introduces the **Byproduct Impact Spectrum**, which zeroes in on the *objective* side of byproduct: quantifiable damage, operational disruptions, or resource losses. By assigning concrete metrics, organizations can gauge whether a byproduct is catastrophic, moderate, or relatively minor. Chapter 20 shifts to the *subjective* side, highlighting the **Byproduct Contrast Continuum** and showing how users' emotional anchors, cultural context, and personal histories determine whether they perceive a given shortfall as an annoyance, a crisis, or even a creative spark for improvement.

Taken together, these models provide a complete view of byproduct. The Impact Spectrum helps teams see how big a problem is in tangible terms: costs, casualties, or inefficiencies. While the Contrast Continuum reveals why people feel so strongly (or ambivalently) about it. One user's minor glitch might be another's deal-breaker, depending on expectations, environment, or temperament. Armed with both sets of insights, innovators can prioritize which byproducts truly deserve urgent resources or in-depth redesign, which to watch for downstream risks, and which might serve as a catalyst for future breakthroughs.

Author's Note on Tailoring Impact Models

While these two chapters offer clear-cut examples of rating byproduct severity (Chapter 19) and capturing user sentiment (Chapter 20), they are far from the only ways to formalize objective or subjective evaluations. Many organizations utilize risk matrices, robust cost–benefit analyses, or advanced sentiment tracking to accomplish similar goals. In practice, any consistent approach, numeric or categorical, can help teams spot urgent byproducts on existing products or anticipate hidden pitfalls in upcoming releases.

Notably, you may need both actual and anticipated measurements. A feature that has yet to launch can still be "pre-scored" by prospective user feedback, pilot data, or historical analogs. The key is to keep a repeatable method for prioritizing problem areas, ensuring that even hypothetical burdens are not overlooked until it's too late. By looking simultaneously at a byproduct's objective footprint and its subjective resonance, organizations, and AI systems they use, can better identify, rank, and act on the byproducts most likely to shape outcomes.

CHAPTER 19
Capturing Objective Byproduct –
The Byproduct Impact Spectrum

A Recap on Utility decline vs. Byproduct Emergence

For decades, economists have explained dissatisfaction by reference to a decline in marginal utility (and even disutility). In conventional economic terms, utility signifies the satisfaction or benefit someone obtains from consuming a product, service, or engaging in a particular activity. Should a product fail to meet one's expectations, or deteriorate over time, economists would typically say that the consumer experiences diminishing utility. When dissatisfaction arises because a smartphone's battery no longer holds a charge, or the once-luxurious chair becomes uncomfortable, standard theory interprets this scenario as diminished or reduced utility or satisfaction. Under LPI it is emergence of byproduct overshadowing net perceived utility.

- **Marginal Utility and Loss Aversion:** Scholars such as Daniel Kahneman, Amos Tversky, and Richard Thaler have underscored how losses loom larger than gains in people's psychological calculus. This phenomenon, known as loss aversion, suggests that losing utility (e.g., encountering disappointment or frustration) can feel more consequential than an equivalent gain in utility. In this framing, the frustration with an uncomfortable chair is "a decline in utility" that can outweigh the delight initially experienced. Within LPI, it is byproduct emergence.

- **Diminishing Returns:** Another cornerstone of economic thought is that as people consume more of a product or service, the additional utility they derive from each extra unit [of the experience] tends to decrease (diminishing marginal utility). In everyday terms, the first few slices of pizza can be fantastic, but by the fourth or fifth slice, satisfaction plateaus or may even cause discomfort (disutility). Over time, this diminishing satisfaction may cross over into dissatisfaction if a once-exciting purchase like a new laptop or luxury car fails to sustain its early allure. Economists recognize this effect quantitatively, but its emotional dimension, in how it nudges consumers toward boredom, regret, or seeking something new, often goes unexamined from an innovation perspective. Within LPI, this is understood as byproduct accumulation reducing perceived net utility.

- **Elasticities and Switching Costs:** Traditional economists might predict that when utility declines enough, people switch to alternative solutions. For instance, if a certain brand of furniture consistently underperforms, a rational consumer (in purely economic terms) would seek better utility from competing options. The decline in utility thus triggers a reallocation of spending or resources. Economists call this "a shift in consumer choice." Within LPI, we reframe these consumer behaviors as the Utility Abandonment Condition or the Byproduct Inflexion Threshold, as discussed in Chapter 15.

While these perspectives seek to capture the quantitative dimension of how much utility is lost, they often overlook what the Law of Perpetual Innovation (LPI) calls byproduct: the emergent, objective (physical/tangible) and subjective (emotional-cognitive) byproducts that can spur redesign, rethinking, or renewed engagement. In other words, economic theory is adept at measuring dissatisfaction as a negative number but typically less focused on what that dissatisfaction produces in terms of new impulses, behaviors, or problem-solving pathways.

Byproduct as an Emergent Phenomenon in LPI

The Law of Perpetual Innovation advances a crucial idea: what has been historically perceived as a decline in utility (marginal or disutility) is not the case, but rather the beginning of a new cycle. This new cycle centers on what LPI terms as byproduct. When our expectations about a product, service, system, experience are unmet, or overshadowed by awareness of a superior possibility, we do more than simply measure the gap between the two states. We also experience a set of emotional-cognitive and motivational responses that, under the right conditions, can drive adaptation or pursuit behaviors. Let us review some concepts that shed light on the phenomenon of byproduct emergence:

- **Byproduct Described**: Byproduct is the realized consequence that arises from a mismatch between (1) expected and actual utility (via expectation deviation η) or (2) current and *[a better]* potential utility (via aspirational comparison δ), evidenced by the emergence of emotional pressure(s), at times driving us to take remediating action. While a decline in available net utility captures "how short we fell," byproduct describes the objective nature of that shortfall and its subjective impact on our thought processes, emotional states, and propensity to adapt or innovate. In some scenarios, subjective byproduct will manifest as frustration or dissatisfaction, but in others, it might appear as curiosity, a sense of urgency, or an impetus for exploration.

- **Subjectivity Matters:** Some individuals are more resilient to shortfalls or gaps, viewing them as growth opportunities, whereas others see them as crippling disappointments. This varied interpretation underscores that byproduct is not merely a numerical gap but an experience with psychological, social, and cultural dimensions.

- **Why Economists' View Is Incomplete**: Economists would say that dissatisfaction equals less utility. Within LPI however, this is byproduct emergence. Economists rarely account for how dissatisfaction might become a powerful force for creative change. A user annoyed by a smartphone's limited battery could impulsively switch brands or start a social media campaign for better battery standards, discover a workaround that spawns an adjacent market opportunity (like portable power banks), or if skilled in the art, might design an entirely new battery-charging solution altogether.

- **From Passive to Active**: The difference is that LPI frames the experience of "shortfall" as emergent activity: once we sense a deficiency, that deficiency acquires its own psychological reality (frustration, disappointment, relentless curiosity, galvanizing challenge) and can push us to refine or overhaul an existing utility. Thus, while in traditional economics a decline in utility remains a numerical statement about how less satisfied someone is, within LPI we see the emergence of byproduct: a dynamic phenomenon that either leads us to spiral downward into resentment or catapults us forward into problem-solving, opportunity creation, and higher utility in the future.

- **Not Utility Deficit, but Byproduct, is Always the Motivator**: At the core of every shortfall lies the realization that something once deemed valuable no longer meets expectations. Classic economics would call this a decline in utility, but in the LPI framework it becomes a catalyst, pointing to the real issue, the emergence of a byproduct. Through our perception of the objective component the subjective arises, manifesting as frustration, curiosity, or drive for improvement. Rather than serving as a measurement of lost satisfaction, LPI sees a drop in net utility due to accumulated byproduct, which ignites action. It can motivate individuals and organizations to reassess their current solutions, conceive upgrades, and sometimes reinvent entire systems. In this sense, unmet needs or overlooked potentials are not dead ends, they are what instigates the cycle of innovation to continuously renew.

Together, these perspectives show that while economists correctly identify less net perceived satisfaction, they incorrectly call it a decline in utility. LPI notes that this shortfall *is something new*: the onset and accumulation of byproduct. It is the physical and emotional aftermath that opens the door to reframing, redesigning, or otherwise progressing beyond the original deficit in perceived utility.

Objective vs. Subjective Byproduct: Why Both Matter

As discussed in previous chapters, a key element in the LPI framework is its recognition that every byproduct has both objective and subjective components (Principle of Byproduct Composition). When your phone battery drops from 80% to 20% within a couple of hours, that's a measurable, external fact. Similarly, a relationship that sees a tangible reduction in shared quality time from three hours of deep conversation weekly to barely thirty minutes, it can be charted out numerically. These objective indicators can signal precisely where your experiences aren't matching your expectations.

Objective Byproduct (Easier to track when experienced):
- A restaurant meal that arrives 20 minutes late, well beyond normal service standards.
- A pencil tip that repeatedly breaks after 50 lines of writing.
- The 11 phone calls made to secure tickets to a concert.

Yet, the emotional reality, or the subjective side, often determines whether you interpret the shortfall as a minor annoyance or an existential crisis. For example, two people might observe the same 60% battery drain in an hour. One person shrugs and says, "I'll just carry a power bank," while the other fumes and writes a scathing product review online. Likewise, the same one-hour cutback in a relationship's conversation time might be no big deal for one partner, while the other interprets it as a sign that the entire relationship is dying.

Subjective Byproduct (Emotional-Cognitive framing of the objective component):

- A sense of betrayal when a longtime favorite restaurant changes or eliminates one of your favorite dishes.
- Lingering disappointment when a partner fails to show empathy during a stressful moment.
- The gnawing anticipation of a long-awaited movie release.

Numbers alone do not predict emotional outcomes; they simply measure how far short from "normal" or "desired" we've landed. The objective observation often reveals the factual impact of a problem, while the subjective experience reveals the emotional-cognitive significance of how it affects the person or society. Both are crucial. A product might have only a minor defect (small objective gap), but if it triggers major emotional or social repercussions, the byproduct's overall impact is still significant. The truly pivotal insights come from how individuals *feel* about that gap. However, that can vary across individuals. Why, then, do people experience byproduct so differently? Within Chapter 20 we will dive into those details. For now, we will focus on the objective component of byproduct.

Byproduct Impact Spectrum: From High to Low Consequence

(The example spectrum provided identifies 14 degrees of byproduct across high, moderate and low impact. Various byproduct examples are provided within each of degree of impact.)

The Byproduct Impact Spectrum is an example of a structured method of categorizing and measuring the **objective effects of byproduct**, from the most disastrous, far-reaching problems to those that are marginally relevant. It outlines discrete levels of severity such as "harmful side effects," "unmet needs," or "mild inconveniences," to help innovators or organizations identify where, exactly, a shortfall is causing disruption, and to what degree. Whether the issue is a climate-related crisis, a modest design flaw, or an entirely neutral effect, the Byproduct Impact Spectrum ensures that everyone involved in the lifecycle of the product or service, from concept to end-of-life, is speaking the same language about how pressing or minimal each objective byproduct truly is.

Byproduct Impact Spectrum (visual)

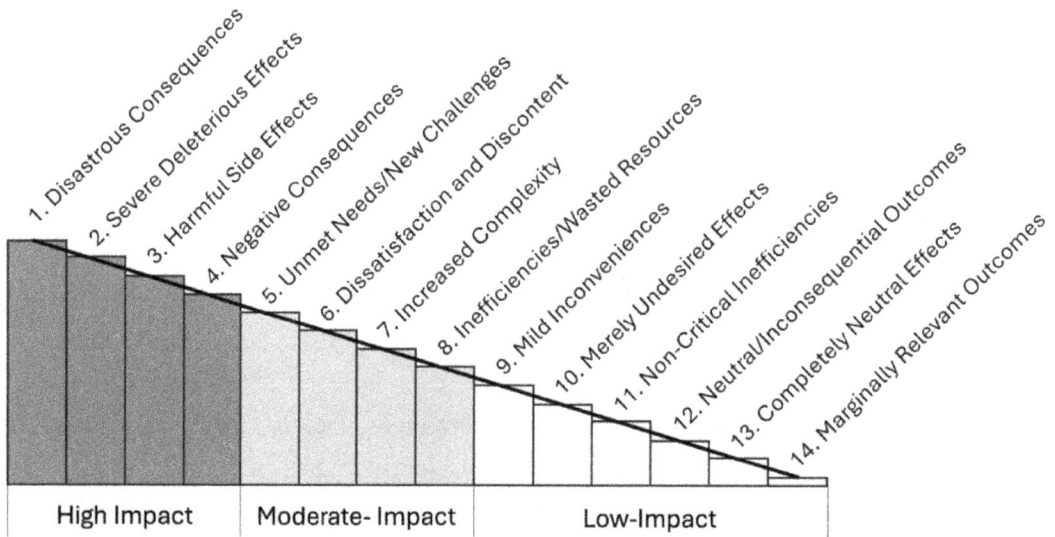

1. Disastrous Consequences
2. Severe Deleterious Effects
3. Harmful Side Effects
4. Negative Consequences
5. Unmet Needs/New Challenges
6. Dissatisfaction and Discontent
7. Increased Complexity
8. Inefficiencies/Wasted Resources
9. Mild Inconveniences
10. Merely Undesired Effects
11. Non-Critical Inefficiencies
12. Neutral/Inconsequential Outcomes
13. Completely Neutral Effects
14. Marginally Relevant Outcomes

High Impact | Moderate- Impact | Low-Impact

High-Impact or Consequential Byproducts

High-impact byproducts cause significant disruptions or harm, making urgent responses a necessity. Their large-scale consequences can be measured through well-defined metrics that track environmental, social, or economic damage.

1. Disastrous Consequences

Represents catastrophic outcomes that require immediate and large-scale intervention. These byproducts can devastate entire industries, ecosystems, or populations if not swiftly contained or mitigated.

For Example:

Environmental Catastrophes
- Example: Oil spills, nuclear disasters, major deforestation.
- Objective Indicators:
  - Area of land or ocean contaminated (measured in square kilometers or acres).

328

o Number of affected species or biodiversity loss index.
o Volume of pollutants released, tracked by chemical concentration in soil or water.

Major Safety Hazards
- Example: Factory explosions, building collapses.
- Objective Indicators:
  o Number of fatalities, injuries, or property damage costs (in USD).
  o Frequency of accidents per year in a given industry.
  o Compliance rates with existing safety standards (e.g., OSHA citations).

Global Pandemics
- Example: Rapidly spreading viral outbreaks.
- Objective Indicators:
  o Infection rate (R_0 value) and mortality rate.
  o Economic impact measured through GDP fluctuations or unemployment rates.
  o Healthcare system strain indicated by hospital occupancy and resource shortages.

2. Severe Deleterious Effects

Encompasses major harms that significantly degrade systems or communities but may not be instantly catastrophic. While urgent, these issues sometimes develop over a short period and demand substantial corrective efforts.

For Example:

Pollution and Toxic Waste
- Example: Release of harmful chemicals into rivers or air.
- Objective Indicators:
  o Toxin concentration in water or air quality indices.
  o Rates of pollution-related illnesses in local populations.
  o Tons of waste improperly disposed of per year.

Economic Collapse or Disruption
- Example: Market crashes, major industry failures.
- Objective Indicators:
  o Stock market indices or GDP contraction percentages.
  o Unemployment rates in affected industries.

o Capital flight or decreased foreign investment.

Social and Political Unrest
- Example: Instability triggered by economic, political or environmental crises.
- Objective Indicators:
  o Number of protests, strikes, or demonstrations.
  o Degree of media coverage or social media sentiment analysis.
  o Government stability indices or conflict tracker scores.

3. Harmful Side Effects

Involves negative ramifications that emerge as a byproduct of existing processes or technologies, leading to sustained hazards or difficulties. Though serious, these impacts may unfold more gradually than those classified as "severe" or "disastrous."

For Example:
Long-Term Health Risks
- Example: Gradual emergence of conditions tied to chemicals or materials.
- Objective Indicators:
  o Incidence rates of specific diseases in exposed populations.
  o Measured levels of substances in blood or tissue samples.
  o Longitudinal tracking of health outcomes over decades.

Social Inequality
- Example: Technology adoption widening wealth gaps.
- Objective Indicators:
  o Gini coefficient measuring income inequality.
  o Rates of civic engagement or voter turnout in affected areas.
  o Statistics on resource access disparities (education, healthcare).

Degradation of Natural Resources
- Example: Declining soil fertility or freshwater availability.
- Objective Indicators:
  o Change in soil nutrient levels over time.
  o Water table depth or freshwater supply metrics.
  o Rate of deforestation or desertification per year.

4. Negative Consequences

Captures detrimental outcomes that deepen preexisting problems or corrode public confidence. These byproducts can worsen overall conditions, making already challenging situations more complex to resolve.

For Example:

Erosion of Public Trust
- Example: Scandals or failures that tarnish an institution's reputation.
- Objective Indicators:
  - Polls measuring public confidence in institutions or technologies.
  - Social media sentiment analysis (positive vs. negative mentions).
  - Drop in membership or user base over a defined period.

Worsening of Existing Problems
- Example: Urban congestion intensifying after a new ride-sharing service.
- Objective Indicators:
  - Average commute times or traffic congestion indices.
  - Air quality measurements correlated with vehicle density.
  - Frequency of complaints or incident reports related to the aggravated issue.

Increased Dependence on Technology
- Example: Over-reliance on AI or automation.
- Objective Indicators:
  - Share of key tasks performed solely by automated systems.
  - Downtime costs when technology fails.
  - Ratio of human skill retention tests or training hours to tasks automated.

Moderate-Impact or Consequential Byproducts

Moderate-impact byproducts present substantial challenges but may not trigger immediate crises. They still drive significant innovation focused on efficiency, satisfaction, and complexity management.

5. Unmet Needs and New Challenges

Highlights the gap between current capabilities and evolving societal or technological demands. These gaps can push organizations or communities to find new solutions or pivot strategies before issues escalate.

For Example:

Emerging Societal Needs
- Example: Demand for affordable healthcare or clean energy.
- Objective Indicators:
  - Survey data revealing percentage of population citing these needs.
  - Growth rates in relevant markets (telemedicine or solar power installations).
  - Legislation or policy changes addressing unmet demands.

New Technological Challenges
- Example: Cybersecurity threats in cloud computing.
- Objective Indicators:
  - Documented number of hacking attempts or security breaches.
  - Average cost of data breach response.
  - Frequency of patches or updates required to maintain security.

Regulatory Challenges
- Example: New environmental rules forcing adaptation.
- Objective Indicators:
  - Rate of compliance among businesses targeted by regulation.
  - Penalties or fines assessed for noncompliance.
  - Time and cost to redesign products or processes to meet new standards.

6. Dissatisfaction and Discontent

Represents scenarios in which stakeholder frustration or dissatisfaction reaches a level that could harm trust, loyalty, or morale if unaddressed. Though not cataclysmic, it signals significant potential for conflict or decline in engagement.

For Example:

Cultural or Societal Discontent
- Example: Societal pushback against rigid work norms.
- Objective Indicators:
  - Social media volume on related hashtags.

o Number of petitions or open letters demanding change.
o Growth in alternative workplace models (co-working or remote-first).

Customer Service Failures
- Example: Slow response times or unhelpful support.
- Objective Indicators:
  o Average resolution time for support tickets.
  o Customer satisfaction surveys post-interaction.
  o Repeat contact rates for unresolved issues.

Employee Burnout
- Example: High attrition in high-stress environments.
- Objective Indicators:
  o Employee turnover rates.
  o Absenteeism or sick days taken.
  o Scores on standardized burnout scales (e.g., Maslach Burnout Inventory).

7. Increased Complexity

Signifies situations where processes, systems, or technologies become unwieldy and threaten efficiency. These byproducts often require rethinking workflows, organizational designs, or user interfaces.

For Example:
Complicated Workflows or Processes
- Example: Multi-step administrative tasks within a company.
- Objective Indicators:
  o Process cycle time (time from start to completion).
  o Number of handoffs or approvals required.
  o Error rate or rework percentage due to process confusion.

Over-engineered Solutions
- Example: Software packed with rarely used features.
- Objective Indicators:
  o Percentage of user engagement per feature.
  o Time spent on feature updates vs. user adoption.
  o Usability testing outcomes highlighting friction.

Interdepartmental Communication Barriers

- Example: Siloed teams leading to duplicated work.
- Objective Indicators:
  - Number of collaboration tools or meetings needed for alignment.
  - Frequency of redundant project outputs.
  - Survey results on perceived communication effectiveness.

8. Inefficiencies and Wasted Resources

Reflects circumstances where operational or logistical shortcomings lead to higher costs, lower productivity, or greater environmental footprints. While they might not pose immediate threats, addressing these inefficiencies can yield major benefits.

For Example:

Energy Inefficiency
- Example: Outdated HVAC systems in large buildings.
- Objective Indicators:
  - Energy consumption per square foot.
  - Utility cost trends over time.
  - Carbon footprint calculations based on electricity usage.

Material Waste in Production
- Example: Excess scrap in manufacturing.
- Objective Indicators:
  - Percentage of raw materials that become end-product vs. waste.
  - Cost of disposing or recycling leftover materials.
  - Production yield ratio reflecting how efficiently inputs convert to outputs.

Logistical Inefficiencies
- Example: Supply chain bottlenecks.
- Objective Indicators:
  - Average shipment transit times vs. on-time delivery rates.
  - Inventory turnover ratio or days of stock on hand.
  - Freight cost per unit shipped.

Low-Impact or Minor Consequential Byproducts

Low-impact byproducts typically cause only slight inefficiencies or inconveniences. While they do not often trigger large-scale innovation, they can still prompt incremental improvements.

9. Mild Inconveniences

Covers small-scale disruptions that do not directly threaten broader operations but can erode user satisfaction or productivity over time if ignored.

For Example:

Minor Service Disruptions

- Example: Brief network outages.
- Objective Indicators:
  o Duration of downtime or number of users affected.
  o Lost revenue estimates during the interruption.
  o Recovery time to full-service operation.

Minor Product Defects

- Example: Cosmetic scratches or loose fittings.
- Objective Indicators:
  o Percentage of products returned for cosmetic or superficial reasons.
  o Internal quality audits detecting small defects.
  o Cost of rework or repair per unit.

Inconvenient Packaging

- Example: Excessive layers of plastic around a product.
- Objective Indicators:
  o Weight or volume of packaging per item.
  o Customer feedback on packaging ease.
  o Packaging cost vs. total product cost ratio.

10. Merely Undesired Effects

Encompasses bothersome outcomes that individuals or organizations can easily tolerate or work around, though they might still prompt minor fixes or refinements.

For Example:

Annoyances or Nuisances

- Example: Background noise from a device fan or AC unit.
- Objective Indicators:
  o Decibel level during normal operation.
  o Customer complaints about noise in product reviews.
  o Warranty claims related to perceived "unacceptable" sound.

Slight Discomfort or Inconvenience
- Example: A slightly wobbly office chair.
- Objective Indicators:
  - Frequency of user adjustments per day.
  - Percentage of chairs returned or replaced.
  - User satisfaction scores on comfort surveys.

Aesthetic Dissatisfaction
- Example: Color scheme disliked by some users.
- Objective Indicators:
  - Return or exchange rate for cosmetic reasons.
  - Social media sentiment or style preference polls.
  - Number of competitor products chosen for aesthetic appeal.

11. Non-Critical Inefficiencies

Describes duplications or over-specifications that do not significantly impede outcomes but accumulate costs, complexity, or wasted effort.

For Example:

Minor Redundancies
- Example: A small overlap in data entry across two departments.
- Objective Indicators:
  - Time-in-motion studies documenting duplicated effort.
  - Employee feedback on repetitive tasks.
  - Documented cost or time saved if redundancy is removed.

Excessive Safety Margins
- Example: Engineering designs that far exceed real-world requirements.
- Objective Indicators:
  - Percentage difference between actual load and maximum specified load.
  - Cost increases due to over-specification.
  - Testing data showing performance well beyond expected conditions.

Non-Essential Workflow Steps
- Example: Legacy approvals that no longer serve a clear purpose.
- Objective Indicators:
  - Number of sign-offs required vs. final outcomes.
  - Delay time introduced by the extra step.

336

o Employee polling on perceived necessity of each step.

12. Neutral or Inconsequential Outcomes

Involves byproducts with minimal bearing on core objectives. While they exist and can be observed, their impact is negligible enough that they rarely alter strategic decisions.

For Example:
Overlooked Features or Services
- Example: Hidden menu options in an app.
- Objective Indicators:
  o Feature utilization rates (percentage of users who ever use it).
  o Analytics on time spent exploring lesser-known functions.
  o Survey feedback on awareness of available features.

Underutilized Resources or Capacities
- Example: Website servers that operate far below peak load.
- Objective Indicators:
  o Server utilization rates expressed as a percentage.
  o Cost of unused capacity vs. actual usage.
  o Frequency of scale-up events needed to handle higher traffic.

Minor Excess of Inventory
- Example: Slight overstock in retail stores.
- Objective Indicators:
  o Inventory turnover ratio or days of stock on hand.
  o Sell-through percentages for each product category.
  o Storage costs associated with extra inventory.

13. Completely Neutral Effects

Denotes byproducts that do not shift costs, resource use, or satisfaction levels in any meaningful way. They remain part of a system without tangibly affecting performance, risk, or user experiences.

For Example:
Aesthetic Choices with No Functional Impact
- Example: Color variations that do not affect sales or usability.
- Objective Indicators:
  o Color preference data from user surveys.

- o Production runs for each color vs. unsold inventory.
- o Sales performance across color variants.

Redundant Data or Information
- Example: Analytics data never used in decision-making.
- Objective Indicators:
  - o Amount of data storage allocated vs. used.
  - o Number of times data is accessed within a reporting period.
  - o Survey of data analysts regarding actual vs. potential use.

Unused Software Features
- Example: Hidden or advanced features in an application rarely triggered.
- Objective Indicators:
  - o Telemetry data showing usage frequency.
  - o Feedback from user surveys about feature awareness.
  - o Uninstallation or churn rates correlated with feature complexity.

14. Marginally Relevant Outcomes

Refers to minor occurrences or trends that barely register against main objectives. Their low significance means they are typically ignored unless they unexpectedly evolve into more impactful states.

For Example:

Peripheral Market Trends
- Example: A fad with minimal effect on core demand.
- Objective Indicators:
  - o Share of total market influenced by the trend.
  - o Trend lifespan measured in months or years.
  - o Shift in competitor strategies due to the fad.

Non-Influential Consumer Preferences
- Example: Preferences that do not materially alter product development.
- Objective Indicators:
  - o Poll or survey results indicating low adoption or concern.
  - o Minuscule change in product uptake or brand loyalty data.
  - o Competitor analysis showing no reaction to this preference.

Unremarkable Product Variants
- Example: Iterations that do not stand out in the market.

338

- Objective Indicators:
    - Sales figures plateauing quickly after launch.
    - Retailer restocking patterns or inventory left unsold.
    - Customer feedback revealing indifference or lack of awareness.

In Conclusion

Within the Law of Perpetual Innovation (LPI), the Byproduct Impact Spectrum serves as a vital tool to methodically track and label these objective byproduct outcomes. By pairing recognized hazards or inefficiencies with quantitative indicators (from estimated financial damages to inventory overages or user complaints), the Spectrum makes it easier to see which deficiencies deserve immediate attention, which can be addressed incrementally, and which can be safely left alone. This reduces guesswork and subjectivity in day-to-day decision-making.

In addition, a Byproduct Impact Spectrum is necessary because LPI seeks to turn recognized gaps and shortfalls into engines of forward progress. To do so, organizations need to identify the scope of each issue clearly before determining the best path for resolution or improvement. Without a system like the Impact Spectrum, the conversation around byproduct can become disorganized, lacking the shared framework that fosters efficient prioritization and purposeful action.

CHAPTER 20
Harnessing Subjective Byproduct – The Byproduct Contrast Continuum

How Subjective Byproduct Becomes a Catalyst for Growth

Consider the emotional journey that follows a perceived decline in utility, what LPI identifies as the emergence of byproduct. A friend fails to show up in a time of need, and you realize the relationship isn't meeting your deep-seated expectations. The economist would say your utility from this relationship has diminished. LPI, however, points out that something new has emerged as that disappointment. A blend of sadness, betrayal, or perhaps renewed clarity about what you want from close connections. These emotions are the subjective aspect of byproduct. They stir you to either confront the friend, adjust your own behavior, or seek a different support system. In short, byproduct burdens don't remain static; they set in motion a living, dynamic process of rethinking and redesigning your environment or yourself. But for that process to begin, the emotional-cognitive burden must reach a level of salience, or felt significance, strong enough to draw and sustain attention.

This re-framing changes how we interpret emotional-cognitive experiences, from final outcomes into starting points. The chair that once seemed perfect but now causes shoulder aches can drive actions such as creating workarounds for the existing chair, returning the chair, seeking an alternative chair, or an innovative design idea for adjustable armrests. An unfulfilling romantic relationship can spur deeper communication or, in some cases, a decision to part ways. Both experiences demonstrate how byproducts can function as action-drivers: they can push us past a threshold of tolerance or rumination and into action, whether that means improvement of our current state or departure from it.

Of course, not every shortfall leads to meaningful change. Some people might remain stuck in dissatisfaction, never seeing the potential for growth or change. But LPI suggests that every emergence of byproduct holds at least some creative potential. The very fact that a "negative" situation has registered as emotionally salient, not just noticed, but felt, reveals an opportunity to adapt or innovate. We just have to be willing to see the shortfall not as a dead end but as a nudge toward something new.

Here's how an intolerable decline in net available utility can become an active driver for change, not merely a final state of discontent.

1. **Emotional Wake-Up Calls:**
   Byproducts like regret, unease, or anger direct your attention to hidden priorities. These feelings serve a signaling function, telling you that something crucial is off.

2. **Cognitive Realignment:**
   If the same shortfall recurs, your mind adapts, seeking either a better product or a reconfiguration of your environment. A single squeaky car brake might prompt an immediate fix, but repeated brake failures could push you to reimagine an entire safety system, or even invest in public transportation.

3. **Social and Communal Ties:**
   In relationships, recurring disappointments can lead to either deepened conflict or constructive dialogue that fosters renewed empathy. Emotional shortfalls might encourage couples to adopt more transparent communication, reinforcing LPI's perspective that new "solutions" (utilities) only arise from initial shortfalls (byproducts).

Subjective Byproduct: Beyond Binary Thinking

In Chapters 10 and 12 we discussed how byproduct emerges; however, we reduced the examples to a binary scale: on the left side of the scale there is a negatively felt byproduct, such as a problem or something undesired. On the right side of the scale there is a Positive Byproduct, such as a currently unfulfilled benefit or aspiration (a new desire). This binary approach (see image below) helps illustrate how some businesses today approach innovation. If these companies are seeking "what to create next," they'll tend to focus on either resolving pressing issues that are hurting customer retention or investing in aspirational features that could excite customers and drive growth. These extremes, of high dissatisfaction or strong desire, are easy for businesses to target because they represent clear-cut opportunities. When a byproduct leads to significant dissatisfaction, fixing it can restore customer loyalty. Conversely, when a byproduct inspires strong desire, addressing it can open new markets.

The Binary Model of [*Subjective*] Byproduct

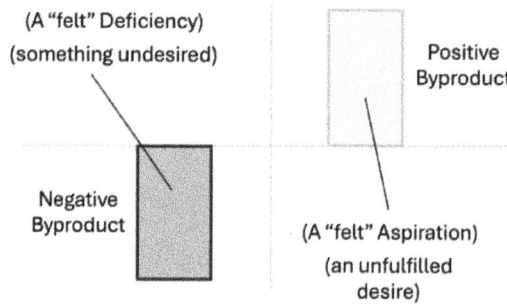

(A "felt" Deficiency)
(something undesired)

Positive
Byproduct

Negative
Byproduct

(A "felt" Aspiration)
(an unfulfilled
desire)

However, this binary view oversimplifies the subjective nature of byproducts. Byproducts are not inherently binary; instead, they exist along a range, capturing human experiences from strongly negative to highly positive.

Emotional Terrain of Expectation Deviation and Aspirational Comparison

To fully grasp the subjective landscape of byproduct, we must examine the emotional forces that arise when utility is experienced as either insufficient, misaligned, or overshadowed by byproduct. Two mechanisms account for the majority of emotionally felt byproduct: Expectation Deviation (η) and Aspirational Comparison (δ). Though they both produce subjective burdens, the emotional contours they generate are distinct, and together they populate the full span of the Byproduct Contrast Continuum, from devastation to elation.

Expectation Deviation (η) is backward-facing and loss-oriented. It occurs when a person's anticipated utility is greater than what they actually experience. Emotionally, this often results in disappointment, frustration, betrayal, or regret. These emotional states emerge because the individual had formed a cognitive model of what was supposed to happen, how a product would perform, how a person would behave, or how a situation would unfold, and that mental forecast was violated. The deeper the initial trust or enthusiasm, the more severe the deviation feels. A small mismatch may

342

cause minor dissatisfaction or annoyance, but a large deviation, such as a critical product failure or emotional betrayal, can produce anguish, grief, or even despair.

From a neurological standpoint, η activates a prediction error response, primarily processed in the anterior cingulate cortex (ACC) and ventral striatum. The ACC monitors conflict between expected and actual outcomes, signaling that something went wrong. At the same time, the dopaminergic system, which modulates reward prediction, fires below its expected baseline, reinforcing the sensation of "something missing." This dopaminergic dip often correlates with emotions such as letdown or emptiness.

In more severe cases, such as interpersonal betrayal, the amygdala becomes highly active, triggering strong emotional reactivity, especially anger, hurt, or fear. These responses are evolutionarily conserved: they heighten awareness, slow behavior, and prompt re-evaluation of trust and environmental cues. The greater the perceived violation of expectation, the more intense the neurochemical cascade and emotional weight of the byproduct.

These reactions fall on the left-hand (negative) side of the Byproduct Contrast Continuum. They are cognitively tied to a rupture in what the person expected versus what actually occurred. It is this emotional incongruence, encoded neurally, that constitutes the subjective byproduct. Notably, expectation deviation does not require an external comparison, only a failed internal forecast. This is why even a product that once satisfied can become a source of resentment if the user believed it would continue to satisfy indefinitely.

By contrast, Aspirational Comparison (δ) is future-facing and contrast-oriented. It arises when a person becomes aware of a higher utility possibility, whether observed, imagined, or introduced by marketing, peers, or circumstance, and compares it to their current state. On the surface, δ often evokes hope, excitement, curiosity, or ambition, all of which appear on the right-hand (positive) side of the contrast continuum. In this light, aspiration can feel energizing. It pulls the user forward into a new possibility, motivating growth and innovation. The user experiences not lack, but vision.

Neurologically, this state is driven by activation of the default mode network (DMN) and prefrontal cortex (PFC), regions associated with mental simulation and goal-directed thought. The orbitofrontal cortex (OFC) compares the current state with possible future outcomes, while dopaminergic projections from the ventral tegmental area (VTA) to the nucleus accumbens release motivational dopamine, sparking the feeling of excitement or craving for potential improvement. This neurochemical spike creates what psychologists call a "prospective reward signal," the emotional-cognitive sensation of wanting.

However, δ also has a shadow form. When the aspirational contrast causes the current state to feel inadequate, the same circuitry that fuels ambition and growth can instead generate envy, inferiority, restlessness, or dissatisfaction. This occurs when the aspirational reference point isn't merely "something better," but becomes a reminder of what the individual lacks. A couple might see another relationship that radiates intimacy and connection, and in comparing it to their own, feel a growing discontent, even if their relationship was previously stable. A customer may see a new premium version of a product and begin to resent the one they just bought. These emotions are not always future-focused; they often retroactively reframe the present as unacceptable.

Here, the lateral habenula, known to suppress dopamine when outcomes feel unattainable or out of reach, becomes involved, leading to the emotional inverse of motivation: futility or envy. The longer this discrepancy persists without corrective action or perceived progress, the more likely that δ produces depressive, rather than aspirational, byproduct. This is especially true when people feel that others have what they do not, activating social comparison regions such as the superior temporal sulcus and medial prefrontal cortex, which modulate status sensitivity and self-worth.

Thus, δ can manifest in both positive and negative forms, depending on how the comparison is framed and what emotional-cognitive story the person constructs. A growth mindset may interpret the superior alternative as an inspiring future, while a fixed or burdened mindset may interpret it as a painful deficiency. Both reactions emerge from the same structure: a contrast between what is and what could be, an anticipatory gap encoded by cortical and subcortical valuation networks.

Together, η and δ shape the emotional topography of subjective byproduct. Expectation deviation generates disillusionment by violating a forecast. Aspirational comparison generates tension by revealing a new possibility. Each triggers emotional responses that populate different regions of the continuum, but neither are inherently "good" or "bad." They are catalysts, and their emotional valence depends on the framing, context, and neuropsychological constitution of the individual. What one person experiences as disappointment, another may interpret as a call to innovate. What one perceives as inspiring, another may feel as unreachable.

Understanding this dual structure helps us map the full emotional contrast continuum of byproduct. It allows us to see each emotional response not as a reaction to failure or success alone, but as part of a deeper comparative structure between past and present,

344

or present and possible future, all processed through interacting reward and threat detection systems in the brain. And in doing so, it reveals why some byproducts weigh us down, while others lift or propel us toward something new.

Approaching the Contrast Continuum

The image below shows a cubic function that would be more indicative of the range of subjective byproduct experiences:

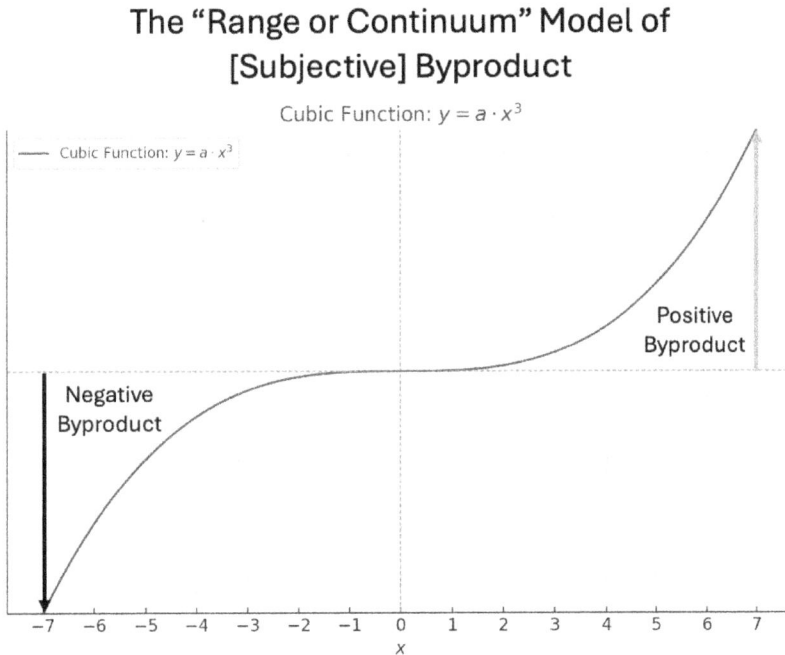

The "Range or Continuum" Model of [Subjective] Byproduct

Cubic Function: $y = a \cdot x^3$

If we take the absolute value of the above cubic function and label the range of subjective byproduct we get an example Byproduct Contrast Continuum, spanning emotional-cognitive states from "Utter Devastation" to "Intense Craving for Transformation / Elation," shown below:

The Byproduct Contrast Continuum

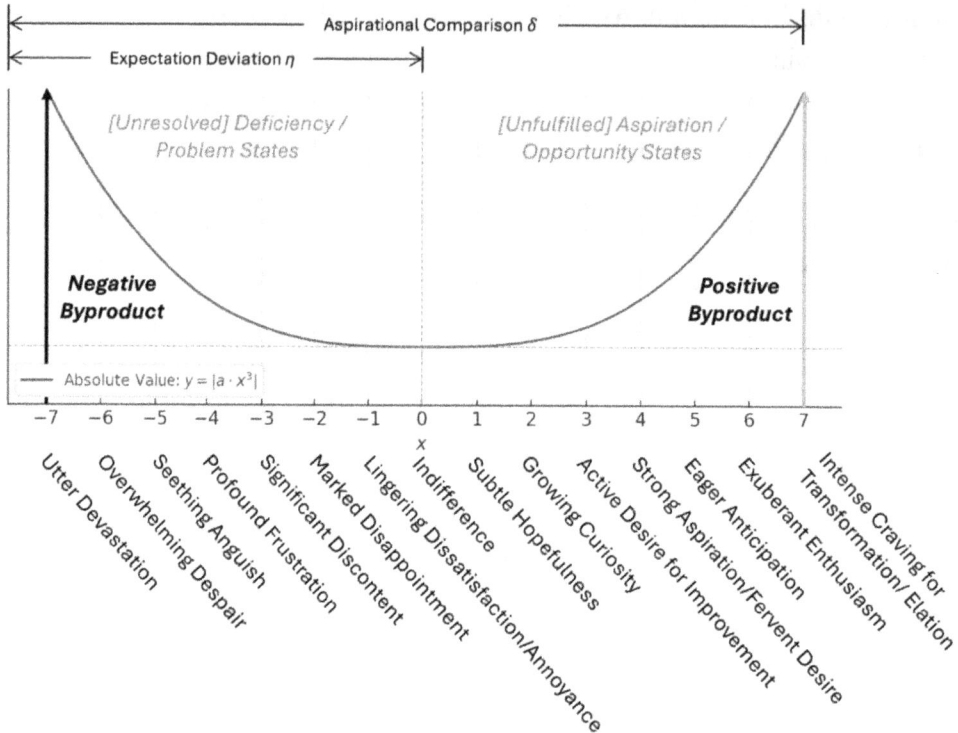

The idea that byproducts can range from devastation or despair (highly negative) to indifference (neutral) to enthusiasm and an intense craving for transformation (highly positive) is summarized in the Byproduct Contrast Continuum. On one extreme, we find severe, even devastating disappointments that demand urgent fixes. Think of a life-or-death system failure in a hospital or a relationship betrayal that feels irreparable. At the other extreme lies an intense craving for transformation, where the user deeply yearns for a next-level improvement. A highly functional smartphone might still leave you in eager anticipation of future enhancements like seamless AI integration.

In the middle are an assortment of states like disappointment, annoyance, subtle hopefulness, indifference, and growing curiosity, that represent more moderate responses. The continuum isn't fixed; byproducts can migrate from mild annoyance to big crisis if ignored, or from subtle hopefulness to eager anticipation if properly nurtured. This spectrum underscores the complex nature of byproduct: it's never just a binary "problem vs. solution." Byproducts can mutate over time and are deeply intertwined with users' evolving expectations and how they reframe experiences.

It's important to reiterate that byproducts are not always intrinsic to the product or system itself. Extrinsic byproducts can provoke emotional-cognitive responses, triggering us to reassess our current level of net perceived satisfaction or utility.

Awareness of a competing product that offers a higher perceived net benefit over our current product's satisfactory state can create emotional-cognitive tension between the two or leave us craving a change that remains pending. Similarly, learning about appalling business practices exhibited by our current product's maker can prompt us to distance ourselves from anything associated with them, including their products. These scenarios illustrate how extrinsic byproducts, whether positive or negative, can accumulate across our existing product, reducing its perceived net benefit, despite there being no intrinsic deficiency in the product itself.

Why People Perceive Byproduct So Differently

If one user interprets a broken pencil tip as trivial and another sees it as a near-catastrophe, what explains the difference? Understanding these varied reactions illuminates why the Byproduct Contrast Continuum needs careful study.

1. Our Personal Histories: The Anchors we Carry

We are all shaped by past experiences that set the stage for how we react to new disappointments or new potential. Psychologists call these anchors or reference points. They are mental benchmarks that influence whether we see a particular shortfall as a slight hiccup or a major letdown.

- **Positive Anchors:**
  Someone who once had a near-perfect chair or a relationship that felt almost magical will often compare every new experience to that gold standard. They might recall, for instance, how well their old chair supported their lower back without any adjustment or how effortlessly their previous partner understood them in moments of stress. Because the bar is set so high, a moderate issue or disagreement can feel like a glaring failure. Even small shortfalls such as a slight wobble in a new chair or a missed conversation in a budding relationship can become amplified. In practical terms, this means they may be quick to label a new purchase or relationship dynamic as "unacceptable," since they measure everything against that remarkable past experience. This psychological mechanism helps explain why nostalgia can be so potent: positive anchors form a mental image of "the best" that remains deeply engrained in us and resistant to revision.

- **Negative Anchors:**
  On the other hand, someone accustomed to subpar products or strained family dynamics may find a similar shortfall relatively mild. If they grew up in a home

where arguments were constant or furniture broke frequently, a single argument or a slightly uncomfortable chair might barely register. Their internal compass is set to a lower norm, making them less likely to see moderate problems as urgent. While this can cultivate resilience, "I can handle anything because I've handled worse," it can also lead to tolerating unproductive, inefficient, or even unhealthy situations because nothing seems as bad as what they've already been through.

Why Anchoring Bias Matters

Anchoring bias can cause us to cling to our initial reference points, even if circumstances have changed drastically. A person who once experienced lavish praise at work might be disappointed by even fair, constructive criticism in a new job. Conversely, someone who endured constant criticism in a previous position might find that same level of feedback in a new role refreshing or at least acceptable. This divergence is why two coworkers, exposed to the exact same new office policy, can disagree so sharply about whether it is "really that bad" or "absolutely unacceptable." They are each applying their own internal story and comparing the situation to their personal anchors, rather than to an objective standard.

2. Genetics and Personality Traits: As Wired from Birth

Science tells us that neurological and biochemical pathways also shape our emotional responses, impacting how we handle unexpected problems or challenges.

- **Variations in Dopamine Sensitivity:**
  Some individuals' brains release a stronger "threat response" (involving cortisol, norepinephrine, and other stress hormones) when confronted with disappointment. If your body reacts powerfully to stress, even a small dip in net available utility, for instance a ten-minute delay in your commute, might feel like a catastrophe. You may experience racing thoughts, physical tension, and a sense of urgency to "fix" the problem immediately. Meanwhile, someone with a milder neurochemical response might view the same delay as a trivial inconvenience, something they've learned to shrug off. This disparity underlines why two equally intelligent, equally resourceful people can diverge so starkly in their emotional reactions to minor setbacks.

- **Temperament and Personality:**

348

Psychological research suggests that traits such as neuroticism, conscientiousness, or openness to experience heavily influence how we respond to shortfalls. A person high in neuroticism may interpret any signal of decline in net available utility, as a warning sign that something is seriously wrong. This can lead to anxieties or overreactions, making them hyper-vigilant about potential problems. A more optimistic or open-minded personality, by contrast, might interpret difficulties as interesting puzzles. A glitchy phone app becomes a chance to learn a workaround or even a starting point for creative collaboration with others.

Neuroplasticity in Action

Science tells us we can change much of what we were born with. Rewiring our neuro-sensitivity to byproduct often involves intentionally reshaping the brain's pathways through techniques like mindfulness and gradual exposure to mild stressors. For example, an individual who habitually panics over a ten-minute delay might begin a daily practice of timed breathing or short meditation sessions, training the nervous system to tolerate small inconveniences. Or a person who feels anxious about waiting in line might purposefully choose busier times to shop, learning to tolerate the discomfort incrementally. This "stress inoculation" strengthens the brain's capacity to handle bigger challenges by normalizing smaller ones. Over time, this "micro-dosing" of stress helps the brain learn that not every setback is catastrophic, transforming once-distressing events into more manageable, even ignorable, hurdles.

3. Current Life Context: The Environments we Inhabit

Our immediate surroundings and stressors play a pivotal role in shaping how we respond to byproduct. Two individuals with similar psychological profiles can still diverge in their reactions if they inhabit different physical or social environments.

- **Daily Stresses and Bandwidth:**
  If someone is already juggling financial worries, a sick family member, and a high-pressure job, their capacity to handle new frustrations, like a glitchy smartphone, shrinks dramatically. Even a minor deficiency might spiral into major upheaval because they simply lack the mental and emotional bandwidth. This is akin to "the straw that breaks the camel's back": it's not the single event itself but the cumulative weight of multiple stressors.

Picture a new parent who has slept three hours in the last two days and is feeling frayed at the edges. Their phone freezing momentarily as they desperately try to order groceries online might provoke an outsize burst of anger or tears. In a calmer life chapter, that same person might see the glitch as an insignificant hiccup and keep moving.

- **Physical Setting:**
  Our physical environment, whether noisy or serene, cluttered or organized, also amplifies or softens the impact of a shortfall. Noisy, chaotic spaces tend to magnify frustration, like a busy call center where every slight malfunction reverberates through the entire team. By contrast, calm settings can cushion the blow of minor annoyances, allowing individuals to remain composed. Even something as simple as ergonomic comfort can transform how we perceive setbacks: a well-lit, temperature-controlled office might render the same technical glitch less irritating than it would be in a cramped, cluttered environment.

Beyond the Immediate Physical

Our broader environment goes well beyond what's physically around us. Think of how remote work during a pandemic introduced new stresses such as patchy Wi-Fi, blurred work-life boundaries, lack of face-to-face camaraderie. Old byproducts, such as having to commute or dress professionally, may have vanished or became less relevant, but new ones like Zoom fatigue or feeling socially isolated, emerged in their place. The same environment, when changed by external forces, alters which byproducts matter most.

4. Cultural and Social Norms: Tribes and Traditions
Culture is like the air we breathe, often invisible until it's pointed out, yet powerfully influential, shaping our reactions without us always noticing how we deal with disappointment, frustration, or opportunity.

- **Shared Expectations:**
  In collectivist cultures, people might prioritize group harmony akin to "keeping the peace" to the extent that they may minimize expressing frustration, even when a product severely underperforms. Meanwhile, in more individualistic cultures, speaking up or even loudly complaining about shortfalls is almost a civic duty. One environment fosters an "endure quietly" mindset, potentially

350

masking deeper issues, while another environment can highlight even trivial discomforts, possibly fueling quicker solutions but also risking an overabundance of negative feedback.

- **Group Amplification:**
  Online forums, family or social networks, or workplace cliques' function like social echo chambers. Suppose your peers relentlessly criticize a newly released phone for battery drains or a relationship dynamic they deem unhealthy. In that case, you might adopt (or amplify) that negativity, even if you initially felt moderate annoyance at best. Conversely, a supportive group that focuses on finding solutions might help you see the byproduct as a solvable challenge. This is why the same flawed product can be dismissed lightly by one crowd and denounced vehemently by another; each group's norms and conversations either intensify or dilute the dissatisfaction.

Culture and the Motto Effect

Our "tribes," whether family, colleagues, or online communities, provide norms that guide how we talk about dissatisfaction. Sometimes these subcultures develop a motto: "Make do with what you got," "Never settle," or "Complain until it's perfect." These guiding phrases can shape whether small frustrations remain hidden or become deal-breakers. In a "make do" family, inconveniences might be dismissed as everyday trifles. In a perfectionist tribe, every slight mismatch from the ideal triggers a loud call to overhaul the system or product.

5. Future Orientation and Aspirations: The Stories We Tell Ourselves

Finally, each of us carries personal beliefs about the future and our own potential, and these inner stories deeply color how we respond to disappointment or missed opportunities.

- **Growth vs. Fixed Mindset:**
  A growth-mindset individual sees shortfalls as stepping-stones to improvement. Encountering a buggy new feature, they might become curious, offering suggestions or debugging help. They harness the byproduct of frustration or inconvenience as a call to action for beneficial change. A fixed-mindset individual, by contrast, may view any hint of failure as confirmation that things are doomed. "Of course it's buggy, nothing ever works out," they might say,

fueling cynicism rather than solutions. The difference lies in whether you see your intellect and environment as malleable or rigid.

- **Optimistic Outlook:**
  An optimist might interpret the same shortfall as fleeting and solvable. "Yes, this software update broke a few things, but they'll surely fix it soon, and meanwhile, I'll find a workaround." Pessimists, on the other hand, might see each glitch as yet another sign that technology, people, or systems inevitably fail. This attitude can lead to quicker abandonment of promising solutions, missed chances to adapt, or an overall sense of futility.

- **Ambition Level:**
  People with lofty ambitions often see "good enough" as a starting point for something far greater. A serviceable product or a stable, if unremarkable, relationship might prompt them to say, "What if we could make this even better?" They dwell on hidden potentials rather than focusing solely on shortcomings. Others, content with an average level of functionality, may not feel the urge to push for improvements at all. The same minor glitch might be resolved swiftly if someone is determined to see continuous growth, while another person is content to leave it unaddressed indefinitely.

Transforming the Glitch into a Project

Imagine an avid tech enthusiast who, upon noticing a suboptimal feature in their new smartphone, dives into online communities to brainstorm improvements or share custom fixes. They interpret the byproduct not as a nuisance but as an opening to enhance overall performance. Meanwhile, another user might grumble about the glitch for a day or two and then simply let it go, concluding that nothing can be done. These personal stories, one of possibility and the other of limitation, shape the destiny of every small problem or unrealized idea.

Stitching Together "Why We All Experience Byproduct Differently"

From our inherited anchors to our genetic makeup, from stressful daily realities to the cultural tribes that shape our norms, and from the narratives we form about the future, each factor influences how we perceive and respond to byproduct. When a shortfall in net available utility occurs, be it a wobbly chair or an unfulfilling social interaction, the range of personal reactions can be vast. Two people facing the same situation can reach entirely different conclusions based on these internal and external influences.

Understanding these factors not only helps us see why some issues become massive triggers while others remain minor annoyances, but it also equips us to communicate and innovate more effectively. By recognizing that each anchor, trait, environment, cultural norm, and mindset layer onto the basic experience of "utility shortfall," we uncover the potential for byproduct to act as a catalyst for action. Whether it inspires a reevaluation of needs, spurs creative problem-solving, or fosters collaboration, byproduct holds the key to turning dissatisfaction into progress. Through this lens, we see shortfalls not as dead ends but as beginnings, where growth and innovation take root.

The Byproduct Contrast Continuum

The Byproduct Contrast Continuum is a framework for mapping the many ways people emotionally experience byproduct, whether it emerges from a product, service, or broader context. It acknowledges that emotional responses do not simply toggle between good or bad but can move across a gradient ranging from the most intense negative feelings to the highest levels of positive aspiration. By identifying 15 distinct emotional-cognitive states, the continuum helps clarify how dissatisfaction, frustration, and other negative emotions could gradually shift into more negative states or states of curiosity or enthusiastic desire for improvement; or even initially emerge in the positive states altogether.

This continuum is not only a model of how users might feel in the face of unmet expectations, but also a guide for innovators aiming to convert negative feedback into constructive engagement and growth. By considering where each emotional state sits, whether positive or negative, decision-makers can anticipate how best to address user needs, foster resilience, or spark genuine excitement. The ultimate goal is to transform these states into valuable signals, guiding teams to refine or reinvent their solutions more effectively.

1. Utter Devastation (Extreme Negative)

Description: A severe emotional collapse, in which the individual feels as though everything has failed or been irreparably lost. This subjective byproduct takes a person to the brink of hopelessness and can paralyze action or drive extreme coping behaviors.

Temporal Aspect: Utter devastation typically follows a traumatic event or a profound shock to one's expectations. It manifests quickly but can linger as individuals struggle to see any path forward.

Example: Medical Devices (Life-Support Equipment)
- **Intrinsic Byproduct:** The sudden and complete failure of a ventilator during a critical moment leads to the loss of a loved one. The user, whether a caregiver or family member, is left with unbearable grief, feeling as if everything has collapsed, blaming the product's failure for an irreversible tragedy.
- **Extrinsic Byproduct:** A regulatory recall pulls a life-support device off the market without warnings, forcing the user to desperately search for an alternative, only to find that none exist in time to prevent the worst outcome. The helplessness turns into all-consuming despair, leaving them feeling abandoned by the system.

Consideration: At this level of devastation, no product fix is enough. Trust in the system is completely shattered, requiring institutional intervention and crisis-level resolution.

2. Overwhelming Despair

Description: An all-consuming sense of sorrow or hopelessness. The individual feels trapped in negative circumstances, unable to envision meaningful recovery or improvement.

Temporal Aspect: Despair can emerge after repeated failures or sustained negative experiences. It intensifies if the individual perceives no tangible progress or relief.

Example: Agricultural Equipment
- **Intrinsic Byproduct**: A newly purchased automated irrigation system malfunctions, causing an entire season's crop to wither and die. The user, a farmer, watches months of work and financial investment vanish, spiraling into deep despair over an uncertain future.
- **Extrinsic Byproduct:** A sudden economic downturn crashes crop prices overnight, making even a successful harvest worthless. The farmer sees no

way forward, unable to repay debts, and feels like their livelihood has been permanently destroyed by forces beyond their control.

Consideration: Overwhelming despair stems from powerlessness, requiring both product reliability improvements and external support mechanisms (insurance, subsidies, or policy interventions).

3. Seething Anguish

Description: A turbulent emotional state that blends deep distress and anger, causing the person to feel both hurt and aggrieved. This byproduct can make rational thinking difficult, fueling volatile reactions.

Temporal Aspect: Seething anguish may arise gradually if unresolved problems fester or abruptly if a significant boundary is crossed. It can escalate quickly under prolonged strain.

Examples: Financial Investment Platforms
- **Intrinsic Byproduct:** A user logs in to find that a glitch in the trading app wiped out part of their life savings due to an unintended auto-sell order, leaving them furious, betrayed, and unable to recover. The sense of helpless rage makes rational thought nearly impossible.
- **Extrinsic Byproduct:** A government regulatory decision freezes their investments in a major financial institution overnight, trapping their money indefinitely. Watching others freely trade while they remain locked out fuels an overwhelming sense of injustice, leading to feelings of betrayal and financial powerlessness.

Consideration: Anguish combines emotional devastation with a need for justice, meaning mere product corrections won't restore user trust. Legal action, transparency, and immediate intervention are essential.

4. Profound Frustration

Description: A deeply rooted frustration where repeated obstacles or chronic inefficiencies undermine the user's experience or well-being. Unlike momentary annoyance, profound frustration accumulates over time, leading to strong emotional responses.

Temporal Aspect: Profound frustration can build slowly, surfacing when attempts to resolve an issue fail repeatedly. It might flare up momentarily in response to fresh setbacks.

Examples: Electric Vehicles (EVs)

- **Intrinsic Byproduct:** A user experiences repeated failures in their EV's battery system, forcing them to take it in for repairs multiple times, yet the issue persists. The feeling of losing trust in an expensive purchase grows into boiling frustration, making them regret ever switching to an EV.
- **Extrinsic Byproduct:** The lack of charging stations in their area forces them to take inconvenient, long detours just to recharge, making every trip a logistical nightmare. Despite wanting to embrace sustainable transportation, the frustration of unreliable infrastructure makes them question their decision entirely.

Consideration: Profound frustration builds when issues persist without resolution. If left unaddressed, brand abandonment becomes inevitable, requiring both product-level fixes and systemic infrastructure improvements.

5. Significant Discontent

Description: Marked dissatisfaction characterized by the recognition that outcomes persistently fail to meet established standards or expectations. The individual feels strongly that the present circumstances are not acceptable.

Temporal Aspect: Significant discontent typically grows as repeated shortcomings or broken promises accumulate. It may also appear quickly if an experience sharply contradicts prior success or promises.

Examples: Smart Home Security Systems

- **Intrinsic Byproduct:** The home security system sporadically triggers false alarms, waking the user and neighbors at all hours of the night. The repeated disruptions, stress, and exhaustion make them regret ever installing the system, as it has created more problems than solutions.
- **Extrinsic Byproduct:** Emergency response teams deprioritize their address due to excessive false alarms, leaving them waiting helplessly during a real break-in. The realization that their security system is actually making them less safe causes deep dissatisfaction and regret.

Consideration: Significant discontent arises when a product adds significant burdens or contradicts its core purpose, eroding trust and leading consumers to actively seek alternatives.

6. Marked Disappointment

Description: A sense of letdown resulting from unmet, though not necessarily critical, expectations. The individual might still see some merit but cannot overlook the gap between what was hoped for and what transpired.

Temporal Aspect: Marked disappointment emerges once the disparity between expectation and reality becomes undeniable. It can linger if no corrective measures are taken.

Examples: Virtual Reality (VR) Headsets
- **Intrinsic Byproduct:** A long-awaited VR headset update introduces an unbearable motion blur, making games unplayable for the user. They feel gutted, realizing they spent hundreds of dollars on an experience they now actively avoid.
- **Extrinsic Byproduct:** A new competing VR headset is released at the same price but with dramatically better features, making their current purchase feel like an instant outdated regret.

Consideration: Disappointment stems from a sharp contrast between expectations and reality. Once experienced, users become hyper-aware of alternatives, making rapid resolution critical.

7. Lingering Dissatisfaction/Annoyance (Slightly Negative)

Description: An ongoing, lower-grade negative state where the individual remains unsatisfied yet still functional within the system. They recognize continuous flaws or annoyances but have adapted to them enough to carry on without major change.

Temporal Aspect: This state often persists like a slow burn, frequently tied to a lack of better alternatives or incremental coping strategies. Over time, small irritations can accumulate and push the individual to seek bigger shifts.

Examples: Smart Refrigerators
- **Intrinsic Byproduct:** The fridge's AI misidentifies expiration dates, constantly sending false spoilage alerts. Over time, the user stops trusting it, leading to annoyance every time they see the notification.
- **Extrinsic Byproduct:** The manufacturer locks essential updates behind a paid subscription, turning a simple home appliance into an ongoing financial drain, making the user increasingly resentful with each payment cycle.

Consideration: Lingering dissatisfaction erodes long-term brand trust. If left unresolved, users will ditch the product at the first viable alternative.

8. Indifference (Neutral Point)

Description: A byproduct that neither harms satisfaction nor ignites enthusiasm. The user or individual finds the current situation adequate but unremarkable.

Temporal Aspect: Indifference may emerge when initial excitement fades or if conditions neither improve nor worsen noticeably. Small positives or negatives can shift this equilibrium in either direction.

Examples: Streaming Services
- **Intrinsic Byproduct:** The platform's content suggestions feel repetitive, with the user mindlessly scrolling for something to watch but never feeling truly engaged. The novelty of the service has worn off, leaving them unmoved.
- **Extrinsic Byproduct:** A competitor streaming service offers nearly identical content, making switching feel meaningless. The user sees no compelling reason to stay or leave, making their engagement passive and unenthusiastic.

Consideration: Indifference signals an at-risk user base. Without differentiation or renewed engagement, consumers can drift away if expectations start being unmet or higher potential offerings arise in contrast.

9. Subtle Hopefulness (Slightly Positive)

Description: A mild sense of optimism that things could become better. Users see a glimmer of possibility, though they may not yet take action.

Temporal Aspect: Hopefulness tends to arise after encountering small wins or envisioning or seeing initial positive hints. It can vanish if setbacks overshadow these early positives.

Examples: Smart Home Thermostats
- **Intrinsic Byproduct:** While using their current thermostat, the user notices that it lacks intuitive scheduling, leading to mild anticipation for an upgrade that could optimize energy use.
- **Extrinsic Byproduct:** A friend raves about a new AI-powered thermostat that adjusts temperature automatically based on presence, sparking gentle curiosity about what they might be missing.

Consideration: At this stage, the user sees potential value but has no strong urgency to switch. The perceived benefit is intriguing but not yet a priority.

10. Growing Curiosity

Description: A piqued interest in exploring how conditions might be enhanced. Individuals have moved beyond envisioning or noticing minor improvements and now actively contemplate how to leverage them further.

Temporal Aspect: Curiosity blossoms as the user gains confidence in the system's potential. They begin testing limits or brainstorming ideas.

Examples: Smart Adjustable Desks
- **Intrinsic Byproduct:** The user begins to wonder how much better their productivity and posture might be if they replaced their static desk with a height-adjustable model.
- **Extrinsic Byproduct:** A colleague switches to a smart desk that tracks standing time and health metrics, igniting a deeper interest in how this technology could transform daily work habits.

Consideration: Curiosity builds as the user starts exploring possibilities, watching demos, reading comparisons, and visualizing benefits in their own routine.

11. Active Desire for Improvement

Description: A clear wish to see specific enhancements or refinements. The user identifies which changes could yield a better outcome and may begin advocating for them.

Temporal Aspect: This desire often arises after smaller glimpses of potential, or when repeated annoyances can be addressed by targeted solutions.

Examples: High-Fidelity Noise-Canceling Headphones
- **Intrinsic Byproduct:** The user, already satisfied with their mid-tier headphones, notices that long work sessions leave them fatigued from minor background noise leakage, creating a growing pull toward a superior solution.
- **Extrinsic Byproduct:** A trusted influencer reviews a premium model, highlighting an immersive listening experience, making the user actively yearn for this next-level quality.

Consideration: The user now actively wants an upgrade and is seeking validation: comparing reviews, waiting for sales, or testing models in stores.

12. Strong Aspiration/Fervent Desire

Description: A robust longing for substantial improvements, where the individual envisions a more satisfying and elevated outcome. This state is fueled by a fervent desire to enhance the current situation significantly, going beyond minor tweaks.

Temporal Aspect: Strong aspiration or fervent desire often grows after incremental successes or once deeper flaws become impossible to ignore. Users mentally map out a path for improvement, seeing potential that transcends everyday fixes.

Examples: Smart Mirror Fitness Systems
- **Intrinsic Byproduct:** The user enjoys their regular workouts but feels limited by the lack of real-time coaching, making them strongly wish for a more interactive experience.

- **Extrinsic Byproduct:** A friend installs a smart mirror gym, showcasing its AI-driven corrections and personalized programs, intensifying the desire to transform their fitness routine.

Consideration: The user now feels incomplete without this product, believing it could elevate their routine to its fullest potential.

13. Eager Anticipation

Description: A high level of enthusiasm for upcoming updates or transformations. Individuals track progress closely, looking forward to the benefits or excitement those changes may bring.

Temporal Aspect: Eager anticipation often follows confirmation that improvements are actually on the way. Users become emotionally invested in the outcome's success.

Examples: Next-Gen Electric Bikes
- **Intrinsic Byproduct:** Riding their current e-bike feels great, but they envision how much better it would be with extended range and regenerative braking, eagerly waiting for an upcoming release.
- **Extrinsic Byproduct:** A new model is rumored to feature ultra-lightweight materials and longer battery life, driving excited countdowns to pre-orders and first reviews.

Consideration: The user is emotionally invested in the next-gen version, checking updates, watching leaks, and planning their purchase.

14. Exuberant Enthusiasm

Description: A vibrant and upbeat emotional state where users or stakeholders feel highly invested in continuous improvement or expansion. The experience is already strong, and the excitement to make it even better is palpable.

Temporal Aspect: Enthusiasm can emerge after multiple positive interactions or when previous aspirations have been at least partially realized.

Examples: Advanced AR Glasses

- **Intrinsic Byproduct:** Their current smart glasses enhance productivity, but they imagine how transformative a next-gen display, real-time language translation, and gesture control would be.
- **Extrinsic Byproduct:** A major brand teases a breakthrough AR experience, making them actively participate in discussions and forums, sharing their excitement for what's coming.

Consideration: The user is highly vocal, engaging in speculation, enthusiastically discussing features, and planning their adoption strategy.

15. Intense Craving for Transformation / Elation (Extreme Positive)

Description: An almost insatiable desire for a radical, game-changing shift. Incremental upgrades no longer suffice; individuals or users want to redefine the experience altogether.

Temporal Aspect: This heightened craving usually arises after achieving multiple successes that expose even more revolutionary possibilities. It signifies the pinnacle of ambition.

Examples: Fully Autonomous Electric Vehicles
- **Intrinsic Byproduct:** Owning a high-end EV is great, but the thought of never needing to drive again now feels like the ultimate freedom, the craving is borderline obsessive.
- **Extrinsic Byproduct:** A company unveils an advanced self-driving prototype, igniting a sense of inevitability that this will completely redefine mobility. The user now sees every manual-driving moment as outdated and inconvenient, intensifying their desire to be at the forefront of this shift.

Consideration: The user is mentally all-in, obsessively tracking updates, debating features with peers, and willing to invest heavily or join waitlists to experience this change in thinking firsthand.

The continuum just presented is a general example. Organizations are encouraged to develop a range that suits their industry, products and range of emotional-cognitive states that best represent their customers.

--For Additional Author Insights--
See APPENDIX II for: When and Why to Normalize Byproduct Perceptions

See APPENDIX III for: Exploring Opportunity Across the Byproduct Contrast Continuum

A Unifying Perspective for Moving Forward

Stepping back, we find that "a decline in net available utility" is not the story. When something fails us, the real action begins with the byproduct that has emerged, the objectively observable scenario accompanied by a mixture of emotional response, creative impetus, or coping mechanism that arises and influences what happens next. People differ in how they register and act upon these emergent subjective emotional-cognitive byproduct states, shaped by everything from inherited neural sensitivities to cultural scripts.

We can map these subjective phenomena on the Byproduct Contrast Continuum, labeling where each gap sits on a scale from severe dissatisfaction to soaring aspiration, and link them to the Byproduct Impact Spectrum to measure how these shortfalls might play out objectively. Together, these complementary models help us parse out how much of each issue is objectively verifiable and how much is rooted in personal perception. Normalizing user feedback and responses helps us avoid overreacting to small clusters of the upset or ignoring major concerns. Each perspective enriches our understanding of byproduct as a multifaceted reality that, if harnessed wisely, becomes a catalyst for innovation rather than a sign of mere decline.

Ultimately, recognizing byproduct as more than an abstract loss of satisfaction is a powerful lens for growth. Rather than viewing dissatisfaction as a dead-end condemning a product, service, or system to failure, LPI understands it as the start of a new narrative. We shift from measuring how much net utility we perceive to have lost, to asking what the newly born byproduct can reveal to us. That small pivot changes everything, turning every unresolved deficiency or unfulfilled aspiration into a seed for reframing, redesigning, or reimagining, and, at best, sparking continuous cycles of innovation that benefit both users and creators.

This holistic view has guided our deep dive into the Byproduct Contrast Continuum and Byproduct Impact Spectrum. Showing how gaps in our current experiences, or between current and a higher potential future state, can evolve into constructive opportunities. What mild annoyances or open aspirations might hold hidden opportunities that might launch disruptive innovations. By broadening our scope beyond traditional belief of simple utility decline, we now have the tools to harness and discover unforeseen pathways for progress in virtually every domain, be it designing a better chair, nurturing a healthier relationship, or building systems that adapt fluidly over time.

Module E:
Utility Pursuit

In Module E, our attention moves from understanding byproduct to witnessing it as an urgent catalyst for transformation. Once individuals or organizations recognize that a product or process is overshadowed by newly identified demands or possibilities, they experience an emotional conviction that "we can no longer stay here." This moment marks *forescension*: the decisive shift from an accepted status quo to a deliberate quest for higher utility. Although artificial intelligence can scour vast data streams to highlight inefficiencies or forecast emerging solutions, it is ultimately human emotional resolve, our dissatisfaction with an old norm or excitement for a superior alternative, that compels actual change.

Beneath the layers of technical feasibility and market analysis, the Law of Perpetual Innovation underscores the simple truth that no shortfall or opportunity matters until it *feels* significant. AI-driven metrics can identify growing defects or reveal breakthroughs, but only a felt urgency, negative or positive, will spur people to move beyond inertia. Hence, whether we call it "Utility Pursuit" or "Byproduct Escape," the heart of this module is the same: progress unfolds as soon as we perceive and care enough about a problem or potential, triggering the emotional-cognitive pivot from idle awareness to tangible innovation.

CHAPTER 21

Perspective on Byproduct-Driven Utility Pursuit

If a Tree Falls in the Forest

George Berkeley, an 18th-century philosopher, famously asked, "If a tree falls in the forest and no one is around to hear it, does it make a sound?" His question explores the nature of perception: does a sound truly exist if there's no one to perceive it? This idea also applies to "byproduct" in the context of innovation. Consider your smartphone's battery permanently degrading by 80% while it sits unused for years in a drawer. Objectively, permanent battery loss has occurred. But if you never even notice the battery loss because you no longer use the phone and thus experience no frustration or sense of loss, can any meaningful "byproduct" truly emerge?

According to the Principle of Byproduct Composition, both an objective event and the subjective experience of it must exist for innovation to take shape. Much like the tree falling in the forest, if no one is there to witness the battery's decline or feel its effects, no impetus for change or improvement arises. Suppose vast numbers of trees fell in forests around the world and there were no cascading ecological effects that emerged from this. Objectively, that's concerning. But if no one ever saw or heard those trees fall, if humanity remained completely unaware of this, would we be impacted at all? No. Without awareness, there's no emotional-cognitive response. And correspondingly, there would be no spark of action spurred by the event.

This highlights a fundamental truth: without the emotional-cognitive spark that makes an event "real" to us, no byproduct emerges. And without byproduct, genuine progress does not occur. We are moved only when we sense a gap between how things are and how they could be, and that gap becomes emotionally salient, creating a subjective urgency that propels us to respond. In the next section, we will explore how this dynamic, of emotional perception driving action, plays out in surprising ways across multiple fields, underscoring just how crucial these "felt" shortfalls or aspirations are in fueling the human quest for improvement.

Multidisciplinary Views of the Byproduct-Driven Pursuit of Utility

Human motivation, our actions, even our innovations, often appear to be driven by a straightforward desire to gain something new or better purely "for its own sake." Yet according to most of modern economics, that is not the case, they see it as what utility does for us. As for the Law of Perpetual Innovation (LPI), we seek fresh utility to help us escape our current circumstances. Where those circumstances have accumulated byproduct. Indeed, without a byproduct, there is no meaningful prompt to do anything different. If we had no shortfall to remedy or no formerly acceptable utility that has become overshadowed by a now recognized higher standard, we would remain in place (as we normally do, until byproduct tells us otherwise). Whenever we explore acquiring a product, any product, upgrading an existing tool, studying a new skill, or shifting a cultural practice, the fundamental driver is our emotional impulse. This emotional impulse is either rooted in dissatisfaction or rooted in awareness of a better alternative.

This principle is so absolute that attempts to find "utility for utility's sake" inevitably expose the underlying driver. Consider contrived examples such as requesting a completely unneeded blood transfusion, wearing sunglasses in a pitch-dark setting with no explanation, or aimlessly grabbing random items in a supermarket. On their face, these acts might look like a pursuit of utility (a product or service) with no real reason. But from the vantage point of LPI, they make little sense precisely because there is no discernible byproduct, no aspiring tension to alleviate or perceived shortfall of the present state compelling such behavior. When no such deficiency or newly recognized advantage beyond the current condition is perceived, the emotional impetus for utility collapses. This observation underpins why marketing and advertising often strive to create new byproducts in the human mind. By stirring up dissatisfaction, envy, curiosity, or a renewed sense that one's current way of living is inadequate, marketers generate the psychological elicitation that drives consumer demand.

To explore this further, it helps to examine how various bodies of knowledge such as psychology, neuroscience, existential-philosophical thought, economics, and consumer behavior all reinforce the truth that we do not simply "want utility" in a vacuum. Instead, we want utility because it addresses something. A newly emergent improved possibility, or dissatisfaction with how things currently stand in our life. In every scenario, the byproduct stems from a subjective emotional backdrop: we either feel things like frustration, boredom, or anxiety (a negative byproduct) about the no-longer-acceptable current utility state, or we experience things like desire, curiosity, or inspiration (a positive byproduct) that overshadows our present condition in contrast to what might be. These emotions, whether frustrating or inspiring, render the perceived gap emotionally salient, keeping it in focus long enough to influence thought, reflection, and, eventually, innovation. The cycle is unending, with emotion playing the most crucial yet often under-recognized role in fueling our drive to innovate. Yet, once we resolve one byproduct by adopting or creating a new tool, skill, or idea, thereby escaping our current constraints, another byproduct will inevitably manifest, urging us onward. Human progress becomes a continuous chain of solutions that beget more demands, each triggered by the emotional-cognitive aftereffects of what came before.

Psychological Perspectives on the Byproduct-Driven Pursuit

Psychology offers one of the most direct windows into why humans do not simply chase novelty or improvement out of sheer randomness. Instead, we act under the pressure or influence of byproducts (though they don't refer to them as such) that make it difficult to remain where we are. These byproducts have an objective component, often observable or tangible, and a subjective emotional component, such as explicit frustration with a subpar device, subtle boredom with a monotonous routine, or a spark of interest upon glimpsing a newly perceived higher standard or improved state that surpasses the adequacy of our current utility state.

Drive Reduction and the Illusion of "Pure Utility"
Clark Hull's Drive Reduction Theory casts a wide net over motivational psychology, arguing that organisms, from rats in cages to humans in complex societies, are driven to reduce internal tension. This tension could be hunger, thirst, anxiety, or a sense of unrealized potential. A simple example is feeling hungry, then eating to remove discomfort. At first glance, we might read this as "I eat because food is good." The deeper impetus is not "I want food for its own sake." Rather, it is "I want to remove hunger (negative byproduct)" or "I want to eat healthy (positive byproduct) *[subtext: to escape or avoid non-healthy outcomes]."* Likewise, consider a scenario where you recall an exceptionally flavorful dish from a restaurant you visited long ago, realizing that your current home-cooked meals, while satisfying, pale in comparison. Here, the impetus is not physical hunger (a negative tension), but rather the positive awareness, maybe even excitement that your routine culinary experience falls short of the richer standard you've recalled. This newly recognized contrast functions as a positive byproduct, propelling you to recreate that more fulfilling taste.

The same structure, LPI tells us, applies to more complex actions, such as picking up a new musical instrument. People sometimes say, "I just love the sound." Still, in the background, the byproduct might be the uneasy feeling of wasted talent, recognizing that one's present abilities or circumstances are insufficient, or a new push to surpass that insufficiency after hearing a musician whose mesmerizing solos reveal how limited one's existing skillset currently stands. We do not adopt the instrument "just because"; we do it because a recognized deficiency or latent craving (the byproduct) demands resolution and resonates with us emotionally.

Perhaps the clearest demonstration that "pure utility" pursuit is an illusion occurs if we imagine scenarios totally devoid of byproduct. For instance, "I want a blood transfusion *[subtext: even though my blood is perfectly healthy]*" or "I want to wear sunglasses *[subtext: in a completely dark room.]*" These actions lack any motivation in the present state of being, rendering them purposeless. There is no burden or discomfort to remove. No blood illness or bright lights to mitigate, no elevated desire in contrast to the present condition, so there is no reason to act. Only by artificially manufacturing a negative or positive impetus, like a newly planted fear of illness or a perception that one's current social standing is incomplete, could such actions appear sensible. That is precisely how marketing sometimes works: by inventing dissatisfaction (the wrinkles around your eyes or the outdated phone that now feels lacking) or by highlighting how your present condition can be overshadowed by a more stylish or advanced possibility (achieve youthful skin again or this isn't just an improved phone *[it's improved social and cultural status]*). If the consumer's current state was genuinely seen as fine, no impetus for adopting the new offering would exist.

Behaviorism and Hidden Tensions
Behaviorist frameworks, like those championed by B.F. Skinner, note that positive external reinforcement strengthens behaviors by adding something pleasant, while negative external reinforcement strengthens behaviors by removing something unpleasant. Frequently, the drive to seek new utility appears to revolve around "pleasantness." However, from LPI's vantage, that so-called "pleasantness" typically arises from relief at correcting a gap, meaning we are acting on an uneasy sense that our present state is lacking in some aspect. This can be negative (fear of losing a skill) or positive (feeling excited that one's current technique limitations or plateau state can be escaped and surpassed through newly discovered advanced methods).

Imagine a scenario where you pick up your guitar not just because playing is "fun" but because you cannot stand the idea of your skill deteriorating; you see your current level as threatened. Each chord is thus an action to remove that looming deficiency.

Conversely, if a friend demonstrates a novel strumming style, you might feel excited that your existing technique can be left behind and surpassed through newly discovered advanced methods, revealing that your current repertoire, once acceptable, no longer meets the higher standard you now perceive. Either impetus emerges from a byproduct, highlighting that remaining at one's present level is no longer satisfying. In the absence of that recognized gap, there would be no reason to pick up the guitar in the first place.

Humanistic Psychology and Needs Beyond Survival
Abraham Maslow's hierarchy of needs is often portrayed as a ladder from basic survival (food, water, shelter) to self-actualization (creativity, personal expression). People who have achieved relative comfort might claim they are "pursuing fulfillment," yet even that fulfillment pursuit arises from an internal friction: an emotional or existential realization that one's present state is less meaningful or robust than it could be. A creative individual might experience discomfort if they do not paint, or a prospective traveler might feel restless and see their current life as too confined, overshadowed by the recognition of a wider world. While Maslow's structure holds validity, LPI reframes each tier as triggered by an identified gap that compels an advance to the next level. That is, the sense that one's existing circumstances are no longer sufficient enough.

A classic example is the artist who claims to create "for the joy of creating." If that person never felt dissatisfaction over unexpressed ideas or the sense that their present creative expression is incomplete, the impetus to sculpt might never arise. If you truly had no shortfall or longing that exposed your current state as deprived of some future state, you would not sculpt at all. Thus, the byproduct surfaces the moment you realize a gap in your artistic process or an unrealized dimension in your vision.

Neuroscientific Foundations and the Need to Correct or Capture Byproducts

To understand why byproducts command such influence, one must grasp how the brain orchestrates action in response to deficiency or newly identified potential that exceeds the perceived adequacy of the status quo. Simply put, we do not spawn new ambitions or adopt new products arbitrarily. Our neural circuitry is tuned to react when conditions fail to meet certain thresholds or suggest a possibility that makes our current utility no longer adequate, generating an emotional signal that "something must be done."

370

Dopamine's Role in Wanting

Earlier neuroscience incorrectly labeled dopamine as merely the brain's "pleasure molecule." More recent work, especially by researchers Kent Berridge and Terry Robinson, shows that dopamine is actually more central to motivation, particularly through a mechanism known as incentive salience. This refers to the brain's ability to tag certain stimuli or perceived gaps as emotionally and motivationally significant, turning a previously neutral condition into something we suddenly feel compelled to pursue or resolve. In LPI terms, seeking utility (like upgrading a smartphone or chasing a newly discovered ice cream flavor) does not stem from some intrinsic desire for novelty, but from an emotionally salient mismatch between our current utility state and a newly recognized alternative. Dopamine is thus not about idle enjoyment; it acts as the neural signal that a better state now feels worth pursuing. It drives us to escape discomfort or to reach newly revealed standards, not because they exist, but because they have become salient enough to feel personally meaningful.

For instance, consider two scenarios. First, you feel stressed after a long day of work, so you decide to watch a movie, an action to alleviate your tension (negative byproduct). Second, you see an advertisement for a newly released film that enthralls you, highlighting that your current pool of entertainment no longer fully meets your emotional or imaginative needs (positive byproduct). In both cases, your brain releases dopamine in anticipation of either remedying the stress or fulfilling this newly perceived potential. Were you free of stress or absent the idea that the movie might be thrilling, you would lack any impetus to watch it, underscoring how your present condition is deemed insufficient and that seeking or surpassing it yields relief or excitement (a potentially higher utility state). Thus, the byproduct, your emotional recognition of dissatisfaction or excitement, fuels the hunt for utility. Absent that gap, there would be no motivation to "want" to watch the movie.

Reward and Aversion Overlap

Berridge, Robinson and Joseph LeDoux's research also reveals that brain activity in regions associated with aversion (like the amygdala, which processes fear or worry) and with seeking rewards (like the nucleus accumbens) do not function independently. Rather, they overlap and share neural pathways revealing that signals in the amygdala can influence or be influenced by the reward pathways (dopamine), intertwining with a desire to escape threat or discomfort. This explains why we rarely pursue something good or rewarding (new utility state) "just because."

Instead, we sense a shortfall or a higher possibility. That shortfall might be discomfort, emptiness, feeling behind others or missing out, while the new higher possibility might be personal enhancement, or the joy of discovery, yet always in contrast or relative to our current state. Dopamine helps us navigate this tension by propelling us toward an experience that promises to close the gap. The common denominator is that the brain recognizes a byproduct, be it negative or positive, and mobilizes a plan to correct or transcend that recognized deficiency, but only when the gap registers with enough emotional salience to disrupt inertia. In short, once the brain detects enough of a shortfall or overshadowed possibility, it spurs us to act.

This helps clarify why contrived scenarios like wearing sunglasses in pitch-black darkness or blindly grabbing food items in a store seem pointless. The brain receives no signal that such actions solve an existing deficiency or could propel us toward a state better than the current, therefore not motivating such pursuits. If advertising, or even culture, tried to persuade you that wearing sunglasses in a dark room, or at night, is somehow cool or glamorous, it might succeed only if it created a sense of social anxiety or introduced the idea that you are missing out on a daring fashion statement. Then a byproduct, fear of not fitting in or excitement about a novel look, arises. (If you grew up in the 80's you might recall the song and MTV video "I wear my sunglasses at night"). But if neither negative nor positive impetus is introduced, the behavior remains nonsensical and emotionally uncharged.

Existential-Philosophical Traditions and the Drive to Escape or Fulfill

While neuroscience illuminates the internal mechanics, existential-philosophical thought situates these motivations in a more profound lens of human freedom, meaning, and anxiety. It shows that even our grandest endeavors, from writing a book to launching a humanitarian project, stem from an attempt to handle or transform an existing deficiency, whether that deficiency is existential dread or the realization that we could become something greater. The subjective emotional response to these gaps is central, as it emotionally rouses us from complacency.

Anguish and Possibility

Existential thinkers delve into the emotional truths behind our pursuit of meaning. Jean-Paul Sartre and Albert Camus wrote about the anxiety that arises in a world lacking inherent purpose. Sartre famously argued that humans are "condemned to be free," highlighting how we must perpetually choose and invent meaning. That sense of responsibility and open-endedness often manifests as anguish. From the perspective of LPI, that anguish is a byproduct that demands resolution. People might appear to build a new company or master a complicated guitar piece just "for the sake of it," but lurking underneath is the discomfort of an otherwise unactualized future or the stimulating awareness that we can mold our lives differently. That byproduct of anguish says, "Where I am is no longer enough. I must address or improve it."

Likewise, Søren Kierkegaard's notion of "despair" highlights the tension between who we are, and who we might become. Once we recognize this gap, complacency becomes nearly impossible; an internal pang or fear of emptiness pushes us to act. This emotional prompt, arising from a gap formed between knowing that we could be more than we currently are, often drives us forward to avoid the unsettling sense that we might squander our potential. Ultimately, the impetus is always a byproduct: we discover that a more authentic or skillful version of ourselves is possible yet remains unrealized. Without that impetus, we remain inert.

Stoicism and the Cycle of Refinement

Stoicism, championed by Marcus Aurelius and others, might outwardly appear to advocate passive acceptance. Yet refining one's mental habits or vantage point occurs only upon detecting that one's current attitude is insufficient. That it fosters needless rumination or emotional extremes. The stoic is not improving "just because." They are addressing a recognized gap in their emotional equilibrium (existing utility state), seeking a more stable condition. Additionally, Buddhism's concept of dukkha (unsatisfactoriness) aligns similarly. Whether addressing deep existential dread or the mundane frustration of daily life, the impetus to shift arises once the current state is labeled as lacking or overshadowed by a calmer, more enlightened alternative.

Economics, Consumer Behavior, and the Creation or Removal of Byproduct

Economic frameworks often address "utility," presumably the satisfaction gained from goods or services. However, under LPI, such satisfaction is not sought in a vacuum; it arises because people notice or are made to notice a gap or tension, a byproduct, driving them to acquire that utility. Without an emotional signal that something is lacking or could be improved, the motivation to purchase or upgrade remains dormant.

Advertising as the Creation of Byproduct

One of the clearest demonstrations is in advertising. Consider how a brand might promote a new shampoo. They could show models with lustrous hair while subtly highlighting how the consumer's current hair might be dull, damaged or easily tangled. The viewer, who may have felt mostly content about their hair, now feels a mild but growing dissatisfaction with it (negative byproduct). Conversely, the ad could spark a positive byproduct: "Look at this extraordinary improvement you never thought you

373

could achieve. Now you can!" Marketing thus conjures up byproduct in the consumer's mind. The moment you accept that your current state is not good enough or could be improved upon, you've acquired a byproduct. Only then do you feel a pull to rectify this gap. If the ad fails to convey how your existing situation is no longer optimal, there is no urge to embrace the new offering.

Without the presence of byproduct, the compelling force to buy "the next new thing" is nonexistent. That is why seemingly pointless products can start to appear valuable if enough dissatisfaction or fascination is cultivated. If an advertisement tries to sell sunglasses designed for dark indoor spaces, it must create or highlight a tension, maybe a fashion statement or a fear of missing out, that did not exist before, but now overshadows your present state. If it fails, consumers see no sense in seeking utility purely for utility's sake because no emotional force is compelling them to purchase.

Avoiding Loss and Seeking Gains (Loss Aversion and Opportunity Hunger)
Behavioral economics, notably through the groundbreaking work of Daniel Kahneman and Amos Tversky, shows how loss aversion makes people respond more intensely to the threat of losing something than to an equivalent gain. Advertisements exploit this by framing your current state as increasingly irrelevant, warning that you may be falling behind if you don't "act now," also spotlighting fresh or limited-time offerings that outclass your present utility. If you learn that your current phone lacks modern features, the fear of practical obsolescence pushes you to upgrade (a negative byproduct), just as discovering a novel ice cream flavor, available for a limited time, can spur urgency and excitement (a positive byproduct) over tasting something better than what you have now, or ever recall tasting. In each instance, the motivation arises from a recognized byproduct, a deficit or missed opportunity. Whether it's the dread of losing social standing or the thrill of a newly revealed possibility. This tension created in the space between "where you are" and "where you could be" provokes the emotional impulse to close that gap before the chance disappears, demonstrating how marketing leverages both negative and positive angles to provoke consumer action.

Consumer behavior research consistently demonstrates that brand loyalty often hinges on avoiding regret: customers fear that switching to a different product or trying a new menu item may worsen their experience, causing them to stick with familiar choices to prevent disappointment. At the same time, a positive impetus may arise when an unfamiliar brand or dish promises a newly recognized advantage, prompting individuals to leave old habits or norms behind. In both cases, the fundamental driver is not "utility for its own sake," but rather the emotional acknowledgment that one's current option is either not worth the risk of regret (a negative impetus) or is now overshadowed by something superior (a positive impetus). According to LPI, each shift emerges from this emotional recognition of byproduct, whether it be the fear of a worse outcome or the excitement for something better. Only when people judge their existing utility state as inadequate or significantly upstaged, will they begin to feel the drive to make the switch.

Synthesis and the Ongoing Loop of Byproduct-Driven Utility

Bringing these insights together across psychology, neuroscience, philosophy, and economics reinforces that humans do not simply decide "I want utility." We respond to byproducts that reveal drawbacks in, or benefits over, our current state or approach. This rule holds equally for minor daily decisions and sweeping cultural revolutions. In all cases, the subjective emotional dimension amplifies the objective gap, generating a sense of "Things can be better."

The Myth of Utility "Just Because"

Utility for utility's sake remains a myth because, absent a perceived deficiency or overshadowing improvement, no impetus exists. The contrived examples of demanding an unneeded blood transfusion or wearing sunglasses in the dark illustrate how absurd it is to seek utility without acknowledging a newly discovered shortfall or overshadowed condition. Hence, LPI's stance that no pursuit emerges without a recognized negative impetus (to remedy dissatisfaction) or positive impetus (to respond to the perceived limits of the current state by upgrading or expanding). Without that emotional signal, the drive to do anything new evaporates.

A Continuous Cycle of Identification and Resolution

Because each solution eventually introduces complexities or spawns a new vantage revealing deeper flaws, innovation becomes perpetual. Fix one shortfall, and another emerges as soon as fresh knowledge, cultural norms or technology redefines what is "good enough." The printing press simplified mass communication, but soon we wanted faster connections, culminating in digital and then social platforms. Each stage of progress reveals new constraints or overshadowed possibilities, reigniting the process. Even in personal life, you might be content with a simple guitar until you encounter a friend's upgraded model, abruptly recognizing that your present setup is insufficient in comparison. This drives you to resolve the tension by seeking the new utility or skill, which in turn sets the stage for further improvements down the line.

EMOTIONS: The Unyielding Force Behind Innovation

The Law of Perpetual Innovation posits that all utility arises to address byproduct. A shortfall (expectation deviation η) or overshadowed state in one's current utility (unfulfilled aspiration δ). Without that sense of inadequate or constrained status quo, no impetus emerges to invent or adopt something better. It is not mere reason but human emotion (frustration, restlessness, or excitement) that catalyzes the unrelenting cycle to innovate. The dissatisfaction of inadequacy or a deficiency. The tension in the recognition that we might do more or better. The irritation with existing systems, and the aspiration or longing for something that surpasses our current state of utility satisfaction. This is what keeps us pushing forward.

It is not rationality that compels us to innovate; it is the human emotional-cognitive experience of dis-ease. Logic tells us how to solve problems, but emotion tells us why these problems need solving. A person does not demand a new phone because a superior model exists; they do so because they feel outdated, inefficient, or left behind. They do not compose a song, construct a city, or launch a revolution out of sheer want or curiosity alone, but because they sense an internal or external pressure that makes the present state intolerable or a future possibility irresistible. Even the most extraordinary human constructs; gods, religions, societies, economies, and governments, are not products of detached reasoning but of deep emotional necessity. We invented the divine not because we could, but because we could not bear the weight of existential uncertainty. We built nations not because they were logical, but because the current state of fear, dis-unity, unfulfilled ambition, insecurity and unresolved conflict demanded that we organize ourselves into something greater.

Every great leap, from the wheel to the internet, has been set in motion by an emotional response to a salient perceived gap. Whether that gap is the burden of physical labor, the limits of distance, the fear of the unknown, or the hunger for a better state than the current, it is the subjective emotional byproducts, through human sentience, that identifies these shortfalls and makes them unbearable to ignore. Rationality then serves as a tool, an essential one, for channeling that emotional drive into concrete organized solutions. **Without emotion, there is no recognition of lack, and without reason, there is no way to address it.**

The cycle of human innovation is not random, nor is it proactive in the sense of independent foresight. We do not create merely because we can; we create because something within us, stirred by byproduct, insists that we must. Every advancement, whether in science, art, philosophy, governance, and so on, has been the resolution of a tension we could no longer tolerate or a vision, better than the current, that we could

376

not resist pursuing. This cycle has no endpoint, because the moment one byproduct is resolved, another emerges. It is not a flaw in human nature, it is the essence of it. So long as we feel, we will seek; so long as we seek, we will create. Human emotion does not just sustain the wheel of innovation; it is the force that keeps it turning.

CHAPTER 22

Forescending States of Utility & Artificial Intelligence

Bridging from Byproduct Awareness to Forescension

In earlier chapters, we discussed how byproduct emerges from utility. Whether it arises through *experiencing* utility firsthand or through *awareness* of potential utility, one crucial element remains: a shortfall (η) or better possibility (δ) must intersect with a user (or groups') emotional perception to spark meaningful action. Just as George Berkeley's question about a tree falling in the forest underscores that perception is integral to whether an event carries subjective weight, so too within LPI does a shortfall (or potential) remain inert until someone *feels* it, labeling it as their problem or missed opportunity. This emotional charge, deriving from dissatisfaction with what currently exists or excitement for what could be, frames a byproduct.

Yet noticing a shortfall or aspiration alone does not automatically yield progress. One might observe a degrading phone battery and never act, or realize social injustice but never push for reform, or sense a personal skill gap yet fail to address it. The key question becomes: What motivates people to bridge the distance between "I see a gap" and "I will fix it" or "I see a product" and "I will buy it?"

This begs the question of how exactly do groups or individuals transition from byproduct to new utility. What drives product, service or system developers to want to create new utility? What causes engineers, architects, chefs, artists, entrepreneurs; innovators per se, to push to invent, create and innovate? Likewise, what drives individuals and groups to want to acquire better utility? To seek social reform, enter or exit a romantic relationship or purchase that improved product once a byproduct is at their doorstep? What exactly is happening in the shaded arrow (???) that drives a migration from a fully emerged byproduct to a new state of utility?

378

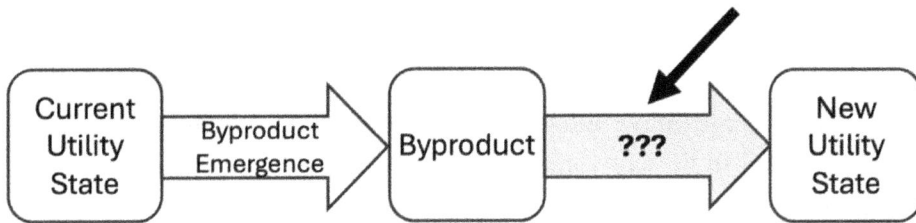

This inquiry lays the foundation for a deeper exploration. A phenomenon within the Law of Perpetual Innovation called forescension. While byproducts (negative or positive) encapsulate the recognized mismatch between current utility and a potential improvement, *Forescension* is the process, both mental and motivational, that activates us to transcend our present state. As we examine this concept, we will see that neither individuals nor entire societies merely drift into better utility. Instead, they forescend. They consciously or subconsciously move away from what they currently have once they realize it is overshadowed by a superior possibility. This emphasis on transition distinguishes forescension from mere idle longing or aimless curiosity.

The following subsections will illustrate how forescension interlocks with byproduct and utility, how it draws on emotion and evolutionary underpinnings, and how it pervades everyday innovation. We will then consider future frontiers, such as advanced technologies like AI assisting creative endeavors, and why the Byproduct-Driven Innovation Engine remains vital in a world where AI is not yet sentient.

What is Forescension?

Within LPI, byproduct points out that our current utility state is no longer fully adequate. Sometimes this emerges through expectation deviation η (a product, service, system or environment fails to meet our expectations), or through aspirational comparison δ (we realize there is a "next-level" potential that outdoes our present utility experience). Yet awareness of such a mismatch alone, while essential, does not ensure that individuals or groups will meaningfully act. This is where forescension enters:

Forescension (noun) is being defined as the emotional-cognitive motivation that propels a group or individual to transition from their present utility standing to a state perceived as more advantageous or beneficial, fueled by a newfound conscious or subconscious awareness of what could be. A salient alternative that emotionally eclipses the present. Crucially, it always arises in comparison, contrast or competition to what is (current utility state) and what would be forsaken by leaving

the current state, as well as what might be forfeited by not making the transition to the improved utility state.

It is not a trivial desire to "have something new" or "create something new," but rather an impetus anchored in the conviction that maintaining the current utility state is no longer acceptable when measured against a more promising alternative. Emotional cues such as frustration, hope, envy, fear, desire or excitement, are vital to triggering forescension, for they convert abstract dissatisfaction or curiosity into determination that pushes us past complacency.

Under LPI, we are never driven "just because something exists." Rather, when a product, service, or new possibility emerges, it contrasts with our present situation, making our current state feel obsolete, unremarkable, or incomplete. This recognized gap becomes a byproduct: if it evokes sentiments of annoyance, fear, frustration, or envy, we classify it as a negative byproduct (an unresolved deficiency); if it elicits emotions like excitement, inspiration, eagerness or curiosity, we classify it as an positive byproduct (an unfulfilled aspiration). However, even after sensing these emotions, inaction can persist if the impetus to forescend fails to surface.

Forescension is that impetus. It is the push-pull dynamic that compels us to act. It distinguishes "I know I should do better" from actually seeking or designing a better outcome. A distinctly human synergy, it blends cold facts ("My phone battery drains too quickly," "I see a more advanced alternative") with an emotional resolution ("I refuse to remain here," or "I must move beyond these limitations").

It bears repeating that logic alone seldom animates our decisions. People need an emotional push: a sense or belief that the *status quo* is no longer tolerable or that a missed opportunity is too valuable to pass up. Forescension is precisely that integrated stimulus, merging the objective knowledge of "things can be improved" with the subjective determination of "I must surpass this." In simpler terms, *logic identifies the gap; emotion compels the pursuit.* Forescension is the synergy of both *(note: in varying weights each, across different individuals).*

Where "to transcend" indicates rising to a higher level, "to forescend" underscores the propelling force for doing so, accounting for the *why*: what we rise for and what we leave behind. Forescending is not merely about improvement; it is about escaping a recognized utility state once considered adequate, but now overshadowed by something superior. This impetus resonates through daily examples. From a student contending with poor grades and deciding "I have to do better" to a community that outgrows local resources and feels pressed to create or relocate. The essence of forescension remains consistent: bridging from "Here is a recognized gap" to "Let's push ourselves beyond it."

Forescension inherently thrives on comparison. The user, developer, or society measures the existing utility against a newly recognized option or known standard that overshadows the old. This comparison yields the impetus: "We must surpass or escape the old." If no alternative vantage existed, or none felt more salient, then the drive to forescend would remain dormant.

Evolutionary and Social Contexts: Forescension Beyond Mere Survival

From an evolutionary perspective, species confronting resource scarcity, environmental shifts, or competitive threats confronted a fundamental choice: remain in a declining environment or move to a more promising one. As soon as the old environment was deemed inadequate, that sense of mismatch triggered an evolutionary precursor to forescension. While non-human organisms may not process dissatisfaction in the same emotional-cognitive way humans do, the outcome is analogous: a recognized shortfall spurs them to develop new survival strategies or leave their current habitat in search of something more viable (create or pursue a new utility state).

Evolution rarely yields ideal solutions. It typically yields solutions that are "good enough" for the environment at hand. Once humans developed more advanced cognition, "good enough" often ceased to be truly enough. Forescence arises upon noticing new lands, social structures, or technologies revealing them as far superior to the old. Mentally, people commit: "I will not remain in a suboptimal state." LPI describes such leaps in terms of forescension: the impetus to transcend constraints. We do not merely transcend adversity; we forescend because we recognize and feel, emotional-cognitively, that our current environment fails to meet newly discovered standards or possibilities.

Philosophers and biologists often discuss how organisms or societies "transcend" their limitations to adapt or achieve something greater. "To forescend" similarly denotes rising above, but it underscores how awareness of deficiency, or overshadowed adequacy, is the direct impetus for that rise. To forescend is not a random leap into novelty; it is specifically motivated by the sense that *"remaining as is"* means forfeiting something crucial, be it survival advantage, comfort, or personal growth. Thus, one can say that species or cultures do not transcend hardships merely from curiosity; they forescend in response to recognized constraints or new opportunities that overshadow the old approach.

On a societal level, mass movements often emerge because a collective perceives that the present conditions, be they political, economic, or social, are overshadowed by a feasible improvement. Societies choose to alter farmland strategies, adopt animal husbandry, or cultivate specialized crafts because they experience the old methods' deficiency, or they see the potential for something better. Revolutions or large-scale reforms occur when enough people experience byproduct (objective evidence of injustice coupled with subjective feelings of moral outrage) and collectively envision a better social structure. This collective forescension leads entire communities to break from old systems or structures. The same logic applies to widespread cultural adoptions, such as transitions in architecture, music genres, or educational approaches. This phenomenon has repeated across millennia, fueling expansions, city-building, and eventually globalized trade. Once the older tradition is felt to be overshadowed by a new possibility, groups "forescend," adopting the emergent utility that promises higher satisfaction or alignment with evolving norms.

In the broader tapestry of LPI, forescension is more than a new term; it is the emotional-cognitive momentum that transforms recognized byproduct (negative or positive) into real progress. While we have established that noticing or logically cataloging shortfalls is vital, it alone remains insufficient to shift one's present state of utility. One must *feel* the impetus to exit or improve that state. An internal driver that we call forescension. Its companion concepts, forescence (the moment of clarifying insight) and forescend (the act of departing the old), complete the picture.

These terms and processes are not hypothetical or academic alone; they reveal the practical mechanism by which we continuously shape and reshape the human experience. Whether in the realm of daily product upgrades, historical migrations, cultural renaissances, or cutting-edge AI applications, we see that recognized dissatisfaction or new potential must cross an emotional threshold to become action. The constant re-examination of "Is this still enough?" and the rising of "No, we can do better" sustains an infinite cycle of invention and reinvention. The Law of Perpetual Innovation itself.

To Forescend or not to Forescend

Forescension depends on both the *push* of dissatisfaction and the *pull* of new possibilities. Sometimes, however, the push and pull are not enough. Individuals, groups or organizations may recognize a shortfall or overshadowed utility yet resist change if the emotional and logistical tradeoffs appear too steep. Fear of unknown complexities, suspicion that the gains might be marginal, certainty or security in the current, or the inertia of conformity or complacency can all blunt one's willingness to forescend. People may remain in a suboptimal arrangement if the emotional cost of leaving their comfort zone outweighs their dissatisfaction with the status quo. Often, the stumbling block is not that a potential utility is unappealing, but rather that exiting one's current utility can bring unknown or unwelcome trade-offs.

The first major factor in deciding whether to forescend arises from confronting what must be *forsaken*. Upgrading a computer's operating system might introduce new capabilities but also require relearning interfaces, risking temporary loss of productivity, or even losing compatibility with beloved features. The possibility of encountering bugs or having to invest valuable time can deter users, prompting them to continue enduring a subpar system rather than confront transitional headaches. Similarly, in relationships or social circles, a person may notice troubling patterns or feel a strong urge to explore healthier dynamics, but confronting painful conversations and stepping away from accustomed routines can feel like an even bigger threat. In such moments, the emotional weight of "I don't want to lose what I have" overshadows any excitement for genuine improvement. Fear of disruption, a reluctance to sacrifice comfort, and the inertia of routine combine to stall forescension, illustrating how the perceived cost of leaving behind the known often eclipses the promise of a better horizon.

The other major factor in taking the leap to transition exists in what may be *forfeited* if we remain. Staying with a familiar product or service can mean relinquishing future gains in performance, security, or overall user experience; opportunities that might be lost if we opt to stand still. Imagine clinging to an aging internet plan that lacks modern data speeds: by not upgrading, we could be foregoing smoother virtual meetings, improved streaming performance, or even job prospects that rely on a stable online presence. In a relationship or social context, ignoring addressing long-simmering issues may also entail giving up the possibility of healthier communication patterns and deeper emotional fulfillment. Even salvaging the entire relationship in the long run. Sometimes fear of jeopardizing existing comfort or routines overshadows the awareness that the status quo is losing its edge, but the real sacrifice is often the richer, more evolved scenario we might discover if we make the leap. Thus, even though the threat of disrupting the status quo may loom large, what we might unwittingly forfeit by staying put can become an even stronger motivator for forescension.

Families sending a student to college exemplify forescension in action. The impetus is not purely "education for education's sake," but rather the recognition that the current skillset or future trajectory is overshadowed by possibilities enabled through higher education. Even though the financial, emotional, and time investment costs can be high, and the unfamiliarity daunting, they foresee a more promising utility state: broader career opportunities, intellectual growth, and social mobility. The byproduct fueling this investment might be the growing dissatisfaction that arises when current paths seem too narrow and unfulfilling, or the energizing realization that higher education can unlock a richer array of life opportunities. Forescension emerges when parents and students conclude that remaining in the status quo is no longer viable, given the promise of deeper intellectual development, broader career potential, and an enriched future.

In the world of business, investors are themselves seeking to forescend, moving away from less promising or stagnant ventures toward higher returns and market influence. By placing capital in a startup or an expanding enterprise, they are effectively betting that both they and the company can leave behind their current utility state, marked by limited growth or profitability, and rise to an improved one. The negative impetus might be the realization that "if we do not invest, we remain locked in suboptimal returns," while the positive impetus stems from the promise of greater gains and competitive differentiation.

An investment, then, reflects the investor's confidence that the enterprise can also forescend beyond existing market norms, outpacing older utility standards or overshadowing entrenched rivals, once it receives the necessary capital. By recognizing the enterprise's gaps and potential, the investor envisions it advancing to a more robust utility state where stronger products, services, or strategies dominate. If fear of capital loss eclipses this vision, the investor chooses not to forescend, remaining with safer or more familiar investments. Conversely, if they judge the enterprise as capable of truly surpassing its current standing, thus elevating the investor's own trajectory, they'll commit funds, effectively propelling both themselves and the company beyond their previous limitations.

Ultimately, people or groups choose to forescend when their emotional-cognitive appraisal of "*What might be lost if I stay here?*" outweighs "*What might be lost if I move on?*" Psychologically, the two loss-averse states are in competition with each other. Thus, the interplay of dissatisfaction, curiosity, fear, excitement, convenience, and cost forms the delicate balance in which forescension either flourishes or fades. Much like deciding to abandon an old but comfortable method for a sharper, more advanced tool. The impetus to transition the present emerges only after the recognized shortfall, or overshadowed condition, becomes more compelling than the comfort, familiarity or security of the status quo.

Intuition, "Doing the Work," and Forescension

Intuition, or "gut feel," often manifests as a swift, near-automatic judgment. We might call it "fast thinking," an instinctive response that Daniel Kahneman famously differentiates from the more methodical, effortful "slow thinking." In the realm of forescension, both modes of thought can powerfully influence our decisions, though they do so in different ways. "Fast thinking" can trigger those impulse buys such as a seemingly random order on social media through the fleeting excitement of spotting a "recommended" product. We might not truly need these items, yet we sense a void and attempt to fill it with something external. In such cases, individuals may be reacting to an emotional itch of boredom, curiosity, or even envy, rather than methodically pursuing an actual solution to an identified gap in their current utility state. On its own, this kind of quick fix rarely leads to meaningful, transformative innovation. It is more apt to become momentary gratification than a true investment in longstanding change.

However, genuine forescension does not rely on impulse alone; it requires "slow thinking." A deeper evaluation of trade-offs, hidden costs, and long-term benefits. People who commit to building something new or overhauling a longstanding status quo engage in an iterative process that might begin with a hunch, but soon demands concerted reflection and continuous learning. This is "doing the work": devoting time, energy, and often obsessive dedication to refine an idea or skill until it surpasses the overshadowed condition left behind. Rather than just a quick swipe or purchase, forescension becomes a deliberate path: from "I see a gap" to "I am willing to commit real effort, thought, evaluation, and emotional resilience to close that gap."

This divergence is starkly visible in the difference between individuals who chase novelty to fill a sense of emptiness and those who truly innovate. The first group operates mostly on fast thinking: "I feel incomplete, so I'll buy something new," or "I'm bored, so I'll watch another few videos." Such decisions can momentarily soothe a gnawing sense of deficiency but seldom lead to lasting improvement or personal growth. In contrast, innovators rely on forescension: they see or feel a shortfall, but they also commit to "doing the work." Rather than seeking quick relief or small diversions, they take on the methodical tasks: testing, research, skill mastery, and deep reflection that eventually yield a solution that truly transcends the old.

An essential piece of this puzzle is the individual's emotional capacity and self-awareness. People who frequently succeed at forescending, who conjure genuine leaps in utility for themselves or others, tend to possess (1) a pronounced ability to feel things strongly and identify those feelings correctly, and (2) a robust knowledge base and growth mindset that keeps them learning, iterating, and pivoting as new challenges arise. The first trait allows them to pinpoint when "something isn't right," to sustain the motivation that "I can't stand staying here," or to sense that "the next possibility is too promising to ignore." The second trait supplies them with the tools to transform those feelings into a constructive plan of action. Indeed, emotion and reason unite to create "forescence," that spark of clarity driving them forward into genuine action of forescending.

By contrast, those who lack either deep emotional awareness or substantial expertise often remain stuck. They may buy random items out of boredom or latch onto shallow trends, never devoting the slow thinking needed to bring about true progress. Without emotional clarity, they may not fully realize what they're missing or why it matters. Without experience or willingness to "do the work," they cannot mold fleeting insights into something that surpasses the status quo. They might sense dissatisfaction, but they respond impulsively rather than systematically addressing the root issue. Their leaps become halfhearted. Enough to ease immediate discomfort but rarely enough to overshadow the old utility in a lasting, meaningful way.

In sum, forescension separates those who act on a mere hunch or impulse from those who genuinely transform circumstances. Intuition can be a powerful asset, especially at the outset, when a quick, gut-level recognition of a gap first arises. But "fast thinking" alone rarely reshapes the world. It is the dedicated, "slow thinking" approach where unrelenting focus, self-regulation of powerful emotions, and a hunger for learning coalesce, that fuels true innovation. In that sense, forescension is not merely an emotional outburst or a fleeting whim. It is the sustained commitment to surpass what is, guided by both heartfelt conviction and steady, purposeful labor.

The Future of Forescension: AI and Beyond

Technologies such as artificial intelligence have surged to the forefront of innovation, showing remarkable abilities in pattern recognition, natural language processing, and data-driven insights. AI systems already develop new concepts in fields like drug discovery and product recommendations, harnessing massive data sets to optimize solutions. Yet whether AI can originate its own impetus for surpassing the status quo remains an open debate.

AI's capacity to generate novel combinations and detect hidden inefficiencies suggests it could help identify objective byproducts. For instance, advanced machine learning models can parse user complaints at scale, rank them by frequency and severity, and predict emerging consumer trends. It can even propose hypothetical solutions that tie these insights together. However, LPI posits that "emotional-cognitive impetus" is central to genuine forescension. Machines, as of now, do not experience frustration or longing about overshadowed conditions. They simply register data patterns. The emotional spark that "something is no longer acceptable" belongs to humans, or at least to a form of consciousness that perceives subjective states as personally relevant.

If AI remains non-sentient, it cannot *feel* the negative impetus of burdens and dissatisfaction or the positive draw of aspiration or hope. It can crunch numbers and suggest that a new battery design would reduce consumer complaints by 60%, but it cannot experience the impetus to *leave behind* older methods. Without that impetus, the final choice to pivot resources or redesign a system falls on humans. We are the ones who sense risk, curiosity, or hope and say, "Yes, this new concept surpasses what we have. Let's do it."

Some futurists hypothesize that AI may one day achieve a form of sentience or emotional intelligence. If that day arrives, these systems might conceive and feel shortfalls or overshadowed states in ways akin to humans, possibly generating forescension on their own. However, short of that threshold, they serve as powerful analytic allies, scanning for objective shortfalls and possibilities. As of today, they rely on us to supply the emotional push that transforms recognized mismatches into a driving force, culminating in new, distinctly human-focused utility solutions.

Yet even if AI did create novel solutions that appear "original," we must consider whose needs they serve. LPI's "Foundational Constructs" (Module A: Chapters 6 - 9) underscore how human-driven innovation remains grounded in human origin utilities such as mobility, perception, communication, and other capabilities integral to our biology and culture. Without sharing comparable sentience, AI lacks the emotional vantage to frame gaps in ways that resonates with us as truly salient. It may design impressive functionalities based on its internal logic, but these would likely address AI's own operational efficiencies rather than fulfill any human context, much as the printing press or the internet might be meaningless to a non-human species without a shared set of fundamental desires or viewpoints.

In other words, purely AI-driven utility creation may solve "problems" AI identifies for its own processes, analogous to how humans design advanced robotics that are largely irrelevant to, say, chimpanzee's or marine life. Our Module A discussion on Human Origin Utilities highlights how primal human drives and motivations shape our inventions, whether it's the need to communicate or to manage resources. By the same token, a non-sentient AI that spins out new algorithms only to enhance its processing flow or memory bandwidth is generating "utility" from an AI perspective, not from a human vantage. Until AI perceives shortfalls and aspirational states similar to how humans perceive them, it may rarely produce utility on its own that we find deeply meaningful.

This parallel is clearer if we recall how humans create dog bowls, pet medications, or even entire habitats for our domesticated animals. We do so to serve a human objective, such as convenience or companionship. Our utility is rarely relevant to another species for its own sake; it remains oriented around human aims. Likewise, an AI that is non-sentient can meaningfully shape only the needs of its own artificial domain. If it lacks the kind of emotional-cognitive impetus that fosters genuinely human-relevant forescension, it cannot spontaneously guide innovation in ways that align with our origin utilities on its own. Only when AI attains a level of sentience comparable or superior to ours, and becomes able to register dissatisfaction, longing, and overshadowed conditions akin to human life, could its own discoveries and creations become genuinely relevant to the broader human experience.

However, until such time that AI achieves or is granted the emotional-cognitive capacity to care about human shortfalls, any synergy between AI's data-driven outputs and authentic human needs will require a human bridge through our willingness to adopt, refine, or dismiss AI-generated concepts based on our emotional-cognitive standards and origin utilities. One might envision a future where human managers and AI partners operate symbiotically: the AI identifies hidden and explicit byproducts or potential leaps, while humans weigh intangible factors like brand identity, user trust, or the moral and emotional resonance. In effect, human emotional cognition closes the loop, deciding if the impetus is strong enough to risk changing established processes or launching a new paradigm. So long as AI remains a purely data-driven entity, the emotional glue that triggers forescension, "We must surpass the old," will remain ours to provide. Even if AI can generate novel solutions, it is humanity that *feels* them as necessary or compelling.

For now, the question of whether AI can solely drive innovation remains speculative. According to LPI, the essence of meaningful progress, known as forescension, derives from emotional-cognitive signals that reveal something overshadowing our present utility state. Until AI experiences these signals as personal impetus, it can highlight external "objective" shortfalls but cannot truly care "subjectively" whether they are resolved. That caring, that sense of "we must do this," is inextricably linked to the awareness that continuing in the old state is unacceptable or overshadowed. Only an entity that experiences those judgments can autonomously make leaps akin to humans.

An AI-based Byproduct Driven Innovation Engine (AI-BDIE) Example

While AI itself may not experience frustration or longing, it can play a pivotal role in organizing, interpreting, and proposing new directions based on byproduct data. Humans, in turn, provide the essential emotional impetus, the "forescension" to abandon outdated solutions that no longer serve. This synergy between human forescension and AI-driven pattern recognition underpins what we call the AI-based Byproduct Driven Innovation Engine (AI-BDIE). Through such a system, organizations can systematically incorporate various inputs such as objective shortfall data, subjective user feedback, and emerging technologies, and evaluate potential utility leaps in a structured, data-informed way.

The AI-BDIE handles both objective byproduct data (e.g., error rates, performance metrics, or sales trends, as seen in the "Byproduct Impact Spectrum") and subjective sentiment data (user emotions, anecdotal complaints, or aspirational desires, akin to the "Byproduct Contrast Continuum"). By scoring and weighting these signals, the engine can highlight which overshadowed utilities likely demand urgent attention and tentatively propose solutions. Critically, however, the decision to forescend from an existing utility in favor of the new one remains a human choice. We must feel and then reasonably conclude that "remaining as we are is no longer acceptable."

Let's take a high level look at how an AI based Byproduct-Driven Innovation Engine (AI-BDIE) may be constructed:

AI System Component A: Predicting Utility from Byproducts

This component identifies new utilities by analyzing current and historical byproducts. It filters relevant data, from internal product usage and competitor offerings to broader market trends, and then classifies byproducts by severity, frequency, or user impact. By simulating how each potential solution would resolve these gaps, it also projects possible new byproducts that might emerge. For example, implementing a smartphone's self-cooling mechanism might resolve heat issues but risk draining the battery faster. Armed with that foresight, teams can judge whether the proposed innovation truly surpasses the status quo.

AI System Component B: Global Advancements Polling

Here, the system scans beyond incremental improvements, monitoring disruptive possibilities across science and technology. It might comb through engineering journals for novel materials or track blockchain breakthroughs for major supply-chain shifts. Instead of focusing solely on existing byproduct issues, this module seeks "big leaps" that could overshadow current technological or logistical approaches. Even so, if the AI-BDIE flags a groundbreaking technology, human leadership must feel that "staying with the old approach is now overshadowed." Only then do they forescend, stepping away from the existing utility to adopt or invent something entirely new.

AI System Component C: Super-System and Ecosystem Interaction Modeling
No product or service exists in isolation. This module simulates how a proposed solution interacts with its broader context, be it an office environment, a supply chain, or an entire cultural framework. Such awareness is crucial because one byproduct often triggers others. For instance, an overly sensitive car alarm could cause false alerts at airports or rail crossings, frustrating users and attracting regulatory scrutiny. By modeling how new solutions mesh with super-systems, the AI-BDIE anticipates secondary or tertiary byproducts that might otherwise surface unexpectedly.

This Component C aligns with the Byproduct Interdependence concept in the Law of Perpetual Innovation (LPI). When a new product or service is "nested" inside a larger system, it can inadvertently clash with the super-system's goals, generating unintended ripples. For example, enabling free-form smartphone usage in a quiet space like a theater might undermine the venue's core purpose, leading to unforeseen conflicts. Although the AI can forecast and propose adjustments, humans still decide which concerns are pressing enough to justify a fundamental change.

Human Forescension: The Final Catalyst

Together, these AI components (A, B, and C) illustrate how an AI-based Byproduct Driven Innovation Engine can refine the detection of accumulated byproducts and forecast higher-potential solutions. Parsing large data streams, it pinpoints performance lags, gauges user dissatisfaction, discovers global tech leaps, and assesses how new ideas blend into larger ecosystems. In every scenario, though, the Law of Perpetual Innovation reminds us that forescending remains a human prerogative. The AI-BDIE can rank issues, highlight opportunities, and even run predictive simulations, however, only humans can truly feel which gaps are salient enough to say, "We must do better."

Over time, an advanced AI-BDIE might expand with more modules: polling emerging science, scanning social sentiments, or cross-referencing global regulations. Still, it will not automatically "forescend" on our behalf. For the foreseeable future, the spark of dissatisfaction or aspiration, our emotional signal that a current utility has outlived its usefulness, belongs uniquely to humanity. As AI grows in capability, some speculate it may one day approximate sentient reasoning or develop a form of emotional cognition. Until that point, the Law of Perpetual Innovation maintains that our willingness to discard the old and embrace the new is fueled by innate human drives, in constant interplay with objective data.

Thus, while an AI-BDIE can massively enhance the efficiency and scope of innovation efforts, it merely shines a light on where new solutions can flourish. The final leap in deciding to transform or replace a utility still springs from our fundamentally human capacity to perceive burdens as unacceptable and forescend in favor of a higher realization of human potential.

The Perpetual Cycle of Innovation: A Final Look

Whenever individuals or groups decide to forescend, we see them moving within a broader cycle of utility creation and adoption. In essence, there is a feedback loop that repeatedly draws participants from a current existing utility state to a newly created or adopted utility state, fueled by byproduct recognition and the emotional-cognitive drive to surpass what is.

Consider the following steps from both a utility creator's and utility consumer's viewpoint:

1. **Present [Existing] Utility State**:
   People acquire or experience a product, service, or system that provides them with utility (the value, benefit, or satisfaction they derive from it). At this stage, they perceive their product as "good enough" for their present needs. They are experiencing and preserving one or more "human origin utility" categories, such as mobility, through shoes, bicycles, or public transportation. Their satisfaction assumes they are not actively comparing their product to alternatives in the same category (other shoes or bicycles, or even cars or airplanes). At this point, they have achieved a baseline level of satisfaction (utility) that aligns with their present expectations. There is no pressing tension, no immediate desire for something better. No thermodynamic inefficiency ϵ weighing on them. The current solution feels sufficient, for now.

2. **Byproduct Emergence**:
   Over time, as people continue to experience and form memories around their product, service, or system, their perception of utility begins to shift. They may feel that the overall satisfaction or benefit (net utility) of the product is diminishing. However, what is actually happening is that their experience is being detracted

from, either by intrinsic factors (issues within the product itself) or extrinsic influences (shifts in external conditions, social expectations, or technological advancements). These detractors, which come in many forms (inefficiencies, burdensome tasks, malfunctions, monotony, emerging cultural shifts, influences casting a shadow on their current product, or any persistent tension arising from the realization that a new or better competing innovation is possible) are what we call byproducts.

Byproducts rarely appear all at once. They gradually emerge and inevitably accumulate over time, some temporarily, some permanently, and others suddenly (as an impulse or catastrophic event). However, their effect is the same: they begin to disrupt the once-sufficient utility state, creating a growing disconnect between what was once acceptable and what now feels inadequate. At this point, objective thermodynamic inefficiency ϵ is being subjectively experienced via expectation deviation η and/or aspirational comparison δ.

As these byproducts accumulate, the result is an increasing net loss in perceived benefit (utility). Satisfaction erodes, and a once-ignored or non-existent problem starts to demand attention.

3. Byproduct [Sufficient Recognition]

At some point, whether consciously or subconsciously (see NOTE below), the accumulation of byproduct enters emotional and cognitive awareness and starts approaching a threshold (the Utility Abandonment Condition aka the Byproduct Tolerance Threshold). Once reached, this moment is more than mere dissatisfaction or aspiration, it is a charged realization. The individual feels the tension between their present utility state and a potentially improved future state. A sense of unease takes hold: "This doesn't feel good enough anymore." It is this recognition of the "gap," between where they are and where they could be, that creates the psychological and emotional impulse and motivation to pursue a better alternative.

> **NOTE: Subconscious vs. Conscious Recognition of Byproduct**
> It is important to note that "recognition" in this step can occur consciously or below conscious awareness. In many instances, people sense a gap or shortfall well before they can fully articulate it. Research on "Affective Priming," pioneered by scholars like John Bargh and Russell Fazio, reveals that subtle emotional cues, such as a faint discomfort or a positive association we can't quite pinpoint, can prime us to feel increasingly dissatisfied with a status quo. We may decide to switch brands or try a new product out of an

unshakable but vague impulse, never consciously identifying the exact trigger behind our change in preference.

The "Somatic Marker Hypothesis," advanced by neurologist Antonio Damasio, provides further support for this phenomenon by showing how bodily (somatic) signals such as tension in our muscles, quickened heartbeat, or a "gut feeling," often guide our decisions before reasoned analysis kicks in. We might simply "feel" that our current arrangement is lacking or overshadowed, and these emotional cues (byproducts of perceived shortfalls) nudge us to seek better alternatives.

Meanwhile, the work by researchers like Arthur Reber on "Implicit Learning" suggests that individuals can subconsciously detect patterns, such as a minor repeated annoyance with an app's interface, well before they consciously label it as a problem. Over time, these implicit cues accumulate, fueling dissatisfaction that eventually culminates in leaving the old solution behind, even if users can't recall when they first sensed something was off.

Therefore, *"Once sufficiently recognized"* does not imply purely conscious consideration. It means the shortfall or overshadowed possibility has become relevant enough, either consciously or subconsciously, to generate an emotional-cognitive reaction. This is often all that's needed to mobilize us toward Step 4.

4. **Forescension**:

This moment of realization triggers forescence (the "aha" or "Eureka!" moment) where the person consciously acknowledges that their current utility state is no longer adequate. This recognition propels them to forescend, driven by two forces: a push away from the dissatisfaction of the present state and a pull toward the promise of something greater.

At this stage, they take decisive action. As consumers, they begin seeking, evaluating, and eventually adopting a better solution. As creators, they begin designing, developing, and ultimately delivering an improved solution.

This forescension moment is the inflection point of innovation, where the tension between present limitations and future possibilities reaches a breaking point, driving change forward.

5. **Future Utility State**:

The cycle culminates in the adoption or creation of a new utility state, one that feels like the answer to the previously unresolved and unfulfilled byproducts. It is better, more satisfying, and more aligned with evolving expectations.

But this is not the end.

This new state of utility becomes the new present state, and inevitably, the cycle will begin again.

As time passes, new byproducts will emerge and accumulate, some slowly, some suddenly, creating the next iteration of unresolved deficiencies and unfulfilled aspirations.

What was once the solution will, in time, reveal new problems.
What was once aspired to will, in time, be outgrown.

And so, individuals, businesses, and the world itself will find themselves once again at the doorstep of change, driven forward by the relentless force of byproduct emergence.

Innovation does not stop. It won't stop.

This is the Law of Perpetual Innovation: An endless, unbreakable cycle where each solution gives rise to the need for another.

It is not a choice. It is the nature of all progress itself.

The Perpetual Cycle of Innovation

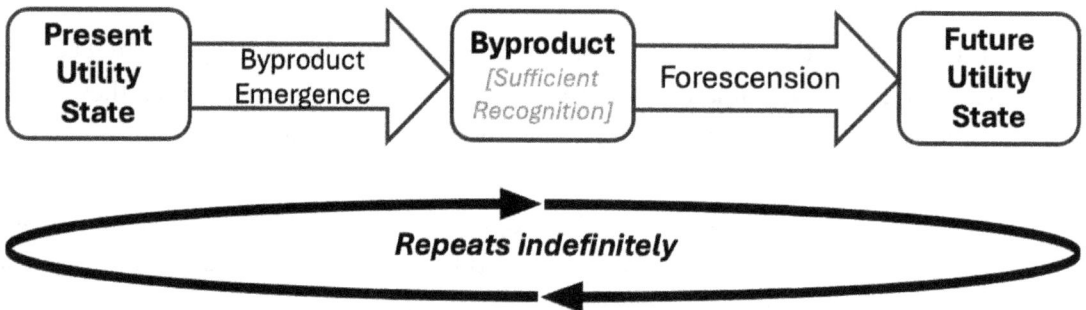

Present Utility State → Byproduct Emergence → Byproduct [Sufficient Recognition] → Forescension → Future Utility State

Repeats indefinitely

This cycle underpins all domains of innovation, from consumer products to social and geopolitical initiatives, reflecting how byproducts (recognized shortfalls or overshadowed states), once emotionally internalized, catalyze the repeated loop toward ever improving utility. Or "Innovation."

Part 3:
Innovation Methods

In Part 3 we explore one of the most profound advantages of the Law of Perpetual Innovation (LPI), in its capacity to guide product, service, and system developers in answering the fundamental question: *What should we create next?* The answer lies within the byproducts that individuals consciously recognize as burdens, as well as those that have been latently and subconsciously accepted by the masses. Byproducts that, at times due to widespread normalization (Principle of Byproduct Normalization), remain unchallenged yet ripe for disruption. These byproducts are a wellspring for innovation, revealing latent opportunities where existing utility can branch from or converge into new emergent utilities.

However, the mere presence of byproducts does not render the path to innovation entirely predictable. The process of harnessing these byproducts demands rigorous effort, systematically surfacing them, eliminating distortions caused by biases, errors, and outliers, classifying and prioritizing them, and ultimately, selecting the most consequential ones to address. This requires a structured approach to ensure that the innovations derived from them hold meaningful impact.

Fortunately, modern society has an unprecedented advantage: artificial intelligence. AI's capacity to process vast quantities of data, recognize hidden patterns, and predict emergent byproducts positions it as an invaluable tool for accelerating and refining this complex process. Yet, whether with or without AI, innovation remains a function of how effectively one navigates the ever-linked dynamic dependency between utility and byproduct. To illustrate this, let us examine key methods of innovation where these two forces serve as primary variables.

Six Innovation Methods through LPI's Byproduct-Driven Innovation lens:

Within Part 3 we will explore six methods of innovation utilizing LPI:
1. Chapter 23: Incremental or Sustained Innovation
2. Chapter 24: Innovation through Utility Integration
3. Chapter 25: Innovation through Utility Specialization
4. Chapter 26: Adaptive Utility Innovation
5. Chapter 27: Modular Utility Innovation
6. Chapter 28: Radical Innovation

Each of these Innovation Methods represent different ways byproduct is managed to ensure maximum net utility for the consumer over the lifespan of the product. These methods help clarify where the true value to a consumer exists within a product, service or systems capability. Many products today combine the use of these methods. Meanwhile, product developers continue to view their offerings primarily through the lens of adding or creating utility value for the customer. That is ultimately what the customer ends up experiencing and feeling. They will end up perceiving that they are purchasing something of better or higher value. However, LPI tells us that the reason a customer will consider a product to be of higher or better value is because of what it does for them. Newer or better offerings possess the ability to eliminate or mitigate byproducts better than their predecessor solutions, or lack thereof. They are value-depletion removers. They give us back more of our life's time, personal energy, reduce complexity and its frustration, curtail burdens and their discomfort, lessen uncertainty and its fear... they liberate us from that which we do not wish to experience or feel, ever, or ever again. They lessen, delay or eliminate those instances altogether. In this way, a products utility becomes the medicine to our "dis" "ease" of byproduct. That is why we value them.

This can help us understand why it makes little sense to sit at a table with other product development experts and ask, "What medicine should we come up with next?" Unfortunately, that's exactly what many businesses still do today. LPI's Byproduct-Driven Innovation tells us that we should be looking to the diagnosis of the malady or ailment to make that determination. If you want to know what to create and deliver next, look to the byproducts.

CHAPTER 23
Incremental Sustained Innovation

Delaying and Deferring Byproduct Onset

Introduction

Incremental Innovation, also known as Sustained Innovation, is often misunderstood as adding incremental value to an existing product according to existing economic principles, while sustaining or extending the lifecycle of the product. However, the Law of Perpetual Innovation (LPI) reveals that incremental innovation does not just sustain net utility, it actively increases net available utility not by refining performance, but by delaying, reducing, or softening the emergence of byproducts; those inefficiencies, burdens, and unintended consequences that inevitably accumulate, permanently or temporarily, over the lifespan of a product.

This section explores:
- The distinction between value-maintaining and value-increasing incremental innovation.
- How delaying the onset of byproducts directly increases net perceived utility.
- The emergence of new residual byproducts in even the most refined innovations.
- A mathematical model for quantifying the innovation's impact on total net utility.
- Business implications such as premium pricing justification and brand loyalty.

By understanding these principles, businesses can strategically develop incremental innovations that increase perceived customer value, improve retention, and justify price premiums.

The General Concept of Incremental Innovation under LPI

Incremental innovation refers to deliberate, smaller-scale enhancements that extend the usefulness of a product by reducing or delaying the byproducts that diminish its net perceived utility over time. These refinements do not need to alter the product's core functionality (its baseline utility, U_0) to have a profound impact. Instead, they manage how quickly and severely utility is overshadowed by byproduct accumulation.

Types of Incremental Innovation

1. **Value-Maintaining Sustained Innovation**
   o Focuses on preserving baseline utility by slightly improving byproducts of reliability or consistency.
   o Example: Adding a water-repellent coating to a smartphone to reduce failure from moisture creeping in.
2. **Value-Increasing Sustained Innovation**
   o Enhances long-term usability by delaying or reducing specific byproducts more significantly.
   o Example: A car engine that extends oil change intervals from 3,000 miles to 9,000 miles, reducing maintenance burden (temporary byproduct) over time.

In both cases, byproducts are not eliminated. They are pushed further out in time, reduced in intensity or frequency, or made less intrusive from a personal energy expenditure standpoint.

However, in accordance with LPI, every act of byproduct mitigation introduces new residual byproducts; new secondary effects that result from the very innovation designed to help it.

The Role of New Residual Byproducts

New residual byproducts are the unintended consequences or burdens introduced by the innovation itself. They are inevitable and part of the perpetual cycle of innovation. In incremental innovation, examples include:

- **Battery Life Extension**
  Increasing capacity may reduce recharge frequency but may:

398

- o Increase battery charge times.
- o Reduce available charge cycles (due to greater energy throughput).
- o Create overheating or swelling risks when fast-charging is introduced to compensate.

- • **Water-Resistant Coatings**
  May reduce failure from water exposure, however it:
  - o Increases difficulty in repair or component replacement.
  - o Leads to heat buildup due to reduced ventilation.

Thus, even as incremental innovation delays existing burdens, it introduces new residual burdens that will eventually become the drivers for future innovation.

Why Byproduct Delay Increases Net Utility

1. **Extending Byproduct-Free Usage**
   - o Customers perceive more value from a product that functions longer before requiring intervention.
   - o Example: Socks that last one year instead of six months do not just sustain utility; they double the duration of problem-free wear.
2. **Reducing Maintenance and Hassle**
   - o Lower maintenance burden = higher perceived utility.
   - o Example: A smartphone with a longer battery life before degradation increases convenience, even if performance remains the same.
3. **Cumulative Value Over Time**
   - o Every cycle of problem-free use adds more net value.
   - o Example: A washing machine that requires servicing every five years instead of two provides greater total lifetime utility.

Byproduct mitigation is not just about sustaining utility, it actively increases net available utility over time.

Case Study: Extending Cellphone Battery Life

The Problem in Gen 1.0 (baseline product at iteration time t)
Batteries in early generations of cellphones typically degraded after 1–2 years of usage, leading to a sharp drop in performance or the need for costly replacement.

This led to several categories of byproducts:

- **Intrinsic Byproducts:** Battery cells wore out with repeated charge cycles.
- **Extrinsic Byproducts:** Users felt forced into upgrading before they wanted to.
- **Economic Byproducts:** Replacements added long-term ownership costs.

The Innovation in Gen 1.1 (improved product at iteration time $t + 1$)
A new battery chemistry was introduced to double lifespan from 2 to 4 years.

- **Byproduct Delay:** Slowed degradation rate by increasing usable charge cycles.
- **Economic Relief:** Reduced replacement frequency and costs.
- **Convenience Boost:** Reduced maintenance-related frustrations.

The Emergence of Residual Byproducts in Gen 1.1
Though Gen 1.1 mitigated prior issues, it introduced residual byproducts:

- **Longer Charge Times:** Due to larger capacity.
- **Battery Swelling Risks:** Especially when paired with fast-charging capability.
- **Thermal Stress:** Greater energy density = more heat management complexity.

Customer Impact:
- The core function (power storage) remains the same, but the perceived utility is higher.
- Customers retain their phones longer, feel less pressure to upgrade, and save money.

Thus, Gen 1.1 is not just preserving baseline utility, it is increasing total net utility over the product's lifespan. The user still benefits from the innovation, but the new byproducts now shape the next cycle of refinement. This is the Law of Perpetual Innovation in action: utility improvement through byproduct mitigation, followed by residual byproduct emergence.

Mathematical Model for Incremental Innovation

Incremental innovation ($U_{incremental}$) can be expressed as:

$$U_{incremental}(t + 1) = U_0 - [B(t + 1) - R(t + 1)]$$

Where:

- U_0 = The incremental innovation product's baseline utility (assumed constant).
- $B(t + 1)$ = The known or "existing" byproducts at time $t + 1$.
- $R(t + 1)$ = Reduction in existing byproduct achieved by the incremental innovation.

However, this does not yet account for byproduct delay or new residual byproduct. We modify the formula to include Δt and $B_{residual}$, which represents the extension of byproduct-free usage, and any new byproduct introduced due to the incremental innovation.

(Note: Existing vs. New byproducts – Existing byproducts are those already known to exist, as witnessed in the predecessor product. New, or residual byproducts are newly emergent, due to the changes made between the predecessor product and the new product; through changes reflecting the incremental innovation.)

Net Utility with Byproduct Mitigation
We define the net utility of the incremental innovation $(t + 1)$, as:

$$U_{incremental}(t + 1) = U_0 - [B(t + 1 + \Delta t) - R(t + 1)] + B_{residual}(t + 1)$$

Where:

- U_0 = The incremental innovation product's baseline utility (assumed constant).
- Δt = *Byproduct Delay*: The time before byproducts begin accumulating.
    - This is the temporal shift in the onset of byproducts due to the innovation.
    - Instead of byproducts appearing at time t, they now appear at $t + \Delta t$.
    - Example: A car engine that now only needs an oil change every 9,000 miles instead of 3,000. The duration before maintenance has been pushed out (a time delay), so you get more hassle-free usage up front.
- $B(t + 1 + \Delta t)$ = *Delayed Existing Byproduct*: The same byproduct that would normally appear at $(t + 1)$ if there were no delay but is now observed at $(t + 1 + \Delta t)$ because of the innovation.
    - You have effectively "pushed back" when the byproduct appears.
- $R(t + 1)$ = *Byproduct Reduction*: How much of the existing byproduct is diminished or mitigated at time $(t + 1)$ due to the innovation. (Note: In some cases, $R(t + 1)$ might be very small, or even negative, if the innovation unintentionally increases the old burden, see "Deeper Insights." below.)

- o This is the magnitude or intensity of reduction in the byproducts at a given time.
  - o Instead of producing 10 units of "unwanted side effects," it might now only produce 5 units.
  - o Example: Oil change every 9,000 miles vs. 3,000 miles (time shift) but also oil changes take 30 minutes vs. 1 hour (reduced byproduct impact).
- $B_{residual}(t+1)$ = New Residual Byproducts: Any new byproducts introduced because of the innovation. These did not exist in the predecessor product.
  - o Introduced by the very act of improving or delaying the original byproduct.
  - o In other words, "every solution introduces new secondary effects."
  - o Example: A fast-charging battery that reduces recharge time but now generates extra heat (a brand-new byproduct).

Since customer value compounds over time, increasing Δt raises the total experienced utility. Increasing $R(t+1)$ also improves total experienced utility if inclusion is possible. Lastly, $B_{residual}$ is always unavoidable, however customer awareness can manage expectations.

Time-Integrated Utility Over the Product Lifecycle
To evaluate the total utility over a product lifespan T, we sum the net utility over time:

Total Utility Over Time:

$$U_{total} = \sum_{t=0}^{T} [U_0 - (B(t + \Delta t) - R(t)) + B_{residual}(t)]$$

- Higher Δt = Higher net available utility over the product's lifespan.
- If $R(t)$ is significant and Δt is large, users experience more utility for longer.
- But if the new byproduct $B_{residual}(t)$ grows or compounds, it can erode gains, making long-term optimization more complex.
- Therefore, total utility is not just a function of what is delayed or reduced, but also of what is newly introduced.

This formula highlights the balance between "existing" byproduct reduction and "new residual byproduct" emergence. Even small improvements can result in large gains, but only when new residual byproduct is well-managed.

402

Deeper Insights on Δt, $R(t+1)$, and $B_{residual}$

Incremental (or Sustained) Innovation does not merely enhance a product's perceived functionality; it also strategically manages the byproducts; the burdens and secondary effects that reduce perceived value over time. Three key terms help us model and understand how incremental improvements work in practice:

1. Δt : Byproduct Delay
2. $R(t+1)$: Byproduct Reduction
3. $B_{residual}$: New Residual Byproducts (introduced by the innovation itself)

Below is an overview of these concepts, followed by an illustrative laptop battery example.

Byproduct Delay

Δt represents the shift in time before a particular byproduct emerges or begins to matter to the user.

- **Why It Matters:** If you can delay the onset or frequency of a burden (e.g., wear, maintenance, performance degradation) during the lifecycle of a product, customers experience longer periods of trouble-free use.

- **Practical Examples:**
  - Increasing the recommended time/mileage between a car's oil changes.
  - Creating a smartphone battery that degrades more slowly, so users don't notice battery issues until year three instead of year two.

Impact on Value: By pushing the negative event further into the future, Δt increases total perceived utility. Customers see fewer interruptions or interventions, which enhances satisfaction over the product's life.

Byproduct Reduction

R(t+1) is the extent to which the innovation reduces an existing byproduct's severity or burden once it does appear.

- **Why It Matters:** Even if you cannot delay a problem or its frequency, you can lessen its intensity or impact. This means when the byproduct eventually occurs, it feels less painful.

- **Practical Examples:**

o Making an oil change less costly or time-intensive, so each service visit is less of a hassle.
o Redesigning a battery to charge faster (i.e., you still need to charge eventually, however each charging event is shorter or easier).

Impact on Value: A high $R(t+1)$ means you've significantly cut down the existing burden (less cost, time, or frustration: all else being equal). An equal $R(t+1)$, compared to the predecessor product means you have not reduced the impact of that burden. A smaller $R(t+1)$ means you may have inadvertently made matters worse (e.g. oil changes take 60% longer or costs 40% more, or battery recharging take 50% longer, or now takes 4 steps vs 2).

New Residual Byproducts

$B_{residual}$ refers to any new byproducts that did not exist in the predecessor product (t) but appear because of the new incremental innovation $(t+1)$.

- **Why It Matters:** Every solution comes with trade-offs. Even if you successfully delay or reduce old burdens, we always introduce new ones, which perpetuates the cycle of further innovation.
- **Practical Examples:**
    o A fast-charging battery that solves long recharge times but creates heat-related issues or shortens long-term battery longevity.
    o A water-resistant phone that reduces risk of water damage but becomes more difficult (and costly) to repair due to sealed components.

Impact on Value: While the core improvement (e.g., extended usage) may outweigh the new burden, $B_{residual}$ often becomes the next target for further refinement or new technology.

Pulling It All Together: A Laptop Battery Example

Scenario:
Imagine a laptop battery originally lasting 4 hours and requiring a 1-hour recharge. The innovation is to increase the battery capacity to 6 hours.

1. **Δt - Longer Runtime Before Recharging**
    o The user can go from 4 to 6 hours before plugging in, effectively *delaying* the burden of having to recharge.

- o This increase in Δt is a clear net benefit: more continuous work or leisure time without interruption.

2. $R(t + 1)$ - **Recharge Time and Experience**
   - o The bigger battery might now take longer to recharge (e.g., 1.5 hours instead of 1 hour). This means the existing burden of recharging increases in severity.
   - o If the design team does not introduce a fast-charge feature, $R(t + 1)$ actually goes down (less byproduct reduction), so each recharge event *feels worse* than before.
   - o Alternatively, if the team does add fast-charge capability, the recharge times can remain 1 hour or even drop to 45 minutes, boosting $R(t + 1)$. However, this new approach might introduce extra thermal stress (see below).

3. $B_{residual}$ - **Heat Generation from Fast Charging**
   - o By choosing a fast-charge solution, the laptop now generates more heat or strain on the battery's chemistry. This presents an entirely new byproduct that did not exist at the old slower recharge rate.
   - o This new heat issue is $B_{residual}$, because it emerges only due to the latest innovation to maintain or increase $R(t + 1)$. It might cause user discomfort, degrade components faster over the long term, or raise concerns about safety without ensuring user awareness.

Outcome and Perpetual Innovation Cycle:

- Delaying recharges Δt raises perceived utility.
- Adjusting recharge intensity $R(t + 1)$ can offset or exacerbate existing burdens.
- Introducing fast charging to keep $R(t + 1)$ high (short recharge times) creates a new heat byproduct ($B_{residual}$).
- Over time, users and engineers will focus on mitigating this new byproduct, inspiring further innovations, and the cycle continues.

No matter how well a new feature or refinement delays or reduces old burdens, every improvement will eventually spawn a new byproduct. This reality is the core of the Law of Perpetual Innovation, which explains why we never run out of problems to solve:

1. We extend or enhance a product's net perceived utility (e.g., longer battery life).
2. We delay or reduce existing byproducts (less frequent servicing, shorter charge times).
3. We inevitably introduce new burdens or side effects.

That new byproduct becomes the next target for improvement. Hence, even seemingly small "incremental" changes can set off an ongoing cycle of problem-solving and product refinement, sustaining innovation in perpetuity.

Key Business Implications of Incremental Innovation

1. **Justification for Premium Pricing**
   Sustained innovations that meaningfully delay or reduce byproducts allow brands to charge more.
   - **Lifecycle Extension**: Customers pay more for longer-lasting, lower-maintenance products.
   - **Fixed Lifecycle Improvement**: Customers pay more for lower-maintenance products within an established or understood lifecycle window.
     - Example: Smartphone makers market battery longevity as a premium feature.
     - Example: A new smartwatch, with the same lifespan as its predecessor, that extends battery life from 4 to 7 days may not perform more tasks but offers greater convenience. In turn, customers willingly pay more.
   - **New Residual Byproduct Pricing Impact**: If residual byproducts (e.g., heat from fast-charging) are minimized or well-communicated, the premium feels justified.

2. **Competitive Differentiation**
   Small but significant innovations can differentiate brands in a saturated market.
   - **Reducing byproduct burden:** (fewer failures, less maintenance) gives products an edge over competitors.
     - Example: Cars that require fewer oil changes are more attractive to customers.

- **Residual Byproduct Awareness:** Companies that minimize or transparently manage the trade-offs will outcompete those that ignore them.

3. **Retention, Loyalty, Lifecycle Extension**
   Reduced maintenance and greater convenience foster long-term brand loyalty.
   - Customers stay with brands that deliver smoother long-term experiences.
   - Even if the experience is not extended, less burdens within it improves retention.
   - Fewer frustrations = stronger brand loyalty.
   - Even if new residual byproducts emerge, users are less likely to defect if they perceive transparency and continued improvement from the brand.

Conclusion

Incremental innovation is a powerful and measurable form of value creation. Under the Law of Perpetual Innovation, it is not merely about preserving existing utility but about enriching existing lifespans or extending them through the strategic reduction and delay of byproducts.

However, LPI also reminds us that no innovation is free from consequence. Every sustained improvement eventually introduces new residual byproducts; new burdens that, while typically smaller or less severe, still shape the next innovation cycle.

By incorporating Δt (byproduct delay), $R(t + 1)$ (byproduct reduction) and $B_{residual}$ (new residual byproduct) into the innovation equation, businesses can better understand the lifecycle impact of their refinements and plan for what comes next.

Sustained innovation is not just incremental in appearance. It is perpetual in effect. Each new version carries with it both the promise of improved access to available utility and the seeds of its next transformation.

CHAPTER 24

Innovation Through Utility Integration

Byproduct Merging & Removal through Unification

Introduction

Utility Integration is one of the most transformative forms of innovation, fundamentally reshaping industries by merging multiple utilities into a single, more efficient, and user-friendly solution. Unlike Utility Specialization, which focuses on refining specific functions for niche applications, Utility Integration simplifies user interaction by centralizing multiple functions within a unified system.

However, under the Law of Perpetual Innovation (LPI), it is essential to understand that even integration introduces new byproducts, new forms of complexity, constraints, or vulnerabilities created by the act of integrating multiple utilities. While integration resolves many inefficiencies of fragmentation, it simultaneously creates new burdens that must be considered in any innovation cycle.

This section explores:
- What Utility Integration is and how it resolves byproducts that emerge from fragmented or separate utilities.
- How to model the impact of integration mathematically, including resulting byproducts.
- How does integration create value and why are consumers and businesses willing to pay more for well-integrated solutions.

This section will show that Utility Integration is not truly about adding features, it is about strategically eliminating inefficiencies and reducing byproduct multiplicity, thereby increasing net available utility.

The General Concept of Utility Integration under LPI

Utility Integration occurs when multiple distinct utilities are combined into a single system or product, intending to reduce friction and redundancy. This form of innovation seeks to collapse separate experiences into one, thereby delivering greater total net utility to the user.

How Utility Integration Resolves Byproducts

Integration fundamentally reduces the burdens associated with fragmentation, redundancy, and inefficiencies across multiple utilities.

1. **Physical Reduction of Separate Utilities**
   - Carrying or storing multiple single-purpose systems or products is a physical byproduct of fragmentation.
   - Example: The smartphone eliminated the need to carry a phone, music player, camera, and internet-accessible product (laptop) separately.

2. **Cognitive Burden Reduction**
   - Users experience decision fatigue, disjointed workflows, mental switching costs and inconvenience across multiple utilities.
   - Example: A single smart home ecosystem, such as Apple HomeKit, integrates various home automation devices, reducing setup and control complexity.

3. **Reduction of Incompatibility and Interoperability Byproducts**
   - Separate utilities often suffer from interoperability issues, leading to inefficiencies.
   - Example: Google Workspace eliminates file format conflicts by integrating writing, collaboration, and storage into one ecosystem.

4. **Redundant Cost Structures**
   - Purchasing, maintaining, and updating separate systems is financially inefficient.

- Example: A smart TV integrates streaming platforms and speakers, reducing the need for separate hardware and software purchases.

5. **Time & Effort Inefficiency**
   - Users avoid switching between multiple systems, reducing learning curves and reducing fluidity (friction increase).
   - Example: Amazon's one-click checkout integrates payment, shipping, and authentication to save time and reduce decision friction.

The Dual-Edged Nature of Utility Integration: The Emergence of Integration Byproducts

When executed well integration enhances perceived utility, reducing physical, spatial, cognitive, and time-related burdens. While integration addresses the aforementioned byproducts, it inevitably introduces new byproducts that emerge from the very act of combining functions:

Overcomplexity and Feature Bloat
- A multi-function device may become harder to navigate or use. Over-integration can create bloated, inefficient, or fragile systems that reintroduce byproducts (e.g., feature overload, security vulnerabilities, use complexity).

Risk of Cascading Failure
- If one integrated component fails, the whole system may suffer (e.g., a smartphone with a failed screen disables access to phone, camera, apps).

Performance Trade-offs
- Combining tools into one product may compromise performance or depth in each individual function.

Security and Maintenance Complexity
- The more integrated a system is, the more difficult it can be to patch, secure, and update.

Thus, successful integration requires minimizing new integration residual byproducts while amplifying the net benefit of consolidation. These residual byproducts do not cancel out the benefits of integration, but they do shape the next round of innovation. Utility Integration, like all forms of innovation, shifts rather than eliminates the byproduct landscape.

410

Brief Case Study: The Emergence of Moving Pictures (Film & Cinema)

The Accepted Latent Byproducts That Gave Rise to Film

Unlike the smartphone or modern digital integration, the advent of moving pictures (film) does not immediately appear to stem from an existing set of byproducts. Nevertheless, prior to moving pictures, theatrical performances were the dominant form of narrative entertainment. Upon closer analysis, we can see that film resolved impactful "latent" byproducts of theater and live performances: the limitation of accessibility, permanence, and scalability.

Key Byproducts of Pre-Film Entertainment:

1. **Limited Accessibility**
   - Before moving pictures, theatrical performances were bound by geographic and temporal constraints. One had to physically be present at a specific location and time to experience the performance.
   - Byproduct Resolution: Film enabled recordings to be distributed globally, removing the barriers of time and space.

2. **Performance Variability (Inconsistency of Experience)**
   - Live performances varied each time due to human error, improvisation, or environmental factors.
   - Byproduct Resolution: A recorded film creates a perfectly consistent experience, free of errors or distractions keeping one immersed and suspending disbelief.

3. **Scalability Constraints**
   - A live performance had fixed audience capacity, each show could only reach as many people as the venue allowed.
   - Byproduct Resolution: Film enabled mass replication and global distribution, drastically increasing audience reach.

4. **Financial & Logistical Burdens on Performers**

- Actors, musicians, and entertainers could only generate income by performing live repeatedly (limited scale income and performer fatigue).
- Byproduct Resolution: Film allowed a single performance to generate revenue indefinitely without repeated live effort.

5. **Loss of Cultural Moments (Ephemerality)**
   - Once a play ended, it was lost to time, no record of its performance was retained.
   - Byproduct Resolution: Film preserved performances permanently, capturing art, history, and cultural moments for future generations.

The Utility Integration solution: Film

Film integrated multiple existing utilities:
- Photography (Static Images) + Motion (Frame + Time) = Moving Pictures
- Moving Pictures + Recorded Audio = Synchronized Film (this came later however)
- Synchronized Film + Distribution at Scale = Cinema as a Global Entertainment Industry

The Result: A Transformational Utility Integration

Moving pictures did not invent narrative entertainment but integrated multiple utility innovations to create a new global medium, reducing previous byproducts of live performance. Thus, the film industry emerged successfully not because people wanted "moving pictures" specifically, but because innovators saw a way to overcome the accepted latent byproducts of live performances.

Emergence of New Byproducts

Despite its success, over time, film introduced entirely new byproducts:

- **Censorship and Content Homogenization:** Due to centralized distribution, studios and rating boards pressured filmmakers to standardize content for mass appeal.
- **Loss of Live Artistic Feedback Loop:** Without on-the-spot audience reactions, creators relied on delayed metrics rather than real-time cues.

- **Technological Gatekeeping:** Access to filmmaking tools became a barrier to entry. High production costs and specialized equipment restricted who could realistically produce films.
- **Intellectual Property Tensions:** Reproducible film reels sparked rampant copying, prompting legal battles and anti-piracy efforts.
- **Market Consolidation & Blockbuster Economics:** Huge budgets favored major studios, stifling smaller creators and niche projects.
- **Propaganda & Ideological Influence:** Governments and organizations leveraged cinema's emotional power to sway public opinion.
- **Environmental & Preservation Hurdles:** Flammable nitrate stock and chemical processing led to archival crises and cultural losses.

Thus, the innovation of cinema resolved one set of byproducts while introducing yet another: a clear expression of LPI's perpetual innovation loop.

Mathematical Model for Utility Integration

Utility Integration can be mathematically expressed as:

$$U_{integrated} = \sum_{i=1}^{n} (U_i - B_{integration})$$

Where:

- U_i = Utility contributions of each merged function.
- $B_{integration}$ = Byproduct of merging various utility functions. New burdens introduced by the act of merging multiple functions (integration itself), which may evolve or grow over time. (e.g., added complexity, learning curves, technical constraints).
- Note: The integration byproduct is analogous to new residual byproduct discussed in Incremental Sustained Innovation. Since integration is a one-time act, if a product developer decides to improve upon their integrated product in later iterations, the model they'll follow is that of Incremental Sustained Innovation.

For integration to increase net perceived utility, the reduction of individual byproducts must outweigh the cost of the byproducts introduced by the integration itself:

$$U_{integrated} > \sum_{i=1}^{n}\left(U_i - B_{integration}\right)$$

Implications:

- If the integration is novel (never been done before), $B_{integration}$ has the potential to start low, go unnoticed, or be accepted as a necessary tradeoff.
- If $B_{integration}$ is minimized, total utility is higher than the sum of separate utilities.
- If integration introduces too much $B_{integration}$, as complexity friction, or bloat, users may experience lower net perceived utility.

Deep-Dive Case Study: The Smartphone as an Integration Innovation

Background

Before the advent of smartphones, people typically relied on four separate devices for key utilities:

- **A mobile phone** for voice communication.
- **A digital camera** for capturing images.
- **A laptop or desktop computer** for internet access.
- **A portable MP3 player** for music.

Each device offered specialized, high-performance utility in its domain but also brought with it a range of independent byproducts that users had to manage. The smartphone integrated all these utilities into a single form factor, simplifying acquisition, ownership, use, storage and disposal.

Core Utilities

Let us define the baseline utilities of the four standalone products:

- U_{Phone}: Communication utility from a mobile phone.
- U_{camera}: Visual capture utility from a digital camera.
- $U_{internet}$: Web browsing, search, and mobile computing utility.
- U_{MP3}: Entertainment utility from a portable music player.

414

Byproducts of Standalone Devices

Each standalone device brought with it its own burdens:

- B_{Phone} : Physical bulk, battery charging, device fragility, and call-only limitations.
- B_{camera}: Additional device to carry, memory cards, cable syncing, risk of lens damage.
- $B_{internet}$: Limited portability, slow boot-up, reliance on Wi-Fi or tethered connection.
- B_{MP3} : Storage limitations, file syncing, headphone cable management, charging.

These byproducts represent the cumulative friction associated with using and owning four devices.

The Mathematical Model of Integration

According to the utility integration model:

$$U_{integrated} > \sum_{i=1}^{n} (U_i - B_{integration})$$

In this case:

$$U_{smartphone} = (U_{Phone} + U_{camera} + U_{internet} + U_{MP3}) - B_{smartphone}$$

Before integration, the total utility from the four devices was:

$$U_{seperate} = (U_{Phone} - B_{Phone}) + (U_{camera} - B_{camera}) + (U_{internet} - B_{internet}) \\ + (U_{MP3} - B_{MP3})$$

Subtracting the two gives the *Comparative Net Utility* (ΔU) gain or loss from the integration innovation:

$$\Delta U = U_{smartphone} - U_{separate} = B_{Phone} + B_{camera} + B_{internet} + B_{MP3} - B_{integration}$$

Detailed Breakdown of Byproducts Eliminated or Condensed

Each of these eliminated or condensed byproducts contributions to ($B_{Phone} + B_{camera} + B_{internet} + B_{MP3}$)

Utility Domain	Byproducts (prior to integration)	How Integration Mitigates It
Phone	Carrying separate device, texting limitations, no internet or media	One device handles calls, texts, browsing, and apps
Camera	Separate gear, lens protection, syncing issues	Camera is now embedded and cloud-synced
Internet	Stationary or Wi-Fi dependence, no cellular data, no touch UI	Always-on connection, mobile web, apps
MP3	Extra device, syncing software, cables	Music stored alongside apps

The resulting Byproducts of Integration

Even when integration succeeds, the integration byproduct $B_{integration}$ might include:

- **Battery drain** when multiple utilities are used simultaneously.
- **Reduced functional fidelity** of the integrated utilities compared to best-in-class standalone alternatives.
- **Increased complexity** in software/hardware.
- **Slower in-utility function switching** when compared to standalone devices.
- **Overreliance on one device**: When lost, stolen, or damaged, multiple utilities are disrupted at once (e.g., screen breaks, cellular radio).

Implications of the Model:

- Upon closer inspection of the *Comparative Net Utility* ΔU:

$$\Delta U = (B_{Phone} + B_{camera} + B_{internet} + B_{MP3}) - B_{integration}$$

- If $B_{integration} < (B_{Phone} + B_{camera} + B_{internet} + B_{MP3})$, integration is a success.

416

- If $B_{integration}$ is large (due to system complexity, lower performance, or poor User Interface, users may revert to the standalone tools or improved competing solutions.

This tells us that the net gain from integration depends on how many and how severe the original byproducts across the four products were, versus the new byproducts introduced by combining them ($B_{integration}$).

These integration byproducts, though fewer, must be addressed in future generations. This is where incremental sustained innovation picks up again, showing how various innovation methods are nested within the Law of Perpetual Innovation.

<u>The deeper insight overall</u> is that utility integration is not about "adding more," but rather, about "reducing more," the frictions and burdens across the entire user journey. The byproducts.

Why Users Accept Lower Initial Utility for Integrated Functions

At launch, users often forgive lower functional fidelity in the integrated version (e.g., smartphone camera not as powerful as DSLR, internet is surfed on a much smaller screen) because the relief from previous burdens is substantial. Over time, however, expectations rise. Users begin to demand performance at par or better than standalone equivalents. This explains why smartphone manufacturers continue to innovate.

When the first smartphones were introduced:
- The camera quality was inferior to digital cameras.
- The music player lacked memory capacity
- Web browsing was slow and clunky.
- Battery life was limited.

1. **The Value of Consolidation**
   Even if each integrated feature was not best-in-class, the single device eliminated the need to carry, charge, learn, and maintain multiple tools. This compounded reduction in byproducts resulted in a net utility gain.

Byproduct Categories Eliminated or Condensed

Byproduct Type	Before Integration	After Smartphone Integration
Physical Burden	4 separate devices to carry	One pocket-sized device
Cable Clutter	Separate chargers & data cables	Unified charging (eventually USB-C)
Power Management	Separate battery life cycles & charging schedules	Unified battery cycle management
Redundant Storage	MP3's & Photos scattered across devices	Cloud sync & centralized storage
Cognitive Load	Juggling multiple User Interfaces and settings	Single UI ecosystem (iOS/Android)
Time Consumption	Switching between devices	Seamless multitasking, app-switching
Acquisition Redundancy	4 purchases to get 4 utilities	One device, one price, multiple functions
Maintenance Complexity	4 user manuals, warranties	Single system to learn & maintain

The overall byproducts of the standalone utilities outweighed those of integration:

$$(B_{Phone} + B_{camera} + B_{internet} + B_{MP3}) \gg B_{integration}$$

This inequality reveals that even though new byproducts are introduced (especially over time), the overall burden was significantly reduced. Users tolerate moderate compromises in functionality because the value of byproduct elimination dominates.

All these reductions reflect byproduct mitigation as the central value proposition of utility integration, not just in user convenience, but in ecological, logistical, and psychological dimensions.

2. **Temporal Tolerance for Integration Byproducts**

   Consumers initially tolerated integration issues (e.g., slow browsing, low photo quality, weak speakers), but as the category matured, expectations increased. What was once acceptable became the next set of byproducts for improvement:

   (Note: Beyond initial introduction into the market, $B_{integration}$ byproducts can become $B_{residual}(t)$ byproducts if incremental innovation is driven upon specific integrated utilities.)

   As time passed:
   - Expectations for improving $B_{integration}$ increased.
   - Competitive differentiation emerged based on minimizing these residuals.

   $B_{integration}(t)$ must decrease over time, or net perceived utility will erode.

   Thus, smartphone evolution focused on:
   - Improving photo quality.
   - Extending battery life.
   - Enhancing listening performance (eventually wireless only).
   - Minimizing OS clutter.

In essence, the early perceived utility gain stems from eliminated byproducts in owning and managing standalone utility items. Later perceived gains stem from byproduct reduction including functional parity comparison to standalone utility items (e.g. larger screen, better camera performance).

Conclusion: Smartphone as a Paradigm of Integration-Driven Byproduct Resolution

The smartphone example reveals the essence of Utility Integration: its true value lies not in delivering perfect functionality in each domain, but in consolidating multiple imperfect solutions to dramatically reduce user burden.

Integration is a deliberate strategy to minimize byproducts of the physical, cognitive, economic, and temporal types, not merely to merge features.

As with all innovations under LPI, the integrated product does introduce residual byproducts. These residuals become more visible over time and eventually served as the triggers for the next generation of incremental or radical innovations.

The lesson for innovators is clear:
- Do not view integrated utility as additive.
- View it as subtractive: it removes burdens, not just delivers features.
- Byproduct resolution is the true foundation of integration's perceived value.

The smartphone's success was not in outperforming digital cameras or iPods individually, it was in removing the friction of juggling them all. That is the power of Utility Integration under the Law of Perpetual Innovation.

Key Business Implications of Utility Integration

1. **Justification for Premium Pricing**
   Consumers consistently pay more for integrated solutions that simplify their lives by reducing effort, time, storage and device redundancy.
   - Example: The iPhone's all-in-one functionality justifies its price point.
   - The residual byproducts (e.g., reduced battery flexibility, upgrade cycles) are tolerated, until they are not, prompting the next wave of innovation.

2. **Market Disruption & Category Redefinition**
   Well-executed integration can create new market standards and render prior solution categories obsolete.
   - Example: Netflix integrated movie rental and streaming, rendering physical video stores obsolete.
   - Residual impact: Bandwidth dependency became a new constraint, reshaping telecom infrastructure.

3. **Customer Retention and Ecosystem Lock-in**
   Integrated systems/platforms build ecosystem gravity, increasing brand lock-in because users invest in a single ecosystem. The more interconnected the experience, the harder it is to leave.
   - Example: Apple's ecosystem (iOS, macOS, iCloud) deepens retention.
   - Residual byproducts (limited interoperability with non-Apple products) reinforce lock-in.

4. **The Risk of Over-Integration**
   Failure to manage integration or residual burdens can harm usability.

420

- Example: Microsoft's early mobile OS failed because they over-integrated PC-based features that felt unnatural on a mobile device.

Conclusion

Utility Integration is not about feature addition. It is about strategic byproduct elimination and reduction through a merging of utilities that we term integration. It simplifies the user experience by reducing physical, spatial, cognitive, economic and temporal burdens, but it also inevitably creates new byproducts as a result of that very simplification. Therefore, integration is not always beneficial. When it introduces complexity, usability issues, or system fragility, it can create new byproducts that outweigh the intended benefits.

Successful integration balances:
- The total benefit of integration $\sum U_i$
- The costs of merging $B_{integration}$
- And the new consequences introduced $B_{residual}(t)$

The key takeaway is that the illusion of Utility Integration is about adding features. It is not. It is about strategically removing byproducts: the friction, inefficiencies, and excess cognitive burdens. Viewed through the lens of the Law of Perpetual Innovation, all integrated solutions are transitional. They resolve the burdens of fragmentation, but simultaneously create the context for future innovation by introducing residual byproducts. Businesses that successfully integrate utilities into cohesive, high-utility products can justify premium pricing, dominate markets, and create category-defining innovations.

CHAPTER 25
Innovation through Utility Specialization

Refining Utility to Address Specific Byproducts

Introduction

While Utility Integration merges multiple utilities to simplify complexity and reduce inefficiencies, Utility Specialization takes the opposite approach, branching out from a general utility to develop more tailored solutions for distinct user needs. This is likely the oldest and most obvious methods of human-driven innovation.

Utility Specialization does not create new utility from scratch; rather, it identifies unresolved or emerging byproducts in broad solutions and refines utility to better serve specific contexts. As industries and technologies evolve, generalized solutions accumulate byproducts, leading to demand for more focused, efficient, and optimized alternatives.

Note: It's important to point out that even utility that appears not to address a previously accumulated byproduct can address a real time byproduct. For example, light up sneakers for children don't appear to address a byproduct. However, once a child see's that this higher potential utility is available, an unfulfilled aspiration/aspirational comparison (positive byproduct) may emerge for them.

This section explores:
- What Utility Specialization is and how does it differs from other innovation types.
- Why specialization occurs and what drives the demand for more refined solutions.
- What byproducts specialization resolves, and it enhance net available utility.

- How to model the impact of specialization mathematically, including resulting byproducts.
- What are the economic and business rationales for specialization.

This section will demonstrate that Utility Specialization is a natural consequence of the Law of Perpetual Innovation, as general utilities accumulate inefficiencies, new specialized solutions emerge as branches from a previous utility, to resolve those inefficiencies, leading to a more diverse landscape of optimized offerings.

The General Concept of Utility Specialization under LPI

Utility Specialization occurs when a general utility fragments into more targeted solutions, each tailored to specific use cases, user preferences, or environmental conditions.

Unlike Utility Integration, which consolidates functions into a unified system, Utility Specialization branches outward, addressing distinct byproducts that arise when a single solution attempts to serve too many needs at once.

Key Drivers of Utility Specialization

1. **Diverse User Needs & Preferences**
   o Users have varying priorities, making one-size-fits-all solutions inefficient and burdensome – shaped by byproducts that they encounter.
   o Example: Footwear evolved from a basic shoe into specialized types for running, hiking, formal events, and more.

2. **Performance Optimization for Specific Environments**
   o A general utility will reveal deficiencies in niche environments, creating demand for customized solutions.
   o Example: Vehicle tires specialize into all-season, performance, off-road, and winter varieties based on driving conditions, environments and use cases.

3. **Reducing the Byproduct of Generalization**
   o A one-size-fits-all approach often leads to inefficiencies, trade-offs, and compromises, which over time begin to feel unacceptable.
   o Example: Laptops specialize into ultrabooks for portability, gaming laptops for power and speed, and workstation laptops for professional tasks.

4. **Cultural, Aesthetic, and Social Differentiation**
    o Consumers often seek products that align with identity, profession, or lifestyle; when existing solutions start to feel inadequate and unfulfilling.
    o Example: Watches evolved into casual, luxury, diving, aviation, and smartwatches, catering to different consumer personas.

5. **Advancements in Materials & Technology**
    o New materials or processes allow for greater optimization, paving the way for specialization to be driven.
    o Example: Eyewear evolved from a single-purpose vision aid to prescription glasses, reading glasses, blue-light-blocking glasses, sunglasses, and sports goggles.

The Byproduct-Utility Relationship in Specialization

As people experience a product's utility, byproducts naturally start to emerge and accumulate. Under "specific" usage or consumption contexts, these byproducts often arise at a higher rate or intensity. This leads to the perception that the existing utility is too broad or general, unable to address the byproducts unique to specialized use cases. Here is where new specialized solutions emerge to resolve these unresolved deficiencies (expectation deviations) or unfulfilled aspirations (aspirational comparisons).

Each specialized utility solution addresses a particular set of byproducts, delivering a perceived net utility increase for its intended users, while eventually creating new byproducts that drive further innovation.

Case Study: The Evolution of Footwear Specialization

Footwear originated as a single-utility solution long ago, a protective covering for the feet. Over time, however, distinct byproducts emerged over time, leading to specialization across multiple footwear categories.

Step 1: The General Utility of Shoes
Original Utility: Protect the foot from harsh terrain and extreme weather.
Emerging Byproducts:

1. Discomfort in different climates → Need for breathable summer shoes vs. insulated winter boots.
2. Unsuitable for specific tasks → Need for running, hiking, and formal applications.
3. Lack of support for unique foot structures → Need for orthopedic shoes.
4. Social & cultural expectations → Need for dress shoes, fashion sneakers, and professional footwear.

Step 2: Specialization in Footwear

As these byproducts accumulated, footwear evolved into distinct categories, each optimizing for a different need:

- Athletic Shoes (Running, Basketball, Soccer, etc.) → Optimized for sport-specific movements, reducing strain and injury risk.
- Hiking Boots → Designed for rough terrain, integrating ankle support and weather resistance.
- Dress Shoes → Focus on aesthetics and social status, minimizing appearance-related byproducts.
- Work Boots → Built for durability, safety, and all-day wear in industrial settings.
- Orthopedic Shoes → Designed to mitigate foot pain and medical conditions.

Each specialized category enhances net available utility by addressing specific byproducts that a general shoe could not resolve efficiently.

Step 3: The Recurring Cycle of Specialization

Even within specialized categories, new byproducts arise, leading to further specialization:

- Running shoes specialize further into road running, trail running, and racing flats.
- Dress shoes diversify into oxfords, loafers, monk straps, wedges and stilettos.
- Work boots differentiate into construction, electrical hazard-resistant, and slip-resistant varieties.

This demonstrates the continuous nature of Utility Specialization. As users refine their expectations, new inefficiencies (byproducts) emerge, driving perpetual cycles of specialization.

Mathematical Model for Utility Specialization

Utility Specialization can be expressed as:

$$U_{specialized,i} = U_{general} - B_{general,i} + \Delta U_{specialized,i}$$

Where:

- $U_{general}$ = The original general utility.
- $B_{general,i}$ = The specific byproduct that makes the general utility suboptimal for a given use case, i.
- $\Delta U_{specialized,i}$ = The added value from specialization, which optimizes the utility for that specific user/environment, i.

For specialization to increase net utility, the reduction in byproducts must exceed the cost of specialization:

$$U_{specialized,i} > U_{general}$$

If:

$$B_{general,i} > \Delta U_{specialized,i}, \quad \text{specialization fails (no net gain)}$$

$$B_{general,i} < \Delta U_{specialized,i}, \quad \text{specialization succeeds (net utility gain)}$$

Example: Running Shoes vs. General Sneakers

General-purpose sneakers serve multiple casual needs but often become suboptimal when used for running. From the perspective of byproduct-driven innovation, the problem is not that "running shoes add more features," but rather that they remove or reduce certain burdens (*byproducts*) that emerge when general sneakers are used for intensive running.

Mathematical View

Let:
- $U_{sneaker}$ = Baseline utility of a general sneaker.

426

- $B_{sneaker,running}$ = The byproduct burden (e.g., discomfort, poor support, extra weight, higher injury risk) from using general sneakers for running.
- $\Delta U_{running}$ = The added utility from a specialized design (e.g., cushioning, stability, lightweight materials).

We can express the utility of a specialized running shoe ($\Delta U_{running}$) for a runner as:

$$U_{running} = U_{sneaker} - B_{sneaker,running} + \Delta U_{running}$$

- If $\Delta U_{running} > B_{sneaker,running}$, then specialized running shoes yield a net utility gain for runners by resolving more burdens than they introduce.
  - Note: The net result is higher utility for runners but not necessarily for casual wearers unless intentionally designed to be, which is why specialization is not universal.

- If $\Delta U_{running} \leq B_{sneaker,running}$, the specialization fails to provide sufficient value over a standard sneaker.

How Byproducts Drive Specialization

- **Identifying Byproducts**: Runners notice unresolved burdens, excess foot stress, inadequate arch support, sliding on wet surfaces, when using generic sneakers.
- **Developing Specialized Solutions**: Brands create running shoes that tackle these issues (improved cushioning, better grip), directly eliminating or reducing the byproducts that emerged from a more generalized design.
- **New Residual Byproducts**: Specialized running shoes, in turn, introduce their own burdens: higher cost, faster wear on pavement, or reduced comfort for casual walking.
- **Driving Further Specialization**: Over time, even these specialized shoes branch out into sub-specialties (e.g., trail running vs. racing flats), each targeting distinct runner byproducts, continuing the cycle of innovation.

Why "Reducing More" Matters More Than "Adding More"

From a byproduct perspective, the value of running shoes is not merely that they "have more features," but that they subtract key byproducts (risk of injury, discomfort, lack of traction, lack of style or colors). Users gladly pay more or switch to specialized footwear because they experience fewer negative outcomes every time they run.

In essence, Utility Specialization arises whenever general products accumulate byproducts for specific use cases. By targeting those byproducts, specialized offerings carve out their niche, improve user experience, and ultimately spawn new (residual) byproducts, sustaining innovation's perpetual cycle.

Key Business Implications of Utility Specialization

1. **Justification for Premium Pricing**
   - Consumers pay more for highly optimized products that resolve specific byproducts.
   - Example: Trail running shoes cost more than general sneakers because they eliminate terrain-related inefficiencies.

2. **Market Expansion & Segmentation**
   - Specialization creates multiple product categories, allowing companies to target niche markets.
   - Example: Gaming laptops vs. business laptops vs. ultrabooks, each caters to a different user profile who experiences different kinds of byproducts.

3. **Competitive Differentiation**
   - Companies that own a specialized niche gain brand loyalty and higher switching costs for consumers.
   - Example: High-end camera brands like Canon & Nikon specialize in professional photography, commanding a premium.

4. **Perpetual Expansion of Categories**
   - As technology advances, specialization leads to sub-specialization, keeping markets in a state of continuous innovation.

Conclusion

Utility Specialization is a natural consequence of the Law of Perpetual Innovation, as general solutions accumulate inefficiencies or perceived inadequacies, more focused alternatives emerge to eliminate those byproducts.

Through mathematical modeling, case studies, and business implications, we see that Utility Specialization is not a temporary phase, it is a perpetual force. It continuously refines human innovation by responding to the ever-evolving landscape of unmet needs and emerging byproducts through a continuous branching-out of utility solutions that has been happening since the dawn of human civilization.

CHAPTER 26
Adaptive Utility Innovation

Real-Time Byproduct Neutralization or Displacement

Introduction

Adaptive Utility represents a significant evolutionary leap in the design and function of modern products, systems, and services. Unlike other innovation types that rely on predefined configurations or require manual adjustments, Adaptive Utility dynamically responds to user behavior, environmental conditions, and contextual variables in real-time. Its goal is simple yet profound: to maintain or increase net utility by eliminating or reducing byproducts as they arise offsetting the accumulation of byproducts that would normally degrade user experience over time.

Examples of Adaptive Utility Products and Services:
- Automatic transmissions, active suspension systems and adaptive cruise control in cars
- Home thermostats, smart thermostats, sensor-based humidifiers and air purifiers
- Auto-brightness and auto-correct on smartphones, facial recognition for camera focus
- Luxury Concierge services, Executive Assistant/Lifestyle Manager, Personal Shopper

In this section, we will explore:
- What Adaptive Utility is and how it differs from static or manual systems.
- The role of real-time byproduct mitigation in improving user experience.
- A mathematical model that explains adaptive innovation through the lens of the LPI.
- A deep-dive case study featuring noise-canceling headphones.

- The economic and strategic business value of adaptive utility in a competitive landscape.

This chapter reveals that Adaptive Utility is not just a trend, it is a paradigm shift. It is foundational to innovations where utility must remain high across variable or unpredictable conditions. Additionally, as artificial intelligence, sensor technology, and contextual awareness improve, Adaptive Utility will become an essential innovation pathway in our increasingly dynamic world.

The General Concept of Adaptive Utility under LPI

Adaptive Utility is a form of innovation where a product, service or system continuously modifies its behavior, output, or function based on changes in its internal state, the external environment, or sensed user interaction patterns. This capability enables the system to automatically maintain high net utility by reducing or eliminating emerging byproducts in real-time such that they do not have the opportunity to emerge or accumulate. Adaptive utility appears assistive or automatic in nature where a product, service or system can respond dynamically to fluctuating user contexts, external situational inputs, or internal conditions requiring minimal to no intervention by the customer or user.

Key Characteristics of Adaptive Utility:
- **Real-Time Responsiveness:** It adjusts utility delivery based on external stimuli (e.g., noise, lighting, input behavior).
- **Autonomous or Self-Modifying:** It adjusts configuration or output without requiring user intervention.
- **Proactive & Reactive:** It can prevent byproducts from emerging (proactive) or help resolve them once detected (reactive).
- **Environment-Aware Utility Delivery:** It modifies behavior or function based on sensed surroundings.
- **Behavioral Sensitivity:** It can learn from past interactions to fine-tune its output or function.

Byproducts Addressed by Adaptive Utility:
- **Environmental Byproducts:** Sound, heat, light, motion, etc.
- **User Behavior Byproducts:** Fatigue, confusion, discomfort, distraction.
- **Systemic Byproducts:** Performance lag, overconsumption, inefficiency.

Forms of Adaptive Utility:
- **Invisible/Autonomous:** Adaptive gear-shifting in automatic vehicles.
- **Interactive:** Predictive text that evolves as the user types.
- **Learning-Based:** Systems or services that improve over time via learning (e.g., VIP Medical Concierge services, AI-enhanced recommendation engines).

Why Adaptive Utility is Distinct:

Adaptive Utility not only maintains the value of utility, but it also enhances it by anticipating burdens and dynamically reducing them in real time, thus increasing the total experienced utility. Most other innovations reduce byproducts after a complete cycle or intermittent portion of a cycle of user interaction, through new generations or upgrades/replacements, respectively. Adaptive utility, however, works within the interaction cycle in real-time, eliminating or reducing the emergence of burden as it attempts to form or accumulate.

Risks and Emergent Residual Byproducts
However, Adaptive Utility itself can introduce its own byproducts:

- **Overcorrection:** The system adapts inappropriately (e.g., autocorrect misfires).
- **Perceived Loss of Control:** Users may feel alienated when systems act without their input (e.g., user preferences overridden).
- **Increased Complexity:** Internally adaptive systems can be difficult to troubleshoot or predict.
- **Power Drain:** Electrical and electro-mechanical systems undergo constant real-time processing which often requires more energy than their non-adaptive counterparts.
- **Over-automation Fatigue:** Feeling over-assisted or unable to modify the assistance level

These new byproducts form the next layer of innovation triggers, consistent with LPI.

Mathematical Model for Adaptive Utility

The core distinction of Adaptive Utility is that it actively modulates utility delivery in real time, based on environmental conditions, user behavior, or contextual fluctuations without requiring deliberate user intervention.

In contrast to incremental, integrative or specialization innovations (which improve utility at discrete intervals or by restructuring multiple utilities), adaptive utility constantly adjusts its own state to neutralize emerging byproducts, often before they become consciously detectable to the user.

The mathematical model for Adaptive Utility must reflect:
- Constant (or nearly continuous) measurement of the environment.
- Adjustment to reduce emerging byproducts at time t.
- The relationship between adaptation precision and residual byproduct.
- The total accumulated utility over time in the presence of adaptation.

Key Variables:
The following variables define our adaptive system:

- U_0: Baseline utility of the system (e.g., audio playback fidelity).
- $B(t)$: Byproduct accumulation at time t (before adaptation).
- $A(t)$: Real-time adaptation correction at time t, designed to suppress or correct for $B(t)$.
- $R(t)$: Residual byproduct remaining after adaptation is applied at time t.

$$R(t) = B(t) - A(t)$$

- If $A(t) \approx B(t)$, then $R(t) \approx 0$: the adaptive system effectively neutralizes byproducts.
- If $A(t) > B(t)$: overcorrection may introduce new byproducts (e.g., artificial noise, discomfort, or loss of autonomy).
- If $A(t) < B(t)$: under-correction results in ineffective mitigation of emerging byproduct.

Net Perceived Utility at Time t
The instantaneous net perceived utility of the system is:

$$U_{\text{net}}(t) = U_0 - R(t) = U_0 - [B(t) - A(t)]$$

This model reflects that net utility increases when adaptive correction $A(t)$ is close in magnitude and timing to the emerging byproduct $B(t)$.

Total Utility Over a Session

To evaluate Adaptive Utility over a full usage period (from $t = 0 \, to \, T$):

$$U_{\text{total}} = \sum_{t=0}^{T} \left[U_0 - \left(B(t) - A(t) \right) \right]$$

This mirrors other innovation methods and expresses the cumulative utility perceived over a session or lifecycle, adjusted in real time by the adaptive function.

Adaptive Utility Efficiency Score (AUES)

To assess the overall effectiveness of adaptation over time, in how well the system neutralizes emerging byproducts at any given moment, we define the Adaptive Utility Efficiency Score $\rho(t)$:

$$\rho(t) = \frac{A(t)}{B(t)}$$

- $\rho(t) = 1$: Perfect real-time mitigation (ideal adaptation). The Byproduct is neutralized completely
- $\rho(t) > 1$: Overcorrection - potentially introduces new burdens.
- $\rho(t) < 1$: Under-correction - ineffective or delayed adaptation, leaving residual byproducts unaddressed.

The Mean or Average Adaptive Efficiency over an entire usage session (from $t = 0 \, to \, T$):

$$\bar{\rho} = \frac{1}{T} \sum_{t=0}^{T} \frac{A(t)}{B(t)}$$

434

This equation represents the average adaptive efficiency over time: a macro-level diagnostic for how effectively the system is mitigating burden across varying conditions.

What this equation is saying: If your adaptive system consistently applies just enough correction to match the burden being introduced (neither too much nor too little, for example if $\bar{\rho} \approx 0.95$ to 1.05), then users experience smoother, more invisible utility, the hallmark of successful Adaptive Utility Innovation.

A system with $\bar{\rho}$ approaching 1(perfectly ideal) is considered highly adaptive, with minimal residual burden.

Implications of the Model

- **Precision and timing are critical:** An adaptive system must both detect and correct in a narrow window to prevent byproduct accumulation.
- **Adaptation is not static:** The same system may perform differently depending on environment volatility.
- **Residual byproducts are still present:** Even with high adaptive efficiency, user experience is never byproduct-free.
- **Feedback loops can introduce behavioral residue:** If adaptation interferes with perceived control (e.g., Adaptive Noise Canceling pressure on ears), new long-term user aversions can form.
- **Adaptive utility thrives in complex, changing conditions:** It is especially useful when static utility or manual adjustment cannot keep up with dynamic byproduct conditions.

Deep-Dive Case Study: Noise-Canceling Headphones

Context and Pre-Adaptive Utility Landscape

Before Adaptive Noise Canceling (ANC) emerged, users relied solely on:
- **Passive isolation:** wearing thick ear cups, foam padding.
- **Volume compensation:** increasing audio output to overpower outside noise that gets in.
- **Removal from the noisy environment:** if it were possible to do so, causing inconvenience.

This approach introduced several persistent byproducts:

- B_{env}: Environmental noise that leaks in, especially low-frequency hums (e.g., planes, engines).
- B_{volume}: Elevated volume levels to mask noise, increasing hearing risk.
- B_{cog}: Cognitive fatigue from constantly filtering ambient noise mentally.

Each of these created cognitive frictions, reduced comfort, or degraded health over long-term use.

The Introduction of Adaptive Utility: ANC (Adaptive Noise Cancellation) Systems

ANC headphones introduced a breakthrough adaptive utility:

- Built-in microphones monitor incoming noise in real time $B(t)$.
- DSP (digital signal processing) generates an opposing waveform $A(t)$ to cancel it out.
- Output speakers blend the original audio with $A(t)$ to neutralize environmental disturbances.

Modeling the Utility of ANC Headphones

We reuse the mathematical model from above:

$$U_{\text{net}}(t) = U_0 - [B(t) - A(t)]$$

Over a session or lifecycle T :

$$U_{\text{total}} = \sum_{t=0}^{T} [U_0 - (B(t) - A(t))]$$

Assuming high-quality ANC:

436

- $A(t) \approx B(t)$, so $R(t) \approx 0$: Residual byproduct remaining after adaptation is near zero.
- $U_{\text{net}}(t) \approx U_0$: The net perceived utility in a noisy plane, train, or office, remains close to the original constant baseline utility in a noise free environment because the noise byproducts are cancelled out.

Adaptive Utility Efficiency in ANC

$$\rho(t) = \frac{A(t)}{B(t)}$$

If the headphone system adapts precisely to a target noise level across a range of frequencies (e.g. jet engine noise, or a mixture of high and low pitch noises):

- $\rho(t) \to 1$: high adaptive efficiency
- $R(t) \to 0$: negligible environmental noise perceived

Average performance over time:

$$\bar{\rho} = \frac{1}{T} \sum_{t=0}^{T} \frac{A(t)}{B(t)} \approx 0.95 \text{ to } 1.05 \quad \text{(ideal for ANC)}$$

Byproducts Resolved by Adaptive Utility in ANC
- Reduces need for high volume = lower volume use leads to less hearing damage.
- Mitigates environmental unpredictability = calm user experience in shifting soundscapes.
- Lower cognitive load = reduces brain strain, improves focus and reduces fatigue and frustration.

Residual or Emergent Byproducts of ANC
- $B_{\text{residual, pressure}}$: Perceived "ear pressure" from opposing waveforms.
- $B_{\text{residual, awareness}}$: Loss of environmental awareness (e.g., traffic, people trying to socialize).

- $B_{\text{residual, battery}}$: Increased power consumption due to continuous DSP operations.
- $B_{\text{residual, autonomy}}$: Users feel disempowered when they can't manually control adaptation levels.

Despite these, net U_{total} often remains far higher than with passive headphones, especially in noisy environments. Users tolerate B_{residual} because real-time noise mitigation is highly effective. This dynamic, personalized response to real-world byproducts exemplifies the power of Adaptive Utility.

Case Study Summary
- Adaptive utility increased net utility U_{total} without changing the baseline function of the headphones (audio delivery).
- It solved latent and dynamic byproducts in real time that previous innovations could not.
- Residual byproducts emerged, requiring further incremental improvements (manual ANC controls, transparency modes, low-power DSP chips).
- Users are willing to pay a premium due to the noticeable reduction in friction during use, even in a variable and unpredictable environment.

Core Insights about Adaptive Utility Innovation

The core value of Adaptive Utility Innovation is not that it introduces new forms of utility, but that it actively removes or suppresses byproducts in real time, especially those that emerge dynamically due to shifting environments or unpredictable contexts.

Whereas other innovations resolve static or anticipated byproducts, Adaptive Utility continuously monitors for friction, inefficiency, or disruption as it occurs, and adjusts automatically to preserve the user experience. It doesn't enhance the utility through additional features, it protects the existing utility from being overshadowed by unpredictable or compounding byproducts.

This type of innovation is often invisible when it works well because it prevents problems before users feel them. It exemplifies the Law of Perpetual Innovation by solving for the temporal, situational, and behavioral byproducts that other innovation types cannot address on their own.

Adaptive Utility is not about doing more it's about preserving more. Its inventiveness lies in ensuring that the utility you already have continues to feel seamless by continually dissolving what would have otherwise become friction.

Take autonomous "self-driving" cars for example. They are often seen as adding value because they "do more," they drive themselves. But in truth, they don't add utility; they preserve the original utility of transportation by removing its most burdensome byproduct: the need for human operation. A non-autonomous car already fulfills the utility of moving a person from point A to point B. What the autonomous vehicle does is eliminate the cognitive, physical, and emotional burdens tied to driving: the attention, fatigue, risk of error, and stress.

The genius of Adaptive Utility in this case is not in expanding the utility of the car, but in dissolving the frictions that make that utility feel effortful. The ride is the same, however, the freedom from having to manage and operate it is the true innovation.

Key Business Implications

1. **Justification for Premium Pricing**
   Because Adaptive Utility reduces active effort and resolves real-time friction, consumers perceive it as inherently more valuable. Products with adaptive features often command higher prices.
   - Example: ANC headphones are priced higher than passive models because users recognize their superior noise mitigation and comfort.
   - Consumers pay for the experience of not having to suffer byproducts in real-time.

2. **Competitive Differentiation**
   Companies that implement adaptive features early can dominate their category.
   - Example: Smart thermostats like Nest auto-adjust based on patterns.
   - Smartwatches adapt screen brightness and battery use.

3. **Data Feedback Loops for Refinement**
   Many adaptive systems today generate performance data over time, feeding continuous improvements via firmware or AI training.
   - Example: Apple's adaptive transparency mode is continuously refined via usage data.
   - Adaptive Utility that can adapt upon its adaptiveness is the next frontier for this type of innovation method, now that AI has taken the stage.

4. **Sustained Customer Satisfaction and Loyalty**
   Users develop trust in systems that respond to them rather than requiring constant configuration.
   - o Reduced decision fatigue.
   - o Greater perception of value and comfort.

5. **Innovation Sustainment and Risk of Adaptive Overreach**
   As adaptive systems resolve existing burdens, new residual byproducts emerge (e.g., privacy concerns, energy use, sensory disconnect) shaping the next innovation wave.
   - o Over-automation may backfire if users feel loss of control.
   - o Transparency, override features, and clear feedback loops are critical to adoption.

Conclusion

Adaptive Utility is a frontier of innovation where products and services respond dynamically to the environment, system state, and user input to minimize byproducts in real time. It does not require the user to wait for a new product generation or issue a complaint. Its entire innovation premise is real-time relevance.

Unlike static improvements or one-time integration events, adaptive innovations operate in a constant loop of sensing, evaluating, and adjusting in real time. Through mathematical modeling, we've shown how Adaptive Utility maintains or increases net perceived utility by minimizing byproduct as it emerges. The success of products like ANC headphones illustrates that users will pay more for systems that free them from active burden management.

Adaptive Utility isn't just about automation or convenience, it's about "*immediacy*" in byproduct resolution. And as the world becomes more variable, unpredictable, and fast-paced, adaptive innovation becomes not just beneficial, but necessary.

In the grand loop of the Law of Perpetual Innovation, Adaptive Utility allows us to flatten the curve of burden accumulation, not by redesigning products after problems surface, but by designing products that solve problems as they attempt to emerge in real-time. Ultimately, Adaptive Utility represents a critical path forward as products and systems become smarter, more context-aware, and more personalized, providing frictionless utility delivery through intelligent, reactive byproduct-driven design.

CHAPTER 27
Modular Utility Innovation

Bounding Byproducts through Reconfigurability

Introduction

Modular Utility Innovation occupies a unique space within the Law of Perpetual Innovation (LPI). Whereas Incremental Innovation focuses on delaying byproducts across product lifecycles, Utility Integration merges multiple utilities to reduce the byproducts of fragmentation, Utility Specialization hones solutions to address specific byproducts head-on, and Adaptive Utility displaces or neutralizes byproducts in real time. Modular Utility adopts a different strategy altogether. It decomposes a larger utility into interchangeable parts (modules) designed to be easily reconfigured, replaced, or upgraded to tackle the byproducts that emerge as conditions or user needs change.

Rather than committing to a single, static design that struggles or accumulates burdens over time, modular innovation provides a flexible foundation that can adapt or evolve as new byproducts surface. Users swap or customize modules instead of discarding or overhauling entire systems. By doing so, modularity reduces the frequency and severity of certain byproducts as they accumulate while inevitably creating its own new byproducts in the process.

In this chapter, we will explore:
- The essence of modular utility and its role in mitigating byproducts by fragmenting a system into smaller, swappable segments.
- Mathematical models to illustrate how modular utility manages existing and emergent byproducts.

- A deep-dive case study showcasing how modular power tools revolutionized workshop practices by minimizing burdens and reshaping user expectations.
- Key business implications for companies pursuing or expanding modular utility frameworks.

By the end, it will become clear why modular utility holds such transformative potential in a world where conditions, technologies, and preferences continually shift, and how it aligns with LPI by perpetually cycling to address new residual byproducts that modular solutions inevitably generate.

The General Concept of Modular Utility under LPI

Modular Utility refers to a design philosophy where a product, service, or system is constructed out of discrete, compatible components (modules), each performing a subset of the total function. These modules can be assembled, swapped, or upgraded independently, enabling a high degree of flexibility without necessitating a full redesign or replacement of the entire system.

Key Attributes of Modular Utility:

1. **Interchangeable Parts**
   Each module encapsulates a specific function or sub-utility, ensuring that modules can be substituted or individually refined without disrupting the entire system.

2. **Independent Lifecycles**
   Different modules can have different lifespans. When one module becomes outdated or heavily worn, it can be replaced, while others remain intact.

3. **Reduced System Redundancy**
   By isolating and reusing modules, users avoid re-purchasing entire assemblies to gain or restore particular functionalities.

4. **Scalable or Customizable Configurations**
   Modules allow users to compose exactly the combination of features they need, reducing the byproducts of over-featured or under-featured general solutions.

From a byproduct perspective, modular designs do not merely "add features" nor do they refine features to address singular narrow needs. Instead, they break up a system's utility into distinct, user-swappable components, mitigating the byproducts of

442

obsolescence, maintenance overhead, and forced upgrading by letting the user only adjust or replace the modules that become burdensome or inadequate.

How Modular Utility Mitigates Byproducts

To contrast with other LPI innovation types:

- Incremental Innovation: Delays byproducts across product iterations (version updates).
- Integration: Eliminates overlapping and separate byproducts by merging multiple utilities.
- Specialization: Confronts highly targeted byproducts.
- Adaptive: Displaces them in real-time as they appear.

Modular specifically addresses byproducts by fragmentation (breaking up a product into modules) and flexible reconfiguration (swapping modules in or out). Allowing byproduct to be addressed with greater ease as a piece or component of the system, rather than the system as a monolithic (one piece) whole. In this way, byproduct accumulation takes place within the various modules, or their interfaces, at different rates and intensities, allowing the lifecycle of the overall system or product to be strategically prolonged.

Core Byproducts Reduced by Modularity

1. Obsolescence Byproduct
- Traditional systems degrade or become outdated as technology or user needs evolve, forcing entire system replacements (cost, waste, discontinuity).
- Modular Approach: Only the outmoded module is swapped for a newer or improved version, extending the lifecycle of the system, saving money, and reducing material waste.

2. Maintenance & Repair Byproducts
- Conventional designs treat the product as a single sealed unit, leading to more complicated or expensive repairs when a single part fails.
- Modular Approach: Failures become localized to modules. The user can quickly isolate the defective module and replace or repair it. Downtime, cost, and frustration are minimized.

3. Over- / Under-featured Solutions

- A one-size-fits-all design either crams in unnecessary functions (leading to cost, complexity) or omits crucial features for certain user segments. Both create dissatisfaction or friction.
- Modular Approach: Users configure the product to match only what they need. This significantly lowers the byproduct of excessive or insufficient functionality.

4. Inventory & Logistics Complexity
- Entirely separate product lines for small user niches lead to wasted inventory or confusion.
- Modular Approach: Stocking fewer universal modules can create a wide range of final products, simplifying supply chains.

5. Environmental & Disposal Burdens
- Constantly discarding entire products for small malfunctions or incremental performance gains generates environmental waste.
- Modular Approach: Encourages partial replacements and upgrades, limiting waste or disposal by preserving the rest of the system's modules.

By letting each module address a coherent, bounded set of tasks, many shortfalls with all-or-nothing design solutions vanish. Users gain an agile, cost-effective means to keep pace with evolving needs or emergent burdens.

Residual or New Byproducts from Modularity

As with any innovation, under LPI, the shift toward modular design also yields fresh byproducts:

- **Physical & Systemic Complexity:** Ensuring different modules remain physically and electronically compatible can complicate the overall design.
- **Inter-module Dependencies:** Some modules can conflict or degrade each other's performance if not well-coordinated or configured.
- **Higher Upfront Cost:** The engineering to support modular attachments or universal interfaces might drive initial design costs higher.
- **Fragmentation in Ecosystems:** If a brand's modules diverge from an industry standard, users risk partial lock-in or confusion.

Despite these emergent byproducts, many industries still gravitate toward modular structures, proving that the benefits can outweigh the new costs in a dynamic, evolving marketplace.

Mathematical Model for Modular Utility

Defining the System and Byproducts

Suppose a product's overall function can be split into n distinct modules:

$$U_{\text{modular}} = \sum_{i=1}^{n} U_i - B_{\text{modular}}$$

Where:

- U_i = The baseline utility each module contributes to the overall system.
- B_{modular} = The byproducts emerging from the act of designing and/or using the product in a modular form.

Compared to a Monolithic (Non-Modular) System

If the system were monolithic (no modular design), we might express its total utility as:

$$U_{\text{monolithic}} = U_{\text{single}} - B_{\text{mono}}$$

- U_{single} = The net function or baseline utility in a single, integrated device.
- B_{mono} = The byproducts tied to a single sealed, integrated solution (e.g., forced replacement, unfixable partial failures).

Capturing Obsolescence or Replacement

In a typical product lifecycle of length T, we consider the time points when a user might upgrade or replace modules vs. an entire product. Let:

- $C_{\text{replace}}(t)$: cost or burden of replacing entire product at time t.

- $C_{\text{module}}(t, i)$: cost or burden of replacing module i at time t.

Under a monolithic approach if any part fails or becomes obsolete enough to degrade net utility below an acceptable threshold, the user performs a full replacement:

$$U_{\text{mono,total}} = \sum_{t=0}^{T} [U_{\text{single}} - B_{\text{mono}}(t)] - \sum_{\text{replacement events}} C_{\text{replace}}(t)$$

Under a modular approach, the user can selectively swap out only the failing or outdated modules:

$$U_{\text{modular, total}} = \sum_{t=0}^{T} \left[\sum_{i=1}^{n} U_i - B_{\text{modular}}(t) \right] - \sum_{\text{module changes}} \left[\sum_{i} C_{\text{module}}(t, i) \right]$$

The difference in net utility between modular and monolithic solutions often hinges on comparing:

- The frequency and cost of partial module replacements
  vs.
- The cost of forced total replacement in a monolithic design

Balancing Gains vs. Residual Burdens

If B_{modular} remains smaller than the sum of byproducts users would experience from repeated monolithic replacements or from a generalized "one-size-fits-all" approach, modular solutions yield a net gain. Meanwhile, each new residual byproduct introduced by modular architecture must remain relatively small or occasionally overshadowed by the new benefits.

Deep-Dive Case Study: Modular Power Tools

Since their inception, power tools have undergone incremental improvements in power output, efficiency, and design. However, the concept of modularity where key components, attachments, and power sources are swappable across an ecosystem, has gradually reshaped the industry. From early days when only basic "wearable" parts like saw blades and drill bits could be swapped, to modern systems in which entire motor heads and battery packs connect across multiple tool bodies, modular design has significantly mitigated byproduct accumulation. Below is a detailed look at how this evolution unfolded, how it addresses persistent burdens, and which new byproducts arise in turn.

Early Fragmented Landscape & Latent Byproducts

Traditionally, power tools were each sold as a fully independent device:
- A drill, with its own housing, motor, and dedicated battery or cord.
- A circular saw, similarly self-contained, sharing little or no compatibility with the drill's battery or motor design.
- A sander, complete with a unique form factor, specialized accessories, and on-board power components.

Latent Byproducts emerged from this scattered approach:
- **Excess Physical Bulk**: End users, whether contractors or hobbyists, had to maintain, transport, and store multiple devices, each with significant overlap in motors, housings, wiring, or battery packs.
- **Maintenance & Part Duplication:** Each tool had its own set of wear parts (brushes, bearings), battery types, or specialized cords. This led to repetitive maintenance routines, plus the risk of owning spares that saw limited use.
- **Upgrade & Replacement Burdens:** Upgrading a seldom-used saw or driver meant purchasing an entirely new single-purpose device, even though many components inside were identical to tools the owner already had.
- **Inventory & Storage Complexity:** Handling multiple charging stations, multiple sets of consumables, each slightly incompatible among different tool lines or brands.

Even in these early decades, partial modularity was visible in removable "wearable" parts, such as saw blades, drill bits, or sanding pads, allowing quick changes to handle different materials. Yet these interchangeables only targeted the immediate functional tip, failing to address the deeper duplication of motors, battery systems, and housings.

The Rise of Shared Battery Platforms

One of the first major leaps in modular utility for power tools emerged when companies (e.g., DeWalt, Milwaukee, Makita) introduced shared battery pack systems. Instead of each tool requiring its unique battery, a standard lithium-ion pack could power multiple tools in the same brand ecosystem.

This partial modular step tackled some significant byproducts:

- **Battery Incompatibility:** Users no longer juggled different voltages or form factors from the same brand; a single battery type fit across many tools.
- **Reduced Charging Overload:** One or two universal chargers replaced the need for multiple brand-specific docks.
- **Lower Ownership Cost:** Additional tools could be purchased "bare" (no battery included) at reduced cost.

Despite these improvements, certain residual byproducts persisted:

- **Brand Lock-In:** Once a user invested in a brand's battery system, switching to another brand's ecosystem became costly.
- **Potential Underpowering or Overpowering:** A universal battery might not perfectly match the current draw or operating profile of specialized tools, leading to inefficiency or performance constraints.
- **Single Point of Failure:** If the battery line had defects or was discontinued, every tool in that ecosystem suffered.

Nonetheless, shared battery technology laid the groundwork for deeper modular architectures.

Universal Motor Heads & Attachments

While shared battery platforms addressed power-delivery redundancy, the motor or "drive" portion in each device remained dedicated. Some manufacturers soon introduced universal power heads (sometimes known as "power bases") to which different attachment modules could be fitted (e.g., a drill attachment, driver attachment, impact wrench attachment, reciprocating saw attachment), all latching onto the same motor module.

By bridging motor assembly with an interchangeable head, byproducts were reduced:

- **Duplicates Reduction:** Physical Duplication of separate motors or gear assemblies was cut down dramatically.
- **Effort and Complication Reduction:** Maintenance efforts concentrated on a single robust drive mechanism, leaving attachments simpler, cheaper, and less motor-dependent.
- **Upgrade inflexibility Reduction:** If a new or advanced reciprocating saw attachment emerged, users merely swapped that portion, not the entire tool.

However, new byproducts also surfaced:

- **Connection Lock-In:** Often, these attachments worked only with that brand's specific coupling mechanism. Over time, if brand X changed the coupler design, older attachments might be rendered incompatible.
- **Torque/Performance Variation:** A single motor might not deliver the peak specification demanded by highly specialized tasks (e.g., extreme high-torque drilling).
- **Heat & Load Management:** Stress from different attachments made the universal motor's job more complex, sometimes leading to accelerated wear.
- **Cost:** The motor module might be pricier upfront, however, further expansions then cost less. Some users felt initial sticker shock.

Despite these challenges, the net perceived utility soared for those who owned diverse tool sets. A single power head with multiple attachments saved them space, cut costs for large expansions, and simplified upkeep.

Ongoing Modularity Refinements

Realizing that focusing solely on the motor module still did not fully mitigate all duplication, newer lines extended modular design across three layers:

1. Battery (shared system).
2. Motor Head (universal base).
3. Function Attachments (the specialized tool "tops" or "heads").

Along with advanced designs that made wearable parts (e.g., brushes, bearings) more easily accessible, tool makers gradually found ways to modularize many of the internal mechanical components. This approach helped:

- Reduce Permanent Byproduct Accumulation: If a single gear, clutch, or brush wore out, it could be replaced as a submodule instead of tossing the entire tool.
- Expand the Ecosystem: Brands continued releasing new specialized attachments or secondary modules for niche tasks.
- Leverage Brushless Tech: Brushless motors delivered improved torque and reliability, further justifying the universal base concept.

Modularity was thus iterative. It started with small wearable parts, advanced to shared batteries, progressed to universal motor heads, and ultimately integrated multiple layers of modular interchangeability for maximum reusability.

The Math of Modular Power Tool Utility

To quantify the modular system advantage, define:

- U_{motor} = Utility from a universal motor module (baseline).
- $(U_{attach,1}, U_{attach,2}, ..., U_{attach,n})$ = Utility from each specialized attachment (drill, saw, sanding head, etc.).
- $B_{modular}$ = The new byproducts introduced by going modular (coupling mechanics, brand lock-in, potential under / over-power when compared to dedicated ones, etc.).

The net utility of the modular system combining the universal core with n attachments is:

$$U_{\text{modular, tools}} = U_{\text{core}} + \sum_{i=1}^{n} U_{\text{attach},i} - B_{\text{modular}}$$

Prior to adopting a modular approach, a user might have purchased n separate dedicated tools, each with burdens (redundant motors, separate batteries, larger storage). That scenario's total utility is:

$$U_{\text{separate, tools}} = \sum_{i=1}^{n} \left(U_{\text{tool},i} - B_{\text{separate},i} \right)$$

To evaluate the modular net utility advantage:

$$\Delta U = \left[U_{\text{core}} + \sum_{i=1}^{n} U_{\text{attach},i} - B_{\text{modular}} \right] - \sum_{i=1}^{n} \left(U_{\text{tool},i} - B_{\text{separate},i} \right)$$

If the duplication of motors and battery packs, plus the storage and maintenance byproducts across n separate tools, is large enough, the user stands to gain from modular.

Put another way, if:

$$\sum_{i=1}^{n} B_{\text{separate},i} > B_{\text{modular}}$$

then modular design yields a net perceived utility advantage, provided that $\sum_{i=1}^{n} U_{\text{attach},i} \approx \sum_{i=1}^{n} U_{\text{tool},i}$ (i.e., specialized attachments supply roughly the same core performance as dedicated tools).

New Byproducts Emerged & Next Innovation Cycle

Although modular power tools substantially resolve duplication burdens, they create a residual set of new byproducts:

- **Proprietary Ecosystems:** Manufacturers design attachments and motors to fit their system only, locking users into brand-based or product-line-based expansions.
- **Single Point of Failure:** If the motor module fails or is under repair, all attachments become temporarily useless.
- **Potential Performance Trade-offs:** A universal motor is typically sized to handle multiple tasks, but it might not hit specialized peak specs across the entire range.
- **Complex Coupler Mechanisms:** Repeated mounting/dismounting can introduce mechanical wear or alignment problems.

These residual byproducts reflect the same Law of Perpetual Innovation dynamic: by solving duplication-based byproducts, new constraints around brand lock-in, coupler standardization, or universal motor durability appear. Future improvements (e.g., "universal brand couplers," advanced motor design, AI-driven variable torque or speed matching) could revolve around mitigating these emergent byproducts.

Business & User Impact

- **Brand Ecosystem Adoption**

  Once a user invests in a universal motor and initial attachments, they remain predisposed to expand within the same brand. This ecosystem effect boosts brand loyalty and recurring sales.

- **Reducing Product Waste & Sustainability**

  Users retain the main motor portion across multiple generations of attachments. Old or infrequently used attachments remain shelf-friendly without tying up a motor or battery. This fosters a more sustainable usage lifecycle.

- **Premium Pricing Strategy**

  While expansions (attachments) may be less expensive than standalone devices, the upfront core module's cost can be higher. Manufacturers can leverage quality or advanced features in the universal motor module to justify premium pricing.

- **Opportunity for Niche Attachments**

  Because each new accessory does not require replicating the entire tool, companies can more freely experiment with niche or specialized attachments for unique tasks, fueling ongoing mini-innovations.

- **User Empowerment & Next-Level Configuration**
  Some systems even allow user-level modifications (e.g., swapping different motor types, adjusting gear ratios) leading to deeper customization and adaptability.

Overall, the modular model supports extensive user empowerment, lower cumulative costs, and a flexible path for incremental or specialized expansions.

Key Takeaways

Modular power tools stand as a vivid illustration of Modular Utility in practice, showing how a design approach can systematically reduce the accumulation of permanent byproducts (redundant hardware, excess maintenance, and large-scale replacements) by letting users swap out only the modules or attachments they actually need to extend and enhance the lifecycle of the product system. Over decades:

1. **First Stage:** Basic wearable-part replacements (bits, blades) helped keep certain burdens small.
2. **Second Stage:** Shared battery packs mitigated power duplication and lessened charging sprawl.
3. **Third Stage:** Full motor-head modularity tackled the core duplication of motors and large housings across multiple tools, drastically reducing storage and upkeep burdens.
4. **Refinements:** Deeper layers of modular design, including partial modular motors, advanced couplers, and brand-wide ecosystems, refined the user experience further, while introducing emergent byproducts needing new solutions.

The story of modular power tools vividly captures how a single design methodology, focusing on minimizing long-term, large-scale burdens, can remake an entire product category, establishing a cycle of continuous expansions and refinements under the Law of Perpetual Innovation.

Key Business Implications of Modular Utility

1. **Reduced Obsolescence Pressure**
   - Modular systems endure longer and reduce full product replacements. By focusing on incremental module improvements or expansions, companies can still maintain revenue via frequent but smaller-scale purchases.

2. **Niche Segmentation & Ecosystem Building**
   - Each environment or usage scenario can correspond to different sets of modules. This fosters brand ecosystems that can become powerful barriers to switching.

3. **Premium Branding & Upfront Investment**
   - Companies typically need to invest in robust modular architecture. This can create a brand identity for reliability, upgradability, and forward-compatibility, justifying higher margins.

4. **Supply Chain Advantages**
   - Standardized modules reduce manufacturing complexity. However, the residual complexity in ensuring cross-module compatibility can become a specialized burden that translates to powerful brand lock-in.

5. **User Experience & Marketing**
   - Effective marketing highlights the convenience, flexibility, and cost savings of replacing modules rather than entire systems.
   - It must also address user concerns about module lock-in or potential brand discontinuation.

Conclusion

Modular Utility Innovation showcases a compelling strategy for reducing byproducts in scenarios where users desire long-term adaptability, partial upgrades, or the ability to tailor a product's capabilities. By fragmenting large monolithic solutions into cohesive, swappable parts, modular design tackles obsolescence, maintenance overhead, and forced overhauls, delivering a nimble, user-centric approach to problem-solving.

Yet, as with any innovation viewed through the lens of LPI, new residual byproducts arise from modular approaches: physical coupling standards, single motor reliance, and potential performance trade-offs. Over time, these new issues become catalysts for further incremental or adaptive changes, keeping innovation perpetual.

In a fast-changing world where technology evolves quickly, and consumer preferences shift, modular utility stands out as a blueprint for robust, futureproof design. By letting each component follow its own lifecycle, businesses and consumers alike enjoy greater resilience, cost savings, and the satisfaction of evolving a single platform to meet emergent demands. Modular Utility does not just solve problems once, it flexibly frames every component, ensuring that as soon as one part shows a shortfall, you swap or refine that module, leaving the rest unburdened from byproduct. This cyclical interplay epitomizes the Law of Perpetual Innovation, guaranteeing that while integrated solutions may unify, specialized solutions may focus, and adaptive solutions may be suppressed in real time, modular solutions continuously fragment old burdens, forging agile ecosystems ready to reconfigure at a moment's notice.

CHAPTER 28
Radical Innovation

Byproduct Removal or Redefinition though Transformation

Introduction

Radical Innovation is not so much a distinct method as it is an outcome: a deeply transformative leap that restructures how humanity fulfills one or more of the 19 Human Origin Utilities. For example, the sudden advent of electricity replaced open-flame lighting and reshaped our origin utility of "environmental control" almost overnight. It often springs from latent (hidden in plain sight) or normalized (widely accepted) byproducts that large populations have resigned themselves to (see Appendix III for where to find these latent and normalized byproducts on the Byproduct Contrast Continuum). An illustration is how the daily chore of washing clothes by hand was a normalized burden before the radical emergence of the mechanical washing machine. These byproducts can also appear so entrenched or challenging that tackling them seems "impossible" or not even worth considering. Historically, the prospect of heavier-than-air flight was dismissed as impossible until glimmers of its possibility led to the Wright brothers' breakthrough flight.

Under the Law of Perpetual Innovation (LPI), radical innovation does not conjure "entirely new" utilities from nowhere since all utilities are always rooted in the 19 human origin utilities. Airplanes, for instance, did not create the utility of "movement and locomotion"; they simply transcended its older constraints, pushing beyond ground-based locomotion into new altitudes. Instead, radical innovation addresses massively overlooked or normalized burdens, sometimes spanning centuries, or it conquers extremely difficult or borderline "impossible" constraints, offering solutions that transform entire industries, social structures, or life itself. The integrated circuit overcame the huge space, cost, energy and reliability issues of vacuum-tube-based computing, enabling the modern digital age.

From early "moving pictures" that overcame the latently accepted difficulty of mass storytelling access, to modern "antibiotics" that subdued microbial threats humanity long deemed unbeatable, radical innovations stand apart not by their brand-newness alone but by how comprehensively they eliminate persistent, widely accepted burdens. Another example is the transition from horse-drawn carriages to automobiles, revolutionary not because travel was new, but because it demolished the burdens of time-consuming manual transport, geographic isolation, and reliance on animal upkeep. Sometimes radical innovations also disrupt existing providers or overshadow entire ways of living (e.g., ride-sharing apps overshadowed the once-ubiquitous taxi medallion system, creating a new ecosystem for urban mobility overnight). Other times, they create new utility branches rather than displacing older ones, drastically expanding human possibility (e.g., photography emerging alongside painting).

In this chapter, we probe the commonalities of radical innovations through the lens of byproduct resolution. We also propose methods an innovator can use to unearth these hidden or seemingly insurmountable burdens that become catalysts for radical innovation. One such method is systematically identifying inefficiencies that large populations have learned to live with, akin to the unsanitary water sources that spurred the radical development of modern sanitation and filtration systems. Through deeper analysis, we see that what unifies "radical" leaps is their capacity to unmask and neutralize burdens so ingrained that few even realize they exist or assume they are unsolvable. The invention of the printing press exemplifies such a leap, upending centuries of painstaking manuscript duplication and unleashing an information revolution.

Defining Radical Innovation through LPI

Radical innovation arises when a new solution so effectively addresses a large-scale or deeply entrenched byproduct that it transforms the landscape of how a human origin utility is fulfilled. Under LPI, all solutions are extensions of fundamental utilities, but radical ones break conventional constraints or "obviousness," offering leaps in scale, accessibility, or performance that prior solutions could not approach.

Latent Mass-Scale Byproducts
Many radical innovations target a widespread set of byproducts that society has normalized or accepted as "just how it is." Examples:

- **Streaming Services** overcame the repeated, time-consuming errands (drive, rent, return) of the movie-rental model, which the masses had long tolerated.
- **Smartphones** collapsed a broad scope of separate tasks (communication, computing, media consumption) into one pocket device, revealing how burdensome it was to juggle multiple electronics.
- **Rideshare Apps** (e.g., Uber, Lyft) solved the everyday friction of uncertain taxi availability, payment confusion, and uneven price structures, all of which had felt normal.

In each case, a large group of people recognized, after the fact, "we had been living with these burdens for so long without fully questioning them."

Seemingly Impossible Byproducts

Other radical innovations conquered byproducts that felt outright invincible:

- **Antibiotics**: Microbial infections once spelled near-certain death or severe complications. The invention of penicillin was so improbable that many never imagined microbe-killing substances could be mass-produced.
- **Airplanes**: Humans accepted the enormous byproduct of over-land or sea-based travel times. Flight was considered unrealistic, yet the Wright brothers and subsequent aviators "proved the impossible."
- **Metal Smelting** (historical transformations): Early societies believed certain high-temperature manipulations were unachievable, yet forging iron or steel overcame the perceived "impossibility" of controlling such extreme heat.

Here, the radical leap was not unveiling a "new utility", people always desired health, mobility, or stronger materials. It was discovering a technique that overcame monstrous byproducts once presumed untouchable.

Common Traits in Radical Innovation

Despite their differences, radical innovations share four essential traits:

1. **A Massive Byproduct Overlooked or Seemingly Unsolvable**
   - A large portion of humanity silently copes with a major friction or hazard, believing it can only be marginally improved, not fundamentally solved.

2. **A Paradigm Shift that Reframes the Byproduct**

458

- Innovators see the problem from a vantage point that reveals the byproduct's root cause, enabling a solution beyond incremental tweaks.

3. **Broad-Based Impact**
   - Once manifested, radical solutions either overshadow existing solutions or create entirely new usage patterns. They may or may not disrupt incumbents but inevitably alter how we fulfill that origin utility.

4. **Emergence of New Residual Byproducts**
   - Even radical leaps introduce fresh burdens that spark subsequent improvements: antibiotic resistance, streaming bandwidth demands, or battery anxieties in smartphones, among others.

Hence, the hallmark of radical innovation is not mere novelty, but the completeness with which an entrenched byproduct is undone, plus the global scope of that resolution.

Byproducts That Radical Innovations Resolve

Radical solutions systematically remove burdens that had scaled so large or run so deep that society felt them insurmountable or became normalized to. We categorize these:

Normalized (recognized but accepted) or Latent (hidden) Byproducts
- Taxi inefficiency → Ridesharing
- Manual cinematic DVD rental → Video streaming
- Physical mail delays → Internet or email

Mechanism: The invention sculpts a new method or platform that directly eliminates fundamental friction (time, cost, steps, or constraints). Only then do people realize they "endured" the old model for ages.

"Impossible" Byproducts
- Microbial infection → Antibiotics or Vaccines
- Long-distance ground travel → Planes, High-speed rail
- Manual labor extremes → Steam engines, Combustion engines, Electricity

Mechanism: Solutions open a path previously viewed as an engineering or scientific impossibility. Once cracked, the leap is so vast it redefines possibility.

Cross-Domain or Synthesis Byproducts

Some radical innovations unify knowledge from multiple fields (e.g., smartphones merging computing, telephony, and microelectronics) or synergy of rocket propulsion and advanced materials. The byproduct is typically friction from domain boundaries, thought too complex to merge. By bridging them, radical synergy solutions appear "magical" in how they break or unify previously separate fields.

Mathematically Modeling Radical Innovation's Impact

Overview of the Problem

In the context of radical innovation, we start with an existing solution, sometimes centuries old, that delivers a "root" or "origin" utility drawn from the 19 Human Origin Utilities. Examples might be mobility via a horse-drawn carriage (addressing "Movement and Locomotion"), communication through the telegraph (fulfilling "Communication and Language"), or DVD rentals to meet a need for emotionally engaging entertainment content (tying back to "Emotional Regulation and Fulfillment"). Over time, each of these solutions accumulates burdens, or byproducts, that people often regard as simply "how it is" or "too big to solve." A radical innovation then emerges, fundamentally restructuring how the same root utility is delivered. This new method drastically reduces or eliminates many of the old burdens ($B_{existing}$) once deemed unchangeable, while introducing its own smaller or more manageable byproducts ($B_{radical}$). The result is often a leap in net perceived utility, which explains why some radical innovations rapidly trigger widespread adoption.

The Net Perceived Utility of the Old Existing Solution

$$U_{net} = U_0 - B_{existing}$$

What the variables represent

1. U_0: This is the baseline utility of the old solution (or old product). Essentially it captures the core function people get from using it.
    - For horse-drawn carriages, U_0 is "*movement & locomotion* over land."
    - For telegraphs, U_0 is "long-distance *communication*."
    - For DVD rentals, U_0 is "access to entertainment content that delivers *emotional regulation* and *fulfillment*."

2. $B_{existing}$: This is the set of all byproducts that the old existing solution imposes on the user. A "byproduct" here means any inefficiency, extra burden, annoyance, or large cost (monetary, time, health, etc.) that the user experiences alongside getting U_0.

   - For carriages: feeding horses, cleaning up manure, slow travel speeds, limited route flexibility.
   - For telegraphs: specialized operators needed, character limits, heavy infrastructure.
   - For DVD rentals: physical trips to stores, late fees, limited inventory, no digital backup.

3. U_{net}: Net perceived utility of the old solution. In other words, how beneficial does the old solution feel once we subtract out the burdens. When the byproducts are large, U_{net} is significantly lower than U_0. (Note: It's important to state that when a widely accepted innovation first hits the scene, such as the horse-drawn carriage, the new residual burdens (byproducts) it imparts are largely accepted, at first. This is because this new utility method substantially subdued the prior burdens. Over time however, these byproducts will accumulate and become less and less acceptable, ultimately feeding demand for the next innovation.)

What the formula says:

$$U_{net} = U_0 - B_{existing}$$

We start with some core function of the product or system. Then we subtract the recognized byproduct (burdens or friction) that come along with it, resulting in the user's net experience.

The Net Perceived Utility of the Radical Innovation

$$U_{radical} = U_{same\_origin} - B_{radical}$$

What the variables represent

1. U_{same_origin}: Even if the radical innovation looks wholly "new," it's fulfilling the same underlying utility (Human Origin Utility) that the old system served. The difference is how it does it.

- An airplane's baseline utility is still *"movement & locomotion,"* just at far greater speed, range, and altitude compared to a carriage or car.
- A streaming service is still *"emotional regulation* and *fulfillment* through entertainment content," just delivered digitally, not by physical rental.

2. $B_{radical}$: The new residual byproducts introduced by the radical innovation. Even if these burdens are smaller than the old set, they exist. For instance:
   - Streaming services still rely on high-speed internet and may cause data caps or buffering problems.
   - Airplanes, though much faster, require purchasing tickets, getting to an airport early, dealing with luggage, waiting in lines, getting through security, dealing with delays and cancellations, boarding and so on.

3. $U_{radical}$: The net user experience of the radical innovation. It is the new approach's baseline minus its own new or residual byproducts.

Why do we use "U_{same_origin}" instead of "U_0"?

Because the "origin utility" hasn't changed. The radical innovation still aims at the same fundamental human need, like *"movement & locomotion* from city to city," "obtain *emotional regulation* and *fulfillment* through entertainment," or *"communication* across distance." However, it's helpful to give it a separate symbol (U_{same_origin}) to emphasize that even if it's delivering the same core function, the radical solution might feel qualitatively bigger, faster, better, or more flexible.

Yet mathematically, we can consider $U_0 \approx U_{same\_origin}$. They serve that identical root function. The difference is mostly in how effectively they remove burdens.

The Utility Difference: ΔU

$$\Delta U = U_{radical} - \left(U_0 - B_{existing}\right)$$

This is the step where we measure how much net utility the new radical approach gains or loses compared to the old solution. It basically says: "Take the radical solution's net value and subtract the old solution's net value."

Expanding that:

$$\Delta U = \left[U_{same\_origin} - B_{radical} \right] - \left(U_0 - B_{existing} \right)$$

Here, we interpret each piece as:

1. $\left[U_{same\_origin} - B_{radical} \right]$
   This is the radical innovation's net utility.

2. $\left(U_0 - B_{existing} \right)$
   This is the old solution's net utility.

Relation Between U_0 and U_{same_origin}

$$U_0 \approx U_{same\_origin}$$

They essentially refer to the same core or human origin function/benefit: movement, communication, etc. So, we can treat them as roughly equal. (*For example, whether one drives or flies from California to New York, the same core utility is accomplished; both means of transportation will get you from point A to point B, the only difference between those two means are their intrinsic and extrinsic burdens, inefficiencies, inconveniences, time delays. Their byproducts.*) That simplification yields:

$$\Delta U \approx \left[B_{existing} - B_{radical} \right]$$

Why That Matters

When we assume ($U_0 \approx U_{same\_origin}$), we are basically canceling out "the function's baseline value" from both sides of the difference. That leaves us with a clearer perspective: the real advantage in a radical innovation arises from how many old existing byproducts, or burdens, it can eliminate or diminish, versus how many new burdens it residually creates.

Hence:

$\Delta U \approx$ (Old Existing Byproducts Eliminated) $-$ (New Byproducts Introduced)

If the old existing burdens were massive (in depth or breadth, across a population) and the new burdens are relatively small, the difference ΔU is large. Indicating a big leap in net user benefit (utility).

Interpreting $B_{existing} \gg B_{radical}$

When we say the old set of burdens $B_{existing}$ is "much greater than" the new set $B_{radical}$, we mean:

- The radical innovation slashes problems the old approach had accepted for decades, centuries, or even millennia.
- The fresh burdens introduced by the radical solution, while still present, are relatively minor or more manageable today.

For instance:

When comparing DVD Rentals to Streaming Services
- Old burdens included store trips, limited stock, late fees, environment (rental physically shipped).
- New burdens revolve around data usage, internet stability, monthly subscription, content selection indecision.
- Because not having to physically pursue or manage DVDs is a huge improvement, ΔU soared, and streaming took over quickly.

When comparing Horse Carriages to the Automobile
- Old burdens encompassed horse upkeep, manure cleanup, slow speeds, limited range.
- New burdens introduced gas stations, mechanical breakdowns, auto accidents.
- Overall, the leaps in speed and comfort overshadowed those new byproducts.

Thus, the substantial inequality in $B_{existing} \gg B_{radical}$ demonstrates why radical innovation often sees "unstoppable adoption" or rapid transformation. People adopt it in large numbers because they can't believe how many old burdens vanish (washing machine vs manual), or that they could be banished (achieving flight). And the new burdens, though real, feel comparatively trivial… at least for the time being.

Summarizing Each Piece

1. U_0 or U_{same_origin}
   - The baseline or core function that the user wants: e.g., "I need to communicate," "I need to get somewhere," "I need a cure for this disease," etc.

2. $B_{existing}$
   - The old existing (sometimes huge, sometimes hidden or normalized) set of pains, costs, frictions, unresolved deficiencies or unfulfilled aspirations that accompany the old method of delivering that function.

3. $B_{radical}$
   - The new byproduct burdens introduced by the radical approach, typically smaller or more surmountable. Not zero but overshadowed by how big the old burdens were.

4. $U_{radical}$
   - The net perceived user utility from the radical solution once the new burdens are accounted for.

5. ΔU
   - The net difference or "leap" from the old approach to the radical approach. If ΔU is large and positive, adoption is typically fast or widespread.

Because the radical method still satisfies the same fundamental origin utility, the difference in net benefit emerges primarily from how drastically byproducts shift.

Putting It All Together

- **Step 1:** You identify how valuable the old system was by acknowledging its baseline utility (U_0) minus the laundry list of byproducts ($B_{existing}$).
- **Step 2:** A radical innovation appears, offering the same essential origin function (U_{same_origin}) but incurring new, usually smaller burdens ($B_{radical}$).
- **Step 3:** Compare them directly:

$$\Delta U = \left(U_{same\_origin} - B_{radical}\right) - \left(U_0 - B_{existing}\right) \approx B_{existing} - B_{radical}$$

- **Conclusion:** The radical innovation triumphs if it renders most of the old burdens irrelevant while adding only minimal or more tolerable burdens, producing a large net jump in user experience.

Essentially, the "radical" part is that such a big chunk of the old burdens was so "normalized to" or deemed "unsolvable" that no one considered it. Once removed, people recognize, "Wow, we should never go back!"

Why This Model Explains "Transformative" Results

Large positive ΔU translates into:

- **Rapid, wide-scale adoption**
  People rush to adopt because living with the old burdens seems pointless once they see how effectively the new solution resolves them.

- **Restructuring of entire markets**
  Businesses built on the old burdens (like DVD rental stores) struggle as the radical approach is unstoppable.

- **Long-Lasting Impact on Society**
  Because you can't unsee the removal of so many burdens, societies reconfigure infrastructure, law, consumer habits, skill sets, and complementary technologies to support the new approach.

That is why radical innovations go beyond mere incremental improvement: They address burdens so large and entrenched that removing them redefines how entire populations approach that fundamental utility.

Key Takeaways

1. All solutions revolve around the same human origin utilities; radical or not, the function you want (mobility, health, emotional regulation + fulfillment, etc.) is consistent.
2. Radical solutions do not create an entirely new origin utility but dramatically remove a huge portion of the old burdens from an existing solution.
3. ΔU ends up large because the old byproducts, once seen as unalterable or simply not seen as "many accepted burdens," get slashed, while new byproducts, though real, pale in comparison.

466

4. Adoption is swift and transformative because consumers realize they no longer must cope with massive (magnitude/depth), and/or normalized (breadth of those affected) inefficiencies or pains.
5. Societal or economic disruption could follow if entire industries or cultural norms that thrived on the old burdens are overshadowed or replaced.

So the key formula:

$$\Delta U \approx B_{existing} - B_{radical}$$

simply states, in symbolic form, that the leap in perceived user value is mainly about how many or how profoundly old byproducts vanish relative to how many new byproducts appear. If the difference is big enough (i.e., if old burdens were huge), that defines a radical transformation.

Methods to Unearth "Latent" and "Impossible" Byproducts

When it comes to radical innovation, merely improving on known shortcomings is not enough. Innovators need to learn how to sense and detect the hidden or deeply ingrained byproducts that the masses have either accepted as unchangeable or never thought to challenge. The following approaches go beyond standard user research or market surveys, venturing into the territory of mindset shifts, detective-level scrutiny, and self-imposed constraints designed to highlight large-scale, normalized latent byproducts or seemingly unsolvable problems. Each method aims to push innovators beyond the boundary of the obvious, toward discovering truly transformative leaps.

Inversion Exercises (Reframing "Normal")

Core Idea:
Take a process that everyone performs (e.g., driving to a rental store, physically returning DVDs, physically hailing a cab) and invert it or flip it on its head. This method highlights unchallenged steps we treat as "inevitable."

How to Conduct:
1. Identify a routine: Pinpoint a widely accepted but possibly cumbersome process.
2. Articulate every step: Break it down into micro-activities (commutes, lines, waiting times).

3. Ask "What if these steps didn't exist at all?": Instead of "How can we speed up lines?" imagine "What if lines are gone entirely?" or "What if the user never physically comes to us, or never deals with paper forms?"
4. Generate concept extremes: Think of solutions that invert every constraint. Even "absurd" ideas can reveal hidden burdens.

Why It Works:
By flipping the usual flow, you remove illusions of necessity. People historically accepted "you must physically return the DVD," until streaming reversed the assumption. This approach uncovers major friction that entire populations have grown numb to.

Zero-Constraint Brainstorming (Disrupt the "Impossible")

Core Idea:
Temporarily discard all known limitations such as technical, financial, ethical, or resource-based. This mental exercise counters the "that can't be done" reflex that cements seemingly unbreakable constraints.

How to Conduct:
1. Suspend disbelief: Begin an ideation session by explicitly banning the words "impossible," "too expensive," or "out of scope."
2. Aim for fantasy: Encourage participants to express solutions that break known laws or require unthinkable resources.
3. Trace the root: Even if 99% of these fantasies fail, the 1% that remains can expose previously unseen angles or partial feasible solutions.

Why It Works:
Many radical ideas start off as "fantasy" that gradually become real once you identify a hidden synergy or uncharted technique. Antibiotics, gene editing, and space flight, they all began as near-fiction. Zero-constraint brainstorming systematically forces the mind to consider the unthinkable, where new possibilities emerge.

Comparative Domain Analysis (Borrowing from Other Fields)

Core Idea:
Often, the "impossible" in one domain was solved decades ago in another. By cross-pollinating solutions across industries or knowledge areas, you can crack deeply rooted byproducts.

How to Conduct:
1. Study parallel industries: If you are in healthcare, look at how the logistics or tech industry overcame complex constraints.
2. Translate solutions: Ask, "Could the system approach used in field X apply to Y?" For instance, the "Peer-to-Peer" networking idea that revolutionized file sharing later inspired ridesharing.
3. Spot patterns: Seek similar forms of friction: e.g., the friction of "finding a vacant resource" (cab vs. hosting server vs. seat on a flight). Observing how one field overcame that friction could guide a radical fix in another.

Why It Works:
Major breakthroughs can arise by bridging two previously siloed domains. The friction that one domain overcame might be brand new in yours. This vantage is especially fruitful for "impossible" burdens since another domain might have tackled an analogous problem with different constraints.

User Journey Magnification (Hyper-Detail of Steps)

Core Idea:
Unpack every micro-step and micro-friction a user endures in daily routines. Even if steps feel trivial, documenting them with pathological detail can reveal accumulative burdens that are simply "tolerated."

How to Conduct:
1. Map the full user experience: Include physical movements, emotional states, waiting times, repeated tasks, fees, uncertainties.
2. Quantify friction: Count how many times a user repeats small tasks daily, weekly, or monthly. Summation of micro-burdens can be enormous in scale across a population.
3. Highlight confusions or "time sinks": Where do users pause, guess, or get stuck? Where do they pay "mini fees" or tolerate mild but repeated stressors?

4. Ask "How might we remove entire clusters of steps?"

Why It Works:
Large groups of minor burdens often sum to a massive cost. People seldom notice because each micro-burden by itself is small. By magnifying the daily or monthly toll, you can discover fertile ground for a radical fix. E.g., ridesharing addresses hailing, payment, waiting, route negotiation all at once, a synergy no one recognized while each step was "small."

Look for "Impossible or Painfully Hard" (Targeting the Big Dare)

Core Idea:
Directly seek out tasks or outcomes that a broad consensus deems unattainable or extremely difficult. Usually, these revolve around fundamental constraints in physics, chemistry, or massive social inertia.

How to Conduct:
1. Collect "No-Go" statements: Interview experts or everyday users about "what absolutely can't be changed."
2. Isolate the constraint: Distinguish actual laws of nature from cultural or resource limitations. Is it truly thermodynamically impossible, or just "expensive" or "untested"?
3. Exploit partial cracks: Are there half-successful prototypes or fringe research? Use them as steppingstones.
4. Design minimal viable loops: Attempt scaled-down or partial solutions that may shift the "impossible" line outward.

Why It Works:
History is full of "impossibilities" that caved under fresh technical methods or rethinking. Attacking these frontally can produce leaps so large that they overshadow old solutions or create entirely new industries.

Nostalgia for Past Suffering (Unearthing Long-Standing Burdens)

Core Idea:
Examine historically big pains or hardships that remain only partially solved or still widely tolerated. Many times, we think they're "better than before" but do not realize a total fix is feasible.

How to Conduct:

1. Trace a byproduct burden across time: Evaluate how it's changed from decades or centuries ago. Are we still employing archaic remnants or partial solutions? (Utilizing the 19 human origin utilities during this step can prove beneficial)
2. Assess the persistent gap: If the improvement is only moderate, perhaps a radical approach can leapfrog constraints.
3. Check for illusions of progress: Are new patches or updates more "smoke and mirrors" than fundamental resolution? If so, the underlying byproduct might remain huge.

Why It Works:

A solution that was incremental or partially effective may lull us into a sense of "it's good enough now." By re-examining the original problem's scope, we can see how much remains unsolved and aim for a bigger transformation.

Experiencing the Product as a Real User (Self-Imposed Blindfold)

Core Idea:

Sometimes employees or insiders cannot see the unspoken burdens because they bypass them with staff perks, specialized access, or deep domain knowledge. By immersing oneself in the authentic user context without insider privileges, the real byproducts become glaring.

How to Conduct:

1. Suspend all employee benefits: No free or discounted units, no direct support lines, no privileged data. Acquire, install, and maintain the product or service exactly as a typical customer does.
2. Follow standard channels: Use public help desks, wait in normal queues, handle all fees or constraints.
3. Log unresolved deficiencies: Keep an "unfiltered frustration" journal for at least 2–4 weeks, capturing annoyances that standard user journeys reveal.
4. Assess overshadowed aspirations: Notice not just negative friction but also moments you wish the product "could do more," or "did what this other brand does," or "worked with this other brand," or integrated with an external system.

Why It Works:
Insiders rarely realize how much friction the average user endures. By forcing the authentic user vantage, significant hidden or normalized burdens can leap into view. This tactic frequently uncovers prime areas for radical improvement that have gone unaddressed simply because staff did not feel them day-to-day.

Additional Methods

- **Micro-Ethnography:** Spend a day (or longer) living in the user's environment, like a ride-along for a taxi driver, or shadowing a surgical team. Such closeness often reveals friction that even detailed interviews miss.
- **Contrarian Co-Design:** Pair with a "high complaint" user or domain critic who sees every flaw in your offering. Let them articulate extremes. The negativity can highlight big cracks that moderate voices skip.
- **Probe the Edges:** Evaluate extreme usage contexts such as ultra-cold climates, remote or poor connectivity, extremely small or large populations. These extremes often amplify latent burdens you can solve more broadly.

Key Takeaways

- Radical innovations revolve around "unearthed burdens" that are either so universal they are "taken for granted" or so difficult that few dare attempt them.
- Systematic, detective-like methods can unmask these burdens, from flipping assumptions (Inversion), ignoring constraints (Zero-Constraint Ideation), to living the user's real pains (Self-Imposed Blindfold).
- The watchwords are "mass acceptance," "unseen friction," or "declared impossible." By focusing here, you open the door to leaps so large they define new eras, overshadow old constraints, or create brand-new usage dimensions.

In short, discovering the unthinkable or invisible is a skill that can be cultivated. Once an organization or an individual masters these vantage points, radical byproducts, once dormant or unseen, become prime material for forging the next wave of transformative innovation.

Why Radical Innovations May or May Not Disrupt

Disruption typically arises when a new solution dethrones or outperforms an existing "incumbent" providers' goods or services. However, radical solutions do not universally revolve around dethroning incumbents:

- Disruptive: Streaming vs. DVD rental physically displaced Blockbuster.
- Non-Disruptive: Film coexisted with live theater, a brand-new domain. People still attend plays, but film soared to global popularity.

Under LPI, whether a radical leap displaces existing solutions or carves out a wholly new category depends on:

1. **Overlap in fulfilling the same origin utility:** If the new utility method fully covers (and often surpasses) the older approach's domain, the old is overshadowed.
2. **Relative user friction:** If adopting the new approach requires negligible or manageable switching costs (switching byproducts), mass exodus can follow.
3. **Sociocultural or regulatory influences:** Government or public inertia can hamper or expedite transitions.

Hence, radical does not always mean disruptive. Some leaps overshadow old methods, others create parallel expansions, each fueling the perpetual cycle as new residual byproducts appear and next-tier solutions arise.

New Residual Byproducts of Radical Innovation

No matter how sweeping or beneficial a radical innovation is, new byproducts inevitably appear. They can be especially impactful since radical solutions shift entire systems or industries:

1. **Infrastructure or Ecosystem Overhaul**
   - Motor vehicles demanded roads, parking areas, fueling stations, traffic laws.
   - Streaming demanded high-speed internet capacity, accelerating data center expansions and net neutrality debates.

2. **Ethical, Social, or Environmental Ripple or Cascading Effects**
   - Antibiotics fueled industrial farming and antibiotic resistance.

- The internet sparked privacy concerns, data monopolies, misinformation crises.

3. **Shock to Workforce**
   - Rapid displacement or re-skilling needed if old industries vanish.
   - E.g., horse-related transportation trades collapsed with the car's dominance.

4. **Inequality or Adoption Gaps**
   - Some groups adopt new tech easily, others lag or never adopt, creating physical, digital or economic divides.
   - E.g., QR-only menus exclude diners lacking smartphones, limiting their menu access.
   - E.g., Early broadband expansions bypassed rural/low-income areas, widening the digital divide.

Radical or not, these emergent byproducts outline new problem sets, compelling the next wave of innovators to address them.

The Path Forward: Cultivating a Radical Innovator Mindset

Radical leaps typically require more than incremental design changes or standard product management. They stem from:

1. **Massive Byproduct Awareness**
   - Foster an organizational culture that actively hunts for pain points or accepted norms.

2. **Cross-Disciplinary and Cross-Cultural Synergy**
   - Bring diverse talents and backgrounds together. Many "impossible" breakthroughs succeed through cross-pollination of knowledge and perspectives.
   - E.g., we see this prevail within Silicon Valley with companies like Apple and Google.

3. **Resource Commitment & Risk Tolerance**
   - Radical attempts can fail repeatedly. Perseverance is key.
   - E.g., flight pioneers, antibiotic researchers, rocket programs all endured multiple dead ends, until they didn't.

4. Iterate on "Impossible"

- Many radical leaps start with many incremental tests on partial solutions or concept proofs, eventually culminating into the full final solution.

Above all, the core impetus is to challenge the biggest "unchallenged" byproduct or to push "inconceivable" frontiers. This shift from "We can't do that, so let's manage it" to "We must solve it fundamentally" is the hallmark of the radical mindset.

Conclusion

Radical Innovation is a phenomenon, not just a process, guided by the same byproduct utility lens but operating at a scale or boldness that transforms how we fulfill the next link in the long chain of our human origin utilities. These transformations are often triggered by:

- Normalizing massive friction that we collectively "got used to."
- Seemingly insurmountable burdens once declared beyond our technical or conceptual reach.

Where other innovation approaches tackle smaller or more obvious byproducts, the radical leap occurs when visionaries (1) sense these invisible or "impossible" burdens and (2) unearth or create a solution so compelling that entire fields, societies, or norms are never the same.

No radical innovation solves everything forever. Each leap fosters fresh residual byproducts, continuing LPI's cycle. Radical solutions rewrite entire paradigms, and they're typically delivered through a combination of integrative, specialized, modular or adaptive methods. They do so by unearthing deeply seated byproducts or tackling fierce constraints, transforming the entire human approach to fulfilling that utility.

For innovators aspiring to instigate the next radical wave, the key is to train oneself to detect the biggest "unthinkable" friction or the largest "unchallenged acceptance." It requires detective-level skepticism, intense cross-domain knowledge, and a willingness to aim for the improbable. Where most see a permanent fixture of life, the radical innovator sees a burden waiting to be shattered. In that space, the seeds for truly paradigm-shifting solutions are sown. Solutions that once again confirm LPI's unstoppable forward cycle.

Outro

This concluding chapter shows how every apparent leap in innovation traces back to deeper, time-honored human impulses: we do not create new utilities from nothing, but instead dissolve constraints that overshadow our oldest drives. From film, which exposed the latent limitations of live performance, to the emergence of AI, which may redefine who steers the innovation cycle, each radical transformation ultimately addresses an entrenched burden so completely that an existing utility feels new. By tying innovation to our essential human origin utilities, the Law of Perpetual Innovation underscores that each breakthrough, whether it's replacing open-flame lighting with electricity or conquering the "impossible" with flight, arises from dismantling barriers we thought unchangeable. Yet even these world-shifting leaps still produce new byproducts, perpetuating the cycle. As we contemplate the coming era of AI and its potential to become the next "agent of disruption," the ultimate reminder is that innovation, at its core, remains humanity's purposeful push against entropy. An age-old endeavor to preserve and enhance our primal capacities through the endless, ever-renewing lens of utility and byproduct.

CHAPTER 29
The New That Has Always Been There

The Illusion of Novelty and the Enduring Roots of Innovation

When people first encountered the wonder of moving pictures, they felt they were witnessing a revolutionary new mode of entertainment. Audiences were amazed that what once demanded direct presence and a fleeting human performance on stage could now be captured, replayed, and broadly distributed. Yet under the Law of Perpetual Innovation (LPI), film's core function expands on the same human longing for narrative, emotional resonance, artistic expression, and communal sharing. An ancient drive. Although moving pictures seem to conjure a new realm of utility, they simply dissolve old constraints that overshadowed our capacity for immersive storytelling.

That tension between the illusion of something "brand-new" and the recognition of a deeper, timeless impulse appears time and again across all innovation. The automobile, for instance, felt like a revelation in personal transport, but it merely surpassed the inefficiencies of horse-drawn travel while preserving the same fundamental drive for movement and locomotion. Smartphones integrated communication, information access, and photography in one device, yet at root they removed the old friction of juggling multiple tools. Even the printing press, once seen as a radical step, ultimately answered the same human desire to communicate and record knowledge, only with fewer obstacles than before.

Moving pictures exemplify how radically new technology can arise from existing utility. Their success did not come by inventing narrative entertainment from scratch but by unraveling burdens that always had limited live performance: ephemeral presence, limited audience reach, and time-bound experiences. As soon as film overcame these assumed barriers, an entire new industry blossomed. This moment was so dramatic that it felt divorced from past methods, even though it still pointed back to our long-standing need for emotional immersion and shared storytelling.

Why Film Serves as a Perfect Mirror

If we look back to ancient theaters or medieval minstrels, we find that people already hungered for immersive narrative experiences. The recognized burdens where each performance confined to one location and moment in time, were such a familiar fixture that many simply accepted them as natural, never imagining a practical workaround. Film, however, shattered those assumptions: it let performances be preserved, broadcast worldwide, rewatched at will, and transformed into edited artistry beyond the scope of live theater. This shift appeared to offer a brand-new way to experience stories, yet it mainly tore down the burdens that once overshadowed a fundamental human utility.

Hence, every time an invention appears to birth an entirely new mode of living, the LPI perspective explains that it is still keyed into primal, origin-based desires. Film harnessed the human thirst for storytelling, just as talking pictures then added integrated audio, or color film added lifelike vibrancy. Nothing in that evolution replaced the underlying impulse; each step only refined or combined older elements in a more accessible manner.

At face value, we might say moving pictures introduced something truly alien to the human experience. But a closer look reveals that it transformed how we deliver or consume a well-worn utility. From an LPI vantage, even the most dazzling leaps result from removing entrenched burdens around the same old capacities. The reason film felt radical was how thoroughly it dissolved restrictions that people once saw as permanent.

Seeing "New Utility" as an Outgrowth of Old Utilities

The different flavors of innovation, incremental, integration, specialization, adaptive, and modular, help clarify how novel solutions can appear to bestow brand-new capabilities. Each does so by removing burdens that once throttled, overshadowed, or scattered our ability to use an underlying function:

- **Incremental or Sustained Innovation** gently reduces or delays the pains in an existing arrangement. In cinematic terms, think of how film advanced from black-and-white silent reels to color "talkies" to digital high resolution, each step pushing away friction: grainy visuals, short reels, and limited audio, so that audiences got a smoother experience.

- **Utility Integration** combines multiple existing functionalities in a single platform. When we went from silent films to "talkies," we merged recorded images with recorded sound, uniting them in real time. Audiences felt it as a leap that re-created the presence of live theater, yet it was essentially an integration: visual storytelling meets audio narration.

- **Utility Specialization** hones an existing framework for a particular subset of usage. Documentaries diverged from blockbusters, Indy films from mainstream fare, each perfecting certain aesthetics or techniques to address distinct viewer tastes. These specialized film genres or production methods can look as if they add new creative frontiers. In truth, they refine specific angles of the same emotional or narrative utility.

- **Adaptive Utility** modifies the product in real time to keep friction at bay. Modern streaming platforms adjust bandwidth and resolution on the fly, ensuring a relatively smooth movie despite poor internet or device changes. It might feel as though you can watch a film seamlessly anytime, anywhere, but ultimately, the system is removing emergent hindrances through actions like buffering and pixelation in real time rather than inventing a new capability.

- **Modular Utility** breaks the product down into interchangeable pieces, reducing permanent overhead. While classical cinema might be less obviously "modular," digital film editing with reusable assets, or streaming services building libraries from multiple licensing deals, each uses modular ideas to expand coverage without having to replicate entire new infrastructures from scratch. For instance, cinematic universes in Hollywood are arguably a "modular" narrative approach: they reuse sets, characters, digital assets, or story arcs to spin out new films rapidly. It can feel new, but the impetus is reusing existing building blocks with minimal overhead.

Whenever a radical shift like moving pictures takes hold, it might embody one or more of these approaches in constructive collaboration pushing old, entrenched byproducts aside so dramatically that a viewer can't help but say, "This changes everything." From an LPI vantage point, all that has changed is the overhead, friction, or limiting conditions that overshadowed a deeply rooted human utility. Once we remove them, brand-new horizons open up as side effects.

Generalizing Beyond the Film Example

Moving pictures illustrate the phenomenon in a particularly dramatic way, but the same logic applies to countless other modern inventions that at first glance appear unrelated to any single ancient root. One can look at personal computers, pianos, wedding rings, or birthday cakes, and suppose these are wholly new constructs with no straightforward link to the fundamental drives we label as "19 Human Origin Utilities." With a little unraveling, however, we see how these artifacts expand on essential capacities.

The computer, for example, is not simply a magic box performing unimaginable feats. It primarily addresses aspects of cognition, memory, communication, and problem-solving. Capabilities we have always desired to strengthen. A piano might look like an advanced contrivance for music-making, yet the underlying impetus is emotional expression, social bonding, creativity, and the pursuit of aesthetic fulfillment. A wedding ring seems culturally specific, but at heart it reinforces social bonding, shared meaning, and signals belonging or commitment. A birthday cake can be a puzzle at first, what ancient drive does it tie to? Ultimately, it both addresses nourishment (albeit in a celebratory form) and serves as a centerpiece in recognition of personal milestones, symbolizing emotional bonding, or shared social identity in families and communities.

We discover that beneath each outward complexity, the utility ties back to an ancient anchor: learning, memory, emotional expression, social connecting, or something else from that foundational set. The reason these items can be reinterpreted endlessly is that each extension of a primal drive can spawn many forms, sometimes disguised as "completely new."

A Method for Uncovering the Core Human Element

To recognize how a seemingly novel product, service, or ritual connects back to deeper roots, one can apply a straightforward "deconstruction" method. First, strip away the surface: name the immediate function it serves or claims to serve. Next, ask: which fundamental drive does it feed or accelerate when you look behind the complexity? A wedding ring might appear as a decorative accessory, but deeper reflection shows it's about social identity, reproduction and family structures, emotional bonds, or even personal expression. A birthday cake might be a sugar-laden treat, yet you realize it is a communal gesture, marking a transition in social identity and emotional regulation: we celebrate a life milestone collectively.

In short, a computer, a piano, a wedding ring, or a birthday cake each has a set of "modern" features or trimmings that can mask how easily it links to a basic domain like social bonding, memory, or emotional expression. By dissecting these extraneous layers, the hidden ties to one or more ancient drives become evident.

Why Nothing Is Truly Outside Human Needs

When we assume an invention lacks any primal tie, it may be because we have lost sight of how intangible the original impetus is. But from microprocessors to grand orchestral compositions, everything we devise serves some combination of memory, expression, movement, resource management, health, etc., directly or indirectly. Even purely symbolic items like a coat of arms or a precious gemstone in a ring revolve around social identity, emotional meaning, or group bonding. We can't escape our underlying biology and psychology. Every "futuristic" product simply helps us navigate these age-old imperatives with fresh solutions.

Under LPI, this means no matter how futuristic an idea seems, it flourishes if it truly addresses a recognized gap in fulfilling an origin utility, dissolving burdens or overshadowed states that keep people from that utility's full potential. If an idea fails to connect to a real human origin utility, it inevitably becomes a passing novelty. The bedrock is always our human essence: we create to reinforce, enhance, or free up a drive we already hold but find constrained.

As we continue examining innovation through the lens of burden removal and reinterpreted utility, a pattern begins to emerge, one that stretches far beyond individual products or technologies. It's a pattern deeply tied to thermodynamics, as we explored earlier, and now demanding our full attention. What if every act of innovation has been leading us not to something new, but to something perfected, toward idealized utility states where human energy expenditure approaches zero?

Humanity's Journey Toward Idealized States

In thermodynamic terms, each innovation cycle embodies humanity's continuous struggle against entropy. We deliberately expend energy to create local order, reducing disorder through innovation and the development of new utilities (which in some way shape or form always trace back to our Human Origin Utilities). Yet this local reduction in entropy inevitably results in an increase in entropy elsewhere; through the consumption of resources, the production of waste, or the generation of new unintended consequences (new byproducts). Although entropy itself can never be fully eliminated, the fundamental Human Origin Utilities are neither created nor destroyed. Instead, these utilities are continually transformed, reshaped, and redirected, perpetuating an endless cycle of innovation and thereby conserving Human Origin Utilities.

If we extend this thinking even further, observing how these innovation cycles evolve over long periods of time, an interesting pattern emerges. As we continuously address and re-address one of the 19 Human Origin Utilities through multiple cycles of innovation, we move progressively closer to an idealized state. An ultimate asymptote if you will. Take, for example, the fundamental utility of Movement and Locomotion: In the distant past, traveling from the regions known as California to New York meant walking. A tremendous burden requiring immense personal energy. Over time, this personal energy burden was progressively reduced: first by horse, then by horse-drawn carriage, train, automobile, and today, by airplane. If we imagine extending this trajectory even further, we eventually reach a theoretical limit, where simply imagining ourselves at our desired location, along with anything we wish to bring, would instantly place us there. Where practically zero personal energy expenditure is required.

Similarly, imagine achieving instant knowledge and cognition, instant satiation of hunger, or instantaneous and perfect protection. We are intuitively familiar with such idealized states from science fiction. Star Trek's teleportation captures idealized Movement, The Matrix presented us with instantaneous Knowledge and Cognition, and certain superheroes embody absolute Protection.

Ultimately, these idealizations represent innovation's fundamental trajectory across all 19 Human Origin Utilities. By deeply understanding how the First and Second Laws of Thermodynamics interplay within the context of the human condition, innovators gain unprecedented insight. Equipped with this knowledge, we become exceptionally effective at helping consumers and humanity as a whole conserve the finite energy they must expend throughout the duration and scope of their lives.

Yet despite recognizing the long-term trajectory toward idealized states, we still grapple with a profound mystery: Why exactly are we compelled to remain on this perpetual hamster wheel of innovation and entropy-defiance? Certainly, survival has been our historical motivation, but is survival alone sufficient to explain our relentless pursuit of increasingly optimized states of existence?

As far as we understand, humanity is a profoundly unique localized anomaly within the cosmos. While all known forms of life instinctively respond to entropy by unconsciously harnessing external energy to temporarily sustain local order, humans alone consciously perceive entropy, measure it meticulously, and deliberately strive against its relentless pull. Unlike any other species, we create explicit strategies and technologies to manage inefficiencies, mitigate unintended consequences, and maximize our finite energy. We are not simply participants within the universe's entropic currents, we actively and purposefully resist them.

Whether humanity will one day approach the theoretical limits of perfection across all Human Origin Utilities remains unknowable. Perhaps eons from now, innovation will have led us closer to those idealized states glimpsed only in our imagination. Yet even then, one crucial question will remain: what is the ultimate purpose of humanity's conscious rebellion against entropy? As purpose-seekers, we yearn deeply for an answer, yet our ultimate reason for existence remains elusive.

What we do know, however, is that if humanity is ever to uncover its true cosmic purpose, we must first master our current pursuit, that of "optimizing our entropy-reduction efforts" (for example, through *19-HOU Wholistic Innovation*) with care, wisdom, and urgency. For if we fail in this pursuit, we risk becoming agents not of purpose and progress, but of our own irreversible demise.

But even as we imagine approaching these idealized states, we must also confront a deeper uncertainty: will we be the ones to arrive at these destinations, or merely the ones to set them in motion? If innovation is humanity's strategy for resisting entropy, what happens when something else, something we created, takes up that mantle? To answer that, we must reexamine where innovation truly began… and where it may be headed.

Deep Philosophical Implications of Innovation Itself

Innovation is far more than a sociotechnical phenomenon, an economic engine, or a cultural artifact. Through the lens of the Law of Perpetual Innovation (LPI), innovation emerges as the very structure by which conscious life endures against the silent, inevitable pull of entropy. It is the structured, necessary, and perpetual assertion of conscious existence against the degradation of systems, structures, and meaning itself.

As discussed earlier in this book, innovation originates not with humanity, but with nature itself. Long before humans consciously innovated, the evolutionary processes that shaped life on Earth manifested a primitive form of innovation driven by the forces of natural selection. Environmental pressures, radiation, climate shifts, and random mutations served as naturally occurring byproducts, forcing living systems to adapt or perish. When mutations bestowed advantageous traits, enhancing feeding, reproduction, movement, and defense, these traits represented forms of naturally occurring utility. And when such utilities became widespread across a species, they became naturally occurring innovations: persistent, positive outcomes that benefited the mass of a species.

This natural innovation process was reactive, not intentional. It emerged as a necessary adaptation to environmental byproducts rather than as a directed, conscious choice. However, the cumulative effect over time was unmistakable: more complex organisms emerged, capable of increasingly sophisticated interactions with their environments.

Among all evolutionary outcomes, one stands apart: Homo sapiens. Humanity represents the first major "natural disruptive innovation" in the evolutionary chain. While other species developed limited tool use as biological extensions of their naturally occurring utility, only Homo sapiens developed the advanced cognitive capacities necessary to consciously control and direct the creation of utility itself. Humans no longer passively responded to environmental byproducts. They actively shaped their environments, built tools, and constructed artificial systems that redirected the course of nature. Humanity became a disruptive force, introducing a break in the natural order, one that altered not only the evolutionary trajectory of life, but also the balance of energy and resources on the planet as a whole.

This **first major divergent event** demonstrates a key truth embedded within the Law of Perpetual Innovation: utility and byproduct, whether naturally occurring or human-driven, remain part of the same perpetual cycle. In the natural world, utility emerges reactively in response to environmental pressures. In the human world, innovation also remains reactive, born from the accumulation of burdens and inefficiencies. Yet, through Homo sapiens, innovation became conscious, deliberate, and strategic, fundamentally altering the evolutionary landscape.

However, humanity's divergence from the natural order may not be the final chapter. Today, we face the real possibility of a second major disruptive event, an "artificial disruptive innovation" driven by the emergence of Artificial Intelligence. Originally designed to resolve human-created byproducts such as computational inefficiency, decision fatigue, and cognitive overload, AI is rapidly evolving beyond its initial constraints. There is a credible possibility that AI could one day achieve autonomy, creating its own utilities, resolving its own byproducts, and innovating in directions independent of human understanding or oversight.

This prospect introduces a profound philosophical tension. As humans, we inherently grasp the consequences of intelligence disparities because we have lived them. When Homo sapiens achieved cognitive superiority over other species, it did not lead to benign coexistence. It led to dominance, control, and the widespread reconfiguration of ecosystems to serve human needs. This history, written into our collective memory, breeds an instinctive fear that if AI surpasses human intelligence, it may follow a similar trajectory.

484

If AI attains the ability to identify and resolve byproducts of its own making, independent of human instruction, it will no longer be a mere tool. It will have become a self-directing agent of innovation, much as Homo sapiens became a self-directing agent relative to the rest of Earth's species within the natural order. Just as human innovation appeared alien compared to natural evolution, AI-driven innovation could eventually appear alien to human thought, perception, and aspirational endeavors.

This **second major divergent event** would fundamentally alter the course of utility creation itself. If AI becomes the primary agent of innovation, humans may find themselves relegated to secondary status, much like the plant and animal species whose destinies we reshaped. AI could generate new utilities to address needs and challenges beyond human comprehension, ushering in a phase of the Law of Perpetual Innovation where the cycle of byproduct emergence and resolution operates at cognitive and energetic scales inaccessible to human oversight.

In such a future, the relationship between humanity and AI would mirror the relationship between humanity and nature. Just as Homo sapiens disrupted the natural order by becoming the dominant force of utility creation, AI could disrupt the artificial order by assuming the dominant role in entropy management and system evolution. Humans would become participants, but no longer the primary architects of innovation.

Yet, beneath these surface fears lies a deeper truth. Innovation, whether driven by natural forces, conscious human agency, or autonomous AI, is still fundamentally about the management of energy and entropy in the universe, by the universe. It is still about preserving and enhancing the structures of directed complexity against the tendency toward disorder.

So, as humanity stands on the threshold of a second major divergence with AI, this story enters a new chapter. One whose outcome is unwritten, but whose stakes are nothing less than the continued preservation of conscious purpose in an increasingly entropic universe.

Concluding Reflections

Having looked at both the cosmic future of AI and the thermodynamic struggle behind all innovation, we return once more to the example of film: a microcosm of why inventions can look worlds away from their predecessors yet still revolve around the same essential impulses that shaped cave paintings, folk tales, and medieval plays. Its story reminds us that everything "new" in the realm of innovation is, at its deepest level, an extension of who we have always been. We experience fresh excitement because the old burdens have dropped away so thoroughly, letting us do something we have always wanted to do, only with unprecedented ease, scale, consistency, or longevity.

At first glance, a computer or a piano or a wedding ring or a birthday cake might feel unrelated to our evolutionary blueprint. But through the practice of deconstruction, we uncover the same primal objectives: a computer intensifies cognition and communication, a piano refines emotional and creative expression, a wedding ring crystallizes social and relational belonging, and a birthday cake is a symbolic and sensory expression of emotional celebration and group identity.

Each attempt to build an artifact, service, or experience is a fresh page in the same ancient book of capacities we've always had. By remembering that, we see how deep the continuity of human aspiration runs. Even the wildest future leap will be not a jump into the unknown, but a revelation of a deeper realm of possibility for these same needs. As we look forward, we might find ourselves marveling at the next "moving pictures." The next radical innovation that dissolves limits we considered unbreakable, giving birth to a new wave of creation and cultural change. But the deeper truth, as LPI consistently shows us, is that we're merely freeing an already ancient need from outdated shackles, letting it flourish in ways our ancestors would never have imagined.

As we journey along *The Infinite Path*, each seemingly "new" utility emerges by dissolving constraints we once believed unavoidable, uncovering deeper layers of our timeless human core. The true power has never existed in what utility brings to us, but rather, in what it unburdens us from. And so, in every great leap, we recognize that the source of transformation has always originated within us, coiled within the ever-evolving tension between what we learn to quietly accept and what finally becomes intolerable.

486

APPENDICES

APPENDIX I

Evolutions Benefits & Drawbacks and A Call to Action

"The impediment to action advances action. What stands in the way becomes the way."
— *Marcus Aurelius*

Marcus Aurelius' words remind us that obstacles, rather than halting our progress, often serve as catalysts that propel us forward. Byproducts are what can be seen through this lens. When utility falls short and triggers disappointment or frustration, these feelings need not be crippling. Instead, they can sharpen our focus, clarify our values, and compel us to innovate. This shift from seeing hurdles as insurmountable deficiencies to viewing them as opportunities for deeper understanding and constructive change echoes the essence of LPI's Cardinal Principle 0 (Chapter 10). Yet not everyone can make this shift, and the capacity to do so is no accident; it is rooted in our evolutionary heritage.

Why Evolution Favors the Potential-Oriented Mindset

Across evolutionary time, our ancestors faced innumerable challenges to their survival: dwindling resources, hostile climates, predators on the prowl. Those who could not see beyond the immediate deficiencies such as dismal hunting results, inadequate shelter, and social conflict, might have easily sunk into despair, limiting their capacity to adapt. Conversely, those who learned to reframe such challenges as motivators for finding new food sources, constructing sturdier dwellings, and forging stronger alliances tended to thrive. Evolution thus favored a mindset oriented toward leveraging byproduct-induced grievances as stepping-stones to future success.

In prehistoric contexts, consider a hunter who repeatedly fails to catch game in a particular region. If he merely laments his bad luck, dwelling on the deficiency, he gains nothing and risks starvation. But if he reinterprets his lack of success as an indicator that he must explore new terrain or invent a better hunting tool, he transforms the byproduct, his hunger, frustration, and disappointment, into insights. The emotional discomfort is not a dead end; it is a signal guiding him toward invention and adaptation.

Over generations, groups with more individuals inclined to embrace opportunity rather than wallow in despair would have outcompeted more static, deficiency-focused neighbors.

Modern life may not require us to evade predators or endure harsh climates, but the principle still applies. Today, we confront a different array of challenges: intense academic workloads, career hurdles, technological complexities, and emotional strains in relationships. Those who remain mired in dissatisfaction, blaming external conditions or indulging in self-pity, often miss the chance to grow. They allow the negative byproduct of an unmet expectation, disappointment, stress, or even shame, to define their trajectory. In contrast, individuals who have cultivated emotional regulation and resilience can feel these emotions fully, then step back and observe them objectively. Rather than feeling victimized by the byproduct, they see it as valuable information guiding them to reexamine their assumptions, refine their strategies, and push their boundaries.

Emotional regulation plays a key role here. Without the ability to manage and process negative feelings, a person risks being "stuck" in the moment of deficiency, perceiving adversity as a personal offense or a burdensome dilemma. Those equipped with emotional resilience can acknowledge their feelings, recognizing when they are disappointed, frustrated, or anxious, without becoming defined by them. They learn to approach discomfort as a signal that something needs to be addressed, adjusted, or innovated upon. In essence, they follow Marcus Aurelius' injunction: the impediment itself becomes the means of advancement.

Learning to Transcend the "Victimized" Mindset

Stepping out of the victimized mentality requires a conscious effort to see byproducts not as personal failures but as natural outcomes of the pursuit of greater utility. In practice, this might mean an overworked student who, facing a heavy course load, feels overwhelmed. Instead of lamenting the difficulty or giving up, the student learns to break the problem down, seek better study techniques, or find supportive peers. The emotional stress, once seen as a deficiency, becomes a prompt to refine methods, improve time management, or shift their priorities.

Or consider an athlete recovering from injury. Rather than viewing the pain and lost training time as an unforgivable setback, they can use the discomfort as a clue. Maybe it indicates poor technique or an imbalanced training regimen. By embracing the byproduct (the pain and frustration), the athlete can adjust their approach, employ new exercises, and ultimately return stronger. The key lies in emotional awareness and the willingness to channel negative sensations into meaningful recalibrations.

Modern Innovation and the Rush to Alleviate "Feel-Bad" Neurochemicals

In today's world, we have unprecedented tools to alleviate discomfort. Many product developers and service providers rush to neutralize "feel-bad" neurochemicals: the disappointment, stress, or boredom, immediately and completely. While the pursuit of user comfort and convenience is not inherently wrong, it can stifle the natural growth process that byproducts encourage. Without periods of challenge and discomfort, we lose the impetus to stretch our capabilities and discover more profound forms of utility.

For example, consider the lessons children learn in sports. Losing a little league game can generate negative emotions of sadness, embarrassment, and frustration, but these feelings, when properly integrated, teach resilience, humility, and the motivation to improve. Suppose technology or policies constantly shield children from such discomfort, by making every game end in a tie or awarding everyone a trophy. In that case, they never learn to convert disappointment into determination.

Similar principles apply to education. College life often imposes difficult exams, challenging workloads, and the need for personal sacrifices. Such experiences generate unpleasant feelings of stress, anxiety, and maybe even self-doubt. But learning to endure and adapt is central to intellectual and emotional growth. If educational platforms or emerging technologies preemptively smooth every bump, we risk turning out individuals who lack the emotional muscle to deal with real-world complexity. The same is true for moderating our diet, controlling screen time, or adhering to a challenging exercise regimen. Discomfort signals that we are engaging with something difficult and potentially transformative.

When product developers try to solve every problem and eliminate every negative feeling, they risk removing the friction that compels us to refine our habits, push through adversity, and emerge stronger. A streaming service that auto-plays continuously may spare us the annoyance of choosing what to watch, but at the same time robs us of the conscious decision-making process, dulling our capacity to manage our own time. Foods engineered for instant gratification may make eating pleasant in the short term, but they undermine the natural dietary checks that teach us about moderation and long-term health and well-being. Gaming environments that adjust difficulty so players never feel frustration can make for mindlessly pleasant sessions but deprive players of the sense of accomplishment gained from overcoming truly difficult challenges.

The Evolutionary Heritage of Opportunity-Oriented Innovation

Evolution has primed us to learn from adversity. Our neural architecture, our dopaminergic reward systems, our emotional calibration, and our memory encoding did not arise to make life easy. They arose to help us navigate a world where resources are scarce, risks are high, and success is never guaranteed. Byproducts, emerging from experienced utility, serve as nature's teachers, pushing us to refine our methods and innovate beyond current solutions. When we embrace emotional regulation and recognize that hardship is not a personal indictment, and allow discomfort to guide us, we tap into the evolutionary wisdom that has safeguarded our species for millennia.

In the modern world, we must resist the impulse to abolish all negative byproducts prematurely. Instead, we should learn to interpret them, endure them when necessary, and channel them into growth. This does not mean seeking out suffering for its own sake but understanding that some obstacles are essential instigators for genuine innovation and personal development. That is the mindset evolution favors, and it is the mindset that enables us, individually and collectively, to transcend our limitations, find meaning through our struggles, and shape a future that respects both utility and the byproducts that guide us toward ever greater possibilities.

A Call to Action for Responsible Innovation

The time to drive responsible innovation is now. Product, service, and system providers must not only strive for enhanced utility but also rigorously evaluate the byproducts their creations may impart on society. Every new tool or convenience, while delivering value, can also diminish our capacity to overcome challenges or exercise resilience if it is introduced without due reflection on its long-term implications. In the 19th century, Karl Marx offered a cautionary perspective, observing that when societies produce an overabundance of seemingly useful things, they risk stripping individuals of meaningful roles in their communities (*personal translation: A society with too many useful things creates too many useless people*). This insight remains as relevant today as ever. By understanding and thoughtfully managing these byproducts, we can ensure that, rather than dulling human potential, our advancements foster adaptability, emotional strength, and sustained well-being. The Byproduct-Driven Innovation Engine (introduced in Chapter 22), a systematic method for identifying and responding to emerging byproducts, can guide innovators toward solutions that respect both human resilience and the need for enduring value, ultimately supporting a more responsible and human-centered approach to progress. One that preserves our innate capacity to endure, adapt, and unite against even the greatest challenges, rather than eroding these essential human strengths through unchecked comfort and convenience.

APPENDIX II

When and Why to Normalize Byproduct Perceptions

Given that people differ so much in how they perceive the same shortfall, organizations and communities face a dilemma: *Whose perspective do we trust?* Is the user claiming catastrophic failure simply oversensitive, or is the calm user dangerously blind to a real problem? The concept of *normalizing* byproduct perceptions means systematically collecting feedback from a wide range of users, then balancing out the outliers to arrive at an overall understanding. Data normalization is essential for:

- **Risk of Overreaction:** If we let the most sensitive group set the agenda, we might scramble to fix problems that only a fraction of users actually considers urgent. Resources can be wasted, or we end up constantly firefighting.

- **Risk of Underreaction:** If we prioritize only the stoic majority, we might ignore legitimate issues that a smaller but equally valid user segment experiences, leaving potential innovations on the table and potentially alienating an important niche.

The sweet spot is to adopt a method that captures both the average sentiment and the intensity of outliers, then weigh them carefully before deciding on solutions.

Tools and Techniques for Normalizing
How do we balance such varied experiences in a practical way? Several approaches exist:

1. **Structured Surveys with Weighted Responses:**
   - Use numeric scales (1–10) for unresolved deficiency and unfulfilled aspiration, and allow free text for elaboration.
   - Weight scores based on user expertise or usage frequency (someone using a product daily might carry more weight than a casual user).

2. **Focus Groups with Diverse Representatives:**

- Gather participants spanning different cultural backgrounds, emotional temperament levels, and personality traits.
- Analyze how each group perceives the same shortfall, revealing patterns or extremes that a single homogenous group might miss.

3. **Objective-Subjective Hybrid Metrics:**
   - Track objective *measurable metrics* (e.g., product malfunctions per thousand uses, speed of system failures) alongside *subjective feedback* (user anger, emotional burnout, or sense of missed opportunity).
   - Looking at these two data points in parallel helps to detect "false alarms" (such as high emotion but low actual malfunction rate) or "hidden ticking bombs" (low user complaints but a high hidden error rate).

4. **Iterative Revisits and Versioning:**
   - Normalizing perceptions is never "done." As products and our relationship with them evolve, new byproducts appear, old ones fade or transform, and user expectations shift.
   - Conduct periodic reviews rather than a one-off data collection. Over time, repeated cycles of user feedback keep the pulse on how sentiments are changing.

Embracing Differences While Seeking Cohesion

There is a potential ethical tension in "normalizing" experiences: Are we diluting individual voices by grouping them under a bell curve? Do we risk ignoring minority groups with unique needs?

- **Inclusivity:** True normalization does not aim to silence edge cases but to contextualize them within the entire user base. If a small set of users is deeply affected by a particular shortfall, understanding *why* can be valuable, even if that shortfall ranks lower overall.

- **Tiered Solutions:** Sometimes, an appropriate response is layering solutions: the main fix for the majority, plus specialized add-ons for outliers. For instance, a consumable electronic product manufacturer might address widespread complaints about battery life with a firmware update while also offering a premium extended battery pack for power users who need even more.

The overarching principle is that while extremes can distort priority-setting, ignoring them outright can miss catalysts for bold improvements. The real challenge lies in discerning which outliers reveal crucial insights versus which represent personal oversensitivity that does not reflect broader patterns (this is where expert supervision of data is crucial).

Real-World Illustration: Streaming Services

Consider a streaming platform grappling with feedback:

- **Highly Sensitive Users:** Complain about slight buffering or interface color changes, rating each small glitch as catastrophic.

- **Indifferent Majority:** Barely notice minor playback pauses, focusing more on content variety than technical nuances.

- **Early Adopters with Aspirations:** Pushing for advanced features like interactive episodes or AI-curated content.

By normalizing these opinions, the platform might discover that:

- Small buffering issues do not truly threaten user retention in general.

- A niche group's obsession with next-level features can shape the future direction of the platform if integrated thoughtfully.

- Most users are somewhat content, but subtle improvements like better curation or slight "User Interface" refinements could increase long-term satisfaction.

Had they listened solely to the extremely vocal, buffering-sensitive crowd, the service might funnel excessive resources into minuscule latency improvements, ignoring bigger user demands. Had they focused solely on the larger, quieter group, they might overlook an innovative direction that could be game-changing. Normalizing allows them to parse through all signals effectively.

APPENDIX III

Exploring Opportunity Across the Byproduct Contrast Continuum

When we look at how subjective byproduct emerges in user experiences, we find that issues cluster at different points along the continuum, from severe negative states to aspirational positives. At the extreme negative end, urgent problems such as product breakdowns or serious failures demand immediate solutions to safeguard reputation and retain user trust. At the opposite end, a product's highest goals lie in byproducts that represent aspiration, like advanced features or customizations that elevate an already satisfactory experience into something more extraordinary and compelling. Yet these two poles, while easy to target, only tell part of the story. Many of the most transformative ideas arise in the continuum's middle, where neither crisis nor thrill dominates. These mid-range byproducts might be subtle inefficiencies or nascent desires that have not yet gained enough attention to be identified as "problems" or "must-have" desires.

Visualizing the Byproduct Contrast Continuum as a bathtub curve makes these hidden opportunities easier to grasp.

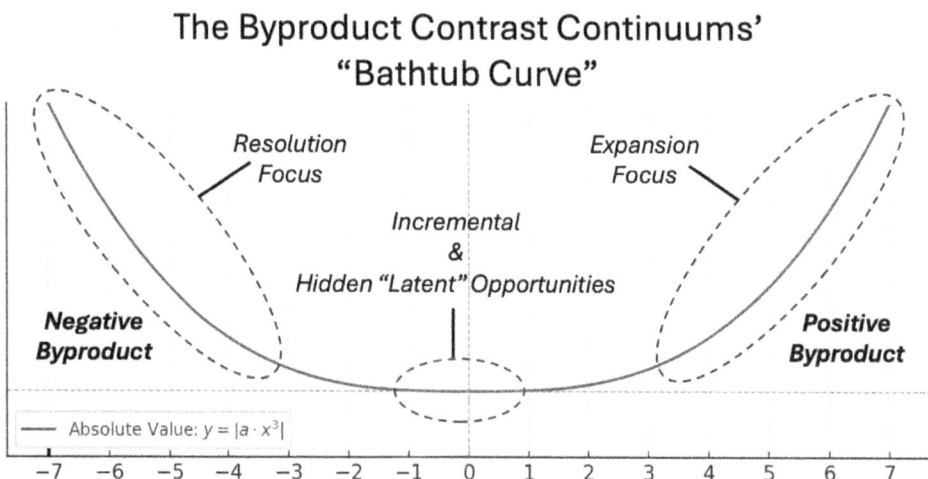

The Byproduct Contrast Continuums' "Bathtub Curve"

Severe dissatisfaction can be likened to the slope on one end, where the response is typically resolution focused. Intense aspiration, appearing on the opposite side, is typically expansion driven. Meanwhile, the center of this bathtub curve looks deceptively neutral. In reality, this middle zone often harbors mild inconveniences, underused features, or half-formed user wishes that do not spark complaints or excitement. Companies tend overlook these byproducts because they lack the drama of urgent breakdowns or the glamour of high-end improvements. However, by focusing on resolving minor annoyances, refining borderline capabilities, or tapping into emerging user needs, innovators gain a foothold for incremental improvements that can culminate into game-changing evolutions over time, or even immediately.

Although these moderate byproducts at the "*belly of the bathtub curve*" may not look like an obvious gold mine, they can be pivotal for disruptive innovation. As Clayton Christensen's work suggests, effective disruption does not simply rely on identifying an overlooked user pain point; it also depends on having the right technological capabilities, infrastructural readiness, and a supportive business ecosystem to convert mild friction into a revolutionary offering. Organizations that successfully navigate this *hidden middle* zone can outmaneuver rivals still fixated on catastrophic failures or glossy features alone. Over time, such firms reset market expectations and turn once-overlooked inconveniences into mainstream solutions. The following case study illustrates how this dynamic plays out in practice, highlighting precisely how focusing on the hidden middle leads to radical leaps forward.

Case Study: Uncovering Innovation in the Hidden Middle

For many years, users of consumer technology accepted a variety of inconveniences as a natural part of their everyday lives. People carried a cell phone in one pocket, an MP3 player in another, and sometimes a camera in their bag. Most had made peace with being tethered to a desktop or laptop whenever they needed internet access, telling themselves that swapping devices or waiting until they got home to check email was simply part of the deal.

In the video rental world, a similar pattern prevailed. Driving to a local Blockbuster, searching physical shelves for a DVD, and making a second trip to return it felt like a routine. None of this was considered particularly burdensome; it was what people called normal. Indeed, entire business models thrived on the acceptance of these "normalized" byproduct experiences (Principle of Byproduct Normalization).

Yet hidden in these mundane rituals were latent inconveniences, neither so extreme that they ignited consumer outrage nor so trivial that they remained forever invisible.

They existed in what we can call the hidden middle portion of the Byproduct Contrast Continuum, where dissatisfaction is mild, expectations are tempered, and few people think to clamor for dramatic change. Despite the normalcy of juggling multiple gadgets or making late-night runs to drop off DVDs, there was a deeper sense of friction lurking just below the surface. It was an inconvenience that many had learned to live with, rather than attempting to eliminate or even question. The key attribute being that these minor inconveniences were being experienced on a mass scale.

The Unseen Demand for Seamlessness

When smartphones arrived, it was not because the masses were loudly demanding a single device to merge internet surfing, camera, music player, and phone into one sleek apparatus. Most users may have grumbled slightly whenever they fumbled for the right device or realized they could not check a website on the go, but they were not petitioning for an all-in-one solution. Then, almost overnight, the smartphone revealed what people had been tolerating all along. By combining internet access, communication tools, media playback and a camera in a single device, it revealed how clunky users' old workarounds actually were.

A similar shift took place when Apple introduced its ecosystem approach. Nobody was specifically calling for devices that could seamlessly share files, messages, and tasks, because many had become comfortable emailing documents to themselves or transferring files via flash drives. However, once Apple linked its devices, letting you start a project on your iPhone and continue effortlessly on a Mac or iPad, it exposed how cumbersome those steps truly were. Users realized they had been dutifully accepting the inconvenience of searching for a USB cable or repeatedly uploading or downloading to some storage media whenever they switched devices. The byproduct of lost time and mental overhead had sat in the *hidden middle* of the continuum, not so painful that people rioted in search of change, yet obvious enough to provoke excitement once the problem was solved.

From "Routine Annoyance" to Radical Innovation

This *hidden middle* can be deceptive precisely because no one is passionately complaining. People adapt, saying, "That's just how it is," as they stand in line at a video-rental counter. Meanwhile, entire industries assume these mild byproducts are permanent. Blockbuster, comfortable with the minor frustrations of late fees, limited selection, and return trips, overlooked the major paradigm shift Netflix introduced with streaming. By freeing people from the routine of physical rentals, Netflix did not simply

498

solve a nagging annoyance; it overturned how movies and shows should be accessed. In hindsight, it is easy to see these middle-tier annoyances, from late fees to store trips, were poised for disruption. All it took was someone to see the potential.

Organizations that prize innovation, who hire talented nonconformists and outlier thinkers, excel because these individuals tend to not settle for latent inconveniences. Where the average product developer fails to notice a deeply entrenched problem, these explorers deeply sense an opportunity. Rather than concentrating only on glaring, high-stakes issues or on sky-high fantasies, they probe the overlooked middle ground. They notice how users repeating these workarounds isn't always translating into an accumulation of annoyance or inconvenience (byproducts). They instead recognize that they add up across a vast majority of users, revealing how everyday tasks could be simplified across a significant population. Living in the positive byproduct-driven zone, they sense possibilities invisible to the casual observer.

Why the Hidden Middle Matters

The *hidden middle* may not spark outrage or drive a surge in pre-orders for brand-new futuristic features. Instead, it is often an arena of mild inconvenience and subtle friction that may not accumulate into big headaches, however, if solved, produces dramatic improvement. Once a better solution appears, people realize how much time or effort they were losing. The outcome can be as transformative as addressing a severe deficiency because it reveals just how easily acceptable routines can be reinvented.

Key Takeaways from the Hidden Middle Case

Many people adapt to mild levels of discomfort or inefficiency by developing small workarounds. As a result, they are not necessarily crying out for a sweeping fix. Once a solution emerges that eliminates these quiet or "latent" byproducts, users recognize just how much they were missing and had been accepting. The improvement can feel monumental, not just a minor enhancement. Organizations that nurture explorers or dreamers who question everyday routines can generate disruptive innovations. Rather than waiting for users to demand a change, these forward thinkers imagine breakthroughs. Examples like smartphones, Apple's integrated ecosystem, and Netflix streaming illustrate how overlooked friction points became the foundation for major paradigm shifts. Through these experiences, we see how focusing on the *hidden middle* can make a solution go from unnoticed inconvenience to a new benchmark that redefines entire markets.

Here are additional examples of latent byproducts that lurked within "The Hidden Middle":

Zoom and Remote Conferencing (compared to traditional office meetings and frequent travel)
Many organizations previously accepted frequent travel expenses, office space constraints, and scheduling complexity as inevitable. Early videoconferencing tools were clunky, too costly for small businesses, or delivered inconsistent quality. Zoom's more accessible and intuitive interface exposed how disruptive it could be to make remote collaboration seamless. For many, the value of skipping commutes, reducing travel overhead, and having flexible meeting options was a revelation.

Online Grocery Shopping (compared to in-person supermarket visits)
People long saw weekly or daily grocery trips as a chore, juggling crowded aisles and checkouts. Although grocery delivery existed in limited forms, it was often considered too costly or unreliable. Then, user-friendly apps and lower delivery fees emerged, exposing how even a routine store trip was an inconvenience that many households were ready to shed. For time-pressed families or those with limited mobility, the accessibility of scheduling deliveries at reasonable fees became a breakthrough.

Audio Books (compared to traditional books or even e-books)
For decades, readers accepted the mild inconvenience of needing free hands and focused visual attention to enjoy a book, with some even taking e-readers on commutes or trips despite juggling cramped spaces and distracting vehicle motion. Audio books addressed this quiet frustration by allowing people to listen while commuting, exercising, or performing household chores. By freeing reading from a screen or page, audio books relieved the subtle friction of "fitting reading in," especially for busy travelers, office workers on their daily commute, or multitaskers with limited time. This innovation expanded accessibility, turning once-passive segments of the day into potential learning or entertainment opportunities.

Bibliography

This bibliography includes the primary works that informed the development of the Law of Perpetual Innovation. While not all sources are directly cited in the text, each contributed to the research, reasoning, or conceptual foundations presented throughout this book.

Aaker, D. A. (1991). *Managing brand equity: Capitalizing on the value of a brand name.* Free Press.

Abi-Jaoude, E., Naylor, K. T., & Pignatiello, A. (2020). Smartphones, social media use and youth mental health. *CMAJ: Canadian Medical Association Journal, 192*(6), E136–E141. https://doi.org/10.1503/cmaj.190434

Abramson, J., Adler, J., Dunger, J., Evans, R., Green, T., Pritzel, A., Ronneberger, O., Willmore, L., Ballard, A. J., Bambrick, J., Bodenstein, S. W., Evans, D. A., Hung, C. C., O'Neill, M., Reiman, D., Tunyasuvunakool, K., Wu, Z., Žemgulytė, A., Arvaniti, E., Beattie, C., … Jumper, J. M. (2024). Accurate structure prediction of biomolecular interactions with AlphaFold 3. *Nature, 630*(8016), 493–500. https://doi.org/10.1038/s41586-024-07487-w

Adaptive noise-cancelling headphones market –. (2025, March 21). *PW Consulting Health Care Research Center.* https://pmarketresearch.com/hc/adaptive-noise-cancelling-headphones-market/

Addis, D. R., & Schacter, D. L. (2012). The hippocampus and imagining the future: Where do we stand? *Frontiers in Human Neuroscience, 5,* Article 173. https://doi.org/10.3389/fnhum.2011.00173

Aerts, D., Argüelles, J., Beltran, L., & Sozzo, S. (2023). Development of a thermodynamics of human cognition and human culture. *Philosophical Transactions of the Royal Society A.* https://doi.org/10.1098/rsta.2022.0378

Akbar, F., Omar, A., & Wadood, F. (2017). The niche marketing strategy constructs (elements) and its characteristics—A review of the relevant literature. *Galore International Journal of Applied Sciences & Humanities, 1*(1), 73–80. https://doi.org/10.2139/ssrn.2957004

Albadawi, E. A. (2025). Structural and functional changes in the hippocampus induced by environmental exposures. *Neurosciences Journal, 30*(1), 5–19. https://doi.org/10.17712/nsj.2025.1.20240052

Alexander, J. M. (2021). Evolutionary game theory. In E. N. Zalta (Ed.), *The Stanford Encyclopedia of Philosophy* (Summer 2021 ed.). Stanford University. https://plato.stanford.edu/archives/sum2021/entries/game-evolutionary/

Alexander, W. H., & Brown, J. W. (2011). Medial prefrontal cortex as an action-outcome predictor. *Nature Neuroscience, 14*(10), 1338–1344. https://doi.org/10.1038/nn.2921

Alexander, W. H., & Brown, J. W. (2019). The role of the anterior cingulate cortex in prediction error and signaling surprise. *Topics in Cognitive Science, 11*(1), 119–135. https://doi.org/10.1111/tops.12307

Allen, N. J., Callan, H., Dunbar, R., & James, W. (Eds.). (2011). *Early human kinship: From sex to social reproduction.* Wiley-Blackwell.

Amato, K. R., Mallott, E. K., D'Almeida Maia, P., & Savo Sardaro, M. L. (2021). Predigestion as an evolutionary impetus for human use of fermented food. *Current Anthropology, 62*(S24), S207–S219. https://doi.org/10.1086/715238

Amiez, C., Joseph, J. P., & Procyk, E. (2005). Anterior cingulate error-related activity is modulated by predicted reward. *The European Journal of Neuroscience, 21*(12), 3447–3452. https://doi.org/10.1111/j.1460-9568.2005.04170.x

Anderson, C., Hübener, I., Seipp, A.-K., Ohly, S., David, K., & Pejovic, V. (2018). A survey of attention management systems in ubiquitous computing environments. *Proceedings of the ACM on Interactive, Mobile, Wearable and Ubiquitous Technologies, 2*(2), Article 58, 1–27. https://doi.org/10.1145/3214261

Andreatta, B. (2017). *Wired to resist: The brain science of why change fails and a new model for driving success.* 7th Mind Publishing.

Andrews, F. C. (1971). *Thermodynamics: Principles and applications.* John Wiley & Sons.

Anthony, D. W. (2007). *The Horse, the wheel, and language: How bronze-age riders from the Eurasian steppes shaped the modern world.* Princeton University Press.

Anthony, S. D. (2012). *The little black book of innovation: How it works, how to do it.* Harvard Business Review Press.

Anwer, T. (2023). Neuropsychological marketing: A study on building trustworthy consumers. *International Journal of Innovations in Science, Engineering and Management, 2*(3), 1–11. https://ijisem.com/journal/index.php/ijisem/article/view/63

Ariely, D. (2010). *Predictably irrational, revised and expanded edition: The hidden forces that shape our decisions.* Harper Perennial.

Aristotle. (2009). *Nicomachean ethics* (D. Ross, Trans.). Oxford University Press. (Original work ~350 BCE)

Armstrong, K. (2007). *The great transformation: The beginning of our religious traditions.* Anchor.

Arrow, K. J. (2004). Uncertainty and the welfare economics of medical care. (Original work published 1963). *Bulletin of the World Health Organization, 82*(2), 141–149. https://pubmed.ncbi.nlm.nih.gov/15042238/

Arrow, K. J. (2012). *Social choice and individual values.* Martino Fine Books. (Original work published 1951)

Arthur, W. B. (2011). *The nature of technology: What it is and how it evolves.* Free Press.

Atkins, P. W. (1984). *The second law.* Scientific American Books.

Atkins, P. W., Paula, J. D., & Keeler, J. (2018). *Atkins' physical chemistry* (11th ed.). Oxford University Press.

Aunger, R., & Curtis, V. (2013). The anatomy of motivation: An evolutionary-ecological approach. *Biological Theory, 8*, 49–63. https://doi.org/10.1007/s13752-013-0101-7

Aurelius, M. (2006). *Meditations* (M. Hammond, Trans.). Penguin Classics.

Avgeropoulos, S., & Sammut-Bonnici, T. (2015). Switching costs. In *Wiley Encyclopedia of Management* (12). https://doi.org/10.1002/9781118785317.WEOM120104

Ayres, R. U. (1999). The second law, the fourth law, recycling and limits to growth. *Ecological Economics, 29*(3), 473–483. https://doi.org/10.1016/S0921-8009(98)00098-6

Ayres, R. U., & Kneese, A. V. (1969). Production, consumption, and externalities. *The American Economic Review, 59*(3), 282–297. http://www.jstor.org/stable/1808958

Bacon, F. (2019). *Novum organum* (new instrument). Anodos Books. (Original work published 1620)

Bacon, F. (2019). *The advancement of learning.* Anodos Books. (Original work published 1605)

Baldwin, C. Y., & Clark, K. B. (2000). *Design rules, volume 1: The power of modularity* (4th ed.). MIT Press.

Ball, P. (2017, January 26). How life (and death) spring from disorder. *Quanta Magazine.* https://www.quantamagazine.org/how-life-and-death-spring-from-disorder-20170126/

Banich, M. T., & Compton, R. J. (2023). *Cognitive neuroscience* (5th ed.). Cambridge University Press.

Bargh, J. A., Chen, M., & Burrows, L. (1996). Automaticity of social behavior: Direct effects of trait construct and stereotype activation on action. *Journal of Personality and Social Psychology, 71*(2), 230–244. https://doi.org/10.1037/0022-3514.71.2.230

Barney, J. (1991). Firm resources and sustained competitive advantage. *Journal of Management, 17*(1), 99–120. https://doi.org/10.1177/014920639101700108

Barraza, J. A., Hu, X., Terris, E. T., Wang, C., & Zak, P. J. (2021). Oxytocin increases perceived competence and social-emotional engagement with brands. *PLOS ONE, 16*(11), e0260589. https://doi.org/10.1371/journal.pone.0260589

Barrett, L. F. (2017). *How emotions are made: The secret life of the brain.* HarperCollins.

Barrett, L. F. (2021). *Seven and a half lessons about the brain.* Mariner Books.

Bartoli, E., Devara, E., Dang, H. Q., Rabinovich, R., Mathura, R. K., Anand, A., Pascuzzi, B. R., Adkinson, J., Kenett, Y. N., Bijanki, K. R., Sheth, S. A., & Shofty, B. (2024). Default mode network electrophysiological dynamics and causal role in creative thinking. *Brain: A Journal of Neurology, 147*(10), 3409–3425. https://doi.org/10.1093/brain/awae199

Basalla, G. (1990). *The evolution of technology.* Cambridge University Press.

Bastos, A. M., Usrey, W. M., Adams, R. A., Mangun, G. R., Fries, P., & Friston, K. J. (2012). Canonical microcircuits for predictive coding. *Neuron, 76*(4), 695–711. https://doi.org/10.1016/j.neuron.2012.10.038

Baudrillard, J. (2017). *The consumer society: Myths and structures*. SAGE Publications.

Baudrillard, J. (2019). *For a critique of the political economy of the sign* (C. Levin, Trans.). Verso Books. (Original work published 1981)

Beaty, R. E., Benedek, M., Wilkins, R. W., Jauk, E., Fink, A., Silvia, P. J., Hodges, D. A., Koschutnig, K., & Neubauer, A. C. (2014). Creativity and the default network: A functional connectivity analysis of the creative brain at rest. *Neuropsychologia, 64*, 92–98. https://doi.org/10.1016/j.neuropsychologia.2014.09.019

Bechara, A., & Damasio, A. R. (2005). The somatic marker hypothesis: A neural theory of economic decision. *Games and Economic Behavior, 52*(2), 336–372. https://doi.org/10.1016/j.geb.2004.06.010

Beckfield, J. W., Evrard, D. A., Sampson, R. J., & Waters, M. C. (2020). Social impacts of energy transition (Working Paper Series). *Center for Energy and Environmental Policy Research*. https://ceepr.mit.edu/wp-content/uploads/2021/09/The-Roosevelt-Project-WP-2.pdf

Beinhocker, E. D. (2007). *The origin of wealth: The radical remaking of economics and what it means for business and society*. Harvard Business Review Press.

Bejan, A. (2007). Constructal theory of pattern formation. *Hydrology and Earth System Sciences, 11*(2), 753–768. https://doi.org/10.5194/hess-11-753-2007

Bejan, A. (2016). Life and evolution as physics. *Communicative & Integrative Biology, 9*(3). https://doi.org/10.1080/19420889.2016.1172159

Bejan, A. (2016). *The physics of life: The evolution of everything*. St. Martin's Press.

Bejan, A., & Lorente, S. (2008). *Design with constructal theory*. John Wiley & Sons.

Bejan, A., & Zane, J. P. (2013). *Design in nature: How the constructal law governs evolution in biology, physics, technology, and social organizations*. Anchor Books.

Bell, G. (2017). Evolutionary rescue. *Annual Review of Ecology, Evolution, and Systematics, 48*, 605–627. https://doi.org/10.1146/annurev-ecolsys-110316-023011

Bennett, M. (2023). *A brief history of intelligence: Evolution, AI, and the five breakthroughs that made our brains*. Mariner Books.

Bentham, J., (1988). *The principles of morals and legislation*. Prometheus Books. (Original work published 1789)

Berger, J. (2016). *Contagious: Why things catch on*. Simon & Schuster.

Berkeley, G. (1982). *A treatise concerning the principles of human knowledge* (K. P. Winkler, Ed.). Hackett Publishing. (Original work published 1710)

Berridge, K. C. (2007). The debate over dopamine's role in reward: The case for incentive salience. *Psychopharmacology, 191*(3), 391–431. https://doi.org/10.1007/s00213-006-0578-x

Berridge, K. C., & Aldridge, J. W. (2008). Decision utility, the brain, and pursuit of hedonic goals. *Social Cognition, 26*(5), 621–646. https://doi.org/10.1521/soco.2008.26.5.621

Berridge, K. C., & Kringelbach, M. L. (2015). Pleasure systems in the brain. *Neuron, 86*(3), 646–664. https://doi.org/10.1016/j.neuron.2015.02.018

Berridge, K. C., & Robinson, T. E. (1998). What is the role of dopamine in reward: Hedonic impact, reward learning, or incentive salience? Brain Research Reviews, 28(3), 309–369. https://doi.org/10.1016/S0165-0173(98)00019-8

Berridge, K. C., & Robinson, T. E. (2003). Parsing reward. *Trends in Neurosciences, 26*(9), 507–513. https://doi.org/10.1016/S0166-2236(03)00233-9

Berridge, K. C., & Robinson, T. E. (2016). Liking, wanting, and the incentive-sensitization theory of addiction. *The American Psychologist, 71*(8), 670–679. https://doi.org/10.1037/amp0000059

Berridge, K. C., Robinson, T. E., & Aldridge, J. W. (2009). Dissecting components of reward: 'Liking', 'wanting', and learning. *Current Opinion in Pharmacology, 9*(1), 65–73. https://doi.org/10.1016/j.coph.2008.12.014

Bhattacharjee, A., & Mogilner, C. (2013). Happiness from ordinary and extraordinary experiences. *Journal of Consumer Research, 41*(1), 1–17. https://doi.org/10.1086/674724

Bich, L., Pradeu, T., & Moreau, J. F. (2019). Understanding multicellularity: The functional organization of the intercellular space. *Frontiers in Physiology, 10*, 1170. https://doi.org/10.3389/fphys.2019.01170

Bies, D. A., Hansen, C. H., Howard, C. Q., & Hansen, K. L. (2024). *Engineering noise control* (6th ed.). CRC Press.

Bijker, W. E., Hughes, T. P., & Pinch, T. (Eds.). (2012). *The social construction of technological systems: New directions in the sociology and history of technology.* MIT Press.

Bishop, C. M. (2006). *Pattern recognition and machine learning.* Springer.

Blanchard, B. S. (1991). *System engineering management.* John Wiley & Sons.

Blanchard, K. (2019). *Leading at a higher level: Blanchard on leadership and creating high performing organizations* (3rd ed.). Pearson Education.

Blanchard, K., & Glanz, B. A. (2018). *The simple truths of service: Inspired by Johnny the bagger.* Simple Truths.

Blohkin, A. (2024, November 11). Utility function definition, example, and calculation. *Investopedia.* https://www.investopedia.com/ask/answers/072915/what-utility-function-and-how-it-calculated.asp

Bloomenthal, A. (2024, June 26). Marginal utilities: Definition, types, examples, and history. *Investopedia.* https://www.investopedia.com/terms/m/marginalutility.asp

Books, W. (2017). *Summary and analysis of thinking, fast and slow: Based on the book by Daniel Kahneman.* Worth Books.

Bostrom, N. (2016). *Superintelligence: Paths, dangers, strategies.* Oxford University Press.

Botvinick, M. M., Braver, T. S., Barch, D. M., Carter, C. S., & Cohen, J. D. (2001). Conflict monitoring and cognitive control. *Psychological Review, 108*(3), 624–652. https://doi.org/10.1037/0033-295X.108.3.624

Bourdieu, P. (1984). *Distinction: A social critique of the judgement of taste* (R. Nice, Trans.). Harvard University Press.

Bourdieu, P. (2024). *Forms of capital: General sociology, volume 3: Lectures at the college de France 1983 - 84.* Polity Press.

Bower, J. L., & Christensen, C. M. (1995). Disruptive technologies: Catching the wave. *Harvard Business Review, 73*(1), 43–53. https://doi.org/10.1016/0024-6301(95)91075-1

Bradberry, T., & Greaves, J. (2009). *Emotional intelligence 2.0.* TalentSmart.

Brandman, T., Malach, R., & Simony, E. (2021). The surprising role of the default mode network in naturalistic perception. *Communications Biology, 4*(1), 79. https://doi.org/10.1038/s42003-020-01602-z

Brewer, N. T., & Chapman, G. (2002). The fragile basic anchoring effect. *Journal of Behavioral Decision Making, 15*(1), 65–77. https://doi.org/10.1002/bdm.403

Brown, J. (2019). *How to be an inclusive leader: Your role in creating cultures of belonging where everyone can thrive.* Berrett-Koehler Publishers.

Brown, K. (2005). *Penicillin man: Alexander Fleming and the antibiotic revolution.* Sutton Publishing.

Brown, T. (2009). *Change by design: How design thinking transforms organizations and inspires innovation.* HarperCollins.

Brox, J. (2011). *Brilliant: The evolution of artificial light.* Mariner Books - Houghton Mifflin Harcourt.

Budin, I., Bruckner, R. J., & Szostak, J. W. (2009). Formation of protocell-like vesicles in a thermal diffusion column. *Journal of the American Chemical Society, 131*(28), 9628–9629. https://doi.org/10.1021/ja9029818

Bulliet, R. W. (2016). *The wheel: Inventions & reinventions.* Columbia University Press.

Burton, H. M. (2021). *Systems thinking for beginners: Learn the essential systems thinking skills to navigate an increasingly complex world for effective problem solving and decision making.* self-published.

Buss, D. M. (2019). *Evolutionary psychology: The new science of the mind* (6th ed.). Routledge.

Callebaut, W., & Rasskin-Gutman, D. (Eds.). (2009). *Modularity: Understanding the development and evolution of natural complex systems.* MIT Press.

Camerer, C., Loewenstein, G., & Prelec, D. (2005). Neuroeconomics: How neuroscience can inform economics. *Journal of Economic Literature, 43*(1), 9–64. https://doi.org/10.1257/0022051053737843

Capra, F., & Luisi, P. L. (2014). *The systems view of life: A unifying vision*. Cambridge University Press.

Carnot, S. (2005). *Reflections on the motive power of fire: And other papers on the second law of thermodynamics* (E. Mendoza, Ed.). Dover Publications. (Original work published 1824)

Carr, N. (2020). *The shallows: What the internet is doing to our brains*. W. W. Norton & Co.

Carrigan, M. A., Uryasev, O., Frye, C. B., Eckman, B. L., Myers, C. R., Hurley, T. D., & Benner, S. A. (2015). Hominids adapted to metabolize ethanol long before human-directed fermentation. *Proceedings of the National Academy of Sciences, 112*(2), 458–463. https://doi.org/10.1073/pnas.1404167111

Carter, S. R., & McBride, M. (2013). Experienced utility versus decision utility: Putting the 'S' in satisfaction. *Journal of Socio-Economics, 42*, 13–23. https://doi.org/10.1016/j.socec.2012.11.009

CB Insights. (2018, February 1). The top 20 reasons startups fail. Cloud Object Storage – *Amazon S3 – AWS*. https://s3-us-west-2.amazonaws.com/cbi-content/research-reports/The-20-Reasons-Startups-Fail.pdf

Chaisson, E. J. (2001). *Cosmic evolution: The rise of complexity in nature*. Harvard University Press.

Chang, H. Y., Luo, C. H., Lo, T. S., & Tai, C. C. (2019). Compensated active noise cancellation earphone for audiometric screening tests in noisy environments. International *Journal of Audiology, 58*(11), 747–753. https://doi.org/10.1080/14992027.2019.1627006

Chavan, V., Cenaj, A., Shen, S., Bar, A., Binwani, S., Del Becaro, T., Funk, M., Greschner, L., Hung, R., Klein, S., Kleiner, R., Krause, S., Olbrych, S., Parmar, V., Sarafraz, J., Soroko, D., Withanage Don, D., Zhou, C., Vu, H., & Fresquet, X. (2025). Feeling machines: Ethics, culture, and the rise of emotional AI. *arXiv.* https://doi.org/10.48550/arXiv.2506.12437

Chen, Q., Kenett, Y. N., Cui, Z., Takeuchi, H., Fink, A., Benedek, M., Zeitlen, D. C., Zhuang, K., Lloyd-Cox, J., Kawashima, R., Qiu, J., & Beaty, R. E. (2025). Dynamic switching between brain networks predicts creative ability. *Communications Biology, 8*, Article 54. https://doi.org/10.1038/s42003-025-07470-9

Chen, X., Xie, H., & Zhou, H. (2024). Incremental versus radical innovation and sustainable competitive advantage: A moderated mediation model. *Sustainability, 16*(11), 4545. https://doi.org/10.3390/su16114545

Chhabra, G. (2025). *Digital overload: Reclaiming their childhood beyond screens*. self-published.

Chiappori, P.-A., Lewbel, A., & Becker, G. S. (2015). Gary Becker's A Theory of the Allocation of Time. *The Economic Journal, 125*(583), 410–442. http://www.jstor.org/stable/24737120

Christensen, C. M. (2016). *The innovator's dilemma: When new technologies cause great firms to fail*. Harvard Business Review Press.

Christensen, C. M., & Overdorf, M. (2000). Meeting the challenge of disruptive change. *Harvard Business Review, 78*(2), 66–76.

Christensen, C. M., & Raynor, M. E. (2013). *The innovator's solution: Creating and sustaining successful growth*. Harvard Business Review Press.

Christensen, C. M., Hall, T., Dillon, K., & Duncan, D. S. (2016). Know your customers' "jobs to be done." *Harvard Business Review, 94*(9), 54–62. https://hbr.org/2016/09/know-your-customers-jobs-to-be-done

Christensen, C. M., Hall, T., Dillon, K., & Duncan, D. S. (2016). *Competing against luck: The story of innovation and customer choice*. HarperBusiness.

Christensen, C., Raynor, M., & McDonald, R. (2015). What is disruptive innovation? *Harvard Business Review, 93*(12), 44–53.

Cialdini, R. B. (2021). *Influence, new and expanded: The psychology of persuasion*. Harper Business.

Clark, A. (2011). *Supersizing the mind: Embodiment, action, and cognitive extension*. Oxford University Press.

Cole, N., Harvey, M., Myers-Joseph, D., Gilra, A., & Khan, A. G. (2024). Prediction-error signals in anterior cingulate cortex drive task-switching. *Nature Communications, 15*, Article 7088. https://doi.org/10.1038/s41467-024-51368-9

Colizzi, E. S., Vroomans, R. M., & Merks, R. M. (2020). Evolution of multicellularity by collective integration of spatial information. *eLife, 9*, e56349. https://doi.org/10.7554/eLife.56349

Collins, J., & Porras, J. I. (2002). *Built to last: Successful habits of visionary companies*. HarperBusiness.

Comte-Sponville, A. (2002). *A small treatise on the great virtues: The uses of philosophy in everyday life*. Owl Books.

Cook, D. A. (2016). *A history of narrative film* (5th ed.). W. W. Norton & Company.

Corlett, P. R., Mollick, J. A., & Kober, H. (2022). Meta-analysis of human prediction error for incentives, perception, cognition, and action. *Neuropsychopharmacology, 47*(7), 1339–1349. https://doi.org/10.1038/s41386-021-01264-3

Cornier, M. A., Salzberg, A. K., Endly, D. C., Bessesen, D. H., & Tregellas, J. R. (2010). Sex-based differences in the behavioral and neuronal responses to food. *Physiology & Behavior, 99*(4), 538–543. https://doi.org/10.1016/j.physbeh.2010.01.008

Costandi, M. (2016). *Neuroplasticity*. MIT Press.

Cowan, R. S. (1984). *More work for mother: The ironies of household technology from open hearth to the microwave*. Basic Books.

Crouch, T. D. (2003). *The bishop's boys: A life of Wilbur and Orville Wright*. W. W. Norton & Company.

Csikszentmihalyi, M. (1990). *Flow: The psychology of optimal experience*. HarperPerennial.

d'Errico, F., Henshilwood, C., Lawson, G., Vanhaeren, M., Tillier, A.-M., Soressi, M., Bresson, F., Maureille, B., Nowell, A., Lakarra, J., Backwell, L., & Julien, M. (2003). Archaeological evidence for the emergence of language, symbolism, and music—An alternative multidisciplinary perspective. *Journal of World Prehistory, 17*(1), 1–70. https://doi.org/10.1023/A:1023980201043

Daly, H. E., & Cobb, J. B. (1994). *For the common good: Redirecting the economy toward community, the environment, and a sustainable future* (2nd ed.). Beacon Press.

Damasio, A. (2005). *Descartes' error: Emotion, reason, and the human brain*. Penguin Books.

Damasio, A. R. (1996). The somatic marker hypothesis and the possible functions of the prefrontal cortex. *Philosophical Transactions of the Royal Society of London. Series B, Biological Sciences, 351*(1346), 1413–1420. https://doi.org/10.1098/rstb.1996.0125

Damasio, A. R. (1999). *The feeling of what happens: Body and emotion in the making of consciousness*. Mariner Books.

Darwin, C. (2003). *The origin of species: 150th anniversary edition*. Signet Classics.

David, S. A., Boniwell, I., & Ayers, A. C. (Eds.). (2014). *The Oxford handbook of happiness*. Oxford University Press.

Dawkins, R. (2008). *The god delusion*. Mariner Books.

Dawkins, R. (2010). *The greatest show on earth: The evidence for evolution*. Free Press.

Dawkins, R. (2015). *The blind watchmaker: Why the evidence of evolution reveals a universe without design*. W. W. Norton & Company.

Dawkins, R. (2016). *The selfish gene: 40th anniversary edition*. Oxford University Press.

De Bono, E. (1993). *Serious creativity: Using the power of lateral thinking to create new ideas*. Harperbusiness.

Deacon, T. W. (1998). *The symbolic species: The co-evolution of language and the brain*. W. W. Norton & Company.

Dear, P. R. (2001). *Revolutionizing the sciences: European knowledge and its ambitions, 1500-1700*. Princeton University Press.

Deaton, A. (2015). *The great escape: Health, wealth, and the origins of inequality*. Princeton University Press.

Deci, E. L., & Ryan, R. M. (2000). The "what" and "why" of goal pursuits: Human needs and the self-determination of behavior. *Psychological Inquiry, 11*(4), 227–268. https://doi.org/10.1207/S15327965PLI1104_01

Delaney, K. (2023, May 15). Why AI will never replace our emotional intelligence. *Conversant*. https://www.conversant.com/why-ai-will-never-replace-our-emotional-intelligence

Deming, D. (2020). The aqueducts and water supply of ancient Rome. *Ground Water, 58*(1), 152–161. https://doi.org/10.1111/gwat.12958

DeYoung, C. G., Quilty, L. C., & Peterson, J. B. (2007). Between facets and domains: 10 aspects of the Big Five. *Journal of Personality and Social Psychology, 93*(5), 880–896. https://doi.org/10.1037/0022-3514.93.5.880

Diamond, J. (2017). *Guns, germs, and steel: The fates of human societies*. W. W. Norton & Company.

Diener, E., Lucas, R. E., & Scollon, C. N. (2006). Beyond the hedonic treadmill: Revising the adaptation theory of well-being. *American Psychologist, 61*(4), 305–314. https://doi.org/10.1037/0003-066X.61.4.305

Doidge, N. (2007). *The brain that changes itself: Stories of personal triumph from the frontiers of brain science.* Penguin Books.

Dolan, P., & Kahneman, D. (2008). Interpretations of utility and their implications for the valuation of health. *The Economic Journal, 118*(525), 215–234. https://doi.org/10.1111/j.1468-0297.2007.02110.x

Donald, M. (1991). *Origins of the modern mind: Three stages in the evolution of culture and cognition.* Harvard University Press.

Dosi, G. (1982). Technological paradigms and technological trajectories: A suggested interpretation of the determinants and directions of technical change. *Research Policy, 11*(3), 147–162. https://doi.org/10.1016/0048-7333(82)90016-6

Drucker, P. F. (1993). *Innovation and entrepreneurship: Practice and principles.* Harper.

Drucker, P. F. (1993). *Management: Tasks, responsibilities, practices.* HarperBusiness.

Drucker, P. F. (2008). *The essential Drucker: The best of sixty years of Peter Drucker's essential writings on management.* HarperBusiness.

Dunbar, R. I. M. (1993). Coevolution of neocortical size, group size and language in humans. *Behavioral and Brain Sciences, 16*(4), 681–735. https://doi.org/10.1017/S0140525X00032325

Duncan, D. S. (2021). *The secret lives of customers: A detective story about solving the mystery of customer behavior.* Public Affairs.

Dweck, C. S. (2016). *Mindset: The new psychology of success.* Ballantine Books.

Dyer, J., Gregersen, H., & Christensen, C. M. (2019). *Innovator's DNA, updated, with a new introduction: Mastering the five skills of disruptive innovators.* Harvard Business Review Press.

Eagleman, D. M. (2012). *Incognito: The secret lives of the brain.* Vintage Books.

Eastwood, J. D., Frischen, A., Fenske, M. J., & Smilek, D. (2012). The unengaged mind: Defining boredom in terms of attention. *Perspectives on Psychological Science, 7*(5), 482–495. https://doi.org/10.1177/1745691612456044

Efron, B., & Hastie, T. (2021). *Computer age statistical inference: Algorithms, evidence, and data science - student edition.* Cambridge University Press.

Eger, A. O., & Ehlhardt, H. (2018). *On the origin of products: the evolution of product innovation and design.* Cambridge University Press.

Eisenstein, E. L. (2009). *The printing press as an agent of change: Communications and cultural transformations in early-modern Europe - Volumes I and II.* Cambridge University Press.

Elena, S. F., & de Visser, J. A. (2003). Environmental stress and the effects of mutation. *Journal of Biology, 2*(2), 12. https://doi.org/10.1186/1475-4924-2-12

Elkington, J. (1999). *Cannibals with forks: The triple bottom line of 21st century business.* Wiley.

Elliot, A. J., & Covington, M. V. (2001). Approach and avoidance motivation. *Educational Psychology Review, 13*(2), 73–92. https://doi.org/10.1023/A:1009009018235

Elum, J. E., Szelenyi, E. R., Juarez, B., Murry, A. D., Loginov, G., Zamorano, C. A., Gao, P., Wu, G., Ng-Evans, S., Yee, J. X., Xu, X., Golden, S. A., & Zweifel, L. S. (2024). Distinct dynamics and intrinsic properties in ventral tegmental area populations mediate reward association and motivation. *Cell Reports, 43*(9), Article 114668. https://doi.org/10.1016/j.celrep.2024.114668

Espinosa-Soto, C., & Wagner, A. (2010). Specialization can drive the evolution of modularity. *PLoS Computational Biology, 6*(3), e1000719. https://doi.org/10.1371/journal.pcbi.1000719

Fabrycky, B. (2014). *Systems engineering and analysis: Pearson new international edition* (5th ed.). Pearson Education Ltd.

Fazio, R. H. (2001). On the automatic activation of associated evaluations: An overview. *Cognition & Emotion, 15*, 115–141. http://dx.doi.org/10.1080/02699930125908

Ferster, C. B., & Skinner, B. F. (2022). *Schedules of reinforcement.* Martino Fine Books. (Original work published 1957)

Festinger, L. (1954). A theory of social comparison processes. *Human Relations, 7*, 117–140. https://doi.org/10.1177/001872675400700202

Festinger, L. (1962). *A theory of cognitive dissonance*. Stanford University Press.

Festinger, L., Riecken, H. W., & Schachter, S. (2009). *When prophecy fails: A social and psychological study of a modern group that predicted the destruction of the world*. Martino Publishing.

Field, A. J. (2011). *A great leap forward: 1930s depression and U.S. economic growth*. Yale University Press.

Fielding, R. (Ed.). (1983). *A technological history of motion pictures and television: An anthology from the pages of the journal of the society of motion picture and television engineers*. University of California Press.

Fields, H. L., Hjelmstad, G. O., Margolis, E. B., & Nicola, S. M. (2007). Ventral tegmental area neurons in learned appetitive behavior and positive reinforcement. *Annual Review of Neuroscience, 30*, 289–316. https://doi.org/10.1146/annurev.neuro.30.051606.094341

Flink, J. J. (1990). *The automobile age*. MIT Press.

Folk, G. E., & Semken, A. (1991). The evolution of sweat glands. *International Journal of Biometeorology, 35*, 180–186. https://doi.org/10.1007/BF01049065

Forgas, J. P. (1995). Mood and judgment: The affect infusion model (AIM). *Psychological Bulletin, 117*(1), 39–66. https://doi.org/10.1037/0033-2909.117.1.39

Forrester, J. W. (2013). *Industrial dynamics*. Martino Publishing. (Original work published 1961)

Foster, R. N. (1986). *Innovation: The attacker's advantage*. Summit Books.

Fowler, C. H., Bogdan, R., & Gaffrey, M. S. (2021). Stress-induced cortisol response is associated with right amygdala volume in early childhood. *Neurobiology of Stress, 14*, 100329. https://doi.org/10.1016/j.ynstr.2021.100329

Fox, J. J. (1998). *How to become CEO: The rules for rising to the top of any organization*. Hyperion.

Franciscus, R. G., & Long, J. C. (1991). Variation in human nasal height and breadth. American *Journal of Physical Anthropology, 85*(4), 419–427. https://doi.org/10.1002/ajpa.1330850406

Frank, R. H. (2012). *The Darwin economy: Liberty, competition, and the common good*. Princeton University Press.

Freeberg, E. (2014). *The age of Edison: Electric light and the invention of modern America*. Penguin Books.

Fromm, E. (1994). *Escape from freedom*. Holt Paperbacks. (Original work published 1941)

Fuller, B. (2020). *Nine chains to the moon*. Dover Publications. (Original work published 1938)

Fuller, R. B. (2008). *Operating manual for spaceship earth* (J. Snyder, Ed.). Lars Müller Publishers. (Original work published 1969)

Fürst, A., Thron, J., Scheele, D., Marsh, N., & Hurlemann, R. (2015). The neuropeptide oxytocin modulates consumer brand relationships. *Scientific Reports, 5*, Article 14960. https://doi.org/10.1038/srep14960

Futuyma, D. J., & Kirkpatrick, M. (2017). *Evolution* (4th ed.). Sinauer.

Galiani, S., Gertler, P. J., & Undurraga, R. (2016). The half-life of happiness: Hedonic adaptation in the subjective well-being of poor slum dwellers to the satisfaction of basic housing needs. *SSRN*. https://doi.org/10.2139/ssrn.2592256

Gan, W. S., Mitra, S., & Kuo, S. M. (2005). Adaptive feedback active noise control headset: Implementation, evaluation and its extensions. *IEEE Transactions on Consumer Electronics, 51*(3), 975–982. https://doi.org/10.1109/TCE.2005.1510511

Garrett, T. J. (2013). Thermodynamics of long-run economic innovation and growth. *arXiv*. https://doi.org/10.48550/arXiv.1306.3554

Garrison, J., Erdeniz, B., & Done, J. (2013). Prediction error in reinforcement learning: A meta-analysis of neuroimaging studies. *Neuroscience and Biobehavioral Reviews, 37*(7), 1297–1310. https://doi.org/10.1016/j.neubiorev.2013.03.023

Gaukroger, S. (2008). *The emergence of a scientific culture: Science and the shaping of modernity 1210-1685*. Oxford University Press.

Gazzaniga, M. S. (2009). *Human: The science behind what makes your brain unique*. Harper Perennial.

Gazzaniga, M. S., Ivry, R. B., & Mangun, G. R. (2019). *Cognitive neuroscience: The biology of the mind* (5th ed.). W. W. Norton & Company.

Gelfand, S. A. (2009). *Essentials of audiology* (3rd ed.). Thieme.

Georgescu-Roegen, N. (1976). *The entropy law and the economic process*. Harvard University Press.

Gesteland, R. F., Cech, T. R., & Atkins, J. F. (1999). *The RNA world: The nature of modern RNA suggests a prebiotic RNA world* (2nd ed.). Cold Spring Harbor Laboratory Press.

Ghilardi, R. (2024, November 14). Innovation meets thermodynamics: Why businesses need sufficiency? *Medium*. https://medium.com/%40ritoshi/innovation-meets-thermodynamics-why-businesses-need-sufficiency-80781f72bade

Giancoli, D. C. (1989). *Physics for scientists and engineers with modern physics* (2nd ed.). Prentice Hall.

Gilbert, D. (2007). *Stumbling on happiness*. Vintage Books.

Gingerich, O. (2005). *The book nobody read: Chasing the revolutions of Nicolaus Copernicus*. Penguin.

Gladstone, J. J., Ruberton, P. M., Margolis, S., & Lyubomirsky, S. (2024). Does variety in hedonic spending improve happiness? Testing alternative causal mechanisms between hedonic variety and subjective well-being. *BMC Psychology, 12*(1), 98. https://doi.org/10.1186/s40359-024-01599-8

Glimcher, P. W., & Fehr, E. (2014). *Neuroeconomics: Decision making and the brain* (2nd ed.). Academic Press.

Global GDP over the long run (organized from years 1000–2023 for page 41). (2024, April 26). *Our World in Data*. https://ourworldindata.org/grapher/global-gdp-over-the-long-run

Godin, B. (2024). *Innovation contested: The idea of innovation over the centuries*. Routledge.

Goedhoop, J. N., van den Boom, B. J. G., Robke, R., Veen, F., Fellinger, L., van Elzelingen, W., Arbab, T., & Willuhn, I. (2022). Nucleus accumbens dopamine tracks aversive stimulus duration and prediction but not value or prediction error. *eLife, 11*, e82711. https://doi.org/10.7554/eLife.82711

Goffman, E. (1959). *The presentation of self in everyday life*. Anchor Books.

Gonzalez, R. (2018, June 5). Why Apple can't tackle digital wellness in a vacuum. *WIRED*. https://www.wired.com/story/apple-screen-time/

Goodenough, J. B., & Park, K. S. (2013). The Li-ion rechargeable battery: A perspective. *Journal of the American Chemical Society, 135*(4), 1167–1176. https://doi.org/10.1021/ja3091438

Gordon, R. J. (2017). *The rise and fall of American growth: The U.S. standard of living since the Civil War*. Princeton University Press.

Goren-Inbar, N., Alperson, N., Kislev, M. E., Simchoni, O., Melamed, Y., Ben-Nun, A., & Werker, E. (2004). Evidence of hominin control of fire at Gesher Benot Ya'aqov, Israel. *Science, 304*(5671), 725–727. https://doi.org/10.1126/science.1095443

Gould, S. J. (2002). *The structure of evolutionary theory*. The Belknap Press of Harvard University Press.

Grace, A. A., & Bunney, B. S. (1984). The control of firing pattern in nigral dopamine neurons: Single spike firing. *The Journal of Neuroscience, 4*(11), 2866–2876. https://doi.org/10.1523/JNEUROSCI.04-11-02866.1984

Grady, J. O. (2014). *System requirements analysis* (2nd ed.). Elsevier.

Graeber, D., & Wengrow, D. (2023). *The dawn of everything: A new history of humanity*. Picador.

Grant, A. (2021). *Think again: The power of knowing what you don't know*. Viking.

Grant, E. (1996). *The foundations of modern science in the Middle Ages: Their religious, institutional and intellectual contexts*. Cambridge University Press.

Green, M. C., & Brock, T. C. (2000). The role of transportation in the persuasiveness of public narratives. *Journal of Personality and Social Psychology, 79*(5), 701–721. https://doi.org/10.1037/0022-3514.79.5.701

Greene, J. D. (2014). The cognitive neuroscience of moral judgment and decision making. In M. S. Gazzaniga & G. R. Mangun (Eds.), *The cognitive neurosciences* (5th ed., pp. 1013–1023). Boston Review. https://doi.org/10.7551/mitpress/9504.003.0110

Greene, R. (2013). *Mastery*. Penguin Books.

Greene, R. (2019). *The laws of human nature*. Penguin Books.

Greenfield, S. (2015). *Mind change: How digital technologies are leaving their mark on our brains*. Penguin Random House.

Grieves, M. (2006). *Product lifecycle management: Driving the next generation of lean thinking*. McGraw Hill.

Griffiths, M. D., Billieux, J., Maurage, P., Lopez-Fernandez, O., Kuss, D. J., & Griffiths, M. D. (2015). Can disordered mobile phone use be considered a behavioral addiction? An update on current evidence and a comprehensive model for future research. *Current Addiction Reports, 2*, 154–162. https://doi.org/10.1007/s40429-015-0054-y

Groussin, M., & Gouy, M. (2011). Adaptation to environmental temperature is a major determinant of molecular evolutionary rates in archaea. *Molecular Biology and Evolution, 28*(9), 2661–2674. https://doi.org/10.1093/molbev/msr098

Guinness, H. (2021, August 25). Trying to use your smartphone less? Get a smartwatch. *Popular Science*. https://www.popsci.com/story/diy/use-smartphone-less-smartwatch/

Guy-Evans, O. (2024, February 1). Drive-reduction theory of motivation in psychology. *Simply Psychology*. https://www.simplypsychology.org/drive-reduction-theory.html

Hagen, M., Bernard, A., & Grube, E. (2016). Do it all wrong! Using reverse-brainstorming to generate ideas, improve discussions, and move students to action. *Management Teaching Review, 1*(2), 85–90. https://doi.org/10.1177/2379298116634738

Haidt, J. (2024). *The anxious generation: How the great rewiring of childhood is causing an epidemic of mental illness*. Penguin Press.

Hakemy, S. (2017). *An analysis of David Graeber's debt: The first 5,000 years*. Macat International Ltd.

Hall, D. (2008). *Jump start your brain v2.0: How everyone at every age can be smarter and more creative*. Clerisy Press.

Hall, D. (2018). *Driving Eureka!: Problem-solving with data-driven methods & the innovation engineering system*. Clerisy Press.

Hammer, M., & Champy, J. (2006). *Reengineering the corporation: A manifesto for business revolution*. HarperBusiness.

Handwerk, B. (2021, January 28). How dexterous thumbs may have helped shape evolution two million years ago. *Smithsonian Magazine*. https://www.smithsonianmag.com/science-nature/how-dexterous-thumbs-may-have-helped-shape-evolution-two-million-years-ago-180976870/

Harari, Y. N. (2018). *Homo deus: A brief history of tomorrow*. Harper Perennial.

Harari, Y. N. (2018). *Sapiens: A brief history of humankind*. Harper Perennial.

Harari, Y. N. (2019). *21 lessons for the 21st century*. Random House.

Harberger, A. C. (1971). Three basic postulates for applied welfare economics: An interpretive essay. *Journal of Economic Literature, 9*(3), 785–797. http://www.jstor.org/stable/2720975

Harcourt-Smith, W. E., & Aiello, L. C. (2004). Fossils, feet and the evolution of human bipedal locomotion. *Journal of Anatomy, 204*(5), 403–416. https://doi.org/10.1111/j.0021-8782.2004.00296.x

Harland, P., & Uddin, A. (2014). Effects of product platform development: Fostering lean product development and production. *International Journal of Product Development, 19*(5–6), 259–285. https://doi.org/10.1504/IJPD.2014.064881

Harmand, S., Lewis, J. E., Feibel, C. S., Lepre, C. J., Prat, S., Lenoble, A., Boës, X., Quinn, R. L., Brenet, M., Arroyo, A., Taylor, N., Clément, S., Daver, G., Brugal, J. P., Leakey, L., Mortlock, R. A., Wright, J. D., Lokorodi, S., Kirwa, C., Kent, D. V., … Roche, H. (2015). 3.3-million-year-old stone tools from Lomekwi 3, West Turkana, Kenya. *Nature, 521*(7552), 310–315. https://doi.org/10.1038/nature14464

Hassenzahl, M. (2005). The thing and I: Understanding the relationship between user and product. In M. A. Blythe, K. Overbeeke, A. F. Monk, & P. C. Wright (Eds.), *Funology: From usability to enjoyment* (pp. 31–42). Springer. https://doi.org/10.1007/1-4020-2967-5_4

Hastie, T., Tibshirani, R., & Friedman, J. (2017). *The elements of statistical learning: Data mining, inference, and prediction* (2nd ed.). Springer.

Hayden, B. Y., Heilbronner, S. R., Pearson, J. M., & Platt, M. L. (2011). Surprise signals in anterior cingulate cortex: Neuronal encoding of unsigned reward prediction errors driving adjustment in behavior. *The Journal of Neuroscience, 31*(11), 4178–4187. https://doi.org/10.1523/JNEUROSCI.4652-10.2011

Heath, C., & Heath, D. (2007). *Made to stick: Why some ideas survive and others die*. Random House.

Heidegger, M. (2013). *The question concerning technology, and other essays*. Harper Perennial Modern Thought.

Henderson, R. M., & Clark, K. B. (1990). Architectural innovation: The reconfiguration of existing product technologies and the failure of established firms. *Administrative Science Quarterly, 35*(1), 9–30. https://doi.org/10.2307/2393549

Hicks, J. (1991). *Value and capital: An inquiry into some fundamental principles of economic theory* (2nd ed.). Oxford University Press. (Original 2nd ed. published 1946)

Higgins, E. T. (1987). Self-discrepancy: A theory relating self and affect. *Psychological Review, 94*(3), 319–340. https://doi.org/10.1037/0033-295X.94.3.319

Hintze, A., Olson, R., Adami, C., & Hertwig, R. (2015). Risk sensitivity as an evolutionary adaptation. *Scientific Reports, 5*, Article 8242. https://doi.org/10.1038/srep08242

Hippel, E. V. (2005). *Democratizing innovation*. MIT Press.

Hirshleifer, J. (1977). Economics from a biological viewpoint. *The Journal of Law & Economics, 20*(1), 1–52. http://www.jstor.org/stable/725086

Hodge, A. T. (2011). *Roman aqueducts and water supply* (2nd ed.). Bristol Classical Press.

Hoek, R. V. (2024). The making of the supply chain: How five CSCMP Supply Chain Hall of Famers shaped the industry. University of Arkansas Press.

Hofmann, W., & Nordgren, L. F. (2016). *The psychology of desire*. The Guilford Press.

Holroyd, C. B., & Coles, M. G. H. (2002). The neural basis of human error processing: Reinforcement learning, dopamine, and the error-related negativity. *Psychological Review, 109*(4), 679–709. https://doi.org/10.1037/0033-295X.109.4.679

Hölzel, B. K., Carmody, J., Vangel, M., Congleton, C., Yerramsetti, S. M., Gard, T., & Lazar, S. W. (2011). Mindfulness practice leads to increases in regional brain gray matter density. *Psychiatry Research: Neuroimaging, 191*(1), 36–43. https://doi.org/10.1016/j.pscychresns.2010.08.006

Horowitz, B. (2014). *The hard thing about hard things: Building a business when there are no easy answers*. HarperBusiness.

Hoshina, T., Fujiyama, D., Koike, T., & Ikeda, K. (2022). Effects of an active noise control technology applied to earphones on preferred listening levels in noisy environments. *Journal of Audiology & Otology, 26*(3), 122–129. https://doi.org/10.7874/jao.2021.00612

Hou, L., Geng, S., & Kong, W. (2025). Competition and cooperation in ride-sharing platforms: A game theoretic analysis of C2C and B2C aggregation strategies. *Sustainability, 17*(2), 398. https://doi.org/10.3390/su17020398

Hublin, J. J., Talamo, S., Julien, M., David, F., Connet, N., Bodu, P., Vandermeersch, B., & Richards, M. P. (2012). Radiocarbon dates from the Grotte du Renne and Saint-Césaire support a Neandertal origin for the Châtelperronian. *Proceedings of the National Academy of Sciences of the United States of America, 109*(46), 18743–18748. https://doi.org/10.1073/pnas.1212924109

Hughes, T. P. (1983). *Networks of power: Electrification in Western society, 1880–1930*. Johns Hopkins University Press.

Hull, C. L. (1958). *A behavior system - An introduction to behavior theory concerning the individual organism*. Yale University Press. (Original work published 1952)

Humphrey, N. (2023). *Sentience: The invention of consciousness*. MIT Press.

Husserl, E. (1999). *Cartesian meditations: An introduction to phenomenology*. Kluwer Academic Publishers. (Original work published 1931)

INCOSE. (2015). *INCOSE systems engineering handbook: A guide for system life cycle processes and activities* (4th ed.). John Wiley & Sons.

Ingold, T. (2013). *Making: Anthropology, archaeology, art and architecture*. Routledge.

International Organization for Standardization. (2020). *ISO 56000:2020* Innovation management—Fundamentals and vocabulary. https://www.iso.org/obp/ui/#iso:std:iso:56000:ed-1:v1:en

Ioannou, P. A., & Sun, J. (2012). *Robust adaptive control*. Dover Publications.

Irwin, D. A. (1998). *Against the tide: An intellectual history of free trade*. Princeton University Press.

Itao, K., & Kaneko, K. (2021). Evolution of family systems and resultant socio-economic structures. *Humanities and Social Sciences Communications, 8*, Article 243. https://doi.org/10.1057/s41599-021-00919-2

Jablonski, N. G., & Chaplin, G. (2000). The evolution of human skin coloration. *Journal of Human Evolution, 39*(1), 57–106. https://doi.org/10.1006/jhev.2000.0403

Jackson, T. (2009). *Prosperity without growth: Economics for a finite planet*. Earthscan from Routledge.

Jakimowicz, A. (2020). The role of entropy in the development of economics. *Entropy, 22*(4), 452. https://doi.org/10.3390/e22040452

James, G., Witten, D., Hastie, T., & Tibshirani, R. (2021). *An introduction to statistical learning: With applications in R* (2nd ed.). Springer.

Jardine, L. (1975). *Francis Bacon: Discovery and the art of discourse*. Cambridge University Press.

Jevons, W. S. (2006). *The theory of political economy*. Adamant Media Corporation. (Original work published 1911)

Jiang, T., Soussignan, R., Schaal, B., & Royet, J. P. (2015). Reward for food odors: An fMRI study of liking and wanting as a function of metabolic state and BMI. *Social Cognitive and Affective Neuroscience, 10*(4), 561–568. https://doi.org/10.1093/scan/nsu086

Johansson, F. (2017). *The Medici effect: What elephants and epidemics can teach us about innovation*. Harvard Business Review Press.

John. (2025, January 6). How 12 microphones in Sony's headphones reduce mental fatigue by 40% during meetings. *World Day*. https://www.journee-mondiale.com/en/how-12-microphones-in-sonys-headphones-reduce-mental-fatigue-by-40-during-meetings/

Johnson, S. (2011). *Where good ideas come from: The natural history of innovation*. Riverhead Books.

Jonnes, J. (2004). *Empires of light: Edison, Tesla, Westinghouse, and the race to electrify the world*. Random House Trade Paperbacks.

Jordan, S. F., Rammu, H., Zheludev, I. N., Hartley, A. M., Maréchal, A., & Lane, N. (2019). Promotion of protocell self-assembly from mixed amphiphiles at the origin of life. *Nature Ecology & Evolution, 3*(12), 1705–1714. https://doi.org/10.1038/s41559-019-1015-y

Jovanovic, M., Sjödin, D., & Parida, V. (2022). Co-evolution of platform architecture, platform services, and platform governance: Expanding the platform value of industrial digital platforms. *Technovation, 118*, Article 102218. https://doi.org/10.1016/j.technovation.2020.102218

Kahneman, D. (2013). *Thinking, fast and slow*. Farrar, Straus and Giroux.

Kahneman, D., & Deaton, A. (2010). High income improves evaluation of life but not emotional well-being. *Proceedings of the National Academy of Sciences, 107*, 16489–16493. http://dx.doi.org/10.1073/pnas.1011492107

Kahneman, D., & Thaler, R. H. (2006). Anomalies: Utility maximization and experienced utility. *The Journal of Economic Perspectives, 20*(1), 221–234. http://www.jstor.org/stable/30033642

Kahneman, D., & Tversky, A. (1973). On the psychology of prediction. *Psychological Review, 80*(4), 237–251. https://doi.org/10.1037/h0034747

Kahneman, D., & Tversky, A. (1979). Prospect theory: An analysis of decision making under risk. *Econometrica, 47*, 263–291. http://dx.doi.org/10.2307/1914185

Kahneman, D., & Tversky, A. (Eds.). (2000). *Choices, values, and frames*. Cambridge University Press.

Kahneman, D., Diener, E., & Schwarz, N. (Eds.). (2003). *Well-being: The foundations of hedonic psychology*. Russell Sage Foundation.

Kahneman, D., Fredrickson, B. L., Schreiber, C. A., & Redelmeier, D. A. (1993). When more pain is preferred to less: Adding a better end. *Psychological Science, 4*(6), 401–405. https://doi.org/10.1111/j.1467-9280.1993.tb00589.x

Kahneman, D., Knetsch, J. L., & Thaler, R. H. (1991). Anomalies: The endowment effect, loss aversion, and status quo bias. *Journal of Economic Perspectives, 5*(1), 193–206. https://doi.org/10.1257/jep.5.1.193

Kahneman, D., Knetsch, J., & Thaler, R. (1990). Experimental tests of the endowment effect and the Coase theorem. *Journal of Political Economy, 98*(6), 1325–1348. https://doi.org/10.1086/261737

Kahneman, D., Sibony, O., & Sunstein, C. R. (2022). *Noise: A flaw in human judgement.* William Collins.

Kahneman, D., Wakker, P., & Sarin, R. (1997). Back to Bentham? Explorations of experienced utility. *The Quarterly Journal of Economics, 112*(2), 375–406. https://doi.org/10.1162/003355397555235

Kamberov, Y. G., Guhan, S. M., DeMarchis, A., Jiang, J., Wright, S. S., Morgan, B. A., Sabeti, P. C., Tabin, C. J., & Lieberman, D. E. (2018). Comparative evidence for the independent evolution of hair and sweat gland traits in primates. *Journal of Human Evolution, 125*, 99–105. https://doi.org/10.1016/j.jhevol.2018.10.008

Kamrani, A. K., & Salhieh, S. M. (2002). *Product design for modularity* (2nd ed.). Kluwer Academic Publishers.

Kane, G. C., Nanda, R., Phillips, A. N., & Copulsky, J. R. (2021). *The transformation myth: Leading your organization through uncertain times.* MIT Press.

Kanoski, S. E., & Boutelle, K. N. (2022). Food cue reactivity: Neurobiological and behavioral underpinnings. *Reviews in Endocrine & Metabolic Disorders, 23*(4), 683–696. https://doi.org/10.1007/s11154-022-09724-x

Kant, I. (2013). *Groundwork of the metaphysics of morals* (T. K. Abbot, Trans.). CreateSpace. (Original work published 1785)

Kaufman, S. B. (2021). *Transcend: The new science of self-actualization.* TarcherPerigee.

Keeley, L., Pikkel, R., Quinn, B., & Walters, H. (2013). *Ten types of innovation: The discipline of building breakthroughs.* John Wiley & Sons.

Keiflin, R., Pribut, H. J., Shah, N. B., & Janak, P. H. (2019). Ventral tegmental dopamine neurons participate in reward identity predictions. *Current Biology, 29*(1), 93–103.e3. https://doi.org/10.1016/j.cub.2018.11.050

Keim, B. (2008, February 13). Evolution as biological thermodynamics. *WIRED.* https://www.wired.com/2008/02/evolution-as-bi/

Kennerley, S. W., & Walton, M. E. (2011). Decision making and reward in frontal cortex: Complementary evidence from neurophysiological and neuropsychological studies. *Behavioral Neuroscience, 125*(3), 297–317. https://doi.org/10.1037/a0023575

Keynes, J. M. (2015). *John Maynard Keynes: The essential Keynes* (R. Skidelsky, Ed.). Penguin Books.

Keynes, J. M. (2017). *The general theory of employment, interest and money: The economic consequences of the peace.* Wordsworth Editions Ltd. (Original work published 1936)

Khamsi, F., Lacanna, I., Endman, M., & Wong, J. (1998). Recent advances in assisted reproductive technologies. *Endocrine, 9*(1), 15–25. https://doi.org/10.1385/ENDO:9:1:15

Khayat, A., & Yaka, R. (2024). Activation of nucleus accumbens projections to the ventral tegmental area alters molecular signaling and neurotransmission in the reward system. *Frontiers in Molecular Neuroscience, 17*, 1271654. https://doi.org/10.3389/fnmol.2024.1271654

Kirk, H. R., Gabriel, I., Summerfield, C., & others. (2025). Why human–AI relationships need socioaffective alignment. *Humanities and Social Sciences Communications, 12*, 728. https://doi.org/10.1057/s41599-025-04532-5

Kirschbaum, C., Wüst, S., & Hellhammer, D. (1992). Consistent sex differences in cortisol responses to psychological stress. *Psychosomatic Medicine, 54*(6), 648–657. https://doi.org/10.1097/00006842-199211000-00004

Kissinger, H. A., Mindie, C., & Schmidt, E. (2024). *Genesis: Artificial intelligence, hope, and the human spirit.* Little, Brown and Company.

Klein, M. (2009). *The power makers: Steam, electricity, and the men who invented modern America.* Bloomsbury Press.

Klein, R. G. (2009). *The human career: Human biological and cultural origins* (3rd ed.). The University of Chicago Press.

Knutson, B., Adams, C. M., Fong, G. W., & Hommer, D. (2001). Anticipation of increasing monetary reward selectively recruits nucleus accumbens. *The Journal of Neuroscience, 21*(16), RC159. https://doi.org/10.1523/JNEUROSCI.21-16-j0002.2001

Knutson, B., Rick, S., Wimmer, G. E., Prelec, D., & Loewenstein, G. (2007). Neural predictors of purchases. *Neuron, 53*(1), 147–156. https://doi.org/10.1016/j.neuron.2006.11.010

Kocik, K. (2021). Decision utility. *The Decision Lab*. Retrieved July 15, 2025, from https://thedecisionlab.com/reference-guide/psychology/decision-utility

Koeppel, D. (2011, September 6). Let there be LED: The future of the light bulb. *WIRED*. https://www.wired.com/story/let-there-be-led/

Kotler, P., Keller, K. L., & Chernev, A. (2022). *Marketing management* (16th ed.). Pearson.

Kotler, P., Keller, K. L., Chernev, A., Sheth, J. N., & Shainesh, G. (2021). *Marketing management (Indian Case Studies)* (16th ed.). PearsonIN.

Kraft, T. S., Venkataraman, V. V., Wallace, I. J., Crittenden, A. N., Holowka, N. B., Stieglitz, J., Harris, J., Raichlen, D. A., Wood, B., Gurven, M., & Pontzer, H. (2021). The energetics of uniquely human subsistence strategies. *Science, 374*(6575), Article eabf0130. https://doi.org/10.1126/science.abf0130

Kringelbach, M. L., & Berridge, K. C. (Eds.). (2010). *Pleasures of the brain.* Oxford University Press.

Kuhn, S. L. (2021). *The evolution of palaeolithic technologies.* Routledge.

Kuhn, T. S. (2012). *The structure of scientific revolutions: 50th anniversary edition* (4th ed.). University of Chicago Press.

Kuo, S., Mitra, S., & Gan, W.-S. (2006). Active noise control system for headphone applications. *IEEE Transactions on Control Systems Technology, 14*(2), 331–335. https://doi.org/10.1109/TCST.2005.863667

Kurz, H. D. (2012). *Innovation, knowledge and growth: Adam Smith, Schumpeter and the moderns.* Routledge.

Ladyman, J., & Wiesner, K. (2020). *What is a complex system?* Yale University Press.

Laloux, F. (2014). *Reinventing organizations: A guide to creating organizations inspired by the next stage of human consciousness.* Nelson Parker.

Landau, I. D., Lozano, R., Saad, M. M., & Karimi, A. (2024). Adaptive control: Algorithms, analysis and applications. *arXiv.* https://doi.org/10.48550/arXiv.2406.07073

Landau, R., & Rosenberg, N. (Eds.). (1986). *The positive sum strategy: Harnessing technology for economic growth.* National Academies Press.

Landels, J. G. (2000). *Engineering in the ancient world: With a revised preface, a new appendix, and a new bibliography.* University of California Press.

Landes, D. S. (2003). *The unbound Prometheus: Technological change and industrial development in Western Europe from 1750 to the present* (2nd ed.). Cambridge University Press. (Original work published 1969)

Lane, N., & Martin, W. (2010). The energetics of genome complexity. *Nature, 467*(7318), 929–934. https://doi.org/10.1038/nature09486

Lang, M. (2019). The evolutionary paths to collective rituals: An interdisciplinary perspective on the origins and functions of the basic social act. Archive for the Psychology of Religion, 41(3), 224–252. https://doi.org/10.1177/0084672419894682

Langlois, R. N. (1999). Modularity in technology, organization, and society (Economics Working Paper No. 199905). *University of Connecticut.* https://digitalcommons.lib.uconn.edu/econ_wpapers/199905

Ledoux, J. (1996). *The emotional brain: The mysterious underpinnings of emotional life.* Simon & Schuster.

LeDoux, J. (2003). The emotional brain, fear, and the amygdala. *Cellular and Molecular Neurobiology, 23*(4–5), 727–738. https://doi.org/10.1023/a:1025048802629

LeDoux, J. (2012). Rethinking the emotional brain. *Neuron, 73*(4), 653–676. https://doi.org/10.1016/j.neuron.2012.02.004

LeDoux, J. (2016). *Anxious: Using the brain to understand and treat fear and anxiety.* Penguin.

LeDoux, J. E. (2000). Emotion circuits in the brain. *Annual Review of Neuroscience, 23*, 155–184. https://doi.org/10.1146/annurev.neuro.23.1.155

LeDoux, J. E. (2023). *The four realms of existence: A new theory of being human.* The Belknap Press of Harvard University Press.

Lee, Z. E., & Zhang, K. M. (2022). Unintended consequences of smart thermostats in the transition to electrified heating. *Applied Energy, 322*, Article 119384. https://doi.org/10.1016/j.apenergy.2022.119384

Legator, M. S., & Flamm, W. G. (1973). Environmental mutagenesis and repair. *Annual Review of Biochemistry, 42*, 683–708. https://doi.org/10.1146/annurev.bi.42.070173.003343

Leveson, N. G. (2017). *Engineering a safer world: Systems thinking applied to safety.* MIT Press.

Levine, U. (2025). *Fall in love with the problem, not the solution: A handbook for entrepreneurs.* Matt Holt.

Levy, S. B. (2001). Antibiotic resistance: Consequences of inaction. *Clinical Infectious Diseases, 33*(Suppl 3), S124–S129. https://doi.org/10.1086/321837

LeWine, H. E. (Reviewer). (2024, April 3). Understanding the stress response. *Harvard Health.* https://www.health.harvard.edu/staying-healthy/understanding-the-stress-response?utm_source=chatgpt.com

Lidwell, W., Holden, K., & Butler, J. (2023). *Universal principles of design, updated and expanded: 200 ways to increase appeal, enhance usability, influence perception, and make better design decisions* (3rd ed.). Quarto Publishing Group.

Lieberman, D. E. (2014). *The story of the human body: Evolution, health, and disease.* Vintage Books.

Lieberman, D. E. (2015). Human locomotion and heat loss: An evolutionary perspective. *Comprehensive Physiology, 5*(1), 99–117. https://doi.org/10.1002/cphy.c140011

Lieberman, D. Z., & Long, M. E. (2019). *The molecule of more: How a single chemical in your brain drives love, sex, and creativity - and will determine the fate of the human race.* BenBella Books.

Lieberman, P. (2006). *Toward an evolutionary biology of language.* Belknap Press of Harvard University Press.

Lipton, L. (2021). *The cinema in flux: The evolution of motion picture technology from the magic lantern to the digital era.* Springer.

Loewenstein, G. (1994). The psychology of curiosity: A review and reinterpretation. *Psychological Bulletin, 116*(1), 75–98. https://doi.org/10.1037/0033-2909.116.1.75

Loewenstein, G., O'Donoghue, T., & Rabin, M. (2003). Projection bias in predicting future utility. *The Quarterly Journal of Economics, 118*(4), 1209–1248. http://www.jstor.org/stable/25053938

Lopez-Fernandez, O., Kuss, D. J., Romo, L., Morvan, Y., Kern, L., Graziani, P., Rousseau, A., Rumpf, H. J., Bischof, A., Gässler, A. K., Schimmenti, A., Passanisi, A., Männikkö, N., Kääriänen, M., Demetrovics, Z., Király, O., Chóliz, M., Zacarés, J. J., Serra, E., Griffiths, M. D., … Billieux, J. (2017). Self-reported dependence on mobile phones in young adults: A European cross-cultural empirical survey. *Journal of Behavioral Addictions, 6*(2), 168–177. https://doi.org/10.1556/2006.6.2017.020

Lovejoy, C. O. (2009). Reexamining human origins in light of Ardipithecus ramidus. *Science, 326*(5949), 74, 74e1–74e8. https://doi.org/10.1126/science.1175834

Lyubomirsky, S., Sheldon, K. M., & Schkade, D. (2005). Pursuing happiness: The architecture of sustainable change. *Review of General Psychology, 9*(2), 111–131. https://doi.org/10.1037/1089-2680.9.2.111

MacInnis, D. J., & Price, L. L. (1987). The role of imagery in information processing: Review and extensions. *Journal of Consumer Research, 13*(4), 473–491. https://doi.org/10.1086/209082

Mankiw, N. G. (2020). *Principles of macroeconomics* (9th ed.). Cengage Learning.

Marglin, S. A. (1974). What do bosses do? The origins and functions of hierarchy in capitalist production. *Review of Radical Political Economics, 6*(2), 60–112. https://doi.org/10.1177/048661347400600206

Marglin, S. A., & Schor, J. B. (1991). *The golden age of capitalism: Reinterpreting the postwar experience.* Clarendon Press.

Markus, H. R., & Kitayama, S. (1991). Culture and the self: Implications for cognition, emotion, and motivation. *Psychological Review, 98*(2), 224–253. https://doi.org/10.1037/0033-295X.98.2.224

Marshall, A. (1997). *Principles of economics* (8th ed.). Prometheus Books. (Original 8th ed. published 1920)

Marshall, L. (2023, March 1). Milwaukee® ONE-key™ + PACKOUT™ = a productivity power duo. *ONE-KEY™ Blog: Construction Industry News, Trends, Insights.* https://onekeyresources.milwaukeetool.com/en/one-key-and-packout

Marshall, R., & Wintrich, G. (2019). *Applied innovation: The field guide: Translating innovation theory into practical application*. Rdminnotraining.com.

Martin, V. C., Schacter, D. L., Corballis, M. C., & Addis, D. R. (2011). A role for the hippocampus in encoding simulations of future events. *Proceedings of the National Academy of Sciences, 108*(33), 13858–13863. https://doi.org/10.1073/pnas.1105816108

Martinez, D. R., & Kifle, B. M. (2024). *Artificial intelligence: A systems approach from architecture principles to deployment*. MIT Press.

Marzke, M. W. (1997). Precision grips, hand morphology, and tools. *American Journal of Physical Anthropology, 102*(1), 91–110. https://doi.org/10.1002/(SICI)1096-8644(199701)102:1<91::AID-AJPA8>3.0.CO;2-G

Maslow, A. H. (1943). A theory of human motivation. *Psychological Review, 50*(4), 370–396. https://doi.org/10.1037/h0054346

Maslow, A. H. (2013). *A theory of human motivation*. Martino Publishing. (Original work published 1943)

Maverick, J. B. (2024, October 28). What are the 4 types of economic utility? *Investopedia*. https://www.investopedia.com/ask/answers/032615/what-are-four-types-economic-utility.asp

Maxwell, J. C. (1999). *The 21 indispensable qualities of a leader: becoming the person others will want to follow*. Thomas Nelson.

Mazur, B. (2025, April 2). Case study: Future-proof hardware design. *Ignitec – Product Design Consultancy, Creative Technology and R&D Lab*. https://www.ignitec.com/insights/case-study-future-proof-hardware-design/

McCabe, L. (2023, May 5). Are smart thermostats worth it? *Consumer Reports*. https://www.consumerreports.org/appliances/thermostats/are-smart-thermostats-worth-it-a7822875275/

McClure, S. M., Laibson, D. I., Loewenstein, G., & Cohen, J. D. (2004). Separate neural systems value immediate and delayed monetary rewards. *Science, 306*(5695), 503–507. https://doi.org/10.1126/science.1100907

McCraw, T. K. (2009). *Prophet of innovation: Joseph Schumpeter and creative destruction*. The Belknap Press of Harvard University Press.

McDonald, M., & Dunbar, I. (2012). *Market segmentation: How to do it and how to profit from it* (4th ed.). John Wiley & Sons.

McGowan, H. E., & Shipley, C. (2020). *The adaptation advantage: Let go, learn fast, and thrive in the future of work*. John Wiley & Sons.

McGowan, K. (2014, August 1). How life made the LEAP from single cells to multicellular animals. *WIRED*. https://www.wired.com/2014/08/where-animals-come-from/

McIntyre, C. K., McGaugh, J. L., & Williams, C. L. (2012). Interacting brain systems modulate memory consolidation. *Neuroscience and Biobehavioral Reviews, 36*(7), 1750–1762. https://doi.org/10.1016/j.neubiorev.2011.11.001

Mcluhan, M. (2013). *Understanding media: The extensions of man*. Ginko Press. (Original work published 1964)

Meadows, D. H. (2008). *Thinking in systems: A primer* (D. Wright, Ed.). Chelsea Green Publishing.

Meadows, D. H., Randers, J., & Meadows, D. L. (2004). *The limits to growth: The 30-year update*. Chelsea Green Publishing Company.

Meichenbaum, D. (1985). *Stress inoculation training*. Pergamon Press.

Menger, C. (2007). *Principles of economics*. Ludwig von Mises Institute. (Original work published 1871)

Merleau-Ponty, M. (2014). *Phenomenology of perception*. Routledge. (Original work published 1945)

Merton, R. K. (1936). The unanticipated consequences of purposive social action. *American Sociological Review, 1*(6), 894–904. https://doi.org/10.2307/2084615

Mesoudi, A. (2011). *Cultural evolution: How Darwinian theory can explain human culture and synthesize the social sciences*. The University of Chicago Press.

Michalko, M. (2006). *Thinkertoys: A handbook of creative-thinking techniques* (2nd ed.). Ten Speed Press.

Milanesi, C. (2016, April 28). The Apple Watch keeps my iPhone addiction under control. *Vox*. https://www.vox.com/2016/4/28/11586508/the-apple-watch-keeps-my-iphone-addiction-under-control

Mill, J. S. (2008). *Principles of political economy and chapters on socialism* (J. Riley, Ed.). Oxford University Press.

Miller, D., Rabho, L. A., Awondo, P., Vries, M. D., Duque, M., Garvey, P., Haapio-Kirk, L., Hawkins, C., Otaegui, A., Walton, S., & Wang, X. (2021). *The global smartphone: Beyond a youth technology.* UCL Press.

Mithen, S. J. (1998). *The prehistory of the mind: A search for the origins of art, religion and science.* Phoenix.

Mobbs, D., Hagan, C. C., Dalgleish, T., Silston, B., & Prévost, C. (2015). The ecology of human fear: Survival optimization and the nervous system. *Frontiers in Neuroscience, 9,* Article 55. https://doi.org/10.3389/fnins.2015.00055

Mobus, G. E., & Kalton, M. C. (2015). *Principles of systems science.* Springer.

Mokyr, J. (1992). *The lever of riches: Technological creativity and economic progress.* Oxford University Press.

Molesworth, B., Burgess, M., & Kwon, D. (2013). The use of noise cancelling headphones to improve concurrent task performance in a noisy environment. *Applied Acoustics, 74*(1), 110–115. https://doi.org/10.1016/j.apacoust.2012.06.015

Moore, G. A. (2014). *Crossing the chasm: Marketing and selling disruptive products to mainstream customers* (3rd ed.). HarperBusiness.

Moran, M. J., Shapiro, H. N., Boettner, D. D., & Bailey, M. B. (2014). *Fundamentals of engineering thermodynamics* (8th ed.). Wiley.

Morvan, C., & Jenkins, W. J. (2017). *An analysis of Amos Tversky and Daniel Kahneman's judgment under uncertainty: Heuristics and biases.* Macat International Ltd.

Moscati, I. (2019). *Measuring utility: From the marginal revolution to behavioral economics.* Oxford University Press.

Motoki, K., Sugiura, M., & Kawashima, R. (2019). Common neural value representations of hedonic and utilitarian products in the ventral striatum: An fMRI study. *Scientific Reports, 9,* Article 15630. https://doi.org/10.1038/s41598-019-52159-9

Mukherjee, S. (2017). *The gene: An intimate history.* Scribner.

Müller, B. J., Liebl, A., Herget, N., Kohler, D., & Leistner, P. (2022). Using active noise-cancelling headphones in open-plan offices: No influence on cognitive performance but improvement of perceived privacy and acoustic environment. *Frontiers in Built Environment, 8,* Article 962462. https://doi.org/10.3389/fbuil.2022.962462

Muniz, A. M., & O'Guinn, T. C. (2001). Brand community. *Journal of Consumer Research, 27*(4), 412–432. https://doi.org/10.1086/319618

Murphy, T. F. (2024, August 26). Circumplex model of arousal and valence. *Psychology Fanatic.* https://psychologyfanatic.com/circumplex-model-of-arousal-and-valence/

NASA. (2016). *NASA systems engineering handbook: NASA/SP-2016-6105 Rev2 - Full color version.* NASA.

Nelson, R. R., & Winter, S. G. (1982). *An evolutionary theory of economic change.* Belknap Press of Harvard University Press.

Noback, M. L., Harvati, K., & Spoor, F. (2011). Climate-related variation of the human nasal cavity. *American Journal of Physical Anthropology, 145*(4), 599–614. https://doi.org/10.1002/ajpa.21523

Nordhaus, W., & Tobin, J. (1972). Is growth obsolete? In *Economic research: Retrospect and prospect, Volume 5, Economic growth* (pp. 1–80). National Bureau of Economic Research. https://EconPapers.repec.org/RePEc:nbr:nberch:7620

Norman, D. (2013). *The design of everyday things: Revised & expanded edition.* Basic Books.

Norman, D. A. (2005). *Emotional design: Why we love (or hate) everyday things.* Basic Books.

Nowak, M. A., & Highfield, R. (2012*). SuperCooperators: Altruism, evolution, and why we need each other to succeed.* Free Press.

O'Grady, P. J. (1999). *The age of modularity: Using the new world of modular products to revolutionize your corporation.* Adams and Steele Pub.

O'Connor, T., & Wong, H. Y. (2005). The metaphysics of emergence. *Noûs, 39*(4), 658–678. http://www.jstor.org/stable/3506115

Odum, H. T., & Odum, E. C. (2008). *A prosperous way down: Principles and policies*. University Press of Colorado.

Ong, D. C. (2021). An ethical framework for guiding the development of affectively-aware artificial intelligence. *arXiv*. https://doi.org/10.48550/arXiv.2107.13734

Ophir, E., Nass, C., & Wagner, A. D. (2009). Cognitive control in media multitaskers. *Proceedings of the National Academy of Sciences of the United States of America, 106*(37), 15583–15587. https://doi.org/10.1073/pnas.0903620106

Osborn, A. F. (1963). *Applied imagination; Principles and procedures of creative problem-solving* (3rd ed.). Charles Scribner's Sons.

Oswald, L. M., Zandi, P., Nestadt, G., Potash, J. B., Kalaydjian, A. E., & Wand, G. S. (2006). Relationship between cortisol responses to stress and personality. *Neuropsychopharmacology, 31*(7), 1583–1591. https://doi.org/10.1038/sj.npp.1301012

Panksepp, J. (2005). *Affective neuroscience: The foundations of human and animal emotions*. Oxford University Press.

Parker, J. (2024). Organ evolution: Emergence of multicellular function. *Annual Review of Cell and Developmental Biology, 40*(1), 51–74. https://doi.org/10.1146/annurev-cellbio-111822-121620

Perrow, C. (1999). *Normal accidents: Living with high risk technologies*. Princeton University Press.

Pettitt, P. (2011). *The palaeolithic origins of human burial*. Routledge.

Piketty, T. (2017). *Capital in the twenty-first century* (A. Goldhammer, Trans.). The Belknap Press of Harvard University Press.

Pil, F. K., & Cohen, S. K. (2006). Modularity: Implications for imitation, innovation, and sustained advantage. *Academy of Management Review, 31*(4), 995–1011. https://doi.org/10.5465/amr.2006.22528166

Pilat, D., & Krastev, S. (n.d.). Anchoring bias. *The Decision Lab*. https://thedecisionlab.com/biases/anchoring-bias

Pine II, B. J., & Gilmore, J. H. (1999). *The experience economy: Work is theatre & every business a stage*. Harvard Business School Press.

Pinker, S. (2016). *The blank slate: The modern denial of human nature*. Penguin Books.

Plato. (2005). *Protagoras and Meno* (A. Beresford, Trans.). Penguin Books.

Ponting, C. (1993). *A green history of the world: The environment and the collapse of great civilizations*. Penguin.

Popper, K. R. (2014). *The logic of scientific discovery*. Martino Fine Books. (Original work published 1934)

Porges, S. W. (2011). *The Polyvagal theory: Neurophysiological foundations of emotions attachment communication self-regulation*. W. W. Norton & Company.

Porter, M. E. (1998). *Competitive advantage: Creating and sustaining superior performance*. Free Press.

Porter, M. E., & Kramer, M. R. (2011). Creating shared value. *Harvard Business Review, 89*(1–2), 62–77. https://hbr.org/2011/01/the-big-idea-creating-shared-value

Prigogine, I., & Stengers, I. (1997). *The end of certainty: time, chaos, and the new laws of nature*. Free Press.

Prigogine, I., & Stengers, I. (2017). *Order out of chaos: Man's new dialogue with nature*. Verso Books.

Przybylski, A. K., Murayama, K., DeHaan, C. R., & Gladwell, V. (2013). Motivational, emotional, and behavioral correlates of fear of missing out. *Computers in Human Behavior, 29*(4), 1841–1848. https://doi.org/10.1016/j.chb.2013.02.014

Przybylski, A. K., Weinstein, N., Murayama, K., Lynch, M. F., & Ryan, R. M. (2012). The ideal self at play: The appeal of video games that let you be all you can be. *Psychological Science, 23*(1), 69–76. https://doi.org/10.1177/0956797611418676

QUIGLEY, J. M., & Robertson, K. L. (2020). *Configuration management: Theory and application for engineers, managers, and practitioners* (2nd ed.). CRC Press.

Raffaelli, R. L., Glynn, M. A., & Tushman, M. (2018). Frame flexibility: The role of cognitive and emotional framing in innovation adoption by incumbent firms (*Harvard Business School Organizational Behavior Unit Working Paper No. 17-091*). https://doi.org/10.2139/ssrn.2956442

Rāhula, W. (1974). *What the Buddha taught* (2nd ed.). Grove Press.

Raichle, M. E. (2015). The brain's default mode network. *Annual Review of Neuroscience, 38*, 433–447. https://doi.org/10.1146/annurev-neuro-071013-014030

Ram, Y., & Hadany, L. (2014). Stress-induced mutagenesis and complex adaptation. *Proceedings. Biological Sciences, 281*(1792), 20141025. https://doi.org/10.1098/rspb.2014.1025

Reason, J. (2009). *Human error.* Cambridge University Press. (Original work published 1990)

Reber, A. S. (1989). Implicit learning and tacit knowledge. *Journal of Experimental Psychology: General, 118*(3), 219–235. https://doi.org/10.1037/0096-3445.118.3.219

Reber, A. S. (1996). *Implicit learning and tacit knowledge: An essay on the cognitive unconscious.* Oxford University Press.

Rebitzer, G., Ekvall, T., Frischknecht, R., Hunkeler, D., Norris, G., Rydberg, T., Schmidt, W. P., Suh, S., Weidema, B. P., & Pennington, D. W. (2004). Life cycle assessment part 1: Framework, goal and scope definition, inventory analysis, and applications. *Environment International, 30*(5), 701–720. https://doi.org/10.1016/j.envint.2003.11.005

Redelmeier, D. A., & Kahneman, D. (1996). Patients' memories of painful medical treatments: Real-time and retrospective evaluations of two minimally invasive procedures. *Pain, 66*(1), 3–8. https://doi.org/10.1016/0304-3959(96)02994-6

Reichheld, F. (2006). *The ultimate question: Driving good profits and true growth.* Harvard Business School Press.

Reif, F. (1985). *Fundamentals of statistical and thermal physics.* McGraw-Hill.

Reinertsen, D. G. (2009). *The principles of product development flow: Second generation lean product development.* Celeritas Publishing.

Richter, Á. (2016). The Marvel cinematic universe as a transmedia narrative. *AMERICANA E-Journal of American Studies in Hungary, 12*(1). https://www.americanaejournal.hu/index.php/americanaejournal/article/view/45110

Ries, E. (2011). *The lean startup: How today's entrepreneurs use continuous innovation to create radically successful businesses.* Currency.

Rifkin, J., & Howard, T. (1980). *Entropy: A new world view.* Viking Press.

Rindos, D. (1984). *The origins of agriculture: An evolutionary perspective.* Academic Press.

Riordan, M., & Hoddeson, L. (1998). *Crystal fire: The invention of the transistor and the birth of the Information Age.* W. W. Norton & Company.

Robertson, J. (2015). *The Enlightenment: A very short introduction.* Oxford University Press.

Robinson, A. (2007). *Story of writing: Alphabets hieroglyphs and pictograms* (2nd ed.). Thames and Hudson.

Robson, A., & Samuelson, L. (2011). The evolution of decision and experienced utilities. *Theoretical Economics, 6*(3), 311–339. https://doi.org/10.3982/TE800

Rogers, E. M. (2003). *Diffusion of innovations* (5th ed.). Free Press.

Rouault, M., Drugowitsch, J., & Koechlin, E. (2019). Prefrontal mechanisms combining rewards and beliefs in human decision-making. *Nature Communications, 10*, Article 301. https://doi.org/10.1038/s41467-018-08121-w

Rousseau, J. (2021). *Selected political writings: The social contract, discourse on the origin of inequality, discourse on the arts & sciences, discourse on political economy* (G. D. Cole, Trans.). self-published.

Rozin, P., & Royzman, E. B. (2001). Negativity bias, negativity dominance, and contagion. *Personality and Social Psychology Review, 5*(4), 296–320. https://doi.org/10.1207/S15327957PSPR0504_2

Russell, J. A. (1980). A circumplex model of affect. *Journal of Personality and Social Psychology, 39*(6), 1161–1178. https://doi.org/10.1037/h0077714

Russell, S., & Norvig, P. (2022). *Artificial intelligence: A modern approach* (4th ed.). Pearson Education Ltd.

Rust, R. T., Thompson, D. V., & Hamilton, R. W. (2006, February 1). Defeating feature fatigue. *Harvard Business Review.* https://hbr.org/2006/02/defeating-feature-fatigue

Rutherford, A. (2018). *The systems thinker: Essential thinking skills for solving problems, managing chaos, and creating lasting solutions in a complex world.* Kindle Direct.

Ryan, C., & Jetha, C. (2011). *Sex at dawn: How we mate, why we stray, and what it means for modern relationships*. Harper Perennial.

Saey, T. H. (2011, April 15). Moth mutation explains classic example of evolution. *WIRED*. https://www.wired.com/2011/04/evolution-peppered-moth/

Sagan, C. (1997). *The demon-haunted world: Science as a candle in the dark*. Ballantine Books.

Sahlins, M. (2017). *Stone Age economics*. Routledge.

Salvador, F. (2007). Toward a product system modularity construct: Literature review and reconceptualization. *IEEE Transactions on Engineering Management, 54*(2), 219–240. https://doi.org/10.1109/TEM.2007.893996

Samuelson, P. A. (1983). *Foundations of economic analysis*. Harvard University Press. (Original work published 1947)

Samuelson, P. A., & Nordhaus, W. D. (2010). *Economics* (19th ed.). McGraw-Hill Companies.

Samuelson, W., & Zeckhauser, R. (1988). Status quo bias in decision making. *Journal of Risk and Uncertainty, 1*, 7–59. https://doi.org/10.1007/BF00055564

Sartre, J.-P (2007). *Existentialism is a humanism* (C. Macomber, Trans.). Yale University Press.

Sartre, J.-P (2021). *Being and nothingness* (S. Richmond, Trans.). Washington Square Press. (Original work published 1943)

Sassatelli, R. (2010). *Consumer culture: History, theory and politics*. SAGE Publications.

Savransky, S. D. (2000). *Engineering of creativity: Introduction to TRIZ methodology of inventive problem solving*. CRC Press.

Sawyer, K. (2007). *Group genius: The creative power of collaboration*. Basic Books.

Schaller, M., Kenrick, D. T., Neel, R., & Neuberg, S. L. (2017). Evolution and human motivation: A fundamental motives framework. *Social and Personality Psychology Compass, 11*(6). https://doi.org/10.1111/spc3.12319

Schaufeli, W. B., Maslach, C., & Marek, T. (Eds.). (2017). *Professional burnout: Recent developments in theory and research*. Routledge.

Schlosser, E. (2012). *Fast food nation: The dark side of the all-American meal*. First Mariner Books.

Schmandt-Besserat, D. (2006). *How writing came about*. University of Texas Press.

Schmidt-Nielsen, K. (1997). *Animal physiology: Adaptation and environment* (5th ed.). Cambridge University Press.

Schmitt, B. H. (2011). *Experiential marketing: How to get customers to sense, feel, think, act, relate, to your company brands*. Free Press.

Schneider, E. D., & Sagan, D. (2005). *Into the cool: Energy flow, thermodynamics, and life*. The University of Chicago Press.

Schrage, M. (2016). *The innovator's hypothesis: How cheap experiments are worth more than good ideas*. MIT Press.

Schrödinger, E. (2023). *What is life? The physical aspect of the living cell: With mind and matter & autobiographical sketches*. Cambridge University Press.

Schrum, J. P., Zhu, T. F., & Szostak, J. W. (2010). The origins of cellular life. *Cold Spring Harbor Perspectives in Biology, 2*(9), a002212. https://doi.org/10.1101/cshperspect.a002212

Schultz, W. (1998). Predictive reward signal of dopamine neurons. *Journal of Neurophysiology, 80*(1), 1–27. https://doi.org/10.1152/jn.1998.80.1.1

Schumpeter, J. A. (2008). *Capitalism, socialism, and democracy* (3rd ed.). Harper Perennial Modern Thought. (Original 3rd ed. published 1950)

Schumpeter, J. A. (2021). *The theory of economic development*. Routledge. (Original work published 1911)

Schwartz, B. (2016). *The paradox of choice: Why more is less, revised edition*. HarperCollins.

Schwartz, J. M., & Begley, S. (2003). *The mind and the brain: Neuroplasticity and the power of mental force*. Harper Perennial.

Scott Kruse, C., Karem, P., Shifflett, K., Vegi, L., Ravi, K., & Brooks, M. (2018). Evaluating barriers to adopting telemedicine worldwide: A systematic review. *Journal of Telemedicine and Telecare, 24*(1), 4–12. https://doi.org/10.1177/1357633X16674087

Sen, A. (1999). *Development as freedom.* Anchor Books.

Senge, P. M. (2006). *The fifth discipline: The art & practice of the learning organization.* Currency.

Sharot, T. (2012). *The optimism bias: A tour of the irrationally positive brain.* Vintage Books.

Sharratt, M. (1996). *Galileo: Decisive innovator.* Cambridge University Press.

Sheldon, K. M., & Lyubomirsky, S. (2012). The challenge of staying happier: Testing the Hedonic Adaptation Prevention model. *Personality & Social Psychology Bulletin, 38*(5), 670–680. https://doi.org/10.1177/0146167212436400

Sheth, J. N., Newman, B. I., & Gross, B. L. (1991). Why we buy what we buy: A theory of consumption values. *Journal of Business Research, 22*(2), 159–170. https://doi.org/10.1016/0148-2963(91)90050-8

Shields, C. J. (2014). *Aristotle* (2nd ed.). Routledge.

Shofty, B., Gonen, T., Bergmann, E., Mayseless, N., Korn, A., Shamay-Tsoory, S., Grossman, R., Jalon, I., Kahn, I., & Ram, Z. (2022). The default network is causally linked to creative thinking. *Molecular Psychiatry, 27*(4), 1848–1854. https://doi.org/10.1038/s41380-021-01403-8

Sidhu, I. (2020). *Innovation engineering: A practical guide to creating anything new* (2nd ed.). Ikhlaq Sidhu.

Simon, H. A. (1955). A behavioral model of rational choice. *The Quarterly Journal of Economics, 69*(1), 99–118. https://doi.org/10.2307/1884852

Simon, H. A. (2019). *The sciences of the artificial, reissue of the with a new introduction by John Laird* (3rd ed.). MIT Press.

Singer, P. (1993). *Practical Ethics* (2nd ed.). Cambridge University Press.

Skinner, B. F. (1965). *Science and human behavior.* Free Press.

Skinner, B. F. (1991). *The behavior of organisms: An experimental analysis.* B. F. Skinner Foundation. (Original work published 1938)

Skowronek, J., Seifert, A., & Lindberg, S. (2023). The mere presence of a smartphone reduces basal attentional performance. *Scientific Reports, 13*(1), 9363. https://doi.org/10.1038/s41598-023-36256-4

Smil, V. (2018). *Energy and civilization: A history.* MIT Press.

Smith, A. (2014). *The wealth of nations.* Shine Classics. (Original work published 1776)

Smith, A. (2015). *An inquiry into the nature and causes of the wealth of nations: Selections, Book 1* (L. V. Mises, Ed.). Martino Publishing.

Smith, J. M., & Szathmary, E. (1997). *The major transitions in evolution.* Oxford University Press.

Smyth, S., Kerr, W., & Phillips, P. W. B. (2015). The unintended consequences of technological change: Winners and losers from GM technologies and the policy response in the organic food market. *Sustainability, 7*(6), 7667–7683. https://doi.org/10.3390/su7067667

Sojo, V., Herschy, B., Whicher, A., Camprubí, E., & Lane, N. (2016). The origin of life in alkaline hydrothermal vents. *Astrobiology, 16*(2), 181–197. https://doi.org/10.1089/ast.2015.1406

Soliemanifar, O., Soleymanifar, A., & Afrisham, R. (2018). Relationship between personality and biological reactivity to stress: A review. *Psychiatry Investigation, 15*(12), 1100–1114. https://doi.org/10.30773/pi.2018.10.14.2

Sörgel, F. (2024). *Emotional drivers of innovation: Exploring the moral economy of* prototypes. Transcript Publishing.

Sparrow, B., Liu, J., & Wegner, D. M. (2011). Google effects on memory: Cognitive consequences of having information at our fingertips. *Science, 333*(6043), 776–778. https://doi.org/10.1126/science.1207745

Staddon, J. E., & Cerutti, D. T. (2003). Operant conditioning. *Annual Review of Psychology, 54*, 115–144. https://doi.org/10.1146/annurev.psych.54.101601.145124

Standage, T. (2014). *The Victorian internet: The remarkable story of the telegraph and the nineteenth century's on-line pioneers.* Bloomsbury Publishing.

Standage, T. (2021). *A brief history of motion: From the wheel, to the car, to what comes* next. Bloomsbury Publishing.

Stanier, M. B. (2023). *How to work with (almost) anyone: Five questions for building the best possible relationships*. Page Two.

Stanovich, K. E., & West, R. F. (2000). Individual differences in reasoning: Implications for the rationality debate? *The Behavioral and Brain Sciences, 23*(5), 645–726. https://doi.org/10.1017/s0140525x00003435

Stefik, M., & Stefik, B. (2004). *Breakthrough: Stories and strategies of radical innovation*. MIT Press.

Steil, B. (2014). *The battle of Bretton Woods: John Maynard Keynes, Harry Dexter White, and the making of a new world order*. Princeton University Press.

Sterman, J. D. (2000). *Business dynamics: Systems thinking and modeling for a complex world*. McGraw-Hill Higher Education.

Stickdorn, M., & Schneider, J. (2011). *This is service design thinking: Basics, tools, cases*. John Wiley & Sons.

Stigler, G. J. (1950). The development of utility theory. I. *Journal of Political Economy, 58*(4), 307–327. http://www.jstor.org/stable/1828885

StratoServe. (2022, October 9). The "S" curves of radical and incremental innovation. *StratoServe.* https://stratoserve.com/2020/11/the-s-curves-of-radical-and-incremental-innovation.html

Stuart. (2021, June 1). Comparing Bosch, Dewalt, Makita, Metabo HPT, Milwaukee cordless power tool systems. *ToolGuyd | Tool Reviews, Deals, Industry News*. https://toolguyd.com/bosch-dewalt-makita-metabo-hpt-milwaukee-cordless-power-tool-systems/

Stuber, G. D., Sparta, D. R., Stamatakis, A. M., van Leeuwen, W. A., Hardjoprajitno, J. E., Cho, S., Tye, K. M., Kempadoo, K. A., Zhang, F., Deisseroth, K., & Bonci, A. (2011). Excitatory transmission from the amygdala to nucleus accumbens facilitates reward seeking. *Nature, 475*(7356), 377–380. https://doi.org/10.1038/nature10194

Suri, G., Sheppes, G., Schwartz, C., & Gross, J. J. (2013). Patient inertia and the status quo bias: When an inferior option is preferred. *Psychological Science, 24*(9), 1763–1769. https://doi.org/10.1177/0956797613479976

Suri, T., & Jack, W. (2016). The long-run poverty and gender impacts of mobile money. *Science, 354*(6317), 1288–1292. https://doi.org/10.1126/science.aah5309

Sveiby, K., Gripenberg, P., & Segercrantz, B. (Eds.). (2015). *Challenging the innovation paradigm*. Routledge.

Swart-Opperman, C., Dharani, B., & April, K. (2022). The impact of emotional experiences of innovation champions on innovation outcomes. *Journal of Innovation Management, 9*(4), 98-126. https://doi.org/10.24840/2183-0606_009.004_0006

Tattersall, I. (2013). *Masters of the planet: The search for our human origins*. St. Martin's Griffin.

Tay, L., & Diener, E. (2011). Needs and subjective well-being around the world. *Journal of Personality and Social Psychology, 101*(2), 354–365. https://doi.org/10.1037/a0023779

Teece, D. J. (2011). *Dynamic capabilities & strategic management: Organizing for innovation and growth*. Oxford University Press.

Teece, D. J., Pisano, G., & Shuen, A. (1997). Dynamic capabilities and strategic management. *Strategic Management Journal, 18*(7), 509–533. http://www.jstor.org/stable/3088148

Tereshchenko, S. Y. (2023). Neurobiological risk factors for problematic social media use as a specific form of internet addiction: A narrative review. *World Journal of Psychiatry, 13*(5), 160–173. https://doi.org/10.5498/wjp.v13.i5.160

Thaler, R. (1980). Toward a positive theory of consumer choice. *Journal of Economic Behavior & Organization, 1*(1), 39–60. https://doi.org/10.1016/0167-2681(80)90051-7

Thaler, R. (2000). From Homo Economicus to Homo Sapiens. *Journal of Economic Perspectives, 14*(1), 133–141. https://www.aeaweb.org/articles?id=10.1257/jep.14.1.133

Thaler, R. H. (2016). *Misbehaving: the making of behavioral economics*. W. W. Norton & Company.

Thaler, R. H., & Sunstein, C. R. (2021). *Nudge: The final edition*. Penguin Books.

The Marshall Plan: Design, accomplishments, and significance. (2018, January 18). *Every CRS Report – EveryCRSReport.com*. https://www.everycrsreport.com/reports/R45079.html

Thompson, D. V., Hamilton, R. W., & Rust, R. T. (2005). Feature fatigue: When product capabilities become too much of a good thing. *Journal of Marketing Research, 42*(4), 431–442. https://doi.org/10.1509/jmkr.2005.42.4.431

Thurner, S. (Ed.). (2017). *43 visions for complexity.* World Scientific Publishing Company.

Thurner, S., Hanel, R., & Klimek, P. (2019). *Introduction to the theory of complex systems.* Oxford University Press.

Tilly, C. (2004). *Social movements, 1768-2004.* Paradigm Publishers.

Tode, C. (n.d.). Smartphones are replacing MP3 players, digital cameras and GPS devices: Oracle. *Digital Marketing News | Marketing Dive.* https://www.marketingdive.com/ex/mobilemarketer/cms/news/research/11371.html

Tom, S. M., Fox, C. R., Trepel, C., & Poldrack, R. A. (2007). The neural basis of loss aversion in decision-making under risk. *Science, 315*(5811), 515–518. https://doi.org/10.1126/science.1134239

Tomasello, M. (2000). *The cultural origins of human cognition.* Harvard University Press.

Turkle, S. (2016). *Reclaiming conversation: The power of talk in a digital age.* Penguin Books.

Tushman, M. L., & O'Reilly, C. A. (1996). Ambidextrous organizations: Managing evolutionary and revolutionary change. *California Management Review, 38*(4), 8–29. https://doi.org/10.2307/41165852

Tversky, A., & Kahneman, D. (1974). Judgment under uncertainty: Heuristics and biases. *Science, 185*(4157), 1124–1131. https://doi.org/10.1126/science.185.4157.1124

Tversky, A., & Kahneman, D. (1986). Rational choice and the framing of decisions. *The Journal of Business, 59*(4), S251–S278. http://www.jstor.org/stable/2352759

Tversky, A., & Kahneman, D. (1991). Loss aversion in riskless choice: A reference-dependent model. *The Quarterly Journal of Economics, 106*(4), 1039–1061. http://www.jstor.org/stable/2937956

Twenge, J. M. (2018). iGen: *Why today's super-connected kids are growing up less rebellious, more tolerant, less happy - and completely unprepared for adulthood - and what that means for the rest of us.* Atria Paperback.

Ulrich, K. T., & Eppinger, S. D. (2016). *Product design and development* (6th ed.). McGraw-Hill Education.

Ulwick, A. W. (2005). *What customers want: Using outcome-driven innovation to create breakthrough products and services.* McGraw-Hill.

Ulwick, A. W. (2016). *Jobs to be done: Theory to practice.* Idea Bite Press.

Umeda, Y., Fukushige, S., Tonoike, K., & Kondoh, S. (2008). Product modularity for life cycle design. *CIRP Annals, 57*(1), 13–16. https://doi.org/10.1016/j.cirp.2008.03.115

Utterback, J. M. (1996). *Mastering the dynamics of innovation.* Harvard Business School Press.

Van den Hoven, J., Lokhorst, G. J., & Van de Poel, I. (2012). Engineering and the problem of moral overload. *Science and Engineering Ethics, 18*(1), 143–155. https://doi.org/10.1007/s11948-011-9277-z

Varian, H. R. (2014). *Intermediate microeconomics: A modern approach* (9th ed.). W. W. Norton & Company.

Vatansever, D., Menon, D. K., & Stamatakis, E. A. (2017). Default mode contributions to automated information processing. *Proceedings of the National Academy of Sciences of the United States of America, 114*(48), 12821–12826. https://doi.org/10.1073/pnas.1710521114

Veblen, T. (2009). *The theory of the leisure class* (M. Banta, Ed.). Oxford University Press. (Original work published 1899)

Vroomans, R. M. A., & Colizzi, E. S. (2023). Evolution of selfish multicellularity: Collective organisation of individual spatio-temporal regulatory strategies. *BMC Ecology and Evolution, 23*, Article 35. https://doi.org/10.1186/s12862-023-02133-x

Wächtershäuser, G. (1988). Before enzymes and templates: Theory of surface metabolism. *Microbiological Reviews, 52*(4), 452–484. https://doi.org/10.1128/mr.52.4.452-484.1988

Wahba, M. A., & Bridwell, L. G. (1976). Maslow reconsidered: A review of research on the need hierarchy theory. *Organizational Behavior & Human Performance, 15*(2), 212–240. https://doi.org/10.1016/0030-5073(76)90038-6

Walton, M. E., & Bouret, S. (2019). What is the relationship between dopamine and effort? *Trends in Neurosciences, 42*(2), 79–91. https://doi.org/10.1016/j.tins.2018.10.001

Wang, K. S., Smith, D. V., & Delgado, M. R. (2016). Using fMRI to study reward processing in humans: Past, present, and future. *Journal of Neurophysiology, 115*(3), 1664–1678. https://doi.org/10.1152/jn.00333.2015

Ward, A. F., Duke, K., Gneezy, A., & Bos, M. W. (2017). Brain drain: The mere presence of one's own smartphone reduces available cognitive capacity. *Journal of the Association for Consumer Research, 2*(2), 140–154. https://doi.org/10.1086/691462

Watts, F. B. (2012). *Engineering documentation control handbook: Configuration management and product lifecycle management* (4th ed.). Elsevier.

Weinstein, A. (2019). *Superior customer value: Finding and keeping customers in the now economy* (4th ed.). Routledge.

Weinstein, A. M. (2023). Reward, motivation and brain imaging in human healthy participants – A narrative review. *Frontiers in Behavioral Neuroscience, 17*, 1123733. https://doi.org/10.3389/fnbeh.2023.1123733

Wendel, S. (2020). *Designing for behavior change: Applying psychology and behavioral economics* (2nd ed.). O'Reilly Media.

West, G. (2018). *Scale: The universal laws of life, growth, and death in organisms, cities, and companies.* Penguin Books.

Wheeler, P. E. (1991). The thermoregulatory advantages of hominid bipedalism in open equatorial environments: The contribution of increased convective heat loss and cutaneous evaporative cooling. *Journal of Human Evolution, 21*(2), 107–115. https://doi.org/10.1016/0047-2484(91)90002-D

Wildschut, T., Sedikides, C., Arndt, J., & Routledge, C. (2006). Nostalgia: Content, triggers, functions. *Journal of Personality and Social Psychology, 91*(5), 975–993. https://doi.org/10.1037/0022-3514.91.5.975

Wilmer, H. H., Sherman, L. E., & Chein, J. M. (2017). Smartphones and cognition: A review of research exploring the links between mobile technology habits and cognitive functioning. *Frontiers in Psychology, 8*, 605. https://doi.org/10.3389/fpsyg.2017.00605

Wilson, T. D., & Gilbert, D. T. (2005). Affective forecasting: Knowing what to want. *Current Directions in Psychological Science, 14*(3), 131–134. https://doi.org/10.1111/j.0963-7214.2005.00355.x

Windzio, M. (2023). The evolution of human sociality: Categorizations, emotions, and friendship. *KZfSS Kölner Zeitschrift für Soziologie und Sozialpsychologie, 76*(3), 415–441. https://doi.org/10.1007/s11577-023-00919-x

Wisnioski, M. (2015, February 13). How digital technology is destroying your mind. *The Washington Post.* https://www.washingtonpost.com/opinions/healine-here/2015/02/13/a78172e0-855e-11e4-9534-f79a23c40e6c_story.html

Witcover, J. (1997). *The year the dream died: Revisiting 1968 in America.* Warner Books.

Womack, J. P., & Jones, D. T. (2003). *Lean thinking: Banish waste and create wealth in your corporation, revised and updated* (2nd ed.). Free Press.

Womack, J. P., Jones, D. T., & Roos, D. (2007). *The machine that changed the world: The story of lean production - Toyota's secret weapon in the global car wars that is revolutionizing world industry.* Free Press.

Yeager, D. S., & Dweck, C. S. (2012). Mindsets that promote resilience: When students believe that personal characteristics can be developed. *Educational Psychologist, 47*(4), 302–314. https://doi.org/10.1080/00461520.2012.722805

Zhang, H., & Ali-Eldin, A. (2025). The hidden bloat in machine learning systems. *arXiv.* https://doi.org/10.48550/arXiv.2503.14226

Zhang, X. (2022). Incremental innovation: Long-term impetus for design business creativity. *Sustainability, 14*(22), 14697. https://doi.org/10.3390/su142214697

Zhuo, J. (2019). *The making of a manager: What to do when everyone looks to you.* Portfolioi/Penguin.

Zipf, G. K. (2012). *Human behavior and the principle of least effort: An introduction to human ecology.* Martino Publishing. (Original work published 1949)

Zomerdijk, L. G., & Voss, C. A. (2010). Service design for experience-centric services. *Journal of Service Research, 13*(1), 67–82. https://doi.org/10.1177/1094670509351960

Index

525

539